The Diary of Sigmund Freud
1929–1939

The Diary of Sigmund Freud 1929–1939

A Record of the Final Decade

Translated, Annotated, with an
Introduction by Michael Molnar

The Freud Museum, London

Designed by Martin Moskof

A ROBERT STEWART BOOK

SCRIBNER

SCRIBNER
1230 Avenue of the Americas
New York, NY 10020

Copyright © 1992 by Freud Museum Publications, Limited, London
Introduction copyright © 1992 by Michael Monar
Freud material copyright © 1992 by A. W. Freud et al.
by arrangement with Sigmund Freud Copyrights

SCRIBNER and design are trademarks of Jossey-Bass, Inc.,
Used under license by Simon & Schuster, the publisher of this work.

Designed by Moskof Associates / Design Assistant: George Brady

Manufactured in the Unites States of America

10 9 8 7 6 5 4 3 2

Front end paper:
Freud's desk, May 1938. "Statues and images helped stabilize the evanescent idea or
keep it from escaping altogether." *(Photo:
E. Engelman)*

Page i:
Freud in London, summer 1938, at work
on *Moses and Monotheism.* "When I sit
down to write and take my pen in my
hand, I am always curious what will
then follow. . . ."

Pages ii–iii:
The consulting room at Berggasse 19,
Vienna, in 1938. *(Photo: E. Engelman)*

Frontispiece:
Freud in the garden of sculptor Oscar
Nemon, July 1931.

Back end paper:
Freud's desk, The Freud Museum, London.
"Looking back, then, over the patchwork
of my life's labours, I can say that I have
made many beginnings and thrown out
many suggestions. Something will come
of them in the future. . . ." *(Photo
N. Bagguley)*

Library of Congress Cataloging-in-Publication Data

Freud, Sigmund, 1856–1939.
The diary of Sigmund Freud, 1929 to 1939 : a record of the final decade
translated and annotated by Michael Molnar.
p.   cm.
"A Robert Stewart book."
Includes bibliographical references and index.
ISBN 0-684-19329-9
1. Freud, Sigmund, 1856–1939—Diaries.   2. Psychoanalysts—
Austria—Diaries.   3. Psychoanalysts—England—Diaries.
4. Psychoanalysis.   I. Molnar, Michael.   II. Title.
BF109.F74A3   1992   91-16503   CIP
150.19′52—dc20
[B]

CONTENTS

20, Maresfield Gardens, London. Freud's final home, now the Freud Museum.

ACKNOWLEDGEMENTS

This book owes its existence to the Freud Museum, London. Its genesis coincided with the museum's opening in 1986, and it has been researched and written almost entirely in the Museum, over its first five years. My primary acknowledgment must be to The New-Land Foundation Inc., and The Sigmund Freud Archives Inc., both of New York, who together form the present organization of the Museum and are its trustees. To them I owe especial thanks for their continued support, and their faith in the work of the Museum.

The Sigmund Freud Collection of the Sigmund Freud Archives provided indispensable primary documentation. I offer my particular thanks to Dr. Harold Blum, the Director of the Sigmund Freud Archives, and to Allan Teichrow and the staff of the Manuscript Room in the Library of Congress, where the Sigmund Freud Collection is housed, for their kind cooperation. Here I should also mention the essential derestriction of Freud's *Kürzeste Chronik*, in accord with the present policy of The Sigmund Freud Archives of derestricting previously classified documents.

It was the first deputy curator of the Freud Museum, Steve Neufeld, who nursed this project through its earliest and most vulnerable stages. Furthermore he set up the library, photographic and collection catalogues. These have been invaluable in my work. In thanking him for them too, I must also thank those who have continued documenting the museum's holdings: J. Keith Davies who has compiled an essential catalogue of the library, (now being prepared for publication), Brendan King who drew up the photograph inventory, Andrea Awde and Tony Clayton who set up a vital database for the newspaper, print and Anna Freud archive listings, David Newman and Nick Bagguley, who photographed the entire collection. Nick Bagguley also took the fine pictures of the museum interior that illustrate this book.

By establishing the post of researcher in the Museum, the previous director, Richard Wells, enabled me to continue my work on the book and I must thank him for all the encouragement he gave me. And it has been thanks to the energy and curatorial skill of his successor, Erica Davies, at present Acting Director of the Museum, that this project eventually reached completion. Moreover, during the hectic final stages of research, both she and J. Keith Davies, sacrificed time from their own work to assist me. I am indebted to them for this vital help, as also to Barrie Cash and the photography department of the National Maritime Museum, who somehow managed to produce copies of our photographs at ridiculously short notice.

During the long gestation of this book, the rest of the museum staff have all been in some way involved in my work and I must therefore express my sincere gratitude and thanks to Alex Bento, Paul Cobley, Allison Green, Susan O'Cleary and Ivan Ward for their tolerance and support.

Beyond the museum, but within the Freud family, Freud's first grandson W. Ernest Freud, helped me more than I dared hope by writing himself the notes to those entries in which he is mentioned. Another grandson, Stephan Gabriel Freud, donated some of his mother's papers, including letters from the 1930s, to the Freud Museum. I am grateful to him and Ann Freud for the gift and for permission to use this new material. A third grandson, Anton Walter Freud, shared with me memories of his grandfather and of his father, Martin Freud. Other first-hand witnesses of the events recorded include Dr. Josefine Stross, Mrs. Katrina Burlingham Valenstein and Mrs. Aviva Harari. I must thank them all warmly for agreeing to be talk to me.

I am especially grateful to Dr. Johannes Reichmayr and Dr. Karl Fallend for their lively research on my behalf. Not only did they clear up a number of obscure references, they also procured some photographs at very short notice. Peter Swales and Professor G. Fichtner, together with Dr. A. Hirschmüller and Dr. C. Törgel, were outstandingly helpful in sending me detailed answers to a long list of inquiries. Ronnie Aked's kind invitation to give a lecture to Bankers Trust International in Vienna indirectly sponsored research that opened a number of doors. And there have been many others who have answered queries or generously assisted in various ways. I would like to offer my thanks to Dr. Jean-Pierre Bourgeron, Dr. Christine Diercks, Dr. Kurt Eissler, Dr. Volker Friedrich, Dr. Ludger Hermanns, Dr. Han Israëls, Dr. Anton O. Kris, Hanns Lange, Dr. Hans Lobner, Elke Mühlleitner, Dr. Cathrin Pichler, Professor Paul Roazen, Anthony Stadlen, Jane Turner and Dr. Margaret Whitford.

In London the archive of the Institute of Psycho-Analysis was a vital source and I must thank its Honorary Archivist, Pearl King, for granting access, and Jill Duncan and Sonu Shamdasani for showing me round its holdings and its computer catalogue. I was also grateful for the use of the Sigmund Freud Copyrights archive at Wivenhoe and must warmly thank the archivist Tom Roberts for his welcome and his consistent helpfulness. And I am indebted to Mark Paterson, director of Sigmund Freud Copyrights, for permission to quote unpublished Freud material, and to Mervyn Jones for the extracts from his father's diary. I also owe thanks to Professor Peter Gay for taking the time to make a number of valuable suggestions.

In addition to all of this, I was lucky in finding an editor who has himself done original research in the field. My thanks to Robert Stewart, therefore, for giving me the benefit of his experience in our discussions and for letting me hear the tapes of his interviews with Anna and Ernst Freud, Max Schur and Robert Waelder—and, of course, for taking on this unwieldy project. And here I must also thank the literary agents, Mary Clemmey, Susanna Nicklin and F. Joseph Spieler, for their work in getting this publication placed, and the designer Martin Moskof for ensuring its fine presentation.

Finally, this book could not have been compiled without the work done by numerous Freud scholars, historians and biographers. Their publications are credited in the end notes, which may be regarded as an extension of these acknowledgements.

—*Michael Molnar*
Freud Museum 1991

INTRODUCTION

I n June 1986, a month before the Freud Museum was opened in London, some documents from Freud's desk were being catalogued. Among them were twenty folio-sized sheets containing a list of dates and brief notes written in Freud's unmistakable Gothic handwriting. At the top of the first sheet was the underlined title *Kürzeste Chronik* ("Shortest Chronicle"). The assistant curator, Steve Neufeld, asked me to look them over. I began deciphering the notes and was immediately fascinated and intrigued.

Not that the document in question was a new discovery. It had always been known that Freud kept brief diary notes. Freud's colleague and biographer, Ernest Jones, mentions this diary. In a subsequent biography the historian Ronald Clark refers to "an unbound diary" and cites a few entries. Peter Gay, has also used this "laconic diary" as an important historical source for his recent biography of Freud. Kurt Eissler, the psychoanalyst and founder of the Sigmund Freud Archives, referred to it in his introduction to the picture biography compiled by Freud's youngest son, Ernst, and a couple of pages of this "abbreviated diary" are even reproduced in the picture section.

Finally, it was Freud's eldest son, Martin, who provided the most complete description of the document: "Father kept on his desk a kind of unbound diary in the form of large sheets of white paper upon which he recorded in a most laconic way those events of each day that seemed to him of importance."[1] But, despite all these references to it, this diary had never yet been published in its entirety. I wondered why.

When Freud fled from Nazi Austria in 1938, he took this document with him into exile, along with the rest of his books and papers. He came to London and bought a house at 20 Maresfield Gardens in Hampstead, where he died a year later, in September 1939. During that final year in England he continued updating the diary. At his death the house, with papers, library, furniture, and Freud's extensive collection of antiquities, remained in the family. His daughter Anna continued to live and work there until her death in 1982. In her will she bequeathed the house to a charitable trust to be turned into a museum. In 1986 the papers stored all over the house were assigned to an archive. It was at this point that the diary was handed to me.

Because it was already evident that the notes constituted an important primary historical source for Freud's final decade, the Museum requested me to transcribe and translate them. I set to work, seated at a trestle table in a sunny upstairs room, which had once been the bedroom of Dorothy Burlingham, Anna Freud's companion. Around me the Freud Museum was rapidly taking shape, under the eye of its first curator, David Newlands. In the study, Steve Neufeld was supervising the unpacking and cataloguing of Freud's antiquities, while in the library Freud's books were being catalogued and in the large room at the top of the house (which had previously been Anna Freud's consulting room), the Freud family photograph albums were being listed. And as I worked, it gradually became clear to me that all this activity around me related in some way to the diary I was transcribing.

At the same time I began to understand why it had never been published in its entirety. Because so many of the entries relate to domestic and everyday life, historians and Freud scholars appear to have regarded the diary as a curiosity, something not quite relevant to the "real Freud." Moreover, a

The study. Freud Museum, London.

A corner of the study.

Freud, 1918.

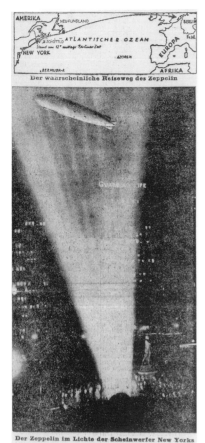

Der Zeppelin im Lichte der Scheinwerfer New Yorks

number of the entries remained cryptic, if not totally incomprehensible, to anyone with no access to Freud's collection of antiquities. Yet now I found that virtually all the objects and books Freud mentions were standing around me. More and more pictures of his family and the acquaintances who are mentioned were turning up in the photograph albums upstairs, many of their unpublished letters lay in a safe in the corner of the room. All that was necessary, it seemed, was to bring this scattered material together and most of the diary's cryptic allusions could be restored to life. The result is this book and it will, I hope, provide a unique documentary background to Freud's own commentary on his last ten years.

I: "A Reliable Chronicler"

On September 19, 1930, a week after his mother's death, Sigmund Freud wrote a letter to his daughter Anna. She was now in St. Moritz, on holiday after attending the funeral, but she and her father kept in daily contact by cards, letters and telegrams. His letter speaks first of their dogs, a subject that is to recur many times in this diary. His chow Jofi had an upset stomach but was playing happily with Anna's Alsatian, Wolf. He then mentions that a sirocco was blowing and as a result his wife, sister and sister-in-law all had headaches. He himself, he added, had a heart ailment, but his stomach troubles were almost cured. His doctor, Max Schur, had not visited, but a medically qualified patient of his, Ruth Mack Brunswick, was looking after his health instead. And Freud concludes this motley bulletin with the disarming words: "I am only reporting, true to my promise, as a reliable chronicler."[1]

It was now almost a year since Freud had begun his final "chronicle." Reading it, we are faced with something much like his letter report to Anna—a strange jumble of disparate events. No distinction is made between the trivial and the momentous. In addition to visits and meetings, it documents Freud's health and that of the people around him, family affairs, political events, deaths, anniversaries, celebrations, work and holidays, the growth of his antiquities collection. And apart from this regular miscellany, now and then an odd event intrudes, such as a dream or the sighting of a Zeppelin. In effect, this journal presents an unexpected side of Freud—Freud the reporter. (At this period the daily newspaper Freud read, the *Neue Freie Presse*, included a section entitled "Small Chronicle"—*Kleine Chronik*—a medley of miscellaneous news items).

But more importantly, the title he gave his diary had significant personal connotations, for this was not Freud's first "chronicle." In 1882 he became engaged to Martha Bernays. During their long engagement they decided to keep a joint record—their *Secret Chronicle (Geheime Chronik)*. It was begun in January 1883, when both were living in Vienna, and it was meant to be both a substitute for the letters they would otherwise have written and a record for future times. Written by each in turn, it was " . . . a combination of diary and self-confession."[2]. Apparently their intention was to destroy all their love letters (and a diary Freud kept of that period) on their wedding day and to keep this "chronicle" alone as the authoritative record of that period of their lives.[3] But by January 10, 1884, when Martha was back in her native Hamburg, Freud was complaining that the diary had been abandoned because "one of them" had failed to keep their side of it going.[4]

There is no evidence of Freud keeping any sort of diary during the early years of married life that followed the end of the "Secret Chronicle." Other records document his life through much of the 1890s, above all an intimate correspondence with his friend, the Berlin nose specialist Wilhelm Fliess. (The correspondence covers 1887 to 1904 and was at its most intense from 1892 to 1902.) At this period Freud was sifting his experience through his pioneering self-analysis. Both his correspondence and his scientific writing played a part in this process. He had also begun recording his dreams for *The Interpretation of Dreams*. There was probably no space left in his life for any sort of personal

Newspaper report, October 29, 1928. *Graf Zeppelin* crosses the Atlantic.

Martha Bernays at the time of her engagement to Freud, c.1883.

journal, either now or during the intensely busy years up to World War I. A passage in the *Psychopathology of Everyday Life* (1901) does, it is true, refer to " . . . a sheet of paper containing short daily notes mainly of a business kind . . . ." But this sounds more like an account book than a diary.[5]

The war restricted travel and social life and fragmented Freud's family. These may be some of the reasons for the next "diary." In 1916, when all three of his sons were away fighting and one of his daughters was in distant Hamburg, Freud occasionally jotted notes on family or current affairs in a set of mass-produced calendar books called *Prochaskas Familien-Kalender*.[6] In style and content the entries have a great deal in common with the final chronicle of 1929-39. Death is in the background of these earlier notes, too, both the universal slaughter of the war and the possibility that Freud's three sons might be killed. Not only these deaths, but Freud's own, since he had a superstitious premonition he would die in February 1918.[7]

When he abandoned his "family-calendar books" in December 1918 he had survived that date—and his sons had survived the war. But when, in 1929, he took up the final chronicle, death was even closer. He was now seventy-three years old and living under a deferred sentence of death, either from cancer or heart trouble. There may be more than a hint of this in the diary's title: "Shortest" may well refer to more than just the brevity of the entries. After his cancer had been diagnosed in 1923, Freud was given five more years to live.[8] By 1929 six years had passed. There was no telling how short his chronicle might be.

That is one descriptive aspect of the title. But it is also prescriptive. The extreme brevity of the entries signals Freud's refusal to report more than the absolute minimum about his own affairs. His attitude on that matter may have been summed up elsewhere, in the epigraph to another history (*History of the Psychoanalytical Movement*) where he quotes a Goethe couplet as epigraph: "Mach es kurz / Am Jüngsten Tag ist's nur ein Furz."[9] ("Make it short/On Doomsday it's just a fart")

The chronicle would be brief because it was written against the background of a last judgment. As far as Freud was concerned Doomsday was not too distant. From 1929 on he was living beyond his predicted end. In that sense this "shortest chronicle" was a posthumous record even as it was being written. But we might be misled into taking its flat objectivity as a sign of detachment from human affairs. In fact, the entries themselves point toward an engrossing and engaged life. They must be read as signposts directing our attention elsewhere, toward other evidence.

The general question, why Freud chose to keep this diary, remains unanswered. Was it simply to "mark time?" What then of the blanks? A chronicler should be obsessive and on the evidence of this diary Freud was far from that. Sometimes illness accounts for the lack of entries; mostly there is no clear reason and one can only assume either that the record was filled in haphazardly and according to the whim of the moment, or that a covert system underlies the entries, and only certain categories of event are included.

Perhaps we can best find out what types of event are noted by examining a few entries in greater detail. I have taken the month of October 1935 as a random sample:

Mon [Tues]* 1.10.1935   Large Kannon
This first entry refers to a new addition to Freud's collection of antiquities. A *"Kannon"* or *"Kuan-yin"* is a figure of the Bodhissatva of Compassion, in meditation, its eyes closed. This object, now in the Freud Museum, takes its place among a growing group of Buddhist figurines acquired during the 1930s. Beyond its intrinsic interest as an antiquity, it could also serve as a source of speculation—on Buddhism and Nirvana and their connection with Freud's concept of the death drive.

Tues [Wed]* 2.10.1935   Beginning of war in Abyssinia
This political entry might appear remote from Freud's immediate interests. But

Freud, 1925.

The large Kannon, acquired on October 1, 1935. WK

---

* Freud gives the first two days of this month incorrectly, probably as a result of filling in the entries at a later date.

Mussolini's distant colonial war had a direct bearing on Austrian affairs. During the 1934 general strike in Austria, it was only Mussolini's intervention that had prevented a German Nazi invasion of Austria. The more he now became involved overseas, with Germany's collusion, the less likely he would be to protect Austria in the future. (And incidentally, we might also wonder here about the lack of another political entry around this period. There is no mention in the diary of the antisemitic "Nuremberg laws," passed only two weeks earlier in Germany.)

Thurs 10.10.1935   Subtleties of a Faulty Action
The entry directs us to Freud's paper of this title and to the autobiographical episode it describes. The essay tells of a gift of an antique ring for Dorothy Burlingham (whose birthday was the following day) and of Freud's own interpretation of a slip of the pen he made while writing the gift note; afterwards Anna added her own interpretation to Freud's.

Fri 11.10.1935   Pichler operation
This is the eleventh operation since the beginning of the chronicle and the fourth that year. These grim figures are some indication of the torture Freud endured during this period.

Sun 13.10.1935   Thornton Wilder
The visit by the American writer is documented both in Freud's own letters and Wilder's diaries. Their meeting was the occasion for a fascinating discussion on literature and psychoanalysis that ranged from Franz Werfel to James Joyce.

Wed 16.10.1935   Mathilde 48 yrs.
This is the birthday of Mathilde Hollitscher, Freud's eldest child, who lived with her husband around the corner from the Freud family. Freud was seriously concerned over her illhealth that year.

Fri 18.10.1935   Berggasse
Berggasse 19 was Freud's address in Vienna. The entry designates the Freud family's return from their regular six months' summer residence in a villa in the Viennese suburb of Grinzing, and the resumption of their winter way of life.

Tues 22.10.1935   + Richard Wahle
Like any other deaths, that of the philosopher Richard Wahle necessarily implies memories. Wahle belonged to a group of Freud's friends who met in the Cafe Kurzweil in the early 1880s, before Freud's marriage. One of Wahle's brothers, Fritz, was in love with Martha and had thus aroused Freud's frantic jealousy.

Mon 28.10.1935   Autobiographical Study
The final entry this month registers Freud's receipt of the English translation of his book, *An Autobiographical Study*. The book was first published in German as part of a series devoted to the life and work of scientists. The series aimed to present the author's own view of the relation between his life and work—and no more. In the postscript Freud wrote to this English translation in January 1935, he states, however, that the story of his life and the history of psychoanalysis are "intimately interwoven."[10]

That statement brings us to the question: what new aspects of Freud's life and work may be revealed in this diary? Glancing through these entries for October 1935, we see that they refer to a wide range of topics—Freud's collection of antiquities, world and national politics, his own writing and publications, illnesses, visitors, family birthdays and domestic affairs, deaths. Some of these have already been recorded in biographies or histories of the period, others have remained unknown or obscure.

But there is a vital difference between this diary and any other sources. This is Freud's own view of the times, in which he has noted those events that seemed to him of importance. Each entry, therefore, has a dual significance—its historical value as news in its own right and its autobiographical implications. Taken overall, the entries present us with a curious weave of impressions. One side of the pattern shows us Freud in history, the other

A small room at Berggasse 19, scene of innumerable consultations and minor operations. EE

View of the desk. NB

side gives us something even more fascinating—a view of history in progress through Freud's eyes.

II: " . . . the language in which one lived and thought . . . "

The paradox of this "*Shortest Chronicle*" is the apparent absence of the familiar Freud the writer, the subtle intelligence behind the published works. There is no sign of that elaborate language here, all we have is a chronological series of words and phrases. The reason is that in its writing Freud did not have to take any outside reader into account.

But the exclusion is not absolute, for the diary was not written in cipher or kept secret; it lay open on Freud's desk. To his family, at least, it spoke of their history. For that particular readership, explanations were not necessary, since they were to be found in their own social lives or those of their visitors, in the antiquities and library, in the surrounding world. Such are the areas of experience that may begin to speak to us through this diary—if we listen with empathy.

Beyond the bald facts we catch frequent glimpses into Freud's family and social concerns. The diary itself may seem off-center to thoughts or emotions, yet it constantly directs attention toward that inner life. There are implicit meditations in the anniversaries and the deaths of old friends; newly acquired antiquities point towards the contemplative silence of the collection; notes on the dogs evoke their companionship during these years; the pleasure Freud took in young children's company lies behind grandchildren's names.

Various unwritten stories emerge from the margins of this diary. Where possible, I have tried to write some of them, either briefly within a single annotation or woven through a number of annotations over the years, so that they can be reconstructed as one reads. If an entry can be explained in Freud's own words, or those of another participant, I have quoted directly wherever necessary. In doing so I have made the most of all the unpublished or little-known material to which I have had access at the Freud Museum. As will be seen from the photographs, I have also used the collection to illustrate the numerous references to antiquities. Where no direct evidence for a specific incident can be found, I have tried to give general information about personalities or issues which might give background to the entry. Inevitably there is sometimes an element of conjecture, and some notes will be far more informative than others.

Apart from all the incidental episodes and parallel lives, there is one overwhelming story that does eventually develop of its own accord. This is the advance of Nazism and the Freuds' emigration. If the diary had been a work of fiction, it could hardly have displayed more craft as far as the construction of that particular "plot" is concerned. After mundane beginnings, the desultory preoccupations of an old man—medical care and sickness, card games, worries about the state of the international psychoanalytical publishing house, visits of acquaintances—it begins registering political drumbeats in the background, and these gradually rise to the crescendo of 1938. By then all the dispersed themes have come together in Freud's penultimate act, the struggle to get out of a trap which had snapped shut. And after the dramatic escape, a last act or coda brings about the fulfilment of a childhood wish to live in England and the adult wish "to die in freedom."[1]

When Freud was an infant, his two half-brothers emigrated to Manchester. As a young man Freud visited them and was impressed by England. But for all his links with the country, for all his anglophilia and deep knowledge of the language and literature, there remained a snag. A few days after emigration, on June 11, 1938, Freud wrote to the French psychoanalyst Raymond de Saussure: " . . . perhaps you missed out the one point which the emigrant experiences so particularly painfully. It is—one can only say: the loss of the language in which one lived and thought and which one will never be able to replace with another, for all one's efforts at empathy. With painful comprehension I observe how otherwise familiar terms of expression fail me in English and how It [*Es*] even

View over the desk. NB

Through the study, London. NB

tries to resist giving up the familiar Gothic script."[2]

The "It" Freud refers to in this last sentence is the Id, the term he had adopted to describe unconscious forces. Here, therefore, he presents the strange phenomenon of his unconscious balking at Latin script. Yet much of the chronicle from 1929 onward is written in that script. When writing Gothic it was the convention that names of places and proper names were written in Latin script. Consequently the diary is an unforced mixture of the two alphabets. Curiously, even in its limited register, there are small reflections of the "exile from language" Freud complained of to de Saussure. The German invasion, the beginning of Austria's dark age, is marked by a Latin epitaph—'Finis Austriae." (This catch phrase is overloaded with implications: it buries an entire country and culture, as if there were nothing more to be said, while at the same time it seems to offer the bleak consolation of a universal perspective on miserable times.) And on 10 November 1938—the infamous "*Kristallnacht*" attack on Jews and their property—Freud simply writes "Pogroms in Germany" in English, as if he were a foreign reporter distanced even from the native language of those unspeakable events.

However, the diary continues after that date in German, it does not switch to English. The final page and year, it is true, seems to be making a very half-hearted attempt to change languages. For 1939 most of the months and a few days are written in English. But that is all. Even at this minimal level of utterance, the inertia of the native language prevails. Written or spoken, words still carry too much hidden weight to be nonchalantly transposed.

The question of the native language that Freud broaches in the de Saussure letter goes beyond simple language ability. Freud's English was excellent. He had been reading it all his life; he corresponded and frequently analyzed in the language. Yet there was still an inner distance to be overcome. It was one of the most sensitive of his patients, the poet H.D., who recalled the disparity between the acquired and the native language: "He might have been talking Greek. The beautiful tone of his voice had a way of taking an English phrase or sentence out of its context (out of the associated context, you might say, of the whole language) so that, although he was speaking English without a perceptible trace of accent, yet he was speaking a foreign language."[3]

H.D.'s analysis began in March 1933. By that time the majority of Freud's analyses had long been with English or American patients. Already in 1921, when he was seeing nine analysands a day, six of them were English-speaking.[4] The chronicle is not a work diary, so these patients remain unmentioned, apart from those with whom he also had some sort of social contact, such as Dorothy Burlingham, Edith Jackson or Mark and Ruth Brunswick. The need for foreign patients was dictated by the unstable Austrian economy after World War I and the high value of hard currency. Long before politics drove Freud into exile, economics imposed a foreign language on him in his working life.

Even apart from that, like most educated inhabitants of the Austro-Hungarian Empire, Freud had lived a polyglot life. As an infant he heard Slovak as well as German around him; as a 16-year-old boy he and his friend Eduard Silberstein taught themselves Spanish and corresponded in the language; he corresponded in English with his Manchester relatives and translated John Stuart Mill into German; studied in Paris and translated Charcot from French; spoke Italian on trips to Italy. But evidently he never felt entirely *himself* in these various languages.

Also, there were the dead languages. School had given Freud Latin and Greek. In a short essay on his schooldays, Freud wrote in 1914 that the culture of antiquity was to be " . . . an unsurpassable consolation in the battles of life . . . ."[5] Like the collection of antiquities, they offered rest, refuge and encouragement—a sort of posthumous perspective on present times. Their "consolation" is analogous to that of dispassionate knowledge, the "life-in-death" of the scientific viewpoint.

But how much has language to do with this "*Shortest Chronicle?*" The diary is, basically, a skeletal grid of isolated words. On the one hand, that fact tells us something significant about the writer's intentions. Freud has chosen the most objective notation possible to record these years. His decision to keep a type of

"She is perfect . . . only she has lost her spear. . . ." The Athena Freud showed H.D. NB

Egyptian stelae from the collection. NB

ledger report represents a refusal of elaborated speech—and of the wider social relationship it implies. The bare "scientific" data connect directly with the lived experience of the reader - if that reader happens to be Freud himself or his family. We outsiders are bypassed. It is not a question of intrusion or secrecy, simply that we have not been taken into account. Because of the lack of backgrounding, there may be a risk of leaning too heavily on the sparse material for clues about Freud's thought and of ignoring the actual point of the diary, which is his everyday life.

In his letter to de Saussure, Freud speaks of living and thinking in a language. This chronicle is a lived record, not a literary creation. Perhaps it should remind us of the obvious, that Freud also lived *outside* the specific consciousness that a literary style evokes. To some extent, events themselves have produced this script, such as it is. Everything it records made some sort of an impression on the writer. The diary remains as a verbal residue of memories, a sort of halfway house between the experience and the full consciousness of elaborated language.

In the summer of 1938 Freud sketched his *Outline of Psycho-Analysis*, an unfinished summary of his life's work. As always, he was concerned that psychoanalysis should be treated as a science and he drew parallels between the nature of psychoanalytical observation and that of the physical sciences. In the end, he stated, reality is unknowable: in both physics and psychoanalysis " . . . everything new that we have inferred must be translated back into the language of our perceptions . . . ."[6]

In this analogy, the experience of reality is seen as an act of translation. That schema may be applied to these diary notes. We may read them as one of Freud's many translations of his experience. This language is more primitive than that of the other writings because it translates a different set of perceptions. This is a world of physical and social phenomena—illnesses, people coming and going, objects or books appearing. It is a perspective on time passing; not so much a language in which one could live or think as a first draft for Freud's own history of the times.

III: *"The Curve of Life"*

Twelve days before beginning the chronicle, on October 19, 1929, Freud wrote to Ernest Jones from the Tegel sanatorium in Berlin, where he was undergoing treatment: "The periodic differences between holiday and work are fast disappearing for me behind the slowly and steadily increasing decline of the curve of life. I think I can claim the right to rest."[1]

During the first two years of the diary, Freud marked his moves to summer residences or to Berlin with a red or blue crayon line in the margin. Thus, he could see these "periodic differences" at a glance. This practice was abandoned in 1932. From then on until 1938 Freud's annual cycle settled into a regular pattern—six summer months spent on the outskirts of Vienna and six winter months at home in Berggasse.

The diary may not chart Freud's conscious or intellectual life in close detail, nor does it display Freud as a "personality," but it does give us a visible chronology that represents the rhythms of his life during his final decade. To keep a diary is to mark time. In one sense, this means that the register of events constitutes a base line, or constant, to which we return daily. By writing a new entry, repeating yet not repeating, we assure ourselves of a minimum of continuity in our lives. In another sense, it is the words we write that actually divide one day from another.

In his letter to Jones, Freud mentioned his right to rest, and not for the last time. During the 1930s he often spoke of abandoning his therapeutic work and devoting himself to writing. But it was the analysands, primarily the foreign ones, who brought in the essential income for himself and his dependants. Although the average number of patients levelled out at four or five, Freud continued work

Freud looking at the roses, Pötzleinsdorf, summer 1931.

Notes on the nature of sex and death drives, 1918.

until the very end. It was not until August 1939 that he was finally forced to stop. If, in 1929, the difference between work and rest was disappearing, this was partly because his treatment of patients overlapped into holiday periods.

But on a more basic level, the "rest" he spoke of to Jones denotes release from tension and "the most universal endeavour of all living substances—namely to return to the quiescence of the inorganic world."² This was a formulation of his disputed "death drive." The death Freud reclaimed for theory was one thing, another was the real death he claimed as his right. Both are in some way a continuum in the background of this last, and longest, chronicle.

The diary begins with the return to Vienna in late October 1929, marking a return to the old surroundings and a resumption of the old work. But this period also brought Freud a sense that his creative life was now over and his actual life rapidly approaching its end. A scientist is bound by the duty of recording events objectively. In the chronicle he could at least tabulate the stages of his own inevitable decline. Perhaps even fight against it? The numerous mistakes in dating over the first full month seem to indicate that those dates, and possibly the attached entries, were filled in at some later period. If entries were indeed sometimes filled in at the end of a month or a week, or even a few days after the event, then the act of writing them down would have served to exercise and test memory. This activity would be a form of "anamnesis"—the recalling of memories, which is the foundation of psychoanalysis.

Whatever the case, the diary starts out, apparently, as a predominantly personal record. But only a week after its beginning came violent "*antisemitic disturbances.*" That ominous entry was the first one not to be directly concerned with Freud's own life. For a full year there are no more such intrusions from outside. Then Freud reports the elections of November 1930. After that, public events begin encroaching—at first distantly, as in the entry "*Republic in Spain*" on April 15, 1931, then nearer home with "*Putsch in Styria*" on September 13, 1931, until finally the entry "*Burning in Berlin*" on May 11, 1933, shows all hope of a purely private life going up in flames.

One could say it was not the diary which changed its private nature, but the state of the world that intruded more and more into Freud's—and everybody else's—personal lives. In this respect, this presents a reliable graph of those dark times. Nor is it surprising it should have been started the moment Freud completed *Civilization and its Discontents*—the book that raises the question of whether civilization can control its self-destructive forces. As a largely domestic and personal record, the diary looks like the antithesis of that universal cultural survey—or like a modest reaction to the violence and aggression he had examined. Whether seen as sequel or shadow of *Civilization and its Discontents*, it inevitably parallels its central theme, the struggle that each individual supposedly reflects, between libido and death drive, Eros and Thanatos.

That opposition could be restated in more mundane terms. One could regard this "chronicle" as a sort of balance sheet. On the face of it, we have nothing more than a record of disparate events, an *aide-mémoire*. But it is also possible to read that record as a statement of accounts. For instance, each anniversary, each birthday, seems to mark a credit for life; on the debit side are all the crosses (signifying death) against names of old friends and acquaintances. Troubles with the psychoanalytical publishing house are weighed against the steady flow of works appearing in foreign translation; the painful sequence of operations and illnesses is balanced against the growth of the antiquities collection.

The prospect of death may be the beginning of other lists, too, since it is a reason for drawing up accounts. For example, exactly six years before the start of the diary and just before the radical operation on his jaw, Freud drafted a will. And a few days later, on November 5, 1923, he began a systematic list of the translations of his works and continued to update it until 1935. Many of the translations are also listed in the diary, hence the two records overlap.

That was not the only parallel record Freud was keeping during the 1930s. He also kept a register of letters received and sent. The only pages of this listing to have survived relate to 1938-39, the period in England. They show how meticulously he kept track of his mail and how rapidly he responded to letters.

Pötzleinsdorf where Freud spent summer 1931 and 1932.

Oskar Rie, died September 17, 1931.

Sándor Ferenczi, died May 22, 1933.

This conscientious register is in Freud's hand until August 27, 1939, and then continues in Anna Freud's hand until September 15, a week before his death. Yet another parallel record is found in a small notebook in which he listed his patients, marking off the number of hours and the amount of payment due. A further notebook lists visitors in England. From June 1938 to May 1939 more than 100 names are recorded in it, a number of them strangers or casual visitors, and less than a tenth of these names, (presumably the most significant of the guests), feature in the chronicle.

All these lists serve a clear purpose. They are ways Freud kept track of his work and social life. In the context of this dispersed documentation, the "chronicle" is a sort of "list of lists," bringing together aspects of all the others. Hence the intersections. The other listings are merely automatic registers, whereas the diary is the trace of a mind selecting, or excluding, items of experience. It also displays apparently arbitrary or inconsistent features. For example, again and again it reports arrivals of guests without any corresponding departure (or vice versa); visitors, birthdays or anniversaries are omitted; entire weeks left unrecorded. After 1930, the first complete year and the best recorded, the mean number of entries declines to average out at only 79 days per year recorded. Yet, despite these irregularities, the record was never totally abandoned. This fact alone argues that it answered some constant need, for it continues steadily, if sporadically, until within a month of the very end.

And far beyond Freud's predicted end. Ever since his early 40s he had been trying to calculate his life expectancy, according to biorhythms, heredity or superstition. Now cancer and old age had reduced the odds. The sheer fact of continued survival arouses the only exclamation marks in the entire record— '81yrs!' and "Mother would have been 100!." (Freud's father had died at $81\frac{1}{2}$; consequently it was the age at which he, too, might expect to die.) The curve of his life is charted on a grid, whose visible axis is regular calendar time, the other, hidden one, is constructed from the secret periodic forces by which we are governed. Between these two axes, the diary notes plot Freud's life in terms of achievements, acquisitions and anniversaries on the one hand, deaths, diseases and deprivations on the other. And behind each entry, even the most banal, one can hear an underlying refrain—"I have survived."

The curve Freud spoke of in his letter to Jones was an abstraction—the idea of life as a geometrical line. But the details of a life form their own patterns. It would be a mistake to read the chronicle as a single line of events or even as a closed system. If it is to be visualized schematically, it should, at the very least, be seen as a series of interwoven curves. Some of them are partly plotted by other documents, such as the correspondences or the parallel lists that also chart his activities during this time. This "chronicle" is a miscellany, but it is not random. As I have indicated, it only includes particular types of events. Internal evidence also shows that sometimes entries were filled in retrospectively. This means that events and people have already been sieved through memory, many to be excluded or censored out. Therefore, this is not anything as innocent as a direct, unmediated account. Each entry has been weighed and only those of a certain importance are registered.

With that in mind, it is worth noting how frequently various names are mentioned in the diary. Not surprisingly, it is Anna's name which absolutely dominates the record, for it was during these years of sickness that she became Freud's constant companion, his "faithful Anna-Antigone"[3]. The following list includes the only personal names that occur more than ten times:—Moses (12), Oliver (12), Mathilde (12), Martha (13), Ernstl (13), Pichler (20), Eitingon (20), Minna (22), Ernst (26), Princess (28), Martin (28), Anna (49).

Leaving aside the "fictional" Moses, all but the surgeon Hans Pichler, Max Eitingon and Princess Marie Bonaparte are family members. Pichler had saved Freud's life, his continuing care was a basic necessity. Eitingon and the Princess were devoted heart and soul both to Freud and to the cause of psychoanalysis: their role outside the family was symmetrical with Martin and Anna's within it, both of whom were likewise involved in the business

Visitor list, 1939.

Freud's mother with his sister Mitzi.

"Anna-Antigone" and her father.

affairs of the psychoanalytical movement and the publishing house. Martha, Minna and Mathilde formed the female core of the family. Ernst, like Martin, helped with practical affairs, Oliver and Ernstl were to some degree cast in the role of dependants. Thus the main "dramatis personae" form a fascinating network of functions and interdependent relationships around Freud's central absent-presence.

Even such a concise "diary-chronicle" as this cannot evade the peculiarities of individual consciousness. As one reads, one becomes aware that a very specific set of contacts with the world is being charted. Even the most physically "internal"—the cancer and prosthesis, the heart and stomach upsets—are transmuted into social events, calling for consultations with Freud's small retinue of doctors and specialists. It is as if the entries mapped the no-man's-land between his own intimate life and his public face.

In this respect the diary can even be read as a sort of psychological document. We can then ask questions about its choices. Why, for instance, is "*Mrs Gunn with Egyptian antiquity*" recorded on June 25, 1938, but not H. Loewenstein or Malinowski (the names Freud recorded before and after that of Mrs. Gunn, on his visitors' list for that period)? Was it because neither of them brought such a desirable gift? Why is the "Princess" (who probably accompanied Malinowski) only mentioned in the diary, not the visitors' list? Or, the following month, what was the nature of Mr. Kent's business, that he should be recorded, whereas neither the old friend Wolf Sachs nor the old antagonist Melanie Klein (who both appear next to Kent on the list) are mentioned? And why is Chaim Waizmann omitted, though Martin Freud said his father greatly enjoyed his visit? And why is the visit by some Jewish scientists on November 7, 1938, also absent—yet "*Pogroms in Germany*" a few days later are recorded? Historians and psychoanalysts will be able to collate this record against Freud's life as known from other sources and they will certainly be able to draw new conclusions about him from the comparison.

But perhaps such a "psychological reading" goes against the grain of the material? After all, a "chronicle" claims to be an objective historical record. Strictly speaking a personal chronicle is a contradiction in terms. The source of the word chronicle is *chronos*, time itself. And in Freud's diary, individuals feature mainly in terms of their birthdays, anniversaries and deaths. Mental activity as such is not part of the picture. Instead, we are given human beings in their relation to the passing of time.

In the context of time and change, the antiquities Freud mentions are of special significance. What is noticeable is that the new acquisitions were by no means all Greek, Roman and Egyptian. Two "Kannons," three Buddhas, Chinese camels, horses, figurines and various jade pieces, a statuette of Vishnu—all point to a growing oriental collection during this period. At the same time, psychoanalysis was spreading eastward. Japanese is the most frequently mentioned foreign language in the diary; Japanese translations were flooding in and Japanese psychologists coming to Europe to study. It was with one of them, Yaekichi Yabe, that Freud discussed *Beyond the Pleasure Principle* in the late evening of May 7, 1930. During the discussion Yabe spoke of affinities between the death drive and Buddhism. Freud was so struck by this comment that he called Anna from the next room to come and hear these words.[4]

This meeting with Yabe, and the Buddhist figures Freud acquired during the 1930s, are both, therefore, reminders of an important speculative aspect of his later work, the disputed "death drive." That concept had first appeared in 1920, in *Beyond the Pleasure Principle*. Freud had initially adopted the term "the Nirvana Principle" to describe a basic principle of psychical life, namely the effort to reduce or remove internal tensions. In different ways the sex and death drives both work in the service of this "principle of constancy."

Marie Bonaparte, Anna Freud, and Max Eitingon.

Showcase of Egyptian antiquities in Freud's study. NB

This level of Freud's thought is not as distant from the diary as might at first appear. The most abstract speculation is grounded in mundane existence. In the simple activity of recording events chronologically, one is, by

Two Tang-style camels from the collection. NB

implication, linking concrete fact with the most abstruse and elusive idea of all—the notion of time. In effect a "chronicle" is time made visible. In *The Mystic Writing Pad* (1925), Freud showed that jotting notes (on a child's toy writing block) could even become a model for the nature of perception. He depicted our perception/consciousness system as continually "sending out feelers" to the external world and withdrawing them, thus producing a momentary impression. Freud saw the discontinuous nature of these "jottings" as the origin of our concept of time.[5] The imprint that is left in the mind, the memory trace, replaces the "moving finger" of consciousness.

This streak of "metapsychological speculation" continued to figure in Freud's writing during the 1930s. It emerges explicitly in some notes he made in 1938. On August 22, he wrote: "Space may be the projection of the extension of the psychical apparatus. No other derivation is probable. Instead of Kant's *a priori* determinants of our psychical apparatus. Psyche is extended; knows nothing about it." A further note with the same date, and as if to complement the previous one, states: "Mysticism is the obscure self-perception of the realm outside the ego, of the id."[6]. Like the previous hypothesis on the nature of time, this speculation about space is a response to the philosophy of Immanuel Kant. Kant set up time and space as the final objective coordinates of perception. Freud stands that structure on its head. Instead he presents time and space as effects of the act of perception. Thus experience is granted primacy over metaphysical abstractions.

The diary provides us with a link between Freud's own experience of the world and his work. It shows, for example, that the above note on the nature of space was written just after he had visited his new house in London for the first time. The same group of notes includes one that returns us to the theme of the death drive: "The individual perishes from his internal conflicts . . . ."[7] This was noted on July 20, 1938. From the diary, we find that on July 17, 1938, three days earlier, Freud had drawn up his final will, and that, on July 28, eight days later, it was signed.

Such correspondences are intriguing, though it would be risky to try to draw any facile conclusions from them. When Freud's death drive was first published, people ascribed it to the effect of his daughter Sophie's death. Freud made it clear that, however attractive that inference was, it was false, for the concept had been developed while she was still alive. It is not always possible to demonstrate causative links between single incidents in the diary and other aspects of Freud's life and work. But the record as a whole may be seen as a reliable chart of his dying years.

In this diary Freud was tracing the declining curve of his own life. His image of a geometric curve conjures up the idea of a graph, and of a life plotted between the axes of advancing time and gradually diminishing energy. That would be the mathematical viewpoint. But in terms of immediate experience, the curve may be reduced to its lowest common denominator—a single perception, an isolated entry in the diary. From this point of view, time and space become, as Freud hinted, vast extrapolations of our mode of perception. Their origin is the single point that forms the curve on this imagined graph, the fleeting moment of consciousness—"a fact without parallel, which defies all explanation or description . . . ."[8]

IV: "This Bit of Good Luck"

The diary begins a week after the Wall Street Crash, it ends a week before the outbreak of World War II. Between these two points fascist and totalitarian regimes had taken over much of Europe. The declining curve of Freud's life coincided with a collapse of European civilization. He was denied a calm background to his final years. Even if we wish to regard this diary as a distanced record, it is too painful on a purely personal level to read dispassionately. One operation succeeds another, the list of illnesses and complaints lengthens. This

Jottings on time and perception, 1918. "Concept formation makes discontinuity from continuity, conversely to time & space."

Sophie, the daughter who died in 1920.

Earth-touching Buddha. Figure from Freud's collection. NB

"chronicle" is also—to borrow the name of another medieval genre—a "Book of Dying."

Its times were catastrophic. Looking back on the Nazi period, Europeans run the risk of extracting it from history and seeing it as a unique irruption of evil. There is even a spurious consolation in this view—that there can be no return to such depths. Freud's own perspective was risky in another sense. What he saw developing had all happened before and would happen again. It was his very distance from political affairs, his cultural pessimism, that deprived him of a reliable yardstick to assess the unprecedented aspects of the German situation. How near he and his family came to the concentration camps as a result of his obstinacy in disregarding warnings should not be forgotten. Nor should it be forgotten that four of his sisters were murdered in the camps.

At the eleventh hour, when flight was inevitable, Freud disbanded the Vienna Psychoanalytical Society. At its final board meeting on March 13, 1938, he told the members that they would do what Rabbi Johanan ben Zakkai had done after the destruction of the Temple in Jerusalem by the Emperor Titus. The rabbi had fled to the town of Jabneh; there he had continued the Jewish traditions by opening a Torah school. Freud's use of this story was a self-consciously historical gesture—a counterpart to the magisterial image projected by his scowling, official portrait photographs.

This was one role he was playing. But there were other self-images apart from that "public relations" version. One of these emerges in an endearing anecdote recorded by Freud's nephew, the poet Ernst Waldinger. On finally receiving his emigration papers in May 1938, Freud apparently called out " . . . gaily, with a whiff of recollection of the folk-lore of his childhood: 'Now I'm Hans im Glück!' "[1]

When he emigrated in June 1938, Freud's possessions remained behind for the time being in Vienna. The Nazi authorities had promised to send the household goods and furniture on afterwards, but one could hardly trust such promises. There was no guarantee that Freud would ever again see his library or collection. Like the character he refers to, the hero of the Grimms' tale *Hans in Luck* (*Hans im Glück*), he would arrive at his new home empty-handed, with no possessions to show for his long years of labor.

It is worth briefly summarizing this tale, since other references show it to be of particular significance. It runs as follows. Hans has finished his years of apprenticeship and is sent home by his master with a "lump of gold as big as his head" as payment. As he trudges homeward under the hot sun, the gold begins to weigh down more and more heavily and his tiredness grows. When he sees a man on a horse, he cannot resist bartering the gold for the horse. Happily he starts trotting back, but the horse is restive and throws him. A man leading a pig passes him as he lies ruefully by the roadside and he decides that a pork dinner would be a far better bargain than an unridable horse. But the pig also turns out to be unmanageable and is swapped for a goose . . . And so Hans' journey proceeds through a series of diminishing exchanges until he finally ends up with nothing but two stones, which he accidentally knocks into a well. And then runs home happily to his mother.

The story carried more than just "a whiff" of Freud's distant childhood, as Waldinger puts it. The Freuds' maid, Paula Fichtl, remembered it as one of the stories he would recite to his grandchildren. In his letters Freud compares his relief at finishing his work to Hans' joy at ridding himself of his possessions.[2] Most interestingly of all, one of his letters to his friend Sándor Ferenczi compares the Grimms' story to the practice of psychoanalysis. In analysis, Freud says, a piece of the infantile complex becomes the transference—emotions the patient discards and gives to the analyst like a shed skin. Freud adds: "Our therapeutic gain is a barter, as in the 'Hans im Glück' story. The last piece falls into the well only with death itself."[3] In the final phrase of this variant, the progress of psychoanalysis, and of "Hans in Luck," blends into an image of the journey toward death.

This diary, too, charts a journey toward a death. On the way, Freud, like Hans, gives away his treasures, both material and intellectual. And for all his terrible suffering, there remains in his life that vital element of "luck" or "happi-

Freud in London, summer 1938. His books and collection were still in Austria.

The study where Freud died in September 1939. NB

ness." (The German word *Glück* means both "happiness" and "luck".) "Happiness [*Glück*] is the deferred fulfillment of a prehistoric wish . . . " Freud once wrote to Wilhelm Fliess.[4] He felt himself to be a *Glückskind*—a lucky fellow—for he had struck gold, he had unearthed one of nature's secrets. When Freud recorded a broadcast for the BBC on December 7, 1938, he referred to his discovery of psychoanalysis as a "bit of good luck."[5]

The beauty of the Grimms' tale is that with each of Hans' payments, with each absurd barter as he becomes objectively poorer and poorer, his happiness grows. Like a holy fool or an infant, he reverses accepted standards and makes nonsense of the supposed joy of possession. The gold was a mere burden, the horse a liability—only his immediate appetites and the approach home bring Hans pleasure.

At first sight, this characteristic would seem to have little in common with Freud. After all, his achievement was, it seems, founded on self-discipline and self-denial, and, above all, on an immense capacity for work. But what was it that fuelled this drive? When his friend Ludwig Braun asked him that question, he replied: "When I sit down to write and take my pen in my hand, I am always curious what will then follow and that drives me imperatively on to work."[6]. The answer sounds mischievous. But it does not mean he simply let the works write themselves; on the contrary, the writer was too involved in the process of writing to stand aside and survey it. It was the final moment of abandoning the work that was the goal and reward of his laborious curiosity.

In its way this abbreviated chronicle could also be a by-product of the same curiosity and ignorance, but on a different time scale. Unaware of their significance at the time, Freud simply noted meetings and events so that he could later look back and fit them into some pattern. It was that overall pattern that concerned him, not his own feelings. If we desire the emotions and reactions to these events, we should bear in mind that, as in psychoanalysis, the events must first announce themselves. The reader should not, therefore, be surprised by the apparent absence of Freud the analyst and theoretician from this record. If the virtually toneless recording of events reminds us in some ways of a child's first diary, perhaps that impression should not be ignored. The writer—the naive but "reliable chronicler"—has recorded these years of life in this diary without commentary or criticism. This simplicity is both childlike and scientific. By plotting this graph of his last years, Freud was also, by default, sketching a diagrammatic self-portrait in time.

It was once suggested to Freud that psychoanalysis had made life a complicated puzzle. He responded: "Psychoanalysis simplifies life. Psychoanalysis supplies the thread that leads a man out of the labyrinth."[7] In the end the figure this diary depicts is not the labyrinthine self produced by time. It shows us something far more schematic, another faint trace of a creative force working through time. Its essence is the deceptively simple urge to record and discard. Its image is the *Glückskind*, the lucky fellow who achieved his greatest desire—to return to his origins empty-handed.

FOOTNOTES
(*See* NOTES & REFERENCES *for a key to the abbrevations.*)

INTRODUCTION.
1. Jones, III.239.
Clark, p.502.
Gay p.552.
Eissler, Kurt "Biographical Sketch" *in Pictures and Words* p.33.
Pictures and Words, p.271, N.311.
Martin Freud, p.205.

Part I: "A Reliable Chronicler."
1. *Freud-Anna Freud 19.9.1930* [FM] ("Ich berichte nur dem Versprechen getreu als verlässlicher Chronist.")
2. Jones, I.131.
3. Jones, I.109.
4. *Freud-Martha Bernays 10.1.1884* in *Letters*.
5. "The Psychopathology of Everyday Life," S.E., VI.116. These "business notes" may refer to the *Kassabuch* or account book, of which a page is reproduced in *Pictures and Words*, Pl.133, p.147.
6. *Prochaskas Familien-Kalender*. Like the manuscript of the *Kürzeste Chronik* (1929-1939), these books now form part of the Sigmund Freud Collection at the Library of Congress, Washington.
7. *Freud-Ferenczi 20.11.1917* in Jones, II.218.
8. Sterba, pp.115-6.

The penitent, walking Buddha. NB

9. "On the History of the Psychoanalytical Movement," *S.E.*, XIV.
10. "Postscript (1935)" *S.E.*, XX.71.

Part II: " . . . the language in which one lived and thought . . . '
1. *Freud-Ernst Freud 12.5.1938* in *Letters*.
2. *Freud-de Saussure 11.6.1938* [LoC] (" . . . vielleicht haben Sie den einen Punkt ausgelassen, den der Emigrant so besonders schmerzlich empfindet. Es ist—man kann nur sagen: der Verlust der Sprache in der man gelebt und gedacht hat und die man bei aller Mühe zur Einfühlung durch eine andere nie wird ersetzen können. Mit schmerzlichen Verständnis beobachte ich wie sich mir sonst vertraute Mittel des Ausdruckes im Englischen versagen, und wie Es sich sogar sträuben will, die gewohnte gothische Schrift aufzugeben.")
3. *H.D.* p.69.
4. *Freud-Ernst Freud 24.10.1921* [LoC]
5. "Some Reflections on Schoolboy Psychology," *S.E.*, XIII.241.
6. "An Outline of Psycho-Analysis," *S.E.*, XXIII.196.

Part III: "The Curve of Life'
1. *Freud-Jones 19.10.1929* [LoC] ("Die periodischen Unterschiede von Ferien und Arbeitszeit verschwinden bereits bei mir hinter der langsam und stetig fortschreitenden Senkung der Lebenscurve. Ich glaube ich habe ein Recht auf Ruhe.")
2. "Beyond the Pleasure Principle," *S.E.*, XVIII.62.
3. *Freud-Arnold Zweig 2.5.1935* in *Zweig Letters*.
4. Y. Yabe, *A Meeting with Professor Freud*, Typescript, p.11 [LoC] (Originally published in Japanese as appendix pp.1-19 in Vol. 5. of Freud's *Collected Works on Psychoanalysis*, Shunyodo Publishing Company, Tokyo, 1931).
5. "The Mystic Writing Pad," *S.E.*, XIX.231.
6. "Findings, Ideas, Problems," *S.E.*, XXIII.299-300.

Part IV: "This Bit of Good Luck'
1. Ernst Waldinger, "My Uncle Sigmund Freud," in *Books Abroad*,
Vol.15., No.1, Jan. 1941, p.4. (The anecdote of *Hans im Glück* does not feature in Jones's biography of Freud, but did appear in an earlier biography by Helen Puner Walker.)
2. Detlef Berthelsen, *Alltag bei der Familie Freud: Die Erinnerungen der Paula Fichtl*, Hamburg, 1987, p.52.
Freud-Martha Bernays 28.1.1884 in *Letters*.
'I am not yet free enough to experience entirely the blessedness of Hans in Luck. But that will come." (*Freud-Ferenczi 29.6.1918*) [FM] ("Ich bin noch nicht so frei, das selige Gefüls Hans im Glück ganz zu empfinden. Aber es wird kommen.")
3. *Freud-Ferenczi 10.1.1910* in Jones, II.496.
4. *Freud-Fliess 16.1.1898* in Masson.
5. *Freud 7.12.1938*, Transcript in Freud's handwriting of BBC talk [FM]. ("I started my professional activity as a neurologist, trying to bring relief to my neurotic patients. Under the influence of an older friend and by my own efforts I discovered some new and important facts about the Unconscious in psychic life, the role of instinctual urges and so on. Out of these findings grew a new science, Psycho-Analysis, a part of Psychology and a new method of treatment of the neuroses.

I had to pay heavily for this bit of good luck. People did not believe in my facts and thought my theories unsavoury. Resistance was strong and unrelenting. In the end I succeeded in acquiring pupils and building up an International Psycho-Analytic Association. But the struggle is not yet over.")
6. Hugo Knoepfmacher, "Zwei Beiträge zur Biographie Sigmund Freuds" in *Jahrbuch der Psychoanalyse*, Band XI, p.70.
7. *London Weekly Dispatch*, 28.7.1927 (Freud: Interview with George Viereck) [Transcription: LoC B28].

Attaché case on Freud's desk containing his diary and letter list. NB

1929	*Shortest Chronicle**
31 Oct	Passed over for the Nobel Prize
Sat 2 Nov.	First Tarock party—Visit Rickman
Tu 4 " "	at Schnitzler's with infected finger
We 5 "	Almanach
	Preface for Eitingon
Th 6	Kris and mounts—Flournoy
Fr 7	Antisemit. disturbances—Dioscori ring—
Mo 11	Neuralgia. Adda given away.
Tu 14	Heart warmth attack. Dr Altmann
Sa 16	Rothschild hospital, Anna's book
We 20	First evening Yvette
Th 21	At Yvette's hotel
Fr 22	Dedication Th. Mann. Second evening Yvette
	At Gottlieb's.
Sa 23	False alarm with Pichler
Mo 25	Adda fetched
Sa 30	Princess left, Eitingon's mother +

Tu 3 Dec.	Anna's birthday 34 yrs.
Sa 7 Dec.	Martin 40 yrs.
Sa 7–Tu 10	Bad heart days
We 11	Emerald ring
Th 12	Society evening.
Tu 17	Anna to Essen—cut stones bought
Sa 21	Anna back
Tu 24	Christmas—Eitingon "Discontents"
Fr 27	Pearls for Martha
Mo 30	Adda died

——————————————— 1930 ———————————————

Fr 3 Jan	Cigars from Landauer
Mon 6 Jan	Conference Martin—Drucker
Th 9 Jan	Society evening.
Fr & Sa 10 & 11	cut stones
We 15 Jan	Mounted terracotta figures arrived
Sa 18 Jan	Felix Wiener in N.Y. +
Th 16 Jan	Books from R. Rolland
Tu 21 Jan	Mrs. London, Gall attack
Fr 24 Jan	Schur. Museum. Acrobat bought

Mon 3 Feb	Visit Prof. Rojas B-Aires
Tu/Fr 6/7 Feb	Dream of Nestroy
Sa 8 Feb	Tom +
Su 9 Feb	Arnold Zweig
Th 13 Feb.	Evening with Alexander—Staub
Fr 14	Jade necklace for Anna. Hypnoanalysis
Sa 15	Egypt. half-bust.
Su 16	Ruth's birthday, opal necklace.
Mo 17	Margaretl's dead child, Roheim's book
Su 23	Mitzi in Vienna
We 26	Prof. Berman Cordoba Argent.
Fr 28	Dr Trebitsch & without prosthesis
	Eisinger about Angela

*For the German text see NOTES & REFERENCES.

1929

Kürzeste Chronik

31 Okt. in Hochzreis übergangen
So. 2 Nov. Erste Tarokpartie — Besuch Reikman
Di. 4 " " mit Augereiterung bei Schnitzler
Mi. 5 " Almanach für Eitingon
Do. 6 " Kris u. Montirungen. Flournoy
fr. 7 Antisemit. Unruhen – Dioscurenring –
Mo. 11 Neuralgie. Adda weggegeben
Do. 14 Herz-Darmanfall. Dr Altmann
Sa. 16 Rothschildspital. Anna's Buch
Mi. 20 Erster Abend Goethe
Do. 21 im Hotel bei Goethe. Goethe zweiter Abend
fr. 22 bei Widmung. Th. Mann.
Sa. 23 bei Gottlieb. bei Pichler
Mo. 25 blinder Lärm. Adda geholt. Eitingon's Mutter †
Sa. 30 Prinzessin abgereist.

Anna's Geburtstag 34 J.

Di. 3 Dez. Martin 40
Sa. 7 Dez. schlechte Herztage
Di. 10 Smaragdring
Sa. 7 — Vereinsabend. Heim gekauft
Mi. 11 Anna nach Essen – u. gestohlen
Do. 12 Anna zurück. Eitingon. Uebehagen
Di. 17 Weihnacht. – Martha
Sa. 21 Perlen für Martha
Di. 24 Adda gestorben
fr. 27
Mo. 30

1930. von Landauer

fr. 3 Jan. Reparatur Martin – Dracker
Mo. 6 Jan. Konferenz. Heim
Do. 9 Jan. Vereinsabend
Sa. 10 u. 11 gestohlen. Thonfiguren gekommen
Mi. 15 Jan Montirte
Sa. 18 Jan felix Wiener in R. Rolland
Do. 16 Jan Besuch von R. Gallenanfall
Di. 21 Jan aus London. Akrobat gekauft
fr. 24 Jan Schur. Museum.

Besuch Prof. Rosas B.-Aires

Mon 3 febr Traum von Nestroy
Do/fr 6/7 feb Tom †
Sa 8 febr Arnold Zweig
So 9 febr Abend mit Alexander – Staub
Do 13 febr Jadekette für Anna. Hypnoanalyse
fr 14 Aegypt. falbütza
Sa 15 Rieth Geburtstag. Opalkette
So 16 Margaret's todtes Kind. Rokeim's Buch
Mi 17 Mitzi in Wien
So 23 Prof Berman Cordoba Argent.
Mi 26 Prof Trebitsch u. ohne Prothese
fr 28 Singer über Abhgola

So 2 März. Konzeption Darmzustand
Di 4 M. Idde gekauft
Mi 5 M. Auftrag preuss. Kultusministeriums
So 9 M. Jo-Fi angekommen
Di 11 M. Ernst 16 Jahre
So 16 M } Joette
Mo 17 M }
Mitt 19 M Neue Vorlesungen. Verlag $1000
Do 20 M. Abend über Unbehagen
Di 25 M. Norwegische Vorlesungen
Mi 26 M Anna nach Bpest. Eitingon aus Paris
Do 27 M Anna zurück — Eitingon aus Paris
Fr 28 M Mela schwer erkrankt. Martha nach Berlin
Sa 29 M Lampe aus Bpest — bei Die
So 30 M $5000 Marton zum Ankauf

Mi 2 April Walter 9 Jahre
Do 3. " nächtlicher Herzanfall. Braun.
Sa 5/So 6 Bob operirt. Dr Hans Zweig
Mo 7 " Rob. Math. abgereist. Dr Stefan Zweig
Do 10 " Witz komposiert
Sa 12 Ferenczi über Sonntag. Prinzen abends
So 13 Martha zurück. Ferenczi. Illusion weg
Mo 14 Feder gebrochen. Anna u. Dorothy nach Paris
Die 15 Anna u. Dorothy zurück
Do 17.18. Anna " Caligula Sach 5 — Caligula
Fr 18. Cottage Sanator.
Di 22 Tabak abstinenz
Fr 25 Japan. übersetz. Jenseits, Lustprinz.
Mai Fr. 2 Zurück K. Sanator.
Sa 3 Ankunft in Tegel
Berlin Mo 5 14 Jahre
KU 6 Gabe aus Japan — Lederer 1 Besuch
Mi 7 Lederer 2 Besuch
Do 11 Operation an Prinzessin
Mi 14
Martha nach Kärnten
Besuch in Caputh. Bullitt
Sa 17 Max auf Besuch
So 25. Lederer 3 Besuch
Mo 26
Do 29 } Hiddensee
Sa 31 }

So 2 March	Congested intestinal condition
Tu 4 M.	Jade bought
We 5 M.	Inquiry of the Prussian Ministry of Culture.
Su 9 M.	Jo-Fi arrived
Tu 11 M.	Ernstl 16 yrs.
Su 16 M/ ⎫	
Mo 17 M. ⎭	Yvette
We 19 M.	New Lectures. Press $1000
Th 20 M.	Evening on Discontents
~~Tu 25 M.~~	~~Norwegian Lectures~~
We 26 M.	Anna to Bpest. Elkuss +
Th 27 M.	Anna back—Eitingon from Paris
Fr 28 M.	Mela fallen seriously ill.
Sa 29 M.	Martin to Berlin
Su 30 M.	Lajos on visit—At Rie's

We 2 April,	$5000 Martin for purchase
Th 3 April,	Walter 9 yrs.
Sa 5/Su 6	Nocturnal heart attack. Braun.
Mo 7	Bob operated. Dr Hans Zweig
Th 10	Rob, Math left. Dr Stefan Zweig
	Jokes in French
Sa 12	Ferenczi over weekend.
Su 13	Martha back, Ferenczi. Princess evening—
Mo 14	Spring broken. Illus. Russ.
Tu 15	Anna & Dorothy to Paris
Th 17	Anna & Dorothy back
Fr 18	Sachs—Caligula
Tu 22	Cottage Sanator.
Fr 25	Tobacco abstinence

May Fr 2	Japan. translation "Beyond Pleasure Principle."
Sa 3	Back fr. Sanator.
Berlin [in red] Mo 5	Arrival at Tegel
Th 6	74 yrs.
We 7	Yabe from Japan—Lederer 1 visit
Su 11	Lederer 2 visit
We 14	Operation on Princess
	Martha to Carinthia
Sa 17	Visit to Caputh—Bullitt.
So 25	Max on visit.
Mo 26	Lederer 3 visit
Th 29 ⎫	
Sa 31 ⎭	Hiddensee

June 1930	
We 4	Third visit to Lederer
Su 8	Robert Fliess
Fr 13	Mrs Mercedes—Renting on Grundlsee.
	Trude Hammerschlag +
Sa 14	Fourth visit Lederer
Tu 17	Dr Alexander
We 18	Dr Weinmann Minna's birthday
Fr 20	Dr Staub.
Sa 21	Lucie—Jackson & David B. dismissed.
	Zeppelin at night.
Tu 24	Max arrived, Dorothy left
We 25	Interpretation 8 ed.
Mo 30	Attack heart neuralgia with diarrhoea
July	
Tu 1	Last visit to Lederer. Royalties
	Interpretation divided
Th 3	Arnold Zweig—Goethe Prize turned up.
Fr 11	Liebman £20 Hogarth f. Discontents
Mo 14	Neuländer £81 Hogarth f. Collected Pap.
We 23	Parting fr. Schröder
[red line] Fr 25	Arrival in Vienna
[blue line] Su 27	Arrival in Grundlsee
Tu 29	Goethe Prize
August Sa 2	Visit Federn, Meng, Hollos
We 6	Mathilde arrived
Fr 8	at Ischl with Mother
Sa 16	F. Salten—Alex Sophie Harry
Su 17	Ischl with Mother B. 95 yrs.
Tu 19	Stands
Su 24	Dr Michel & Goethe Prize. Parting fr Mother
Mo 25	Mela Rie +
Th 28	Anna in Frankfurt
Fr 29	News Martin appendix. Anna
	back.
Sa 30	Math. left
Su 31	Simmel & Laforgue
Sept Tu 2	Sachs.
We 3	Bernfeld evening, Paquet also
Su 7	Eitingon, Simmel, Federn, Weinmann
Fr 12	+ Mother died 8 am
Su 14	Anna at mother's burial.
We 15	Anna left with Dorothy
Tu 16	Princess left
We 17	Dolfi arrived.
Th 18	Ernst & Jofi to Vienna. Eva moved in
[blue line] Su 28	Arrival in Vienna
Mo 29	Anna back. Dr Bondy
Th 30	X-ray with Schwarz

Juni 1930
Mi 4 — dritter Besuch bei Lederer
So 8 — Robert Fliess — Miete in Grundlsee
Fr 13 — Frau Mercedes — †
Trude Hammerschlag †
Sa 14 — Abschiedsbesuch Lederer
Di 17 — Dr Alexander — Minna's Geburtstag
Mi 18 — Dr Weinmann
Fr 20 — Fr Stross — Jackson. David b. entlassen
Sa 21 — Lucie —
Zeppelin nach St. Romu. Dorothy abgereist
Di 24 — Max aus Romu.
Mi 25 — Traumdeutung 8. Aufl. mit Diarrhoe
Mo 30 — Anfall Herzneuralgie. Honorar
letzter Besuch b. Lederer.
Juli
Di 1 — Traumdeutung bestellt
Do 3 — Arnold Zweig — Goethepreis aufgetaucht
Fr 11 — Liebman — Hogarth b. hubehagen
Mo 14 — Neulander — Hogarth f. collect. Pap.
Mi 23 — Abschied v. Schröder
Fr 25 — Ankunft in Wien
So 27 — Ankunft in Grundlsee
Di 29 — Goethepreis
August Sa 2 — bekam Federn. Menz. Kollos.
— angekommen
Mi 6 — Mathilde
Fr 8 — in Ischl bei Mutter Alex Sophie Harry
Sa 16 — J. Salten — Mutter g. 95 J.
So 17 — Ischl bei
Di 19 — Ständchen Goethepreis abschied v. Mutter
So 24 — Dr Michel u. †
Mo 25 — Mela Rie Frankfurt
Do 28 — Anna zu Martin Eindkorn. Anna
Fr 29 — Nachricht zurück
Sa 30 — Math abgereist
So 31 — Simmel u. Laforgue

Sept. Di 2 — Sachs
Mi 3 — Bernfeld abend, Paquet dazu
So 7 — Eitingon Simmel federn Weinmann
Fr 12 — † Mutter gestorben 8ʰ früh
So 14 — Anna bei Mutters begräbnis
Mo 15 — Anna mit Dorothy abgereist
Di 16 — Princess abgereist
Mi 17 — Doebes angekommen. Eva eingezogen
Do 18 — Ernst u. Sofi nach Wien
So 28 — Ankunft in Wien
Mo 29 — Anna zurück Dr. Bondy
Do 30 — Röntgen bei Schwarz

Okt Fr 3 Alle Ärzte bei Pichler neue Vitrine
    Di 14 Operation bei Pichler
    Fr 17 Fieberhafte Erkrankung – Bullitt –
    Mi 29 Arbeit aufgenommen
Nov Fr 2 Erste kleine Zigarre
    So 5 Fortsetzg des Grabreliefs von Rom
    Mi 5 Der Nobelpreis endgiltig übergangen
    Do 6 Wahlen – Exercize
    So 9 Relief montiert Goethe
    Do 20 Erster Abend Goethe
    Di 25 Eitingon
    Sa 29 Der Goethe Nobel
    So 30 Anna 35 J.
Dez Mi 3 Wilson beendigt
    Do 4 Ed. Weiss – Herzing
    Do 11 Anna nach Paris
    Sa 13 Halsmann in 91. Irene
    So 14 Hebraeische Vorreden
    Mi 17 bei Max Pollak
    Fr 26 Unbehagen f. 2 Aufl. corrigirt
    Di 30 Japanisches Selagsleben

1931

Jan Do 8 Ernst „Lux" dots fig. Lux
    Sa 10 ernst abgereist Joh. Wiederkunft
    Mo 12 Einladung London, Huxley Lecture
    Mi 14 Bericht b. Schwierzen Nacht b.
    Do 15 Anna in Prag
    Sa 17 Prozess eingetreten
    Mo 19 Röntgen bei Dr. Kreiser
    Di 20 Martha Grippe
    Mi 21 Martha außer Bett
    So 25

Febr Mi 4 Consult Wagn bei fröhlich
    Sa 7 Electrobution bei Pichler
    Mo 9 † Mathilde Breuer
    Mi 11 mundprama St. Zweig Heilung d. Geist
    Mo 16 Arbeit aufgenommen
    Do 17 Oli 40 Jahre
    Fr 20 Gutachten f. Bernfeld
    Sa 28 Eitingon Besuch
    Fr 27 Abend Bernfeld

März Fr 20 Lux Operation überstehen
    Sa 21 Ehrenmitglied Ges. Ärzte
    Fr 27 Abend mit Radó

April Fr 3 Pötzleinsdorf genannt Grusel nach Scharfenberg
    So 12 Tausky – nach Scharfenberg
    Di 14 Consil Pichler
    Mi 15 Republik Spanien
    Fr 22 Consil Kohlknecht
    Di 24 Auersperg Operation

Oct Fr 3	All doctors at Pichler's. New glass case
Tu 14	Pichler operation
Fr 17	Feverish sickness—Bullitt
We 29	Work recommenced

Nov Su 2	First small cigar
We 5	Continuation of Rome burial relief
Th 6	Finally passed over for Nobel Prize.
Su 9	Election—Ferenczi
Th 20	Relief mounted
Tu 25	First evening Yvette
Sa 29	Eitingon
Su 30	at Yvette's Hotel

Dec We 3	Anna 35 yrs.
Th 4	Wilson finished
Th 11	Ed. Weiss—Session
Sa 13	Anna to Bpest
Su 14	Halsmann in N. Presse
	Hebrew Introductory Lectures
We 17	At Max Pollack's
Fr 26	Discontents f. 2 ed. corrected
Tu 30	Japanese Everyday Life.

——————————————————— *1931* ———————————————————

Jan Th 8	Ernst & Lux, necklace for Lux
Sa 10	Ernst left. Jofi lodging.
Mo 12	Invitation London, Huxley Lecture
We 14/Th 15	Periostitis. Pain at night
Sa 17	Anna in Prague
Mo 19	Princess entered
Tu 20	X-ray at Dr Presser
We 21	Martha flu
Su 25	Martha out of bed

Feb We 4	Corinth vase from Fröhlich
Sa 7	Electrocution at Pichler
Mo 9	+ Mathilde Breuer
We 11	Lockjaw St. Zweig. Healing thr. Spirit
Mo 16	Work taken up
Tu 17	Oli 40 yrs.
Fr 20	Testimonial for Bernfeld
Sa 28	Eitingon visit
Fr 27	Evening Bernfeld

March Fr 20	Lux underwent operation.
Sa 21	Honorary Member Soc. Physicians
Fr 27	Evening with Radó

April Fr 3	Poetzleinsdorf rented
Su 12	Tansley—Ernstl to Scharfenberg
Tu 14	Consultation Pichler
We 15	Republic in Spain
Tu 22	Consultation Holzknecht
Th 24	Auersperg operation

May Th 5	back home again
We 6	75 birthday
Sa 9	Session Poetzl—Gomperz
Th 14	Oli's visit.
June	
[P & line in red] Mo 1	Move to Poetzleinsdorf
Tu 3	Edith Rischawy burial
Sa 6	Japan. translation—Otto Fleischl
Sa 13/Mo 15	Eitingon
Sa 20/Tu 23	Ernst
Su 28	Storfer—Tarock with Fleischl
July Tu 14	Sculptor Juran for Freiberg
Sa 19	+ Johanna Rie
Th 23	at Alfred Rie—v.d. Hoop
Fr 24	Sculptor O. Neumann—Graf portrait
	—Alex & Lilli evening—Congress cancelled
Su 26	Martha 70 yrs.
Tu 28	+ Forel
Fr 31	Armenian dentist from Boston
August Sa 1	Anna ill. New prosthesis Kazanjean
Fr 7	Dr Stein because of nose bleeding
Mo 10	Kazanjian work begun
Th 13	Ernstl accepted at Scharfenberg
Tu 25	Tegel will close
Th 27	Turning point
Fr 28	Ricarda Huch Goethe Prize
Sa 29	Kazanjian left. New prostheses
Mo 31	Minna's accident on street.
Sept Tu 1	Oscar Rie fallen ill.
We 2	Libidinal types begun.
Mo 7	Dr Alexander
Fr 11	Eitingon
Sa 12	Princess left
Su 13	Nunberg taken leave. Putsch in Styria,
	Eitingon left
We 16	Minna to Merano
Tu 17	+ Oscar Rie, Emden
Fr 18	at Nunberg
[red line] Sa 26	at Berggasse
We 30	Fem Sexuality finished
	—Rickman—
Oct Su 4	Lampl—Friedjung
Mo 5	+ Tattoan
Tu 6	Kannon & Tang figure bought
Th 8	Federn—Priest bought
Fr 9	Currency regulation
Mo 12	Juran plaster plaque
	Album of Poetzleinsdorf
We 14	Gold exchanged
Th 15	Minna back
	Rider and Guard bought

Mai Di 5 nach Sanh zurück
Mi 6 75. Geburtstag
Sa 9 Sitzung Poetzl-Gomperz
Do 14 Oli's Besuch

Juni
Mo 1 Überfindung Pötzleinsdorf
Di 3 Edith Kischausy Begräbnis Fleischl
Sa 6 Japan übersetzt Otto Fleischl
Sa 13 Mo 15 Sitzungen
Sa 20 Di 23 Storfer Zarek mit Fleischl
Vo 28

Juli Di 14 Bildhauer Juran hier Freiberg
So 19 + Johanna Rie
Do 23 bei Alfred Rie - v.d. Hoop
Fr 24 Bildhauer O. Neumann - Graf'sches Portrait
Alex, Lilli abd. Kongress abgesagt
So 26 Martha 70 J
Di 28 + Forel Zahnarzt aus Posten
Fr 31 + Altmenier Neue Prothese Kazanjan

August Sa 1 Anna krank. Neue Prothese Kazanjan
Fr 7 Dr Stein wegen Nasenbluten
Mo 10 Kazanjian Arbeit begonnen
Do 13 Ernst in Scharfenberg aufgenommen
Di 25 Segel wird Herren
Do 27 Wendepunkt
Fr 28 Riccarda Huch Goethepreis
Sa 29 Kazanjian abgereist Neue Prothesen
Mo 31 Minna's Unfall auf Reise

Sept. Di 1 Oscar Rie erkrankt
Mi 2 Libidinöse Typen begonnen
+ Alexander
Mo 7 11 Sitzungen
Fr Sa 12 Nürnberg abgeschickt Putsch in Steier-
So 13 Eilungen abgereist
mark Mi 16 Minna nach Meran Emden
Do 17 + Oscar Rie
Fr 18 bei Nürnberg Berggasse
Sa 26 Weibl Sexualität beendigt
Mi 30 Dickman

Okt. So 4 Lampl - Friedjung
Mo 5 + Tattwan
Di 6 Kwannon u. Tanzfigur gekauft
Do 8 Jederan - Priester gekauft
Fr 9 Devisenordnung
Mo 12 Juran Figurplakette
Album v. Pötzleinsdorf
Mi 14 Gold eingewechselt
Do 15 Minna zurück
Reiter u. Wachter gekauft

Fr 16   Mathilde 44 J
Sa 17   Ernst angekommen
Mi 21   Arthur Schnitzler †
Do 22   Albr. Schaeffer u Frau
So 25   Feier in Freiberg
Mi 28   Ferenczi — Martin nach Zürich
Do 29   Zwei Büsten von Nemon
Sa 31   Holzknecht † — Nepenthe-
         Jeanne überreicht
         Magendarmzustand

Do 5/6 XI   Stockrot wird
So 8/11   Rolik — Bondi   Kameeltreiber, Jade
Di 10/11   Vortrag XIV u XV — Einkäufe Croation
Fr 13/18   Marianne Kind getauft
Mi 18   Stolzer "   Martin nach Berlin
Do 19   Bleuler — Martin   Prometheussage
Sa 21   Oppenheimer —   in d. Presse
So 22   Tandlerbrief
Mo 30   Yvette

                Dezember
Do 3   Perlen f Anna J — 36 Geburtstag Schlachtbei
        Ernst's Kindern
Fr 4   Lou Salomé ; Vauk
Mi 9   Vishnu von Calcutta
Di 22   Japanische Übersetzen.

                1932   Januar
Fr 1   Langer Magenanfall — Kritik gegen Reich
Sa 16   Astragon   Martin an Walter Storfer's
So 17   Anna Grigri — sehr schön abgereist
Mo 18   £ 2500 von Shillit
Di 26   Anna auf Semmering ; Brill
Sa 30 $ 1000 von Jackson u von Brill
                Februar
Mo 1   Anna zurück
Fr 5   Chinesische Reiterin
Mi 10   Aufsatz zu unserer Vorlesungen
Do 18   Geschenk Fujiyama von Rosawa
Fr 19   Morosov Verlag
Mo 22   Inschab Schumsad bei Anna u mit
Di 23   Prospekt. Bücher im Goethehaus
                März
Mo 7   Operation an Sattler
Di 8   Ernst — rosa Klebe von fröhlich gemacht
So 13   Plakette von Kreuger
Mo 14   Wahl in Deutschland unaufgeklärt
Do 17   Besuch Thomas Mann
Fr 22   Goethe Tag — französ. Illusion

Fr 16	Mathilde 44 yrs.
Sa 17	Ernst arrived.
We 21	Arthur Schnitzler +
Th 22	Albr. Schaeffer & wife
Su 25	Celebration in Freiberg
We 28	Ferenczi—Martin to Zurich
Th 29	Three busts from Nemon
Sa 31	Holzknecht +—Nepenthe—
	Jeanne departed

Th 5/Fr 6 XI	Gastro-intestinal state
Su 8/XI	At Hochrotherd
Tu 10/XI	Colic—Bondi
Fr 13	Obras XIV & XV—Acquisitions Camel Driver, Jade
We 18	Marianne child & operation
Th 19	Pearls & rings bought.
Sa 21	Bleuler—Martin to Berlin
Su 22	Oppenheimer—Prometheus legend.
Su 29	Tandler's letter in N. Presse
Mo 30	Yvette

December

Th 3	Pearls for Anna on 36th birthday—Ernst's children with scarlet fever.
Fr 4	Lou Salomé's Thanks
We 6	Vishnu from Calcutta.
Tu 22	Japanese translations.

1932 January

Fr 1	Long gastric attack—Step against Reich
Sa 16	Eitingon—Martin in Storfer's place.
Su 17	Anna flu—first Portug. translation.
Mo 18	£2500 from Bullitt
Tu 26	Anna on Semmering
Sa 30	$1000 from Jackson & from Brill.

February

Mo 1	Anna back
Fr 5	Chinese woman rider
We 10	Preface to new Lectures.
Th 18	Gift Fujiyama from Kosawa
Fr 19	Morator. f. publishing house
Mo 22	Anna and I have infect. cold
Tu 23	Project of busts at the Goethe House

March

Mo 7	Operation at Pichler
Tu 8	Briand +
Su 13	Large kelebe bought from Fröhlich Kreuger suicide
Mo 14	Election in Germany undecided
Th 17	Visit Thomas Mann
Tu 22	Goethe Day —French Illusion

Easter 1932

27 March	46 yrs. practice. Circular for publishing house
Mo 28 March	Dr. Stockert. Meynert's grandson. Circular finished.

April

Mo 4/4	Martha to Berlin—Four Case Histories
We 6/4	Roheim on visit. Martha at Ernst's birthday
Su 10/4	Hindenburg elected.
Sa 16/4	Rivista italiana—Ed Weiss
Su 17/4	At Hochrotherd.
Tu 19/4	Martha from Berlin, Martin to Leipzig
Fr 22/4	Binswanger

May

Fr 6/5	76 birthday
Su 8/5	Day at Hochrotherd
We 11/5	Editorial staff meeting
Sa 14/5	Poetzleinsdorf
Mo 23/5	Hungarian translation
Tu 31/5	Psa. Quarterly—Mitzi gone—

June

Mo 6/6	Discontents Swedish
We 15/6	Psychology of Love Japanese
Tu 21/6	Invitation Steinig—Einstein
Fr 24/6	Lux & Gabi
Tu 28/6	Large horse bought. $2000 from Jackson

July

Mo 11/7	Jakob Bernays by Fränkel
We 13/17	Mathilde Halberstadt +
Sa 16/17	Eva scarlet fever at Mallnitz—Jofi back
Tu 26	Birthday at Hochroterd

August

Mo 1/8	Steinig with Einstein's letter
We 10/8	Martin kidney colic
Su 14/8	Geometrical pyxis
Mo 15/8	Jeanne as guest.
We 22/8	Brill
Tu 23/8	Ferenczi's refusal
Sa 27/8	Ernst's visit—Radó
Tu 30/8	Ernst departed
We 31/8	Lectures finished

Sept.

Th 1/9	Anna to Göttingen—Congress
Fr 2/9	Ferenczi with Brill.
Su 4/9	Wiesbaden Congress
Tu 6/9	Discussion Einstein ended
Th 8/9	Anna back
Fr 9/9	+ Chr Ehrenfels
Mo 12/9	Obras XV & XVI
Sa 17/9	Berggasse

Ostern 1932.

27 März   467 Praxis. Rundbrief für Verlag
Mo. 28/3   Dr Stockert Sokal u. Meynert, Rundbrief fertig
                        April
Mo 4/4   Martha nach Berlin — Vier Krankengeschichten
Mi 6/4   Kohn auf Besuch. Martha bei Ernst's Geburtstag
Do 10/4   • Hindenburg gewählt.
Sa 16/4   Rivista italiana Ed. Weiss
Do 17/4   In Kochroterd
Di 19/4   Martha von Berlin, Martin nach Leipzig
Fr 22/4   Thiernanger
                        Mai
Fr 6/5 —   76 Geburtstag
So 8/5   Tag in Kochroterd
Mi 11/5   Redaktionssitzung
Sa 14/5   Pötzleinsdorf
Mo 23/5 Psa. ungarische Übersetzungen
Fr 31/5   Quarterly - Mitri abgegangen
                        Juni
Mo 6/6   Unbehagen schwedisch
Mi 15/6   Ueberleben japanisch
Di 21/6   Aufforderung Steinig — Einstein
Fr 24/6   Alex u. Gabi
Di 28/6   Grosses Pferd gekauft. $2000 Jackson
                        Juli   Fränkel
Mo 11/7   Jakob Bernays von
Mi 13/7   Hassfeld, Ueberstadt Sofi zurück
Sa 16/7   Eva Barlach in Malbritz
Di 26   Geburtstag in Kochroterd
                        August   Einstein's Brief
Mo 1/8   Steinig mit innere Politik
Mi 10/8   Martin
Do 14/8   geometrische Pyxis
Mo 15/8   Jeanne als Gast.
Mi 22/8   Brill
Di 23/8   Ferenczi's Absage - Radó
Sa 27/8   Ernst Besuch —
Di 30/8   Ernst abgereist. Vorlesungen fertig
Mi 31/8   Sept.
                        Göttingen — Kongress
Do 1/9   Anna nach
Fr 2/9   Ferenczi mit Brill
Sa 4/9   Kongress Wiesbaden
Di 6/9   Diskussion Einstein beendigt —
Do 8/9   Anna zurück
Fr 9/9   † Chr. Ehrenfels
Mo 12/9   Obras XV, XVI
Sa 17/9   Berggasse

Fr 20. Mathilde krank
Sa 24/9 Minna nach Meran — Martin zurück
So 25/9 Kochrotherd
Di 27/9 bei Anna in Imperial. Uraufr. Brücke's
                    Oktober
So 2/10 Kochrotherd mit Ruth. Werk
          Anna nach Berlin geflogen. — Felisch Jackson
Di 4/10 Anna zurück. Gersberg — nochige Operation b. Pichler
Do 6/10 Minna von Meran
Fr 14/10 Alfred Rie † Unfall u. Tod.
Sa 29/10 – So 30/10 November
          Grippe und Ohrenentzündung
Di 1/XI Parazentese Rutin
Do 3/XI Roosevelt in USA gewählt.
Di 8/XI bei Goette im Nobel
Mi 30/XI Dezember
Sa 3/XII Anna 37 J — Neue Vorlesungen.
          Operation bei Pichler
Do 8/XII 1933

                    Januar
Mi 4/1 — Dr May — Martin nach Berlin
Do 5/1   g. Anton †
Mi 18/1   L. Tiffany † New York
Fr 27/1   Eljugon
So 29/1   Ruth kriegen; Hitler Reichskanzler
Di 31/1   Galsworthy † ; Sofi Lagrün
                    Februar
So 12/2   Arnold Zweig
Mo 13/2   Brief — Traumdeutung
Di 14/2   vier japan. Übersetzungen
Fr 17/2   Tessener Buddha
Di 21/2   Leonardo czechisch brand
Di 28/2   Parlament Berlin in Brand
                    März
                         Roosevelt
Fr 4/3   Dollarmoratorium in Deutschland.
So 5/3   Hitlerwahl in Deutschland
Mo 13/3   Egypt. Stoffmalerei
Mi 15/3   Harry proanotion —
Fr 1?/3   farbige Chinesin —
Mi 24/3   Warum Krieg —
Sa 25/3   Selbstreik
Mo 27/3   Bourgeoi Guerre? — neulich ferencei — Sofi Gaul
Mi 29/3   besuch Barbara
Fr 31/3   Bryher

Tu 20	Mathilde ill
Sa 24/9	Minna to Merano—Martin back
Su 25/9	Hochrotherd
Tu 27/9	with Anna in the Imperial. Brücke's great grandson.

October

Su 2/10	Hochrotherd with Ruth & Mark
Tu 4/10	Anna flown to Berlin—Jackson fetish
Th 6/10	Anna back—Gerstberg—Thorough operation at Pichler
Fr 14/10	Minna to Merano
Sa 29/10—Su 30/10	Alfred Rie + Accident & death.

November

Tu 1/XI	Flu and ear inflammation
Th 3/XI	Paracentesis Ruttin
Tu 8/XI	Roosevelt elected in USA.
We 30/XI	at Yvette's hotel

December

Sa 3/XII	Anna 37 yrs.—New Lectures.
Th 8/XII	Operation with Pichler

1933

January

We 4/1	Dr May—Martin to Berlin
Th 5/1	G. Anton +
We 18/1	L. Tiffany + New York
Fr 27/1	Eitingon
Su 29/1	Ruth flu, Hitler Reichs Chancellor
Tu 31/1	Galsworthy +; JoFi Kagran

February

Su 12/2	Arnold Zweig
Mo 13/2	Brill—Interpretation of Dreams
Tu 14/2	four Jap. translations
Fr 17/2	Iron Buddha
Tu 21/2	Czech Leonardo
Tu 28/2	Berlin parliament on fire

March

Sa 4/2	Dollar moratorium—Roosevelt
Su 5/3	Election of Hitler in Germany.
Mo 13/3	Egypt. fabric painting
We 15/3	Harry graduation
Fr 17/3	painted Chinese lady
We 27/3	Warum Krieg?
Sa 25/3	Typesetters' strike
Mo 27/3	Pourquoi Guerre?—Ferenczi news—Jofi injured
We 29/3	Visit Barilari
Fr 31/8	Bryher

April

Su 2	Ernst from Berlin—Arn. Zweig—.
Mo 3	Jofi's dangerous birth—Norman Douglas
We 5	Ernstl with Mabbie to Sicily
Sa 8	Oli—Henny from Berlin
Mo 10	Italian Moses—Why War?
Su 16	Easter. 47 yrs practice
Mo 17	Boehm & Federn
Sa 22	Klemperer
Tu 25	Dr Ed Weiss—Forzano

May

Mo 1	City closed to marches.
Th 4	Move Hohe Warte
Fr 5	Ernst & Klemens
Sa 6	77 birthday—attack of vertigo
Th 11	Burning in Berlin
Tu 15	Ernst departed. Operation P.—Arn. Zweig
We 16	Jeanne house visit
Su 21	Colitis. Jeanne departed—van Vriesland
Mo 22	Ferenczi +. Serbian Lectures
Tu 23	Japan. journal No. 1
We 24	Ruth & Mark from Paris
Th 25	Anna & Martin from Bpest
Fr 26	Diathermy of lower jaw—
Su 28	Oli—Henny in Paris
Mo 29	Poe by Marie Bonaparte
Tu 30	Buddha head

June

Su 4	Ferenczi obituary finished
Mo 5	H.G.Wells on visit
Fr 16	Eitingon
Mo 26	Paul Hammerschlag + Wittels' journey.
Fr 30	Ernstl's tonsil operation

July

Sa 8	Ruth operation—Martin's furunculosis.
Su 9	60 yrs Matura with Knöpfmacher & Wagner

August

Tu 1/8	Holidays—Hochroterd
We 2	Bullitt
Th 10	Institute for the Blind
Fr 11	Eitingon
Sa 12	Hochrotherd—Stephen Wise
Th 17	Princess—Essais de psych. appliquée
Fr 18	Dorothy back & Lampl
Th 24	Jeanne operated
Fr 25	Ruth to America

April

<table>
<tr><td>So 2 —</td><td>Ernstl von Martin — Arn. Zweig</td></tr>
<tr><td>Mo 3 —</td><td>Jofi's geschäftliche Geburt — Norman Douglas</td></tr>
<tr><td>Mi 5 —</td><td>Grosse Not, Mabbie nach Sizilien</td></tr>
<tr><td>Sa 8 —</td><td>Oli — Henny auf Berlin</td></tr>
<tr><td>Mo 10 —</td><td>Moses italienisch — Why war?</td></tr>
<tr><td>So 16 —</td><td>Ostern. 477 Praxis</td></tr>
<tr><td>Mo 17 —</td><td>Boehm u. Federn</td></tr>
<tr><td>Sa 22 —</td><td>Klemperer</td></tr>
<tr><td>Di 25 —</td><td>Dr Ed Weiss — Forzano</td></tr>
</table>

Mai

Sperre der Stadt gegen Umzüge

<table>
<tr><td>Mo 1 —</td><td>Umzug Kohe / Wärter</td></tr>
<tr><td>Do 4 —</td><td>Ernst u. Klemens</td></tr>
<tr><td>Fr 5 —</td><td>77 Geburtstag. Schwindelanfall</td></tr>
<tr><td>Sa 6 —</td><td>Verbrennung in Berlin X — Arn. Zweig</td></tr>
<tr><td>Do 11 —</td><td>ernst abgereist. Gratulation X</td></tr>
<tr><td>Di 15 —</td><td>Jeanne Jausenbuch</td></tr>
<tr><td>Mi 16 —</td><td>Cotitis. Jeanne abgereist — van Vriesland</td></tr>
<tr><td>So 21 —</td><td>Ferenczi † Serbische Vorlesung</td></tr>
<tr><td>Mo 22 —</td><td>Japan Zeitschrift X — Paris</td></tr>
<tr><td>Di 23 —</td><td>Ruth Mack von Paris</td></tr>
<tr><td>Mi 24 —</td><td>Anna u. Martin von Bpest</td></tr>
<tr><td>Do 25 —</td><td>Diathermie u. Unterkühler —</td></tr>
<tr><td>Fr 26 —</td><td>Oli u. Henny in Paris Bonaparte</td></tr>
<tr><td>So 28 —</td><td>Oe von Marie</td></tr>
<tr><td>Mo 29 —</td><td>Budha Kopf</td></tr>
<tr><td>Di 30</td><td></td></tr>
</table>

Juni

<table>
<tr><td>So 4 —</td><td>Nachruf Ferenczi beendigt.</td></tr>
<tr><td>Mo 5 —</td><td>H. G. Wells auf Besuch — Wittels Rede</td></tr>
<tr><td>Fr 16 —</td><td>Eitingon</td></tr>
<tr><td>Mo 26 —</td><td>Paul Hammerschlag †</td></tr>
<tr><td>Fr 30 —</td><td>Ernstl's Tonsillenoperation</td></tr>
</table>

Juli

<table>
<tr><td>Sa 8 —</td><td>Ruth operation — Martin Tuberkulose</td></tr>
<tr><td>So 9 —</td><td>60 fache Matura und Knopfmacher u. Wagner</td></tr>
</table>

August

<table>
<tr><td></td><td>Ferien Kochrohrerd</td></tr>
<tr><td>Di 1/8</td><td>Brill</td></tr>
<tr><td>Mi 2/10</td><td>Blindeninstitut</td></tr>
<tr><td>Do 3 —</td><td>Eitingon</td></tr>
<tr><td>Fr 11 —</td><td>Kochrohrerd — Stephen Wise</td></tr>
<tr><td>Sa 12 —</td><td>Prinzessin — Essais de psych. appliquée.</td></tr>
<tr><td>Do 17 —</td><td>Dorothy zurück u. Lampl</td></tr>
<tr><td>Fr 18 —</td><td>Jeanne operiert</td></tr>
<tr><td>Do 24 —</td><td>Ruth nach Amerika</td></tr>
<tr><td>Fr 25 —</td><td></td></tr>
</table>

September 1933

So 3 — Laforgue. Sitzung später
Di 5 — Operation. Herzanfall. Beginn d. Krankheit
Sa 16 — Ernst u. Lux gekommen
Di 19 — Pichler; Consilium. Lux abgereist
Sa 30 — Berggasse

Oktober 1933

Di 3 — Attentat auf Dolfuss
Mi 4 — Dr Ludwig Bauer
Do 5 — Martin Unregelmäßig bestanden
Mo 9 — Erste Ausfahrt — Zwergfigur u. Jade f. Dorsey
Sa 14 — Deutschland tritt aus Völkerbund aus
Mo 16 — Mathilde 46?
Mi 19 — Martin nach Zürich

November

Sa 4 — Martin zurück
Do 8 — Asthmatisch. Pichler Besuch deutsche Masken
So 12 — 10 Jahre seit Bronchien. deutsche ...
Di 14 — Nachricht Simmels Verhaftung
Do 16 — New Lectures (sprott) — ... Flegel u. Funde
Ernst von Berlin abgereist
Sa 25 — Eitingon

Dezember

So 3 — Anna 38? — Mittl. Herzanfall
Mo 11 — fall bei den Langen

1934

Januar

Hebräische Vorlesungen I
Di 2 — Martin's Nierensteinoperation
Fr 5 — Prozess abgereist Oscar Philipp
Sa 6 — Röntgen im Hause
Mi 24 — Februar

Mi 7 — Silberne Hochzeit Math-Robert u. Alex-Soph
Sa 10 — Martin nach Hause
Mo 12 — Generalstreike
Sa 17 — Ehrenfels sein
So 18 — Buckingham's nach Italien
Mo 19 — König Albert †

März

Sa 3 — Lux ...
Do 8 — G. Earle — ...
Fr 9 — Mussolini...
Mo 12 — Katarrh
Mi 14 — † Zänker
Fr 23 — ...

September 1933

Su 3	Laforgue—Bryher Foundation
Tu 5	Operation—Heart attack—Beginning of illness
Sa 16	Ernst & Lux come.
Tu 19	Pichler for consultation. Lux departed.
Sa 30	Berggasse

October 1933

Tu 3	Attempted assassination of Dollfuss.
We 4	Dr Ludwig Bauer
Th 5	Martin passed Bar exams.
Mo 9	First outing—Dwarf figure & jade for Dorothy
Sa 14	Germany wants to leave League of Nations.
Mo 16	Mathilde 46 yrs
Th 19	Martin to Zurich

November

Sa 4	Martin back
Th 8	Stomatitis—Pichler visit
Su 12	10 years since operation—German elections
Tu 14	News of Simmel's arrest
Th 16	New Lectures (Sprott)—Cypriot seal & trove
	Ernst left Berlin
Sa 25	Eitingon

December

Su 3	Anna 38 yrs—Mitzi heart attack
Mo 11	Accident at the lamp

1934

January

Tu 2	Hebrew Lectures I.
Fr 5	Martin's kidney stone operation
Sa 6	Princess departed—Oscar Philipp.
We 24	X-ray at home.

February

We 7	Silver wedding Math—Robert & Alex—Soph
Sa 10	Martin gone home
Mo 12	General strike
Sa 17	Ehrenfels jun.
Su 18	Burlinghams to Italy
Mo 19	King Albert +

March

Sa 3	Lux in car accident.
Th 8	G. Earle—Mummy mask
Fr 9	Mummy case
M 12	Catarrh
We 14	+ Läufer
Fr 23	Radium

1934

April

Th 5/4	Census commission
Fr 13/4	House Strassergasse seen and rented
Fr 20/4	Oli from Paris.
Sa 21/4	Daly
Mo 23/4	Second radium
Tu 24/4	Nestroy's works
We 25/4	Jekels' departure
Th 26/4	Ur excavations—Oli departed—vdLeeuw evening
Sa 28/4	Strassergasse 47

May

Tu 1/5	New constitution
Su 6/5	78 years Gisela Ferenczi—
Mo 7/5	Ivory Buddha & stone Dog of Fo
Fr 18/5	Gardenia

June

Mo 4/6	Sarapis and fountain bull
Th 14/6	+ Groddeck and + Frau Zweig
Sa 30/6	S.A. revolt in Germany

July

We 4/Th 5	Ophthalm. migraine with illness
Mo 9	Meteor stone—Harry Karlsbad
Th 12	Ernstl on tour—Lion dragon
Fr 13	Sarasin
Mon 16	Chinese lectures
Tu 17	Dr Sachs, Johannesbg.
Sa 21	Ernst fr. Berlin
We 25	+ Dollfuss; Putsch in Ballhaus
Th 26	Martha 73 yrs—Son to Marianne

August

Th 2/8	+ Hindenburg.
Sa 18/8	Eitingon
Mo 20/8	Nunberg
We 22/8	Jones
Sa 25/8	Alexander—Anna to Lucerne
We 29/8	+ v.d.Leeuw

September

Sa 1/9	Anna from Lucerne
Tu 3/9	Radó
We 6/9	Eros Myrina
Fr 14/9	XII volume Ges. Ausgabe
Su 23/9	Moses ended

1934

April

Do 5/4 Volkszählungscommission
Fr 13/4 Wohnung Strasserg gesehen u. gemietet
Fr 20/4 Oli aus Paris.
Sa 21/4 Daly zweites Radium
Mo 23/4 Nestroy's Werke
Di 24/4 Jekels' Aufsatz
Mi 25/4 Ur Excavations - Oliabgereist - otheeuev abds
Do 26/4 Ur Strassergasse 47
Sa 28/4

Mai

Di 1/5 Neue Verfassung
So 6/5 78 Jahre - Gisela Ferenczi
         Elfenbeinbuddha u. stein. Hohund
Mo 7/5 Gardenia
Fr 18/5

Juni

         Sarapis und Brunnenstier
Mo 4/6 Groddeck und † Frau Zweig
Do 14/6 † S.A. Revolte in Deutschland
Sa 30/6

Juli

Mi 4/7 Migraine ophthalm. mit Krankheit
Do 5/7 Meteorstein - Harry Karlsbad
Mo 9/7 Ernst auf Wanderung - Löwendrache
Do 12   Sarasin
Fr 13   Chinesisch Vorlesen
Mo 16, 17 Dr. Sachs, Johannesbg.
Di 17   Ernst v. Berlin
Sa 21   † Dollfuss, Putsch im Ballhaus
Mi 25   Martha 73 - Sohn bei Marianne
Do 26

August

Do 2/8 † Hindenburg
Sa 18/8 Sittingen
Mo 20/8 Nürnberg
Mi 22/8 Jones
Sa 25/8 Alexander - Anna nach Luzern
Mi 29/8 † v.d. Leeuw

September

Sa 1/9 Anna von Luzern
Di 3/9 Radó Myrina
Mi 5/9 Eros
Fr 14/9 XII Band Ges. Ausgabe
So 23/9 Moses bräuchtl.

Oktober 1934

Di 9/10 Attentat in Marseille –
Sa 13/10 n. Berggasse
Di 16/10 Mathilde 47 J.

Nov 1934

Sa 3/x1 Lux
Mo 26/x1 Dozentur erloschen – Hormoninjektion

Dezember 1934

Mo 3/x11 Anna 39 J. 45 J.
Fr 7/x11 Martin 45 J. Fleischer
Fr 14/x11 flimmern – Dr
So 16/x11 Vagusanfall

1935

Januar

Di 1/1 Magenanfall-Erbrechen
Mi 9/1 Martin zurück vor Nizza
So 13/1 Saarabstimmung Anna's Vortrag
Mi 23/1 + Anna v. West –
So 27/1 Nachschrift zu Selbstdarstellung

Februar

Mi 6/2 Levy-Brühl. Anna's II Vortrag
Di 18/2 Dr Gerard
Mi 19/2 Oli 44 J.
Fr 22/2 Minna nach Meran (Nachkur)
Do 28/2 + Otto Fleischl

März

Mo 11/3 Ernste Erkrankung gemischt
Sa 16/3 Haus in Grinzing
So 17/3 allgemeine Wehrpflicht in Deutschland
Sa 23/3 Operation bei Pichler
Fr 29/3 Elektrische Uhr.

April

Sa 6/4 Minna zurück. Ernst 43 J.
Do 11/4 Neue amerik. Vorlesungen
Sa 13/4 Martin aus Zürich
So 18/4 Strassergasse
Sa 20/4 Reik u Landauer
So 21/4 Ostern 49 J Preis – Jones u Familie
Mo 22/4 Neuralgie – Federn u Meng
Di 23/4 Schmiedeberg
Do 25/4 Jones abreist Maria Anna
Fr 26/4 Schale von Wedgwood – Gegenstück zu geh. Drachen
von Leeuw –
So 28/4 Brief an Thomas Mann
Mo 29/4 Ruth operirt
Di 30/4 Operation bei Pichler

October 1934

Tu 9/10	Assassination in Marseilles
Sa 13/10	At Berggasse
Tu 16/10	Mathilde 47 yrs.

Nov 1934

Sa 9/XI	Lux
Mo 26/XI	Dozent position annulled—Hormone injection

December 1934

Mo 3/XII	Anna 39 yrs
Fr 7/XII	Martin 45 yrs
Fr 14/XII	Fibrillation—Dr ~~Fischer~~ Fleischer
Su 16/XII	Vagus attack

1935

January

Tu 1/1	Stomach attack—Vomiting
We 9/1	Martin back from Nice
Su 13/1	Saar plebiscite
We 23/1	+ Anna v Vest—Anna's lecture
Su 27/1	Postscript to Autobiographical Study.

February

We 6/2	Levy-Brühl. Anna's II lecture
Tu 18/2	Dr Gerard
We 19/2	Oli 44 yrs
Fr 22/2	Minna to Merano
Th 28/2	+ Otto Fleischl (News)

March

Mo 11/3	Ernstl majority
Sa 16/3	House in Grinzing rented
Su 17/3	Universal conscription in Germany
Sa 23/3	Operation with Pichler
Fr 29/3	Electric clock.

April

Sa 6/4	Minna back. Ernst 43 yrs
Th 11/4	New American Lectures.
Sa 13/4	Martin from Zurich
Th 18/4	Strassergasse
Sa 20/4	Reik & Landauer
Su 21/4	Easter, 49 yrs. practice—Jones & family
Mo 22/4	Neuralgia—Federn & Meng
Tu 23/4	Schmiederberg
Th 25/4	Jones in the evening
Fr 26/4	Bowl from McCord. Marie Stuart by Zweig —Counterpiece to yellow dragon
Su 28/4	Letter to Thomas Mann
Mo 29/4	Ruth operated
Tu 30/4	Operation with Pichler

May 1935

S 5/5	Beginning of prosthesis misery
Su 6/5	79 yrs
Mo 20/5	Bullitt
Fr 24/5	Honorary Member of ~~London Medical Society~~
	Royal Society of Medicine

June

Su 9/6	Four Nation Conference in Vienna
Mo 10/6	Hollos Ed Weiss
Tu 11/6	Chatterji
Tu 18/6	Minna 70 years
Sa 22/6	Anna to Prague. New prosthesis
Th 27/6	Ernstl Matura

July

Mo 8/7	+ Albert Hammerschlag
Sa 13/7	Schuschnigg accident
Su 14/7	Th. Reik
We 17/7	Heart attack extra systole
Mo 24/7	Princess
Fr 26/7	Martha 74 yrs.

August

Fr 2/8	Rockefeller jr.—Isis with Horus
Su 4/8	Robert 60 yrs.
Tu 6/8	Eitingon
We 14/8	Ernst with Lucian
Su 18/8	Mother would be 100 years old!
Mo 19/8	Operation on scabs.

September

Su 1/9	Sarasin—Kempner
Tu 3/9	Greetings of the "Wien" B.B. on 40th anniversary
Th 5/9	Jade bowl and camel
Su 15/9	Emden—Stefan Zweig—Willy Haas
Su 29/9	Jeans

October

Mo 1/X	Large kannon.
Tu 2/X	Beginning of war in Abyssinia.
Th 10/X	Subtelties of a Faulty Action
Fr 11/X	Operation w Pichler
Su 13/X	Thornton Wilder
Mo 16/X	Math 48 years
Fr 18/X	Berggasse
Tu 22/x	+ Richard Wahle
Mo 28/X	Autobiographical Study

November

We 6/XI	+ Victor Dirsztay
Su 10/XI	Visit from Yvette Guilbert
Th 21/XI	Almanach 1936

Mai 1935

So 5/5 Anfang des Prothesenlands
Mi 6/5 79 Jahre
Mo 20/5 Bullitt — Ehrenmitglied der London Medical Society
Fr 24/5 - Royal Society of Medicine

Juni
So 2/6 Vierländertagung in Wien
Mo 10/6 Notlos. Ed. Weiss.
Di 11/6 Chatterji 70 Jahre
Di 18/6 Anna nach Prag — Neue Prothese
Sa 22/6 Ernst Matura
Do 27/6

Juli
Mo 8/7 + Albert Hammerschlag
Sa 13/7 Unfall Schuschnigg
So 14/7 Th. Reik
Mi 17/7 Herzanfall Extrasystole
Mo 22/7 Pfneudl?
Fr 26/7 Martha 74 J.

August
Fr 2/8 Rockefeller jr. — Jesinek Morus
So 4/8 Robert 66 J.
Di 6/8 Lisingen
Mi 14/8 Ernst mit Lucian
So 18/8 Mutter wäre 100 Jahre
Mo 19/8 Operation der Prothese

September
Sarasin — Kempner
So 1/9 Begrüssung der "Wien" B.B. z. 40 Jubil.
Di 3/9 Sachschütze und Kampel — Willy Haas
Mo 23/9 Emden — Stefan Zweig
So 15/9 Franz
So 29/9

Oktober
Mo 1/x Grosse Kwannon
Di 2/x Beginn d. Krieges in Abessinien
Do 10/x Aufheit e. Fehlleistung
Fr 11/x Operation b. Pichler
So 13/x Thornton Wilder
Mi 16/x Math 48 Jahre
Fr 18/x Berggasse
Di 22/x + Richard Wahle
Mo 28/x Autobiographical Study

November
Mi 6/xi + Viktor Tausk?
So 10/xi Besuch von Yvette Guilbert
So 24/xi Almanach 1936

Sa 23/11. Oli von Nizza
Dezember
Di 3/XII Anna 40 J. – Große Hausbücher
Sa 7/XII Martin 46 J Palaestina
Di 10/XII Ernst nach zurückgefallen
Sa 14/XII Masaryk zurückgetreten
Mo 23/XII Paul Hollitscher †

1936

Do 2/1 Ernst
Mo 13/1 Ernst abgereist Akropolis fertig
Di 14/1 Unglaube auf Akropolis Operation 6 Pichler
Do 16/1 Georg v. † Königsberger
Mo 20/1 Nemon z. Zweiten
Di 21/1 von Brüssel
Mi 22/1 Februar
Sa 1/2 Eine Woche Nemon — Max
Di 4/2 Abschied von Max.
So 9/2 † Rob. Breuer
Do 20/2 Bischowski Operation Pichler
März
Di 3/3 † Pineles Schriftgruß von Alex.
Di 10/3 Operation 6 Pichler
Mi 25/3 Minna's Glaukom — Angela
Konfiskation unserer Bücher in Leipzig
Migraine April
Fr 3/4 Großes Totenstift
So 5/4 Henny mit Eva
Mo 6/4 Erpt 44 J. Praxis- Angret Ausnahme
So 12/4 Ostern 50 J über
Di 14/4 Minna nach Eva abgereist
Mi 15/4 Henny in Sanatorium
Sa 18/4 Strassergasse
Do 23/4 £5000 von Brill
Mi 29/4 Minna aus Sanat.
Mai
Mo 4/5 Adresse von Mann Wells Rolland u. A.
Mi 6/5 50 Jr Geburtstag Eroberung
Do 7/5 Thomas Mann v. Abessinien
Fr 8/5 Vortrag Th. Mann † L. Braun

Sa 23/XI	Oli from Nice

December

Tu 3/XII	Anna 40 yrs—large Han box.
Sa 7/XII	Martin 46 yrs
Tu 10/XII	Ernstl to Palestine
Sa 14/XII	Masaryk resigned
Mo 23/XII	Paul Hollitscher +

1936

Th 2/1	Ernst
Mo 13/1	Ernst departed
Tu 14/1	Disbelief on the Acropolis finished
Th 16/1	Princess departed. Operation w Pichler
Mo 20/1	George V +
Tu 21/1	Nemon & Königsberger
We 22/1	van Wulfften

February

Sa 1/2	One week Nemon—Max
Tu 4/2	Max's departure
Su 9/2	+ Rob. Breuer
Tu 20/2	Bischowski—Operation Pichler

March

Tu 3/3	+ Pineles—Osiris group from Alex.
Tu 10/3	Operation w Pichler
We 25/3	Minna's glaucoma.—Angela
	Confiscation of our books at Leipzig
	Migraine

April

Fr 3/4	Large funerary barge
Su 5/4	Henny with Eva.
Mo 6/4	Ernst 44 yrs
Su 12/4	Easter 50 yrs practice—Egypt. ploughing scene
	Minna still ill
Tu 14/4	Henny Eva departed
We 15/4	Minna to the sanatorium
Sa 18/4	Strassergasse
Th 23/4	£5000 from Brill
We 29/4	Minna out of sanat.

May

Mo 4/5	Addresses from Mann Wells Rolland among others
We 6/5	80th birthday conquest of Abyssinia
Th 7/5	Thomas Mann
Fr 8/5	Lecture Th. Mann + L. Braun—

1936

June

Fr 5/6	Visit to the new premises Berggasse 7
Su 14/6	Lecture by Thomas Mann at our home.
Th 18/6	Minna 71 years
Mo 29/6	Painter Krausz, Ella Braun
Tu 30/6	foreign member Royal Society

July

Sa 11/7	Agreement with Germany
Fr 14/7	Operation with Pichler
Sa 18/7	Sanatorium operation
Su 19/7	Back with bandaged eye.
Th 23/7	Out of serious illness
Fr 31/17	Anna Marienbad, Congress

August

Th 6/8	Anna back from Congress
Fr 14/8	Arn. Zweig and H. Struck
Tu 18/8	Moses with Arn. Zweig
Th 20/8	Anna on the Rax—Plaquette by Willy Levy
Tu 25/8	Tandler + —Bullitt to Paris
Fr 28/8	Jones with family—Ernstl to Russia

September

Sa 6/9	Kadimah
Sa 12/9	Ernst & Lux—Wolf again
Mo 14/9	50th wedding anniversary

Oct.

Sa 17/10	Berggasse
Su 18/10	Beer-Hofmann
Th 22/10	Arnold Zweig
Sa 24/10	Eitingon & date of Fliess's birthday.
Tu 27/10	Nose bleed.
Fr 30/10	New horse.

Nov

Su 1/11	Meeting with Boehm
Su 15/11	Director v Dehmel
Sa 21/11	Oliver
Su 22/11	+ Etka Herzig
Th 26/11	Oli departed

December

Th 3/12	Anna 41 years.
Mo 7/12	Martin 47 years.
Th 10/12	Eduard VII abdicated
Sa 12/12	Operation with Pichler
Su 20/12	Prof. Otto Loewi
Fr 24/12	Christmas in pain
Su 27/12	Stefan Zweig

1936

Juni

Fr 5/6 Besuch im neuen Lokal Berggt.
So 14/6 Vorlesung von Thomas Mann bei uns.
Do 18/6 Minna 71 Jahre
Mo 29/6 Maler Krausz   Ella Braun
Di 30/6 foreign member Royal Society

Juli

Sa 11/7 Verständigung mit Deutschland
Di 14/7 Operation bei Pichler
Sa 18/7 Sanatorium Operation
So 19/7 Zurück mit verbundenem Auge.
Do 23/7 aus schwerem Kranksein
Fr 31/7 Anna Marienbad Congress

August

Do 6/8 Anna zurück von Congress
Fr 14/8 Arn. Zweig und H. Struck
Di 18/8 Moses nach Arn. Zweig
Do 20/8 Anna auf Rax - Plaquette von Willy Levy
Di 25/8 Sandler + Bullitt nach Paris
Fr 28/8 Jones mit familie - Sachs nach Russland

Sept.

So 6/9 Radium
Sa 12/9 Grust u. Lux - Doof noch einmal
Mo 14/9 50 jährige Ehe

Okt.

Sa 17/10 Berggasse Hofmann
So 18/10 Beer - Hofmann
Do 22/10 Arnold Zweig Fliess' Geburtstag
Sa 24/10 Einigung in Sachen F. Fliess' Nabenblutung.
Di 27/10 Neues Pferd.
Fr 30/10 Tod   Bockow

So 1/11 Versammlung mit
So 15/11 Sinclair v. Wettmel
Sa 21/11 Oliver Ella Kerrig
So 22/11 + Ella Kerrig
Do 26/11 Oli abgereist

December

41 Jahre.

Anna 41 Jahren
Do 3/12 Martin 48 Jahren
Mo 7/12 Edward VIII abgedankt
Do 10/12 Operation bei Pichler
Sa 12/12 Prof Otto Loewi
Sa 20/12 Weihnacht in Schmerzen
Di 24/12 Stefan Zweig
So 27/12

1937

Januar

Sa 2/1 — Prinzessin, nach Korrespondenz mit Fliess

Mo 11/1 — Sofie ins Spital zur Operation

Do 14/1 — + Sofie zur Narzgespräch

Fr 18/1 — Thomas Mann — Lien ausgenommen

Februar

Mo 18/1 —

Mi 3/2 — Kl. Moses beendet

Do 11/2 — + Lou Salomé, geb. 5/2 ?

So 28/2 — Ralf Sachs aus Johansburg

März

So 7/3 — Jul. Wagner 50 Jahre — Montessori Krippe

Di 23/3 — Japanische Medaille

April

So 4/4 — Beer-Hofmann auf Besuch

Di 6/4 — Ernst 45 Jahre

Do 22/4 — Operation und Grippe, + Hallam

Sa 24/4 — von Sanat. nach Grinzing

Fr 30/4 — „Unendliche Analyse" beendigt.

Mai

Do 6/5 — 81 Jahre! Ernst abgereist

Mi 12/5 — Coronation

Do 13/5 — Antiquit. aus Athen

So 16/5 — Fürsten Anna i Bpest

Fr 28/5 — + A. Adler in Aberdeen

Juni

Sa 5/6 — Oberholzer — Weil

Fr 11/6 — Anna's Unfall — Schwanzau — Großstehen

Sa 26/6 — Kittsee von McCord

Juli

Moses II

Di 27/7 — Eitingon

Mi 28/7 — arm Weil, Prozess abgereist

August

So 8/8 — Moses II beendigt

Mi 18/8 — Haematurie

Di 24/8 — + Kallich

1937

January

Sa 2/1   Princess buys correspondence with Fliess
Mo 11/1   Jofi in hospital for operation
Th 14/1   + Jofi from heart failure
Fr 15/1   Thomas Mann—Lün taken on
Mo 18/1   Heart condition

February

We 3/2   Small Moses finished
Th 11/2   + Lou Salomé, died 5/2?
Su 28/2   Wolf Sachs from Johannsburg

March

Su 7/3   Jul. Wagner 80 years
Tu 29/3   Japanese medal—Montessori nursery

April

Su 4/4   Beer-Hofmann on visit
Tu 6/4   Ernst 45 years
Th 22/4   Operation with Evipan
Sa 24/4   from sanat. to Grinzing, + Halban
Fr 30/4   "Interminable Analysis" terminated.

May

Th 6/5   81 years!
We 12/5   Coronation—Ernst departed
Th 13/5   Antiquit. from Athens
Su 16/5   Whitsun, Anna in Bpest
Fr 28/5   + A.Adler in Aberdeen

June

Sa 5/6   Oberholzer—Weil
Fr 11/6   Anna's accident—Pain—Great heat
           Otitis
Sa 26/6   Bust from McCord

July

           Moses II
Tu 27/7   Eitingon
We 28/7   Arn. Zweig, Princess left

August

Su 8/8   Moses II finished
We 18/8   Hematuria
Tu 24/8   + Kallich

Sept 1937

We 1/9	Emanuel Loewy 80 yrs
Tu 14/9	+ Masaryk—51 yrs. since marriage
We 15/9	Lou Jones
Th 23/9	Idea about delusion and construction

Oct

Fr 15/X	New teeth
Sa 16/X	Mathilde 50 yrs.—Back Berggasse
Tu 19/X	Queen Elisabeth of Belgium
Th 21/X	+ Wilh. Knöpfmacher
Fr 22/X	Dorothy fallen ill—Eitingon

November

Fr 5/XI	in bed with bronchitis. + Gärtner
Th 11/XI	Oli
Su 14/XI	Princess film show
Tu 23/XI	Lecture Dr Bienenfeld
Su 28/XI	Stefan Zweig
Tu 30/XI	Prosthesis broken,

December

Fr 3/XII	Anna 42 yrs.
Tu 7/XII	Martin 48 yrs.

1938 January

9/1	Anna Lichtheim +.
Sa 22/1	Operation Auersperg—Atherom. Evipan

February

Fr 11/2	+ Emanuel Loewy
Sa 19/2	Operation Auersperg
Th 24/2	Schuschnigg's speech
— 28/2	Bad days

March

We 2/3	Minna operation
We 9/3	Schuschnigg in Innsbruck
Th 10/3	Wiley from Americ. embassy
Fr 11/3	Minna second operation.
	Ernstl 24 yrs.—Schuschnigg's resignation.
	Finis Austriae
Su 13/3	Anschluss with Germany
Mo 14/3	Hitler in Vienna
Tu 15/3	Search of press and house
We 16/3	Jones
Th 17/3	Princess
Th 22/3	Anna with Gestapo

Sept 1937

Mi 1/9 Emanuel Loewy 80 J.
Di 14/9 † Masaryk — 57 J. zu Privat
Mi 15/9 Roo. Jones
Do 23/9 Vorr. über Wahn u. Konstruktion

Okt
Fr 15/X Neue Zähne 59 J. zurück Berggasse
Sa 16/X Mathilde
Di 19/X Königin Elisabeth v. Belgien
Do 21/X † Wilh. Knopfmacher
Fr 22/X Dorothy u. Kraupl-Eitingon

November
Fr 5/XI mit Bonaparte zu Ott. † Gärtner
So 11/XI Offiziersingklinovorstellung
So 14/XI Vortrag Dr. Bienenfeld
Di 23/XI Stefan Zweig
So 28/XI Prothese gebrochen
Di 30/XI

Dezember
Fr 3/XII Anna 42 J. 48 J.
Di 7/XII Martin

1938 Januar
9/1 Anna Lichtheim †
Sa 22/1 Operation Auersperg - Atherom. Eripan

Februar
Fr 11/2 † Emanuel Loewy
Sa 19/2 Operation Auersperg
Do 24/2 Schuschnigg's Rede
28/2 Schlechte Tage

März
Operation
Mi 2/3 Minna Operation
Mi 9/3 Schuschnigg in Innsbruck
So 10/3 Wiley vom amerik. Gesandtschaft
Fr 11/3 Minna zweite Operation
Ernst 24 J. — Abdankung Schuschnigg
finis Austriae
So 13/3 Anschluss an Deutschland
Mi 16/3 Hitler in Wien
Di 15/3 Kontrole in Verlag u. Haus
Mi 16/3 Jones
Di 17/3 Prinzessin
Di 22/3 Anna bei Gestapo

Mo 28/30. Aufnahme in England gesichert
— Ernste in Paris — Ausreise scheint ermöglicht

<u>April</u>

Fr 1/4   Zweig Arilee in London
Mi 6/4   Ernest 49 J
Sa 9/4   Joneys Übersetzung besucht
So 10/4   Abstimmung
Di 12   Minna aus Sanatorium zurück
          Ostersonntag 52 J. Praxis
So 17/4   Alex 72 J. Amschütz abgereist
Di 19/4   Mahlzeit mit Prinzessin Radziwill
Mo 18/4   Anfall von Taubheit
Di 26/4   Paulets wiedergekommen
Fr 29/4

<u>Mai</u>

So 1/5   Beer-Hofmann mit Prinzess
Do 5/5   Minnat ausgereist — Verhandlg mit Gestapo
Fr 6/5   82 Jahre
Di 10/5   Ausreise in 6 14 Tage?
Do 12/5   Väter bekommen
Sa 14/5   Martin abgereist
Sa 21/5   Schätzung der Sammlung
Di 24/5   Mathilde u Robert abgereist
Mo 30/5   + Emilie Kassowitz

<u>Juni</u>

Do 2/6.   Unbedeutliche Äußerl. Erklärung
Sa 3/6   abreise 3h25. Orient Express. 33/4 am
          Trinität nach Kel
London Sa 4/6 Paris London Marie Ernst Bullik
          empfangen. statt nach London
Mo 5/6   früh Dover-London. Haus
          Minna sehr krank. bekommen
          Haus Zeitungen Manchester
Do 9/6   Sam aus Besuch
Fr 10/6   Len Jahuda
Sa 11/6   Besuch Minna z. Geburtstag zurückgefahren
Sa 18/6   H. Wells
So 19/6   Moses III neu begonnen
Di 21/6   Prinzess-Zyprischer Koffer
Do 23/6   Besuch der R.S. — filme
Sa 25/6   Mrs Gunn mit aegypt. Antiq.

Mo 28/3	Acceptance by England assured
	—Ernstl in Paris.—Emigration appears possible

April

Fr 1/4	Two Ernsts in London
We 6/4	Ernst 47 yrs.
Sa 9/4	Topsy's translation finished
Su 10/4	Plebiscite
Tu 12/4	Minna back from Sanator.
Su 17/4	Easter Sunday 52 yrs. in practice
Tu 19/4	Alex 72 yrs. Princess left
X Mo 18/4	Meal with engaged Radziwil couple
Tu 26/4	Attack of deafness
Fri 29/4	Princess returned.

May

Su 1/5	Beer-Hofmann with Princess
Th 5/5	Minna emigrated—Negotiations with Gestapo.
Fr 6/5	82 yrs.
Tu 10/5	Emigration within a fortnight?
Th 12/5	Received passports
Sa 14/5	Martin left
Sa 21/5	Valuation of the collection
Tu 24/5	Mathilde & Robert departed.
Mo 30/5	+ Emilie Kassowitz

June

Th 2/6	Declaration of no impediment
Sa 3/6	Departure 3h 25. Orient Express—3¾ am
	Kehl bridge
London Su 4/6	Paris 10h, met by Marie Ernst, Bullitt
	in the evening to London
Mo 5/6	9 am Dover—London. New
	house. Minna seriously ill. Columns
	in newspapers.
Th 9/6	Sam from Manchester
Fr 10/6	Lun visited
Sa 11/6	Visit of Jahuda
Sa 18/6	Minna seen for the first time on her birthday
Su 19/6	G.H. Wells
Tu 21/6	Moses III begun again
Th 23/6	Princess—Cypriot head
	Visit of R.S.—films
Sa 25/6	Mrs. Gunn with Egypt. antiq.

July 1938

Fr 15/7	Moses sold to America—Mr. Kent?
	Dr Exner
Sa 16/7	House in Finchley Road viewed
Su 17/7	Moses finished.—Will.
Mo 18/7	Mr Kent—12000 Dutch g. demanded.
Tu 19/7	Deafness—Salvador Dali
Sa 23/7	Dutch press.
Tu 26/7	Martha 77 yrs.
Th 28/7	Will signed
	House purchase concluded.
Fr 29/7	Anna to Congress in Paris

August

Mo 1/8	Greetings from Paris Congress
Tu 4/8	Prospectus of new press
Fr 5/8	News Bäumler of despatch of things.
	Anna back from Paris
Sa 6/8	Princess
Su 7/8 Mo 8/8	Things arrived. Willi Lévy begun.
Sa 13/8	Own house viewed 20 Maresfield Gardens.
We 24/8	Ruth took her leave
Mo 29/8	Minna to nursing home

September

Fr 2/9	Hotel Esplanade—Warrington Crescent
Sa 4/9	Alex Sophie Harry arrived
We 7/9	Sanat. London Clinic.
Th 8/9	Operation Pichler
Tu 27/9	20 Maresfields Gardens
Fr 30	Peace

October

Su 2/10	Minna in the house—Martin in hospital
Tu 11/10	Dr Sauerwald
We 12/10	Arnold Zweig takes leave
	Mathilde 51 yrs.
Su 16/10	Princess & Eugenie—Bronze Venus
Sa 29/10	A Comment on Antisemitism.

November

Th 10/11	Pogroms in Germany—Ban in Franco-Spain
Tu 29/11	H. G. Wells

December

Sa 3/XII	Anna 43 yrs.
Su 4/Xii	Princess on house visit
Tu 6/XII	Lün back—Recital Engel Lund
We 7/XII	Broadcasting—Martin 49 yrs.
Th 8/XII	Princess left—Will. Brown

Fr 15/7 — Moses nach Amerika verkauft — Mr Kent ?
Dr Exner.
Sa 16/7 Haus in Finchley Road besichtigt
So 17/7 Moses beendigt Testament.
Mo 18/7 Mr Kent — 12000 Hollande angefordert.
Di 19/7 Taubheit — Salvador Dali
Sa 23/7 Holländischer Verlag.
Do 26/7 Martha 77 J.
Do 28/7 Testament unterschrieben
Fr 29/7 Hauskauf abgeschlossen.
Anna zum Kongress nach Paris

August
Mo 1/8 Begrüssung von Paris Kongress
Do 4/8 Projekt des neuen Verlags.
Fr 5/8 Nachricht Bäumler v. Abgang v. Sachen.
Anna zurück v. Paris
Sa 6/8 Prinzessin — Sachen angekommen — Willi Levy begonnen
So/8 Mo 8/8 Eigenes Haus besichtigt 20 Maresfield Gardens.
Sa 13/8 24/8 Ruth ... nursing home
Mi 24/8 Minna in's nursing home
Mo 29/8
September

Fr 2/9 Hotel Esplanade Warrington crescent
4/9 Alex, Sophie, Harry angekommen.
Sa 4/9 Sanat London Clinic
Mi 7/9 Operation Pichler
Do 6/9 — 20 Maresfield Gardens.
Di 27/9 Friede
Fr 30/9

October
Minna in's Haus Martha in Spital
Sa 2/10 Dr Sauerwald
Di 11/10 Arnold Zweig z. Abschied
Mi 12/10 Mathilde 51 J.
So 16/10 Prinzessin u. Eugenie — Bronze Venus
Sa 29/10 ein Werk g. Antisemitismus.
Mo 31/10 November
Pogroms in Germany — Rebellion in Franco-Spanien
Do 10/11 H. G. Wells
Di 29/11 Dezember
Anna 43 J.
Sa 3/12 Prinzessin mit Hausbesuch
So 4/12 Eva zurück — Vortrag Engel Zernd
Di 6/12 Broadcasting — Martin 49 J.
Mi 7/12 Prinzess abgereist — Willi Brown
Do 8/12

1939.

January

Lumbago.

Knochenschmerzen

4/31/1

Februar

Do 2/2   Moses unprimirt

So 5/2   Prinzessin

Fr 10/2   + Pius XI – Trotter

So 19/2   Oli 487 Lacassagne

So 26/2   Prinzess mit Lacassagne

Fr 28/2   Probeexcision u Röntgen

March

Fr 3/3   Bescheid von Paris – Pius XII

Mo 6/3   Dr Finzi

Mi 8/3   25 Jahrfeier d. British Society

Do 9/3   Erster Röntgen – Finzi

Sa 11/3   Jahrstag der Nazi-invasion

Mo 13/3   Moses bei Gange – Prinzess u Lacassagne

Mi 15/3   Radium – Prag besetzt

April

Do 6/4   Ernst 47 J.

So 16/4   Sommerzeit

19/4   Alexander 73 J.

Mi / Do 20/4   Schur nach New York

May

Sa 6/5   83st. Geburtstag

Fr 12/5   Tost welshinern

19/5   Moses englisch

Sa 20/5   Anna nach Amsterdam

June

Tue 6/6   Ein Jahr in England

July

So 2/7   Prinzessin Geburtstag bei uns

Mo 10/7   + Havelock Ellis

We 12/7   Schur zurück

Sa 15/7   + Bleuler

Mo 24/7   Evchen – Wells in ärztliches ...

Mi 26/7   Martha 78 J.

August

Tue 1/8   Auflösung d. Praxis – besuche Ruth Preisig

George u Marie Segredaels. Sachs

We 23   Ruth erwachsende

Do 24   Jak von Dänk

Fr 25   Eva nach Wien. Dorothy u York

Kriegspanik

1939

January

2/1	Lumbago.
—31/1	Bone ache

February

Th 2/2	Moses printed
Su 5/2	Princess
Fr 10/2	+ Pius XI—Trotter
Su 19/2	Oli 48 yrs.
Su 26/2	Princess with Lacassagne
Tu 28/2	Trial excision & X-ray

March

Fr 3/3	News from Paris—Pius XII
Mo 6/3	Dr Finzi
We 8/3	25th anniversary celebration of British Society.
Th 9/3	First X-ray—Finzi
Sa 11/3	Anniversary of the Nazi invasion
Mo 13/3	Moses with Lange—Princess & Lacassagne
We 15/3	Radium—Prague occupied

April

Th 6/4	Ernst 47 yrs.
Su 16/4	Summer time
We 19/4	Alexander 73 yrs.
Th 20/4	Schur to New York

May

Sa 6/5	83rd birthday
Fr 12/5	Topsy published
Fr 19/5	Moses in English
Sa 20/5	Anna to Amsterdam

June

Tue 6/6	One year in England

July

Su 2/7	Princess birthday at our house.
Mo 10/7	+ Havelock Ellis
We 12/7	Schur back
Sa 15/7	+ Bleuler
Mo 24/7	Evchen—Wells in citizenship
We 26/7	Marthe 78 yrs.

August

Tue 1/8	Disbanded the practice. Visitors. Ruth Prince George & Marie, Segredakis. Sachs.
We 23	Ruth taken leave
Th 24	Money from bank
Fr 25	Eva to Nice. Dorothy N. York War panic

Freud, with Anna, her aunt Mitzi and niece Angela, Berlin 1929.

1929

The diary opens in bad times, halfway between two world wars and a few days after the Wall Street Crash. The Austrian and German economies had never recovered from the effects of World War I and both suffered drastic inflation during the 1920s. Freud's foreign patients and their hard currency had partly cushioned him from the worst effects, but his three sons were all experiencing difficulties making a living. "Business and public affairs, as you may know, are very bad with us, the young people have a hard life. No sign of improvement . . . " Freud wrote to his nephew, Sam Freud, on December 6, 1929.

The following day, December 7, 1929, the diary records **Bad heart days**. This was the second period of heart trouble Freud had suffered within a month. These two themes, poor health and political disasters, are leitmotifs of the last ten years of his life. Yet he continued working, and his work at this period reflects the problems of the age, seen through the eyes of an old man with a limited faith in progress. A week after the letter to Sam Freud, he wrote to his colleague Max Eitingon that he would be giving him " . . . a *discontenting* Christmas present . . . ." This refers to the book Freud had just completed when the diary opens—*Civilization and its Discontents*—his latest diagnosis of the troubles endemic in culture. Eitingon visited Freud on December 24, 1929, and a diary entry for that day—**Eitingon "Discontents"**—registers the presentation of this gift.

It was now thirty years since Freud had published *The Interpretation of Dreams*, the book that became the cornerstone of psychoanalysis. A series of works had followed, in which he established the power of unconscious drives and forces over the individual. By the late 1920s, he was turning to the analysis of social and cultural behavior. *The Future of an Illusion* (1927) dissected the unconscious components of religious faith, the extent to which deities are adult idealizations of infant images of parents. Now, in *Civilization and its Discontents*, he depicted the fundamental conflict between humanity's destructive urges and the necessary taming of the drives imposed by society.

Although Freud was now 73 years old, a world-famous figure and founder of the international psychoanalytical movement, his work continued to be intellectually scandalous, still rejected by most of the general public and the majority of the medical and scientific establishments. The diary opens on October 31, 1929, with the dry comment:—**Passed over for the Nobel Prize**. Freud knew he was attacking beliefs that were precious and ideas that were generally accepted as "common-sense": he could hardly be surprised by the hostility his work aroused. Though his name was to be proposed many times as a candidate for the Nobel Prize, he remained justifiably sceptical about his chances. Exactly fourteen years before this first diary entry, on October 31, 1915, he had written to a friend: "But it would be absurd to expect a sign of recognition when one has 7/8 of the world against one . . . ."[1]

Undeterred by resistance to his ideas, in these last years he continued his attack on illusions and the institutions founded upon them. His ideal remained scientific truth, a reflection of reality. Through his analysis of civilization's discontents, he was also able to express his own discontent with the dire state of the world around him, and specifically with the failure to understand and master the destructive tendencies within human society.

1. *Freud-Ferenczi 31.10.1915* in Jones, II.213.

Passed over for the Nobel Prize . . .   **[Thurs] 31 October 1929**

The Nobel Prize awards had already been announced the previous week. Christiaan Eijkman and Sir F. Hopkins were awarded the Medicine and Physiology Prize for their work on vitamins: the Literature Prize went to the German novelist Thomas Mann.

But the Nobel Prize—or rather, the lack of it—had figured as a largely irritating factor in Freud's life since at least 1915, when he had written to his friend, the Hungarian psychoanalyst Sándor Ferenczi, complaining that the failure to get the award saddened him, for it indicated his inability to gain the respect of the general public.[1]

By 1917, when the prospect of a Nobel Prize for Freud came under discussion, he was already reacting with scepticism: "I don't think I shall live to see the day," he wrote to his friend, the writer and psychoanalyst Lou Andreas-Salomé (*Freud-Lou Andreas-Salomé 13.7.1917*).

First tarock party . . .   **Sat 2 November 1929**

Tarock was a Viennese card game which Freud had been playing regularly on Saturday evenings since the 1890s. This entry must refer to the first game after his return from holidays. His partners were a devoted circle of old friends, including the pediatrician Oskar Rie, his brother Alfred Rie and Freud's sister-in-law Minna Bernays.[1]

The game could be played with 2, 3 or 4 players: the four-handed version had a different set of rules and was called *Königrufen*.[2]

Visit Rickman* . . .   **Sat 2 November 1929**

The British psychoanalyst John Rickman (1891–1951) was the compiler of the *Index Psychoanalyticus 1893–1926* published by Hogarth in 1928. He began an analysis with Freud in 1920, on the recommendation of the leading British psychoanalyst Ernest Jones. By 1929 he had switched to analysis with Ferenczi. Jones wrote: "Everything goes smoothly except for Rickman who, being in the middle of his analysis with Ferenczi, is naturally in a very difficult and ambivalent mood." (*Jones-Freud 14.10.1929*)

At this time the previously intimate and frequent correspondence between Freud and Sándor Ferenczi in Budapest had become more sporadic: Rickman's visit to Freud brought them indirectly into contact. But in his next letter to Ferenczi, Freud complained that the visitor had now apparently formed an unfavorable judgment of Freud's analysis, because it had failed to unearth some hidden truth: "So e.g. I jokingly complained that Rickman, now your patient, treated me as if I were his grandfather, rationally, with ill-concealed disdain, because in his analysis I did not discover the truth which was however to be discovered in the continuation of the analysis." (*Freud-Ferenczi 11.1.1930*)

At Schnitzler's with infected finger . . .   **Tues [Mon]** 4 November 1929**

Julius Schnitzler (1865–1939), professor of surgery and specialist in the treatment of abdominal disorders, was the brother of the famous Austrian writer Arthur Schnitzler and brother-in-law of Professor Marcus Hajek (1861–1941), who performed the initial, botched operation on Freud's jaw in 1923.[1] It is unclear what the finger infection was.

Schnitzler was another of the tarock regulars. Did this consultation in fact take place before the card party? These early entries are cramped together and from November 2 to 6 it is not clear to which dates entries may apply. This one could be a continuation of Saturday, November 2.

Almanach . . .   **Tues [Mon] 4 November 1929**

The *Almanach der Psychoanalyse* was an annual collection of essays on psychoanalytical themes. Founded in 1926, it was edited by A.J. Storfer and published by the International Psychoanalytical Press in Vienna. The 1930 number that Freud

Freud's friend and "paladin," Sándor Ferenczi, sketched in 1924.

Freud's deck of tarock cards.

John Rickman in 1924, when he was in analysis with Freud. In 1929 he was Ferenczi's patient.

---

* It seems unlikely Rickman's visit would have occured *after* the evening tarock game. Probably Freud noted events for each day as they occured to him later, not chronologically.

** Tuesday was in fact 5th November. All the days this week are incorrectly dated. Thus, the "Antisemitic disturbances" Freud records on "Fri 7" actually took place on *Thursday* 7. (The correct day is in square brackets.) Perhaps Freud filled them in later in the month. He may then have calculated the figure from the first complete date—"So. 2 Nov"—which he misread as "Sunday" (Sonntag) instead of "Saturday" (Sonnabend).

had just received opened with a reprint of his article "Dostoevsky and Parricide," written as an introductory essay for a 23-volume edition of Dostoevsky, published in 1928 by the Piper press and edited by René Fülöp-Miller and Friedrich Eckstein.

Preface for Eitingon . . .   Tues [Mon] 4 November 1929

Max Eitingon (1881–1943) studied medicine in Zurich where he met the Swiss psychiatrist Carl Gustav Jung, through whom he came into contact with Freud. They first met in 1907. He was a member of the "Wednesday Society," the early psychoanalytical discussion group at Freud's house and in 1908 he took part in the first International Psychoanalytical Congress at Salzburg.

In 1910, together with the German psychoanalyst Karl Abraham, Eitingon co-founded the Berlin Psychoanalytical Society of which he was the secretary. In 1919, at Freud's suggestion, Eitingon became a member of the Committee—a small, secret group formed in 1912 to champion the cause of psychoanalysis.[1] In 1920 the Berlin Psychoanalytical Society opened an institute and psychoanalytical polyclinic to train psychoanalysts and treat nervous disorders—the first of its type in the world.

Eitingon had a considerable private income from the family fur business, which he used not only to support this enterprise but also to rescue the international psychoanalytical press (*I.P.V.* or *Internationaler Psychoanalytischer Verlag*) during its frequent crises. In 1925 Eitingon was elected president of the International Psychoanalytical Association to replace Abraham, who had just died.

By 1929 Eitingon had proved himself invaluable both to the psychoanalytical movement and to Freud himself. With the tenth anniversary of the Berlin Polyclinic approaching in 1930, the Hungarian analyst Sándor Radó, editor of the international psychoanalytical journal (*Internationale Zeitschrift für Psychoanalyse*), suggested publishing a brochure in honor of the Polyclinic. Freud agreed, but his preface makes it clear that he felt the publication was actually a tribute to Eitingon himself, who had founded, funded and directed the institution.

Kris and mounts . . .   Thurs [Wed] 6* November 1929

Ernst Kris (1900–1957) was an art historian, curator in the Vienna Kunsthistorisches Museum. He was a student of Freud's friend, the archaeologist Emanuel Löwy, but it was through his future wife, Marianne Rie, a daughter of Freud's tarock partner and old friend, the pediatrician Oskar Rie, that he first met Freud. In 1927, after a training analysis with Helene Deutsch, he joined the Vienna Psychoanalytical Institute: in the same year he married Marianne Rie.

Kris was a world authority on cameos[1] and intaglios. He was an expert in the mounting and display of items and also helped Freud purchase antiquities.

The mounts mentioned in this entry were perhaps prepared by the Greek and Roman antiquities department of the museum where Kris worked. They may have been mounts for the terracotta figures delivered on January 15, 1930.

Flournoy . . .   Thurs [Wed] 6 November 1929

The Swiss psychoanalyst and philosopher Henri Flournoy (1886–1956) was the son of the psychologist Théodore Flournoy. He was analyzed by the Dutch analyst Johan H.W. van Ophuijsen, by Freud and by the Viennese analyst Hermann Nunberg. From 1915 he had a psychoanalytical practice in Geneva.

Antisemitic disturbances . . .   Fri [Thurs] 7 November 1929

From late 1923 onward the Vienna colleges and universities were focal points for confrontations between Jewish and Nazi students. During the week, right-wing students had already interrupted classes and mobbed Jewish students at the Vienna Technical University. On the morning of Thursday, November 7, Nazi students disrupted a lecture at the Anatomical Institute by the (Jewish) professor and city councillor, Julius Tandler, and afterwards the disturbance spilled out into the street and other parts of the building.

---

* A broken line connects "Kris" with Thursday (*Wed*) 6: an unbroken one links his name with Wednesday (*Tues*) 5. Either Kris visited on both days or Freud had second thoughts about the date and added the unbroken line as a correction, assigning Kris to Wednesday. In that case the broken line might refer only to "Flournoy"

Max Eitingon, creator and director of the Berlin Psycho-Analytic Institute. This photo, sent to Freud in 1923, shows the ring Freud gave him.

Ernst Kris, art historian and pupil of Freud.

Antisemitism had long been endemic in the Austro-Hungarian Empire. Two of its earlier proponents, Georg Ritter von Schoenerer, the founder of the German nationalistic Linz program of 1882, and Karl Lueger, the very popular Mayor of Vienna at the turn of the century, served as political models for Hitler. It was antisemitism that had first made Freud aware of his Jewish identity during his youth: he countered discrimination with pride and intellectual independence. In 1930 he wrote: "But I had already felt myself to be a Jew earlier—under the influence of German antisemitism, of which a renewed outbreak took place during my university days." (*Freud-Dwossis 15.12.1930*)

Dioscori ring . . .   Fri [Thurs] 7 November 1929

This ring probably contained an intaglio bearing the figures of the Dioscori, the heavenly twins. It is no longer in Freud's collection of antiquities, but that is not surprising for he often gave items away as gifts, especially rings, which were a frequent token of affection or trust.

When the secret Committee first gathered on May 25, 1913, Freud ceremonially presented each member with a gold ring bearing an antique Greek intaglio. He himself wore such a ring with an intaglio of the head of Jupiter.

Neuralgia . . .   Mon 11 Nov 1929

Pain and illness are a leitmotif of these last years: Freud was now 73 years old and the radical cancer surgery in 1923 had resulted in a series of minor ailments and continual pain from the badly-fitting prosthesis. Neuralgia may have been one among many other side-effects. The psychoanalyst Richard Sterba, watching Freud, noted: "His demeanour was alert and lively, the movement of his hands quick and assertive. However, when he sat silently [. . .] he often touched an area of his upper jaw with his fingers as if this gave him some relief from pain or discomforting pressure."

Adda given away . . .   Mon 11 Nov 1929

Adda seems to have been an animal, given away now, but picked up again on November 25. Neither letters nor personal memories contain any clues about this entry. In August 1929 Freud's first dog, a chow named Lun Yug, was run over. In September Anna wrote: "I would very much like us to have a new Lün. For the time being my father does not want to hear of it." (*Anna Freud-Jones 19.9.1929*) Could Adda have been a substitute dog? Why was she given away?

Heart warmth attack . . .   Thurs 14 November 1929

Freud had suffered from heart trouble for many years: between 1893 and 1895 he had a "severe cardiac episode." Already in 1894 he was writing that burning sensations were among the symptoms. At that time nicotine was being blamed and Freud tried, unsuccessfully, to give up smoking. But he claimed that the trouble had begun organically, after an attack of influenza in 1889.

In 1926 Ferenczi tried to persuade Freud that much heart trouble was conversion hysteria and required psychoanalysis. Freud replied that dying, too, had its psychical root but nevertheless psychoanalysis could not cure it. His own heart trouble was beyond analysis, he said, owing to its toxic etiology and anatomical diagnosis. Freud's doctor, Max Schur, also insisted that the trouble had an organic basis and he reprimanded Freud's biographer, Ernest Jones, for "cavalierly" treating it as neurotic.

Dr. Altmann . . .   Thurs 14 November 1929

This may well have been Professor Dr. Siegfried Altmann (1887–1963), director of the Jewish Institute for the Blind in Vienna, which Freud was to visit on August 10, 1933.[1] It was Anna Freud's friend, Dorothy Burlingham, who had contacted Altmann on her own initiative. She was now beginning the psychoanalysis of "Sylvia", a blind 3-year old, her first analysis, and the start of her life-long involvement with blind children.

Rothschild hospital . . .   Sat 16 November 1929

This may have been a consultation with the heart specialist Dr. Ludwig Braun, Freud's old friend, who was head doctor at the Rothschild Hospital, a Jewish hospital in Vienna.

Students escaping a Nazi attack on Tandler's Anatomical Institute, Vienna. DOW

Anna's book . . .   Sat 16 November 1929

Of all Freud's six children only the youngest, Anna Freud (1895–1982), became a psychoanalyst. By this period she was the only one unmarried and still living at home. She began her working career as a schoolteacher during World War I and this experience enabled her to write the book Freud probably refers to here—*Einführung in die Psychoanalyse für Pädagogen*, published in 1930. It came out in English in 1931 as *Introduction to Psychoanalysis for Teachers: Four Lectures* (Allen & Unwin, London) and in the United States in 1935 as *Psychoanalysis for Teachers and Parents* (Emerson Books, N.Y.).[1]

The book consisted of four lectures which had been given to the staff of the Vienna *Hort* (the day-care center for working mothers). This course had been arranged under the patronage of the progressive city councillor Hugo Breitner and the inspector of schools Anton Tesarek.

Freud sent a copy of Anna's book as a New Year's gift to Ferenczi, who immediately responded: "I read Anna's book with unmixed joy; it combines all the advantages of her writing style: deliberation, sagacity, moderation, intelligence and humanity. Her maturity is downright admirable." (*Ferenczi-Freud 5.1.-1930*)

First evening Yvette . . .   Wed 20 November 1929

Yvette Guilbert (1865–1944), the French singer and *diseuse*, first made her name as a *café-concert* performer in Paris. By the 1890s she had an international reputation. Her repertoire ran the gamut of characters, from songs in which she played the part of an innocent schoolgirl to those in which she was a drunkard or prostitute. Toulouse-Lautrec had portrayed her several times in the long black gloves that were her trademark: Freud's picture collection contains one of the artist's original lithographs of her ("Columbine à Pierrot"). There is also a signed portrait photograph of her hanging in his study. In addition to the glamour that characterized some of Freud's other women friends of this period (Princess Marie Bonaparte and Lou Andreas-Salomé), Yvette Guilbert was a living link with the *Belle Époque* and the Paris of Freud's own youth. He had in fact first heard her in 1889 while attending the first congress on hypnosis in Paris, but did not meet her until the 1920s when Anna Freud befriended Eva Rosenfeld, a niece of Yvette's husband, Max Schiller.

At this period of Freud's life her touring concerts in Vienna were the only form of entertainment that could entice him out in the evening. He presented her with some flowers; in a note of thanks she invited him to have tea with her at her hotel, together with his wife and daughter Anna. In a letter to Ferenczi three weeks later Freud quotes from one of the songs she sang: "This November I heard my dear Yvette again—you know we get on very well together—singing with her inimitable emphasis:

'J'ai dit tout ça? C'est possible, mais
je ne me souviens pas.' "
[I said all that? It's possible, but
I don't remember.] (*Freud-Ferenczi 13.12.29*)

At Yvette's hotel . . .   Thurs 21 November 1929

Yvette Guilbert always stayed at the luxurious Hotel Bristol during her concert tours to Vienna: her invitation to Freud, his wife and Anna is on the hotel's stationery.[1]

Thomas Mann dedication . . .   Fri 22 November 1929

In 1929 Thomas Mann (1875–1955) published an essay on Freud in the first number of the journal *Die Psychoanalytische Bewegung* (May-June 1929). It is entitled "Freud's Position in Modern Intellectual History" and it links Freud with German Romanticism as represented by Novalis, and with Nietzsche. It ends with Mann's verdict on Freud's teaching: "*It is that manifestation of modern irrationalism which unambiguously resists any reactionary misuse. We wish to express our conviction that it is one of the most essential building blocks which have been laid down for the foundation of the future, the home of a liberated and wise humanity.*"

Freud was flattered by the essay but remained sceptical as to its relevance. He wrote to his friend Lou Andreas-Salomé: "Th. Mann's essay is certainly an

Yvette Guilbert, 1927. From her book *The Art of Singing a Song (L'Art de chanter une Chanson)*.

honour. It gives me the impression that he had an essay on Romanticism ready to hand, when he was requested to write something about me, and so he furnished the front and back of the essay with a veneer of psycho-analysis, as the cabinet-makers say; the bulk is of a different material. However, when Mann says something, it has real substance." (*Freud-Andreas-Salomé 28.7.1929*)

In 1930 Mann republished the essay on Freud in a volume of his speeches and essays. He sent Freud a pre-publication copy, now in the library at the Freud Museum, with a handwritten dedication which must be the one referred to in this entry: "Sigmund Freud. With great respect, Munich 17.11.1929."

Second evening Yvette . . .   Fri 22 November 1929

Freud's enthusiasm for Yvette's art was such that he attended two of her concerts in a week. She appeared onstage in a long black dress, with bright red hair and, of course, her long gloves and sang "*Au temps d'Yvette*," '*C'est le mai*," '*Il était trois petits enfants.*" A reviewer for the *Wiener Zeitung* called her "a great actress with genial insight into the human soul."

At Gottlieb's . . .   Sat 23* November 1929

Rudolf Gottlieb (1864—?), a Viennese doctor, had been one of the five registered participants—all of them, incidentally, Jewish—of Freud's first university course in 1886-7, on "The Anatomy of the Spinal Medulla and Medulla Oblongata as an Introduction to the Treatment of Nervous Diseases." It was held in the lecture hall of his eminent teacher, Theodor Meynert. Gottlieb also attended his first *Disputatorium* on April 11, 1889, and was among the donors of a large embossed photograph album given to Freud in honor of the occasion. If this was indeed the same Gottlieb whom Freud now visited, then he was among his very oldest acquaintances.[1]

False alarm with Pichler . . .   Sat 23** November 1929

Dr. Hans Pichler (1877–1949) was the oral surgeon who had been operating on Freud since 1923. During World War I he had been the head of a new department of oral surgery at the Vienna University Hospital: he wrote 125 technical papers, contributed to several textbooks and was a pioneering surgeon. Freud and his "personal doctor" Max Schur trusted him implicitly. His skillful and radical surgery certainly extended Freud's life by several years.

Over the 10 years from 1929 to 1939 the diary records 20 operations by Pichler. Freud did not bother to record the innumerable consultations and examinations. From the time Pichler began treating Freud in 1923 he kept detailed clinical notes on the case history and these include an account of the false alarm to which Freud refers.

Freud visited Pichler with Dr. Joseph Weinmann, who was now attending to him from day to day, in order to gain a second opinion on what Weinmann feared might be a recurrence of the cancer. Dr. Hermann Schroeder in Berlin, who had manufactured Freud's latest prosthesis, had also considered one particular place in the mouth suspicious. In this instance, however, Pichler judged the swelling to be nonpathological, possibly an attack of coryza—hence a "false alarm."

Adda fetched . . .   Mon 25 Nov 1929

A second reference to the mysterious "Adda," given away six weeks previously on October 11.

Princess left . . .   Sat 30 November 1929

Apart from family members, Princess Marie Bonaparte is the most frequently mentioned person in the diary. She is usually referred to either as *Prinzess* or *Prinzessin.*

Princess Marie Bonaparte (1882–1962) was a direct descendant of Lucien

Marie Bonaparte with her friend and translator Rodolphe Loewenstein, speaking to Franz Alexander (left).
TG

---

* "Sat 23"—This entry is ambiguously placed between Friday and Saturday, but a line above "Sat 23" seems to connect it to this latter date.

** The dates from Wednesday 20 to Saturday 23 were initially filled in incorrectly, as *21 to 24*, then corrected. It is improbable Freud would have continued four days in ignorance of the right date. Probably he wrote all these entries together at the end of the week and again miscalculated.

Bonaparte, one of Napoleon's younger brothers. Her husband was Prince George of Greece, younger brother of Constantine I, the King of Greece, and through him she was also related to the royal families of Denmark, Russia and England. Nevertheless she was a woman of great character and lively intelligence.

In 1925 she began a psychoanalysis with Freud which was to change her life. She herself became a psychoanalyst and a leading figure in the international psychoanalytical movement. Freud's friendship with her was one of the most important relationships of his final years. It was based not just on attraction but on compatibility of temperaments. Martin Freud wrote: ". . . she had most of father's chief characteristics—his courage, his sincerity, his essential goodness and kindliness and his inflexible devotion to scientific truth. In this sense the similarity of character was almost startling."

During August 1929 Princess Marie Bonaparte and her daughter Eugénie had stayed with the Freuds at their rented house, "Schneewinkel," in Berchtesgaden. Eugénie was virtually an invalid—she had suffered first from pulmonary tuberculosis, which had been cured, but now had a tubercular cyst in her leg. The visit was arranged in order for her to convalesce.

After her initial psychoanalysis Marie Bonaparte frequently returned to Vienna, not just to visit Freud socially but also for further reworking and training analysis. When she left Vienna on this occasion,[1] Freud gave her one of his famous intaglio rings, a prerogative of his disciples and closest friends.

One of Marie Bonaparte's great interests was criminal psychopathology. In 1929 the journal *Imago* published Dr. R. Loewenstein's German translation of her study of a murderer—*Le Cas de Madame Lefebvre*. This dealt with the case of a woman who in 1925 had murdered her pregnant daughter-in-law. Freud had a copy of the book in his library.

Eitingon's mother + . . .   Sat 30 November 1929

Crosses next to names, denoting death, are a frequent feature in the diary. On the death of Max Eitingon's mother, Freud sent him a letter which touches a theme Freud was to return to less than a year later, on the death of his own mother—the idea that a mother bars the way to one's own death: "I must express our deepest sympathy to you and your family and will not attempt to console you. The loss of a mother must be something very strange, not comparable with anything else and it must arouse emotions which are difficult to grasp. For I have a mother of my own and she bars my way to the desired rest, the eternal Nothing; I could not, so to speak, forgive myself were I to die before her." (*Freud-Eitingon 1.12.1929*)

Anna's birthday 34 yrs . . .   Tues 3 December 1929

During Freud's final decade his youngest child, Anna, became indispensable to him in a number of ways. After his operation he had largely withdrawn from any public activity or business. She was involved in the work of the Vienna Psychoanalytic Institute and in the business affairs of the International Psychoanalytical Association and was thus his day-to-day link with this outside world. Moreover, she became in effect his nurse. As Freud later said, ". . . fate has granted me as compensation for much that has been denied me the possession of a daughter who, in tragic circumstances, would not have fallen short of Antigone." (*Freud-Arnold Zweig 25.2.1934*)

If any further evidence is needed of her paramount importance to her father during his last years, one could point to the fact that each of her ten birthdays from 1929 to 1938 is recorded in the diary. This was by no means the case with other family birthdays. Freud's wife, Martha, and his children Mathilde, Martin and Ernst each have six of theirs mentioned, Minna Bernays, his sister-in-law, has four and his second son, Oliver, three.

Martin 40 yrs . . .   Sat 7 December 1929

Martin,[1] Freud's eldest son, studied law at the University of Vienna. Like his two brothers, he served in the army during World War I. After the war he married and went into banking. But the *Fides Treuhandbank* where he worked went bankrupt, like many others, with the collapse of the Austrian economy in the early 1920s. He then formed the *Autokreditanstalt*, a form of car leasing (many of the Viennese taxis were acquired through this system) and he also took on law cases.

Anna Freud at Schneewinkel, Freud's holiday home in 1929. MH

Anna Freud, aged about 30. For Freud she was "compensation for much that has been denied me. . . ."

He lived on the Franz-Josef-Kai, very near his father, and his offices were in the *Börse*, the Stock Exchange building, two minutes' walk from the Freuds' apartment at Berggasse 19. Most days he visited in the mornings and often spent his evenings there too.

Bad heart days . . .   Sat 7-Tues 10 December 1929

After this attack of heart trouble Freud wrote to Ferenczi: "Privately the situation is such that I must expend the greater part of my energies on maintaining that bit of health that I need for the continued daily work. A true mosaic of measures to force the recalcitrant organs to serve their purpose. In the end my heart intervened with extra systoles, arrhythmia and attacks of fibrillation. My wise personal doctor, Prof. Braun, says however that all of this has no serious significance. He should know. Is he already beginning to deceive me?" (*Freud-Ferenczi 13.12.29*)

Emerald ring . . .   Wed 11 December 1929

Freud's predilection for rings was shown by his use of them as tokens of authority for the members of the Committee: ". . . a privilege and a mark distinguishing a group of men who were united in their devotion to psychoanalysis. . . ." (*Freud-Simmel 11.11.1928*) In that instance he had had them made up from ancient intaglios. The ring he gave Simmel in 1928 is an example—a Roman seal in a modern setting.[1]

Society evening . . .   Thurs 12 December 1929

This was not the Vienna Psychoanalytical Society, for they met fortnightly and on Wednesdays. (This month they met on December 4th and 18th.) Freud had stopped attending meetings after his operation in 1923, being too ill to take part in full sessions. However, he missed the discussions and in their place Paul Federn organized smaller sessions, attended by members of the executive board and a few selected members of the Society. They took place in Freud's waiting room, about five times yearly from 1928 to 1932, then stopped. Generally someone presented a paper or reviewed a recent work of Freud's and this was followed by a discussion, a break, then continued discussion, during which Freud would often speak at length.[1]

Anna to Essen . . .   Tues 17 December 1929

From Essen, Anna went to Göttingen to visit the novelist and critic Lou Andreas-Salomé (1861–1937), who in her youth had fascinated Nietzsche. Later she was Rilke's mentor and lover. Her meetings with Freud, at the Third Psychoanalytic Congress at Weimar in 1911, then in Vienna in 1912, were crucial for her and she subsequently became a practicing psychoanalyst. For many years she had been in correspondence with Freud and Anna, both of whom respected her highly and confided in her. In early December she wrote to Anna of her delight in the success of an analysis of a young girl: ". . . I wanted best to tell your father about it every day and did that too in my thoughts." (*Lou Andreas-Salomé-Anna Freud 1.12.1929*)

Cut stones bought . . .   Tues 17 December 1929

Since Ernst Kris was an expert on cut stones, it is highly likely he played a part in helping Freud obtain and select these gems.

Anna back . . .   Sat 21 December 1929

A series of telegrams home marked each point in Anna's itinerary. The morning after leaving home she sent one from Cologne and another from Essen in the evening; the next day, Thursday, December 19, a telegram from Göttingen informed the family that she would be returning Saturday morning after breaking her return journey in Nuremberg.

Christmas . . .   Tues 24 December 1929

Freud was an atheist and the festivities celebrated in the household were for the sake of the children. Martin Freud wrote: "We were brought up without any traces of the Jewish ritual. Our festivals were Christmas, with presents under a candle-lit tree, and Easter, with gaily painted Easter eggs. I had never been in a

Lou Andreas-Salomé, c.1930. It was "an honour when she joined the ranks of our collaborators . . ." Freud stated.

synagogue, nor to my knowledge had my brothers or sisters." His wife, Martha, also felt the need to celebrate Christmas, which (she wrote to a daughter-in-law) ". . . always costs us a lot of money but also brings great joy." (*Martha Freud-Lucie Freud 7.12.1934*)

Eitingon "Discontents" . . .   Tues 24 December 1929

During the year Eitingon had been kept informed of the progress of Freud's most recent work in progress, *Civilization and its Discontents*: "My work could perhaps be called, if it needs a name at all: Misfortune in Culture. It is not coming easily to me." (*Freud-Eitingon 8.7.1929*) It had been sent to the printers in November, despite Freud's dissatisfaction with it, and a presentation copy was ready for Eitingon when he visited at Christmas: "Of course we would very much like to see you between Christmas and New Year. I will be free from 24–26. I will probably also be able to give you a discontenting* Christmas present." (*Freud-Eitingon 13.12.1929*)

An incidental topic of their conversation was the Japanese psychologist Yaekiche Yabe. Eitingon told Freud that Yabe had made contact with the International Psychoanalytical Association to arrange a training analysis in Europe.

Pearls for Martha . . .   Fri 27 December 1929

Probably these pearls were a New Year's gift from Freud to his wife, Martha. In a number of subsequent photographs she is seen wearing a pearl necklace. This is the only instance where a specific present for her is mentioned. Indeed, she appears relatively seldom in the diary. Ever since their marriage in 1886, she had been a constant factor in Freud's life, providing emotional security and practical support. She had never shared his scientific interests: her sphere was care of the family and the household. It was her temperament and function which he sketched in a letter to his eldest daughter Mathilde about the choice of a wife: "The intelligent ones among the young men know what they must look for in a wife, gentleness, cheerfulness and the ability to make their lives brighter and easier." (*Freud-Mathilde Freud 26.3.1908*)

Adda died . . .   Mon 30 December 1929

This is the final mention of the mysterious "Adda."[1]

---

*"*Unbehaglich*"—literally "discomforting." Freud is playing on the new book's title, *Das Unbehagen in der Kultur*–later translated as *Civilization and its Discontents*, though Freud had suggested "Man's Discomfort in Civilization" as a possible translation.

Martha Freud. "Methodical and observant," she watched over Freud "as inconspicuously as possible."

Freud and his mother. "She bars my way to the desired rest. . . ."

1930

The topic of public recognition came into focus again this year. On November 6, 1930, Freud's diary states: **Conclusively passed over for Nobel Prize**. But though the Nobel Prize once again eluded him, he did receive an important award this summer—the Goethe Prize for 1930, bestowed by the city of Frankfurt. To Freud, and those who shared his cultural background, Goethe embodied the ideal balance between Romantic desire and Classical control. "The fantasy of a closer relationship with Goethe is all-too-appealing . . ."[1] Freud wrote. This honor greatly pleased him, but it placed him in a wider cultural context in which he was not entirely at ease. He had numerous contacts among writers and artists who were frequently more responsive to him than scientists. But Freud disliked being described as an "artist," feeling that belittled the essence of his work, its scientific accomplishment.

The entry for August 28, 1930—**Anna in Frankfurt**—reports Freud's speech of acceptance of the Goethe Prize. He was not strong enough to travel to Germany for the official ceremony, and, as so often during these years, his daughter Anna represented him. In the speech she delivered at Frankfurt, Freud refers to our ambivalence toward great men, fathers and teachers. This can be interpreted as another aspect of the hostility to the father implicit in the Oedipus complex. However, Freud did not discuss the relationship to mothers. A previous study of Goethe, *A Childhood Recollection from "Dichtung und Wahrheit"* (1917), had shown that the poet's success was grounded in confidence of his mother's love. Freud could not but have drawn comparisons with his own situation, as first-born and best-loved child of his own mother. And it was on the very day the Goethe Prize was handed to him at his holiday home on Grundlsee (August 24, 1930), that he saw his mother, Amalia Freud, for the last time. Three weeks later she died. The diary entry for September 12, 1930 simply reports: **Mother died 8 a.m.** He did not mourn her. She was 95 years old and had been painfully ill for some time. Her death was a release, not only from her own sufferings, but to Freud himself. In December 1929 he had written to a friend whose mother had just died: " . . . I

have a mother of my own and she bars my way to the desired rest . . . ."[2] Her existence had laid upon him the obligation to stay alive: now he at last felt free to die.

Ever since the cancer diagnosis in 1923, Freud had faced, with equanimity, the possibility of imminent death. But what irked him most was having to live as an invalid, often in great pain, and forced to pay constant attention to his health. The diary for 1930 opens on January 3 with the words **Cigars from Landauer** - a gift of cigars from a colleague. For Freud smoking was more than just a pleasure, it was an addiction. He had been a "passionate smoker" for fifty years, since the age of twenty-four, and "owed to cigars the greater part of his self-discipline and steadfastness at work."[3] But the entry for April 5/6, 1930, reports a further heart attack. This convinced Freud he would have to stop smoking—literally "cut out" the habit, for he terms it "an act of autotomy [cutting into oneself]."[4] However, the entry for November 2, 1930—**First small cigar**—shows that this "operation" was unsuccessful.

Without smoking, and the work it enabled, life would be hardly worth living. Smoking, like the purchase of an antiquity, was one of the small and constant rewards cultured life could offer. Records of purchases punctuate the entire diary and six visits to the antique dealer, Dr. Lederer, are mentioned during the summer of 1930. When Stefan Zweig published a biographical sketch that portrayed him as a correct bourgeois, Freud pointed out that Zweig had omitted his idiosyncrasies, particularly his smoking and collecting. It might seem that these habits hardly contradict the bourgeois image. Yet they slightly complicate the picture by introducing elements of extra-professional passion. In this respect they may be interpreted as signs or indices of Freud's wider cultural ambition, his *daemon*- that drive which Goethe prefigured in the form of Faust's unrestrained quest for knowledge.

1. *Freud-Arnold Zweig 21.8.1930 in Zweig Letters.*
2. *Freud-Eitingon 1.12.1929* [FM] ("Ich habe ja selbst noch meine Mutter und sie sperrt mir den Weg zur ersehnten Ruhe . . . ")
3. *Freud-Stefan Zweig 7.2.1931 in Stefan Zweig.*
4. *Freud-Ferenczi 7.5.1930* [FM].

Cigars from Landauer . . .   Fri 3 January, 1930

Karl Landauer (1887–1945) studied medicine in Freiburg, Berlin and under Kraepelin in Munich. In 1912 he came to Vienna where he studied psychiatry under Julius Wagner von Jauregg and psychoanalysis with Freud. In 1926 he founded the Frankfurt Psychoanalytical Study Group. This developed into the Frankfurt Psychoanalytical Institute, which he headed, together with the Swiss psychoanalyst Heinrich Meng, from 1929 to 1933. Its status was "Guest Institute" of the University of Frankfurt. Through its links with the Frankfurt Institute for Social Research it was to influence the Frankfurt School sociologists. In 1932 Landauer organized the Wiesbaden International Psychoanalytical Congress, the last to take place in pre-war Germany.

Smoking is one of the leitmotifs of Freud's life. At this period Freud could not obtain high-quality cigars in Austria and relied on foreigners such as Max Eitingon (another cigar smoker) to bring them in from Germany or elsewhere. Clearly, Landauer also knew that good cigars were the most acceptable gifts to Freud.

Conference Martin—Drucker . . .   Mon 6 January 1930

Martin married Ernestine ("Esti") Drucker (1896–1980) on December 7, 1919– his 30th birthday. They had two children, Anton Walter and Sophie, but the marriage was not happy and their estrangement had already begun by 1922. By 1930 Martin was spending more time at Berggasse than with his family.[1]

Esti's father was a well-known barrister and after Martin's return from the war he had found work for him as a secretary in a bank and set the couple up in an apartment. It is possible that this "conference" was a discussion of the couple's situation, or an attempt on the part of the in-laws to heal their differences. It could, however, have been a business consultation.

Esti was an irascible woman and Freud disliked her. It is even possible (though unlikely) that the meeting mentioned here involved the couple alone and that Freud is referring to her as "Drucker" instead of Esti. At the end of 1930 he wrote to his nephew Sam Freud: "Martin you may have heard or guessed is in bad relations with an unreasonable, abnormal wife, his two children are fine. There are several sore spots in the wider range of the family, but we have no right to be exceptions to the most valid rules." (*Freud-Sam Freud 31.12.1930*)

Society evening . . .   Thurs 9 January 1930

Another of the informal discussions organized by Federn. No minutes were kept and the only published record consists of edited notes secretly taken by Richard Sterba. He notes that at one meeting in 1929 or 1930 the brilliant young analyst Wilhelm Reich presented his ideas on the Soviet experiment in rearing children apart from their parents. Reich believed the method could abolish the Oedipus complex and consequent neuroses. Freud reacted cautiously, saying: ". . . the Oedipus complex is not the specific cause of neurosis. There is no single specific cause in the etiology of neurosis. Reich neglects the fact that there are many pregenital drive components that cannot possibly be discharged, even through the most perfect orgasm."[1]

Cut stones . . .   Fri/Sat 10/11 January 1930

The second purchase of gems within a month. Today it is impossible to say how many gems Freud may once have had, not only because many were given away but also because the house at Maresfield Gardens was broken into and burgled during Anna Freud's lifetime, in the 1960s.

Mounted terracotta figures arrived . . .   Wed 15 January 1930

Freud had too many mounted terracottas for us to know which ones he was referring to here. Although he did keep a number of authentication slips written for him by Dr. Banko and Dr. Demel, curators of the Vienna Kunsthistorisches Museum, he himself did not record the sources and dates of acquisition, apart from the references to major pieces in this diary.

According to Ernest Jones, Freud spent the first August of World War I "minutely examining and describing his collection of antiquities. . . ." Marianne Kris also claimed that her husband, Ernst Kris, had catalogued Freud's collection. Unfortunately, no record of either catalogue has survived. However, some

Karl Landauer, head of the Frankfurt Psychoanalytical Institute. TG

Martin Freud's wife, Esti, with their two children. c.1927.

Freud's grandchildren, Anton Walter and Sophie.

Freud's terracottas in his study showcase. NB

The acrobat figurine bought on January 24, 1930. NB

of the mounts and figures do bear red painted numbers that may have referred to a lost catalogue.

Felix Wiener in N.Y. + . . .   Sat 18 January 1930

This was the death of the husband of one of Freud's nieces in America. Freud's eldest sister, Anna, had married Eli Bernays, who had emigrated to New York and become a member of the Produce Exchange. Their second daughter Leah ("Lucy") Bernays married a sales representative, Felix Wiener.[1] His death at the age of 56 had actually occured two days earlier on January 16, 1930.

Books from R. Rolland . . .   Thurs 16* January 1930

Freud had the highest respect for the French writer Romain Rolland. They had been in correspondence since 1923, when Freud commented: "A delightful letter and exchange of books with Romain Rolland. One is always amazed that not everyone is rabble." (*Freud-Ernst Freud 14.3.1923*)

At present Freud's library only contains two plays by Romain Rolland—*Les Léonides* (Paris 1928) and *Liluli* (Paris n.d.). The second bears an authorial dedication dated May 1923 that addresses Freud as *"Déstructeur d'Illusions"* ("Destroyer of Illusions"). This is relevant to the book's content, for its heroine, *Liluli,* represents the beauty of illusion. Freud took up the theme of illusion in 1927 when he sent Rolland his latest work—*The Future of an Illusion* (1927). He later wrote to Rolland: "Mysticism is as closed to me as music." (*Freud-Rolland 20.7.1929*) Rolland responded to Freud's attack on religion by proposing that faith had a valid essence in what he called the "oceanic feeling."

Freud's next book, *Civilization and its Discontents* (1930), opens with a discussion of the religious sentiment as seen by Romain Rolland. A footnote (added in 1931) refers to *Liluli* and two later books—*La Vie de Ramakrishna* (1929) and *La Vie de Vivekananda* (1930). In view of this reference, it is more than likely that these last two are the books Freud now received.

Mrs. London . . .   Tues 21 January 1930

Not known. It might, however, have been a visit from the wife of the American psychologist Louis Samuel London (born 1883), author of *Mental Therapy: studies in fifty cases* (N.Y. 1937) and *Dynamic Psychiatry* (N.Y. 1952).

Gall attack . . .   Tues 21 January 1930

Freud's doctor, Max Schur, records a number of undefined gastrointestinal disorders from which Freud suffered at this period. The source of the complaint, if there was a single one, was never exactly located. Three months earlier Freud had written to him: "The gall attacks—or whatever it is—have become rarer and less severe." (*Freud-Schur 19.9.1929*)

Schur . . .   Fri 24 January 1930

Dr. Max Schur (1897–1969) became Freud's *Leibarzt* (his "personal doctor") in autumn 1929. Princess Marie Bonaparte had recommended him to Freud. She had fallen ill while in Vienna and had been impressed, not only by Schur's treatment but by his involvement in psychoanalysis: he had attended Freud's final university course in the winter of 1918–19, had read all Freud's writings and been in analysis since 1925.

At their first meeting Freud had stated the basic conditions of their relationship: that Schur should always tell him the truth about his condition and that, when the time came, he should not let him be tortured unnecessarily—this being, in effect, a plea for euthanasia.[1]

Museum. Acrobat bought . . .   Fri 24 January 1930

This bronze Roman statuette of an acrobat standing on his hands was originally offered to the Vienna Kunsthistorisches Museum on January 22, 1930, by the art dealer and archaeologist Ludwig Pollak. The museum declined the offer. Freud must have been tipped off by Kris or Pollak or one of his contacts among antiquities dealers. Perhaps he actually visited the museum now to buy the

---

* This note follows the one for January 18, providing further evidence that Freud filled in diary entries retrospectively and as much as several days after the event.

object. The photo in the Vienna museum's records shows the piece intact, but it is now handless and fixed to a metal support. Clearly it suffered an accident at some time.

Visit Prof. Rojas B.-Aires . . .   Mon 3 February 1930

Nerio Rojas (1890-?) was Professor of Forensic Medicine at the University of Buenos Aires from 1924 to 1946, founder and president of the *Sociedad de Medicina Legal* (Society of Forensic Medicine) and in 1931 founder of the *Archivos de Medicina Legal*. It is likely he was on a study tour of Europe at this period, when he visited Freud. At this time there was no psychoanalytical society in Argentina. However, a Brasilian group had been formed in 1927 by J.P. Porto Carrero—the *Société Brésilienne de Psychanalyse*.

Dream of Nestroy . . .   Thurs/Fri 6/7 February 1930

Freud frequently quotes witticisms from the popular farces of the playwright Johann Nestroy (1801–62), whom he called "the Vienna Aristophanes." He was greatly amused, for example, by Nestroy's *Tannhäuser* parody when he saw it in May 1909, and the acquisition of the complete edition of Nestroy for his library in 1934 was significant enough to rate a diary entry.

Nestroy was not only notable for his satirical portrayal of Viennese society. His characters' cast of mind is revealed through their language; its grammar and syntax is symptomatic of their weaknesses. Freud recognized this when he cited Nestroy's jokes in support of his own psychoanalytical insights.[1] This entry is the only reference to a dream in the diary.

Tom + . . .   8 February 1930

Tom Seidmann-Freud (*née* Martha Gertrud Freud) was a daughter of Freud's sister Marie (Mitzi). Anna Freud said of her: "She was an extremely gifted girl, but rather hated to be female and therefore changed her name to a male one . . . "[1] Her death at the age of 37 in a Berlin hospital was the consequence of a deep depression following the suicide of her husband, Jakob ("*Jankef*") Seidmann, on October 19, 1929. Freud described the circumstances that led to the death of the couple in a letter to Sam Freud: ". . . we became involved in the tragic accident of the suicide of Jankef Seidman the husband of Martha who calls herself 'Tom,' the third daughter of your Aunt Marie Freud. He was an honest nice and clever fellow, liked by all of us, but he had undertaken what seems impossible in our days, to build up a 'Verlag' (publishing office) without money and finally he could not stand the burden of debts and the shame of bankruptcy. Tom, his wife, whom perhaps you remember is a very gifted artist, inventor of illustrated books for children, but more than half crazy. She used to be so even before the disaster so you may imagine how she behaves now. They h[ad] a charming blond girl of 7 years Angela [,] in some way we will have to provide for the child." (*Freud-Sam Freud 6.12.1929*)

Arnold Zweig . . .   Sun 9 February 1930

The eminent German novelist Arnold Zweig (1887–1968) first contacted Freud personally in 1927 with a request to dedicate to him *Caliban*, a book on antisemitism.[1] In 1929 he revealed to Freud that it was psychoanalysis which had enabled him to regain his creativity. After Freud's death, Zweig told Jones: "I loved him as a father and benefactor without whose discoveries my talent would have been buried under the ashes of the first world war." (*Arnold Zweig-Jones 22.2.1956*)

In the July-August 1929 number of the journal *Die Psychoanalytische Bewegung* Zweig published an essay—"Freud und der Mensch" ("Freud and Man")—which presents Freud as a liberator from religious and pathological terrors.

Evening with Alexander—Staub . . .   Thurs 13 February 1930

Franz Alexander (1891–1964) studied medicine at Göttingen and Budapest before becoming the first pupil of Karl Abraham's Berlin Psychoanalytical Institute. In 1930 he was invited to the United States to take up the post of visiting professor of psychoanalysis at the University of Chicago Department of Medicine.

Hugo Staub (1885–1942) had been a lawyer and financier, before training as an

Tom Freud with her mother, Freud's sister Mitzi, c.1900.

The novelist Arnold Zweig in 1931. "I loved Freud as a father and a benefactor without whose discoveries my talent would have been buried under the ashes of the first world war."

analyst at the Berlin Institute.[1] Here he collaborated with Franz Alexander.

This was another of the informal discussion groups held in Freud's waiting room. Franz Alexander and Hugo Staub presented new work for discussion.[2] After the meeting, Freud wrote to Eitingon: "Thank you for the cigars you sent with Alexander, I have been waiting for them with great longing. The evening at my house took place with much excitability, Alex. in his paper behaved naively to a certain extent, Staub created a very intelligent impression." (*Freud-Eitingon 15.2.1930*)

Jade necklace for Anna . . .   Fri 14 February 1930

Although Anna Freud chose to dress simply, often in flowing peasant-style dresses, she had a great fondness for necklaces, and to the very end of her life the majority of photos show her wearing various necklaces, particularly bead ones.[1]

Hypnoanalysis . . .   Fri 14 February 1930

The following day Freud wrote to Eitingon: "I received through you a booklet 'Hypnoanalysis' from Lifschitz in Moscow. Have you read it? Do you know the man and have you any idea to what extent he may be suspected of veracity? It seems to me beyond doubt that he is an ass and has subordinated his work to the norms of a culture which officially recognizes reflexology but where psychology is banned. [. . .] He confirms all the psychic characteristics of the dream which I have described, yet for him the dream is without meaning. It does not worry him that it is only when one presupposes the contrary that these characteristics can be found. Happy dolt! And everything turns out well for him, obviously by order of the Soviets. The translation is awful and makes him speak more nonsense than his task justifies—But I will tear open my intestines once again to prove to the world that the dream has a meaning!" (*Freud-Eitingon 15.2.1930*)

The booklet in question—*Hypnoanalyse* by Semyon Lifschitz, a professor of physics—had been published as part of a series (*Abhandlungen aus dem Gebiete der Psychotherapie und Medizinischen Psychologie* Stuttgart 1930 No.12). It included a dedication to Freud by the author, dated 27.1.1930.

Egypt. half bust . . .   Sat 15 February 1930

Probably this entry refers to the basalt bust of an Egyptian official—a Middle Kingdom, 12th Dynasty (1938–1759 B.C) piece, forming the upper part of a statuette. Freud used it as a paperweight on his writing desk. But the term "half bust" might in fact mean "half a bust" rather than one cut off at the shoulders*. If so, this figure could be another basalt bust from the same area and period—the figure of a woman broken off from a group, probably half of a couple.

Ruth birthday, opal necklace . . .   Sun 16 February 1930

Ruth Mack Brunswick (1897–1946) was an American who came to Vienna in 1922 to be analyzed by Freud. At that time she was married to her first husband, a cardiologist named Hermann Blumgart, from whom she separated in Vienna. She began practicing as a psychoanalyst in 1925: in 1926 Freud referred to her one of his most famous patients, Sergei Pankejeff, the "Wolf-Man."[1] By 1927 Freud was writing to his son Ernst that "she almost belongs to the family. . . ." (*Freud-Ernst Freud 28.4.1927*) When she married the composer Mark Brunswick in March 1928, Freud acted as witness at the ceremony.

Her birthday was in fact the next day, Monday, February 17. It may have been celebrated a day in advance to avoid doing so on a weekday: on the other hand this entry might just mean that Freud bought an opal necklace now for the birthday.

Margaretl's dead child . . .   Mon 17 February 1930

Margaretl was Margarethe Rie, the eldest daughter of Freud's friend and tarock

Anna wearing a necklace, c.1930.

Fragments of Egyptian busts from Freud's collection. NB

Freud's patient and pupil, Ruth Mack Brunswick, in the 1920s, with her daughter Mathilda.

---

* Freud's references to his acquisitions in the diary are always cursory. Given the size of his collection, it is frequently not possible to specify the object in question with any degree of certainty. The main criterion for recording any acquisition seems to have been its quality or importance: numerous smaller pieces probably acquired over these years go unmentioned.

partner, Oskar Rie. She was a school-friend of Anna Freud and married to the psychoanalyst Hermann Nunberg. This, their first child, was stillborn. A year later, however, they had a daughter. When Nunberg first announced his marriage Freud complimented him on his good taste and gave him as a wedding present a large sum of money that the couple used to attend the 11th International Psychoanalytic Congress at Oxford in July 1929.

Róheim's book . . .   Mon 17 February 1930

The Hungarian anthropologist Géza Róheim (1891–1953) was analyzed by Ferenczi in 1915–16. He was the first anthropologist to apply psychoanalytical theory to ethnography. Freud and the Hungarian analysts Ferenczi and Vilma Kovács arranged a number of expeditions, financed by Marie Bonaparte, so that he could collect psychoanalytically-orientated ethnographic data. Between 1928 and 1931 he did fieldwork in Somaliland, Central Australia and Melanesia and among the Yuma Indians of Arizona.

There are four of his books at present in Freud's library. The one which, to judge by publication date, Freud may now have received is *Animism; Magic and the Divine King* (Kegan Paul, London 1930).

Mitzi in Vienna . . .   Sun 23 February 1930

Marie Freud (1861–1942)—"Mitzi"—was Freud's third sister. She married her second cousin, Moritz Freud, in 1886, the year Freud himself married. Moritz died in 1920. They had five children, one of whom was stillborn. Her youngest daughter, Tom, had died on February 7 and the problem of the orphaned grandchild, Angela, remained to be settled. This was probably one of the reasons why she travelled now to Vienna.

Prof. Berman Cordoba Argent. . . .   Wed 26 February 1930

Dr. Gregorio Berman (1894–1972), the second South American visitor this month, was Professor of Forensic Medicine at the Medical Faculty of the University of Cordoba, Argentina. He had published a work on drug addiction that Freud possessed (*Toxicomanias. Psicologia de la apetencia tóxica*, Buenos Aires 1926). Berman apparently visited Freud while on a study tour of European clinics in 1929–1930 and his visit may have had some connection with that of Professor Rojas earlier this month, for both South Americans were interested in forensic medicine and toxicology.[1]

Dr Trebitsch & without prosthesis . . .   Fri 28 February 1930

As usual, the prosthesis had been causing trouble and was taken away briefly to be modified. The modifications appear to have been successful, for Freud wrote to Eitingon a few days later: "I was on the point of coming to Berlin already in March because of my prosthesis, but an assistant of Schroeder's, Dr. Trebitsch, who was here on holiday, has brought about such an improvement for me for the time being that I am able to postpone the appointment, perhaps for quite a long time." (*Freud-Eitingon 6.3.1930*)

Eisinger about Angela . . .   Fri 28 February 1930

Angela is Tom Freud's orphaned 7-year old daughter, whose fate was now under discussion.[1] Arpad Eisinger was Tom Freud's executor. Eisinger had a letter from the girl's mother expressly forbidding her adoption by Anna Freud. Tom Freud had wanted her daughter to have a normal family life and did not want her to be subjected to psychoanalysis.

Possible Freud already knew of Tom's antipathy toward this plan. Two weeks earlier, in a letter to the girl's grandmother, he dismissed the possiblility that he or Anna could look after the child adequately.[2]

Angela was instead adopted by her aunt and uncle, Arnold and Lilly Marlé.

Congested intestinal condition . . .   Sun 2 March 1930

Freud had suffered periods of chronic constipation for many years: the cause was never satisfactorily determined. One diagnosis had been appendicitis. Apparently he suffered an attack of this during his stay in the United States in 1909. Two years later Freud was still blaming subsequent disturbances—what he termed his "American colitis"—on the after-effects of American cooking.

Freud, Anna, Mitzi, and Angela photographed in Berlin by her mother Tom.

Schur states that during the 1930s, when Freud was under his care, the attacks of irritable spastic colon were mostly brought on by excessive smoking and relieved by a reduction of smoking and small doses of belladonna.

Jade bought . . .   Tues 4 March 1930

During the first decade of the century Freud already had a collection of Chinese jade bowls that served as ashtrays at meetings of the Wednesday Society. On his visit to America in 1909 a Chinese jade bowl was one of the objects he bought at Tiffany's. From the number of jade items in his collection it is clear Freud was fond of the material, though most of them are not of the highest quality. And although his library contains no more than two or three works on oriental art, there is a large illustrated volume on jade—*Early Chinese Jades* by Una Pope Hennessy (London 1923).

Inquiry Prussian Ministry of Culture . . .   Wed 5 March 1930

Freud was deeply concerned about the survival of the world's first psychoanalytical sanatorium, Schloss Tegel in Berlin, which was now threatened by bankruptcy. On March 15, 1929 the director, Ernst Simmel, had issued an appeal to the Prussian Minister of Culture, Prof. Dr. Becker, asking for moral, rather than financial, support in the setting up of a foundation to ensure the survival of the clinic. Other signatories of the appeal included Freud, Eitingon and Einstein.

Although the Minister did not support the appeal he was interested enough in psychoanalysis to visit Freud in 1930. Possibly Freud here refers to a request to arrange a meeting. It took place in the summer, when Freud was again staying at the sanatorium. At the meeting Becker congratulated him on his scientific achievements and Freud was flattered enough to write, six years later, about Berlin and the possibility that offered itself of actually moving there: "It was all so enticing, I was well regarded in the city, the social democrat minister Dr. Becker paid a friendly visit on me in Tegel, accompanied by two of his councillors . . . ." (*Freud-Hermann 28.2.1936*)

Jo-Fi arrived . . .   Sun 9 March 1930

When Freud's first dog, the chow Lun Yug, was run over in August 1929, he was quite deeply affected. He wrote to Ferenczi that the loss of the dog had cast a shadow over his summer. But this was not the family's first dog. During the 1920s an Alsatian called Wolf had been acquired for Anna Freud so she could go for walks on her own in Vienna. Wolf was still alive and active.

Anna Freud said that they all took Lun as seriously in death as in life and actually mourned it. She had wanted to find an immediate replacement but in September 1929 Freud would still not hear of it. The lapse of time between then and the arrival of Jo-Fi, Lun's sister, may be seen as a measure of the time it took for him to mourn the lost dog. The new animal was to become a dearly loved companion. Only three weeks after her arrival Freud was writing to Martha, who was visiting the children in Berlin: " . . . JoFi daily wins more fondness, she beds down in front of a door instead of making herself comfortable," and a week later he added that JoFi had become everybody's darling. When Freud left for Berlin in May the chow was put in kennels. In an anxious footnote to a letter four days after his arrival he asked: "P.S. Is anybody at all visiting Jofi? I miss her a great deal. The tortoise is a poor substitute."

Ernstl 16 yrs . . .   Tues 11 March, 1930

Ernstl, Freud's eldest grandson, was the son of Sophie Freud and Max Halberstadt. He was the infant mentioned in *Beyond the Pleasure Principle*, who played "*Fort*" . . . "*Da*" with a cotton reel—a game of which he himself preserved no memory.[1] His mother died of influenza in 1920 and his younger brother of tuberculosis three years later. In recent years Freud had been worried by his behavior. In 1928 he and Anna together paid and arranged for Ernstl to be sent to the school run by Eva Rosenfeld in Hietzing, which the four Burlingham children attended. Freud's attitude toward Ernstl was still colored by regret at the loss of his younger brother, Heinerle. He wrote to Max Halberstadt: "For he is the only legacy of our Sophie. Of course, one cannot prevent oneself thinking what was lost in Heinele." (*Freud-Max Halberstadt 9.8.1928*)

Paula Fichtl, the housemaid, holding Jofi.

Yvette . . .   Sun/Mon 16/17 March 1930

Yvette Guilbert's concerts in November 1929 had been a success and she now did two further concerts in Vienna.[1] They took place in the Konzerthaussaal under the direction of Georg Kugel and were sold out. She took as her theme Parisian street life. A reviewer spoke of her features ". . . as if sculpted by all human passions . . . ."

New Lectures . . .   Wed 19 March 1930

These "New Lectures" are not the *New Introductory Lectures*, which were only begun two years later. Freud is here referring to a new edition of the *Introductory Lectures on Psycho-Analysis*, first published in their entirety in German in 1917 and subsequently reprinted several times. The International Psychoanalytical Press (*Internationaler Psychoanalytischer Verlag*–I.P.V.) was now reprinting it in a small octavo edition.

Press $1000 . . .   Wed 19 March 1930

The International Psychoanalytical Press was founded in January 1919 with Otto Rank as the managing director. Adolf Storfer took over, but he lacked financial acumen and by the 1930s the financial standing of the business was critical. Now Storfer, "in an attack of megalomania" (as Freud put it), sent Freud a check in dollars as part payment for his work.[1] Freud wrote to Eitingon that he intended converting the sum into marks and bringing it with him to Berlin.

Evening on Discontents . . .   Thurs 20 March 1930

This was another of the select meetings arranged by Federn (the previous ones were on Thursday, December 12, 1929 and Thursday, January 9, 1930). Federn reviewed Freud's *Civilization and its Discontents*, then Freud responded by severely criticizing his own work. He compared it to Trajan's Tropaeum of Adamklissi—a small monument built on a vast base. He ended by saying: "My book is the outcome of the insight that our theory of instincts was insufficient. [. . .] I wrote the book with purely analytic intentions, based on my former existence as an analytic writer, in brooding contemplation, concerned to promote the concept of the feeling of guilt to its very end." [1]

(Norwegian Lectures* . . .   Tues 25 March 1930)

The Norwegian *Introductory Lectures on Psycho-Analysis*, translated by Kristian Schjelderup, was first published in 1929. Freud's library contains a hardback copy bearing an undated dedication from the translator and also an undedicated paperback copy published in 1930.

Anna to Budapest . . .   Wed 26 March, 1930

Anna Freud's reputation as a psychoanalyst specializing in child analysis was firmly established by this time and she was receiving invitations to appear as a guest speaker. In December 1929 the First International Congress on Mental Hygiene had invited her to come to the United States to address them, in the hope that her presence would have a positive influence on the further development of psychoanalysis there and would in particular further the beleaguered cause of lay analysis.

Because of the distance, she did not go. Budapest, however, was only a few hours by train from Vienna. Also, the invitation to address the Hungarian Psychoanalytic Society on March 26 gave her an opportunity to do Ferenczi a favor.

On Mondays Anna Freud had been holding a seminar in Vienna on child psychoanalysis and her talk in Budapest was based on this work: its theme was methods of case description. (During the 1920s the regular seminar at the Training Institute, which Anna Freud attended, was dubbed the *Kinderseminar* or "children's seminar"—not because it dealt with child analysis, but because its members all belonged to the younger generation.)

Anna the schoolteacher, c.1919, with her 5th class of the Volkschule, Cottage Lyceum, Vienna XIX.

* For some reason this entry and date have been crossed out in blue pencil. Did Freud perhaps now receive a copy of the 1930 paperback edition, then notice he already had the 1929 hardback copy in his library?

Elkuss + . . .   **Wed 26 March 1930**

This refers to the death of Elkuss, Eitingon's younger sister, who had lived in Leipzig. Her husband had suffered for some years from periodic short bouts of depression and in September 1929 Eitingon sent him to Hermann Nunberg in Vienna for psychoanalysis.

Anna back . . .   **Thurs 27 March 1930**

Ferenczi had been looking after Anna in Budapest and Freud afterwards wrote to him: "I cannot neglect thanking you from the bottom of my heart for the reception you prepared for Anna and the respect you showed. Her development appears so gratifying to me that I am also very pleased by any echo." (*Freud-Ferenczi 30.3.1930*)

Eitingon from Paris . . .   **Thurs 27 March 1930**

Eitingon had had to travel to Paris a week before, to act as arbitrator in one of his brother-in-law's business affairs. This relative from New York had done the family favors previously, but his business was now in serious difficulties as a result of the Wall Street Crash.

In his first letter following this meeting with Freud, Eitingon thanks Freud for his friendship during his "very melancholy visit to Vienna" (*Eitingon-Freud 7.4.1930*). Though his sister, Elkuss, is not explicitly mentioned, one assumes her death may at least partially explain his mood.

Mela fallen gravely ill . . .   **Fri 28 March 1930**

Mela (Melanie) Rie was the wife of Freud's friend and tarock partner, Oskar Rie. She and her older daughter, Margarethe, were close friends of Anna Freud's as well. The initial diagnosis of her illness was encephalitis, but this was soon rejected. Writing to Martha in Berlin at the beginning of April, Freud said the trouble seemed likely to be over harmlessly in a few weeks; however, a week later he was writing that there was no improvement and new complications appeared to threaten her.

Martha to Berlin . . .   **Sat 29 March 1930**

Freud was planning to visit Berlin again to have his prosthesis fixed by Dr. Schroeder and Martha was to have accompanied him. But the work done a month previously by Dr. Trebitsch made the prosthesis bearable for the time being and he now intended delaying his departure until after Easter (April 20). Instead, Martha was to go ahead of him, travelling there by way of Prague. One reason for her to go now was to be there for Ernst's birthday on April 6.

In Berlin she stayed in a hotel, in a comfortable room: Freud wrote to her: "I am very pleased you kept your good room in the hotel. We are too old to save money." and ended his letter ". . . have yourself 'a good time'* as they say in America." (*Freud-Martha Freud 1.4.1930*)

Lajos on visit . . .   **Sun 30 March 1930**

Dr. Lajos Lévy from Budapest was a friend and a frequent visitor to Freud. Also he was his advisor on medical matters during the mid-1920s. He had been an analysand of Ferenczi while his wife Katá was analyzed by Freud. Katá Lévy was the sister of Anton von Freund (1880–1920), a wealthy brewer from Budapest, who was psychoanalyzed by Freud during World War I. He donated a large sum of money to the cause of psychoanalysis and with it the *Internationaler Psychoanalytischer Verlag*, the press, was established in 1919.

At Rie's . . .   **Sun 30 March 1930**

Freud's friendship with Oskar Rie (1863–1931) went back a long way. They were colleagues at the Kassowitz Institute for children's diseases, where Freud was director of the department of neurology from 1886 to 1896. Together they wrote an authoritative monograph on unilateral paralyses in children (*Klinische Studie über die halbseitige Cerebrallähmung der Kinder*) published in 1891.

Rie was preoccupied by his wife's illness. Freud wrote to Martha: "On Sunday we went to Rie's. I only spoke with him. He is very depressed although they have

---

*In English in the original.

Freud and his old friend Oskar Rie.

dropped the grim diagnosis of her influenza encephalititis and the whole thing looks much more cheerful. It seems to me not out of the question that the condition will run its course in a few weeks without leaving much damage behind. Margarethe does not look well. The unlucky Nunberg has a severe bout of influenza." (*Freud-Martha Freud 1.4.1930*)

$5000 Martin for purchase . . .   Wed 2 April 1930

Martin Freud was attempting to put the business affairs of the press in order: eventually he was to take over its management. The $5000, wherever it came from, [1] could have been intended to help buy out Storfer's share in the business, since he was causing constant difficulties.

Walter 9 Jahre . . .   Thurs 3 April 1930

This is the only birthday of Anton Walter [1], the son of Martin and Esti Freud, that Freud records. Perhaps the boy visited Berggasse, where his father spent a great deal of his time. Mr. A.W. Freud has no memory of this occasion, but does remember receiving a curious gift from his grandfather on his tenth or eleventh birthday—a year's subscription to the intensely nationalistic German boys' magazine *Der gute Kamerad*.

Nocturnal heart attack. Braun . . .   Sat/Sun 5/6 April 1930

The heart specialist Professor Ludwig Braun (1861–1936) was a good friend of Freud's and a fellow member of the Jewish brotherhood, the B'nai B'rith. It was he who gave a speech in praise of Freud at one of their meetings to celebrate Freud's 70th birthday in 1926. Only a few months before that, on February 19, 1926, he had treated Freud when he suffered an attack of angina pectoris on the street a few steps away from Braun's house. This attack shocked Freud into taking the drastic measures he wrote of to Martha in Berlin: "Late last Saturday evening I was alarmed by a heart attack, but Braun made nothing of it and I have finally come to the conviction that I cannot stand unlimited smoking, since then I have restricted myself to $3\frac{1}{2}$ cigars and since then really feel like a changed person. Except that that changed person also has a great longing for the missing cigars." (*Freud-Martha Freud 9.4.1930*)

Bob operated . . .   Mon 7 April 1930

Robert (Bob) Burlingham (1915–1970) was the eldest son of the American Dorothy Burlingham who lived in the upstairs flat of Berggasse 19. He suffered from asthma and his mother had come to Vienna in 1925 with him and her other children, seeking treatment for his (and her own) problems. He had entered analysis with Anna Freud while his mother had begun analysis with Theodor Reik. Bob was the first of the Burlingham children to be operated on for appendicitis.[1] Two days later Freud speaks of this "latest affair with Bob" passing without a hitch: two months later he is healthy and thriving ". . . like a young god . . . ."

Dr. Hans Zweig . . .   Mon 7 April 1930

Dr. Hans Zweig came from Brünn (Brno) and had published a group report on psychotherapy in Czech literature from 1920–1930 in the February issue of the *Zentralblatt für Psychotherapie*. (There is no available evidence that he was a relative either of Stefan or Arnold Zweig.)

Rob Math left . . .   Thurs 10 April 1930

Mathilde (1887–1978), Freud's eldest child, had a special place in the family's affections. Anna wrote " . . . she fulfilled in a remarkable way the role of the helpful eldest which was thus hoisted on her. Always ready to give advice, support and information her authority amongst the younger ones was unquestioned."

In 1909 she married the textile merchant Robert Hollitscher (1875–1959). The consequences of a botched appendectomy in her youth had left her unable to conceive; after her sister Sophie's death she and her husband adopted her nephew Heinerle, but he died of acute tuberculosis on June 19, 1923, at the age of 5—a death that had also affected Freud profoundly. Though Mathilde lived to the age of 90 her health was not good—Freud wrote in 1929 "Mathilde

Anna, the Burlingham children and dogs, c.1930.

[. . .] is a chronic invalid but behaves in a marvelous normal way." (*Freud-Sam Freud 6.12.1929*)

She and her husband lived in Vienna not far from the Freuds. This departure may have been for reasons of health—a visit to South Tirol or to a spa.

Dr. Stefan Zweig . . .   Thurs 10 April 1930

Stefan Zweig (1881–1942) had known and admired Freud since the turn of the century, when he belonged to a circle of young Austrian writers known as *Jung Wien*. They included Arthur Schnitzler, Hermann Bahr and Hugo von Hofmannsthal. They met in the Café Griensteidl and frequently published their essays in the most cultured contemporary newspaper, the *Neue Freie Presse*, which Freud read regularly. Zweig was deeply committed to the idea of pan-European culture (his autobiography was subtitled *Memoirs of a European*). During World War I he published an anti-war drama, *Jeremias*. Together with Henri Guilbeaux, the editor of the anti-war journal *Demain*, and Romain Rolland, he campaigned against the frantic militarism unleashed by the war. During the 1920s he enjoyed enormous international popularity with his biographies of Mary Stuart, Erasmus, Magellan, Marie Antoinette, Balzac, and also with his historical studies and novels, which made him, at one period, the most translated author in the world.

Like most Austrians of his generation, Freud was meticulous about correct titles and terms of address. Stefan Zweig did indeed have a doctoral degree from the University of Vienna, for his dissertation on Hippolyte Taine. But his name, without any title, was world-famous. Freud does not repeat Zweig's title elsewhere in the diary. He may, of course, be playing off this name against its namesake above—Dr. Hans Zweig. But there is possibly a more devious explanation.

In a letter of August 21, 1930, Freud mistakenly addresses Arnold Zweig as "*Herr Doktor*." When Arnold Zweig objected to this unearned title, Freud explained this slip of the pen as an expression of his anger against his namesake Stefan Zweig, who had given him, he said, "good cause for dissatisfaction." On December 4, 1929, during his daily walk, Freud had come across an advertisement for a book called *Freud's Tragic Complex: An Analysis of Psychoanalysis* by the American Charles E. Maylan. It set out to prove that psychoanalysis was a product of Freud's desire for revenge against life. The author, according to Freud, was a "malicious fool, arian fanatic" who had been rejected as unsuitable by the Berlin Institute before completing an analytic training. The advertisement, however, quoted recommendations from Jung and Stefan Zweig.[1]

French Jokes . . .   Thurs 10* April 1930

This was *Le Mot d'Esprit et ses Rapports avec l'Inconscient*, the title given to the French translation of Freud's *Jokes and Their Relation to the Unconscious*.[1] It was done by Marie Bonaparte in collaboration with Dr. M. Nathan and published by Gallimard, Paris (1930). Freud's copy is specially bound, but is uninscribed.

Ferenczi over weekend . . .   Sat 12 April 1930

Sándor Ferenczi (1873–1933), for a long time Freud's closest friend among his analytical colleagues, had been in constant correspondence with him since their first meeting in 1908. In 1909 Ferenczi accompanied Freud and Jung on their American tour. He founded the Hungarian Psychoanalytic Society in 1913. From 1919 he held the first university professorship in psychoanalysis, at the University of Budapest. During the 1920s Ferenczi had been developing "active therapy," encouraging patients to let actions or behavior as well as their free associations express the unconscious material. This had aroused great interest among other analysts, but when Ferenczi extended the technique into such practices as mutual analysis and mothering his patients it became controversial.

One of the purposes of this visit was to heal the growing rift between Ferenczi and Freud, epitomized by their difference of opinion over the new analytical

---

* A crossed-out line connects this entry to Saturday, April 12, and the underlining of "Thurs 10" ("*Do 10*") has been extended to incorporate this entry. It is as if Freud was uncertain to which date this event belonged. Such corrections, and the poor alignment between dates and entries, offer further evidence that at this period Freud first listed events retrospectively, then added dates.

Mathilde Freud, 1908, the year before her marriage.

techniques. Ferenczi was deeply indebted to Freud, both intellectually and emotionally, and the prospect of offending him was extremely painful: he now hoped that their discussion would set his mind at rest.

Martha back . . .   Sun 13 April 1930

During her stay in Berlin, Martha had led an active social life. Among other things, she had paid a visit to Eitingon and his wife Mirra at their home on the Altensteinstrasse in Berlin-Dahlem: the following day she had also visited the Berlin Psychoanalytical Institute on the Wichmannstrasse. Apart from such visits, she had been able to help organize Ernst's 38th birthday on April 6. Freud wrote to her: "It was with respect and admiration that I heard and read of your social achievements in Berlin. I will not be imitating you." (*Freud-Martha Freud 9.4.1930*)

Freud wrote to his son on her return: "Mama returned today in the best of moods, very content with her Berlin impressions and experiences. It was of course quite right that she went alone and did not wait for me. All parties gained by that." (*Freud-Ernst Freud 13.4.1930*).

Ferenczi . . .   Sun 13 April 1930

This two-day visit marked a brief healing of the rift between the two men. But in his letter of thanks, Ferenczi's justified fears for their friendship are revealed: "Time and again I recollect the friendly and cheerful mood of those hours I spent the Sunday before last in your study which is so dear to me. I left in the conviction that my fear of my rather too independent manner of work and thought leading me into what would be for me a painful opposition to you was greatly exaggerated. So I am resuming work with renewed courage and firmly hoping that these small detours will never lead me away from the high road along which I have been wandering at your side for almost 25 years." (*Ferenczi-Freud 30.4.1930*)

Ferenczi was one of the few colleagues who shared Freud's passion for antiquities. In his thanks after this visit he promised to send Freud an Osiris figure (from the Roman period and unearthed in Hungary).

Princess in the evening . . .   Sun 13 April 1930

Marie Bonaparte had come to Vienna the previous day to consult the surgeon Professor Halban. During the 1920s she had heard of his operation to move the clitoris in order to overcome frigidity. Under the pseudonym "A.E. Narjani" she published an article advocating this procedure (it was titled *Considerations on the Anatomical Causes of Frigidity in Women* and appeared in the journal *Bruxelles Medical*, April 1924). Furthermore, she underwent the operation herself. But sensitivity persisted at the site of the operation. Halban recommended a further operation, to be performed in Paris, during which he would not only try to rectify this but would also perform a hysterectomy as a cure for her chronic salpingitis.

The contrast between the two visitors today is to some extent emblematic. Marie Bonaparte was taking over Ferenczi's roles of friend and exemplary disciple. She was now well established in the psychoanalytical world, through her publications and translations, as well as now being a psychoanalyst in her own right. She had three analysands and Freud supervised her analyses by mail. Her analysands would be brought to their sessions at her house in Saint-Cloud in chauffeur-driven cars. In fine weather the analysis took place in the garden.

Spring broken . . .   Mon 14 April 1930

During 1927 and 1928 the springs on prostheses numbers 3, 4 and 5 supplied by Dr. Pichler had caused constant trouble, cutting into the cheek and breaking. This was a prime reason for Freud's visit to Berlin in the summer of 1929 to be fitted with a new prosthesis by Dr. Schroeder. Between November 23, 1929 and October 3, 1930 Freud did not consult Pichler at all. But now it was Schroeder's work (modified by Trebitsch) that was causing difficulties.[1]

Russian Illusion . . .   Mon 14 April 1930

The Future of an Illusion had first been published in Russian in 1928, in issue 32 of the journal *Ateist* (*The Atheist*). It now appeared as a separate volume and in

Martha Freud in Berlin, with her daughter-in-law Henny and her favorite granddaughter Eva.

a different translation *(Budushchnost' odnoi illyuzii,* Moscow-Leningrad, 1930). From the very beginning the Russians had been receptive to Freud's work. The first of his books to be translated there was *On Dreams* (St Petersburg, 1904), followed by the *Psychopathology of Everyday Life* (Moscow, 1910)—the first translations of both works. During the 1920s there had been an upsurge of interest in psychoanalysis in the Soviet Union—Jones records that 2,000 copies of the Russian translation of the *Introductory Lectures* sold out in Moscow in a single month and in 1923 a new psychoanalytical society was founded in Kazan. *The Future of an Illusion,* the 25th of Freud's works to be translated into Russian, was the last to be published in the Soviet Union before the Stalinist era categorized psychoanalysis as "bourgeois-individualism."

Anna & Dorothy to Paris . . .   Tues 15 April 1930

Dorothy Burlingham (1891–1979) was the daughter of Louis Comfort Tiffany, the wealthy New York decorator and glass designer. In 1914 she had married Dr. Robert Burlingham. They had four children—Robert (Bob), Mary (Mabbie), Katrina (Tinky) and Michael (Mikey). But her husband was a manic-depressive and in 1921 she left him. Though it was primarily in an attempt to cure her son Bob's chronic asthma that she came to Vienna in 1925 with the children, she herself became involved in an analysis with Reik at the same time as Anna Freud was psychoanalyzing both Bob and his sister Mabbie.

A close friendship developed between Dorothy and Anna. In 1928 the Burlinghams moved into the apartment above the Freuds at Berggasse 19 and the two households entered into a symbiotic relationship. In 1929 Paula Fichtl, who had been the Burlingham children's nanny since 1926, moved downstairs and became the Freuds' maidservant: she was to serve them in Vienna and England until Anna Freud's death in 1982. Meanwhile, Dorothy had contracted tuberculosis and required treatment as well as fresh air. Together with Anna she acquired a weekend cottage named Hochrotherd in 1930. Dorothy had a car and they would drive out there most weekends.

Anna and Dorothy back . . .   Thurs 17 April 1930

This brief trip to Paris may have been a visit to Marie Bonaparte. But she was in Vienna consulting Halban only two days earlier and may still have been there. However, Dorothy also had a relative in Paris, Henrietta Brandes (*née* Ely), the chow breeder who provided Freud with his first chow, Lun Yug.

Sachs-Caligula . . .   Fri 18 April 1930

As a law student, Hanns Sachs (1881–1947) had attended Freud's lectures during the first decade of the century, but they first met in 1910, when he presented Freud his translations of Kipling's *Barrack Room Ballads.* He became a lay psychoanalyst and, together with Otto Rank, co-editor of the journal *Imago,* founded in 1911. In 1913 the two co-authored a book—*The Significance of Psychoanalysis for the Humanities (Die Bedeutung der Psychoanalyse für die Geisteswissenschaften).* Freud's great trust in Sachs at this period is demonstrated by the fact that in 1912—and despite their relatively brief acquaintance—he was chosen to be one of the original members of the secret Committee set up to rally around Freud and safeguard the basic tenets of psychoanalysis from corruption or distortion.

Hanns Sachs presented Freud with a dedicated copy of his new book—*Bubi, die Lebensgeschichte des Caligula* (Berlin 1930)—a psychoanalytical study of the Roman emperor Caligula. A comment in a letter to Sachs three years later contains a somewhat slighting reference to the book: "Your work plans arouse my interest, better narcissism than Caligula."

Cottage Sanatorium . . .   Tues 22 April 1930

Cottage was a part of Vienna. The Cottage Sanatorium was an expensive and luxurious establishment founded in 1908 by Rudolf Urbantschitsch [1]; it treated intestinal and nervous disorders and offered special diet and convalescent facilities. Freud had been suffering more frequent and severe attacks of colic and he was now obliged to enter the sanatorium for a diet cure. Professor Braun had insisted that this was more important than the prosthesis and that it was essential for Freud to undergo treatment before leaving for Berlin. Anna accompanied him to the sanatorium.

The Hochrotherd cottage before renovations. "We found it so peaceful," Anna wrote.

Hanns Sachs, previously member of the secret Committee. TG

Tobacco abstinence . . .   25 April, 1930

After the heart attack three weeks previously, Freud had cut down consumption to $3\frac{1}{2}$ cigars a day. Now even that concession had to be sacrificed. Ten days later he wrote to Ferenczi: "This is the news: on 22/4 heart and bowel trouble forced me to take refuge in the Cottage Sanatorium. The recuperation began with the painful recognition that a cigar smoked on 25/4 would have to be the last for a long time. On 4 May I was able to travel to Berlin almost fully I am feeling fairly healthy here, but it was an act of self-mutilation [*autotomy*] [1], as the fox performs in a snare when it bites off its own leg. I am not very happy, but rather feeling noticeably depersonalized." (*Freud-Ferenczi 7.5.1930*)

Japanese translation Beyond Pleasure Principle . . .   Fri 2 May 1930

On April 30, Eitingon sent Freud a Japanese translation of Freud's *Beyond the Pleasure Principle* that he had received from Yaekichi Yabe.[1] His letter explained that it was the 7th volume of a planned 40-volume edition of Freud's complete works in Japanese, edited by Yabe.[2]

Back from sanatorium . . .   Sat 3 May 1930

Freud left the sanatorium, if not totally cured then at least healthy enough to travel to Berlin. For the time being his resolution to give up smoking continued: "I soon made the discovery there that I had gained an absolute intolerance toward cigars and in return for abstention from this long-habitual pleasure I gained a rapid and far-reaching improvement which has lasted. Only my stomach is not yet functioning without disturbances." (*Freud-Jones 12.5.1930*). But two weeks after his return there was already a relapse: "Only yesterday I tried the first timid cigar, for the time being the only one of the day." (*Freud-Jones 19.5.1930*)

Arrival at Tegel . . .   Mon 5 May 1930 *

The psychoanalytical clinic and sanatorium in Berlin, Schloss Tegel, was opened in April 1927 under the direction of Ernst Simmel. Freud's architect son, Ernst, had been in charge of the interior redesign of the building. The clinic was privately run and adapted to treat 25–30 patients with serious psychoneurotic and physical disorders, especially addictions. Simmel's wish to establish a closed section for psychotic patients was vetoed by the von Heinz family from whom the Schloss was rented. Freud had first stayed there while being treated for a new prosthesis by Schroeder in September 1928, and he had two more consultations there with him the following year, in March 1929 and September-October 1929.

Freud wrote home the day after he and Anna arrived in Tegel: "The most important thing is Schröder. Instead of improving the prosthesis he wants to make a new one. How much time have I got? I am 74 today . . . [. . .] So it is not likely we will be home soon. But with the refined affection here in the house, the peace and the beauty of the spring, it is an extension of the holidays for Anna and me." (*Freud-Meine Lieben 6.5.1930*)

74 yrs . . .   Tues 6 May 1930

Freud's opposition to birthdays—which was not incompatible with an appreciation of gifts—found expression in his first letter home: "There was of course no way of evading the nonsense of the birthday. I am stifling in roses, orchids and telegrams as in Vienna. There are fewer visitors there. Predominant is a rose-bunch from Eitingon, I believe there are 74, others think: 120. The nicest thing is a poem in Jofi's name, from Anna of course, in the company of a live little tortoise." (*Freud-Meine Lieben 6.5.1930*)

Jofi was in the care of kennels at Kagran, Vienna. The tradition of the dogs presenting a poem had begun in 1926 with a rhyme from Wolf. Film records show the poems being tied round the dogs' necks. This year, in the absence of any dog, it was left to the tortoise to deliver the following doggerel: "Jo Fie who leaps—and through doors escapes—who slips the leash—and fights with enemies—who stretches out in greeting and—licks your hand—sends herewith—on May the sixth—a symbol that—should indicate—how she wants to change—and act more restrained:—wants to scarcely move when—doors are opened—does

Moshe Wulff and Ernst Simmel (standing), with Anna, Freud and Mrs. Wulff at the Tegel Sanatorium, 1929.

An inscribed portrait Freud gave Simmel: "In memory of the long billeting, summer 1930, to his dear host, Freud."

---

* The word *Berlin* is written in the left-hand margin and linked by a red line to this date.

not want to bark nor scrap—nor run nor leap—hardly wants to drink or eat.
So speaks Jo Fie sad at heart—sorry that we are apart."

Yabe from Japan . . .   Wed 7 May 1930

Eitingon came with Yabe late in the evening to visit Freud; they stayed over an
hour and left after midnight. Freud was curious that one of his first Japanese
translations should be *Beyond the Pleasure Principle* and challenged Yabe about
this. Yabe replied that ". . . the theory that life tends towards death is a Buddhist
idea. Since Buddhism influences Japanese thinking to a great degree, an understanding of psychoanalysis might be easier through this book." Yabe's account
of their meeting continues: "This reasoning pleased Freud tremendously. Since
he had been attacked for this theory, and had modified it somewhat, he was
happy to feel that he had suddenly acquired many colleagues who would agree
with him. He called out to his daughter in the next room: 'Anna, Anna!' " [1]

Lederer 1st visit . . .   Wed 7 May 1930

Dr. Philipp Lederer was an antiquities dealer with a shop on Am Kupfergraben
in Berlin. Freud had already had dealings with him. The previous autumn he
wrote home from Tegel: "It turns out that the news of Dr. Lederer's death is, in
Mark Twain's expression, greatly exaggerated. I am convinced that he will show
himself to be just as avaricious as the previous times and that is a strong sign of
life." (*Freud-Meine Lieben* 18.9.1929)

At various times Freud acquired antiquities explicitly as a compensation for
suffering and as a means of raising his spirits. At this period, when his smoking
was severely restricted, the interplay of his two addictions—cigars and antiquities—is revealed in a comment from a letter home: "I am only missing cigars,
whatever measures I try against that fail, wine drinking, letter writing, eating
dates are no substitute. Antiquities may have been one, but one cannot buy so
many." (*Freud-Meine Lieben* 9.5.1930)

Lederer 2nd visit . . .   Sun 11 May 1930

This and the previous visit to Lederer were clearly a success. In a letter home the
following day Freud is in high spirits: "It would be nice if everything this year
went as well as my purchases from Lederer. It is a pity that after that the long
holidays are coming, during which one must be parted from them *. They are all
standing gathered together on the table here at Tegel. Of course it is then as if
the press had never paid me anything **. But that could easily have been the
case." (*Freud-Meine Lieben* 12.5.1930)

Operation on Princess . . .   Wed 14 May 1930

At her consultation in Vienna on April 12 the surgeon Halban had agreed to
come to Paris to operate. The hysterectomy and the surgery on her clitoris was
performed at the American Hospital in Neuilly. Ruth Mack Brunswick had
come especially to look after her and Max Schur was also in attendance. It is very
likely one of them would have telephoned Freud to keep him informed. The
Princess recovered rapidly and was out of bed two weeks later.

Martha to Carinthia . . .   Wed 14 May 1930

At this time Martha and the rest of the household were still in Vienna, waiting
to find out when Freud's treatment with Schroeder would finish. They had still
not found anywhere to rent for the summer and Martha's trip to Carinthia, the
southernmost province of present-day Austria, was an unsuccessful attempt to
find somewhere suitable. Regretting and condoling this failure Freud invokes the
Biblical "lilies of the field" in a rueful reference to their summer homelessness:
"I am doubly sorry that your brave undertakings remained fruitless. What shall
we do now? One would think that the dear Lord, who is known to manage an
institute for the clothing of lilies, might also run an agency for summer homes,

Ashtrays and antiquities, traces of
Freud's two addictions. NB

* The antiquities would be sent to Vienna. Freud would not take them with him to his summer
home.
** "It is as if the press had never paid me anything." Freud is referring here to his practice of
setting aside extraordinary or bonus sources of income, such as royalty payments, toward his
collection.

but one cannot rely on that." (*Freud-Martha Freud 19.5.1930*)

Visit to Caputh . . .   Sat 17 May 1930

Caputh was at that time no more than a tiny village outside Berlin, situated on a lake shore just beyond Potsdam. Though Albert Einstein was living there at this period, there is no record of a meeting. The outing had been planned for May 12, but the weather was bad that day and in addition Ernst, who was to accompany him, was not free.

Freud had first met Einstein in late December 1926. After that initial meeting he wrote: "Einstein was very interesting, happy and cheerful, we spoke for 2 hours and also had a discussion, more about analysis than relativity. He is reading [it up] at the moment, has of course no convictions. He looks older than me, is coming up to 48 yrs old!" (*Freud-Anna Freud 29.12.1926*)

Einstein and his wife had the house in Caputh built in 1929 just after his 50th birthday: it overlooked the Havelsee where he could sail the boat which was a gift from his friends. It was on the occasion of this birthday that Freud, also in Berlin at the time, had written him a letter calling him a lucky person—for being able to work in the esoteric science of mathematical physics and not psychology, where everybody could have their say.

Eitingon had writtten a book about Einstein which Freud read later this year: in December he wrote to Eitingon that from it he had learned nothing about the man and that his theory remained incomprehensible.

Bullitt . . .   Sat 17 May 1930

William Christian Bullitt (1891–1967) was working in the State Department as an administrative adviser to President Woodrow Wilson in 1919, when he was sent on a mission to Russia. There he came to an agreement with Lenin to establish diplomatic relations between their two countries. On his return, Wilson rejected his proposals and Bullitt resigned. Over the next decade he engaged in journalism, wrote a novel, painted and dabbled in the movie business. He first encountered Freud through his second wife, who was in psychoanalysis with him in Vienna.

At the time of this meeting Bullitt was studying material in the German archives for a book on the 1919 Paris Peace Conference in which he himself had taken part. Reporting their meeting, Bullitt said Freud seemed in a somber mood: "He asked me what I was doing, and I told him that I was working on a book about the Treaty of Versailles which would contain studies of Clemenceau, Orlando, Lloyd George, Lenin and Woodrow Wilson—all of whom I happened to know personally. Freud's eyes brightened and he became very much alive. Rapidly he asked a number of questions, which I answered. Then he astonished me by saying he would like to collaborate with me in writing the Wilson chapter of my book."

Bullitt and Freud shared an antagonism toward Wilson: two days after the meeting, according to Bullitt, they agreed to collaborate on a book-length psychological study of the president.

Max on visit . . .   Sun 25 May 1930

Max Halberstadt (1882–1940), a photographer from Hamburg, had married Sophie Freud in 1913. Freud said of him, before the marriage, that he ". . . is among our most distant relations in Hamburg, is very serious, trustworthy, both seem to be truly in love with each other. The circumstances are respectable middle-class, no wealth, no high rank which does not concern us either." (*Freud-Marie Freud 20.7.1912*).

His photographic business in Hamburg was not flourishing at this period and Freud was now helping to support him financially.

Lederer 3rd visit . . .   Mon 26 May 1930

These visits to the antique dealer were not enough to keep Freud's primary addiction at bay: a week previously he had resumed smoking—"the first timid cigar." (*Freud-Jones 19.5.1930*).

Hiddensee . . .   Thurs 29–Sat 31 May 1930

This was Freud's only visit to his son Ernst's holiday cottage on the island of

Freud's son-in-law, the photographer Max Halberstadt. MH

Hiddensee off the north German coast. Two mishaps occured on the journey out. In Stralsund, where they changed from the train to a ferry, a door slammed on Ernst's left hand, severing the tip of a finger. Secondly, Freud's heart condition recurred and was to last until the following morning. In spite of that the visit was a success and Freud was impressed enough by the scenery and healthy air of the island to consider spending the summer there. However, the problem of accomodation in the high season was a deterrent and he wrote home that, although it would be a paradise of health (*Gesundheitsparadies*) for the children, he doubted whether it could do much for the old.

Anna, who repeated the description of "paradise," was even more impressed and wrote to Eva Rosenfeld: "Now I know exactly what I needed all this time: an island. Only two days of the island have cured me completely and now I am so completely myself again that I don't need to know anything more about myself. That is the best of all. Hiddensee is a real paradise, a combination of everything beautiful in one small patch and with air and wind and sun and freedom." (*Anna Freud-Eva Rosenfeld 3.6.1930*)

Freud, however, had been feeling healthier in Berlin and the heart attack had unsettled him: "Of course, the recurrence of the attack greatly disturbed my confidence and leaves me sometimes thinking a summer holiday is no longer of much use to me. But to live for one's health instead of from it is something very stupid." (*Freud-Meine Lieben 1.6.1930*)

The next letter home elaborated this theme further: "In fact, my heart troubles remind me very much of the time 35 years ago when I first had to give up smoking. But I admit my high spirits have been broken, I no longer feel safe, do not trust myself to undertake any more daring enterprise and would be content with an undemanding summer. Incidentally I feel as if cheated that the great improvement since giving up smoking has not lasted and what with the privation and the troubles of the miserably neglected prosthesis I am not exactly enviable." (*Freud-Martha 4.6.1930*)

Third visit to Lederer . . .   Wed 4 June 1930

A "Lederer third visit" had already been registered on May 26. This is at the bottom of the previous sheet of paper and not visible when Freud wrote this entry. Also the visit to Hiddensee and heart trouble had occured since then, which may help account for the confusion.[1]

Robert Fliess . . .   Sun 8 June 1930

Robert Fliess, son of the Berlin rhinologist Wilhelm Fliess (1858–1928), was born in 1895—the same year as Anna Freud, who would have been named Wilhelm, after Fliess, had she been a boy. Like Anna, Robert became a psychoanalyst. His father had studied his infancy, keeping a record of his behavior and illnesses, in search of periodic patterns: he also communicated to Freud one of his son's hunger dreams, which Freud included in the *Interpretation of Dreams* as a counterpart to the infant Anna's hunger dream of "wild strawberries."

The intense friendship and exchanges of ideas with Wilhelm Fliess during the mid-1890s—their correspondence and their meetings or "congresses"—gave Freud the emotional and intellectual confidence to evolve his own psychology and to perform his self-analysis. But during the late 1890s his vast admiration for Fliess declined and their relationship faded into bitterness and recrimination (for example, over the concept of bisexuality, which Freud adapted from Fliess without adequate acknowledgement). Although there were to be many other good friendships in Freud's life there were none into which he threw himself so whole-heartedly. This was the last one in which both partners were on equal terms; subsequent male friendships were to be unequal, with younger men or disciples.

The break with Fliess left a permanent mark. Robert Fliess later wrote to Siegfried Bernfeld: "You are quite right in mentioning the strongly emotional character of the significance of these two men for each other. I have heard a good deal about this from both of them—over a long stretch of years, of course, from my father, and in a long conversation with Freud in 1929*, in which he spoke

"Air and wind and sun and freedom." Ernst, Lux and Stephan Freud sailing in Hiddensee harbour.

Ernst Freud's holiday home at Hiddensee. "A real paradise. . . ."

---

* This was written 14 years later; it is highly likely Robert Fliess confused the date of this conversation and that it took place on this occasion.

with a frankness apparently not too customary to him in personal matters."
(*Robert Fliess-Bernfeld 28.8.1944*)

Frau Mercedes . . .   Fri 13 June 1930
This may be the name of the Grundlsee landlady (see following note). Alternatively, it could be an unknown visitor.

House rented in Grundlsee . . .   Fri 13 June 1930
Martha Freud had rented a house for the summer at Rebenburg on Grundlsee. It was planned that Freud and Anna would go there after Berlin. On hearing the news, Freud wrote home: "So we have a summer residence thanks to Mama's energy and I am simply satisfied that it is not Ischl or Reichenau (chicken and cauliflower), have made myself a promise not to complain more than once about every little deficiency which may perhaps be found at the castle on Grundlsee." (*Freud-Meine Lieben 14.6.1930*)

Trude Hammerschlag + . . .   Fri 13 June 1930
Trude Hammerschlag (1898–1930), daughter of Albert Hammerschlag, was a grandchild of Samuel Hammerschlag, Freud's schoolteacher whom he had greatly liked and respected and who had frequently helped him with loans of money in the penniless days before his marriage. She was killed in an explosion or fire in a chemistry laboratory at Vienna University where she was working. On hearing the news Freud wrote home: ". . . Trude H.[Hammerschlag]'s horribly inept end shocked me deeply too." (*Freud-Meine Lieben 14.6.1930*).

Fourth visit Lederer . . .   Sat 14 June 1930
Actually the *fifth* visit to the antiquities dealer in Berlin.

Dr. Alexander . . .   Tues 17 June 1930
Franz Alexander was on a visit from the United States where he had been visiting professor of psychoanalysis at the University of Chicago Department of Medicine.[1] Over the year he had been keeping Freud informed of a controversy in which he had become involved. The Dean of the University Clinics, Dr. McClean, had proposed a permanent professorship of psychoanalysis, but this had been resolutely rejected by the faculty board. During the discussion aspersions had been cast about Alexander's personal integrity as well as the fact that his work was offensive to behaviorism.

In February Alexander wrote to Freud: "In all it seems to me that this excursion into the academic world and the medical faculty will only be a new demonstration that psychoanalysis is still unacceptable to medicine. McClean told me that at this session he saw for the first time how deep a resistance prevails against analysis and that people cease behaving correctly under the influence of this resistance." (*Alexander-Freud 1.2.1930*)

Dr. Weinmann . . .   Wed 18 June 1930
Dr. Joseph Weinmann was a dentist and oral pathologist who had studied with Schroeder in Berlin. He treated Freud from 1928 to 1930.

Both Anna and Freud were slightly unwell today. Freud wrote home from Berlin the following day: "Yesterday I again suffered a condition with dizziness, upset stomach, nausea, for the whole day the heart unaffected. Curiously, Anna had exactly the same, the sickness actually worse than mine, so that our diagnosis alternates between an effect of the heat and a mild food poisoning (from what?), today it is almost over. [. . .] Dr. Weinmann visited us yesterday and reaped our thanks." (*Freud-Meine Lieben 19.6.1930*)

Minna's birthday . . .   Wed 18 June 1930
Minna Bernays (1865–1941) was Martha's younger sister who lived with the Freuds. In 1886, the year her sister married Freud, her fiancé, Ignaz Schönberg, had died of tuberculosis. She moved into Berggasse "for a few months" in 1895 and stayed with the Freuds for the rest of their lives. The arrangement suited everyone: she helped Martha run the large household and provided Freud with a level of intellectual companionship he did not find in his wife.

On this, her 65th birthday, Freud demonstrated that his notoriously negative

A view over Grundlsee, 1930.

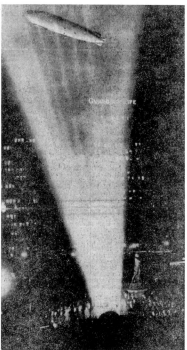

Der Zeppelin im Lichte der Scheinwerfer New Yorks

Die Leidenschaft fürs Fliegen
Prof. S. Freud, der große Psycho-Analytiker, hat heute als Siebzig-
jähriger seinen ersten Flug in Tempelhof unternommen

Minna Bernays talking with Freud's
sister Rosa.

Freud's only flight coincided with the
Atlantic crossing by the *Graf Zeppelin*.
Both were reported on the back page of
the newspaper *Tempo* (29.10.1928).[1]

attitude toward his birthdays extended also to other people's. He wrote to the family in Vienna: "Minna's birthday is a difficult problem. Actually I am for abolishing all birthdays that do not end in a zero but she is free to express her own opinion on that." (*Freud-Meine Lieben 14.6.1930*) However, the question of a present was solved by a lucky chance. A visitor, a lady from Peru, brought him a silver picture frame of Peruvian Indian workmanship. Since the gift came on Minna's birthday, Freud resolved to give her first option on the object.

Dr. Staub . . .   Fri 20 June 1930

Hugo Staub had been a lawyer before training in Berlin as a psychoanalyst. He had worked on crime and psychoanalysis with Franz Alexander—their previous visit to Freud had been together.[1] If Freud and Staub did discuss crime and psychoanalysis at this meeting, they may have mentioned two cases that were in the news at this time—the trial of the mass murderer Peter Kürten, the "Düssel-dorf vampire," and the trial of Hildegard Frenzel. She had accused her father of incest, then withdrawn her charge: the explanation offered was that she had "transferred" sexual experiences with others onto her father. Among the expert witnesses was the sexologist Magnus Hirschfeld.

Lucie . . .   Sat 21 June 1930

Lucie ("Lea") (1886–1980) was Freud's niece, daughter of his eldest sister Anna, and Eli Bernays. When she was seven years old her parents had emigrated to New York and while they established themselves there, Lucie had remained behind with the Freuds for a year in Vienna. Her husband, Felix Wiener, had died earlier this year in New York. She had come to Berlin from Frankfurt and would be travelling back there the following day on her way to Paris, where she intended looking for work in order to avoid returning to the United States. Freud was fond of her and spoke of her as "affectionate and reasonable as ever, in fact the only real person [*der einzige Mensch*] in that whole line." (*Freud-Meine Lieben 22.6.1930*)

Jackson & David B. discharged . . .   Sat 21 June 1930

Freud had come to Berlin with three of his analysands whom he continued to treat there until now. He wrote home: "Yesterday I discharged the Jackson lady and David, only Dorothy will carry on for a further week. So real holidays." (*Freud-Meine Lieben 22.6.1930*). Freud is referring to Edith Jackson, Dorothy Burlingham and David Brunswick (b.1896), brother of Ruth Mack Brunswick's husband, Mark.

Dr. Edith Banfield Jackson (1895–1977) had studied pediatrics and psychiatry in the United States before coming to Europe this year for a training analysis with Freud.

Zeppelin at night . . .   Sat 21 June 1930

The next day Freud described this incident: "Yesterday after 12 o'clock I was torn from sleep by a rising noise, I woke Anna, we opened the door onto the balcony, hurried into the garden and caught sight of the Zeppelin quite low above our house as if it were paying us a special visit." (*Freud-Meine Lieben 22.6.1930*)

Freud was fascinated by flight. When the English writer Bryher visited him in May 1927 she noted that ". . . an amazing life came into his eyes as he questioned us about flying . . . ". On October 29, 1928 he himself went on a 20-minute pleasure flight over Berlin. "I found the sensations startling and rather pleasant," he wrote afterwards to Sam Freud. (*Freud-Sam Freud 6.12.1928*)

Max arrived, Dorothy left . . .   Tues 24 June 1930

Max Halberstadt had come to Berlin for two days on photography business and was staying with Ernst Freud. His son Ernstl, who had now arrived in Berlin, was also staying there and was to accompany his father back to Hamburg for three days.

Dorothy Burlingham was to have continued her analysis until the end of the week, but she left for Vienna in a hurry because her eldest daughter, Mary ("Mabbie"), who had stayed behind, had suddenly developed appendicitis. Her departure left Freud unoccupied and alone with Anna. But with Max and Ernstl around he still had visitors.

Interpretation of Dreams 8 ed . . . Wed. 25 June 1930

Freud had been working on this 8th edition [1] until late into 1929, at the same time as he was writing *Civilization and its Discontents*. In a downcast mood he had told Ferenczi: "Well, the only items of public interest I have to communicate are that the new work will appear early in the new year and that I am boring myself with the 8th edition of the Intepretation of Dreams." (*Freud-Ferenczi 13.12.1929*)

Attack heart neuralgia with diarrhea . . . Mon 30 June 1930

Freud was treating his digestion problems with yoghurt pastilles, but two weeks earlier his supply had run out. He was trying to put on weight and to this end had been eating caviar. The disturbances today meant going without a meal, but by evening he was eating again. In the letter home that evening he noted that whenever he went from one condition to another in this way he remembered that he was approaching 75 years of age.

Last visit to Lederer . . . Tues 1 July 1930

This may have been the last actual visit to the antique dealer, but it was far from being the end of Freud's dealings with him. These continued, with Ernst as intermediary. In September 1931 Freud was writing: "I request you today to send Lederer another 300 mark—probably for the last time . . . " (*Freud-Ernst Freud 20.9.1931*).

Five years later Freud wrote to the German author Georg Hermann: "On the Kupfermarkt resided a Dr. Lederer with whom I was able to convert the larger part of the Goethe Prize of the city of Frankfurt into antiquities." (*Freud-Hermann 28.2.1936*)

Interpretation royalties divided . . . Tues 1 July 1930

Freud had decided to divide the royalties for the 8th edition of the *Interpretation of Dreams* between his sons Martin and Oliver, leaving himself only a small fraction.

Arnold Zweig . . . Thurs 3 July 1930

The novelist Arnold Zweig lived in Berlin-Eichkamp. Bad health may have prevented him making more than this one visit. "On Thursday evening Arnold Zweig visited with his wife. The poor boy is half blinded, he cannot even read any more. In the face of such fates one is silent about one's own. But hopeful it will not last much longer." (*Freud-Meine Lieben 5.7.1930*) Zweig's eyesight may have been damaged by tuberculosis of both eyes in 1926. Freud's final sentence here refers to his own fate at the hands of Schroeder. Initially the treatment was to last only a month, but it had now continued for twice as long and Schroeder would still not give a deadline for its end.

Goethe Prize turned up . . . Thurs 3 July 1930

The Goethe Prize was a prestigious award given by the city of Frankfurt. It had been founded in 1927, was worth 10,000 Reichsmarks and (in the words of the official notification which Freud was only to receive on 29 August) ". . . the prize shall be bestowed upon a person who has achieved eminence through their work and whose creative influence has been worthy of an honour dedicated to the memory of Goethe."

The expression Freud uses in this entry—*aufgetaucht*, "turned up" or (literally) "surfaced"—indicates surprise at something unexpected. At this stage there had been no official announcement and Freud could not have been entirely certain of his chances. It was another week before he mentions it in his letters home, in the form of a newspaper cutting from the *Berliner Tageblatt* of July 9, sent to his wife on July 10: "The Goethe Prize of the City of Frankfurt is soon to be awarded once again. The previous holders were Albert Schweitzer and Stefan George. This year Sigmund Freud is the most promising candidate for the prize. However, the committee has not yet reached a definite decision." (*Berliner Tageblatt 9.7.1930*)

Liebman . . . Fri 11 July 1930

Apparently Julius Liebman was a wealthy American whose son was in analysis with Freud.[1] The previous year Freud had spoken of the Liebmans from New

The Goethe House, Frankfurt.

York having visited the Tegel Sanatorium in spring 1929 at his instigation. A subsequent donation by them saved the Tegel sanatorium from closure. Now, on June 26, 1930, Freud wrote home that Liebman was one factor which would prevent him travelling direct from Berlin to Grundlsee.

£20 Hogarth for Discontents . . .   Fri 11 July 1930

This would have been a royalty for the English translation of *Civilization and its Discontents*, translated by Joan Riviere and published this year by the Hogarth Press and the London Institute of Psycho-Analysis. In 1924, at James Strachey's request, the Hogarth Press took on the publication of Freud's work, because a previous arrangement, by which George Allen & Unwin distributed it on behalf of the International Psycho-Analytical Library, had proved unsatisfactory.

Such a large-scale enterprise was a considerable risk and one which the new publishers undertook against expert advice. Leonard and Virginia Woolf had formed the Hogarth Press in 1917, but in 1924 it was still a comparatively small venture—during the previous seven years it had only published 32 books, albeit of the highest quality. (Its authors included Virginia Woolf, Katherine Mansfield, T.S. Eliot, E.M. Forster and Robert Graves, as well as Chekhov, Bunin, Gorky and Dostoevsky in translation.)

Neuländer . . .   Mon 14 July 1930

There was a Gertrud Neuländer (1878-?), a cancer specialist, but no consultation with her is mentioned in the Pichler Notes. No further evidence is available about who this might have been.

£81 Hogarth for Collected Papers . . .   Mon 14 July 1930

Initially the Institute of Psycho-Analysis bought the rights to Freud's work outright for £50 per volume. The Hogarth Press then bought the rights to the four volumes of the *Collected Papers* already published for £200, but began paying Freud royalties as soon as the books began making a profit.

Leonard Woolf wrote of Freud's attitude toward copyright: "Freud had been incredibly generous and casual with his copyrights. The outright sale of his English rights in the four volumes of *Collected Papers* for £200 was a good example of his generosity; his casualness is shown by the fact that he once simultaneously sold the American rights in one of his books both to the Hogarth Press and to another publisher."

Between 1924 and 1939 Hogarth published English translations of every book produced by Freud and after his death brought out the 24-volume *Standard Edition*.

Parting from Schröder . . .   Wed 23 July 1930

Though Freud had been happy and well-treated in Berlin, he was greatly relieved that the prosthesis was finally ready and he could now leave. Successive prostheses were the bane of his life during these years, not simply because they were painful but also because they required repeated modification. This meant that he was dependent on continual consultations with oral surgeons just to be able to perform such basic functions as eating, speaking and smoking. That sense of dependence galled Freud. Moreover, he had remained sceptical about Schroeder's new prosthesis: "Of course it will be a masterpiece and one cannot yet foretell in what manner it will spoil my life. What is difficult to bear is dependence upon a person one can't actually get hold of. I cannot expect that the new prosthesis will grant me independence." (*Freud-Martha Freud 4.6.1930*).[1]

Schroeder's inability to meet deadlines had been a source of irritation throughout the summer. Freud had originally been led to believe that the work would be ready far earlier and the delay had held up the whole family's plans for the summer, since Martha and Minna had been waiting in Vienna until he would be free to join them. Eventually, in early July, he had suggested they leave for Grundlsee without him. Although he already had the new prosthesis by this time and it was more or less satisfactory, he had pains from a wound in the mouth and could not leave until it was healed. Meanwhile, Schroeder continued to modify his "masterpiece."

View across Grundlsee towards the Totes Gebirge range.

* Arrival in Vienna . . .   Fri 25 July 1930

Freud needed to spend a couple of days in Vienna before following the others to Grundlsee. He had to see his doctors, Braun and Weinmann, and also collect the books he wanted for the summer.

** Arrival at Grundlsee . . .   Sun 27 July 1930

In Berlin there had been a heat wave. Freud feared that the fine weather would end as soon as his real holiday began and this was in fact what happened. Four days after arrival he wrote: "Grundlsee is beautiful, the house comfortable, the weather rainy and unfriendly as everywhere." (*Freud-Eitingon 31.7.1930*).

Martha Freud had arrived at Grundlsee suffering from angina, but was better by the end of the month. The weather, however, did not improve so quickly— two weeks later there was still no change: "es regnet, regnet *every day*" ("it rains, rains every day") he wrote to Jones in mid-August (*Freud-Jones 13.8.1930*).

Goethe Prize . . .   Tues 29 July 1930

Freud had known of the prize since the beginning of the month, but the official notification was only sent on July 26. By this time Freud had already begun working on his speech of acceptance, asking friends for advice on how he could connect Goethe to psychoanalysis. In a letter of August 10 Eitingon informed him of Goethe's psychotherapeutic assistance to an unfortunate man called Kraft. A Goethe specialist, Dr. Rosenfeld, had helped him locate this and other references.

The official notification of the Prize justifies the granting of the award to Freud: "Not only medical science but also the conceptual world of the artist and the pastor, of the historian and the educator, have been stirred up and enriched by your psychology."

In a reply to Arnold Zweig's letter of congratulation, Freud expressed his— measured—satisfaction at this award: "I do not dispute that the Goethe Prize gave me pleasure. The fantasy of a closer relationship with Goethe is all too appealing and the prize itself is rather an obeisance to the person than a judgment of their achievement. But on the other hand at my age such recognition has neither much practical value nor great emotional significance." (*Freud-Arnold Zweig 21.8.1930*)

Visit Federn Meng Hollos . . .   Sat 2 August 1930

Paul Federn (1871–1950) was one of Freud's longest and most faithful disciples— his "Apostle Paul." He had known Freud since 1902 and was a member of the Wednesday Psychological Society. Since World War I he had been one of the leading teaching analysts in Vienna. After Freud largely withdrew from practical affairs because of his cancer, Federn had stepped in as his representative. In 1924 he was elected vice-president of the Vienna Psychoanalytical Society and in 1926 he became co-editor of the journal, *Internationale Zeitschrift für Psychoanalyse*. From this period on he was working closely with Anna Freud, who was a second representative for her father.

Heinrich Meng (1887–1972) was introduced to psychoanalysis by Karl Land-auer during World War I and he did his training analysis with Federn. They co-founded the pedagogical journal, *Zeitschrift für Psychoanalytische Pädagogik*, and collaborated to produce two reference books, *Ärztliche Volksbuch* in 1924 and the *Psychoanalytische Volksbuch* in 1926.

István Hollós (1872–1957) was one of the pioneers of psychoanalysis in Hungary and had published *Zur Psychoanalyse der paralytischen Geistesstörung* (*Contributions to the Psychoanalysis of Paralytic Disorders*) together with Sándor Ferenczi in 1922. He had done psychoanalytical work in asylums on the clinically insane.[1]

Freud invited these three psychoanalysts because he wished to try out on them his acceptance speech for the Goethe Prize. One of them read it out for him, then he asked for criticisms. But they did not have any. Meng said: "It was touching for us to feel how great his joy was and how deeply he was moved by the fact of the first public honor that was about to be paid to his work."

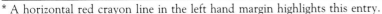

* A horizontal red crayon line in the left hand margin highlights this entry.
** In the left-hand margin there is a blue crayon line next to this entry.

Villa Rebenburg on Grundlsee, where Freud spent the summer of 1930.
". . . in an unusually beautiful environment and in a comfortable house . . ." (*Freud-Jones 13.8.1930*)

Goethe

Goethes Mutter

Mathilde arrived . . .   Wed 6 August 1930

Mathilde came to spend a month with her parents at Grundlsee. She had a reputation in the family for her sense of responsibility toward others and for her practical nature. It was probably this year that she gave Freud the curiously shaped armchair he was to use for the rest of his life.

The designer Felix Augenfeld (a friend of Ernst Freud) wrote that she approached him around this period to design a chair tailor-made to Freud's peculiar requirements: "She explained to me that S.F. had a habit of reading in a very peculiar and uncomfortable body position. He was leaning in this chair, in some sort of diagonal position, one of his legs slung over the arm of the chair, the book held high and his head unsupported. The rather bizarre form of the chair I designed is to be explained as an attempt to maintain this habitual posture and to make it more comfortable." (*Augenfeld-Lobner 8.2.1974*)

At Ischl with Mother . . .   Fri 8 August 1930

Bad Ischl, the spa where Freud's mother stayed every summer, was only a short drive away from Grundlsee and Freud had three cars at his disposal this summer—Dorothy Burlingham's, Ruth Mack Brunswick's and Marie Bonaparte's.

As his mother's favorite, Freud always felt he owed his own success in some measure to her love. That debt of gratitude [1] is implied at the close of Freud's brief essay "A Childhood Recollection from *Dichtung und Wahrheit*" (1917): ". . . if a man has been his mother's undisputed darling he retains throughout life the triumphant feeling, the confidence in success, which not seldom brings actual success along with it. And Goethe might well have given some such heading to his autobiography as:'My strength has its roots in my relation to my mother.' " [2]

F. Salten . . .   Sat 16 August 1930

Felix Salten (1869–1945) was the pen-name of Sigmund Salzmann, author of numerous plays and novels, including *Bambi*, which Walt Disney was later to make world-famous. Though born in Budapest he had grown up in Vienna. Poverty forced him to leave school at 16 and earn his living as a clerk. At the turn of the century he had been one of the young writers associated with Hugo von Hofmannsthal in his battle against a jaded 19th century literature.

Apart from this entry there is no other evidence that he and Freud were personally acquainted. However, the previous year Freud wrote a greeting on Salten's 60th birthday which was published in the yearbook of the Zsolnay press for 1930. (The greetings to Salten included messages from Beer-Hofman, Galsworthy, Hofmannsthal, Heinrich and Thomas Mann, Arthur Schnitzler and others.) This publication may have prompted Salten to pay Freud a visit.[1]

Alex Sophie Harry . . .   Sat 16 August 1930

Alexander (1866–1943) was Freud's only brother [1] and his youngest sibling, born when Sigmund was already 10 years old. Because of the age difference there was apparently no rivalry, in fact Freud played an almost godfatherly role toward him [2]; it was Sigmund, according to family tradition, who had suggested Alexander's name. Alexander had become a Professor at the Vienna Exportakademie and editor of the journal *Tarifanzeiger*. In 1909 he married Sophie Schreiber (1898–1970) and their only son, Harry, (1909–1968) was born the same year.

A week earlier Freud had written to his brother, suggesting he come to Grundlsee after their meeting in Ischl at their mother's birthday.

Ischl with Mother Birthday 95 yrs . . .   17* August 1930

Although her health had been good until quite recently, Amalia Freud was now suffering from gangrene of the leg and in such pain that constant morphia was necessary. Freud wrote to Ernst: "On 17th and 18th of this month we visited grandmother in Ischl. Not much good can be said about her any more. One notes with gratitude whenever she wakes from her apathy, recognizes us and shows interest." (*Freud-Ernst Freud 23.8.1930*).

Freud's armchair, designed by Felix Augenfeld to suit his eccentric reading posture. NB

Freud's mother Amalia, c.1872, with Alexander and Pauline, her two youngest children.

Alexander Freud, his wife Sophie and son Harry, c.1920.

(*Opposite*) Frankfurt 1930. These three pictures form part of a gift box given to Anna Freud as a souvenir of her trip to Frankfurt.

(*Opposite top left*) Goethe.

(*Opposite top right*) Goethe's mother.

---

* Amalia Freud's actual birthday was August 18, but Freud visited her both on that day and August 17. He may have recorded the initial visit [*Ischl bei Mutter*], then added an abbreviated mention of her birthday (*G. 95 J.* i.e. *Geburtstag 95 Jahre*–"Birthday 95 yrs.") after he had filled in subsequent entries and there was no room left to include August 18.

For at least ten years now she had been living a secluded life, looked after by Freud's unmarried sister, Adolfine ("Dolfi"), and kept out of touch with family affairs. Freud wrote to Sam in 1925 after her 90th birthday: "We had made a secret of all the losses in the family: my daughter Sophie, her second son Heinele, Teddy in Berlin, Eli Bernays and your parents." (*Freud-Sam Freud 21.8.1925*)

Stands . . .   Tues 19 August 1930

"*Ständchen*" ("Pedestal," "Stand") can be either singular or plural. Perhaps these were mounts Freud had ordered on his return to Vienna, for the figures bought from Lederer in Berlin.

Dr. Michel & Goethepreis . . .   Sun 24 August 1930

Dr. Michel, a Frankfurt city councillor, brought Freud the Goethe Prize and the check for 10,000 Reichsmark. (At this period 1.44 RM would buy a pound of butter, 4,300 a four-door Opel car.) Freud told Eitingon: "On Sunday councillor Dr. Michel brought me the diploma and the prize. A charming, liberal-minded and still young man. He was accompanied by his wife and—strangely!—by the wife of Little Hans who is now Kapellmeister in Frankfurt. The Lord Mayor of the city Dr. Landmann is a Jew by both parents, although baptized! That explains quite a lot." (*Freud-Eitingon 26.8.1930*)

Parting from Mother . . .   Sun 24 August 1930

Freud's mother was accompanied back to Vienna by Paul Federn. Freud was aware this "parting" (*Abschied*) could well be forever. He wrote to Eitingon: "My mother's condition is bad, we are glad that with Federn's help she arrived alive in Vienna from Ischl." (*Freud-Eitingon 26.8.1930*)

Mela Rie + . . .   Mon 25 August 1930

Mela (Melanie) Rie, *née* Bondy, (1872–1930), the wife of Oskar Rie, was the sister of Wilhelm Fliess's wife Ida; thus she was connected both to a previous and a present friend of Freud's. She had fallen seriously ill in March, soon after her daughter Margarethe had given birth to a stillborn child in February.

Anna in Frankfurt . . .   Thurs 28 August 1930

Freud was too frail to travel to Frankfurt to receive the Goethe Prize in person and Anna went to accept it on his behalf. She read his speech of acceptance in which he defended the attempts of biographers and psychoanalysts to decipher great men. (He speaks of Goethe as a "careful concealer.") The prize even brought Freud a measure of honor in his own country. Radio Vienna transmitted a half-hour broadcast of the ceremony in the evening, preceded by a reading of "Goethe's" *An die Natur*.[1]

News of Martin appendix . . .   Fri 29 August 1930

In the postscript to a letter recording Anna's return from Frankfurt, Freud added: "Martin had to have his appendix operated on suddenly, he is doing fine." (*Freud-Eitingon 30.8.1930*)

Anna back . . .   Fri 29 August 1930

Freud reported to Eitingon: "Anna is back and says it was very nice and an honor to psychoanalysis . . . ." (*Freud-Eitingon 30.8.1930*). But Freud's pleasure at the offer of the prize did not dupe him into thinking he had been accepted by the public in general. In fact he was convinced from the beginning that the award of the prize would only increase resistance to psychoanalysis. He noted, as if with gratification, reports about his ill-health following the award: "You have probably heard or yourself read that foreign newspapers are reporting alarming news about my condition. I think these are consequences of the Goethe Prize which a hostile public opinion cannot accept without signs of resentment. So they promptly murder me. Well, they have to be right some time." (*Freud-Jones 15.9.1930*)

Mathilde departed . . .   Sat 30 August 1930

After spending August with her parents, Mathilde was now perhaps returning to Vienna, where she and her husband lived on the Türkenstrasse, one street away from Freud's Berggasse home.

Alexander and Amalia Freud, 1925.

Amalia Freud with her daughters Mitzi and Dolfi, August 18, 1930.

Simmel & Laforgue . . .   Sunday 31 August 1930

Ernst Simmel (1882–1947) was President of the Society of Socialist Doctors (*Gesellschaft sozialistischer Ärzte*) and from 1926 to 1930 editor of the journal "The Socialist Doctor" (*Der sozialistische Arzt*). His training analyst was Karl Abraham. In 1920 together with Eitingon he founded the Berlin Polyclinic and in April 1927 opened the first psychoanalytical clinic at Schloss Tegel, which had offered Freud such a comfortable haven while he was being treated by Dr. Schroeder.[1]

René Laforgue (1894–1962) was a native of Alsace and bilingual in French and German. In 1923 he entered analysis with E. Sokolnicka and in the same year began corresponding with Freud. He was to be one of the most important promoters of psychoanalysis in France. Also in 1923 he was named assistant and psychoanalytic consultant at the psychiatric clinic of Sainte-Anne and in 1926 he was one of the founder members of the Psychoanalytic Society of Paris. Laforgue was also involved in founding the French Institute of Psychoanalysis, established in 1934. Laforgue came with his wife and movie camera and filmed some surviving footage of his visit.

Sachs . . .   Tues 2 September 1930

Hanns Sachs was soon to emigrate to the United States where he became Professor of Psychoanalysis at Harvard University. After a visit to Europe in 1933 Freud expressed his exasperation with the change America had wrought[1]: "I had a short discussion with Sachs. Unfavourable impression, his vulgar side which was always present has become that much more evident. Like a nouveau riche, fat, self-satisfied, vain, snobbish, delighted with America and in raptures over his great successes there. Anna was right to bring up the question of what one should want for people. Misfortune is not good for them and they cannot stand success." (*Freud-Lampl-de Groot 8.6.1933*)

Bernfeld in the evening, also Paquet . . .   Wed 3 September 1930

Siegfried Bernfeld (1892–1953) organized the Zionist Youth Rally in 1918 and in 1919, together with Willi Hoffer, founded the Baumgarten Children's Home for Jewish war orphans in Vienna. He began his psychoanalytical practice in Vienna in 1922 and in 1924 became Vice-Director (under Helene Deutsch) of the Vienna Training Institute. In 1925 he moved to the Berlin Psychoanalytical Institute: in the same year he published a prophetic book that exposed the methods of a future fascist dictatorship in Germany (*Sisyphos oder die Grenzen der Erziehung*. Freud had a copy in his library.) Like Simmel, Bernfeld believed that Marxism and psychoanalysis were compatible and complementary systems.

Freud's first impressions of Bernfeld were very positive: in 1920 he was recommending him to Eitingon to collaborate in the Berlin Polyclinic: " . . . Dr Bernfeld should be taken into consideration, a first-rate man, a brilliant teacher but who keeps his distance from the pathological . . . ." (*Freud-Eitingon 27.5.1920*)

The German poet, essayist and dramatist Alfons Paquet (1881-1944) was the secretary to the Goethe Prize Commission (*Curatorium des Goethe-Preises*) in Frankfurt and it was he who had persuaded them to bestow the prize on Freud. When Dr. Michel visited Freud at Grundlsee with the award on August 24 Paquet was unable to accompany him[1], but had been invited to call at his convenience.

Eitingon, Simmel, Federn, Weinmann . . .   Sun 7 September 1930

These four visitors each represented important strands of Freud's concerns at this period. As the intermediary between Freud and the International Psychoanalytical Press, Eitingon was preoccupied by its latest financial crisis. Storfer had informed him that August 6 was a critical date for its balance of payments; a loan from a Leipzig bank had averted disaster, but now further debt crises were forecast for the autumn.

Simmel's Berlin psychoanalytical clinic also had pressing financial problems, which worried Freud. As the pioneering psychoanalytical sanatorium, Schloss Tegel was a model of its kind which the movement could ill afford to lose.

Federn, apart from editing the *Internationale Zeitschrift* and being vice-president of the Vienna Psychoanalytical Society, had looked after Freud's mother when she was taken back to Vienna, and may now have brought further news of her condition.

Siegfried Bernfeld with some of the staff of the Baumgarten Children's Home.

Dr. Joseph Weinmann was the dentist who had gone to Berlin, at Max Schur's suggestion, to take care of the minor, day-to-day adjustments of the prosthesis. Freud was impressed by him and called him "intelligent and very willing." (*Freud- Lampl-de Groot 14.3.1931*) (Later he emigrated to the United States, where he became a professor of dentistry at the University of Illinois.)

+ Mother died 8 a.m. . . .   Fri 12 September 1930

Amalia Freud died in her bedroom in Vienna. The death came as no surprise, rather as a relief, given her recent suffering. Furthermore it relieved Freud from the responsibility of being indispensable. Even 12 years earlier he was already concerned she might be unable to bear his death: "My mother will be 83 this year and is no longer very strong. Sometimes I think I would be a little freer were she to die, for there is something about the idea that she would have to be informed of my death from which one recoils in fright." (*Freud-Abraham 29.5.1918*) Consequently he felt no grief at her death, only "an increase in personal freedom." (*Freud-Jones 15.9.1930*)[1]

Anna at Mother's burial . . .   Sunday 14 September 1930

Jewish law forbids funerals and burials on Saturdays. Consequently it was not until today that Freud's mother could be buried, alongside his father, in the main Jewish cemetery in Vienna. Freud's absence from his own mother's funeral seems surprising, but tallies with his firm opposition to religious rites and to "such ceremonies." [1] Also, as he wrote to Ferenczi, he felt "No pain, no mourning . . . ". Instead, he observed his own apparent absence of affect with curiosity: "Somehow in the deepest strata the values of life will have changed perceptibly." (*Freud-Ferenczi 16.9.1930*)

Anna departed with Dorothy . . .   Wed 15 September 1930

After the stresses of the Goethe Prize presentation and her grandmother's illness and death, Anna needed a rest. She and Dorothy Burlingham now left for a tour of northern Italy. Martha Freud and her sister, Minna Bernays, saw them off at the station with flowers. Anna kept in constant correspondence while on holiday. On the very first evening she wrote to her father from Milan: "Instead of being at La Scala we are already in bed for the first day was as full as a whole holiday. Journey excellent, according to your motto: 'You can do it cheaper, but . . . ' Fattening cure in the restaurant car, arrival on the dot, no more perceptible than Vienna-Berlin." (*Anna Freud-Sigmund Freud 15.9.1930*).

Princess departed . . .   Tues 16 September 1930

Marie Bonaparte's arrival at Grundlsee is unrecorded. Her departure, so soon after that of Anna and Dorothy, left Freud feeling abandoned in the beautiful house with its view over the entire lake and the mountains beyond. Two days later he wrote: "The house grows steadily more desolate. Today Anna with Dorothy are between Sulden and Trafoi." (*Freud-Eitingon 18.9.1930*)

Dolfi arrived . . .   Wed 17 September 1930

"Dolfi"—Adolfine Freud (1862–1942)—was the fourth of Freud's five sisters.[1] She had spent her entire life at the service of their mother.[2] The previous months must have been particularly exhausting in view of her mother's suffering. Freud wrote: "Sister Adolfine is recovering at our house from the experiences of the last week. Nature did not accept Mother's 95 years as grounds for clemency; pain from the gangrene in her legs made the morphine of the final days indispensable." (*Freud-Eitingon 18.9.1930*)

Ernst and Jofi to Vienna . . .   Thurs 18 September 1930

Ernst (1892–1970), Freud's youngest son, now an architect in Berlin, was a "lucky fellow" (*Glückskind*). Of the three sons, according to Freud, Ernst was the nearest to him in character and temperament.

A telegram from Anna in Italy had asked how Jofi was. Freud replied the day after this entry: "Today's news, she has an intestinal disturbance and is playing happily with Wolf. Naturally at every turn we miss the little creature." (*Freud-Anna Freud 19.9.1930*) Perhaps Ernst had informed him of this by telephone, after taking Jofi to the Nausch kennels at Kagran, Vienna.

Amalia Freud, c.1900. Her death brought Freud "an increase in personal freedom."

PROF. DR· FREUD

WIEN, IX., BERGGASSE 19

Tegel 22, 7. 30.

[handwritten letter in German]

Freud to Dolfi, 22.7.1930. "Dear Dolfi,
The enclosed is just pocket money for
your birthday on the occasion of which
I send you all the best wishes and my
profoundest thanks for your inestimable
work over all these years. This year we
shall be near Mother, unfortunately I
do not yet know from when onwards.
With love, your Sigm."

Dolfi, 1898, "the sweetest and best of
my sisters. . . ."

Eva moved in . . .   Thurs 18 September 1930

Eva Rosenfeld, a niece of Yvette Guilbert's husband, Max Schiller, was the mother of four children, of whom two boys had died in a diphtheria epidemic while a daughter had died in a mountain-walking accident. Like Dorothy Burlingham, she had formed a very close relationship with Anna over the preceding two or three years. It was she who had helped Martha Freud procure Rebenburg on Grundlsee for the summer. At this time she was in an analysis with Freud, which continued when she moved in. Ruth Mack Brunswick was also living there now, as substitute *Leibarzt* (personal doctor) to Freud in the absence of Max Schur. A letter to Anna the following day details the comings and goings of visitors, the weather and people's health. Both Ruth and Eva felt tired, Freud wrote, because of the sirocco, which caused the three older women headaches and Freud himself a heart condition.

* Arrival in Vienna . . .   Sun 28 September 1930

Grundlsee had been as idyllic as Freud's circumstances permitted. Never had they lived in such beauty, he wrote to his brother; later he told another correspondent: ". . . I have nothing serious to do, am more disposed to be friendly to people that usual . . . ." (*Freud-Viereck 20.8.1930*) Freud had rested and enjoyed the countryside. There is good reason to think the return to Vienna was not especially welcome.[1]

Anna back . . .   Mon 29 September 1930

Anna and Dorothy came back refreshed from their hike through South Tirol. Anna's mood is reflected in a lyrical letter to Eva Rosenfeld: "We are 1500 m. nearer the sun than usual and one can feel it. It slowly burns away everything unnecessary in you.

"It is very beautiful and at every stage I leave behind a little bit of worry.

"I visited a peasant woman who still spins herself and weaves loden cloth.

"But she does not perform analyses at the same time.

"I have everything I need in the rucksack. Perhaps one never needs more." (*Anna Freud-Eva Rosenfeld 18.9.1930*)

Dr Bondy . . .   Mon 29 September 1930

This may be the child psychologist from Hamburg, Dr. Curt Bondy (1894–1972). When Freud was considering sending Angela Seidmann into a home, he mentioned that ". . . we hear good things about the one belonging to a Dr. Bondy near Hamburg." (*Freud-Mitzi Freud 15.2.1930*).

X-ray at Schwarz . . .   Thurs** [Tues] 30 Sept 1930

Dr. Gottwald Schwarz worked in the Institute of Radiology at the Vienna General Hospital. He was also a consultant radiologist to the Cottage Sanatorium where Freud had stayed in April of this year and he now x-rayed Freud's stomach to discover whether there had been any organic basis for the colic attacks he had been suffering earlier this year. Nothing was found.

All doctors at Pichler's . . .   Fri 3 October 1930

It was now almost a year since the "false alarm" that had lead to Freud's last consulation with Pichler. He now returned to the specialist, because Schur had detected a suspicious growth. This marks the beginning of the long decline—from now until 1938 Pichler was to be in charge, constantly consulted and continually operating.

Apart from Schur, the dentist Weinmann may have been present. Possibly Freud's second "personal physician," Ruth Mack-Brunswick, was also there and/or Pichler's assistant Berg. Pichler's notes record the results of this consultation: the discovery of a small leukoplakia behind the prosthesis and an area of

---

* A blue line in the margin marks this entry. There is no apparent reason for the color of the crayon used to underline changes of address—it is probably a matter of which was to hand. The same goes for marginal markings in Freud's books, which are in variously colored crayons or colored pencil.

** Freud wrote *"Do"* (for *Donnerstag*—Thursday) instead of *Di* (for *Dienstag*—Tuesday).

Berggasse 19.

about 1 cm. which he suspected to be a precancerous proliferation of the epithelium. His advice was one week's observation and an operation.

New glass case . . .   Fri 3 October 1930

This must be the small rectangular case next to the study door, which now houses most of the smaller oriental antiquities. The larger, free-standing cases are older, in all likelihood pre-war. At this time there was hardly space in the cluttered rooms for anything of comparable size, but the continuous growth of the collection necessitated at least a table-top case such as this one to stem the overflow of antiquities.

Pichler operation . . .   Tue 14 October 1930

The operation Pichler advised had been set for Friday, October 10, but was postponed because Freud had suffered an attack of coryza. Instead it took place now, with Dr. Weinmann and Pichler's private assistant, Dr. Berg, in attendance. Schroeder's treatment in Berlin had left an area of scar and tissue which Pichler now decided to excise, covering the exposed area with a skin graft from the upper arm. The operation lasted $1\frac{1}{2}$ hours.

The following day Freud wrote to Eitingon: "While stomach and heart complaints were gradually retreating in the face of treatment, Pichler's initiative has shifted the condition of my mouth to the forefront. [. . .] it was highly uncomfortable, as an operation it is obviously not considered serious. The prosthesis will not be put aside for 3–4 days, it is meant to press the piece of flesh to the wound. For that time I cannot chew and speak poorly, consequently I am on holiday from work and feed on liquids. Yesterday I had severe mouth pain, today only pressure." (*Freud-Eitingon 15.10.1930*)

Feverish sickness . . .   Fri 17 October 1930

This illness was an after-effect of the operation. It began as a fever and developed into an attack of bronchopneumonia that lasted ten days.

Bullitt . . .   Fri 17 October 1930

Despite his illness, Freud received Bullitt, who may now have brought him the "1,500 pages of typewritten notes" on Woodrow Wilson's biography, for Freud to digest as a basis to their collaboration on the study of Wilson's character. According to Anna Freud, it is impossible to reconstruct how the two men worked together. Freud kept the matter confidential to protect Bullitt's political career. Also, Bullitt became a patient of Freud's as well as collaborator.

When Bullitt returned to Vienna in late 1931, Freud was still optimistic enough to hope that the projected book could be published soon and might help save the embattled press from bankruptcy. (*Freud-Eitingon 15.11.1931*)

Work taken up . . .   Wed 29 October 1930

Apart from Freud's patients, one specific piece of work that the fever had interrupted was the Woodrow Wilson book. A letter to Arnold Zweig makes a guarded reference to this work: "Also I would prefer not to write anything more at all, yet I am again writing an introduction for something somebody else is doing, I can't say what it is, it is however also an analysis but at the same time highly contemporary, almost political . . . ." (*Freud-Arnold Zweig 7.12.1930*) Here Freud clearly intended providing only the introduction. This contradicts Bullitt's later accounts of closer collaboration. But Freud probably envisaged at least checking or supervising the rest of the manuscript.

First small cigar . . .   Sun 2 November 1930

This probably means the first cigar since the operation. It is evidence of a return to work and health. "Yesterday I covered over the traces of my days of sickness . . . " he wrote to Eitingon the following day.

The ban on smoking during the summer had such a bad effect on Freud's mood and ability to work that by June one of his doctors, Braun, was advising him to resume the habit—even though Freud himself claimed to have lost the desire. But his complaints continued: ". . . since the time I have not been allowed to smoke I also work with great difficulty." (*Freud-Radó 26.9.1930*) But what Freud means here is that he is not allowed to smoke *freely*, for by September 9

The new glass case. NB

he was already smoking two cigars a day. By mid-November he was writing to Eitingon: "I work 4 hours and consume 2 cigars a day." And six days later: "With the approval of my personal doctor Braun I smoke 3–4 cigars a day."

Continuation of funerary relief from Rome . . .   Wed 5 November 1930

This purchase represents a collector's delight—to acquire an additional fragment of an object already in one's possession. Some time in 1930 an unknown lady [Marie Bonaparte?] acquired a fragment of a marble Roman sarcophagus lid, which she gave Freud. This fragment had originally been brought to Vienna by the archaeologist and antique dealer Ludwig Pollak and it was he who discovered the second fragment on the Roman antiques market. He bought it and offered it to Freud.[1]

Conclusively passed over for Nobel Prize . . .   Thurs 6 November 1930

Earlier this year Jones had suggested setting up a Nobel Prize award as a gift for Freud's approaching 75th birthday. The idea was to form an official committee to put their case as strongly as possible to the Nobel authorities ". . . in the hope of removing the scandal of their neglect." (*Jones-Eitingon 26.7.1930*). But it was another Viennese who received the Nobel Prize for Medicine this year, the pathologist Professor Karl Landsteiner, for his discovery of human blood groups. (In fact the award had been announced a week earlier—the *Reichspost* had carried the news on October 30.) The literature prize went to the American Sinclair Lewis.

Why does Freud write "conclusively"? (*endgiltig*–"finally," "conclusively") as if the prize had now eluded him forever, rather than just for this year? Possibly—despite denials—he did feel that the recent Goethe Prize represented a strong argument in his favor and that if the Nobel Prize committee ignored him this year, it signified he would never receive the award. Another undertone might be a premonition of death. In May 1931, after his 75th birthday, Freud "promised" Einstein he would not be there to celebrate his 80th birthday.

Elections . . .   Sun 9 November 1930

These Austrian elections showed how politics had been radicalized by the onset of the Depression. Neither the Communist nor Social Democratic parties could halt the move toward the extreme right. Thus the Social Democratic Party vote gained only by 20,000 against previous figures, as against a 110,000 gain by the Nazis. Two months earlier the German elections showed the same shift, but on a wider scale. On September 14 the German Nazis had increased their share of the poll from 800,000 in 1928 to 6.5 million.

In Austria the Social Democrats took 72 seats in the election, the Christian Social Party together with the Heimwehr and Heimatwehr 66 seats, the National Economic Block and Land League 19 seats and the Heimat Block 8. In Freud's home constituency of Vienna North-West, the Social Democrats still netted 50 percent of the vote (73,177) while the Nazis received only 5,273 votes.

Ferenczi . . .   Sun 9 November 1930

This visit was a further brief interim in Ferenczi's progressive estrangement from Freud and the psychoanalytical community. Also, it was unexpected, for six days previously Freud had written to Eitingon regretting Ferenczi's isolation and silence.

Ferenczi's new "active psychoanalysis" involved much more emotional and even physical interaction between analyst and patient than Freud could accept. At their April meeting Freud had reassured Ferenczi that he had not destroyed their friendship. But the difference of opinion continued to cause Ferenczi great anxiety. From the letter Ferenczi wrote following this visit to Vienna it is clear that they once again discussed their differences and that Freud, at least to some extent, again allayed Ferenczi's fears. "The trip to Vienna did me good. I am glad to see that the things I am working on are not in the end so revolutionary; you know how I dislike differing from you even in matters of detail. I hope you are well; my impression of your state of health was that it was excellent." (*Ferenczi-Freud 23.11.1930*)

The Roman sarcophagus lid showing Hector's mourning parents and his Trojan comrades bearing his ransomed corpse back to Troy for burial. NB

Relief mounted . . .   **Thurs 20 November 1930**

The two heavy marble fragments now in Freud's possession were joined and set
on a wooden base. It was placed on top of the bookshelves in his consulting
room—a striking addition to the collection. (A further missing fragment probably portrayed Hector's father, Priam, kneeling before his son's murderer,
Achilles, to plead for the ransoming of the body.)

First evening Yvette . . .   **Tues 25 November 1930**

It seems Freud again attended Yvette Guilbert's yearly concert tour in Vienna.
After her concerts he would send flowers to her hotel. An undated note on Hotel
Bristol stationery thanks him and his wife: "A thousand thanks for the adorable
flowers received and how flattered and happy I remain that the Great Man has
found some pleasure in my concert!"

Critical reaction to the concert this year was noticeably less enthusiastic than
the previous year. The *Wiener Zeitung* said: "This time Guilbert is vocally out of
sorts. But in her recital song was never the most important thing. She always only
pretended to sing."

Eitingon . . .   **Sat 29 November 1930**

Eitingon had come to discuss his own future as president of the International
Psychoanalytical Association and his troubled relationship with members of his
own group, the Berlin Psychoanalytical Society.[1] There was also an embarrassing
oversight that Eitingon wished to clear up. The brochure—*Zehn Jahre Berliner
Psychoanalytisches Institut*–celebrating the first ten years of the Berlin Psychoanalytical Institute had come out in September, with a forward by Freud praising
Eitingon. Instead of receiving the first advance copy as would normally be the
case, Freud did not get his copy from Eitingon until November: ". . . the question
whether that was really just chance cannot be evaded." (*Eitingon-Freud 19.11.
1930*)

At Yvette's hotel . . .   **Sun 30 November 1930**

After this visit Freud was to complain that his ill-health had prevented him
making more of Yvette's visit to Vienna. However, the discussion he might have
intended to have with her was continued by correspondence. Yvette had announced her intention of writing about herself and her acting technique: a letter
of Freud questions her assumption that her own personality is pushed totally
into the background to make way for the stage persona. Instead, he countered
this idea with the hypothesis that the adopted character is made credible because
it is the expression of repressed wishes.

This discussion continued in a letter to Yvette Guilbert's husband, Max
Schiller ("Onkel Max"), in which Freud answered a possible objection to this
theory: "Now you will point out that Madame Yvette doesn't play just one part,
that she plays with equal mastery all kinds of characters: saints, sinners, co-
quettes, the righteous, criminals, and *ingénues*. This is true and testifies to an
unusually rich and adaptable psychic life. But I wouldn't hesitate to trace back
this whole repertoire to experiences and conflicts of her early youth. It is tempt-
ing to continue on this subject, but something holds me back. I know that
unwarranted analyses call forth antagonism, and I don't want to do anything that
could disturb the warm sympathy that dominates our relationship." (*Freud-Max
Schiller 26.3.1931*)[1]

Anna 35 yrs . . .   **Wed 3 December 1930**

On none of Anna's birthdays does Freud ever record visitors. The day was a
family celebration, apparently closed to outsiders. As for the relationship between Freud and Anna, though it did not exclude others, it was obviously in a
class of its own. As Freud had said to Jones three months previously, after his
mother's death: "Her [Anna's] significance for me can hardly be exaggerated."
(*Freud-Jones 15.9.1930*)

Wilson finished . . .   **Thurs 4 December 1930**

Presumably Freud and Bullitt had been working on the psychological study of
Woodrow Wilson since October 17. In his foreword to the book, Bullitt claimed

Anna. Portrait by her brother-in-law,
Max Halberstadt. MH

that each wrote a first draft of certain portions, then amended the other's drafts until "the whole became an amalgam for which we were both responsible." In the light of the end product, this version appears highly questionable. It is more likely Freud simply corrected and criticized Bullitt's text, for none of the book apart from Freud's introduction bears any trace of his style.

Nevertheless, Freud must have been reasonably content with the manuscript at this point. Three days later he confided in Arnold Zweig that he was ". . . again writing an introduction . . . ." This is evidently an introduction to the Wilson book. (*Freud-Arnold Zweig 7.12.1930*) Whatever draft or version of the book Freud had now finished, it was far from final.[1] Storfer, the director of the press, was counting on the book to save them from ruin and in April 1931 Freud reported a meeting with him: "The press has brilliant prospects if it could only receive from me the new Wilson book (which is still only half finished)." (*Freud-Eitingon 16.4.1931*)

Ed. Weiss . . .   Thurs 11 December 1930

Edoardo Weiss (1889–1971) gained his qualifications as a doctor in Vienna and in 1909 began a training analysis with Federn. On returning to his native city of Trieste he worked in a psychiatric hospital: when Marco Levi Bianchini established the Italian Psychoanalytical Society in 1925 he was a co-founder and the only other member already authorized to practise psychoanalysis. In 1919 Weiss undertook to translate the *Introductory Lectures* into Italian. In a letter of encouragement Freud wrote that he was glad to have him as a champion of psychoanalysis in Italy, but warned him that it would be no easy task. This visit of Weiss's occured just after Freud had received a further Italian translation—*Totem and Taboo*. Thanking him for it in November, Freud praised Weiss as a "true, tough pioneer."

Session . . .   Thurs 11 December 1930

Since this is a Thursday, it is likely Freud and Federn were resuming the informal discussions mentioned the previous winter. Freud refers to them as "Society evening" ("*Vereinsabend*"), but talks here of a "session" ("*Sitzung*"), which might imply something a little more formal. Could this have been an early session of the editorial committee of the *Internationale Zeitschrift?* According to Robert Waelder, one of the editors, these editorial meetings actually began around 1932. But they served the same purpose as the previous evening meetings, by allowing Freud to continue participating in discussions.

The pretext of these "editorial meetings" was to discuss business, but in actual fact they allowed Freud to enjoy scientific discussions. Waelder characterized this ploy by a Jewish joke. On a feast day the synagogue is so crowded one can only enter with a ticket. A man with no ticket was stopped at the entrance by a guard. He pleaded to be allowed to enter only for a moment because he had an urgent message for someone inside. He was let in and stayed for some time. When he emerged the guard shouted at him: "You swindler! You said you had business, but you really wanted to pray!"

Anna to Budapest . . .   Sat 13 December 1930

This was Anna's second guest lecture this year to the Hungarian Psychoanalytical Society in Budapest. Its title was *Detailed Description of the Analysis of a Child Suffering from pavor nocturnus* and it was, according to Freud, a great success.

Halsmann in Neue Presse . . .   Sun 14 December 1930

Philipp Halsmann was a student who had been found guilty of parricide by an Innsbruck court in 1929. An appeal had failed, but a Professor of Jurisprudence at the University of Vienna, Dr. Josef Hupka, was campaigning to clear Halsmann and published a long article in the Vienna newspaper, *Neue Freie Presse*.[1] Hupka had consulted Freud for his views on the case and in response Freud wrote *The Expert Opinion in the Halsmann Case* in which he warned against the careless use of psychoanalysis in a forensic context. The existence of an Oedipus complex in the suspect could not be more than unreliable corroboration: in support of that argument Freud cited the wrongful conviction of Dmitri Karamazov and Dostoevsky's dictum that psychology is a stick with two ends.

Edoardo Weiss, the "tough pioneer." TG

Hebrew Prefaces . . .   **Sun 14 December 1930**

These two prefaces introduce the Hebrew translations of the *Introductory Lectures* and *Totem and Taboo*. (The Hebrew version of the *Introductory Lectures on Psycho-analysis* was published in two volumes in Tel Aviv 1934–5, *Totem and Taboo* in Jerusalem in 1939.) In the preface to the former, Freud remarks sardonically: "The author can well picture the problem which this has set its translator. Nor need he suppress his doubt whether Moses and the Prophets would have found these Hebrew lectures intelligible."

   In the preface to *Totem and Taboo* Freud reveals his attitude toward Judaism. Speaking of himself in the third person, he says that he does not understand the "sacred language," is totally alienated from the religion of his fathers (as from any other religion), cannot participate in nationalistic ideals, and yet still feels himself to be Jewish and would not wish to be otherwise.[1]

At Max Pollack's . . .   **Wed 17 December 1930**

Eitingon had been trying to persuade Freud to have a new portrait etching done, by Professor Orlik, to replace the one done in 1914 by Struck, showing Freud in profile. But Freud refused: "This is not the time to have one's face immortalized, anyway in my opinion the Schmutzer print cannot be surpassed. I have promised Max Pollak in Vienna the 'final face'." (*Freud-Eitingon 5.10.1930*). Max Pollack had already done one of the best-known portraits of Freud. This was an etching done in 1914, showing Freud at his writing desk with a row of his antiquities in the foreground.[1]

Discontents corrected for second edition . . .   **Fri 26 December 1930**

It was on Christmas eve of the previous year that Freud had received his author's copies of the first German edition of *Civilization and its Discontents*. The second German edition came out in 1931 in the same form, again published by the International Psychoanalytical Press.

Japanese Everyday Life . . .   **Tues 30 December 1930**

Two translations of the *Psychopathology of Everyday Life* were published in Japan in 1931. One, translated by Otsuki, was printed by the Shinyodo Press under the supervision of Yaekichi Yabe, the other, translated by Kiyoyasu Marui, came from the publishers "Ars" in Tokyo. (This was republished by Iwanami Bunko in 1952.) This curious situation, where two rival publishers were simultaneously producing translations of his work, bemused Freud. A few days later he wrote to Jones: "A little while ago I received the Japanese translation of the *Everyday Life* but not from Yabe's direction. I have caused a little confusion there." (*Freud-Jones 4.1.1931*) Jones replied: "To have translated the *Alltagsleben* into Japanese must have been a hard task, but presumably they chose Japanese examples." (*Jones-Freud 15.1.1931*)

Freud at his summer home, 1931.

1931

On June 2, 1931, Freud wrote to his British colleague, Ernest Jones, that the previous year's Goethe Prize had altered the public's attitude toward him into "reluctant recognition." He added that he was indifferent to this and would much prefer a "bearable prosthesis which did not try to turn itself into the end and chief aim of existence."[1] The remark alludes to a critical topic and one that was especially relevant in 1931—Freud's cancer and its aftermath.

An echo of this theme had found its way into his latest book, *Civilization and its Discontents*, which in 1931 was republished in a second edition. "Man has, as it were, become a kind of prosthetic God," he wrote. "When he puts on all his auxiliary organs he is truly magnificent, but those organs have not grown on to him and they still give him much trouble at times."[2] The footnote to this passage in the *Standard Edition* of Freud's work tells us that a prosthesis is "an artificial adjunct to the body" such as false teeth or a false leg. It does not tell us that Freud had been condemned to wear an oral prosthesis ever since 1923. In that year a radical operation for cancer of the jaw had removed a tumor, together with part of his upper and lower jaws and a section of the soft palate. To allow him to talk or eat (or smoke), it was necessary for him to wear a cumbersome device in his mouth, which was often painful and frequently a torture.

It was in July 1931 that the tantalizing possibility of physical comfort was offered, through the agency of a man Freud refers to in the entry for July 31, 1931 as **Armenian dentist from Boston**. This was Varaztad Kazanjian, a distinguished oral surgeon who was in Europe this summer. Nevertheless, Freud had to be cajoled into consenting to be treated by him, for the work of making a new prosthesis was extremely expensive and had to be paid in precious dollars. He was not convinced he would live long enough to justify the expense and felt the money would have been better spent propping up the ailing psychoanalytical publishing house. In the end he submitted, but only because he had been "undermined by the long years of torture."[3]

Another concession forced on Freud this year was his consent to submit to a tenth operation on his cancer. Constant consultations, adjustments of the literally unbearable prosthesis (clinical notes for February 13, 1930, speak of the "intolerable" pain it was causing), continual operations (two this year, twenty in the ten years of the diary)—all of this was wearing Freud's patience to the utmost and there were times when he was in favor of simply letting the disease take its course. A consultation with experts was called in April and he put this case to the radiologist Guido Holzknecht, who was also an analysand of his and a member of the Vienna Psychoanalytical Society. Holzknecht, who was to die of radiation poisoning later this year, answered Freud's objections to further treatment by simply stating that he himself was about to undergo his twenty-fifth operation. The example of his stoicism persuaded Freud. He continued fighting the cancer. And continued, with scepticism and even good humor, his search for the "bearable prosthesis." Some time later, after a visit to his tailor, Stefan, Freud wrote to his wife: "The new suit from Stefan is again perfect, I shall ask him whether he doesn't also make prostheses."[4]

---

1. *Freud-Jones 2.6.1931* [Typescript: Inst. of PsA] ("Seit dem Goethepreis im Vorjahr hat sich das Benehmen der Mitwelt gegen mich zu einer immerhin noch widerwilligen Anerkennung gewandelt, nur um zu zeigen, wie gleichgiltig das eigentlich ist. Etwa im Vergleich zu einer erträglichen Prothese, die nicht Selbst- und Hauptzweck der Existenz sein wollte.")
2. *S.E.*, XXI.91-2.
3. *Freud- Lampl-de Groot 11.8.1931* [FM] ("Durch die vieljährigen Quälerei mürbe gemacht . . . ")
4. *Freud-Martha Freud 12.4.1932* [FM] ("Der neue Anzug von Stefan ist wiederum tadellos, ich werde ihn fragen, ob er nicht auch Prothesen macht.")

Ernst & Lux. Necklace for Lux . . .   Thurs 8 January 1931

Ernst Freud, the youngest son, married Lucie Brasch ("Lux") in 1920. She was a favorite in-law; both Freud and Martha found her enchanting. The necklace, like those given to Anna and Martha, was a token of affection. It was not a birthday gift: on March 18 Freud told Ernst to give her 150 Reichsmark from him for her birthday (he was late—her birthday was on March 2).

Ernst departed . . .   Sat 10 January 1931

To return to Berlin? That is not certain. Like Martin Freud, Ernst skied and he may have gone on a skiing holiday after Vienna.

Jofi lodging . . .   Sat 10 January 1931

Probably another stay in the Nausch kennels at Kagran. A possible reason—she may have come on heat. With Wolf, a male dog, also in the house, it may have been thought best to separate them.

Invitation London, Huxley Lecture . . .   Mon 12 January 1931

The invitation to give the prestigious Huxley Commemorative Lecture in London was another honor which greatly pleased Freud. The letter came from David Forsyth, Chairman of the Charing Cross Medical Committee, University of London, who had studied psychoanalysis under Freud in Vienna in 1919. It suggested Freud should deliver a lecture on the theme, "Recent Advances in Science in their Relation to Practical Medicine." The invitation enclosed a list of previous speakers, including the pioneer of scientific pathology, Rudolf Virchow, and Joseph Lister, the founder of antiseptic surgery. It was with real regret that Freud had to refuse.[1]

Periostitis pain at night . . .   Wed 14/Thurs 15 January 1931

Periostitis is an inflammation of the connective tissue that covers bones. The acute form, due to infection, is accompanied by severe pain. Until now Freud's general health had been quite good: in late December 1930 he even said: "If it were not for the prosthesis, the very model of a necessary evil, I could even hazard an attempt at enjoying life." (*Freud-Eitingon 22.12.1930*)

This interim of relative health continued into early January 1931: "In spite of continuing torture with the prosthesis my health is not bad; I put on $6\frac{1}{2}$ kilo in all here and in Berlin. Indulgence in smoking continues to be limited." (*Freud-Jones 4.1.1931*)

The conjunction of periostitis and prosthesis now put an end to this respite. A few days later he wrote: "I am having a particularly bad time at the moment with my jaw and/or the prosthesis." (*Freud-Eitingon 18.1.1931*)

Anna in Prague . . .   Sat 17 January 1931

Possibly another guest lecture. (In 1935 she was to give two lectures there to a study group). Though Anna did not publish this year she was kept as busy as ever.

When she offered to look after her aunt Mitzi's monthly allowance from Freud's fund, which Ernst was supervising on his behalf, Freud would not hear of it: ". . . I do not want her to put herself under even more obligations, she has enough to do and will continue to be in demand for another 35 years." (*Freud-Ernst 1.2.1930*)

Princess entered . . .   Mon 19 January 1931

The verb used here, "entered" (*eingetreten*), rather than "arrived" (*angekommen*) may mean that she entered another brief period of analysis with Freud. But she had another reason to be in Vienna—to be operated on for a third time by Halban in an attempt to cure her frigidity.

Freud was sceptical and noncommittal about the chances of success: "The Princess has been here for two weeks and wants to stay until the beginning of March. She is behaving very well, and very much split between various interests. Her daughter is again suffering from her tubercular bursa infection, is supposed to be coming here for X-ray treatment.[1] She herself wants to undergo another plastic surgery operation with Halban in order to take to the limit her ideas on the anatomical basis of frigidity." (*Freud-Eitingon 8.2.1931*)

Ernst Freud.

Lux with her eldest son Stephan Gabriel, 1922.

Freud and Lux, his favorite daughter-in-law, in 1931.

X-ray at Dr. Presser . . .   Tues 20 January 1931

This consultation is not recorded in Dr. Pichler's notes. If it was connected with the jaw, or a consequence of the recent periostitis, it may have been performed at Weinmann's or Schur's recommendation.

Martha flu . . .   Wed 21 January 1931

Martha was not the only one ill. Freud wrote to Eitingon: " . . . just about all of us are suffering from symptoms we ascribe to the flu. My wife too was in bed for several days with fever and intestinal symptoms." (*Freud- Eitingon 27.1.1931*)

Martha out of bed . . .   Sun 25 January 1931

Martha Freud was only five years younger than her husband, but her health was better than either Freud's or her younger sister's. It was unusual for her to be bedridden, if only for these four days from January 21.

Corinthian vase from Fröhlich . . .   Wed 4 February 1931

Fröhlich[1] was one of the antique dealers with whom Freud was in regular contact during the 1930s. This Corinthian vase could be the black-figured alabastron (an oil or perfume flask) dating from c.600 B.C. It depicts a winged "mistress of animals" deriving from a Near Eastern mother goddess, but associated by the Greeks with Artemis.

Electrocution at Pichler . . .   Sat 7 February 1931

Freud was resigned to this resumption of surgery. He wrote: "Last week the specialists once again discovered that a certain mucous membrane excrescence though not of course malignant is nevertheless suspect, one can never know what it might get up to and therefore it has to go. Summoning up all my passivity I complied and so yesterday I underwent a new small operation by Pichler. This time it was an electrocoagulation, I was given less of a bad time than in October, today I am already free of pain, am smoking as I write to you and will probably only miss 2–3 days of work, if I avoid getting flu and bronchial pneumonia." (*Freud-Eitingon 8.2.1931*)

+ Mathilde Breuer . . .   Mon 9 February 1931

Mathilde Breuer, *née* Altmann, (1846–1931) was the widow of Freud's early friend and collaborator, Josef Breuer (1842–1925). Together the two men had written the first published work on psychoanalysis—the *Studies in Hysteria* (1895). Freud always credited Breuer with having discovered the method—"the talking cure"—through his treatment of the patient Anna O. (Berthe Pappenheim).

Breuer was already a well-established specialist in the 1880s when he and his wife virtually adopted Freud by furthering his career, lending him money and offering him the hospitality of their home. Freud showed his gratitude by dedicating his book *On Aphasia* (1891) to Josef Breuer and by naming his eldest daughter, born in 1887, after Mathilde Breuer.

However, the intellectual and personal distance between them grew during the 1890s and their friendship finally ended in 1896.[1]

Lockjaw . . .   Wed 11 February 1931

Pichler's laconic notes two days after this attack of lockjaw betray the degree to which Freud was suffering: "Pain with prosthesis inserted was intolerable. Have to urge patient to tolerate prosthesis nevertheless since removal would increase later troubles. Agrees finally."

St. Zweig Healing t.t. Spirit . . .   Wed 11 February 1931

Freud now received Stefan Zweig's latest book, "Healing through the Spirit" (*Die Heilung durch den Geist: Mesmer; Mary Baker Eddy; Sigmund Freud*) published by the Insel Verlag, Leipzig. It was translated by Eden and Cedar Paul as *Mental Healers*).

He read the book within a week and sent Zweig his reactions: "It is a common and widely-known fact that one is displeased by one's own portrait or that one does not recognize onself in it. Consequently I hasten to express my satisfaction that you have recognized the most essential aspects of my case. Notably that

Martha, 1931.

Josef and Mathilde Breuer in the 1880s, at the start of Freud's career, ". . . when I could almost count myself a member of your family." (*Freud-Mathilde Breuer 13.5.1926*)

insofar as achievements are concerned, these were not so much a matter of intellect as of character. That is the crux of your interpretation and I think so too. Aside from that I could object that you stress the petit-bourgeois correct element in me too exclusively, the fellow is a bit more complex than that . . . ." (*Freud-Stefan Zweig 17.2.1931*)

Work taken up . . .   Mon 16 February 1931

Clearly the ability to work did not mean freedom from pain: Freud had still not recovered from the small operation on February 7: "The wound from my last operation is not yet healed. All these interventions are presented to me as unavoidable, then however as necessary. Their consequences fill the succeeding weeks with misery." (*Freud-Ferenczi 22.2.1931*)

Oli 40 yrs . . .   Thurs 17 [19]* February 1931

Oliver Freud (1891–1969), Freud's second son, named after one of Freud's culture heroes, Oliver Cromwell, was the "scientific" child who loved figures and machinery and grew up to be an engineer.

He worked in Düsseldorf and Breslau during the 1920s and now lived in Tempelhof, Berlin with his wife and daughter. He was not finding enough work and in July 1931 Freud asked for him to be sent 300 Reichsmark monthly out of the fund Ernst was administering (made up of money from the Goethe Prize).[1]

Testimonial for Bernfeld . . .   Fri 20 February 1931

Siegfried Bernfeld, now living in Berlin, was trying to procure a university appointment as professor of education and psychology at Braunschweig. (The previous year he had hoped for a post at the University of Berlin.) At this time Freud had a high opinion of Bernfeld.[1]

In January he wrote a letter of recommendation: "He is an outstanding expert of psychoanalysis. I consider him perhaps the strongest mind among my students and followers. In addition he is of superior knowledge, an overwhelming speaker and an extremely powerful teacher." (*Freud-Olden 22.1.1931*)

Freud now sent a testimonial direct to Dr. Richter, head of department, at the Berlin Ministry for Science, Art and Education.

Eitingon visit . . .   Sat 28 February 1931

One of the chief topics under discussion must have been the continuing crisis in the International Psychoanalytical Press. Storfer was now asking Eitingon for a rise in salary despite the press's financial difficulties. Eitingon responded by pointing out the press's immediate projects, which would presumably be endangered by further outlays at that moment. These included Princess Marie Bonaparte's book on Poe and Freud and Bullitt's book on President Wilson, which, it was hoped, would be finished in the spring and could appear in the autumn of that year.

The result of this exchange was a threat of resignation from Storfer and a demand that he be repaid that portion of the press's credit for which he had been personally responsible. Since this would have led to the collapse of the press, Eitingon was forced to accede to his demands: "So I simply had to buy him off for this year . . . " (*Eitingon-Freud 13.4.1931*)

Evening Bernfeld . . .   Fri 27** February 1931

Freud wrote to Eitingon that Bernfeld would be speaking "at my house" (*bei mir*). This sounds as if he were presenting a paper to one of the informal discussion groups held at Berggasse 19 during 1929–30.

Lux undergone operation . . .   Fri 20 March 1931

Probably minor surgery, since no other mention can be found. When Freud wrote to Ernst two days previously he appears unaware of anything amiss.

Oliver Freud, his wife Henny and their only daughter Eva, on holiday, late 1920s. "Much cheerfulness and modesty will be demanded of the young lady," Freud commented when the couple married (*Freud-Ferenczi 17.4.1923*)

*Freud first wrote "Tues 17," then corrected it to "Thurs" without, however, altering "17" to "19."

** This misplaced entry has been tagged on after 28 February.

Siegfried Bernfeld. Freud's testimonial for him concluded ". . . we deeply regretted it when he left for Berlin." TG

Honorary membership Society Physicians . . .   Sat 21 March 1931

Since the beginning of his career Freud had despised the Vienna *Gesellschaft der Ärzte* (the ruling body of the Austrian medical profession), which he saw as representing Christian conservatism.[1] They had ignored his 70th birthday celebrations in 1926 and Freud commented: "I would not have taken their greetings and honors for honest." (*Freud-Marie Bonaparte 10.5.1926*)

The *Gesellschaft* had now nominated Freud and the Nobel Laureate Karl Landsteiner to Honorary Memberships. "A cowardly gesture at the appearance of success, very disgusting and repulsive." (*Freud- Eitingon 20.3.1930*) So as not to attract attention, Freud intended responding only with a cool message of thanks.

Evening with Radó . . .   Fri 27 March 1931

Sándor Radó (1890–1972) had done his training analysis with the first German analyst, Karl Abraham, and become a member of the Berlin Psychoanalytical Society. Among his analysands were Otto Fenichel, Heinz Hartmann and Wilhelm Reich. During the 1920s he was editor of the *Zeitschrift* (the International Journal)—a job Freud considered of the greatest significance. In general he had great respect for Radó's intelligence and ability.

Later this year Radó became first director of the newly-opened New York Psychoanalytical Training Institute.[1] Before leaving he was due to present a paper in Vienna and Freud also had a good talk with him about his plans for America.

This entry follows exactly a month after the "Bernfeld evening" and might be either another of the informal discussion evenings or simply a private talk with Radó.

Poetzleinsdorf rented . . .   Fri 3 April 1931

This was the large house and garden which the Freuds rented for the summer—the Mauthnervilla, Khevenhüllerstrasse 6, in the Viennese suburb Pötzleinsdorf. Like most middle-class Viennese, the Freuds had always spent their summers in the country. Even after Freud's operation they had stayed at Berchtesgaden or on the Semmering.

However, his health was now more precarious and they had to remain in easy reach of expert medical help. From now until 1938, all the summers had to be spent on the outskirts of Vienna.

Tansley . . .   Sun 12 April 1931

The botanist Arthur Tansley (1871–1955) was analyzed by Freud in 1922. Freud wrote of him: "I find a charming man in him, a nice type of the English scientist. It might be a gain to win him over to our science at the loss of botany." (*Freud-Jones 6.4.1922*). He became a member of the British Psycho-Analytical Society in 1926. In 1927 he was made Sherardian Professor of Botany at Cambridge University.

Ernstl to Scharfenberg . . .   Sun 12 April 1931

Scharfenberg was Ernstl's new school. In a letter of April 21, Freud reminded his son Ernst not to forget to pay Ernstl his "school money" monthly.

W. Ernest Freud ("Ernstl") writes about his educational career: "I had been at the very progressive Burlingham-Rosenfeld School in Hietzing (Viennna), but it had no facilities for sitting the official examination (Matura) which qualified for entry into university. For that purpose I had to find another school. After casting around Anna Freud located for me the Schulfarm [farm school] Insel Scharfenberg on an island in the Tegeler See, Berlin. How she found it I do not know, but I would assume that Ernst Simmel, who ran the psychoanalytic Sanatorium Schloss Tegel at the side of the Tegeler See, might have had something to do with it; or Anna Freud may have been in touch with the director of the progressive girls' school in Vienna,, the Schwarzwald Schule, who might have known of Scharfenberg. I would be interested to know how she found Scharfenberg. I have no recollection of going to Scharfenberg for the purpose of having a look at it before I was accepted there, but the date—12.4.1931–may well refer to such an occasion."

The beautiful villa where Freud spent the summers of 1931 and 1932. Its garden was like a small park.

Pichler consultation . . .   Tues 14 April 1931

The reason for this consultation was that Schur had discovered a new lesion. Pichler's examination proved that the tumor was once again growing and required an operation. Pichler's notes of this incident reveal a new turn of events— Freud pleading with the doctor for a respite from treatment: "Considerable lockjaw, ca.15mm. Since after-effects of diathermy-operation are reported to have lasted throughout these 2 months, advise excision and Thiersch-graft. Guttapercha supplied to prosthesis. Patient to celebrate his 75th birthday soon, has had coryza. Would like postponement. I advise against such long postponement. I believe soft tumor still precancerous but am against waiting (in view of fast growth not mentioned to patient). Asked whether tumor could be left alone and malignancy risked, I advised against it. " *(Pichler notes 14.4.1931)*

Though Pichler did not tell Freud about the rapid growth of the tumor, Schur did, bound as he was by his promise to his patient.

Republic in Spain . . .   Wed 15 April 1931

King Alfonso XIII of Spain (1886–1941) abdicated after elections on April 12, announcing: "Sunday's elections have shown me that I no longer enjoy the love of my people." He left the country and a republican administration was formed under Niceto Alcalá Zamora, president until his resignation in 1936.

Freud had more than a casual interest in Spain. As a schoolboy he and a friend, Eduard Silberstein, taught themselves Spanish. They called themselves the "Academía Castellana" and corresponded in Spanish from 1871 to 1881.

Consultation Holzknecht . . .   Tues [Wed] 22 April 1931

Professor Guido Holzknecht (1872–1931) had devoted his life to the use and improvement of X-ray techniques. He had made the X-ray department of the Vienna General Hospital world-famous and published a number of works on diagnosis through X-ray. He also invented the chromoradiometer to measure dosages.

But like other pioneers he himself fell victim to cancer from overdoses of radiation. This had led to the amputation of his right arm and he was now in hospital awaiting further surgery. Holzknecht was an old acquaintance of Freud's and a member of the Vienna Psychoanalytical Society.

In an attempt to avoid more operations Freud now wished to investigate the possibility of radium therapy. Schur suggested consulting Professor Rigaud of the Institut Curie in Paris, who was at that time in Locarno. But Rigaud advised against the use of radium except against undeniably malignant tissue, which was not the case here.

As a last resort, following Pichler's suggestion, Professor Holzknecht, the leading Viennese radiologist, was consulted. The Viennese analyst Richard Sterba describes the meeting: " . . . Pichler showed Holzknecht the X-ray of Freud's new lesion. After Holzknecht had examined the plate, he said: 'Freud, you have to be operated on,' to which Freud repeated his refusal to undergo a tenth operation. Holzknecht simply remarked: 'What should I say? I will be operated on tomorrow for the twenty fifth time.' Then the conversation turned to other, unrelated matters. After the three visitors left Holzknecht's sick-room, Freud said to Pichler and Weinmann: 'We have visited a real hero. Of course, I will be operated on tomorrow.' "

Auersperg operation . . .   Thurs 24 [23]* April 1931

The Auersperg Sanatorium, used for surgery by several doctors including Pichler, was just around the corner from his office on Lichtenfelsgasse. Drs. Berg and Weinmann assisted him with the operation and Drs. Schur and Ruth Mack-Brunswick were also in attendance. Apart from the excision of the tumor, a skin-graft from the upper arm was involved. Quite severe arterial bleeding occured, but the operation was a success and Freud recovered fairly rapidly.[1]

The report on the tumor was written by the eminent pathologist Jakob Erdheim and, according to Max Schur, was "a masterpiece of pathological examina-

---

* The operation in fact took place on Thursday, April 23. Probably Freud did not write up this and the previous entry until after his return home, at least eleven days later, which would explain the mistakes.

Pelikangasse 18, the psychoanalytical Ambulatorium (out-patient clinic) that Guido Holzknecht helped found in 1922.

tion." It characterized the tumor as precancerous and it laid stress on the fact that it was caused by smoking. Apparently Freud merely shrugged his shoulders on hearing this authoritative condemnation of his addiction.

Home again . . .   Tues 5* May 1931

"I have brought home a peculiar tiredness or exhaustion . . . " Freud wrote to Eitingon. (*Freud-Eitingon 7.5.1931*) Ordinary tiredness would be natural after the operation and the pulmonary complications that had followed it. But this peculiar exhaustion may have been linked to the discovery of precancerous tissue, which disturbed the equilibrium Freud had established with his affliction. A month later he told Jones: "The last illness has ended the security I enjoyed for 8 years . . . ." (*Freud-Jones 2.6.1931*)

75 Birthday . . .   Wed 6 May 1931

Under normal circumstances this birthday would have required public celebrations, but since Freud had only just returned from the sanatorium and was still weak, only the immediate family took part. This suited Freud perfectly. He wrote to Eitingon[1]: "I was very glad to be home on my birthday, it was easier and nicer for my harrassed nurses. In all the day passed cheerfully . . . ." (*Freud-Eitingon 7.5.1931*)

But there were, as usual, many congratulatory messages and telegrams, including one from Einstein and—the one that gave him most pleasure—from Romain Rolland.

There was also the regular birthday poem from the dogs. This was attached to a pink ribbon tied round the dog's neck and signed by "the union of quadrupeds—Wolf—Jofie—Tattoun." Among the gifts was a Greek vase from Marie Bonaparte. Thanking her, Freud commented " . . . it is a pity one cannot take it into ones's grave." It is this vase, according to Jones, which now holds Sigmund and Martha Freud's ashes at the Golders Green Crematorium.

Session Poetzl—Gomperz . . .   Sat 9 May 1931

This entry can be read two ways. Either there was a meeting or seminar, followed by the two visitors, or they themselves constituted the "session."

Both were old acquaintances, sympathetic to psychoanalysis, but now working in other areas. The neuropathologist Otto Pötzl (1877–1962) began his career as Freud's student and was among the first to use experimental methods in psychoanalysis.[1] The positivist philosopher Heinrich Gomperz (1873–1942) was the son of the eminent classicist Theodor Gomperz—an early benefactor of Freud.[2]

In 1899 Heinrich Gomperz offered himself as a guinea-pig to test Freud's dream theory, apparently without any success. From 1920 to 1935 he was professor of philosophy in Vienna. During the 1920s he wrote psychological observations of the Greek philosophers Parmenides and Socrates for publication in *Imago*.

Oli's visit . . .   Thurs 14 May 1931

No record of the visit can be found. Oliver was short of money and possibly he came alone, without wife or daughter, since their names are not mentioned.

** Move to Poetzleinsdorf . . .   Mon 1 June 1931

In a letter to Eitingon Freud described the move: "It is not comfortable to settle down among the relics of a connoisseur and collector of old furniture and Austrian folklore, but it worked and you will definitely like some pieces of the new furnishings. Anyway, when I open my door I am in a spacious park-like garden which for the safety of Wolf and Jofi, who are expected tomorrow, has been fenced across. Acacias are still fragrant, the lime trees are just beginning, blackbirds and larks are going or flying for walks, no loudspeakers or car horns disturb the peace. One could be very happy here. Of course I am not. I have still

Freud and Martha, 1931.

---

* According to Max Schur, Freud returned home on May 4. Even if Freud did write the entry up later, it would be curious if he had confused the dates so near to his birthday. However, if he arrived back in the evening of May 4 he might have treated the next day as his real return.
** "P." [*Poetzleinsdorf*] written in red and a line in the left margin mark this entry.

not regained my strength, the prosthesis has still not been definitively built up. I am again giving five hours [analysis]." (*Freud-Eitingon 1.6.1931*)

Edith Rischawy burial . . .   Tues [Wed] 3 June 1931

Edith Rischawy was the niece of Robert Hollitscher, Mathilde's husband. She had suffered a mental breakdown and been in analysis with Hermann Nunberg. In 1929 she visited Freud in Berlin. She was, as he put it ". . . very meschugge [mad], completely inaccessible, dominated by the conviction she had to kill herself and silly enough to demand the means from other people." (*Freud-Meine Lieben 18.9.1929*)

The cause of her distress turned out to be an unhappy love affair with an older woman, and fear of madness was driving her to suicide. She did not, however, kill herself directly, but rather let herself die after a wound to her hand became infected. It can be taken for granted Freud himself did not attend the burial.

Japanese translation . . .   Sat 6 June 1931

In 1931 at least seven Japanese translations of Freud appeared from the two rival publishers. This may have been another volume of the 40-volume Japanese edition edited by Yabe.

Otto Fleischl . . .   Sat 6 June 1931

Otto Fleischl (1849–1935) was a younger brother of Freud's friend and mentor, Ernst Fleischl von Marxow. Otto Fleischl was a doctor and when younger had worked in Rome. He also edited his brother Ernst's collected papers, published in Leipzig in 1893.

Ernst Fleischl von Marxow (1846–1891) was one of the scientists Freud took as his model in his youth: his portrait hung in Freud's study all his life. He was a brilliant physiologist (and physicist) who worked at Ernst Brücke's Institute, where Freud did anatomical research from 1876 to 1882. An infection had led to the amputation of Ernst Fleischl's right thumb. Unbearable pain drove him to morphine addiction, which Freud attempted to cure by cocaine treatment; as a result Fleischl became addicted to cocaine instead.

Eitingon . . .   Sat 13–Mon 15 June 1931

Freud arranged this visit to occur after Martin Freud's return from his holidays so that his son could discuss his plan of taking over from Storfer as manager of the International Psychoanalytical Press. Freud recommended Martin to Eitingon, the director of the press, as "efficient and reliable in everything he undertakes." (*Freud-Eitingon 12.5.1931*)

This year was Eitingon's 50th birthday. Freud wrote a letter of congratulation this month, thanking Eitingon for everything he had done for psychoanalysis.[1]

Ernst . . .   Sat/Tues 20/23 June 1931

The second of three visits by Ernst this year. In both 1930 and 1932 he visited only once.[1]

Storfer . . .   Sun 28 June 1931

From 1921 onward Adolf Joseph Storfer (1888–1944) managed the International Psychoanalytical Press together with Otto Rank. In 1925 he replaced Rank as managing director. Complaints about Storfer recur throughout the correspondence with Eitingon during 1931. The press's financial predicament was dire; Storfer's mismanagement was to blame.[1]

One current cause of friction was the Hungarian edition of Freud's work. The translation had long been ready (the *Interpretation of Dreams* for 15 years!) but Storfer was creating difficulties over selling the manuscripts and rights to the Hungarian publisher.

In March Freud was talking of Storfer's "rascally malicious" behavior (*lausbübisch-boshaft*) and in April he approved Eitingon's schemes to protect himself and the publishing house against Storfer's activities. But later that month Storfer's behavior changed and became "buttermilk, rose-honey" (*Buttermilch, Rosenhonig*). In line with his apparent willingness to rescue the press he announced his intention of publishing the Wilson book.

Meanwhile, Eitingon was hoping to buy Storfer out and for someone else to

Freud reading in the garden. "One could be very happy here. Of course I am not." (*Freud-Eitingon 1.6.1931*)

The portrait of Ernst Fleischl von Marxow in Freud's study.

František Juřan unveiling his plaque at Freud's birthplace, 1931.

Freud's mummy portraits from the Graf collection. WK

Freud and his brother Alexander.

Oscar Nemon sculpting Freud "angry with humanity", 1931.

take over his functions. At the recent meeting with Eitingon (June 13–15, 1931), Martin Freud had declared himself a candidate for the post. Probably Storfer was now informed of the decisions that had been reached at that meeting.

Tarock with Fleischl . . .   Sun 28 June 1931

Probably Otto Fleischl again. Since this was Sunday, the card game mentioned here may have been been in addition to the habitual one on Saturday evening. Or Freud may have belatedly tagged a reference to a Saturday game onto an already written Sunday entry.[1]

Sculptor Juran for Freiberg . . .   Tues 14 July 1931

The Czech sculptor František Juřan was sculpting the relief plaque for Freud's birthplace in Freiberg (Příbor), which was to be unveiled at a formal celebration on October 25 of this year.

Anna Freud wrote: "Papa is playing cards and one can look in through the window and outside the wind is blowing and cooling off the terrible heat. A sculptor was here the whole day and did an image of Papa for his birthplace in Freiberg. It came out very lifelike." (*Anna Freud-Eva Rosenfeld n.d.*)

+ Johanna Rie . . .   Sat 19 July 1931

This was the death of a friend's wife—Johanna Rie (1871–1931), *née* Karplus, married in 1895 to Alfred Rie, an older brother of Oskar Rie.

To Alfred Rie . . .   Thurs 23 July 1931

Alfred Rie (1862–1932) was a lawyer and one of Freud's regular tarock partners. This is likely to be a visit of condolence after the recent death of his wife.

v.d.Hoop . . .   Thurs 23 July 1931

J.H. van der Hoop (1887–1950) was a co-founder and president of the Dutch Association for Psychotherapy (*Nederlandsche Vereeniging voor Psychotherapie*) and had come to Vienna to study psychoanalysis.[1] He was a university lecturer in Amsterdam: in 1937 the International Psychoanalytical Press published his book *Bewusstseinstypen* ("Types of Consciousness").

Sculptor O. Neumann . . .   Fri 24 July 1931

The sculptor is in fact Oscar Nemon (1906–1985)—Freud has germanicized the name here. Nemon delivered the three busts he had produced in October. (In 1936 he was to work on some more busts of Freud.)

In a letter to Eitingon Freud reports: ". . . someone is making a bust of me, the sculptor Oscar Neumann from Brussels, from his appearance a slavic eastern Jew, Khazar or Kalmuck or something like that. Federn, who is usually highly inept in discovering unacclaimed geniuses, forced him on me. But this time there is something or rather quite a lot in it. The head which the gaunt, goatee-bearded artist has fashioned from the dirt—like the good Lord[1]—is a very good and an astonishingly lifelike impression of me. He has kept quiet about how he intends valuing the work, but I didn't order it from him." (*Freud-Eitingon 3.8.1931*)

The clay bust became the model for three further busts in wood, stone and bronze. Paula Fichtl, the Freuds' housekeeper, commented that the sculptor had made the professor look too angry. Freud's response was: "But I am angry. I am angry with humanity."

Graf portrait . . .   Fri 24 July 1931

Freud now acquired a 4th century A.D. Egyptian mummy portrait of a bearded young man. The purchase was a stroke of luck, for he already had one of these portraits.[1] He hung the new one above his chair, behind the couch. Both originated from the collection of the Austrian dealer Theodor Graf.

Graf had acquired a great number of similar portraits discovered in the cemetery of ancient Philadelphia, el-Rubaiyat in Fayyum; some of these he exhibited in Berlin in 1889 and at the Chicago World Fair in 1893.

Alex & Lilli evening . . .   Fri 24 July 1931

These visitors were most probably Alexander, Freud's younger brother, and his niece Lilly ("Lilli" is Freud's spelling), the daughter of his sister Mitzi.

Lilly Marlé, *née* Freud, (1888–1970) was an actress: in 1918 she married the actor Arnold Marlé. She had a son, Omri, born in 1919, and when her niece Angela Seidmann was orphaned in 1930, she adopted her. Freud sent contributions toward the girl's upkeep; in August 1930 he directed Ernst to send the Marlés 500 marks from the "Goethe Prize fund."

Congress cancelled . . .   Fri 24 July 1931

An international psychoanalytical congress had been planned to take place in September at Interlaken, but the grave internal political situation in Germany, the world economic crisis and the collapse of the Vienna Creditanstalt bank were all having their effect. Since many analysts could not have afforded to come, it was postponed until the following year. A further factor was that Eitingon was now too preoccupied by problems of the press to help organize a congress.

Meanwhile, he suggested to Freud that they "take advantage" of those problems as a pretext not to publish a book submitted to the press by Melanie Klein. Freud agreed: "If we have a good opportunity to put off the publication of Melanie Klein's book and to finally repudiate it, we should take it. Out of consideration for Anna I am forced to be partisan, but in the latest studies of the development of the female child I nevertheless came to the conviction that the results of Kleinian play therapy are misleading and its conclusions incorrect. There is really no need for us to champion it." (*Freud-Eitingon 3.8.1931*)

Martha 70 yrs . . .   Sun 26 July 1931

This must have been a celebration tinged with memories of the 45 years Freud and Martha had lived together. She had played a vital role in protecting him from many of the demands of domestic life.

Initially she and his work had been Freud's two guiding principles. During their four-year engagement, from 1882 to their marriage in 1886, he frequently spoke of the ideal life he imagined—to know that she was his and to be able to continue his research and work: "Couldn't I for once have you and the work at the same time?" (*Freud-Martha Bernays 21.10.1885*).

At that period, when his spirits were low, she even outweighed everything else: "I took no pleasure in life before I had you, and now that you are mine 'in principle' the main condition I set on life, which is otherwise of little consequence, is to have you completely." (*Freud-Martha Bernays 19.6.1884*)

+ Forel . . .   Tues 28 July 1931

Auguste Forel (1848–1931), who had died the previous day, was a Swiss psychologist and psychiatrist; Bleuler had been among his pupils.

In its scope his career parallelled Freud's. He had begun his scientific work with research into ants, studied medicine and made discoveries in brain anatomy. As Professor of Psychiatry, he became director of the Burghölzli asylum. In 1887 he visited Hippolyte Bernheim and took up hypnotherapy: he also published works of sexology and was involved in forensic psychology.

Freud had a number of his books in his library, including a dedicated copy of *Gehirn und Seele*.[1]

Armenian dentist from Boston . . .   Fri 31 July 1931

Varaztad Kazanjian was a world-famous oral surgeon, an Armenian who had fled from Turkey as a boy and graduated from Harvard Dental School, where he now taught. During World War I he treated British soldiers in France, specializing in reconstructing jaws. He was now in Europe to attend a world congress of dentists in Paris at the beginning of August.

With the appearance of this "Armenian dentist," Ruth Mack Brunswick resolved that Freud's prosthesis should be improved. She persuaded him, with great difficulty, to come to Vienna briefly before the congress. Kazanjian agreed to look at Freud's prosthesis, but did not make any promises about returning after the congress.

Freud's prosthesis was the bane of his life. He had grown sceptical about the possibility of improvement, but had not entirely given up hope and consented to the consultation. Afterwards he wrote to Eitingon that Kazanjian ". . . inspires great confidence and is a shy man with a smile like Charlie Chaplin." (*Freud-Eitingon 3.8.1931*)

Freud and his niece Lilly Marlé.

Martha, aged 70.

Anna ill . . .   Sat 1 August 1931

This was a sudden fever that must have been, at least partly, precipitated by
tiredness and overwork. After the cancellation of the congress (which she had
been helping to organize), Anna wrote to Ferenczi, two days previously: "Now
one can at least allow oneself to be tired." (*Anna Freud-Ferenczi 29.7.1931*)

New prosthesis Kazanjean . . .   Sat 1 August 1931

Freud's first response to Kazanjian's preliminary work was amazement: "And
now the unbelievable has happened! In 1 1/2 days—Friday and Saturday—today
is Monday, the magician has completed a provisional prosthesis, which is only
half as big and heavy as the previous one, with which I can chew, speak and
smoke at least as well as before." (*Freud-Eitingon 3.8.1931*)

But the hope of an end to long years of torture was no more than a prospect.
"No certainty, all previous efforts and promises only faded away into disappointment." Above all, Freud objected, he might not live long enough to justify the
outlay. The treatment was immensely expensive and he could not be certain it
was worth the $6,000 or so it would cost—a sum that would be more profitably
spent rescuing the press.

Dr. Stein because of nosebleed . . .   Fri 7 August 1931

During the 1890s Freud had paid special attention to nasal symptoms (his own
or those of his family) owing to his friend Wilhelm Fliess's theory about the
connection between the nasal passages and the genitalia. Later, in 1924, nasal
suppuration was the most serious and troubling after-effect of the cancer surgery.
In 1925 he was speaking of "an endless nasal infection." (*Freud-Abraham 21.7.-
1925*)

In this instance there is no record of Dr. Stein or the attack, to indicate what
may have been the cause.

Kazanjian begun work . . .   Mon 10 August 1931

After the congress Kazanjian did not want to return to Vienna, partly because of
his family. However, Ruth and Marie Bonaparte inveigled him into coming,
despite his—and Freud's—resistance: Ruth offered him his equivalent normal
income of $5,000 a month[1] and the Princess escorted him "with wife and daugh-
ter also in tow" (*Freud-Ernst Freud 30.8.1931*) from Paris to Vienna and paid for
their stay at the luxurious Cottage Sanatorium.

Kazanjian was planning to work on Freud only until the last week of August.
After the continual extensions of his treatment with Schroeder in Berlin, Freud
must have welcomed this strict timetable. He submitted passively to the treatment "undermined by the long years of torture" (*Freud- Lampl-de Groot 11.8.-
1931*) and giving in to other people's insistence.

Ernstl accepted at Scharfenberg . . .   Thurs 13 August 1931

W. Ernest Freud draws a sympathetic picture of this unusual school: "The
Schulfarm Insel Scharfenberg was run by the City of Berlin, in the main for
working-class children. The official fee at that time was, I think, 1 Deutschmark
per day. It was a boarding school for about 100 boys (nowadays it is a co-
educational school) and was headed by a remarkable man by name of Blume.
There is a good deal of literature about it. As its name implied, it was also a farm,
albeit of modest measure. It had some cows, a few horses, many chickens, and
there was also some agriculture. The idea was to acquaint the city child with the
ways of the country, and the pupils had to help with planting and harvesting
potatoes, etc. It was intended that I stay there until the Abitur (the German
equivalent of the Austrian Matura) but Hitler's rise to power in 1933 put a
premature end to this."

Tegel will close . . .   Tues 25 August 1931

The Tegel sanatorium had long been in financial difficulties. Simmel appealed for
funds in 1929 and various benefactors stepped in, including Dorothy Burlingham, the Swiss-born French psychoanalyst Raymond de Saussure and Marie
Bonaparte. But to run such a clinic privately was not economically viable because
the staff-patient ratio had to be high.

Now the sanatorium could no longer afford the rent for Schloss Tegel and was

Martha Freud (standing) with her sister
Minna c.1882.

Martha with Mathilde, Oliver and
Martin, 1894.

·forced to close. Eitingon wrote to Freud the next day of the decision[1]: he added "A pity, a great pity." ("*Schade, sehr schade*").

Freud also had reason to regret its closure. Apart from its unique value as the first psychoanalytical clinic, it had provided him with welcome rest, refuge and hospitality during his stays in Berlin in 1928, 1929 and 1930.

Turning point . . .   Thurs 27 August 1931

This entry is not clear. It could refer to a turning point in the weather, for in early August Freud had written; "The heavy heat of the last week has had a bad effect on my general condition." (*Freud-Eitingon 8.8.1931*) But by late August the weather was already cooler. The phrase may therefore be a reference to health, either his own (perhaps in connection with the prosthesis) or Anna's.

The date of Anna's recovery from her fever at the beginning of the month is unrecorded. But it seems to have resulted in complications that may have lasted until now.

She wrote afterwards to Eva Rosenfeld: "Today I am already lying in the garden in Dorothy's green wheelbarrow and trying to be well again. I no longer have a high temperature and if it doesn't return in the afternoon then it is probably all over. My throat is still not quite free and my gall which was slightly infected is also not yet perfect but in all I am much better. The whole thing is curious." (*Anna Freud-Eva Rosenfeld n.d.*)

Ricarda Huch Goethe Prize . . .   Fri 28 August 1931

The award of the 1931 Goethe Prize was naturally a matter of interest to Freud. His successor to the award was Ricarda Huch (1864–1947), a prominent "neoromantic" poet, author and historian.[1]

Kazanjian left. New prosthesis . . .   Sat 29 August 1931

Kazanjian had reduced an existing prosthesis and produced three new rubber ones. Pichler generously lent him his laboratory, but Kazanjian had had to do all the construction work on the plate himself: there were no trained assistants and many unavailable materials had to be sent by Marie Bonaparte from Paris.

The day after his departure Freud wrote: "The magician left me yesterday. I am not feeling so wonderful, but anyway speech is better. I should anticipate further progress on growing accustomed to the new thing. It does not seem possible to do anything more for me." (*Freud-Eitingon 30.8.1931*)

In September Pichler noted that Freud could not smoke with the soft prosthesis and bit his tongue. He spent the following months modifying Freud's new prostheses, but without great success.[1]

Minna's accident on the street . . .   Mon 31 August 1931

No documentation of this accident has so far come to light.

Oscar Rie fallen ill . . .   Tues 1 September 1931

Oskar* Rie, who suffered a heart attack on this day, was one of Freud's oldest friends, among the very few left from preanalytic days. Freud wrote to Marie Bonaparte: ". . . 45 years ago, when as a newly married man (1886) I announced the opening of my office for the treatment of the nervous disorders of children, he came to me first as an intern and then as an assistant. Afterward he became the physician of our children and our friend, with whom we shared everything for a generation and a half. One of his daughters, Marianne [Kris], became an analyst, as you know; the other married the analyst [Dr. Hermann] Nunberg, so that the ties became possibly even closer." (*Freud-Marie Bonaparte 18.9.1931*)

Libidinal Types begun . . .   Wed 2 September 1931

The brief essay *Libidinal Types* attempts to characterize people by their libidinal inclinations. Freud distinguished three main types—*erotic, narcissistic* and *obsessional.* The erotic type seek loving and being loved, they represent the instinctual

Oskar Rie ". . . with whom we shared everything for a generation and a half." (*Freud-Marie Bonaparte 18.9.1931*)

---

* Rie spelled his first name with a "k" in signatures and on his printed notepaper, even before the German spelling reform of 1902. Freud stuck to the old-fashioned variant, but I have followed Rie's own practice. (As far as Freud's own name was concerned, he changed it in adolescence from "Sigismund" to "Sigmund." He, and others, occasionally used the variant spelling "Siegmund.")

demands of the id. The obsessional type are dominated by conscience and the demands of the super-ego. The narcissistic type is independent and centered on self-preservation.

Combinations of these basic forms are more common than pure examples. The *erotic-narcissistic* is the commonest; from a cultural viewpoint the most valuable type is the *narcissistic-obsessional*.[1]

Dr. Alexander . . .   Mon 7 September 1931

In the United States, opposition to Franz Alexander had diminished since 1930 when he became Visiting Professor of Psychoanalysis at the University of Chicago. In January 1931 Alexander gave the Harvey Lecture in New York (on "Psychoanalysis and Medicine") and after the lecture the Dean of the Medical Faculty at Cornell announced that he was now convinced psychoanalysis should be taught to medical students at a relatively early stage of their course.[1]

Another opportunity was the Rosenwald Fund. Its director, E.R. Embree, was interested in psychoanalysis and willing to finance the analysis of criminals, which was Alexander's speciality.

Alexander wanted to discuss with Freud this possibility of opening a psycho-analytical institute in the United States. Earlier that year he had told Freud: "Resistance here is naiver and less malicious than in Europe . . . " (*Alexander-Freud* 18.1.1931).

Eitingon . . .   Fri 11 September 1931

The problems of the International Psychoanalytical Press must have been one inevitable topic during Eitingon's three day visit to Vienna. Probably cigars were also discussed, since Eitingon was now the chief supplier.

In January Freud had told him he was smoking again, but complained about the inferior Austrian cigars. Eitingon contacted the Berchtesgaden dealer, found out the name of Freud's brand there (*Don Pedro*) and ordered several hundred. In May, when Eitingon heard that Freud had given up smoking, he still had a fine supply of *Don Pedros* and *Reina Cubanas* and asked whether Freud could not be tempted. Not much persuasion was necessary.

In August Eitingon's wife Mirra visited the *Festspiele* in Salzburg and brought two boxes of Berchtesgaden cigars across the border. Two months later Eitingon returned from a trip to Holland with two boxes of *Liliputanos* which Freud had asked for.

Princess departed . . .   Sat 12 September 1931

Marie Bonaparte had visited her daughter Eugénie, who was in Switzerland recovering from an operation on her leg. She then travelled on to visit Freud.

She had always been interested in criminal psychology. After her visit to Freud, she intended travelling to Düsseldorf with Raymond de Saussure to collect information on the sadistic murderer Peter Kürten, who had been tried there the previous year and executed at the beginning of August 1931.

Nunberg taken leave . . .   Sun 13 September 1931

Hermann Nunberg (1884–1970) studied under Bleuler and Jung at Zurich but afterwards settled in Vienna where he became a member of the Vienna Psychoanalytical Society. He taught at its Institute from its foundation and his lectures formed the basis of his textbook *Allgemeine Neurosenlehre auf psychoanalytischer Grundlage*, Berne 1932, (*Principles of Psychoanalysis* N.Y. 1955) to which Freud wrote a foreword.

In 1930 the Professor of Psychiatry at the University of Pennsylvania invited Nunberg to introduce the study of psychoanalysis at the Mental Hygiene Institute of Pennsylvania Hospital. He was now saying goodbye to Freud before leaving for Philadelphia to take up this post.

Putsch in Styria . . .   Sun 13 September 1931

This was an attempted march on Vienna by the Styrian *Heimwehr* under Dr. Pfrimer. The *Heimwehr* was an Austrian fascist paramilitary organization; its politics were stated in the "Oath of Korneuburg" adopted at a rally on May 18, 1930: "We repudiate western parliamentary democracy and the party state! [. . .] We are fighting against the subversion of our *Volk* by marxist class struggle

Berchtesgaden, once Freud's holiday resort, now the source for his cigars.

and liberal and capitalist economics." The "patriotic" *Heimwehr* strongly resembled the Nazis at this stage and in fact the Styrian *Heimwehr* later amalgamated with the Nazi Party.

At Pfrimer's subsequent trial in Graz, he and his eight associates were acquitted by a jury. It seems the government had known of his plans and was itself considering a "constitutional *coup*" if the November general election did not give the bourgeois parties a two-thirds majority.

Eitingon departed . . .   Sun 13 September 1931

It had been resolved that Storfer should be replaced by Martin Freud as business manager and a certain Hosemann who should be given power of attorney from November 1, 1931. In late October Eitingon officially informed Storfer of this in a series of propositions, stating that the firm was to be collectively run from November on and that Frau Zweig was also to be included. In addition he requested that the firm be moved to cheaper premises.

Minna to Meran . . .   Wed 16 September 1931

Minna Bernays was now 66 years old and her general health was not good. She regularly visited the resort of Meran to convalesce. It is possible this visit may have had some connection with her accident on August 31.

+ Oscar Rie . . .   Thurs 17 September 1931

Oskar Rie did not recover from the heart attack at the beginning of the month. The day after his death, Freud sent Marie Bonaparte a resigned comment: "It is an inevitable lot to see one's old friends die. Enough if one is not condemned to outlive the young ones." (*Freud-Marie Bonaparte 18.9.1931*) Rie was cremated two days later.[1]

Emden . . .   Thurs 17 September 1931

The Dutch psychoanalyst Jan van Emden first met Freud in Leyden in 1910; he attended the third international psychoanalytical congress at Weimar in 1911. He became a friend of Freud's. In 1929 he even spent a week as a guest of the family.[1]

At Nunberg's . . .   Fri 18 September 1931

Hermann Nunberg had left for Philadelphia alone without his wife and daughter, because of the grave illness of his father-in-law, Oskar Rie. Freud's visit to Margarethe Nunberg was one of condolence on her father's death.

* At Berggasse . . .   Sat 26 September 1931

This marks the move back from the spacious summer quarters to the relatively cramped appartment in the city.

The villa in Pötzleinsdorf had provided a beautiful environment for the summer—"an idyll hardly permissible these days . . . " (*Freud-Eitingon 3.8.1931*) . Freud had managed to continue work, despite the Kazanjian treatment: apart from his own writing he had three analysands (Dorothy Burlingham, Marie Bonaparte, the American Irma Putnam and from mid-August Jeanne Lampl-de Groot).

Moreover, the dogs had enjoyed themselves: "Don't laugh, but our dogs contribute a great deal to the pleasure of Poetzleinsdorf and they keenly enjoy their freedom in the garden. My Jofi is a delightful creature, recuperation after most of the human visitors, her black son is a pleasant rogue. I can no longer imagine summer without these animals." (*Freud-Eitingon 3.8.1931*).

The return to Berggasse nearly coincided with the 40th anniversary of Freud's first move to that address.[1]

Female Sexuality finished . . .   Wed 30 September 1931

In *Some Psychical Consequences of the Anatomical Distinction between the Sexes* (1925) Freud had compared male and female infantile sexuality and suggested that penis envy develops into a desire for a child as a substitute penis for little girls. Boys endure a castration complex which shatters the Oedipus complex,

Dr. Karl Renner, leading Social-Democrat, speaking at a memorial rally for two workers killed in the 1931 Pfrimer putsch. DOW

---

* This entry is marked by a red line in the left-hand margin.

whose sublimated desires now form the core of the super-ego. Girls are spared this stage. As a result their super-ego is less pitiless, their sense of justice less unrelenting and their actions dictated more by emotion.

The paper *Female Sexuality* was a further exploration of this theme[1]—one that aroused a great deal of discussion particularly among analysts with feminist views. It depicts the relationship of girls to their mother. Freud suggests that girls progress directly from an attachment to their mother to one on the father: consequently their Oedipus complex is a later development and one that is often not surmounted.[2]

Rickman . . .   Wed 30 September 1931

John Rickman was returning to England after analysis with Ferenczi. His behavior over the next year convinced Jones that he must have had "a very abnormal primary constitution," which, Jones eventually decided, was an underlying and incurable psychosis.

Lampl . . .   Sun 4 October 1931

The Viennese psychoanalyst Hans Lampl (1889–1958) had been a schoolmate of Martin Freud and had socialized with the Freud family long before he began attending Freud's lectures in 1912.

After graduating from the University of Vienna medical school in 1912 he did research in serology, bacteriology and pathological anatomy under the future Nobel Prize laureate Dr. Karl Landsteiner. In 1920 Lampl took up psychoanalysis and moved to Berlin in 1921, the year his future wife, the Dutch doctor Jeanne de Groot, began a training analysis with Freud. They married in 1925.

Between August and November the Lampls were in Vienna, so that Jeanne could continue her training analysis with Freud.

Friedjung . . .   Sun 4 October 1931

Dr. Josef Friedjung (1871–1946), a Czech pediatrician, joined the Wednesday Psychological Society in 1909 and was among the original members of the Vienna Psychoanalytical Society when it was founded in 1910. After World War I he was active in Austrian revolutionary politics and from 1919 to 1922 was a member of the Diet. From 1920 on he lectured in pediatrics at the University of Vienna. In 1938 he emigrated to Palestine.

+ Tattoan . . .   Mon 5 October 1931

Jofi's first "husband" was a black chow. Her puppy, a male named Tattoan, was also "as black as the devil" but "a pleasant rogue." (*Freud-Eitingon 3.8.1931*) It was only nine months old now when it died, possibly from canine distemper.[1]

It had been named after Tattoun, Marie Bonaparte's first chow, acquired in 1928 when her daughter Eugénie suffered a bout of illness and asked for a dog to keep her company. This Tattoun and the bitch Cheekee had a daughter, Topsy. She was to become famous through a book Marie Bonaparte wrote about her, which Freud and Anna Freud translated in 1938.[2]

Kannon and Tang figure bought . . .   Tues 6 October 1931

A *kannon* (or *kuan-yin*) is a Bodhisattva of Compassion. Originally, in Indian and early Chinese Buddhism, it was a male figure, an equivalent of the Bodhisattva Avalokitesvara, one of the attendants of the Buddha Amitabha. This later assumed female form and became immensely popular as a sort of Buddhist Madonna, a "goddess of mercy." The kannon Freud acquired was a small 19th-century jade seated figurine, on a wooden base.

The Tang figure may be one of two grooms or a female, now on Freud's desk. The Tang dynasty (618–907 AD) saw the spread of Buddhism in China and expansion of the silk trade: Its art reflects its cosmopolitan culture.

Federn . . .   Thurs 8 October 1931

As Freud's deputy, Paul Federn often represented him on public occasions and he was to do so at the unveiling of the plaque at Freud's birthplace in Freiberg on October 25. This visit now may have involved a discussion of his speech.

Entrance to Berggasse 19 where Freud had lived since 1891.

Visiting card, announcing Freud's change of address, September 1891.

Hans Lampl with his two daughters.

Hier lädt der helle Sonnenschein
Dich zum Spazierengehen ein.

Priest bought . . .   Thurs 8 October 1931

Freud's collection includes two Buddhist *Lohan*, priest figures of the Ming dynasty (15th-16th century).

Hard currency regulation . . .   Fri 9 October 1931

In August the Austrian government had asked the League of Nations for help in overcoming the crisis caused by the failure of the *Creditanstalt* bank and the consequent run on the schilling. They were told to save money and balance the budget. Wages and salaries were reduced, government expenditure cut and taxation increased.

Among the credit restriction measures was a foreign currency regulation, published the following day in the official *Wiener Zeitung*. Business with foreign currencies could only be negotiated through the Austrian national bank, which also set the exchange rate. No more than 500 Austrian schillings could be taken out of the country. Flouting the new regulations could involve fines of up to 250,000 Austrian schillings or imprisonment from one month to one year.[1]

Juran plaster plaque . . .   Mon 12 October 1931

In July the sculptor Juřan had sculpted Freud for the plaque that was to be ceremonially unveiled in Freiberg on October 25. The plaque Freud mentions here could have been a plaster cast of the design, which Juřan may have given Freud. There is no indication it was brought to England and its present whereabouts is unknown.

Album of Poetzleinsdorf . . .   Mon 12 October 1931

An album of photographs with a commentary in Anna Freud's handwriting records the summer in the beautiful villa in Pötzleinsdorf. It includes pictures of visitors, house, garden and dogs and forms a visual counterpart to the diary notes for the summer.

Gold changed . . .   Wed 14 October 1931

The currency regulations of October 9 stated that all hard currency worth over 1,000 schillings had to be declared and offered to the national bank within eight days, to be changed into Austrian currency at a rate fixed by the bank.

Possibly Freud is using the word "gold" ironically, for his hard foreign currency which now had to be changed into the debased local currency. But he may have had a stock of foreign gold coins.

Minna back . . .   Thurs 15 October 1931

Minna had returned from Meran, where she had spent a month. Soon after her departure, Freud had written to Ernst: "In Meran Aunt Minna has hit upon the sun, which we are not getting to see here." (*Freud-Ernst Freud 20.9.1931*)

Rider and Guard bought . . .   Thurs 15 October 1931

Among the mounted figures in Freud's collection is an archaic Greek terracotta figurine (c. 550 B.C.). Such figures were typically laid in graves as gifts or comfort to the dead. The collection also includes two terracotta figures of horsemen (one Egypto-Roman, 1st-2nd century A.D., the other perhaps a modern imitation), possibly representations of the Dioscori. In addition there is a terracotta horse and rider, c.500 B.C., possibly Boeotian.

The guard could be either a ceramic standing figure with a sword, a Wei figure of a soldier, or a Ming Dynasty bronze—the head of a tomb guardian. These grimacing Buddhist figures are generally found in pairs guarding entrances.

Paul Federn, Freud's deputy in the psychoanalytical movement.

Mathilde 44 yrs . . .   Fri 16 October 1931

The previous year Freud did not record Mathilde's birthday, but that was probably because two days before it he underwent an operation and on the following day he came down with bronchopneumonia.

Chinese guard (2nd from right) and priest (2nd from left) on Freud's desk. WK

Ernst arrived . . .   Sat 17 October 1931

In autumn 1930 Anna and Dorothy Burlingham bought a country cottage in the village of Hochrotherd. It was near Breitenfurth, only 45 minutes by car from Vienna, and they were able to drive out in Dorothy's car for weekends. Over the

Freud's eldest daughter Mathilde.

Anna wrote, "Here at the sunshine's invitation/You take a short perambulation."

year they had been fixing it up (with advice from Ernst); a series of photographs recorded the alterations. During Ernst's visit plans for the rebuilding were finalized and after his departure Anna kept him informed by letter and telephone of the work in progress. She wrote: "The building brings me great joy and I am only terribly sorry I cannot be out there every day and take part in everything." (*Anna Freud-Ernst Freud 22.11.1931*)

+ Arthur Schnitzler . . .   Wed 21 October 1931*

Arthur Schnitzler (1862–1931) was probably the most famous Austrian dramatist and prose writer of his time. At their first direct contact in 1906 Freud wrote to him, praising his insight into psychological and erotic problems and thanking the novelist for in turn crediting Freud as a source of ideas.

The final communication was a note dated May 1931, thanking Schnitzler for his birthday greetings and congratulating him in advance on his impending 70th birthday in 1932.

Freud revealed the curious nature of his relationship with Schnitzler in a letter congratulating him on his 60th birthday: "I think I have avoided you from a kind of awe of meeting my 'double.' [. . .] Your determinism and your scepticism—what people call pessimism—your deep grasp of the truths of the unconscious and of the biological nature of man, the way you take to pieces the social conventions of our society, and the extent to which your thoughts are preoccupied with the polarity of love and death: all that moves me with an uncanny feeling of familiarity." (*Freud-Arthur Schnitzler 14.5.1922*)

Albrecht Schaeffer and wife . . .   Thurs 22 October 1931

The German poet Albrecht Schaeffer (1885–1950) had recently published an article in *Die Psychoanalytische Bewegung* (Vol.2 1930)—"Der Mensch und das Feuer" ("*Man and Fire*")—which contested Freud's view of the origin of fire in *Civilization and its Discontents*. Probably this was one of the topics of their conversation today, since Freud was again working on this theme. Over the next month he was to write his article "The Acquisition and Control of Fire."

Schaeffer and his wife had translated the Iliad and may have brought Freud the copy still in his library, with the author's dedication dated 1931. During this visit Freud gave Schaeffer a Tanagra figure from his collection.[1]

Celebrations in Freiberg . . .   Sun 25 October 1931

Freud's native town of Freiberg (Příbor) placed a bronze plaque on his birthplace, with the sculptured relief bust of him by Juřan. The street, originally Schlossergasse, was renamed Freudova.

Once again Anna Freud read her father's speech in his absence. Freud noted that he had not returned to his hometown since he was sixteen, but concluded ". . . deeply buried within me there still lives the happy child of Freiberg, the first-born son of a youthful mother, who received his first indelible impressions from this air, from this soil."

Other representatives present at the plaque unveiling ceremony were Martin Freud, Paul Federn and Eitingon who wrote an enthusiastic report of the great number of people who attended and of the excellent speeches.

Freud's reply tempers appreciation with a touch of irony: "Certain indications lead me to believe that the good citizens of Freiberg, being unaware of my position in the world, must have anticipated an overabundance of visitors from all corners of the globe." (*Freud-Eitingon 27.10.1931*).[1]

Ferenczi . . .   Wed 28 October 1931

At this meeting the two men discussed and tried to sort out their growing differences. Afterwards Freud sent Eitingon a resigned letter: "I saw Ferenczi a lot during the three days of his stay. On the first day he was withdrawn and clogged up, also he had the corresponding intestinal disturbance, on the second day he felt at ease ('relaxed') and listened to me quietly while I told him more or less everything I had to say, on the third day he answered with his usual bonhommie and frankness. Since he did not go into a certain point, his personal aliena-

Anna reading her father's speech at the Freiberg ceremony, October 25, 1931.

A view of Freiberg (Příbor), Freud's birthplace where he "received his first indelible impressions. . . ."

---

*Since Schnitzler actually died at 7 pm on 21 October and Freud may not have found out about the death until the next day, this entry seems to have been pre-dated.

tion from me, I am fairly well orientated about the localization of the disturbance. [. . .] Apart from the dangers of his technique I am sorry to know him to be on a track which is scientifically not very productive. The essential thing, however, seems to me to be its neurotically produced regression. But that is how it is with people. What can one do about it?" (*Freud-Eitingon 1.11.1931*)

It was Ferenczi's intimate "mothering" relationship with his patients which worried Freud. A month later he warned him: "But since you like to play the tender mother role toward others, perhaps you are doing it toward yourself. So you should hear the reminder from the brutal father's side that—as far as I remember—you were no stranger to sexual games with patients in your pre-analytical period, so that one could associate the new technique with your old error. Hence I spoke of a new puberty in my previous letter . . ."

Martin to Zurich . . .   Wed 28 October 1931

From January 1, 1932, Martin was to take over the press. He had met Eitingon a few days previously at Freiberg and they had discussed the arrangements. Perhaps this trip now to Zurich was to investigate the press's international business and banking contacts. It could also have involved moving Freud's foreign investments, which Martin did from time to time, to save them from inflation ". . . following political and economical developments." (*Martin Freud-Jones 5.12.1952*)

Three busts by Nemon . . .   Thurs 29 October 1931

Three busts, produced by Oscar Nemon at Federn's request and on behalf of the Vienna Psychoanalytical Society, were presented to Freud, for him to choose the one he preferred for himself: "At the moment my room is uncanny for me, apart from myself it houses three heads on high columns which try to resemble me and between which I have to choose. . . ." (*Freud-Eitingon 1.11.1931*). Freud eventually chose the wooden one ". . . which with its lively and friendly expression promises to be a pleasant room companion." (*Freud-Federn 1.11.1931*)

Holzknecht + . . .   Sat 31 October 1931

Professor Guido Holzknecht, the eminent radiologist, had died of cancer the previous day. Freud visited him for a consultation in April. On that occasion his quiet heroism while dying of terminal cancer deeply impressed Freud.[1]

Nepenthe . . .   Sat 31 October 1931

Perhaps a pitcher plant (*Nepenthacea*) and possibly a farewell gift from Jeanne Lampl-de Groot. (She was to give him an amazing orchid for his next birthday.) Or perhaps a subsidiary gift from the Vienna Psychoanalytical Society, to go with the Nemon bust?

Jeanne departed . . .   Sat 31 October 1931

Jeanne Lampl-de Groot had now finished her period of analysis with Freud and returned to Berlin. Freud was fond of her, and concerned because her husband Hans Lampl was suffering from irrational moods—possibly even psychotic episodes. In a letter a month later, Freud admits that he was afraid Lampl might be opening his wife's mail.

Gastro-intestinal state . . .   Thurs 5/Fri 6 November 1931

An unusually violent intestinal disorder now struck Freud: "If I have to speak of myself, I have had more than a simple upset stomach, it was a severe gastro-intestinal rebellion—cause unknown—in the course of which a colon cramp lasting several hours actually forced me suddenly to break off an analysis hour, which I have only been obliged to do once before in my life." (*Freud-Eitingon 15.11.1931*)

Anna with flowers at the plaque unveiling ceremony.

Freud's print of the house where he was born, done by M. Jungwirth in 1936.

Martin, Alexander and Anna Freud at the Freiberg ceremony.

At Hochrotherd . . .   Sun 8 November, 1931

This was Freud's first visit to Anna and Dorothy Burlingham's country cottage in the village of Hochrotherd. It had now been completely renovated. He was to visit it four times during the following year.

On the anniversary of his first visit, Anna inscribed a series of photographs for the family album. By the photo of the countryside Anna has written: "The view

*Der leere Armstuhl
unter dem Sonnenschirm
wartet auf jemanden,
der sich in ihm
niederläßt.*

8. Nov. 1932.

*Die Aussicht, die
immer gleich schön
ist, im Frühling;
Sommer und Herbst.
Winter ist noch nicht
ausprobiert.*

8. Nov. 1932

The cottage at Hochrotherd. "The empty armchair under the parasol is waiting for someone to sit in it."

"The view that is always equally beautiful . . ."

which is always equally beautiful, in spring, summer and autumn. Winter has not yet been tried out. 8. Nov. 1932." The photo of the house-front is inscribed: "The empty armchair under the parasol is waiting for someone to recline in it. 8. Nov. 1932."

Colic . . .   Tues 10 November 1931

This seems like a recurrence of the disorder that had struck five days earlier.

Bondi . . .   Tues 10 November 1931

The extended Bondi family was friendly both with Freud's family and with his wife's family, the Bernays. Joseph Bondi (born c.1865) was an obstetrician-gynecologist who had treated Freud's wife and mother. His brother, Samuel Bondi (born c.1871), a specialist in Internal Medicine, was living and practicing in Vienna at this time. Freud had probably been his patient previously and this visit may have been a consultation with him—perhaps about the colic?

Obras XIV & XV . . .   Fri 13 November 1931

Volume 14 of the Spanish complete works (*Obras Completas*) was entitled *El Porvenir de las Religiones* and contained the translation of the *Future of an Illusion* as well as a number of other pieces written between 1904 and 1928. Volume 15 (and 16) contained case histories—*Historiales Clinicos I*. Freud records receiving another copy of Volume 15 on September 12, 1932.

Purchases, Camel driver, Jade . . .   Fri 13 November 1931

The camel-driver may refer to an Egyptian standing wooden figure with its right arm extended as if to hold a stick or cord.

Freud's fondness for jade is attested by the number of such pieces in the collection as well as by other references to the material in the diary.

Marianne baby and operation . . .   Wed 18 November 1931

Marianne Kris (1900–1980), the second daughter of Freud's close friend Oskar Rie, married the scholar and analyst Ernst Kris; both became members of the Vienna Psychoanalytical Society in 1930. Freud called her his "adopted daughter" and analyzed her. The child was a girl named Anna in honor of Anna Freud, who said four days later, when child and mother were out of danger, ". . . it is very little but very well formed." (*Anna Freud-Ernst Freud 22.11.1931*)

Freud commented: "I myself have been ill in various ways and heavy demands were made on us all by the dangerous illness of Marianne Kris's newly-born baby—suffering from Melaena neonatorum. Now the child has been saved by a blood transfusion and I am again well enough to be able to write." (*Freud-Lampl-de Groot 29.11.1931*)

Pearls and rings bought . . .   Thurs 19 November 1931

Anna's birthday was two weeks away and she received pearls, very likely these same ones. The rings probably also ended up as gifts for someone.

Bleuler . . .   Sat 21 November 1931

Eugen Bleuler (1857–1939) was Professor of Psychiatry at the University of Zurich from 1898 to 1927 and the director of the Burghölzli asylum—the first official institution to be receptive to psychoanalysis.[1] Bleuler's *Lehrbuch der Psychiatrie* has remained a standard work and some of the terminology he devised has gained common currency, such as autism and schizophrenia.

A number of Freud's followers initially trained at Burghölzli—these included Karl Abraham, Abraham Brill, Max Eitingon, Carl Jung, Hermann Nunberg and Franz Riklin.

Bleuler had been aware of Freud's work since the 1890s—in 1896 he reviewed the *Studies in Hysteria* and in 1904 began a sporadic correspondence with Freud. He attended the first International Psychoanalytical Congress at Salzburg in 1908 and the Weimar Congress of 1911, where he read a paper on autism. However, he did not participate in the International Psychoanalytical Association and distanced himself from psychoanalysis in later years, concentrating his attention on clinical psychology. But in 1925 Bleuler wrote that he was pained by their differences and that Freud's essential ideas were self-evident to him; he could not, however, follow him into his metapsychology.

This entry refers to a visit. A letter from Bleuler some days later tells Freud of the case of a woman with literary fantasies who connected the Jewish Golem legend to the ancient Egyptians. This letter might relate to a discussion they had at their meeting. At any rate it attests reasonable relations between them, although Freud did afterwards speak of Bleuler "fairly disrespectfully" ("*ziemlich despektierlich*").

Martin to Berlin . . .   Sat 21 November 1931

Martin went to Berlin to see Eitingon: together they finalized the arrangements for taking over the press from Storfer. This required paying him an indemnity as well as dealing with the debts he had incurred.

Even so, Freud remained uncertain whether the press could be saved. He was in a dark mood not only about Martin's, but about his other sons' financial prospects: "You know about Martin's visit to Berlin. Yes, during those days I had three healthy, able-bodied sons in that city, not one of whom is able to earn a farthing. Happy times." (*Freud- Lampl-de Groot 29.11.1931*)

Oppenheimer . . .   Sun 22 November 1931

It is possible that this was the painter and illustrator Max Oppenheimer (1885–1954), known as "Maximilian Mopp." He was a member of the Vienna and Prague academies and a well-known portraitist; he painted Thomas Mann and Arthur Schnitzler. In October 1909 he did an oil portrait of Freud, which belonged to Paul Federn. (Federn later donated the picture to the New York Psychoanalytic Institute.)

Edoardo Weiss remembered that it interfered with his psychoanalysis: "On the wall to the right of the analytic couch, as I remember, hung an oil painting of Freud as I had seen him a few months before—beardless, with a trimmed mustache and penetrating eyes. Because this portrait drew too much of my attention during analytic sessions, it was soon replaced by a less interesting picture."

There is, however, another possibility—that this refers to Carl Oppenheimer, who had just published an article on Otto Warburg's theory of malignant tumors. Hence it and its author may have been of direct concern to Freud at this time.

Prometheus legend . . .   Sun 22 November 1931

In a footnote to *Civilization and its Discontents* Freud speculated that the origin of our control of fire involved a renunciation of man's competitive, (homo)sexual urge to extinguish it by urination.

Albrecht Schaeffer, who had visited Freud exactly a month previously, had contested this view in an article published the previous year—"Der Mensch und das Feuer." This, and a reference Freud had read to a Mongolian law against urinating on ashes, led him to return to this theme in a separate article centered on the Prometheus legend—"The Acquisition and Control of Fire." This article, completed today, used the myths of Prometheus and of Herakles and the Hydra as further evidence for the thesis that the control of fire requires an instinctual renunciation.

Tandler letter in N. Presse . . .   Sun 29 November 1931

Julius Tandler (1869–1936), a Professor of Anatomy at Vienna University, became one of the leading progressive politicians of the 1920s; as Commissioner of Health from 1920 to 1934 he helped create the social security system of "Red Vienna."

In two official instances his path had crossed Freud's. Together with the eminent psychiatrist Julius Wagner-Jauregg, they were members of a commission set up in 1918 to study war neuroses that had resulted in breaches of military discipline. Then, in 1925, he was involved in a discussion with Freud over the lawsuit against Theodor Reik, for having practised psychoanalysis without a medical qualification.[1]

In October 1931 the Vienna authorities organised a nonreligious and nonpartisan winter campaign to aid the city's numerous unemployed. Tandler was its chairman. On November 29 the *Neue Freie Presse* published a letter from "Profes-

Freud without a beard, 1909. Portrait by Max Oppenheimer ("Mopp").

sor Siegmund Freud" to Tandler, in which Freud suggested that money could most effectively be raised for the campaign by people pledging to donate a regular sum, which could then be collected from them weekly. Freud himself pledged to donate 20 schillings per day, excepting Sundays.

His letter was followed by the editorial note: "We hope many will be found who will possess the same high degree of awareness of their social obligations as this internationally known Viennese scholar."

Yvette . . .   Mon 30 November 1931

The concert was a triumph. The reviewer in the *Neue Freie Presse* (1.12.1931) praised her for being ". . still the same and yet never the same . . . ." Freud sent her flowers the next day, indicating he probably attended the concert, and Martha, who must also have been there, sent her an (unexplained) "Russian" gift.

Yvette thanked them in a letter on Hotel Bristol notepaper, written in her exuberant style, with abundant underlinings and exclamation marks.

Pearls for Anna on 36th birthday . . .   Thurs 3 December 1931

These are probably the pearls Freud bought on November 19. Anna did not share her father's love for antiquities but she did have a taste for jewelry and continued amassing it—as well as giving it to her friends—to the end of her life. Among her other gifts Anna received the customary poem from her brother Martin, congratulating her on now owning a house in Hochrotherd.[1]

Ernst's children with scarlet fever . . .   Thurs 3 December 1931

All three of Ernst and Lux's sons caught scarlet fever. Martha wrote to Lux that if it had to happen, then it was marvelous that they all had it together. Of her own children, she added, only Ernst and Anna had suffered from it, and afterwards been in quarantine for six weeks. The illness took a mild form, but Ernst's sons still had to endure six weeks' "room arrest." When they were released on January 7, 1932, Lux wrote: "They flew and leapt down the stairs in a way that frightened and alarmed me." (*Lucie Freud-Ernst Freud 7.1.1932*)

Lou Salomé's thanks . . .   Fri 4 December 1931

This refers to Lou Andreas-Salomé's publication *Mein Dank an Freud. Offener Brief an Professor Sigmund Freud zu Seinem 75 Geburtstag.* (My Thanks to Freud. Open Letter to Professor Sigmund Freud on his 75th Birthday) (Wien, I.P.V., 1931). A letter to Freud explained her reasons for writing the book: ". . . while I was lying ill a year ago I was very, very anxious to write a work which should bear the title: 'Mein Dank an Freud' (My Thanks to Freud). It wasn't a really satisfactory form of thanks, because it tried to do too much at once and, for instance, also tried to explain how it was through you that I first became free enough to appreciate those respects in which we feel differently about things." (*Lou Andreas-Salomé—Freud soon after April 3, 1931*)

When Freud proposed substituting "psychoanalysis" for his name, she refused. The whole essay, she said, ". . . has been wholly derived from the man who bears this name; what it would have been as purely factual knowledge without this human experience I simply cannot imagine (I am a woman, after all)." (*Lou Andreas-Salome—Freud mid-July 1931*).

Vishnu from Calcutta . . .   Wed 9 December 1931

This ivory figure was a belated birthday present, sent by Girindrashekhar Bose on behalf of the Indian Psychoanalytical Society. The accompanying letter explained that the present was delayed for so long because it had been made especially for Freud: the figure was modelled on an old stone statue at Travancore.

Freud wrote back: "The Statuette is charming, I gave it the place of honor on my desk. As long as I can enjoy life it will recall to my mind the progress of Psychoanalysis[,] the proud conquests it has made in foreign countries and the kind feelings for me it has aroused in some of my contemporaries at least." (*Freud-Bose 13.12.1931*)[1]

The Indian Psychoanalytical Society was founded in 1922 by Bose (1886–1953), who remained its president until his death. A protocol of its celebration

A monk doles food to the unemployed at a church-run soup-kitchen in Vienna. DOW

Anna Freud wearing one of her bead necklaces.

of Freud's birthday accompanied the gift, and a Sanskrit poem with English translation.

As a collector, Freud was most of all interested in classical and Egyptian antiquities, but he also had a taste for Chinese objects. Indian art, however, remained unrepresented. Ten years previously he admitted knowing very little about India: "In Indian matters I am unfortunately as ignorant as in philosophical ones, but nothing more can be done to cure that now." (*Freud-H. Gomperz 21.1.1921*)[2]

Japanese translations . . .   Tues 22 December 1931

There are more references to Japanese translations than to any other language over these years. Because of the rival publications it is impossible to know which ones Freud had now received.[1] Earlier this year the *Zeitschrift* announced that the Japanese Psychoanalytical group (*Nippon Seishin-Bunteki Gakukei*) founded by Yaekichi Yabe had been provisionally accepted into the International Psychoanalytical Association, pending ratification of the decision by the next international congress.

The White Vishnu statuette, gift of the Indian Psychoanalytic Society. "Can the god, being used to Calcutta, not stand the climate in Vienna?" Freud mused when the wood and ivory developed cracks. NB

The Japanese psychoanalytical group, November 1930. Jones advised them to keep the group small and of high quality and to send two members to Europe for analysis.

Freud at his summer home. In the album, Anna Freud wrote beneath this photo: "When you lie here for your midday rest,/All the dogs watch with interest."

1932

It was now thirty years since Freud had established psychoanalysis as a movement, by founding a small discussion group—the "Wednesday Psychological Society"—in 1902. By 1908 the movement was already large enough to hold its first international congress in Salzburg, and the following year its first journal was published. A series of further journals was to emerge, but it was not until 1919 that the movement finally acquired its own publishing house.

Since that time Freud had considered the International Psychoanalytical Press as a most valuable asset and an essential means of disseminating psychoanalytical ideas. Yet it was badly run and by 1932 its financial situation had become critical. Freud sprang to its defense, appealing to the international movement for funds. The first sum of money Freud recorded this year was £2,500, which represented an advance on royalties, from the American diplomat William Bullitt, who was appointed first American ambassador to the Soviet Union the following year. Freud and Bullitt had been working together on a book about President Woodrow Wilson. Freud had been hoping that the book's sales might save the press, but the collaboration struck difficulties and the possibility of its publication was fast diminishing. Spurred by the urgent necessity of raising money for the press, Freud now embarked on a new book—*New Introductory Lectures on Psycho-Analysis*—which was written over the summer and already in print by the end of the year.

These lectures were a continuation of the *Introductory Lectures* delivered at Vienna University from 1915 to 1917. They resumed themes which Freud had elaborated since that time, such as his model of the mind constructed upon the ego, the id and the super-ego, which he had described in *The Ego and the Id* (1923). The book also dealt with anxiety and the neuroses, psychoanalysis as therapy, and with Freud's new interpretation of early female development, which had been the subject of *Female Sexuality* (1931). As an indication of the continuing vital importance of dream interpretation, the book opens with a revision of the theory of dreams.

The final part of the *New Introductory*

Lectures on Psycho-Analysis asks whether psychoanalysis involves a particular world view (*Weltanschauung*). Freud concludes that it does not, for it is a part of science and therefore bound to the scientific attitude. He contrasts it in this respect with Bolshevism, which had foresaken its scientific basis for the illusions of faith. Consequently, when one of the most brilliant of the younger psychoanalysts, Wilhelm Reich, began combining psychoanalysis and Marxism, Freud felt it necessary to take the measures referred to in the opening entry for 1932—**Step against Reich**—namely, to distance the movement as a whole from this ideology.

The psychoanalytical cause was Freud's life work, his overriding concern was to guard its coherence and intellectual integrity. This was difficult. Over the years a number of eminent psychoanalysts had turned from it to develop their own ideas. One of Freud's closest friends and colleagues, the Hungarian analyst Sándor Ferenczi, had been gradually distancing himself and now in 1932 he declined the presidency of the international association, on the grounds that his present stance was too much at variance with Freud's. It is no surprise that Freud's efforts to rescue the press and keep his disparate movement together were taking their toll and that he should be writing to Ernest Jones on June 17, 1932: "I have gradually grown tired of the efforts it costs to keep together such different and not very willing people."[1]

---

1. *Freud-Jones 17.6.1932* [Typescript Inst. of PsA] ("Ich bin der Anstrengungen, die das Zusammenhalten so verschiedener und nicht sehr williger Personen kostet, allmählich müde geworden.")

Long gastric attack . . .   Fri 1 January 1932

This recurrence of the gastric trouble, which had begun in November 1931, was depressing, especially when combined with the perpetual modifications of the prosthesis. By mid-January Freud was writing: "My stomach is once again in service and with it my general health improved. One is getting no further with the prosthesis." (*Freud- Lampl-de Groot 17.1.1932*)

Step against Reich . . .   Fri 1 January 1932

Wilhelm Reich (1897–1957) became the youngest analyst even before graduating in medicine at the University of Vienna in 1922. He joined the Vienna Psychoanalytical Society in 1920, worked at the psychoanalytical outpatient clinic (Ambulatorium) and conducted influential seminars at the Training Institute from 1924 to 1930. Here he developed the analytic techniques propounded in his seminal work, *Charakteranalyse* (1933). In 1930 he moved to Berlin and founded Sexpol (the German National Association for Proletarian Sexual Politics).

In 1931 Reich submitted a paper entitled "Der masochistische Character" ("*The Masochist Character*") to the *Internationale Zeitschrift für Psychoanalyse*, in which he proposed incorporating Marxist terminology into psychoanalysis. The article (as Freud complained) " . . . culminated in the nonsense that what is considered the death drive is a function of the capitalist system." (*Freud-Ferenczi 24.1.1932*)

Initially Freud wished to add an editorial disclaimer. Eventually the article was published without this, but the issue also contained a refutation by Siegfried Bernfeld.

During the 1920s Reich had been the most brilliant and promising of the younger analysts. His development during the 1930s disturbed Freud, who saw it as evidence of the effect the ominous socio-political atmosphere was having on psychoanalysis and as another blow against scientific neutrality.[1]

Freud wrote: "Annoying, actually worse than that, is the accumulation of experience that nothing can be done about more and more people . First one then another turns out to be unusable or unguidable. Ferenczi's obstinacy with his suspect technique, Reich and Fenichel's attempt to misuse the journals for Bolshevik propaganda [. . .] everything shows that under the corrosive influence of these times characters rapidly decompose." (*Freud-Eitingon 9.1.1932*)

Eitingon . . .   Sat 16 January 1932

On January 8, 1932, Freud sent Eitingon a telegram urgently requesting his presence, owing to the critical situation at the press. A letter the next day speaks of losing sleep over the situation. (Given Freud's usually sound sleep, this was a measure of the severity of the situation.)

Eitingon now arrived to take part in the "cleansing of the press," as Freud put it in a letter to Jeanne Lampl-de Groot.

He added: "It seems that we will succeed in this, though with great financial sacrifices, which are necessary to pay Storfer's personal debts and to impel him to give up his position. His mismanagement has ruined everything. As valuable as he was as editor and intellectual director, to the same extent his foolishness, disorderliness and quest for greatness have had an uncanny commercial effect." (*Freud- Lampl-de Groot 17.1.1932*)[1]

But Eitingon himself was suffering from economic problems. His considerable family fortune had been eroded by the 1929 crash and was now diminishing further. Moreover, his analytic practice was not thriving; analysands were no longer coming to Berlin.

Martin replaces Storfer . . .   Sat 16 January 1932

In his autobiography, Martin Freud wrote: "Something obviously had to be done; but it took a long time to persuade father to make a change and to appoint me as his manager. I found the business side of the press in a shocking state, and I doubt if it would ever have climbed to a sound business basis and avoided bankruptcy without the valuable help given by the International Psychoanalytical Association and its president, Dr. Ernest Jones. As it turned out, the Nazis eventually had the doubtful privilege of taking over something of substance and value and then destroying it utterly."

After Eitingon's departure Freud sent him the first progress report: "My poor

Otto Fenichel, Wilhelm Reich's fellow "Bolshevik." TG

Wilhelm Reich (centre seated) with the director Eduard Hitschmann (at his right) and staff of the Vienna Psychoanalytical Ambulatorium. (Hoffmann, Eidelberg, Bibring, Parker, Betlheim, Bengler, Kronengold, Angel, Jekels, Hitschman, Reich, Bibring-Lehner, Sterba, Reich-Pink)

Freud, c.1932.

boy is walking around with a careworn expression, but has taken up his duties seriously. On the day after his overthrow Storfer is supposed to have been irreproachably tractable. For how long? With calculated politeness Martin left him the manager's room." (*Freud-Eitingon 19.1.1932*)

Anna flu . . .   Sun 17 January 1932

This severe attack of flu lasted a week; afterwards Anna was sent to convalesce in the country.

First Portuguese translation . . .   Sun 17 January 1932

The first Portuguese translation—*Cinco Lições de Psicanalise*—came from Brazil. It was translated by Durval Marcondes and Barbosa Correa and published by Companhia Editora Nacional, São Paulo. The edition was undated but the translators' inscription in Freud's copy is dated December 31, 1931.

£2500 from Bullitt . . .   Mon 18 January 1932

This sum was (ostensibly) an advance on expected American royalties from the joint study of Woodrow Wilson. But since the work was still unfinished and was not to be published until Bullitt's death in 1967, it was in effect a gift.[1]

Anna on the Semmering . . .   Tues 26 January 1932

After her severe flu Anna was sent to the Semmering Kurhaus. The Semmering is a wooded resort in the foothills of the Alps at their nearest approach to Vienna. In the vicinity were two mountains that could be walked up, the Rax and the Schneeberg. Freud spent five summers in this attractive area during the 1920s.

$1000 from Jackson and from Brill . . .   Sat 30 January 1932

These contributions meant the press could be saved. Freud added to them his own contribution and sums from Eitingon. A letter to Eitingon enumerates their assets : "To date the publishing house has received the following assignations:
        5000 Mark—with you
        6000 Mark—contribution from you
        about 6000 Sch.—institution money which was available in Vienna
        [$]1000—collection from Brill
        [$]1000—gift Dr. Edith Jackson
        [$] 200—Alexander, Dr. Putnam, Boston
        [£]2500—from me, which my collaborator on the Wilson book advances against the anticipated American royalties.
I will keep a further $3000 ready in order to advance them to Martin in installments for running costs." (*Freud-Eitingon 12.2.1932*)

The American Dr. Edith Jackson was one of the analysands who had accompanied Freud to Berlin in the summer of 1930. That year she began her training at the Vienna Institute of Psychoanalysis.

Abraham Arden Brill (1874–1948) played a vital pioneering role in introducing and establishing psychoanalysis in the United States. Born in Austria, he had emigrated to the States as an adolescent, without any English, and eventually succeeded in working his way through medical school.

He studied for a time under Bleuler at Burghölzli, attended the first Psychoanalytic Congress at Salzburg in 1908, then travelled on to Vienna with Ernest Jones to visit Freud. It was on this occasion that Freud granted him the rights to undertake the first English translations of his works.

In 1911 Brill founded the New York Psychoanalytical Society: the following year he published the first American book to champion psychoanalysis—*Psychoanalysis: Its Theories and Practical Application*.

Subsequently Brill became Professor of Psychiatry at New York University College of Medicine and Lecturer in Psychoanalysis at Columbia University.

Anna back . . .   Mon 1 February 1932

Freud wrote to Jeanne Lampl-de Groot: "Anna recovered rapidly on the Semmering, too rapidly actually, I would have liked her to have stayed longer. It is the fashion now to get the flu again after a brief interval." (*Freud- Lampl-de Groot 6.2.1932*)

Hotels on the Semmering.

Freud and Brill at Clark University, Worcester, Massachusetts, 1909.

Chinese woman rider . . .   **Fri 5 February 1932**

This is an attractive figure of a leaping horse and rider, a female polo player, probably genuine Tang. Freud placed it on top of a case in the consulting room in front of a print of the Roman Forum. It now stands at the entrance to Freud's library in Maresfield Gardens, on top of a glass case of jade objects.

Preface to new Lectures . . .   **Wed 10 February 1932**

At this time the idea of writing a sequel to the *Introductory Lectures on Psycho-Analysis* (1916–17) had only just occured to Freud—not because of any "inner necessity" but as a means of rescuing the press from bankruptcy. So far he had not even begun writing the new lectures.

A week later he wrote: "I am considering the plan of writing New Lectures in summer as a supplement to the Introductory Lectures, the mercy of fate permitting, of course. For some chapters I may need help, literature, suggestions. Can I count on you as well for that? But keep the matter a secret from everyone. Only Martin and Anna here know about it." (*Freud- Lampl-de Groot 18.2.1932*)[1]

In the published *New Introductory Lectures on Psycho-Analysis* the preface is dated "Summer 1932" when the lectures themselves were completed. This preface may be an earlier version, drafted in advance of the lectures themselves in order to chart the way ahead. Freud appears to have begun it on February 7, the date at the top of his manuscript.

Gift Fujiyama from Kosawa . . .   **Thurs 18 February 1932**

Dr. Heisaku Kosawa was another Japanese who came to Europe to study psychoanalysis. (He had already known Freud's work in 1925, when he first contacted him.) Federn was now advising him on his course of study.

This gift, a print of Mount Fuji by Kiyoshi Yoshida (1876–1950), preceded the beginning of an analysis with Freud. Freud's note of thanks speaks of ". . . the beautiful picture which presents to my eyes what I have read so much about and a sight which I myself have not been granted." (*Freud-Kosawa 20.2.1932*)

Freud hung the print in the waiting room (it now hangs in the dining room at Maresfield Gardens). On March 16 Freud wrote to Kosawa, offering to analyze him at $10 an hour instead of the standard $25.

Moratorium for the publishing house . . .   **Fri 19 February 1932**

Martin Freud's first achievement in managing the press was to obtain from the creditors a moratorium until summer on its debts. Its eventual survival still depended on the economic situation in Germany, but if it were now to collapse it would at least go down—as Freud said—" . . . in an honorable manner." (*Freud- Lampl-de Groot 2.3.1932*)

Of all the press's creditors, Storfer turned out to be the only one to cause difficulties about this arrangement. Freud was now regretting the Kazanjian expenses, which had deprived him of the means to help the press more: "You know I have not grown rich, have spent $7000 on a failed experiment with the Armenian etc." (*Freud-Eitingon 12.2.1932*). (The figure of $7,000 is a further advance on the previous estimate of $6,000 or on Kazanjian's honorarium of $5,000. Perhaps Freud is totalling all expenses and possibly adding the cost of subsequent work on the new prostheses.)

Anna and I have infectious cold . . .   **Mon 22 February 1932**

There was a cold epidemic prevalent. Freud's infectious catarrh meant there had to be a short delay before yet another scheduled operation.[1]

Project of busts in Goethe House . . .   **Tues 23 February 1932**

A project must have been mooted to place busts of winners of the Goethe Prize in the Goethe House at Frankfurt.[1] But a month later, at the memorial celebrations for the centenary of Goethe's death, no mention of this project occurred and three months later Freud was writing: ". . . that my bust has been or will be set up in the Goethe House is, I believe, only a rumor . . . ." (*Freud-Lilly Marlé 11.5.1932*)

Operation with Pichler . . .   **Mon 7 March 1932**

Although this is the first actual mention of Pichler's name this year, Freud had

Tang riding figure. (Above) In Vienna. (Below) In London. EE NB

already had 20 consultations in the two months preceding this operation. His three current prostheses were being constantly modified. This operation, the first since April 1931, was a "precautionary" one.

Afterwards Freud wrote: "My operation and the first week afterwards were really not as bad as usual, in the second week which is now coming to an end the pain was more severe and together with gastro-intestinal upsets have given me a truly uncomfortable time." (*Freud- Lampl-de Groot 19.3.1932*)

Anna was optimistic about her father's condition. She wrote to the writer and therapist Georg Groddeck: ". . . he overcomes all physical difficulties that arise repeatedly with wonderful energy and freshness." (*Anna Freud-Groddeck 25.3.-1932*)

Briand + . . .   Thurs 8 March 1932

The eminent French statesman Aristide Briand (1862–1932) had died the previous day in Paris. He was Prime Minister of France 11 times and served 20 times as Cabinet minister.

Apart from the political significance of this death there was also a personal one of which Freud would have been aware—Briand had been one of Marie Bonaparte's lovers. She had met him at a luncheon for Rudyard Kipling in 1913, when he was 51 and had already been Prime Minister of France four times. Soon after this meeting Marie Bonaparte began a notebook entitled *Le Bonheur d'être aimée*. Their affair had ended in 1919.

Large Kelebe bought from Fröhlich . . .   Sun 13 March 1932

The *Kelebe* is a broad-mouthed, two handled Greek *krater*–a vessel used as a mixing bowl for wine.

Fröhlich and Lederer are the only antique dealers to be mentioned by name in the diary, although it is known that others, such as Robert Lustig, were in regular contact with Freud.

Kreuger suicide . . .   Sun 13 March 1932

Ivar Kreuger (1880–1932), the "Swedish Match-King," had been in control of three-quarters of the world's match production and through the businesses of Kreuger & Toll, Inc., Dutch Kreuger and Toll and the Swedish Match Company had managed a host of subsidiary companies, many of them fictitious. Revelations of his fraudulent dealings resulted in the collapse of his empire and his own suicide in Paris on March 12, 1933.[1]

Elections in Germany undecided . . .   Mon 14 March 1932

This election for the presidency left President Paul von Hindenburg with over $18\frac{1}{2}$ million votes, only 168,000 votes short of the absolute majority he needed. Hitler had over 11 million and the Communist Thälmann almost 5 million.

The Nazi newspaper *Völkischer Beobachter* termed the results a "Pyrrhic victory" for the ruling parties. The liberal British paper *News Chronicle* called it a victory of common sense over the twin absurdities of communism and nationalism.

Eitingon was reassured by the result that the forthcoming international psychoanalytical congress could take place in Germany and recommended it be held in Wiesbaden.

Visit of Thomas Mann . . .   Thurs 17 March 1932

Thomas Mann was in Vienna to give his talk "Goethe as a Representative of the Age of the Bourgeoisie" ("*Goethe als Repräsentant des bürgerlichen Zeitalters*"). It was his first visit to Freud, who was charmed by him. After only five minutes the two men were on intimate terms.

Because his wife and sister-in-law were avid readers of Mann and, like him, from Hamburg, they too felt they had a claim on the visitor: "Thomas Mann's visit was very pleasant. His behavior was sincere and unforced, one was immediately at ease with him and what he had to say gave the impression of being deeply founded. Naturally the women did not leave us alone for long. They are very fond of him as a semi fellow-countryman." (*Freud-Eitingon 20.3.1932*)

Vases in Freud's study. The kelebe may be the one on the left, similar to Freud's eventual funerary urn. WK

Goethe Day . . .   Tues 22 March 1932

Johann Wolfgang von Goethe (1749–1832)—one of Freud's cultural hero figures—died in Weimar on March 22, 1832, and this day marked his centenary
celebration.[1] There were celebrations in Weimar and Frankfurt, where Albert
Schweitzer gave a memorial lecture. Vienna also celebrated the event with a
memorial performance in the Burgtheater.

French Illusion . . .   Tues 22 March 1932

This was Marie Bonaparte's French translation of the *Future of an Illusion–
L'Avenir d'une Illusion*–published by Denoël et Steele, Paris (1932).

46 yrs practice . . .   Sun 27 March 1932

Freud set up in private medical practice on Easter Sunday, April 25, 1886. Since
he always commemorated the event at Easter, it too became a "moveable feast."
Jones calls it an "act of defiance" to open his practice on Easter Sunday when
everything else in Vienna was closed. The symbolic significance of the day has
also given rise to inevitable speculation.

Circular for the publishing house . . .   Sun 27 March 1932

Although the press had been saved from immediate bankruptcy, its situation
remained critical. This prompted Freud to send out this circular, appealing to all
the psychoanalytical societies and influential members. It pleaded that the press
was a common analytical interest and that it should be formally adopted as an
institution by the International Psychoanalytical Association.[1]

    This idea was generally accepted; it remained to be decided how the press
should be managed. Freud felt it should not be run directly by the standing
committee of the International Association, but should retain a certain degree of
independence. He subsequently proposed it should have a supervisory committee made up of Jones, Eitingon, Marie Bonaparte and Brill.

Dr. Stockert grandson of Meynert . . .   Mon 28 March 1932

This visitor was presumably Franz Günther von Stockert. His mother was the
writer Dora Stockert-Meynert, Theodor Meynert's daughter. She wrote a biography of her father, published in 1929.

    During Freud's university studies the brain anatomist Theodor Meynert
(1833–92) was Professor of Psychiatry at the University of Vienna. After Ernst
Brücke, he was Freud's most significant teacher.

    In 1883, at the age of 27, Freud worked as a doctor in Meynert's psychiatric
clinic; in taking up this post he was given quarters in the hospital and left home
for the first time. He worked only five months for Meynert, but in the summer
of 1886 Freud continued his anatomical research in his laboratory.

Circular finished . . .   Mon 28 March 1932

Normally it would have been Eitingon's responsibility to send the circular out
to the chairmen of local groups as well as to such outstanding members as
Princess Marie Bonaparte, Franz Alexander, Nunberg or the American analyst
Smith Ely Jelliffe. But he fell ill in April and Freud and Anna took over this task.

    Meanwhile, Jones and his wife translated the circular into English. Jones wrote
to Freud that he agreed the press should be maintained. But how? The economic
depression was international. Perhaps Brill knew a millionaire?

Martha to Berlin . . .   Mon 4 April 1932

Martha went primarily to visit Ernst and the grandchildren, but while in Berlin
she called on other friends, including the Eitingons.

    On this visit she found out that Max Eitingon was quite seriously ill (this had
been kept secret from Freud). He had suffered a slight cerebral thrombosis,
which had been attributed to smoking (*Nikotinvergeltung*) and which resulted in
a paresis of the left arm.

    Freud refused to credit this diagnosis, preferring to believe something else lay
behind it. However, Eitingon stopped smoking and after three weeks' rest felt
well enough to take on four hours of analysis daily.

Goethe's writing desk in the Goethe
house, Frankfurt.

Theodor Meynert, one of Freud's
scientific mentors.

Ernst Freud.

Four Case Histories . . .   Mon 4 April 1932

The book, a reprint of four early case histories, was published by the International Psychoanalytical Press (I.P.V.). It included the studies of Dora, Little Hans, the Rat Man and Schreber.

"Dora" (*Fragment of an Analysis of a Case of Hysteria*) was first published in 1905 although the case occured in 1900. The patient, an 18-year-old girl, broke off the analysis. Freud afterwards attributed this failure to his ignorance of transference—a phenomenon this case first investigated. (In *transference* previous emotional relationships emerge in the relationship between analyst and analysand: they must be recognized and rightly used for the analysis to succeed.)

"Little Hans" (*Analysis of a Phobia in a Five-Year-Old Boy*), the first child analysis, was actually conducted at a distance, through the intermediary of the boy's father, Max Graf. He was a member of the Wednesday Psychological Society from 1906 to 1908. The case was published in 1909.

The "Rat Man" (*Notes upon a Case of Obsessional Neurosis*), also published in 1909, revealed the anal-erotic sources of a young man's compulsions and his fantasies of being tortured by rats.

"Schreber" (*Psycho-Analytic Notes on an Autobiographical Account of a Case of Paranoia (Dementia Paranoides)*) is an analysis of a book by a German judge describing his madness. Schreber was convinced God was turning him into a woman: Freud's analysis traces the homosexual aspects of his delusion to his relationship with his father, a famous educator. From this Freud infers a repressed homosexual component at the root of male paranoia.

Róheim on visit . . .   Wed 6 April 1932

It was this year that the journal *Imago* published Róheim's *Die Psychoanalyse primitiver Kulturen* and the *International Journal of Psycho-Analysis* published an English version in a special "Róheim Australasian Research Number"—*Psycho-Analysis of Primitive Cultural Types*. In this and future publications Róheim pioneered the introduction of psychoanalytical theory into anthropology.

Martha at Ernst's birthday . . .   Wed 6 April 1932

In Berlin Martha was not staying with Ernst, possibly on Freud's insistence that she needed quiet and isolation at her age, but also because their flat was on the fourth floor.

In his first letter to her, Freud spoke of their communications functioning well, despite his not writing. Perhaps this meant she was writing, but it is possible he could have phoned Berlin, perhaps to congratulate Ernst on his 40th birthday, and thus immediately known of Martha's visit.

Hindenburg elected . . .   Sun 10* April 1932

Paul von Hindenburg (1847–1934) now gained the absolute majority he had failed to get on March 14, 1932–53 percent. Hitler received 36.8 percent and the Communist Thälmann 13.2 percent. But Hindenburg was already 84 years old and his election did not solve any problems. Von Hindenburg's re-election as Reichspresident led to the formation on June 1, 1932 of a second presidial Cabinet under von Papen. The first presidial Cabinet under Brüning had governed without parliament, using emergency powers, from March 30 to September 14, 1930. On that day a Reichstag election gave the Nazi Party 6.5 million votes (increased from 800,000 in 1928), the Communists 4.5 million and the Socialists 8.5 million. Two weeks after his accession von Papen lifted a temporary ban on the SA and SS and on July 31, 1932 there was another Reichstag election. The Nazi Party now had 13.5 million votes, the Communists 5.5 million and the Socialists 8 million.[1]

Rivista Italiana Ed. Weiss . . .   Sat 16 April 1932

In 1931 the Italian psychoanalyst Edoardo Weiss moved from Trieste to Rome and in the same year published his *Elementi di Psicoanalisi*, a course of five lectures on the fundamental principals of psychoanalysis which he had delivered to the Trieste medical association.

---

* The election in Germany actually took place this day. As the results could not have been known the same day, this entry must have been retrospective.

In Rome he founded the journal *Rivista Italiana di Psicoanalisi*. Freud was full of praise both for Weiss and for his new journal: "The personality of the leader is a sure guarantee for the development of the group, he alone is worth a group and one cannot make any further demands upon a society which publishes a Rivista." (*Freud-Eitingon 27.4.1932*)

Freud sent Weiss a message of encouragement: "The journal, your Rivista, creates a very respectable impression both in terms of form and content. Also the civilians in it seem highly relevant. Your collaborator Berroti promises to develop into an effective force. I hope you will long be spared the inevitable disappointments with your collaborators." (*Freud-Weiss 24.4.1932*)

Freud continued in this high opinion. In 1936 he said of the Italian movement that the "name Edoardo Weiss assures it a rich future."[1]

At Hochrotherd . . .   Sun 17 April 1932

The weather was now finally good enough to allow Freud to make the journey to the renovated cottage. Five days earlier he had written: "Anna is blissfully happy with Hochrotherd, proud of her visitors' words of praise: Uncle Deutsch, Marlé and others. My visit out there has not yet been allowed because of the Sunday weather." (*Freud-Martha 12.4.1932*)

Martha from Berlin . . .   Tues 19 April 1932

The economic depression and political threats left traces on Martha's impressions. Freud wrote: "My wife greatly enjoyed her stay in Berlin, even though not everything she saw was nice. The times are actually awfully bad and totally without any guarantee of a bearable future." (*Freud- Lampl-de Groot 24.4.1932*)

During her absence, Freud's tailor Stefan had delivered a new suit. He wrote to her: "The new suit from Stefan is again perfect, I shall ask him whether he doesn't also make prostheses." (*Freud-Martha Freud 12.4.1932*)

Martin to Leipzig . . .   Tues 19 April 1932

In his report to Martha in Berlin Freud spoke of Martin's hard work on behalf of the press. This trip to Leipzig was also on business, for that was the book-distributing center for Germany and Austria and the press's stocks were stored there.

Binswanger . . .   Fri 22 April 1932

Ludwig Binswanger (1881–1966) studied psychiatry under Jung in Zurich and through him came into contact with psychoanalysis. In March 1907 he and Jung took part as guests at the meetings of the Vienna Psychoanalytical Society: in the same year he became a member of the newly-formed Zurich psychoanalytical group and in 1910 became president of the Swiss Psychoanalytical Association. Both his father and uncle were psychiatrists and in 1911 he took over as medical director of his father's sanatorium at Kreuzlingen, where he remained until 1956.

Binswanger had come to Vienna to give a talk to the Academic Society for Medical Psychology. He visited Freud from 5–6 p.m. and found him ". . . intellectually very fresh and completely unchanged in his whole aspect." Freud spoke with great admiration of Marie Bonaparte and her work.

Binswanger's views had evolved away from psychoanalysis toward a practice based on the philosophies of Husserl and Heidegger (*Daseinsanalyse*). It undertook to comprehend the patient's total "being-in-the-world," both in a social and ontological sense, and was concerned with the ability to love as the crucial therapeutic issue. But the personal friendship with Freud continued long after Binswanger had renounced psychoanalysis.

76th birthday . . .   Fri 6 May 1932

For once Freud was able to bypass any celebrations.[1] Illness prevented even the most regular visitor, Eitingon, from attending.

Freud wrote: "Your absence from my birthday this year—undesired as its cause is—will at least enable me to pass the day as I have always wanted to, that is as an ordinary weekday. In the morning a visit to Kagran with the dogs, in the afternoon the usual visit to Pichler, 4 hours of analytical work and a harmless game of cards in the evening. Doubt whether one should be glad at having survived the date and then resignation." (*Freud-Eitingon 4.5.1932*)

Edoardo Weiss (centre) and his collaborator Nicola Perrotti (right). TG

Anna and Dorothy's cottage, from the orchard at the back.

But gifts and greetings continued to arrive. On May 9 he received a belated but "amazingly beautiful" orchid from Jeanne Lampl-de Groot.

Day at Hochrotherd . . .   Sun 8 May 1932

The cottage was now furnished and looked after, in the Freuds' absence, by the neighboring Faddenberger family. Anna Freud was living what she termed a "double life," half of it being Hochrotherd, and she wanted the family and her friends to share her delight in it. To Eva Rosenfeld she wrote: "You must also put down roots in HRE so that we can grow in the same earth." (*Anna Freud-Eva Rosenfeld n.d.*)

But after the end of this year, during which he visited the cottage four times, Freud's health was mostly too poor to risk even such a comparatively short journey into the country.

Editorial staff meeting . . .   Wed 11 May 1932

Storfer left his post as manager of the press on April 24. He had also been editor of *Imago* and was temporarily replaced there by Otto Fenichel.

At the same time there was also the problem of the other international journal—the *Zeitschrift*—to be sorted out. Much depended on the decision of Radó, who was on both editorial boards, but was now in the United States.

Freud wrote to him: "Of course we have missed you greatly here. You can take what I am now going to tell you as a consequence of your absence. I was unable to be satisfied with your substitute Fenichel and taking into consideration both the saving and the advantage of concentration I decided to move the editorial staff to Vienna. Federn and Hartmann are to take over the *International Journal*, Kris and Waelder (two non-doctors) the *Imago*. We are obviously reckoning that you will rejoin the editorial staff if you wish. Otherwise we are concerned, as you know, with worries about the press, of which my son Martin has taken over command. Storfer's disastrous management could not continue any longer." (*Freud-Radó 10.5.1932*).

Meanwhile, Martin negotiated for time with each of the creditors. It was hoped the fund-raising campaign would manage to pay them off by the end of the year.

Poetzleinsdorf . . .   Sat 14 May 1932

The Freuds had been so impressed by the villa on Khevenhüllerstrasse 6, Pötzleinsdorf, which they had rented the previous summer, that they returned there this year.

Soon after moving in Freud wrote to Ferenczi: "I think I am gradually regaining my strength here. Our home in Poetzleinsdorf is ideally beautiful and comfortable. Dogs and people are happy here. One forgets that one is actually living in the XVIII district of a large city. I am doing all of my five hours, am wrestling with the answers I still owe, and have not yet got round to my own work." (*Freud-Ferenczi May/June 1932*)

Hungarian translations . . .   Mon 23 May 1932

This refers to the first volume of the *Collected Papers of Sigmund Freud* edited by Ferenczi and Storfer (I.P.V. & Budapest: Somló 1932). It contained Dr. Imre Hermann's Hungarian translation of the *Introductory Lectures–Bevezetés a Pszichoanalizisbe*.

Psa Quarterly . . .   Tues 31 May 1932

The Psychoanalytic Quarterly was a newly-founded American journal. Its inaugural editorial stated that it had been established ". . . to fill the need for a strictly psychoanalytic organ in America, where, although Freudian analysis has been received more favorably than in any other country, it nevertheless is exposed to the danger of misrepresentation and dilution . . . ."

The editors further justified its founding with an anecdote. Two years previously Freud had written a preface to a special psychoanalytical number of a medical journal, under the impression it was actually the inaugural issue of a monthly. His disappointment on finding out the facts was taken by the editors as a wish which they were now fulfilling.[1]

This first number included three of Freud's latest writings—*Libidinal Types, Female Sexuality* and *The Acquisition of Fire.*

Cattleya labiata var. Dowiana. Print from an orchid album in Freud's library. (Julien Constantin, *Atlas des Orchidées cultivées*, Paris, 1911.)

The Faddenbergers, who looked after Anna's cottage. She wrote: "The pillars of the house are sitting there,/Man, wife and child, dog and Mrs. Hare."

Mitzi gone . . .   Tues 31 May 1932

Evidently Freud's sister Mitzi had paid another visit to Vienna and was now leaving, probably returning to Berlin. On March 22 of this year she had celebrated her 70th birthday and Freud wrote to her: "Now you too are the fourth among us to cross the threshhold which separates careless youth from mature age." (*Freud-Mitzi Freud 20.3.1931*)

Swedish Discontent . . .   Mon 6 June 1932

This was the Swedish translation of *Civilization and its Discontents* (*Vi Vantrivs i kulturen*), translated by S.J.S. and published by Albert Bonniers Förlag, Stockholm.

Psychology of Love Japanese . . .   Wed 15 June 1932

This was a Japanese translation of *Contributions to the Psychology of Love*,[1] which consisted of three essays: *A Special Type of Choice of Object Made by Men* (1910), *On the Universal Tendency to Debasement in the Sphere of Love* (1912) and *The Taboo of Virginity* (1918).

As with the rest of Freud's work in Japanese, there were two rival versions— one published by the Shinyodo Press, translated by Otsuki, the other by "Ars" publishers, Tokyo. Freud's library only contains the Shinyodo version (publication date 1933).[2]

Invitation Steinig—Einstein . . .   Tues 21 June 1932

In 1925 the League of Nations had founded an Institute of Intellectual Cooperation. One of its aims was to encourage and publish exchanges of letters between leaders of thought. One such volume had already been published; it was entitled *A League of Minds* and contained letters from M. Henri Focillon, Salvador de Madariaga, Gilbert Murray, Paul Valéry and others.

Leon Steinig was the League official entrusted with ensuring Einstein's cooperation on a second such volume, but the idea of a discussion of war between himself and Freud had been Einstein's own. The correspondence was eventually to be published under the title *Why War*.

Lux and Gabi . . .   Fri 24 June 1932

Lux, Ernst's wife, brought her 11-year-old eldest son Stephan Gabriel ("Gabi") to visit Freud. Her three sons each bore the name of an archangel—Stephan Gabriel, Lucian Michael and Clemens Raphael.[1] She wrote to Jones: "The reason by the way of giving the children the names of a set was my plan of having three of them and my conviction that I would have nothing but boys." (*Lucie Freud-Jones 23.1.1956*)

Large horse bought . . .   Mon 28 June 1932

The two large horses in Freud's collection are both Chinese imitation Tang antiquities produced for the European market. One of them he placed on top of a case in the consulting room, under a picture of the Egyptian Sphinx.

$2000 from Jackson . . .   Mon 28 June 1932

The fund-raising campaign to save the press was beginning to succeed. This was Edith Jackson's second large donation this year and Brill, on behalf of the New York Society, sent a further $2,500. Meanwhile, the English Society had pledged to raise the same amount as the Viennese.

Jones, at first optimistic about raising the money, was then appalled by the size of the sum which Martin Freud informed him would be needed by September. "We have therefore still to count on the unknown American uncle," he wrote in late May. But by June he was able to promise £500 for the *Verlag* fund.

Jakob Bernays by Fränkel . . .   Mon 11 July 1932

Jacob Bernays (1824–1881), uncle of Martha Freud, was Professor of Classical Philology in Breslau and Bonn. His letters had just appeared in a volume edited by Michael Fränkel and entitled "*Jacob Bernays: A Biography in Letters*" (*Jacob Bernays: Ein Lebensbild in Briefen* Breslau, Marcus 1932). The book was dedicated to Freud.

In September 1931 Freud had asked Ernst to pay the editor 1000 marks out

Kenji Otsuki, Freud's Japanese translator at work on volume X of Freud's complete writings, June 1931.

One of Freud's Chinese horses. NB

Ernst and Lux Freud's "archangel" sons;
Stephan Gabriel, Klemens Raphael and
Lucian Michael.

Eva convalescing from scarlet fever at
Mallnitz.

of the family fund as ". . . an act of gratitude, for with his inheritance we established our house." (*Freud-Ernst Freud 20.9.1931*) This "inheritance" could refer both literally to Martha's dowry and figuratively to the Jewish Enlightenment Jacob Bernays represented. Bernays retained his strict Jewish faith, although antisemitism impeded his academic career. Fränkel depicts his great mission as an effort to unite the Bible with Greco-Roman culture.[1]

Mathilde Halberstadt + . . .   Wed 13 July 1932

This must have been a relation of Freud's son-in-law, Max Halberstadt. No further evidence has yet come to light.

Eva scarlet fever in Mallnitz . . .   Sat 16 July 1932

Freud was extremely fond of Oliver's daughter Eva and concerned by her illness: "My little Eva has gone to Mallnitz (Carinthia) with an apparently very mild case of scarlet fever, but I fear they are not careful enough with her. My army of small complaints grows . . . ." (*Freud-Eitingon 21.7.1932*)

Jofi back . . .   Sat 16 July 1932

Two months after Jofi's return, a sentence in one of Bernfeld's letters speaks volumes about Freud's present relationship with his dogs: "Today I visited Anna F[reud]. Prof. charmingly amiable; spoke neither with nor about the dogs, but was very kind to me." (*Bernfeld-Liesl Neumann-Bernfeld 14.9.1932*)

Birthday at Hochroterd* . . .   Tues 26 July 1932

This was Martha Freud's 71st birthday. She wrote: "In general I have once again been overwhelmed with flowers and attention on my birthday." (*Martha Freud-Ernst Freud 30.7.1932*).

The weather was radiant and in the afternoon everyone drove out to Hochroterd. Frau Josefa had filled the house with flowers and hung a garland of them over the entrance. Marie Bonaparte asked to join the party and she dug up potatoes, picked and cut beans and helped Anna prepare her speciality—*Salzburger Nockerln* (fluffy pancakes).

At the end of the week Freud wrote to Jeanne Lampl-de Groot: "I too am at least working hard, despite many small complaints and treatments. Our weather seems to have been much more merciful than yours. On the 26th we spent a completely beautiful half day at Hochroterd." (*Freud- Lampl-de Groot 30.7.1932*)

Steinig with Einstein's letter . . .   Mon 1 August 1932

Freud had accepted the June invitation to exchange letters about war with Einstein. The League of Nations representative, Leon Steinig, who was in charge of the publication now brought Freud Einstein's letter. Steinig also brought a personal message from Einstein: "I should like to take this opportunity to send you my private best wishes and to thank you for the many hours of pleasure I owe to the reading of your works. It is always amusing for me to observe that even people who consider themselves 'Unbelievers' as far as your teaching is concerned, can put up so little resistance to your ideas that they have the habit of thinking and speaking in your concepts when—they let themselves go." (*Einstein-Freud 30.7.1932*)[1]

By the time *Why War* appeared, Einstein had already severed his connections with the League of Nations and condemned the disarmament conference being held under its auspices in Geneva 1932–34.

Martin kidney colic . . .   Wed 10 August 1932

This attack of kidney trouble was so severe that Martin had to spend some time in hospital. His illnesses were a matter of more than personal concern since he had now become indispensable in the running of the press. He had quickly proved his worth and Freud was soon reproaching himself and Eitingon for both "having tolerated Storfer too long . . . ." (*Freud-Eitingon 5.6.1932*)

---

* Unusually Freud spells "Hochrotherd" here according to the new orthography. Occasionally such inconsistencies appear in letters, too, but generally he remained faithful to the pre-1902 standard rules of German spelling.

Geometrical pyxis . . .   **Sun 14 August 1932**

This is an elegant ceramic cylindrical bowl (Greek) with a lid decorated with geometrical designs.

Jeanne as guest . . .   **Mon 15 August 1932**

Jeanne Lampl-de Groot had been planning to come to Freud for further analysis and he had arranged for her to stay a few days with them in the guest room. However, her husband Hans Lampl had been resisting the idea and it was not clear until the last moment that she would come.

Despite evident problems, she did arrive and afterwards she attended the Wiesbaden Congress where she presented a paper. It was delivered so quietly that the audience objected several times.

Freud interpreted this as an attempt at self-sabotage, to punish herself for resistances during the analysis.

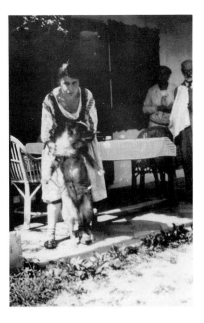

Brill . . .   **Mon 22 August 1932**

One of the main topics of discussion must have been the problem of the new groups in America refusing to recognize Brill's authority: "In no country—it is unbelievable—does organization and collaboration meet with such resistance as in America. It would be very good if Brill could manage to get together a unit with sub-groups but there is no outstanding personality, the New York Society enjoys no respect from the others. Brill has the latently enormous American antisemitism against him. So if Brill cannot carry through his intention we should take up what concerns us and not insist on a form which these redskins refuse." (*Freud-Eitingon 27.4.1932*)

Freud's affection for Brill and his sympathy with his difficult situation did not prevent him from proposing acceptance of new groups by the international association, whether or not they subordinated themselves to Brill's New York group.[1]

Ferenczi's refusal . . .   **Tues 23 August 1932**

After Karl Abraham's death, Max Eitingon succeeded him as President of the International Psychoanalytical Association in 1926. Ferenczi had been the other candidate; during the late 1920s he was hurt by refusals to elect him, but in 1930 Jones and Eitingon agreed he should become the next president. By May 1932 Ferenczi was beginning to express doubts to Freud about taking up that post "in the present difficult times . . . ."

Freud wanted to insist, hoping that the duties of president would rescue Ferenczi from his self-imposed isolation. However, it was too late for that and Freud now received Ferenczi's final refusal of the presidency: "After long and tortured hesitation I have decided to decline the presidential candidacy. In addition to the motives of which I have already informed you, there is also the circumstance that I have reached a definitely critical and self-critical juncture in the course of efforts to structure my analyses more profoundly and effectively and to a certain extent this seems to make it necessary not only to supplement but also correct our practical and in part our theoretical views. I have the feeling that such an intellectual standpoint in no way suits the dignity of the presidency, whose main task is to preserve and strengthen what has been established and my inner sense tells me that it would not even be honest to occupy this position." (*Ferenczi-Freud 21.8.1932*)

Ernst's visit . . .   **Sat 27 August 1932**

On average Ernst visited his father once a year, but in this and the previous year he came to Vienna twice.

He may have combined business with social visits. Apart from advising Anna on the rebuilding of Hochrotherd, it is possible there was other work for him in Vienna. He claimed to have been the first architect to be a specialist in designing psychoanalysts' consulting rooms (he designed rooms for Karl Abraham, Franz Alexander, René Spitz, Sándor Radó and Melanie Klein).

Radó . . .   **Sat 27 August 1932**

Radó, together with Brill, had just visited Ferenczi in Budapest. Freud was concerned by their report on his state: "Ferenczi apparently looks awful, chalk

Anna holding Jofi. Freud and Minna Bernays watch in background.

The Greek geometrical pyxis. NB

pale and deeply depressed. Radó, whose understanding is razor-sharp, thinks he is in an advanced state of sclerotic degeneration. I would prefer to attribute much of that impression to the conflict which is shaking him, its resolution is evidently causing him great difficulties." (*Freud-Eitingon 29.8.1932*)

Ernst departed . . .   Tues 30 August 1932

Though it is unlikely to have been the reason for this visit, Ernst, like Martin, was also involved in his father's financial affairs at this period. He was now administering a fund based on the Goethe Prize award. Every so often Freud would request him to pay someone a sum out of the fund, mostly as a gift or birthday present—apart from payments to the antiquities dealer Dr. Lederer.[1]

Lectures finished . . .   Wed 31 August 1932

Over the year Freud had been complaining of difficulties in writing the *New Introductory Lectures*. He blamed a lack of inner motivation—he was doing it only to make money for the press. But since moving out to Pötzleinsdorf, they had advanced fairly rapidly.

However, he still complained about inner obstacles: "I am writing busily, not finding it easy, my work inhibition could well be physiologically grounded. I also get angry every time I omit or deform words. Nothing like that used to happen." (*Freud- Lampl-de Groot 15.7.1932*)

At that point, in mid-July, Freud had more or less completed the first two chapters and was at work on the third—*The Dissection of the Psychical Personality*. The fourth—*Anxiety and Instinctual Life*–was still only planned, the final chapter, *The Question of a Weltanschauung*, existed in draft form. The rest remained "pretty misty" ("*recht nebelhaft*") but Freud was certain he would not finish it in Pötzleinsdorf.

Nevertheless by mid-August another chapter had been completed—*Femininity*. Finally, toward the end of August he added a further chapter which, he told Eitingon, was " . . . particularly popular and chatty, about attacks, secessionist movements, therapy and so on, entitled: *Explanations, Applications and Orientations . . . .*" (*Freud-Eitingon 24.8.1932*)

Anna to Göttingen—Congress . . .   Thurs 1 September 1932

On her way to the psychoanalytical congress (and, to judge by its date, probably on her return), Anna seems to have paid a visit on Lou Andreas-Salomé at her home in Göttingen. For the past decade Lou had acted as a benevolent aunt or mother to Anna and as a confidante to both her and her father.

Five years previously Freud had confided to her his anxieties about Anna: "Anna is magnificent, good and intellectually independent, but no sexual life. What will she do without a father?" (*Freud-Lou Andreas-Salomé 11.12.1927*).

Ferenczi with Brill . . .   Fri 2 September 1932

Despite Ferenczi's renunciation of the presidency on August 23, Freud had continued pressing him to accept. The final decision was deferred until their meeting, when the Ferenczis would be passing through Vienna on their way to Wiesbaden.

The day after that meeting Freud sent Anna a report: "The Ferenczis came then before 4 o'clock. She friendly as ever, he exuded an icy coldness. Without any further question or greeting he began: I want to read you my lecture. This he did and I listened thunderstruck. He has totally regressed to the etiological views I believed in and gave up 35 years ago, that the gross sexual traumas of childhood are the regular cause of neuroses, says it in almost the same words I used then. No word about the technique by which he obtains this material, in the middle of it all remarks about the hostility of patients and the necessity of accepting their criticism and admitting one's errors to them. The consequences of this confused, tortuously contrived. The whole thing is actually stupid or it seems so since it is so devious and incomplete." (*Freud-Anna Freud 3.9.1932*)

Brill arrived in the middle of Ferenczi's lecture. This disturbed Ferenczi, who felt Freud had deliberately arranged for a third party to witness their discussion.

Wiesbaden Congress . . .   Sun 4 September 1932

Despite the trouble with Ferenczi the Congress ran smoothly. Jones reported:

Ferenczi at Clark University, 1909, at the beginning of his long friendship with Freud.

Jeanne Lampl-de Groot with her husband Hans and daughters Harriett and Edith. His "paranoia" over her analysis with Freud strained their relationship.

"My impression of the Congress was throughout excellent. I have rarely known one with a better Stimmung [atmosphere], friendly and confident." (*Jones-Freud 9.9.1932*).

One reason for Jones's enthusiasm was that the congress had elected him the new President of the International Psycho-Analytical Association to replace Eitingon.

Discussion Einstein finished . . .   Tues 6 September 1932

Of his open letter to Einstein, Freud commented sourly: "Unfortunately it is about how one can avoid the doom of war. I do not think I will receive the Nobel Peace Prize for my contribution." (*Freud-Eitingon 18.8.1932*) Freud's letter—*Why War?*—presented the death drive and the destructive tendencies of mankind as forces still untamed; his conclusions are correspondingly pessimistic about the prospect of lasting peace.

Anna back . . .   Thurs 8 September 1932

Anna returned with Dorothy Burlingham, who had been to the United States. They had met on September 3 during the Congress, at the Hotel Rose in Wiesbaden, where the delegates were staying. Dorothy heard Anna's lecture—"The Neurotic Mechanisms under the Influence of Education." In it she presented some examples of the interaction between inner and outer worlds in the development of infantile neuroses.

On September 6 Anna and Dorothy both took part in a boat trip organized for delegates, along the Rhine from Mainz to the Lorelei rock.

+ Chr Ehrenfels . . .   Fri 9 September 1932

Christian Freiherr von Ehrenfels (1859–1932) had in fact died the previous day at Lichtenau, Lower Austria. His name is associated with Gestalt psychology which he pioneered in an early essay on "gestalt" qualities (*Über Gestaltqualitäten*, 1890). From 1900 until his retirement in 1929 he was Professor of Philosophy in Prague.

Ehrenfels developed the theory that monogamy had led to the decline of the species and he advocated social reforms based on eugenics and the notion of a society where colleges of women would rear the children of selected males.

Freud's " 'Civilized' Sexual Morality and Modern Nervous Illness" (1908) took as its starting point von Ehrenfels' book *Sexual Ethics* (1907), with its distinction between "natural" and "civilized" sexual morality.

Ehrenfels gave two guest lectures to the Wednesday Society and Freud remained in correspondence with him from 1903 to 1915. After a long pause the correspondence was resumed in 1931.

Obras XV & XVI . . .   Mon 12 September 1932

These two volumes of the Spanish complete works contained parts one and two of the case histories (*Historiales Clinicos I & II*).

Berggasse . . .   Sat 17 September 1932

Most years the family returned to Berggasse in late September or early October. This year's return was unprecedentedly early.

Mathilde ill . . .   Tues 20 September 1932

Mathilde's illness is not specified. But her health was not good in general. In 1927 Freud had even written: "Mathilde is sick and giving us for the first time grave cause for concern." (*Freud-Ernst Freud 7.10.1927*)

Minna to Meran . . .   Sat 24 September 1932

Three weeks earlier Minna had spent a day at Hochrotherd, while Anna was away at Wiesbaden. Her trip to Meran followed the pattern of the previous year.

Martin back . . .   Sat 24 September 1932

It is possible Martin had been convalescing after his severe bout of kidney colic in August.

Jones with the Freuds at Belle Vue in 1919. Here, in 1895, Freud discovered the secret of dreams.

Wiesbaden conference, 1932. Anna sits in the front row, third from right, between Marie Bonaparte and Ernest Jones.

The cottage at Hochrotherd.

Hochrotherd . . .   Sun 25 September 1932

The Freud family saw Hochrotherd as an idyllic refuge from the everyday struggle of life in Vienna. Among the poems that Martin wrote for Anna there is one entitled *Hochrotherd* which ends with the following stanza:
> "Still lies the land as though allotted bliss,
> As though the world were not by hate and fear distorted,
> Around the house imbued with grace, rest, peace,
> The beautiful green island: HOCHROTHERD."

To Anna in the Imperial . . .   Tues 27 September 1932

The eldest of Freud's sisters, Anna (1858–1955), married Martha's eldest brother, Eli Bernays (1860–1923), in 1883. In 1892 they emigrated to the United States, where he soon became a successful dealer in grain and founded the main branch of the large Bernays family in the United States.

Freud told Fliess, before a previous visit of hers: "I have never had any special relationship with her, as I had, for instance, with Rosa, and her marriage to Eli B. has not exactly improved it." (*Freud-Fliess 23.3.1900*)

The Imperial Hotel on the Ringstrasse was and is Vienna's grandest hotel, the one used by visiting royalty. Anna's stay there emphasized her rise in the world since leaving Vienna exactly 40 years earlier.

Brücke's great-grandson . . .   Tues 27 September 1932

Ernst Brücke (1819–92) was one of the small group of determinist scientists associated with Hermann Helmholtz (1821–94). They were committed to explaining phenomena in terms of chemical and physical forces and they actively opposed vitalism or other efforts to invoke a "life force" as a basis for science. This attitude survived as an implicit conceptual background to the development of psychoanalysis.

At Vienna University Freud worked from 1876 to 1882 in the physiological laboratory of Ernst Brücke's Institute. Brücke came to personify for him the ideals of science and this visit from a descendant of his early mentor took Freud back 50 years, to the origin of his scientific vocation. Freud called Brücke the greatest authority that had ever influenced him. It was under his influence that he abandoned chemistry and zoology for physiology, the first step toward neurology and psychology.

The great-grandson is either Franz Theodor von Brücke (born 1908), a professor of pharmacology in Vienna, or Hans von Brücke (born 1905), a surgeon in Graz.

Hochrotherd with Ruth & Mark . . .   Sun 2 October 1932

This was the final visit this year to Anna's cottage, in the company of Ruth Mack Brunswick and her husband, the composer Mark Brunswick (1902–1971).[1] The house was by now completely renovated and well-furnished.

Bernfeld, who visited the cottage in November, wrote: "The house of Anna F. and Dorothy Burlingham is very clean . . . with a lot of first-class peasant furniture, beautiful curtains, stoves, chests, a hall. A stall with a cow, a lot of egg-laying hens, butter churns, vegetable gardens, hotbeds—a very tasteful, expensive primitiveness. But really cozy." (*Bernfeld-Neumann 21.11.1932*)

Anna flown to Berlin . . .   Tues 4 October 1932

This was not Anna Freud's first flight. In 1929 she and Dorothy flew from Vienna to Salzburg and back. Freud commented: "Apparently it was a marvelous experience." (*Freud-Ernst Freud 12.5.1929*)

Fetish Jackson . . .   Tues 4 October 1932

The American Edith Jackson was in analysis with Freud. This "fetish" sounds like a gift to Freud, though it might conceivably refer to a discussion on fetishism. Freud did not collect "primitive" art and there are only one or two objects that might be loosely termed "fetishes."

But Freud may have used the term to describe something with fetishistic value—a "fetish" relating to her psychoanalysis with him.[1]

Anna Bernays, Freud's eldest sister.

Anna back . . .   **Thurs 6 October 1932**

Anna had given a talk or seminar in Berlin.[1] Eitingon wrote: "You must have heard what a great success Anna's appearance in Berlin was. This time there was an enormous gathering." (*Eitingon-Freud 19.10.1932*)

Gerstberg . . .   **Thurs 6 October 1932**

Unexplained.

Thorough operation with Pichler . . .   **Thurs 6 October 1932**

This was the second precautionary operation this year. Freud commented: ". . . Pichler again undertook one of those small operations in my mouth which he considers necessary out of caution, this time much more energetically than the previous times. But everything went very well, I only had wound pains for three hours and bore up to the injections well. Today I am going out, Monday I will be working again. There are of course no guarantees that this will be the last of its type." (*Freud- Lampl-de Groot 8.10.1932*).

But this "small operation" had in fact involved a considerable diathermy burning[1]; the wound was still causing pain 17 days after the operation.

Minna from Meran . . .   **Fri 14 October 1932**

Some time after her visit to Vienna, Freud's sister Anna went to Meran. She stayed at the Savoy Hotel and from there she wrote a letter of admiration to Stefan Zweig, on his recent book *Marie Antoinette*, dated November 25 (a doubt remains about this date, since it is not clearly legible). But it is possible that she may have been there earlier and that she and her sister-in-law Minna met there.

Alfred Rie + accident & death . . .   **Sat/Sun 29/30 October 1932**

Freud's previous mention of the lawyer Alfred Rie had involved what was probably a visit of condolence on the death of his wife, Johanna Rie. He only survived her by a little over a year. The accident that led to his death is unexplained.

Like his brother Oskar Rie, Alfred Rie was one of Freud's Saturday evening tarock regulars. His death left a vacant hand at cards. Eitingon inquired about this vacancy and was told: "Jekels has been enlisted to replace Alfred Rie." (*Freud-Eitingon 20.11.1932*)

Flu and ear inflammation . . .   **Tues 1 November 1932**

Schur writes: "In early November, 1932, Freud had his usual cold—this time a more severe upper respiratory infection with otitis media of the right ear." It was rainy weather and Freud was feeling miserable, Schur continues. During the doctor's visit, Freud showed him pictures of Crete and Rhodes and said he was daydreaming of the sunny Mediterranean.

By the middle of November he had recovered from the attack of ear inflammation (otitis) but "gruesome catarrhs" lingered on into December "and reduce the quality of life a bit more." (*Freud-Eitingon 20.11.1932*)

Paracentesis Ruttin . . .   **Thurs 3 November 1932**

Erich Ruttin (1880–1940) was an outstanding Viennese ear, nose, and throat specialist and the author of a monograph on ear inflammations. Paracentesis means the puncture of a cavity with removal of fluid. Ruttin evidently performed this operation to relieve Freud's ear inflammation.

A few days later Freud was feeling better. He wrote: "After a by no means comfortable week of flu and fever, otitis, paracentesis etc. I am today taking up work again in a limited manner from 2 to 5. Naturally [I have] not become very strong. But human again." (*Freud- Lampl-de Groot 7.11.1932*).

Roosevelt elected in USA . . .   **Tues 8 November 1932**

For Freud the immediate effect of this election was that it released Bullitt from his political duties in the United States. Freud was impatient to complete the Wilson book, but could do nothing without Bullitt.

He wrote to Eitingon: "Around 1 December I am expecting my collaborator after the elections in the U.S.A. and will hear from him when the Wilson book can be sent out to be published." (*Freud-Eitingon 20.11.1932*)

Minna Bernays, 1930s.

VERLAG VON W. BRAUMÜLLER, WIEN.   PHOTOGRAVURE VON R. PAULUSSEN, WIEN.

Freud's portraits of two of his scientific
mentors, Hermann Helmholz and Ernst
Brücke.

Bullitt eventually turned up in December, for three days, on a diplomatic tour through Europe. Freud told Marie Bonaparte: "He is expected to be entrusted with an important political post, admits however that he could easily be passed over. In that case our Wilson book could appear without delay."(*Freud-Marie Bonaparte 21.12.1932*).

But Bullitt was in fact given an important post, as the first U.S. Ambassador to the U.S.S.R., and further work on the book was consequently delayed.

At Yvette's hotel . . .   **Wed 30 November 1932**

Yvette Guilbert had returned for her regular late November concerts in Vienna. Over the years she had been widening her repertoire to include historical songs which she herself introduced, so that her recitals began to take the form of illustrated lectures.

A Viennese critic said of this year's concert: "She introduces each little drama with a few witty words. This time she speaks at a table like a humorous and clever, yet learned, university lecturer."[1]

A month later a French concert program appeared, containing a collection of caricatures of Yvette and dated December 24, 1932. Freud's copy is unsigned and may not have been a gift from the artist herself, given her dislike of caricatures, even Toulouse-Lautrec's.

Anna 37 yrs . . .   **Sat 3 December 1932**

From her father Anna received $100 to buy a writing desk of her own choice. This was not the first gift of furniture: in 1925 she had received a chair, with the note "Good(s) to sit on for many hours" ("*Gut um viele Stunden darauf zu sitzen*") (*Freud-Anna Freud 3.12.1925*). Hard currency, too, had been an acceptable gift for some time, but the amount seems to have increased considerably over the years. In 1924 Anna received only one pound and with it a note saying "One year, one pound" ("*Ein Jahr, ein Pfund*"). (*Freud-Anna Freud 3.12.1924*)

A measure of the fame which Anna had by now achieved in her own right is the fact that a Vienna gossip newspaper, *Die Stunde*, featured a front page article with the headline: "Anna Freud—37 years old. A visit to Sigm. Freud's daughter, the famous child therapist."[1]

New Introductory Lectures . . .   **Sat 3 December 1932**

Though Freud received his first copy of the *New Introductory Lectures on Psycho-Analysis* now, the publication date is given as 1933. In this respect the book followed the example of the *Interpretation of Dreams*, which was dated 1900 although it appeared in late 1899. (Publishers often postdate books brought out later in the year, in order to extend the copyright.)

During its composition Freud repeatedly complained that writing had become far more difficult than previously. But now he was at least satisfied with the appearance or general impression of the book: "It looked good" ("*Es sah gut aus*") he said of this advance copy. It came out three days later.

Operation with Pichler . . .   **Thurs 8 December 1932**

On Max Schur's advice this operation had been postponed for a week owing to an attack of coryza and tracheitis. Freud wrote: "On Thursday I again had one of those diathermy burnings with Pichler. It's a bore that the tissue doesn't want to calm down. Each time it is a case of the excised material being of a totally harmless nature, but you know of course that if one had left it there longer, perhaps etc. Since then things have gone as always, at first little pain or complaints and after a few days the troubles of the inflamed reaction, not being able to chew, hardly speak, curiously hardly to write either." (*Freud- Lampl-de Groot 11.12.1932*).

Jofi benefited from Freud's inability to chew. In mid- December Anna Freud wrote that her father could still only bite with difficulty and Jofi was eating most of his food.

Pichler's brief consultation note for Christmas Eve records the continuing after-effects: "Patient complains still. Objectively satisfactory. Orthoform indispensable still."

Newspaper article, December 3, 1932. "A Visit to Sigm. Freud's daughter, the famous child therapist."

Freud on the balcony of his summer home, Hohe Warte 1933.

1933

"Sometimes I am amazed that in such times as the present spring and summer come as if nothing had happened . . . " Anna Freud wrote to Ernest Jones on April 27, 1933.[1] Her father's diary records the terrible political changes that aroused this comment. The entry for January 29, 1933, states simply **Hitler Reichs Chancellor**. A month later, on February 28, Freud reported; **Berlin parliament on fire**. In the aftermath of the burning of the Reichstag building civil rights were suspended and political opponents were rounded up and imprisoned in the first German concentration camps. The grim series of disasters continued. Universities were encouraged to organize the ritual burning of "ungerman" books and on May 11, 1933, the diary states simply **Burning in Berlin**. Freud's own works had been burnt at one such ceremony. The Nazi myth of an antisemitic Aryan "culture" had become the new Germany's official policy.

Antisemitism was, of course, nothing new to central European Jews such as Freud. Born into a Jewish family living in Moravia, he grew up and received his education in Vienna, capital of the Empire and a city with a large Jewish population—and an entrenched tradition of antisemitism. But though it was pervasive, it remained generally low-key. Significantly enough, the first directly political entry in his diary, only a week after Freud began keeping it—**Antisemitic disturbances** on November 7, 1929—gives a foretaste of the violent and systematic forms antisemitism was now taking.

As an atheist, Freud felt no loyalty to the religious traditions of Judaism. But he never hesitated to define himself as a Jew. According to his own account, it was his experience of antisemitism at Vienna University during his youth that had forced him to accept the social identity of "Jew."[2] Later, in 1897, he joined a Jewish debating society, the "B'nai B'rith," which was committed to combating antisemitism by ethical, non-violent means.

Meanwhile, Austria was suffering many of the same economic problems that had led to Nazism in Germany. On March 25, 1933, the diary speaks of a printer's strike and on May 1 of the city being closed to May Day demonstrations. Strikes and political unrest in Austria had produced the home-grown "Austro-Fascism" of Engelbert Dollfuss. Freud felt the Austrian reactionaries would be less savage than their German equivalents and would protect Austria from the Nazis. He was determined to remain in Vienna, in the face of his friends' persistant advice to leave. One of those who had advised him to leave was the Hungarian analyst Sándor Ferenczi, who had once been his closest friend. On May 22, 1933, the diary reports his death. He died after a period of estrangement from Freud and isolation from many of his former colleagues. The entry for June 4, 1933, is telling: **Ferenczi obituary finished**. Freud's struggle to write this obituary had brought to the surface the sense of loss and failure he had experienced with the decline of their friendship.

In a sense, their friendship had been emblematic of the vanishing Austro-Hungarian civilization, soon to be swamped by Hitler's "Aryan culture." Freud in Vienna and Ferenczi in Budapest were at the axis of the old Empire. Their friendship was built on a common heritage. Both had the background of a classical education and were widely read in European literature, both collected antiquities. This hobby displayed their culture in material form. Ancient mythologies and religions formed, quite literally, the furniture of their studies.

In April 1933 Jews were excluded from public office in Germany. Freud's family and friends in Berlin began emigrating—his sons Oliver and Ernst to France and England respectively, his grandson Ernstl to Austria, the writer Arnold Zweig and the analyst Max Eitingon to Palestine. In September, with the formation of a Nazi "Chamber of Culture" (*Reichskulturkammer*), Jews were excluded by decree from journalism and the arts. European culture was visibly disintegrating under the pressure of "cultural regression."[3]

---

1. *Anna Freud-Jones 27.4.1933* [Inst.of PsA: CFA/FO1/30] ("Manchmal wundert mich, dass auch in solchen Zeiten wie den jetzigen der Frühling und Sommer kommt, als wäre nichts geschehen.")
2. "But I had felt myself to be a Jew even before this—under the influence of German antisemitism of which repeated outbreaks occured during my university years . . . " (*Freud-Dwossis 15.12.1930*: FM: ARC/40] ("Ich hatte aber schon früher mich als Jude gefühlt - unter dem Einfluss des deutschen Antisemitismus dessen neuerlicher Ausbruch in meine Universitätszeit fiel.")
3. *Freud-Hermann 1.2.1936* [Baeck] ("Ein Teil der lebenden Menschheit, gewiss nur ein Teil, scheint gegenwärtig eine kulturelle Regression durchzumachen . . . ")

Dr. May . . .   Wed 4 January 1933

Dr. Richard May was a general practitioner from the village of Gross-Schwein-barth, 30 km northeast of Vienna. In late 1932 he had written to Freud about an incident from his medical practice. Freud replied: "We are not particularly astonished by letters full of psychoanalytical interest from somewhere like South Africa. But it is with good reason that a letter like yours from Gross-Schwein-barth in Lower Austria, with so much understanding for the facts and theories of analysis, should cause us surprise." (Freud-May 1.1.1933)

Perhaps Dr. May drove to Vienna to visit Freud and discuss his article, which was printed (at Freud's suggestion) in the journal *Die psychoanalytische Bewegung* (*The Psychoanalytical Movement*). It came out anonymously in the January/February number under the title "Letter from a Country Doctor." The case dealt with a local farmer, son of a miserly father, both typical anal characters. The son had injured himself by inserting a wooden bung into his anus. Freud was particularly interested in this case since it offered a rare example of a doctor applying psychoanalysis in his everyday medical practice.

Martin to Berlin . . .   Wed 4 January 1933

Possibly Martin visited his brothers Ernst and Oliver in Berlin: he saw his old friend Lampl and his wife. If it was a business visit, too, there is no record that he called on Eitingon, who at this time was preoccupied by deaths in his family.

G. Anton + . . .   Thurs 5 January 1933

The death of another of Freud's earliest acquaintances. Fifty years earlier Dr. Gabriel Anton (1858–1933) had, like Freud, been a pupil of Theodor Meynert. From 1894 to 1905 he was director of the Graz hospital, then from 1906 on he was professor of psychiatry at Halle.

L. Tiffany + New York . . .   Wed 18 January 1933

Louis Comfort Tiffany (1848–1933), Dorothy Burlingham's father, died of pneumonia on January 17. The heir to Tiffany & Company, the famous New York jewelry and silver store, he had made his own name as America's foremost artist in stained glass, which came to be highly valued as "Tiffany" glass. Dorothy had visited him the previous summer and did not return to the United States for the funeral.

During Freud's single visit to America in 1909 (long before Dorothy came to Vienna), he went shopping at Tiffany's and bought a Chinese jade bowl and a bronze Buddha bust. But he had no Tiffany glassware in his collection, although he did have a collection of Roman glass.

Eitingon . . .   Fri 27 January 1933

Eitingon's father had recently died and the mother of his wife Mirra died shortly afterwards. Freud invited him to visit as soon as he had once again found peace and quiet. But when he came he had still not fully recovered. Freud wrote: "Eitingon looks ill, but we found him more sociable and talkative than usual." (Freud- Lampl-de Groot 1.2.1933)

At this meeting Freud arranged for Eitingon to examine his correspondence, covering the period from 1907 to 1925, with the first German psychoanalyst, Karl Abraham (1877–1925).

Ruth flu . . .   Sun 29 January 1933

Ruth Mack Brunswick's frequent illnesses were interfering with her analysis with Freud. He complained that she was ". . . a very irregular patient and difficult to grasp owing to organic complications." (Freud- Lampl-de Groot 23.10.1932).

But this time everybody else was ill, too. The weather had turned warm and there was an epidemic of flu. Mark Brunswick was in the Cottage Sanatorium, Marianne Kris had a fever and in the apartment above the Freuds two of the Burlingham children and an American guest lay ill.

Hitler Reichs Chancellor . . .   Sun 29 January 1933

This entry should be for the following day. (In fact Freud appears to have originally written the date as 30, then altered it to 29.) It was on the morning of January 30 that President Hindenburg received Hitler, together with the previous

SS-men picket Jewish businesses. Their placards read: "Germans! Fight back! Don't buy from Jews!" DOW

German Chancellor von Papen, and that Hitler was formally named as new Chancellor. It was still widely believed that Hitler's lack of a coherent political program could lead to his rapid downfall. Freud wrote to Jeanne in Berlin: "We are all curious what will come of the program of Reichs Chancellor Hitler, whose only political theme is pogroms." (*Freud- Lampl-de Groot 1.2.33*)

Galsworthy + . . .   Tues 31 January 1933

The death of the English novelist John Galsworthy (1867–1933) followed only two months after he had received the 1932 Nobel Prize for Literature.

A reference to Galsworthy in *Civilization and its Discontents* (1930) shows that Freud had already read—and been impressed by—at least one work of Galsworthy's: "Among the works of that sensitive English writer, John Galsworthy, who enjoys general recognition to-day, there is a short story of which I early formed a high opinion. It is called *The Apple Tree*, and it brings home to us how the life of present-day civilized people leaves no room for the simple natural love of two human beings."

Another reference, in the recent *New Introductory Lectures*, mentions a patient with a rich English library who lent Freud some authors he had read little until then—Bennett and Galsworthy. Among the novels lent was *The Man of Property*.

JoFi Kagran . . .   Tues 31 January 1933

According to Martin Freud, at Kagran the dogs " . . . enjoyed a second home."

The reason for sending Jofi to the kennels may again have been that she was in heat.[1] But this time a suitable chow had apparently been found to impregnate her. The period of gestation for chows is nine weeks: it was exactly nine weeks after this visit that she gave birth.

Arnold Zweig . . .   Sun 12 February 1933

While on holiday in the Tatra Mountains, Zweig had been reading Freud's *Metapsychological Supplement to the Theory of Dreams* (1917) and *Mourning and Melancholia* (1917) to help him with his self-analysis. He wrote: "With each new essay I read you help me forwards and upwards out of the confusions which as reanimated unconscious residues oppress and overshadow me." (*Arnold Zweig-Freud 30.12.1932*)

Meanwhile Freud had raced through Zweig's latest novel—*De Vriendt Returns Home* (*De Vriendt kehrt heim*, Berlin, 1932). Zweig sent him the first bound copy on November 24, 1932 and by November 27 Freud wrote that he had finished it in one reading and that the impression was so powerful he hardly knew what to say. The hero was based on the Dutch journalist and lover of Arab boys, Jacob Israel de Haan, murdered in Jerusalem in 1924. As so often, Freud was fascinated by the story's factual origins—the fictional equivalent of "day residues" in dream interpretation.

Brill—Interpretation of Dreams . . .   Mon 13 February 1933

Brill's translation of the *Interpretation of Dreams* first appeared in 1913. In 1932 a third, completely revised edition was published by George Allen & Unwin in London and Macmillan in New York. It was a copy of this which must now have reached Freud.

Brill was a native German speaker and had arrived in America as a boy, without a word of English. His translations were widely criticized, but Freud was grateful for Brill's personal devotion and for his pioneering work.

He wrote of the translation: "If psycho-analysis now plays a role in American intellectual life, or if it does so in the future, a large part of this result will have to be attributed to this and other activities of Dr. Brill's."

Concluding his very brief preface, (written on March 15, 1931, for this edition), Freud said of the *Interpretation of Dreams*: "It contains, even according to my present-day judgement, the most valuable of all the discoveries it has been my good fortune to make. Insight such as this falls to one's lot but once in a lifetime."

Four Japanese translations . . .   Tues 14 February 1933

It is likely these included volumes 7–9 of the Shinyodo Press edition of Freud's work.[1] These were all published in 1933 and included *The Ego and the Id* and

Freud with Jofi. "One cannot help feeling respect for animals like this." (*Freud-Lou Andreas-Salomé 8.5.1930*)

Totem and Taboo, translated by Yabuhachi and Tsushima, *Papers on Technique*, translated by Otsuki, and *Contributions to the Psychology of Love*, also translated by Otsuki.

Iron Buddha . . .   Fri 17 February 1933

Freud had two iron oriental pieces, both Ming Dynasty (15–17th century), but neither of them is strictly speaking a Buddha.[1] One is the standing figure of an acolyte, the other the bust of a Bodhisattva, a saintly attendant on the Buddha. It is most likely Freud is talking of the latter figure here.

Czech Leonardo . . .   Tues 21 February 1933

Freud's *Leonardo da Vinci and a Memory of his Childhood* (1910) was translated by Dr. Ladislav Kratochvíl and published as *Vzpomínka z Détství Leonarda da Vinci* by Orbis in Prague.

Berlin parliament on fire . . .   Tues 28 February 1933

The burning of the Berlin Reichstag during the night of February 27 was the pretext for an instant purge of enemies by the Nazis. During the night 10,000 Communists, SPD members and other democrats were arrested. This was followed by a ban on the Communist press and on part of the Social-Democratic press. An international committee was formed to investigate the Reichstag fire. Its chairman was Albert Einstein, who demonstratively resigned his German citizenship on April 1, 1933. The committee cast suspicion on Goering, who was living in the chancellery opposite, connected to the Reichstag by an underground passage. But a show trial convicted the Dutchman Marinus van der Lubbe and he was guillotined in 1934.[1]

Dollar moratorium . . .   Sat 4 March 1933

A bank crisis in the United States had affected 50 million Americans in 18 states. Banks were closed in Texas, Utah, Idaho, Kentucky, Washington, Arizona and Nevada. The financial moratorium resulted in $3 billion in savings being frozen. This was potentially another blow to Freud's American patients, who were an important source of income to him during the postwar years.

Roosevelt . . .   Sat 4 March 1933

This was Franklin D. Roosevelt's inauguration as President of the United States.[1] The inauguration actually took place on March 3.

Election of Hitler in Germany . . .   Sun 5 March 1933

The election gave the Nazi Party 17.3 million votes (43.9 percent), far ahead of their nearest rivals, the Socialists, with 7.2 million (18.3 percent). The Center and Bavarian People's Party followed with 5.5. million (14 percent) and the Communists with 4.8 million (12.3 percent). But on March 9 the Nazis annulled the Communist Party mandate in order to assure their two-thirds majority in the Reichstag. (The Communist Party chairman, Ernst Thälmann, had already been arrested on March 3.)

Hitler was installed as Chancellor over a coalition Cabinet containing two other Nazis—Frick as Minister of the Interior and Goering as Air Minister and Minister of the Interior for Prussia.

In the aftermath of this election, Freud noted: "Something uncanny is happening to our little Austrian state; naturally one does not know what." (*Freud-Lampl-de Groot 9.3.1933*)

It was clear that the German reign of terror threatened Austria, but Freud, like many Austrian Jews, was still under the nationalistic illusion that his countrymen would be less savage: "We hold fast to two points, to the determination not to move out and to the expectation that what happens here will be markedly different from Germany. We are on the way to a dictatorship of the right-wing parties who will ally themselves with the Nazis. This is far from good, but discriminatory laws against a minority are expressly forbidden in the peace declaration, the victorious powers will never permit annexation to Germany and our rabble is a bit less brutal than its German brethren." (*Freud- Lampl-de Groot 8.4.1933*)

The Leonardo cartoon that served as basis to Freud's study of Leonardo's childhood memory.

Iron Buddha standing on showcase in Freud's study.

Shelf in study. The iron Bodhisattva stands third from the right. Next to it is the white stone Buddha bust Freud acquired on May 30, 1933. The stone "Dog of Fo" (4th from left) is mentioned on May 7, 1934. NB

Egyptian fabric painting . . .   Mon 13 March 1933

Two fragments of Egyptian linen mummy bandage inscribed with excerpts from the Book of the Dead fit this description. They are from the Ptolemaic-Roman period (c.100 B.C.—200 A.D.): one contains a representation of Osiris, the other a procession to the tomb of the deceased.

Freud's collection also contains a cartonnage mummy covering of painted linen, glued together in such a way as to resemble board.

Harry doctorate . . .   Wed 15 March 1933

Freud's nephew, the son of his brother Alexander, received his doctorate in law (*Dr. jur.*) at the age of 24. In a letter to his Manchester nephew, Sam, Freud described Harry as "a clever boy and affectionate son . . . ." (*Freud-Sam Freud 1.12.1931*)

Colored Chinese woman . . .   Fri 17 March 1933

Apart from the woman rider, there are four Chinese female figures in the collection, three of them, (two Tang and a Sui,) are standing figures on the desk. Only one of the Tang figures has traces of paint, and there is strong evidence that it and the others were given to Freud in June 1938 by Marie Bonaparte. That leaves a seated glazed ceramic woman, which Freud was to set on top of a case in his consulting room, next to a Chinese horse and under a print of the Egyptian Sphinx.

Warum Krieg? . . .   Wed 22 March 1933

This was the German edition of the League of Nations brochure *Why War?* In private Freud was disparaging about it: "My discussion with Einstein ('Warum Krieg') has been all corrected and can already be published in February. It won't save humanity either. Yes, why does Einstein commit such stupidities like his confession of faith and other unnecessary things? Perhaps because he is so good-natured and otherworldly." (*Freud- Lampl-de Groot 10.2.1933*)

Printers' strike . . .   Sat 25 March 1933

Press censorship and official pressure had been growing in Austria. Proletarian papers suffered worst, being subjected to outside control and intervention. This 24-hour strike called by the printers was a spontaneous protest against infringements of the freedom of the press and the victimization of workers' papers.

Pourquoi Guerre? . . .   Mon 27 March 1933

This was the French edition of *Why War?* Freud informed Eitingon he would not be likely to see the German version in Berlin. Meanwhile, Martin Freud was in charge of distributing the Austrian edition.

Ferenczi news . . .   Mon 27 March 1933

In late November, long after his ill-fated visit to Freud on September 2, 1932, Ferenczi aired his grievances about that meeting: first Freud had allegedly introduced an outsider (Brill) to "arbitrate," and second, Freud had asked Ferenczi to refrain from publication. Following that complaint, Freud received only a brief New Year's greeting. This news about Ferenczi probably came through the intermediary of Ferenczi's doctor, Dr. Lajos Lévy, who was keeping Freud and Eitingon informed about Ferenczi's health and condition.

Only two days after this news about him, Ferenczi resumed direct contact with Freud: "Two immediate motives prompt me today finally to break off the childish sulking and to resume contact with you as if nothing had happened. [. . .] Perhaps you have heard from Dr. Lévy that in recent weeks I have endured a relapse of the symptoms of my previous illness (Anaem. pernic.), but this time less as a worsening of my blood count than as a sort of nervous collapse from which I am only slowly recovering." (*Ferenczi-Freud 29.3.1933*)

Ferenczi ended this letter with excellent advice—an urgent appeal to Freud to leave for a safe country, together with Anna and several patients. He recommended England because of the presence there of good dentists and surgeons. Freud was encouraged by the tone of the letter; he felt that Ferenczi was emotionally on the road to recovery.

Egyptian mummy bandage. NB

Freud's nephew, Harry. Portrait by Max Halberstadt. MH

Jofi injury . . . **Mon 27 March 1933**

No documentation of this injury is available. But Jofi was now pregnant and this injury may have affected the delivery a week later.

Visit Barilari . . . **Wed 29 March 1933**

Perhaps Mariano Barilari (1892-?), who had published a work on the psychosomatic aspect of ulcerous colitis.

Bryher . . . **Fri 31 March 1933**

The writer Bryher (pen name of Annie Winifred Ellerman [1894–1983]) had first met Freud during a flying visit to Vienna in May 1927. She had a letter of introduction to Freud from her friend Havelock Ellis and had flown in from Venice where she was holidaying with her future husband Kenneth Macpherson.[1]

From 1928 to 1932 Bryher was in analysis with Hanns Sachs. On Sachs' recommendation, her friend and companion, the poet H.D. (Hilda Doolittle), entered analysis with Freud at the beginning of this month, on March 1, 1933.

The meeting now must have involved discussions of the payment and practical arrangements which were in Bryher's hands—and Freud's thanks for a contribution Bryher had made two weeks previously towards the Vienna Psychoanalytical Society.

Ernstl from Berlin . . . **Sun 2 April 1933**

Freud's grandson Ernstl's journey to Vienna involved a narrow escape from the Nazis. Freud told Eitingon: "Our Ernstl arrived today on 'premature' Easter holidays. In Dresden he experienced his first brush with contemporary history." (*Freud-Eitingon 3.4.1933*)

W. Ernest Freud ("Ernstl") explains this "brush with history": "In view of the uncertain political situation it was decided that I join Eva Rosenfeld and her son, Victor, who were returning to Vienna from Berlin (where Eva Rosenfeld's mother lived; Eva Rosenfeld may have been working at Simmel's Sanatorium at the time) for the Easter holidays.

In Dresden all Jews were taken from the train and had to spend the night in the Braune Haus in Dresden. The Austrian Ambassador intervened on behalf of the Austrians who had been on the train and the next morning the Austrian Jews were allowed to proceed to Austria by train after an interview. As I felt I belonged to the Austrians I managed to persuade the interviewer of this and was allowed to proceed to Vienna with the Rosenfelds. Technically I was a German subject, but I think I was the only German Jew on that train who was not sent back to Berlin."

Arnold Zweig . . . **Sun 2 April 1933**

As a Jewish writer with left-wing political views, Arnold Zweig had no alternative but to leave Germany. He sent his wife and children to Palestine and was preparing to follow them later. Meanwhile, he was working on a book about the German Jews in order to publicize their plight under the Nazis.

Jofi's dangerous delivery . . . **Mon 3 April 1933**

Jofi had had one previous puppy, which died. This time she ". . . had a dangerous delivery but is now well and proud of her two little, ratlike children." (*Freud-Lampl-de Groot 8.4.1933*) They were named Fo and Tattoun; by July, Freud wrote, they were " . . . almost as large as their mother, very high-spirited and get up to all sorts of tricks." (*Freud- Lampl-de Groot 14.7.1933*)

Norman Douglas . . . **Mon 3 April 1933**

The Scottish writer Norman Douglas (1868–1952) was a friend of Bryher; they had come to Vienna together, in part to visit Freud. She aroused or encouraged Douglas's interest in Freud by sending him one of Freud's books in February. After the meeting Douglas sent Freud some of his own books. Freud replied: "I would like to return the compliment and send you some of my books. You would only have to express the wish; but I fear that my books do not please readers—they annoy or frighten them. I submit to my fate in this respect, but not without envy." (*Freud-Douglas 10.4.1933*)

Jofi's pups, Fo and Tattoun, summer 1933.

Oliver & his wife Henny. Max Halberstadt photo, 1920s. MH

The Moses of Michelangelo (possibly Freud's own sketch).

Anna Freud speaking with Felix Boehm, May 1937.

Freud with Henny and his granddaughter Eva, (July 1927).

Freud read and enjoyed Douglas's *Old Calabria*. Characteristically, in his reponse to the work he picked on an instance of possible confused identities, between Frederick Barbarossa and his grandson Frederick II, of whom Hitler might be seen as a grotesque reincarnation: ". . . so the past always glimmers through the very latest moment in time. It is the Messiah-belief of the Germans." (*Freud-Douglas 10.4.1933*)

Ernstl Bob. Mabbie to Sicily . . .   Wed 5 April 1933

W. Ernst Freud writes: "I think the Sicilian journey was planned to give us a break. A Professor Taglicht, an elderly Viennese Jew, who made a living by giving Nachhilfestunden [private tuition], took Bob and Mabbie Burlingham and myself to Sicily, where we visited several of the big cities, like Palermo and Catania, possibly also Taormina."

Oli—Henny from Berlin . . .   Sat 8 April 1933

This visit by Oli and his wife Henny (*née* Fuchs) was a somber occasion. Freud wrote before their arrival: "My son Oliver whom I have been supporting for a year, since he is unemployed, is coming to Vienna tomorrow to talk about his future. There is little doubt that he will never again find work in Berlin. (He is a civil engineer.)" (*Freud-Jones 7.4.1933*)

After the consultation the outlook remained bleak: "The impression left by Oli's visit was depressing. He behaves well, doesn't moan, is looking round and is prepared to take pains. But his prospects are so bad. He is hesitating between Spain and Palestine but has no point of reference anywhere." (*Freud- Lampl-de Groot 15.4.1933*)

Italian Moses . . .   Mon 10 April, 1933

Edoardo Weiss had translated Freud's *The Moses of Michelangelo* (1914) into Italian. Two days after receiving his copy Freud wrote back: "The Italian 'Moses' has given me particular pleasure. My relationship to this work is something like that to a love child. Every day for three lonely weeks in September of 1913 [1] I stood in the church in front of the statue, studying it, measuring and drawing it until there dawned on me that understanding which in the essay I only dared to express anonymously. Not until much later did I legitimize this nonanalytical child." (*Freud-Weiss 12.4.1933*)

Why War? . . .   Mon 10 April 1933

This was now the English edition of *Warum Krieg?*, translated by Stuart Gilbert.

Easter 47 yrs practice . . .   Sun 16 April 1933

This was the first day of Freud's Easter holidays and also, as he wrote, ". . . incidentally the last day of a 47-year-old practice." (*Freud- Lampl-de Groot 15.4.-1933*)

Boehm and Federn . . .   Mon 17 April 1933

Felix Boehm (1881–1958) became a member of the International Psychoanalytical Association in 1913; he worked at the Berlin Psychoanalytic Institute from 1920–36 and became secretary of the German Psychoanalytical Society in 1931.

In early April the Nazis excluded Jews from the civil service; Jews were also forbidden to sit on the central executive of any medical society. On inquiry, Boehm found out this also applied to psychoanalytical groups. Eitingon, the head of the Berlin Psychoanalytical Society, was a Russian-born Jew with Polish nationality: Boehm, who was German and "Aryan," was next in line.

He now visited Freud to decide what was to be done in Germany. Boehm wanted Eitingon to step down and for Jews to withdraw voluntarily from the German Psychoanalytical Association and he tried to gain Freud's consent to this tactic. Freud refused to be drawn in, feeling this could not prevent the Nazis from banning psychoanalysis. But he agreed that Boehm might take over the leadership (with the backing of a majority vote against Eitingon), so as not to provide the authorities with an easy pretext for clamping down.

This concession was treading a fine line and Freud was grateful for Federn's presence as a witness to guard against distorted reports of the meeting.[1]

Klemperer . . .   Sat 22 April 1933

It appears unlikely that this would have been Dr. Paul Klemperer, a cousin of
Paul Federn and an early member of the Wednesday Society. He left the Society
together with Adler and later became a pathologist.

The German conductor Otto Klemperer also seems a priori unlikely, although
he was acquainted with Gustav Mahler, whom Freud had very briefly "analyzed"
during a four-hour stroll through Leyden in August 1910. He left Germany in
1933 to become musical director of the Los Angeles Philharmonic.

There are a number of other Klemperers known, but no evidence that points
decisively to any particular one.[1]

Dr. Ed. Weiss—Forzano . . .   Tues 25* April 1933

Edoardo Weiss had brought with him an acquaintance, Giovacchino Forzano, to
discuss the analysis of his daughter Concetta Forzano. She was being treated
unsuccessfully by Weiss, who wanted to refer her to Freud.

Inevitably another subject surfaced at this meeting—Mussolini. Forzano was
an intimate of the Fascist dictator with whom he had co-authored three plays
(*Villafranca*, *Cesare* and *Campo di Maggio*). During this meeting Forzano gave
Freud a dedicated copy of *Campo di Maggio*.

Afterwards Forzano embarrassed Weiss by asking Freud for an inscribed copy
of a book for the dictator. Freud took his newly-published dialogue with Einstein—*Warum Krieg*–and wrote the dedication: "Benito Mussolini with the respectful greetings of an old man who recognizes the potentate as culture hero.
Vienna 26.4.1933 Freud." [1]

City closed against marches . . .   Mon 1 May 1933

The Austrian Chancellor, Engelbert Dollfuss, now had dictatorial power, but the
political situation remained volatile. A month earlier Freud wrote to Eitingon:
"Nobody here understands our political situation, people think it unlikely that
it will develop as it has in your country, life carries on here undisturbed but for
marches which are occupying the police. There is no lack of attempts to instill
a sense of panic, but just like you I will only pack up and leave the place at the
very last moment and probably not even then." (*Freud-Eitingon 3.4.1933*)

After the announcement of a ban on May Day demonstrations, the Social
Democrats and Nazis withdrew their intention to march and simply asked sup-
porters to decorate their windows. But the Communists continued their preparations. On the previous day the police had announced that the inner city would
be closed off and entry only allowed through seven designated streets to people
able to prove residence or business. Also, to hinder access, no trams ran on the
Ringstrasse. These measures proved largely effective since May Day passed quietly. The official *Wiener Zeitung* rejoiced in "A Day of Victory for Goverment
Authority."

Move to Hohe Warte . . .   Thurs 4 May 1933

This year the Freuds had found a summer home in Hohe Warte on the outskirts
of Vienna. The contrast of their annual migration with the violent political
upheavals in Germany and Austria prompted Anna Freud to write: "We are
moving on May 3 to Vienna XIX. Hohe Warte 46. Sometimes I am amazed that
in such times as the present spring and summer come as if nothing had happened." (*Anna Freud-Jones 27.4.1933*)

Freud's diary entry is also a wry comment on the times—or perhaps an ironic
note of defiance. The previous entry records a ban on "marches" or "demonstrations" (*Umzüge*) and it is immediately followed by Freud's announcement of his
own "march" or move (*Umzug*). To judge from the spacing of the diary entry,
it is even possible that Freud could have written *"Hohe Warte"* first, then
inserted the word *"Umzug"* in front of it, as a comic afterthought.

Ernst & Klemens . . .   Fri 5 May 1933

Clemens Raphael (born 1924) is the youngest of Ernst Freud's three sons. Now
Sir Clement Freud, he is a British politician, writer and radio performer. He has
served as Liberal M.P. for Ely.

Paul Federn descending staircase.

Edoardo Weiss. TG

The villa at Hohe Warte where the
Freuds spent the summer of 1933.

---

* The date of both book dedications shows that this meeting actually took place on April 26.

Clemens had been staying with his father in Vienna. Ernst, like Oliver, was preparing to emigrate and looking around for a destination. He was considering Palestine.

On July 9, when Freud met some old schoolfriends he told them his grandson in Berlin was summoned at school by the name "Jew Freud" ("*Jud Freud*"). This may refer to Clemens, who possibly related this to him now, for Jones quotes a remark Freud's grandson made during this visit to Freud: "What a different situation I should be in to-day if I were an Englishman."

77th birthday . . .   Sat 6 May 1933

On May 7, the day after his birthday, Freud sent Jones a bitter commentary on aging: "I believe I have discovered that the longing for ultimate rest is not something elementary and primary, but an expression of the need to be rid of the feeling of inadequacy which affects age, especially in the smallest details of life.

"You are right in saying that in comparison with the time of my seventieth birthday I no longer feel anxious about the future of psycho-analysis. It is assured, and I know it to be in good hands. But the future of my children and grandchildren is endangered and my own helplessness is distressing." (*Freud-Jones 7.5.1933*)

Freud discouraged most people from giving him presents, but not Marie Bonaparte, who gave him a camel statuette. Eitingon again had to apologize for his absence. The previous year it was he who he had been ill; this year, he said, it was Germany.

Attack of vertigo . . .   Sat 6 May 1933

Freud wrote to Marie Bonaparte ". . . that morning [i.e., Freud's birthday] I had an attack of dizziness which nearly knocked me over, with no disturbance of consciousness. Dr. Schur, who by chance came in right afterward, did not make much of it. His diagnosis asserted that the dizziness was of a vestibular type and caused by nicotine. Since then I have been restricted to three cigars . . . ."

Burning in Berlin . . .   Thurs 11 May 1933

On May 10 a ritual bookburning was ordered in Berlin by Goebbels. Organized by the university, it took place at 11 p.m. on the Opernplatz and was orchestrated in an operatic manner. SA and SS bands played patriotic music while troops of Nazi students and academic staff paraded with burning torches, which they threw into the bonfire.

Over 20,000 books, passed by the students from hand to hand, were hurled into the flames, while a series of student representatives recited incantations against nine categories of "un-German writing" (*undeutsche Schriftmaterial*). The first was political: "Against class struggle and materialism, for community of the people and an idealistic way of life [*Volksgemeinschaft und idealistische Lebenshaltung*]! I commit to the flames the writings of Marx and Kautsky."

Freud fell into the fourth category: "Against soul-disintegrating exaggeration of the instinctual life, for the nobility of the human soul! I commit to the flames the writings of Sigmund Freud."

Similar book burnings were organized in other university towns. Freud commented: "What progress we are making. In the Middle Ages they would have burnt me: nowadays they are content with burning my books."

Ernst left . . .   Tues [Mon] 15 May 1933

While Oliver had gone to Paris in search of a new home, Ernst set off for London to prepare a home for his family, who for the time being remained in Berlin. By early June, and with help from acquaintances, including Ernest Jones, he was already on the way to establishing himself there.

Jones told Freud: "We have been able to give Ernst some good introductions and he has fully lived up to his reputation of a Glückskind [lucky fellow]. You need have no anxiety about his making his way. We shall be delighted to have him in England, though I have wondered whether his vivacious personality would not be more suited to France." (*Jones-Freud 3.6.1933*)

Hard times in Vienna. Poverty reduced some of the unemployed to begging and busking. DOW

Operation P. . . .   Tues [Mon] 15 May 1933

This operation involved oxygen and perhydral treatment and resulted in severe

Klemens Freud, (left) with his two older brothers, Lucian and Stephan.

pain. Consequently the surgeon, Hans Pichler, followed it up the next day with an electrocoagulation by diathermy, using a novocain anesthetic as well as orthoform. (The two consecutive treatments may have confused Freud's dating of this and the following day.)

Pichler's notes show that this was the 23rd visit since the beginning of the year. This was partly at Freud's own request. On February 28 he told Pichler he wished to visit more frequently to "avoid neglecting himself."

Arn. Zweig . . .   Tues [Mon] 15 May 1933

This was Arnold Zweig's final visit to Freud before he followed his family to Haifa in December 1933. Freud dissuaded him from returning to Berlin, where he would almost certainly have been sent to concentration camp. In the book about the Jews in Germany, which he was now working on—*Bilanz der deutschen Judenheit 1933. Ein Versuch* (Amsterdam 1934) [*Insulted and Exiled. The Truth about the German Jews* London 1937]—Zweig lists the glories and achievements of the Jews; among them Freud figures as "the most significant living scientist."[1]

Jeanne house visit . . .   Wed [Tues] 16 May 1933

In the weeks before this visit Jeanne Lampl-de Groot had been concerned with the problem of where to live and what to do with her property in Germany. She came from a wealthy Dutch, non-Jewish family but was working at the Berlin Institute and she had, as Freud said, " . . . thrown in her lot with the Jews." Jeanne's husband, Hans Lampl, was Viennese and a friend of the Freuds. Over the year Jeanne had been keeping Freud informed of his unbalanced, "paranoid" mental condition. In April 1933, Freud advised her to move with her family to Vienna, but tentatively, since it was uncertain how Hans Lampl would now react to a return to his previous home.

Colitis . . .   Sun 21 May 1933

Two months previously the entry *"Barilari"* (March 29, 1933) may refer to a specialist on ulcerous colitis. Could that have involved a consultation related to a previous attack of this ailment?

Jeanne departed . . .   Sun 21 May 1933

Jeanne's brief visit to Vienna was a preliminary to moving there with her husband and family. They lived in Vienna from the end of August 1933 until May 1938, when they moved to Holland.

van Vriesland . . .   Sun 21 May 1933

The writer Victor Emanuel van Vriesland (1892–1974) was Dutch consul in Palestine, where he was in charge of the finance department of the Jewish Palestine Executive. He was a former analysand of van Ophuijsen. Later in the year, Eitingon refers to him as a strong advocate of psychoanalysis and one who commanded wide respect in the country and also from the Zionists.

Ferenczi + . . .   Mon 22 May 1933

Although this news was not unexpected, Ferenczi had once been Freud's closest friend and virtually his adopted heir. His death aroused contradictory emotions in Freud: "A confused feeling, on the one hand of relief that he has now escaped the terrible decay—in the final weeks he could neither stand nor walk and the delusions were worse than we knew—on the other, only now the pain at the loss of the old, what he meant for us, even though he had withdrawn from us years ago. But there is a particular violence about the conclusive brutal fact." (*Freud-Lampl-de Groot 26.5.1933*)

To Jones, Freud repeated his previous diagnosis—that Ferenczi's physical degeneration had been accompanied by paranoia and that the breakdown of their previously close relationship had been a precipitating factor: "At the center was the conviction that I did not love him enough, did not want to recognize his work, also that I analyzed him badly. His technical innovations were connected to that, he wanted to show me how lovingly one had to treat one's patients in order to help them." (*Freud-Jones 29.5.1933*)

Jeanne Lampl-de Groot and her daughters, Edith and Harriett, April 1933. Freud wrote ". . . in photos it is becoming harder for me to distinguish Jetti from Edith . . ." (*Freud-Lampl-de Groot 15.4.1933*)

Ferenczi, the lost friend. (Portrait sent to Anna at Christmas, 1925.)

Serbian Lectures . . .   Mon 22 May 1933

This was a Serbian translation of the *Introductory Lectures–Uvod u Psihoanalizu* published by "Kosmos," Belgrade 1933 and translated by B. Lorenz.

Japanese journal No.1 . . .   Tues 23 May 1933

The first issue of the new journal the Japanese were now producing—their own *Zeitschrift für Psychoanalyse* in Tokyo—which they started sending to Freud. Two years later Freud wrote to his Japanese translator Kenji Ohtski [Otsuki]: "I do get your Journal regularly . . . [. . .] What you write about the resistance in your country is no surprise to me; it is just as we may have expected, but I am sure you have given psychoanalysis a solid foundation in Japan, which is not likely to be swept away." (*Freud-Ohtski 20.5.1935*)

Ruth & Mark back from Paris . . .   Wed 24 May 1933

On April 15 Mark Brunswick left Vienna for New York, where his father was dying. He may have arranged to meet his wife, Ruth, in Paris on his return journey.

A month previously Ruth Brunswick had had to interrupt her analysis with Freud yet again owing to illness. Freud complained that she was "eternally ill, coughs, is feverish . . . ." (*Freud-Jeanne Lampl-de Groot 15.4.1933*)

Anna & Martin from Budapest . . .   Thurs 25 May 1933

Anna and Martin had been to the burial of Ferenczi in Budapest. Of the Viennese, Paul Federn and Helene Deutsch also attended. Freud wrote: "Anna returned deeply shaken." (*Freud- Lampl-de Groot 26.5.1933*)

Diathermy of lower jaw . . .   Fri 26 May 1933

After the recent operation, pressure had started building up again on the lower prosthesis and Pichler decided to remove some dead skin by another diathermy. But the pain returned a week later in the same place and in early June Pichler tried to eliminate it with further oxygen treatment. By the end of June Pichler reported an overall improvement.

Oli-Henny in Paris . . .   Sun 28 May 1933

Freud now wrote to a friend of the family, Oskar Pfister, who was a Swiss protestant pastor and psychoanalyst: "Three members of my family, two sons and a son-in-law*, are looking for a new country and have not yet found one. Switzerland is not one of the hospitable countries. There has been little occasion for me to change my opinion of human nature, particularly the Christian Aryan variety." (*Freud-Pfister 28.5.1933*)

By July Oliver, Henny and their daughter Eva were living in the seaside village of St. Briac, near St. Malo, but in autumn they were back in Paris, living at 36 Rue George Sand. Here Arnold Zweig paid a visit on them and wrote afterwards to Freud: ". . . I have been thinking very much about this son of yours, who is also too decent to find it easy to adapt himself to life. It was shattering to observe how he too talked most vividly and warmly when speaking about his wartime service. Just like all other men of his generation and of his circumstances who now find that they have to begin all over again at a time when they are firmly set in their ways of thought and feeling, habits and ambitions." (*Arnold Zweig-Freud 21.1.1934*)

Poe from Marie Bonaparte . . .   29 May,1933

Marie Bonaparte's psychoanalytical study of Edgar Allen Poe had just been published in Paris. Freud's foreword to the book cautiously defines the limitations of psychoanalysis when applied to literature: "Such studies do not claim to explain the genius of creative artists, but they show the factors which awakened it and the type of material fate has imposed upon it."

Marie Bonaparte's handwritten dedication on the flyleaf reads: "to my beloved master, these pages inspired by his work and spirit, and in which the author has taken pains, in order to penetrate one of the darkest psyches there has ever been,

The Japanese Psychoanalytical Group in May 1933. Yabe sits front row, third from right, Otsuki, front row, third from left.

---

* Oliver Freud, Ernst Freud and Max Halberstadt.

to follow with deliberation the trails blazed by the first man to penetrate the human unconscious."

Buddha head . . .　　　　　　　　　　Tues 30 May 1933

This is a heavy white stone Buddha bust, Chinese early Tang or a later copy. In Berggasse Freud placed it on a special table in the study with a number of other busts and masks, under the bookshelves. It is now on the shelf facing Freud's desk at Maresfield Gardens.

Ferenczi obituary finished . . .　　　　　Sun 4 June 1933

This brief obituary, written for the *Internationale Zeitschrift* and the *International Journal*, caused Freud great difficulties[1]: "Whitsun was taken up with the obituary for Ferenczi, in no sense an easy job. Now I only feel the emptiness left over from it all." (*Freud-Lampl-de Groot 4.6.1933*) A few days later it was still weighing on him: "I have finished Ferenczi's obituary, it was troublesome to write and has left behind a troubled state of mind." (*Freud-Eitingon 7.6.1933*)

H.G. Wells visit . . .　　　　　　　　Mon 5 June 1933

Afterwards Freud simply described the visit as "interesting"[1], but H.G. Wells' account reveals that one of the conversation topics was death: "When I talked with Sigmund Freud in Vienna this spring, he did not seem to feel as I do about death. He is older than I and he was in bad health, but he seemed to be clinging to life and to his reputation and teaching much more youthfully than I do to mine. But then perhaps he was just drawing me out."

Eitingon . . .　　　　　　　　　　　Fri 16 June 1933

After Boehm's visit on April 17 Freud had immediately sent Eitingon a detailed account of the discussion. Boehm was clearly in a hurry to take over. Alleging that any delay threatened their survival, he wanted Eitingon's resignation to be declared immediately, though Eitingon himself was at the time on holiday in Mentone.

Freud had to agree that Eitingon would eventually have to step down, but he insisted on delaying the measure until a general meeting could at least vote him out. This happened on Eitingon's return to Berlin.

The meeting now was a chance for Eitingon to discuss his idea of moving the German Psychoanalytical Society and its Institute to Vienna. Eitingon's letter before the meeting also mentioned Ferenczi's death and its effect, adding: "I have a great need to talk about all these things with you soon." (*Eitingon-Freud 31.5.-1933*)

Paul Hammerschlag + . . .　　　　　Mon 26 June 1933

The schoolteacher Samuel Hammerschlag taught Freud religious education. He continued to be very friendly and helpful toward Freud after he left school, lending him money several times while he was studying. His son, Paul, also became Freud's friend. Paul married Josef Breuer's eldest daughter Berthe in 1893.

Wittels' journey . . .　　　　　　　Mon 26 June 1933

The journey in question must be Fritz Wittels' trip to Europe from New York. A letter from Wittels in April speaks of hoping to see Freud again soon.

Fritz Wittels (1880–1950) joined the Wednesday Society in 1907. He resigned from the Society in 1910, the year he published a novel (*Ezekiel der Zugereiste*) caricaturing Karl Kraus and implying that he was impotent. This was one factor leading to an estrangement from Freud, another being his close association with Wilhelm Stekel.

In 1924 he published the first biography of Freud. The wealth of marginal notes and interjections in Freud's copy of this book reveal his antipathy toward the work.[1] This was partly because he objected to a biography on principle.

In his *Letter to Fritz Wittels* he said: "It seems to me that the public has no concern with my personality, and can learn nothing from an account of it, so long as my case (for manifold reasons) cannot be expounded without any reserves whatever. But you have thought otherwise."

In 1925 Wittels was readmitted to the Psychoanalytical Society with Freud's

Freud's copy of Wittels' 1924 biography is full of marginal comments. Against this passage on his early career he has scrawled "wrong", "nonsense", "no" and several exclamation marks.

support. But the biography cast a long shadow. On November 19, 1933, Freud wrote to Wittels, who had been living in New York since 1928: "As concerns your brooding and afterthoughts about your misdeed of ten years ago, allow me to remark that absolute undoing is in general a difficult matter and really best left to magic. If in addition you are striving toward a different personal relationship with me, allow me to point out that such conversions are no longer worth it for me. At my age they would not come into effect." (*Freud-Wittels 19.11.1933*)

Ernstl's tonsil operation . . .   Fri 30 June 1933

Freud's grandson Ernstl (W. Ernest Freud) writes: "If I remember correctly, this was my third (and last) tonsil operation. I had already had two tonsil operations in my early childhood but in those days one only capped the tonsils and in time the tissure would grow again. Anna accompanied me to the hospital, and during one of her visits, when she was sitting at my bedside after the operation, she narrowly escaped death, because the electric cord, which held a counterweight to balance the ceiling lamp (which was adjustable for height) suddenly broke and the counterweight landed a few inches beside her on the floor."

Ruth operation . . .   Sat 8 July 1933

Ruth Mack Brunswick was in the hospital for surgery of the cervix. There was no malignancy and she had recovered by the end of the month.

Martin's furunculosis . . .   Sat 8 July 1933

This unpleasant affliction, perhaps a result of blood poisoning, became too serious for the family doctor, Dr. Abels, to deal with by lancing the boils. Eventually, in August, Martin had to go into the hospital for treatment.

60 yrs Matura with Knöpfmacher & Wagner . . .   Sun 9 July 1933

On May 28, 1933, Freud received a letter from his old school (*Bundesrealgymnasium, Kleine Sperlgasse 2c*), congratulating him on the 60th anniversary of the *Matura* (the Austrian school-leaving and university entrance certificate). A short list of surviving schoolfellows included: "Freud Sigmund, University professor
Knöpfmacher Wolf, Lawyer in Vienna
Wagner Julius, Lawyer in Vienna."[1]

The three men celebrated the occasion at Freud's Hohe Warte house. When Freud showed the others the antiquities on his desk, Knöpfmacher told him he only kept them there to make himself seem younger. Whereupon Freud took him aside and, indicating Wagner, said: "He is old, you are young, I am in between."

Knöpfmacher was at Freud's school from 1871 to 1873. In later years he told his son that he and Freud spent many nights studying for the dreaded *Matura* exam at Freud's house, keeping themselves awake with black coffee and grapes.

Holidays Hochroterd . . .   Tues 1 August 1933

This was the first day of Anna Freud's holidays. She was to spend most of August living totally at the cottage, coming on short visits to Vienna only every second or third day. The comparatively long period without work—and without the constant duty of nursing her father—rested her and did her good, she told Jones in a letter later that month. (*Anna Freud-Jones 23.8.1933*)

Bullitt . . .   Wed 2 August 1933

Since Bullitt had now been assigned U.S. Ambassador to the Soviet Union, this is unlikely to have been more than a brief visit. The previous time, Freud spoke of him "again appearing like a meteor." According to Bullitt, the final draft of their Wilson book was complete by spring 1932, at which point the two disagreed over the text and by common consent, set it aside. Bullitt had returned to the United States to take part in Franklin D. Roosevelt's campaign for president and he did not anticipate again finding time to work on the book.

Whatever their disagreements, Freud had great faith in Bullitt's political judgment, for he wrote to Jeanne: " . . . B. is the only American who understands something about Europe and wants to do something for Europe. Therefore I can't trust myself to hope that he will really be given a post in which he could be effective and have his own way." (*Freud- Lampl-de Groot 16.2.1933*)

Anna and Dorothy, with calf and
Lampl children, at Hochrotherd.

Once in Moscow, Bullitt probably had little time for the Wilson book. In December 1933 Freud wrote: "No direct news from Bullitt. Our book will not see the light of day." (*Freud-Marie Bonaparte 7.12.1933*)

Institute for the Blind . . .   Thurs 10 August 1933

Dorothy Burlingham was in contact with Dr. Siegfried Altmann, the director of the Jewish Institute for the Blind (*Israelitische Blinden-Institut* founded 1872) at Hohe Warte. She analyzed three of the blind children at the institute and it is very likely she arranged Freud's visit there.[1]

He signed the guestbook, which contained over 3,000 names of many illustrious visitors—artists, rabbis, politicians, scientists and even royalty, and met the blind children who lived there. They fetched him roses and carnations from the garden and he spoke to them, as they said afterwards, "in an infinitely kind voice . . . " ("*mit einer unendlich liebevollen Stimme*").[2]

Eitingon . . .   Fri 11 August 1933

At the end of July Freud had told Eitingon of Marie Bonaparte's projected visit to see Freud in Vienna during the week following August 17. He mentioned her desire to speak with Eitingon as well. However, Eitingon was now preoccupied with emigration to Palestine; instead of waiting for the Princess, he came earlier to see Freud alone.

Hochrotherd . . .   Sat 12 August 1933

This is the last recorded visit to Hochrotherd; the risk to health precluded further excursions. (However, for Anna and Dorothy Burlingham the cottage remained a haven for holidays and weekends.) It is likely to have been a brief outing, since Freud also had time the same day to write a letter to Jeanne, addressed Grinzing, and probably to meet the American Rabbi Stephen Wise, also presumably at the Hohe Warte house rather than at the cottage.

Stephen Wise . . .   Sat 12 August 1933

Rabbi Stephen Wise (1874–1949) of New York was on a European tour researching the situation of Jews who had suffered as a result of Nazi persecution.

Wise was a grandson of the Chief Rabbi of Hungary and had himself been ordained in Vienna under Chief Rabbi Jellinek. He was the founder of the liberal Free Synagogue of New York[1] and a political activist. As soon as Hitler came to power, he had begun urging governments to take action against his atrocities: in May 1933, after Hitler's book burnings, he organized a protest march in New York against the silence of the British and American governments.

Princess . . .   Thurs 17 August 1933

One of the reasons Freud and Marie Bonaparte had hoped to meet Eitingon at this particular moment was to discuss the post of Vice-President of the I.P.A., left vacant by Ferenczi's death. Freud was now canvassing on behalf of Marie Bonaparte. In a letter to Jones of August 23, 1933, Freud outlined all the advantages to be gained from her election. Not only did she possess acute intelligence and outstanding energy, but she had reached a time of life when these qualities would increasingly fuel her dedication to psychoanalysis.

Moreover, she had an impressive work record and her social position would work to the benefit of the movement.[1] And in addition to all of this she was a lay analyst[2]; this would be a demonstration against the predominance of doctors in positions of authority within the movement, and would show outsiders that psychoanalysis was not just some part of psychiatry.

Essais de psych. appliquée . . .   Fri 18 August 1933

These *Essays on Applied Psychoanalysis* (*Essais de Psychanalyse appliquée*) included work ranging from 1906 to 1923, translated into French by Marie Bonaparte in collaboration with Edouard Marty and published by Gallimard, Paris (1933). Presumably she brought them with her to present to Freud. But the example in his library is not a dedication copy and is uninscribed and uncut.

Dorothy back and Lampl . . .   Fri 18 August 1933

Dorothy had been to Cherbourg and Copenhagen, where she had sent her

Anna, Dorothy and Anna Faddenberger at Hochrotherd.

children Bob and Mabbie to the United States. She returned, alone for the first time in 18 years of motherhood.

Freud had been advising Jeanne Lampl-de Groot to move to Vienna, but had been concerned about her husband Hans Lampl's "paranoia". This appeared to have improved during the spring and Lampl now returned to his home town with Jeanne and their daughters. They were to stay until 1938, when they moved to Holland.

Freud's particular concern was that Hans might lean emotionally on Anna. (Thirteen years earlier he had been her suitor, but she—and Freud—had rejected him.) In July she was so exhausted that Freud was for the first time seriously worried about her. Consequently he requested Jeanne to take care that her husband did not put stress on Anna.

Jeanne operated . . .   Thurs 24 August 1933

This sounds like another appendectomy (all four Burlingham children in turn also had the operation during these years). A month previously Freud wrote to Jeanne Lampl-de Groot: "The illness figures here are improving but the news that you want to increase them is intolerable. One does not need much medical knowledge to think of the appendix from your description . . . ." (*Freud-Jeanne Lampl-de Groot 27.7.1933*). In August she took the waters in Bad Gastein and was feeling well, but a recurrence of the symptoms apparently led to this operation.

Ruth to America . . .   Fri 25 August 1933

Ruth Mack Brunswick went to the United States to see her father who was very ill. While in the States she spoke with members of the New York Psychoanalytical Society and reported back to Anna Freud. The situation there had been causing Jones and Anna Freud grave concern, mainly through reports from Brill about the trouble he had been having with a younger, Russian-born psychoanalyst, Gregory Zilboorg. According to Jones, Zilboorg was a paranoiac, who was tormenting the long-suffering Brill.

In contrast to Jones, Ruth represented Zilboorg as "gifted, harmless and impetuous," but saw Brill, on the other hand, as "autocratic without a sense for the constitution of the society." Anna was intrigued by the different perspectives the two views presented and said so to Jones. He replied that Ruth's sympathies were with the younger members and this had influenced her report.

Laforgue . . .   Sun 3 September 1933

One topic of discussion with the French psychoanalyst, René Laforgue[1], may have been the exclusion of German emigrants from the French Psychoanalytical Society. At this time the French were refusing to accept foreign doctors to membership of the society if they did not have a French license. In theory they had no objections to foreign lay analysts, but apparently preferred to wait a while until accepting them. This went against the resolutions adopted at the 1929 Oxford Congress and contradicted the internationalist aspirations of the I.P.A..

Jones and Anna Freud were both angered by the insularity of the French attitude. Anna contrasted their exclusion of the emigrants with the way the British had immediately accepted them[2] and she cited a list of examples where the German and Austrian societies had accepted doctors who had only a foreign medical license (Radó, Alexander, Harnik, Lampl-de Groot).

Bryher foundation . . .   Sun 3 September 1933

Bryher's father, the immensely rich financier and shipping magnate Sir John Ellerman, had died on July 16, 1933. As heiress to part of a vast fortune, she was able to set up a fund to assist the training of analysts in Vienna.

Bryher also helped finance the Jewish emigration: letters of her companion, the poet H.D., now in analysis with Freud, show that during her analysis H.D. was discussing this problem with Freud.[1]

Operation—Heart attack—Beginning of illness . . .   Tues 5 September 1933

Pichler's note ten days later tersely summarizes this sequence: "15.9. Patient felt very unwell subsequent to small operation, coronary infarct with angina pectoris. Subsequent to this pneumonia of right lower lobe. All right again now."

According to Anna the infection of the lungs that followed two days after the

René Laforgue, 1934. TG

Hans Lampl (standing) on a Sunday outing in 1912 with Sophie, Martin and Ernst Freud and friends.

operation was caused by Pichler's injection of adrenalin. These had frequently been given previously without any ill-effect; this time, however, Freud suffered a fever and was very sick for a week.

On September 20 he was allowed to get up: "I am out of bed, have already been making a modest start at work for a week, feel *'moderately' well**, but the consequences of the thrombosis have not yet been overcome and I paid for a first attempt to climb my stairs with a hefty relapse." (*Freud-Jones 15.10.1933*)

A few days later Anna reported to Jones: "He had gone out for the first time and did not stand the stairs well. But now he has overcome that again. He is well again and has five patients. The only thing is that he cannot go for walks yet, since we have no [. . .] elevator." (*Anna Freud-Jones 18.10.1933*) On October 24 she added that he was well, but still not able to climb the stairs.

The next day Freud told Arnold Zweig that though alive he was not smoking and consequently unlikely to write anything.[1]

Ernst & Lux come . . .   Sat 16 September 1933

This was the final visit Ernst and his family paid on Freud before their emigration. Before this visit, Freud wrote to Oliver and Henny: "We shall have the joy of a visit from Lux and the boys from 12–18 September before they go to London and because of that we are prolonging our stay at Hohe Warte. We would have liked to have had you too, but we have the impression that you remain nearer to us in France than they are in England . . . ." (*Freud-Liebe Kinder* [*Oli & Henny Freud*] *2.9.1933*)

Pichler for consultation . . .   Tues 19 September 1933

Pichler concluded his treatment with unwelcome advice which Freud had heard often enough before: "Rinsing and orthoform. Inflammation of sinus and nasal secretion much better than ever since patient does not smoke. Advice to give up smoking altogether." Later Freud again had heart trouble, which Pichler thought a consequence of the orthoform anesthetic when he came to examine him the following day. He added: "Patient has not smoked for some time and suffers much from being deprived of it."

Lux departed . . .   Tues 19 September 1933

Ernst Freud's family now settled in England. Their first London address was in expensive lodgings in Mayfair, run by Mr. Humble, an ex-butler. Later they moved out to cheaper accomodations in St. John's Wood.

On returning to England after this visit to Vienna, Lux had to find a school for the boys. She decided to send them to Dartington Hall, a progressive boarding school in Devon. Freud approved; he had heard of this school from a patient, a "first-rate Dutchman" (J. J. van der Leeuw?) who had told him that it was the only school in England where the food was good, too.

Ernst himself returned to Berlin to conclude his affairs there, before joining his family in London in November.

Berggasse . . .   Sat 30 September 1933

A month after this move Mathilde wrote to Ernst Freud: "You know that Papa had a fairly severe cold and Mama has direct symptoms of heart fatigue after the move from Hohe Warte; I am now set on the idea of finding a house for the family for the entire year, but what one sees is all completely impossible!" (*Mathilde Hollitscher-Ernst Freud 1.11.1933*)

Attempted assassination of Dollfuss . . .   Tues 3 October 1933

During the afternoon, Rudolf Drtil, a young ex-soldier, walked into a committee session of the Christian Socialist Party and shot at the Austrian Chancellor Engelbert Dollfuss, but merely grazed him. Since taking office on May 20, 1932, Dollfuss (1892–1934) had suspended parliament on March 4, 1933, and inaugurated a dictatorship—"government by emergency decree"—on March 7. He also banned the Communist and Nazi parties, and this was the cause of the assassination attempt, for Drtil was a Nazi sympathizer.

Freud on an outing at Kahlenberg, near Vienna, early 1930s.

* [in English in the original]

Dollfuss's aim was the destruction of parliamentary democracy and the establishment of an authoritarian corporate system under the "Fatherland Front" set
up in May 1933. The chief obstacle to that end remained the Social Democratic
Party, which represented about 42 percent of the electorate and was the strongest
party in parliament.

Meanwhile, the German Nazis clearly had their eyes on Austria. Freud was not
alone among Austrian Jews in reluctantly supporting Dollfuss's local right-wing
dictatorship as the safest protection against a Nazi victory in Austria. In July he
wrote: "Politics only after the dogs. For the time being it is quiet. We may
assume that we are heading for a specific indigenous fascism which will not be
as brutal as the German. But will it be pleasant to live in Vienna?" (*Freud-
Lampl-de Groot 14.7.1933*)

Dr. Ludwig Bauer . . .   Wed 4 October 1933

Freud knew Dr. Ludwig Bauer as a journalist who had written intelligent articles
on the political situation. Bauer had gained his confidence by presenting himself
as a friend of Arthur Schnitzler and Richard Beer-Hofmann. At his visit Freud
treated him as a friend and discussed the situation in Austria. Some weeks later
an article on Austria appeared in several newspapers. Freud was appalled by
Bauer's fabrications[1]: "He described how I, good old man that I am, highly
regarded and helpless, trembling with fear, had seized him by both hands and had
kept on repeating just the one question: "Do you think they will turn me out,
do you think they will take my books away?" [. . .] I still have a nasty taste in
my mouth from this encounter and he is supposed to be on our side!" (*Freud-
Arnold Zweig 28.1.1934*)

Martin passed Bar exams . . .   Thurs 5 October 1933

Martin Freud was now 44 years old. His academic ability was well above average:
on finishing school at the Maximilian Gymnasium in 1908 he had passed his
Matura (university entrance exam) with distinction. At university he gained a
doctorate in law but had not gone on to qualify as a lawyer since this would have
involved a six-year apprenticeship (as *Conzipient*) in a lawyer's office, on a tiny
salary that would not have supported his wife and two children. Consequently,
he had gone into banking and business instead.

Now, however, the demands of his present work for the press permitted him
to take this final qualification and practice law. In his memoirs Martin wrote of
his new job: "The work, I found, was enormously interesting and rewarding and,
what was a great advantage to me personally, it allowed me some time to devote
to my legal profession. I had been admitted to the Bar Association of Vienna, and
father agreed to my using the press office for legal work."

First outing . . .   Mon 9 October 1933

After this outing Freud stayed indoors. The first snow came early. Martha wrote
in mid-November: "Unfortunately Papa does not go out at all although we have
a sedan-chair standing ready. Partly this is his own, partly his doctors' anxiety.
But curiously enough he hardly misses it." (*Martha Freud-Lucie Freud 13.11.-
1933*)

Martha, who had also been incapacitated, had recovered by that time: ". . . I
can run again and bend as before, the machine is working again, thank God!!"
she wrote.

Dwarf figure & jade for Dorothy . . .   Mon 9 October 1933

The entry is ambiguous. Were both items for Dorothy or only the jade? There
is a dwarf figurine in Freud's collection—an Egyptian faience representing Pataikos (Ptah-Sokar), a manifestation of Ptah, creator god of Memphis—which may
be one of the items in question. If so, it was intended for his own collection.

But Dorothy also collected antiquities to decorate her consulting room. H.D.
described her and her apartment: "She was quiet, slim, and pretty in her art-craft
simple consulting room or sitting room that Freud's architect son had decorated
for her. Like the Professor, she had a few Greek treasures."

This gift (or gifts?) was for her 42nd birthday on October 11.

Martin Freud in Switzerland, 1934. TG

Dwarf Pataikos figure from Freud's
collection. NB

Germany wants to leave League of Nations . . .   Sat 14 October 1933

The second session of the International Disarmament Conference had opened in Geneva on February 2. On March 27 Japan left the League of Nations. Because of the discouraging state of the disarmament conference Germany now walked out and five days later, on October 19, followed Japan's lead in formally leaving the League of Nations. The German parliament was dissolved to allow an election on the issue on November 12.

Mathilde 46 yrs . . .   Mon 16 October 1933

Freud's birthday gift was contained in an envelope on which he wrote: "From Papa with best wishes and assurance against sinking exchange rates." (*Freud-Mathilde Hollitscher 16.10.1933*) Presumably the envelope contained the familiar birthday standby of foreign currency. The amount is not stated. (A previous year's envelope does specify the sum—on October 16, 1924, Mathilde received £15.)

Martin to Zurich . . .   Thurs 19 October 1933

Martin went to Zurich, apparently to establish a base from which to conduct the press's business affairs. Negotiations involving his father's foreign investments may also have been involved.

Martin back . . .   Sat 4 November 1933

The following month Freud wrote to Ernst that, from January 1934 on, he intended taking care of the business through Martin in Zurich. In his two-week visit to that city, Martin had presumably now laid the basis for this new phase.

Stomatitis . . .   Thurs 8 [9] November 1933

On Tuesday Anna Freud sent Ernst a brief report on Freud's condition: "Father is in overall good health, with very many small daily complaints and torments . . . ." (*Anna Freud-Ernst Freud 7.11.1933*)

Pichler visit . . .   Thurs 8 [9] November 1933

Pichler had only visited twice since his final September consultation. Freud misdated this entry, since Pichler's notes date this visit to the following day: "9.11. For the last 2–3 days pain, i.e. diffuse sensitivity of oral mucous membrane whether prosthesis is inserted or not. This disturbs sleep."

10 years since operation . . .   Sun 12 November 1933

This anniversary marks the radical operation performed on November 12, 1923 in which part of Freud's upper jaw and soft palate were removed.[1] Freud's hopes and fears at that period of the first two serious operations were reflected in a remark from a letter to Rank: "Emotionally I have really been leaning quite heavily on Professor Pichler, the second operation brought disappointment, loosening of the homosexual bond. Back to women." (*Freud-Rank 26.11.1923*)

At the time Freud was given a maximum of five years to live[2]: this tenth anniversary marked his and Pichler's success. But the price was high in physical discomfort. It is hardly surprising Freud should be thinking back to that time—Martha wrote that he was now ". . . so tortured by the prosthesis as only before during the first period of the first operation." (*Martha Freud-Ernst & Lucie Freud 29.11.1933*)

German elections . . .   Sun 12 November 1933

This was a rigged election for the new Reichstag. The *Neue Freie Presse* commented that there had never before been elections in which one could only vote in favor of the government. There were no opposition candidates and the Nazi list received 96 percent of the vote. Opposition could only be expressed through spoiling the ballot papers and there were 3 million invalid ballots. At the same time a referendum on Germany's withdrawal from the League of Nations was given approval by 95 percent of the vote.

News of Simmel's arrest . . .   Tues 14 November 1933

As a Jew, a psychoanalyst and an active socialist, Ernst Simmel was an obvious target for Nazi persecution. After this news of his arrest, Ruth Mack Brunswick

Ernst Simmel (right) with Freud at the Tegel Sanatorium.

began immediate efforts to raise $1,000 ransom money to get him out of the country.[1] However, the news appears to have been unfounded; there is no evidence Simmel was actually arrested. But he was forced to flee the country. Meanwhile the S.A. group Berlin-Brandenburg took over Schloss Tegel, his previous psychoanalytical clinic.

New Lectures (Sprott) . . .   Thurs 16 November 1933

W.H.J. Sprott (1897–1971) trained as a clinical psychologist at Cambridge and became Lecturer in Psychology at Nottingham University in 1926. It was his English translation of the *New Introductory Lectures* which Freud now received. The translation was revised by James Strachey and Jones before publication. (It was later supplanted by Strachey's new version in 1964.)

Freud did not know Sprott, remembering him only as a lover of Lytton Strachey's, whom he had once met in Bad Gastein. (In the history of the Bloomsbury Group Sprott also features as having been a lover of John Maynard Keynes.)

Cypriot seal and trove . . .   Thurs 16 November 1933

Freud apparently had an unsystematic coin collection of which nothing remains, perhaps because coins make ideal gifts. This trove may be the six rare gold coins from Crete and Cyprus that Freud gave Arnold Zweig in early 1936.

Ernst left Berlin . . .   Thurs 16 November 1933

While Lux stayed near her sons at Dartington Hall School in Devon, Ernst had been in Berlin arranging affairs. He had now succeeded in doing this and returned to England, where he and Lux moved into lodgings in Clarges Street, Mayfair.

Freud and Martha had read that a great deal of building was going on in London and were hopeful that Ernst would quickly find work there as an architect.[1]

Eitingon . . .   Sat 25 November 1933

Eitingon and his wife emigrated to Palestine in mid-September. He had now moved to Jerusalem. On October 5 Freud sent him, at his request, a testimonial addressed to the Hotel King David, where he was in temporary residence, recommending him as one of the "best known, most influential and honored persons in the psychoanalytical movement of our time."

Eitingon was far more enthusiastic about Palestine than Arnold Zweig and immediately set to work. His first undertaking was to found a Palestine Psychoanalytical Society (*Chewra Psychoanalytith b'Erez Israel*), consisting of four ex-members of the German Society—Moshe Wulff, Anna Smeliansky, Ilja Schalit and himself). He then announced his intention of opening a psychoanalytical institute in Jerusalem.

He had delayed his visit to Europe for a few days to see how the recent outbreak of Arab disturbances in Palestine developed. He and his wife travelled to Berlin overland from Istanbul and spent three days in Vienna on the return journey. He told the Freuds about Palestine and the house he was having built, with oil heating and bathroom. Martha said she could not imagine Eitingon's wife Mirra in Jerusalem, but Eitingon insisted that she had been the driving force behind their emigration.

Anna 38 yrs . . .   Sun 3 December 1933

Instead of spending the entire weekend at Hochrotherd, Anna returned on Sunday morning so the family could celebrate her birthday together. Freud's gift was again jewelry with an "authentication note": "Chinese jewelry (previous century) both plates connected by a needle can be parted and used separately. The ornamentation is fine gold. on 3 Dec. 1933 Love Papa." (*Freud-Anna Freud 3.12.1933*) Martha gave her a book rest to set up next to her armchair.

Mitzi heart attack . . .   Sun 3 December 1933

This incident cast a shadow over Anna Freud's birthday. Freud's sister Mitzi had previously been living in Berlin, but had had to leave her home there (which she greatly missed) and come to Vienna. She was at the party, talking to Martha, when she collapsed with angina. Luckily Ruth Brunswick was there and was able

Anna Freud, early 1930s. Behind her left shoulder stands the vase that was to become Freud's funerary urn.

to give first aid. Only in the evening could Mitzi be taken back to her pension in an ambulance.[1]

Accident at the lamp . . .   Mon 11 December 1933

The word Freud uses for "accident" is "Fall," which may literally mean a fall. Could this have been another attack of vertigo, such as he had on his birthday this year? The lamp in question would be indoors; at this period Freud was not going out at all.[1] In January 1934 Dorothy Burlingham wrote: ". . . one feels so sorry for him that he must always stay in the house . . . ." (*Dorothy Burlingham-Lucie Freud 17.1.1934*)

Mitzi Freud at Bad Ischl, 1930.

"Existence is not worth much any more, but earnings are still good." (*Freud-Ernst Freud 18.11.1933*)

1934

"Faced with the new persecution, one asks oneself again how the Jews have come to be what they are and why they have attracted this undying hatred. I soon discovered the formula: Moses created the Jews . . . ."[1] Spurred by the violent upsurge of antisemitism in Germany, Freud now felt compelled to investigate the origins of Jewishness. The first result of this study appears on September 23, 1934—**Moses finished.** But in fact the work was far from finished. Over the next four years there were to be three more entries, all claiming that *Moses* was "finished," for the figure of the founder of the Jewish faith was to obsess Freud's last years.

The work in question here, *The Man Moses, a Historical Novel*, was eventually to be incorporated into Freud's last completed book, *Moses and Monotheism*, eventually published in 1939. It elaborates the hypothesis that Judaism's origin is obscured by traumas—the murder of its founding father, an Egyptian called Moses, who imposed upon the Jews a version of the Pharoah Akhenaten's sun worship; the merging of the Jewish exiles from Egypt with a group of Midianites; and the conflict between their two religions—the intellectual monotheism of the Egyptian branch and the Midianites' worship of their local volcano god Yahweh. In effect, Freud was once again attempting, as in *Totem and Taboo* (1912-13), to trace a repressed source of contemporary culture by applying the model of unconscious drives to history, and pre-history, as well as to individuals.

Therefore, his fascination with archeology and antiquities was no side-track or mere hobby. A book acquired this year on Wooley's excavations at Ur, the native city of Abraham, or a discovery at Akhenaten's Tell el Amarna, might provide a vital clue in his research on the roots of the Jews—and of antisemitism. The antiquities Freud was constantly adding to his collection were not mere decoration; they, too, served as markers or signposts. To one of his patients, he remarked that the " . . . little statues and images helped stabilize the evanescent idea, or keep it from escaping altogether."[2]

The fleeting ideas Freud was now chasing were the connections between distant traumas and contemporary disasters. In Germany, President Hindenburg's death left Hitler free to form an absolute dictatorship. A series of new laws excluded Jews from professional life. Meanwhile, in Austria this was a particularly dangerous year. February finally brought the anticipated clash between the right-wing Chancellor, Engelbert Dollfuss, and the Social Democrats he had been trying to suppress. A general strike and civil war ended with government forces bombarding workers' apartments in Vienna. A curfew confined the Freuds to their home. Unaware of what exactly was going on, they knew that the events could easily result in a Nazi invasion and they would have to flee. Then, in July, Nazis assassinated Dollfuss. Though a German invasion was again averted, it remained a constant threat, kept at bay, it seemed to Freud, only by Catholic reactionaries' hostility to Nazism.

The European culture in which Freud had grown up was disintegrating. To his enemies, it even seemed he himself had contributed to that catastrophe, for it was he who had destroyed the religious (and humanist) concept of personality as an integral whole. But Freud always held that his work was a product of this culture's supreme achievement, which was the scientific viewpoint. However, in his investigation of the Moses story, he was aware of dropping from this cultural vantage point into unprovable speculation. It was a "historical novel" and hard to defend against the inevitable attacks, both from Christians and Jews. For the time being he refrained from publication, concerned that in these politically precarious times, he might harm his one great cause, the psychoanalytical movement.

1. *Freud-Arnold Zweig 30.9.1934* in *Zweig Letters.*
2. H.D., p.175.

Hebrew Lectures I . . .   Tues 2 January 1934

Freud had completed a "cool and direct" foreword for a planned Hebrew edition of his *Introductory Lectures* on December 14, 1930. He only now received the first volume. It was being published in two volumes in Jerusalem by the Stybel Press, translated by Y. Devosis (J. Dwossis).

Martin kidney stone operation . . .   Fri 5 January 1934

Martin had had kidney trouble before. This time it was precipitated by exertion: on New Year's Eve he strained himself carrying luggage home after a 10-day skiing holiday with his son, Anton Walter. Afterwards he was unable to urinate and three days later an emergency operation to remove the stone was performed in the Rothschild Hospital run by Dr. Edelmann. This was followed by high fever and the necessity of day and night care until the crisis passed. The family brought him delicacies and his wife Esti, according to Martha, behaved very well ". . . only he cannot stand her." (*Martha Freud-Ernst/Lucie Freud 15.1.1934*)

Princess left . . .   Sat 6 January 1934

The diary often records departures without arrivals or vice versa and this is another such instance. Though Princess Marie Bonaparte is one of the most frequently mentioned visitors, not all her visits appear. She was in Vienna again from September 28 to October 9, 1934.

At the time of that (unrecorded) visit Anna Freud had wished to discuss questions concerning the psychoanalytical societies with her. However, she afterwards wrote to Jones: "The Princess was in Vienna. But her mind was full of scientific and literary questions and a book she is going to write. So she was not interested in society questions at all." (*Anna Freud-Jones 24.10.1934*)

Oscar Philipp . . .   Sat 6 January 1934

Oscar Philipp was a cousin of Martha and Minna, his father being their mother's brother. Born in Wandsbeck in 1887, he grew up in the same small Jewish community and their relations with him were those of older sisters. In 1909 he came to England and, with his elder brother Julius, founded the firm of Philipp Brothers, dealing in non-ferrous metal. He was probably in Vienna on business: his visit would have been primarily to his cousins and only incidentally to Freud.

The Freuds were greatly interested in England at this moment because Ernst had just moved there with his family. Martha spoke of their unhappiness when the papers reported fog in London. She gave Philipp three scarves to bring back for Ernst's boys.[1]

X-ray at home . . .   Wed 24 January 1934

Since Pichler's last recorded visit on November 8 [9], twelve more consultations had taken place. The January visits record a steady increase in pain. On January 23 Pichler consulted doctors Eisler and Schur and they decided to treat the pain with X-rays. A portable X-ray apparatus (a great innovation in this period) was moved into Minna's room and the treatment was carried out by Dr. Eisler, a radiologist.

A few days later Anna told Jones: "My father had more pains in his mouth lately and they tried an X-ray treatment now which already relieved some of it." (*Anna Freud-Jones 30.1.1934*) (At this time Anna herself was not well. She was suffering from a troublesome facial eczema.) Over two weeks later, Pichler's notes for February 9 report only a slight improvement as a result of the treatment: "So far no effect of X-ray therapy, may come still. Pain, pressure, lock-jaw all as before but improvement of the permanent pain which persisted also when prosthesis was removed."

Silver wedding Mathilde—Robert & Alex—Sophie . . . Wed 7 February 1934

The twenty-fifth wedding anniversary both of Freud's younger brother Alexander and his eldest daughter Mathilde. She had met Robert Hollitscher and become engaged to him in Meran, where she was recuperating after an operation for cysts, the result of the botched appendectomy in 1905. Their marriage coincided with that of Alexander Freud to Sophie Schreiber.

Martha Freud sent a reminder to Ernst and Lux in London to send greetings to both couples. Though the Hollitschers did not advertise the occasion, their

Alexander Freud on the Adriatic, early 1900s. Before his marriage he sometimes went on holiday with his brother. In 1904 they went to Athens together.

maid reckoned she opened the door to 64 visitors that evening. Freud, Anna, Dorothy and Ruth joined together to buy the couple a radio, Minna gave them a tablecloth and Martha household linen. She wrote afterwards: "In short, they were both radiant, which, as is well known, one cannot say of Robert *every day!*" (*Martha Freud-Ernst/Lucie Freud 12.2.1934*) (In the family, Robert Hollitscher was notorious for his gloomy outlook.)

Martin home . . .   Sat 10 February 1934

After his kidney stone operation Martin Freud had been seriously ill, and there was the risk that another operation might be necessary. By the end of January he was recovering, but his wound had not yet healed. He then went to the Sanatorium Gutenbrunn in Baden to recuperate properly and was still there in early March.

In addition to working for the press, Martin was business administrator for the Vienna Psychoanalytical Society. Consequently they had to suspend all their meetings and courses for two weeks until he had recovered.

He was still shaky and had lost about 18 pounds, which, as Martha wrote, suited him very well. But she added: ". . . we are convinced he will do all he can to make them up again speedily." (*Martha Freud-Lucie Freud 12.2.1934*)

General strike . . .   Mon 12 February 1934

The Social Democratic Party had been under attack ever since Dollfuss came to power. It was pledged to call a general strike should he try to dissolve the party or the trade unions, or impose a fascist constitution. But until now he had cunningly eroded their position while avoiding a direct clash.

On February 11, 1934 the *Heimwehr*, the right-wing paramilitary force, decided to attack provincial party headquarters. Against instructions, Socialist activists in Linz resolved, in the early hours of February 12, to resist by force. This action unleashed a general strike and four days of civil war.

Against the overwhelming combined power of the *Heimwehr*, the army and the public security forces the resistance of the Socialists was heroic, but doomed. In Vienna blocks of council flats, the *Karl Marx-Hof*, formed a center of resistance and was bombarded by the government forces' howitzers.

In this first confrontation between socialism and fascism (a prelude to the Spanish Civil War), Freud wished a plague on both their houses: "We passed through a week of civil war. Not much personal suffering, just one day without electric light, but the 'stimmung' [mood] was awful and the feeling as of an earthquake.[1] No doubt, the rebels belonged to the best portion of the population, but their success would have been very short-lived and brought about military invasion of the country. Besides they were Bolshevists and I expect no salvation from Communism. So we could not give our sympathy to either side of the combatants." (*Freud-H.D. 5.4.1934*)

But by destroying the Socialist movement, the only real opposition to the Nazis, Dollfuss was effectively signing Austria's death warrant. And for the first time Freud was forced to consider seriously the possibility of emigration, only to conclude that at his age it would be suicide.

Ehrenfels jun. . . .   Sat 17 February 1934

This must have been Rolf Ehrenfels, who later converted to Hinduism and became Rolf 'Umar Ehrenfels. He was the son of Freud's previous acquaintance, the philosopher and advocate of sexual freedom, Christian Ehrenfels.

The following year, on April 12, 1935, the widow of Christian Ehrenfels wrote to Freud, asking for her husband's letters to him. This visit may have been in some way a preliminary to her request.

Burlinghams to Italy . . .   Sun 18 February 1934

On hearing of the street-fighting in Austria, Dorothy Burlingham's estranged husband cabled from the United States that she should immediately return the children to America. Instead, she sent them on a trip to Italy with their governess Margot Goldschmidt. They went to Florence and Venice and eventually finished up penniless in Paris and had to borrow money from the Paris branch of Tiffany & Company for their return journey to Vienna.

Viennese armed socialists captured after the Civil War, February 1934. DOW

Egyptian mummy masks in Freud's library. NB

The mummy case, made of gilded cartonnage (c. 600BC), displays amulets of Maat, goddess of divine order and cosmic harmony. WK

King Albert + . . .   Mon 19 February 1934

King Albert I of Belgium (1875–1934), a keen mountain climber, was killed in a climbing accident on February 17 while attempting to scale some cliffs at Marche-les-Dames on the banks of the Meuse. He had ascended the throne in 1909 on the death of his father, Leopold I.

His wife Elisabeth, whom he married in 1900, had many acquaintances among scientists and artists, including a number who were also in contact with Freud, such as Stefan Zweig, Einstein and Roman Rolland. It was on a visit to Rolland, after her husband's death, that she supposedly asked him to write a biography of Albert—an appeal he tactfully ignored.

Lux in accident . . .   Sat 3 March 1934

The car accident involving Lucie Freud had happened a week earlier and it had at first been feared that she had fractured her skull. Ernst had kept the news of the accident from his parents until now, in order not to alarm them.

After the accident Jones visited Lucie Freud in the hospital at Yeovil and sent a detailed report to Freud. In his account he stressed the psychological factors that he felt were impeding her recovery, which in his opinion was slower than her apparently minor injuries warranted.[1] Despite Jones's apprehensions she made a complete recovery.

G. Earle . . .   Thurs 8 March 1934

G. Earle was the American ambassador to Austria. Bullitt had instructed him to offer Freud asylum in the American Embassy, should there be any personal danger to him from the Nazis. (Freud was supposedly at the top of their lists.) Earle was now soon to return to the United States to become Governor of Pennsylvania. He visited Berggasse 19 to see Dorothy Burlingham, who had known him from her youth, and also paid an incidental visit on Freud.

Mummy mask . . .   Thurs 8 March 1934

Three mummy masks hang against the bookshelves in Freud's study. Such masks were originally pegged to the lids of anthropoid coffins, which were substitutes for mummies. These coffin masks are Egyptian New Kingdom (19th Dynasty—1292–1190 B.C.).

Mummy case . . .   Fri 9 March 1934

The dealer Robert Lustig sold Freud this piece. According to his account, Freud was taken by its "nice Jewish face." He did not have enough money to pay for it but offered Lustig instead a drawerful of Etruscan mirrors in exchange.

Catarrh . . .   Mon 12 March 1934

Catarrh may refer to any inflammation of the mucous membrane, with excessive formation of mucus. Freud continually suffered from two varieties of this complaint—nasal and stomach catarrh. In the earliest biography, published in 1924, Wittels wrote that Freud had ruined his stomach in the United States in 1909 and never again rid himself of his stomach catarrh. But here Freud simply wrote "*nein*" in the margin of his copy.

This attack is more likely to be nasal catarrh since Freud had been suffering especially badly from it over the previous years—he called it "the immortal nasal catarrh . . . " (*Freud- Lampl-de Groot 25.1.1933*)

+ Läufer . . .   Wed 14 March 1934
Unknown.

Radium . . .   Fri 23 March 1934

The limited success of the X-rays led the doctors to attempt a more powerful irradiation treatment. It involved inserting the prosthesis with a radium case attached.

According to Pichler's notes, the application was tested the day before: "22.3. Prosthesis with inserted case but without radium inserted to test whether tolerable for 1 hour. (Patient retained it without discomfort for $1\frac{1}{2}$ hours.) 23.3. 50 mg radium inserted for 1 hour. All metal parts coated with lacquer and wax."

Census commission . . .   Thurs 5 April 1934

On March 22 there had been a census. From April 3 to 25, 400 inspectors went systematically through Vienna's 21 districts house by house, checking and correcting details submitted in the census forms.

House Strassergasse seen & rented . . .   Fri 13 April 1934

Because of Freud's heart condition, he could no longer climb stairs. Consequently any house for the summer would have to offer bedroom, workroom and bathroom all on the ground floor. This was not easy to find.

The following day Freud wrote: "After a particularly long and difficult search we rented a house for the summer yesterday. It is XIX Strassergasse 47, that is half way up the hill that is called 'Heaven' at the top, not far from Kobenzl etc. The house seems comfortable, the old garden has a level and a climbing part on which I will be able to practise terrain therapy. For the moment I can only manage very little, paying with heart sensations for every small muscular effort." (*Freud-Eitingon 14.4.1934*)

The owners were "not impoverished Jews, but honest patricians" called von Schöller and their house had ten rooms: Martha called it ". . . old-fashioned but enormously comfortable [*behaglich*] and the garden is simply glorious, perhaps even more beautiful than the one in Poetzleinsdorf." (*Martha Freud-Lucie Freud 8.5.1934*)

Oli from Paris . . .   Fri 20 April 1934

Oliver was finding things difficult in Paris. He did not know French and Freud feared he would get no work there. In October 1933 he had written to Lux: "Nothing hopeful from the Paris branch of the family." (*Freud-Lucie Freud 20.10.1933*) A month after that Martha had added: ". . . now they have been sitting over half a year in Paris and not the glimmer of a prospect!" (*Martha Freud-Lucie Freud 13.11.1933*)

Daly . . .   Sat 21 April 1934

Claude Dagmar Daly (1884–1950) was a major in the Indian Army, in which he had served since around 1905. During World War I he suffered a nervous breakdown which led to a short psychoanalysis in London. In 1924 he came to Freud for analysis; in 1928–9 he was in analysis with Ferenczi. There was an attitude of condescending benevolence in discussions of Daly, for example Freud wrote to Ferenczi:—"Daly is a naive person, but right-minded and is a good fellow." (*Freud-Ferenczi 14.4.1925*)

Daly developed the idea of the "menstruation complex" and published "Der Menstruationskomplex" ("The Menstruation Complex") in *Imago* 14 (1928). In 1934 his wife died. He retired from the army and came to Vienna, where he was to live for the next four years, continuing his analysis with Freud and practicing psychoanalysis himself.

Second radium . . .   Mon 23 April 1934

This second radium treatment had been postponed for two weeks to monitor the inconclusive results of the first dose. Pichler noted: "7.4.[1934] No reaction visible. [. . .] Subjective feeling better in first weeks, rather worse in second. Precautionary postponement of second irradiation. [. . .] 23.4.[1934] Insertion of 50 mg radium for 1 hour 12 min."

Nestroy's works . . .   Tues 24 April 1934

This was the 15-volume complete edition of Nestroy, which Freud now acquired. (*Sämtliche Werke: historisch-kritische Gesamtausgabe.* Edited by Fritz Brukner and Otto Rommel, Vienna 1924–1930.)

Freud frequently quotes Nestroy. A characterization of Nestroy by the Austrian poet Richard Beer-Hofmann indicates some of the reasons why he appealed to Freud: "Nestroy can never turn his back on his intelligence, can never give it even a moment's leave. He can never cease being in command—above all in command of language, he likes to unmask it, he keeps a strict eye on it and loves to catch it out in its small or great dishonesties and in the course of the perpetual hearing to which he exposes it, he forces it to act as chief witness for the prosecution against itself."

Oliver with Eva on holiday, early 1930s.

Nestroy's works, on a top shelf in Freud's library, above the complete Nietzsche and the 126-volume complete Goethe. (Above) The library in Vienna. (Below) The library in London. EE NB

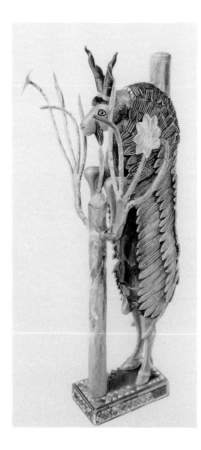

Jekels' departure . . .   Wed 25 April 1934

Ludwig Jekels (1867–1954), one of the first generation of analysts, was of Polish origin. He came to Vienna in 1905, became an analysand of Freud's and a member of the Wednesday Psychological Society. He took part in the First International Congress in Salzburg in 1908. He was primarily responsible for introducing psychoanalysis into Poland and for translating Freud into Polish. After the death of Alfred Rie in 1932 Jekels had joined Freud's Saturday evening games of tarock.

On Freud's recommendation Jekels left for Stockholm to support the newly-founded Finnish-Swedish Psychoanalytical Society, along with Otto Fenichel.[1]

Ur Excavations . . .   Thurs 26 April 1934

The second set of books this week. This was a luxury two-volume set on the Ur excavations, published jointly by the British Museum and the University of Pennsylvania. ("Ur of the Chaldees" was the home town of Abraham, the father of the Jewish race.) Written by the archaeologist Sir Charles Leonard Wooley, the book was entitled *The Royal Cemetery: a report on the predynastic and Sargonid graves excavated between 1926 and 1931.* A volume of photographs depicts some of the spectacular finds from the Great Death Pit, including the famous "ram caught in a thicket," gold and silver lyres, the sledge-chariot, harp and headdress of Queen Shub-Ad.

It is curious that there are only two references to non-psychoanalytical books in the diary—this work and the Nestroy set—and both come within two days of each other.[1]

Oli departed . . .   Thurs 26 April 1934

Oliver's situation was a continuing cause for concern. In September 1933, when Freud heard that he and his family intended moving back from St. Briac to Paris, he advised them not to be over-hasty but to find out first whether there was likely to be any work in Paris.

Freud was also worried that Oliver showed no sign of willingness to adapt and to work in any other speciality than civil engineering, in which he had been trained.

v.d. Leeuw evening . . .   Thurs 26 April 1934

Dr. J. J. van der Leeuw (1893–1934) was a wealthy Dutchman from Rotterdam who set out to apply spiritual laws to contemporary problems. He was General Secretary of the Netherlands Theosophist Society and founder of the Practical Idealist Association for youth and field organizer of the New Education Fellowship. He had also written a number of books, including *The Conquest of Illusion* and *The Dramatic History of the Christian Faith.* His brother was an analysand of Ruth Mack Brunswick and he himself had now come to Freud for a brief period of analysis.

Strassergasse 47 . . .   Sat 28 April 1934

In the morning Freud had an analytical hour in Berggasse 19: in the afternoon, when he moved out to the villa at Grinzing, he was able to sit down at his desk and feel at home: ". . . all his pictures and also the majority of his antiquities were in their places!" (*Martha Freud-Lucie Freud 8.5.1934*) Freud wrote to Lou: "Do not fail to note the address; it indicates the most beautiful garden and the most charming house in which we have ever spent our summer holiday. [. . .] We got out here before 1 May, and the year in its caprice has let us enjoy an uncannily beautiful but unfortunately somewhat premature spring. Here would be the right place—at least for a native of Vienna—'to die in beauty.' " (*Freud-Lou Andreas-Salomé 16.5.1934*)

Freud could now begin his "terrain therapy." He set out to conquer the higher regions of the garden, but gradually. Anna Freud wrote Jones, who was preparing to visit them: "I do not think we have ever been so comfortable in one of our summer places. You will soon see for yourself! He is beginning to walk quite a lot again in the garden and to make up for the lack of sun and air all through the winter." (*Anna Freud-Jones 7.5.1934*)

"The Ram Caught in a Thicket." Plate from Freud's copy of *The Royal Cemetery* by Wooley.

New constitution . . .   Tues 1 May 1934

The new Austrian constitution that was proclaimed on this day laid the legal foundation for an authoritarian régime. In Article 1 of the previous constitution, power was declared as coming from the people: the new constitution was based instead "on the will of God."

At the same time the concordat with the Vatican, signed on June 5, 1933, was ratified to underpin the constitution. Part of the 1920 constitution was preserved, but the Federal Chancellor, Englebert Dollfuss, was granted dictatorial power. Now that left-wing opposition had been crushed, this formal alliance of church and state was seen as Austria's surest defense against the threat of German invasion.

78 years . . .   Sun 6 May 1934

Freud's traditional dislike of birthdays again found expression after this year's birthday, in a note to Eitingon: "Almost everyone who congratulated me on my birthday this year will wait in vain for thanks and acknowledgment. Through this technique I want to train them not to do it again on the next 'occasion.' " (*Freud-Eitingon 27.5.1934*)

Martha, mindful of her husband's well-being, wrote to Lux: "The birthday again brought a rain of flowers but we energetically forbade all visits, even from the family." (*Martha Freud-Lucie Freud 8.5.1934*)

Gisela Ferenczi . . .   Sun 6 May 1934

This appears to contradict Martha's statement about an absolute ban on visitors. (In fact she mentions, as single exception, a visit from Ina Lewisohn with her daughter.)

However, if another exception to the ban was to be made, no doubt it would have been in favour of Ferenczi's widow, Gisela, for the Freuds got on well with her. Freud spoke of her constant amiability (in contrast to Ferenczi's own later moodiness) and he was impressed by her strength in the face of her husband's illness and death.

Ivory Buddha and stone dog of Fo . . .   Mon 7 May 1934

Freud had two ivory Buddhas—both quite rare 16th-17th century figures from the Burmese borders of Thailand. The standing figure represents the penitent, walking Buddha, the other, seated with right hand extended to the ground, is the earth-touching Buddha. *Fo* is Chinese for Buddhism and the "dog" of *fo* was originally a lion—an image that came to China from India in the 3rd century A.D. In the course of time this fearsome guardian figure changed into a playful dog (the Pekinese was bred to resemble them).

Freud's "dog of *fo*" is a heavy stone figure, seated on its hind legs. These pieces are possibly belated birthday gifts.

Gardenia . . .   Fri 18 May 1934

Though Freud's love of orchids was well-known, gardenias were his favorite flowers.[1] For him this flower represented memories of Rome and some of the best times of his life.

In 1912 he wrote from Rome: "I have never looked after my appearance so much nor lived so idly and so much according to my own wishes and well-being. Today I even found and bought a gardenia, whose scent put me in the best of moods. Minna knows the flower, it is even nobler than the Datura." (*Freud-Martha Freud 20.9.1912*)

Sarapis and fountain bull . . .   Mon 4 June 1934

From about 600 BC to the Roman Period in Egypt, Sarapis was one of the most important forms of the god Osiris. He was a Hellenized fusion of the bull-god Hep (the Apis of the Greeks) with Osiris and was sometimes represented as a man with a bull's head or a Zeus-like figure with horns. Freud is probably referring here to a small clay statuette of a male deity bearing on its head a corn pot symbolizing fecundity.[1]

"Fountain bull" (*Brunnenstier*) is unclear. One possibility is a bull drinking vessel or rhyton. There is also a small nephrite figurine of a water buffalo with a boy on its back. This was a favorite Chinese subject: the figure could date from 17th-20th century.

Freud's ivory, earth-touching Buddha. NB

The ivory, penitent Buddha. (See also overleaf.) NB

+ Groddeck und + Frau Zweig . . .   Thurs 14 June, 1934

Georg Groddeck (1866–1934) had founded a sanatorium in Baden-Baden in 1900, where he practiced a form of therapy taken from his Berlin teacher, Ernst Schweninger, and involving a combination of massage, diet, baths, suggestion and lectures. From 1909 his treatment became progressively more influenced by psychoanalysis and in 1917 he published a pioneer work of psychoanalytically-oriented psychosomatic medicine—*Psychical Dependence and the Psychoanalytical Treatment of Organic Diseases* (*Psychische Bedingtheit und psychoanalytische Behandlung organischer Krankheiten* Hirzel, Leipzig, 1917).

Freud respected Groddeck's instinctive grasp of psychoanalysis and borrowed from him the concept of the id which Groddeck had propounded in his controversial novel: *The Book of the It* (*Buch vom Es. Psychoanalytische Briefe an eine Freundin* I.P.V. 1923).

Freud did not dismiss stories that, like their mutual friend Ferenczi, Groddeck had supposedly become unbalanced before his death.[1] He wrote to Jones: "Rumour has it that in the end Groddeck was committed as mentally disturbed. The obituary says he died in Zurich; what business did he have in Z.? Was he then in Burghölzli? The times demand their sacrifice. People die, perhaps more willingly than usual." (*Freud-Jones 16.6.1934*) But Groddeck had simply collapsed and died in a hospital.

Frau Stella Zweig was a highly capable and popular assistant at the International Psychoanalytical Press. Her sudden death, together with Groddeck's, shocked Freud: "Yesterday we learnt that Mrs. Stella Zweig, Martin's invaluable aide at the press, had fallen victim to an attack of poliomyelitis of the Landry type. A difficult predicament for the press. It is fine here in Grinzing but one is not glad to be alive. The foundations are shaking." (*Freud-Jones 16.6.1934*)

S.A. revolt in Germany . . .   Sat 30 June 1934

This was the "Night of the Long Knives." One of Hitler's earliest Nazi comrades, Röhm, was in charge of the S.A.. He and his chiefs had tried to foment a second, "national" revolution and create a "*Volksheer*" (People's army) made up of S.A. bands. In doing so, they threatened Hitler's image as a stable figure upon whom the big industrialists could rely.

Röhm's murder and this purge of the S.A. was carried out by means of their rival organization, the S.S., under Himmler's control.

Two weeks later Freud told Arnold Zweig: " . . . after the news of June 30th I had just one feeling—what, I'm supposed to leave the table after the hors-d'oeuvres! There's nothing more to come? I'm still hungry." (*Freud-Arnold Zweig 15.7.1934*)

Ophthalmic migraine with illness . . .   Wed 4/Thurs 5 July 1934

This was a violent attack of what Pichler described as "flimmer-scotomatous migraine." Freud ascribed it to the radium treatment but Pichler disagreed and advised that the treatment should be continued but with smaller doses over lengthened intervals.

Schur consulted a radium expert, Dr. Schloss, about the side-effects and learned that the metal of the prosthesis could have produced secondary radiation. After that, a specially constructed prosthesis was used during the treatments. This prosthesis was later remodelled into a replacement for the old Kazanjian one which was no longer functioning. The side-effects continued, but the treatment was effective in containing the cancer.

A month later Pichler noted: "9.8.[1934] Had another very bad day: migraine, heart trouble, bad speech and severe local discomfort. Objectively: whole former swelling subsided and smooth." By the end of the month a suspect brown spot had vanished completely.

Meteor stone . . .   Mon 9 July 1934

There is no longer any meteorite fragment in Freud's collection: it may have been left behind in Vienna or given away.

Collection cabinet in Freud's front study in London. The ivory Buddhas stand on the top shelf. NB

Harry Karlsbad . . .   Mon 9 July 1934

A visit by Freud's nephew to Karlsbad (*Karlovy Vary*), the popular spa in Bohemia which Freud himself frequently visited before and during World War I. The entry may mean that Harry paid Freud a visit either before or after his Karlsbad journey.

Ernstl on tour . . .   Thurs 12 July 1934

Evidently Freud's 20-year-old grandson Ernstl set out on some sort of holiday or trip. Unfortunately, W. Ernest Freud no longer has any memory of this tour.

Lion-dragon . . .   Thurs 12 July 1934

This could be a Buddhist jade lion paperweight, (Chinese, Qing Dynasty). It might, however, refer to the heavy stone lion figure, now on the shelf facing Freud's desk at Maresfield Gardens, but that figure is more likely to be the "Dog of Fo" Freud acquired on May 7, 1934.

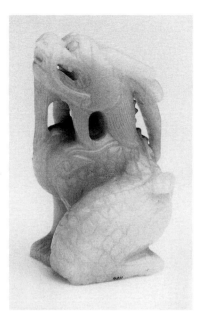

Sarasin . . .   Fri 13 July 1934

Philipp Sarasin (1888–1968) studied psychoanalysis under Freud before World War I and afterwards became a founding member and President of the Swiss Psychoanalytical Society. In 1930 he published *Goethes Mignon, eine psychoanalytische Studie* and presented a copy to Freud with a dedication.

Since 1928 Sarasin had been on the editorial board of the *Internationale Zeitschrift für Psychoanalyse*. In 1932, when problems with the press led to the question of establishing an international supervisory committee to look after its affairs, Freud recommended Sarasin to Jones as a prospective member, but with a proviso: "Sarasin is close to me as a personal pupil, I would also recommend him for any confidential position, only I would not expect business acumen from him." (*Freud-Jones 17.6.1932*)

Chinese Lectures . . .   Mon 16 July 1934

This appears to be the only Chinese translation Freud received. It was the *Introductory Lectures* translated by Kao Chio-Fu and published by The Commercial Press, Shanghai (1933).

Dr. Sachs, Johannesburg . . .   Tues 17 July 1934

Dr. Wulf Sachs (1893–1949) was born in St. Petersburg and studied in the psychoneurological institute of Pavlov and Bechterev. He then took a London medical degree and in 1922 emigrated to South Africa. In 1934 he published *Psychoanalysis—Its Meaning and Practical Applications*, with a foreword by Freud. At this time Sachs was in charge of a small South African psychoanalytical group. In 1933 only two of its members had been in Europe and undergone something like a standard analysis—Sachs himself, who in 1929–30 had spent six months with Reik in Berlin, and MacCrone, who had been analyzed by Dr. Adrian Stephen in London.

Freud, Anna and Jones were intrigued by the idea of a South African group, but wary at first about allowing it immediate independent status. Initially it was to be affiliated to London in 1935 as a Study Group.[1]

Ernst from Berlin . . .   Sat 21 July 1934

Lux was still convalescing after her car accident and Martha Freud had wanted her to come to Grinzing to recover. She offered her the prospect of a garden room shaded by a chestnut tree, walks in the garden with "Papa" [Freud] and card games in the evening. However, in the end Ernst had to come to Vienna, via Berlin, without her.

Dollfuss +: Putsch in the Ballhaus . . .   Wed 25 July 1934

Since the beginning of the year the threat of a German invasion had been hanging over Austria. After Austria registered an offical complaint about German intervention in her affairs, Italy, France and Great Britain signed a tripartite declaration of Austrian independence.

In spite of this, Freud did not trust Mussolini. In June, when Hitler and Mussolini were meeting for the first time in Venice, Freud wrote to Jones: "Perhaps at this very moment the schemer M. has sold us to the robber chieftain H. in Venice." (*Freud-Jones 16.6.1934*) [1]

Meanwhile, the Austrian authorities had been informed of a plot against Dollfuss, but did nothing. The band of Nazi conspirators who broke into the

Chinese jade lion-dragons from Freud's collection. NB

Engelbert Dollfuss's corpse, laid out after the 1934 putsch. DOW

ministry on the Ballhausplatz succeeded in murdering the chancellor, but the uprising was rapidly quelled. At the same time Mussolini forestalled a possible German invasion by mobilizing Italian troops at the Brenner Pass.

Dollfuss was given a hero's burial and turned into the object of a posthumous personality cult. But his appeal was primarily to the peasants and bourgeoisie, not to "Red Vienna."[2] He was succeeded as Chancellor by a young lawyer from Innsbruck, Kurt von Schuschnigg.

Martha 73 yrs. . . .   Thurs 26 July 1934

The previous year Freud had neglected even to note Martha's birthday. But a concern for her health showed through family letters over the year—for example, that she had eczema on her hands and feet, that she was not in good condition and refused to take medical advice.

Son to Marianne . . .   Thurs 26 July 1934

The birth of a son, Anton, to Marianne Kris, the wife of Ernst Kris and Freud's so-called "adopted daughter."[1]

+ Hindenburg . . .   Tues 2 August 1934

With the death of President Hindenburg at the age of 86, the only counterbalance to Hitler disappeared. The German Wehrmacht was immediately declared loyal to Hitler, who by decree became henceforth "Führer und Reichskanzler."

On August 20 a law forced all soldiers and civil servants to swear allegiance to Hitler personally.

Freud was obviously disturbed by the political uncertainty. He wrote to the American, Smith Ely Jelliffe: "This very day the news of the death of the German President Hindenburg has come and nobody can guess what consequences developments in Germany may have for our poor Austria. We would be enjoying beautiful summer peace in a delightful suburb of Vienna if the political situation allowed it." (*Freud-Jelliffe 2.8.1934*)

Eitingon . . .   Sat 18 August 1934

After a long, enthusiastic letter to Freud written in November 1933 soon after emigrating to Palestine, Eitingon did not write again until July 1934, to announce his intention of attending the Lucerne Congress and of visiting Vienna. This letter admitted that it had not been easy to settle down and there had been moments of depression. However, he now felt he had established himself and had several analysands. Also, he was waiting to hear whether a chair of psychoanalysis would be established at the University of Jerusalem.

Nunberg . . .   Mon 20 August 1934

After teaching in Philadelphia from 1931 to 1932, Hermann Nunberg returned to Vienna with his family.[1] When Hitler came to power he realized Austria was doomed and arranged to return permanently to the United States.

On this visit to Vienna Nunberg implored Freud to leave Austria. But Freud thought the government would protect Jews and not give way to the Nazis, and he even tried to persuade Nunberg to stay. (By 1936, when Nunberg paid him another visit, Freud had changed his mind and advised him to keep away.) On his return to the United States Nunberg moved to New York, but continued for a time to lecture in Philadelphia.

Marianne Kris, mid-1930s. Her husband Ernst Kris stands back to the camera.

Max Eitingon speaking with Thomas French, Lucerne 1934. TG

Hermann Nunberg with Anna Freud, Paris 1938.

Jones . . .   Wed 22 August 1934

Jones and Anna Freud had spent many months organizing the imminent International Psychoanalytical Congress at Lucerne Just before his visit she wrote to him: "I think it was an excellent idea of you to come to Vienna *before*, not after the Congress.[1] We will probably be able to have the main points settled before we arrive in Lucerne, as f.i. [for instance] the question of the Beirat [committee], how to deal with the American lay question in Brill's absence, the former German members etc." (*Anna Freud-Jones 18.8.1934*)

Their day-to-day correspondence over the year, as well as the meetings in Vienna and in Lucerne, brought them even closer together. Before the conference she had always addressed her letters "Dear Dr. Jones," afterwards they begin "Dear Ernest." (He, being her senior, always began "Dear Anna"). Each expressed their gratitude to the other with gifts. Jones wrote: "The beautiful Mappe [brief case] you gave me travels every day to Harley Street except when it is raining, for which I keep an older case. I have just procured for you a fountain pen with a nib like mine, only better, and will bring it with me." (*Jones-Anna Freud 2.4.1935*)

Alexander . . .   Sat 25 August 1934

A meeting with Dr. Franz Alexander, not with Freud's brother Alexander. This may be the occasion on which Dr. Alexander brought with him his American analysand, Dr. Karl A. Menninger, who was also in Europe to attend the Lucerne Congress.

Freud's impressions of Alexander were to be strongly coloured by his own hostility to America. On July 20, 1932 there had been another meeting, not recorded in the diary, after which Freud wrote: "I would like to have unwavering confidence in Alexander; I can't quite manage it. His true or pretend simplicity estranges him from me. Or my mistrust for America is not to be overcome." (*Freud-Eitingon 21.7.1932*)

Anna to Lucerne . . .   Sat 25 August 1934

The Congress was due to begin the next day, the culmination of months of organization, done mostly by Jones and Anna Freud. One of the organizational problems had been the large number of papers offered—by June there were 62, of which a third had to be rejected. Since only their titles had been submitted, any rejection could only be on a personal basis. Anna disliked this idea and wanted the branches themselves, not the organizers, to limit the number.

She explained her feelings to Jones: "You know, you must not think that I am too much afraid of not pleasing everybody and of hurting people's feelings. I have learned of course that that is unavoidable. Only what I hate so is the division between 'big' people and 'small' people and even if we try to term them 'interesting' and 'dull' when we think about it, that is the way it may turn out so easily. That really is my main worry about it." (*Anna Freud-Jones 15.6.1934*)

+ v.d. Leeuw . . .   Wed 29 August 1934

Freud had nicknamed J. J. van der Leeuw the "Flying Dutchman." He had flown his own plane to a conference in Johannesburg. On the return flight he crashed in Tanganyika and was killed.

During the spring he had been Freud's analysand and the analysis had revealed desires that were liable to impel him "to fly too high, to fly too quickly . . ." As he told the poet H.D. (Hilda Doolittle), Freud felt he had found the solution after van der Leeuw had left, but by then it was too late.

Anna from Lucerne . . .   Sat 1 September 1934

The Lucerne Congress was a success: Anna wrote to Jones afterwards that the "impression that the Americans made was the only really bad aftertaste from Lucerne . . . ." (*Anna Freud-Jones 20.9.1934*)

Meanwhile, Eitingon reported to Freud that Anna had proved her skill and efficiency in resolving difficult problems. The previous day she had given her paper "On the Problem of Puberty," which dealt with the parallels between the drives during the first period of childhood and those at puberty.

After the long preparations and the Congress itself, she was glad to retreat to her cottage at Hochrotherd: "I cut grass on my clover field as much of one day as my arms would stand it and I felt very good after it. I had all sorts of reactions to the Congress but by now, I think, I have digested it." (*Anna Freud-Jones 20.9.1934*)

One fortunate consequence was that (on Jones's initiative) she was replaced as Central Secretary by Glover. This was one burden removed and a second one was that the Vienna Training Institute relieved her of the task of secretary. She told Jones: "It sounds as if I ought to have a lot of free time now but I am trying to put other work in its place." (*Anna Freud-Jones 24.10.1934*)

Anna Freud and Ernest Jones on the podium at Lucerne. The speaker is Ernst Kris. At the far right sits J. W. van Ophuijsen. TG

Franz Alexander and Marie Bonaparte outside the Lucerne congress hall. TG

Anna Freud speaking at Lucerne. TG

Lucerne congress, 1934. From right, Paul Federn, Ludwig Jekels, Carl Müller-Braunschweig. TG

Radó . . .   Tues [Mon] 3 September 1934

Since emigrating to New York in 1931, Radó had been the first director of the psychoanalytical training institute, set up there on Berlin lines by Bertram Lewin,

Abram Kardiner and Monroe A. Meyer in 1930. He was now one of the "Americans" and Anna wrote: "Radó passed through Vienna still and he came and talked with me for hours. But there is no feeling of security with him either, even though he is surely far above the level of the 'real' Americans." (*Anna Freud-Jones 20.9.1934*)

Later this year Radó sent Anna Freud a report to the International Journal. She would not accept it without drastic alteration. As a protest he resigned in 1935 from his post as Secretary of the International Training Commission, which he had held since 1927, and from all movement business.

Jones feared he was going the way of Rank and would next be starting a new movement in the United States. In March 1935 Radó was accusing Anna Freud and Eitingon of trying to rule the analytic world.[1]

Eros Myrina . . .   Wed 5 September 1934

This dramatic terracotta statuette is the largest of several Eros figures in Freud's collection. Originally the arms held something such as a lyre. It comes from Myrina, c.150–100 B.C.

XII Volume Collected Edition . . .   Fri 14 September 1934

This was the 12th and final volume of the *Gesammelte Schriften*–the first collected edition of Freud's writings. It contained his work from 1928 to 1933, which included *Civilization and its Discontents* and the *New Introductory Lectures* as well as some shorter pieces. Freud was occasionally dismissive of some of his recent writings. Even so, the existence of a collected edition was gratifying. In his postcript to *An Autobiographical Study* (1935) Freud proudly cites this 12th volume as proof that in the ten years since his first operation for cancer he continued both his analytical work and his writing.

Moses finished . . .   Sun 23 September 1934

The first page of the manuscript *The Man Moses: A Historical Novel* (*Der Mann Moses: Ein historischer Roman*) [1] is dated August 9, 1934, presumably the date when it was begun. But a letter to Arnold Zweig from the previous year shows that the themes of this work were already preoccupying Freud: "One protects oneself in every way against castration, a piece of opposition to one's own Jewishness may be concealed here. For our great master Moses was a strong anti-semite and makes no secret of it. Perhaps he was really an Egyptian." (*Freud-Arnold Zweig 18.8.1933*)

A week after finishing this draft Freud wrote to Arnold Zweig: " . . . I have written something myself and this, contrary to my original intention, took up so much of my time that everything else was neglected. [. . .] The starting point of my work is familiar to you [. . .] Faced with the new persecution, one asks oneself again how the Jews have come to be what they are and why they have attracted this undying hatred. I soon discovered the formula: Moses created the Jews. So I gave my work the title: *The Man Moses, a historical novel . . . .*" (*Freud-Arnold Zweig 30.9.1934*)

Freud was convinced the work could not be published, since it would bring about a prohibition of analysis by the Catholic authorities and " . . . it is only this Catholicism which protects us from the Nazis." (*Freud-Lou Andreas-Salomé 6.1.1935*)

Assassination in Marseilles . . .   Tues 9 October 1934

On October 9, 1934, King Alexander I of Yugoslavia and the French Foreign Minister, Jean Barthou, were assassinated in Marseilles. Alexander had been proclaimed monarch of the Serbo-Croato-Slovene State of Yugoslavia in 1918 and in 1929 had taken over as royal dictator. Macedonians and Croats opposed his rule and their terrorist groups were behind this assassination.[1]

At Berggasse . . .   Sat 13 October 1934

Anna Freud told Jones that "moving with us is always a lengthy and strenuous process. . . ." (*Anna Freud-Jones 24.10.1934*) Martha's comments to her daughter-in-law Lux confirm this: "This time we were away for exactly $5\frac{1}{2}$ months, in that time all sorts of things accumulate! And I am really looking forward to the winter traffic regulations." (*Martha Freud-Lucie Freud 12.10.1934*)

Freud, not actively involved in that aspect of the move, simply commented: "Berggasse is not quite so beautiful as Grinzing. Health, falsely so called, could be more enjoyable." (*Freud-Eitingon 27.10.1934*)

Mathilde 47 yrs. . . .   Tues 16 October 1934

Since Mathilde and Robert Hollitscher lived nearby, it is possible they could have visited or eaten with the Freuds, but there is no mention or documentary evidence of that for this year.

Lux . . .   Sat 3 November 1934

Freud and Marthe were extremely fond of Ernst's wife Lux, who had now come from England to stay with them. But when Martha heard that the visit would only last four days, she let Ernst know of her disappointment, for she had expected Lux to stay at least two weeks.

Dozent post annulled . . .   Mon 26 November 1934

Freud had been a *dozent* (lecturer) at the University of Vienna since June 1885. The post, formally entitling the holder to teach, guaranteed status but not income. After Dollfuss's rise to power the university fell under extreme right-wing control. Freud's enemies could now use his age and nonfulfilment of his duties as a legalistic pretext to remove his name from university records.

The letter informing Freud of this decision is dated November 23, 1934, and cites as justification an ordinance of May 23, 1934, according to which a dozent post can be annulled without reason after the holder's 70th birthday.

Hormone injection . . .   Mon 26 November 1934

A remark of Schur's explains this entry: ". . . Freud's general condition was also better. He was receiving injections of male hormone at regular intervals mainly for its anabolic action. (The androgen extracts available at that time were already somewhat effective, although not yet as standardized as they are now.) Whatever their pharmacological effect, he responded quite well to them. [1]

"This [1934] was to be the only year without surgical intervention!"

Anna 39 yrs . . .   Mon 3 December 1934

According to tradition Martin's gift was accompanied by birthday verses. On this occasion he donated an old suit of his, to be worn by her "faithful servant" at Hochrotherd (perhaps Herr Faddenberger, who with his wife looked after the house?):

      "To the country comes the ancient suit
        There to enjoy, 'midst cow and hen,
        Its well-deserved retirement."

Martin 45 yrs. . . .   Fri 7 December 1934

It is very likely Martin celebrated this birthday with the Freuds, since he and his wife Esti were leading completely separate social lives.

Fibrillation . . .   Fri 14 December 1934

Freud began experiencing irregularities of heartbeat—arrhythmia—in 1889, after an attack of influenza. After one such "heart warmth attack" on November 14, 1929, he listed his symptoms as "extra systoles, arrhythmia, attacks of fibrillation [*Flimmern*]." (*Freud-Ferenczi 13.12.1929*) This particular attack is not mentioned elsewhere, either by Schur or Pichler.

Dr. Fleischer . . .   Fri 14 December 1934

Since Freud first wrote the name as "*Fischer*," then crossed it out, this may imply that the visitor was an unfamiliar person. Perhaps this was a doctor called in on account of the heart trouble.

Vagus attack . . .   Sun 16 December 1934

Schur states that Freud was prone to "vasovagal reflex," which resulted in a number of varied symptoms including circulatory and cardiac disorders. (The vagus is the tenth cranial nerve, a major component of the parasympathetic nervous system.)

Frau Faddenberger at Hochrotherd with the cottage's first hen and egg.

Freud in his study, mid-1930s.

1935

"My mood is bad, little pleases me, my self-criticism has grown much more acute . . . " Freud wrote in February 1935[1]. He would have interpreted this as "senile depression" in anyone else, he added. His physical condition may have been partly to blame for this mood. Heart trouble and general bad health had kept him housebound all winter. Another factor may have been the study of Moses. Freud was continuing his research and background reading on this theme, but could make no headway. And of course there was the dire political situation. The Saar plebiscite in January gave back to Germany lost territory and provided Hitler with an enormous propaganda victory. He was now unmistakably preparing for war: soon afterwards a Luftwaffe was created and universal conscription introduced. Consequently, Austria's fragile independence remained under threat. In July the Austrian Chancellor Schuschnigg, who had replaced the assassinated Dollfuss, was injured in a car accident. Had he been killed, the subsequent crisis could easily have precipitated the end for Austria. Small wonder that Freud saw " . . . a cloud of disaster passing over the world, even over my own little world."[1]: his forebodings denoted clarity, rather than clouding, of the intellect.

During 1934 the cancer had been kept at bay by x-ray and radium treatment and the entire year went by without operations. Now they again became necessary; there were four in 1935. Moreover, the existing prosthesis became so agonizing that a new one had to be constructed. In addition to that, Freud suffered further heart trouble during the summer. But he continued working, despite interruptions imposed by bad health and operations: in the summer, however, he was reduced to two analysands. His old age was following what he had once described as the most merciful pattern of decay - " . . . survival of mental life accompanied by physical decrepitude . . . ."[2]

The summer was spent, like the previous four summers, in a rented villa on the outskirts of Vienna. His chow Jofi enjoyed the freedom after the dark Berggasse appartment, and Freud could stroll or lie in the garden. As usual, pieces of Freud's collection were also moved to the summer residence, so that he could work there surrounded by the familiar statuettes. But the domestic routine could not block out the changes in the world. In autumn the Nuremberg Laws were passed in Germany, reducing all Jews to outcasts. "The times are dark . . . ."[3]

1. *Freud-Arnold Zweig 13.2.1935 in Zweig Letters.*
2. *Freud-Pfister 7.2.1930 in Pfister Letters.*
3. *Freud-Arnold Zweig 2.5.1935 in Zweig Letters.*

Gastric attack—vomiting . . .   **Tues 1 January 1935**

Freud had suffered from gastrointestinal symptoms for many years. From 1910 to 1917 he regularly visited Karlsbad to take the waters as a cure for his chronic constipation. Schur diagnosed the complaint that afflicted him during the 1930s as an irritable, spastic colon and he also implied a possible connection with the vasovagal reflex. This present upset stomach might merely relate to something eaten: it could, however, be a further symptom of the disorders signalled by the recent vagus attack.

Martin back from Nice . . .   **Wed 9 January 1935**

After living a short time in Paris and St. Briac, Oliver Freud and his family settled in Nice. Martin had probably visited them there.

Saar plebiscite . . .   **Sun 13 January 1935**

The Treaty of Versailles had taken the rich industrial region of the Saar from Germany, and since then it had been governed by a League of Nations commission. This had crippled Germany's economy after the war and made it impossible to repay the enormous reparation imposed by the allies.

Inevitably, popular feeling both in Germany and the Saar held that the territory should be returned. The plebiscite resulted in over 90 percent voting in favor of union with Germany.

Regaining the Saar was Hitler's first great success in foreign politics. Like succeeding triumphs it was a feat of diplomatic brinkmanship. Ernest Jones wrote to Federn in December 1934: "We may hope for some clearing of the air after the Saar vote and to know whether it is to be peace or war in 1935." (*Jones-Federn 4.12.1934*)

+ Anna v. Vest . . .   **Wed 23 January 1935**

Anna von Vest (1861–1935) had died three days previously, on January 20, in Ebenthal near Klagenfurt where she had spent all her life. She was an early patient of Freud's, who had suffered from a hysterical paralysis of the legs and had come to him for treatment in 1903. The analysis lasted about a year; most of the symptoms cleared up but the patient appears not to have overcome her transference love for Freud. Consequently she was not entirely cured and in 1925 re-entered analysis for a short time. At the time Freud had six analytical hours and could not make space for another. However, one of the hours was his daughter's training analysis and she agreed to sacrifice every second hour to Anna v. Vest. As Freud wrote to her: "In place of one Anna I will get another." (*Freud-Anna v. Vest 26.3.1925*)

Anna's Lecture . . .   **Wed 23 January 1935**

During her Christmas holidays Anna Freud had continued working on the manuscript of her book and also on two lectures for the Vienna Psychoanalytical Society. The society was to devote three evenings to a discussion on "The Usefulness of Psychoanalytic Technique for the Study of the Mental Agencies." The "mental agencies" are substructures of the psychical apparatus, such as the ego, the id and the super-ego. Anna used her lectures to elaborate the theory behind her current work on the ego and defence mechanisms.

Her progress pleased Freud: "My one source of satisfaction is Anna. It is remarkable how much influence and authority she has gained among the general run of analysts—many of whom, alas, have derived little from analysis as far as their personal character is concerned. It is surprising, too, how sharp, clear and unflinching she is in her mastery of the subject. Moreover, she is truly independent of me; at the most I serve as a catalyst." (*Freud-Lou Andreas-Salomé 6.1.-1935*)[1]

Postscript to An Autobiographical Study . . .   **Sun 27 January 1935**

Freud's *Autobiographical Study* (*Selbstdarstellung*) was originally published in 1925 in a series called *Contemporary Medicine in Self-Portrayals* (*Die Medizin der Gegenwart in Selbstdarstellungen*), which aimed at presenting a history of medicine though the accounts of its most important representatives. The *Postscript* was specially written for its republication by W.W. Norton in New York.

The English title—*An Autobiographical Study*–is slightly misleading. In this

Eva on the step of Oliver's photo shop at Nice. Photo inscribed "for grandfather."

Postscript Freud makes it clear that no intimate revelations should be expected[1]: "This *Autobiographical Study* shows how psycho-analysis came to be the whole content of my life and rightly assumes that no personal experiences of mine are of any interest in comparison to my relations with that science."

Lévy-Bruhl . . .   Wed 6 February 1935

The French ethnologist Lucien Lévy-Bruhl (1857–1939) was the author of a series of works on "primitive" thought processes.[1] On this visit to Freud, Lévy-Bruhl gave Freud a dedicated copy of *La Mythologie primitive: le Monde mythique des Australiens et des Papous* (Paris 1935).

The next day Freud wrote to Marie Bonaparte: "He is the real *savant*, especially in comparison with myself." This may be a rueful comment on Freud's own recent work on the genesis of culture. Despite his respect, Freud did not get around to studying the copy of the book Lévy-Bruhl gave him—its pages are uncut.

Anna's 2nd Lecture . . .   Wed 6 February 1935

This was the second of Anna's two lectures to the Vienna Psychoanalytical Society. Later she told Jones: "I have finished my lectures here, that gave me so much to do lately. My subjects were the unconscious activities of the ego or the defense-mechanisms. It was really the theoretical background of the paper about puberty that I read at the Congress." (*Anna Freud-Jones 25.2.1935*)

Her energy continued to delight Freud, who was otherwise in a bad mood: "I would diagnose it as senile depression in anyone else. I see a cloud of disaster passing over the world, even over my own little world. I must remind myself of the one bright spot, and that is that my daughter Anna is making such excellent analytic discoveries just now and—they all tell me—is delivering masterly lectures on them. An admonition therefore not to believe that the world will end with my death." (*Freud-Arnold Zweig 13.2.1935*)

Dr. Gerard . . .   Tues 18 February 1935

The American Dr. Ralph W. Gerard was later to become Director of Laboratories in the Mental Health Research Institute of the Department of Psychiatry at the University of Michigan. He was now visiting various laboratories and centers for the study of neurology, physiology and psychiatry, on behalf of the Rockefeller Foundation.

In Leningrad he had visited Pavlov and discussed his work on the conditioned reflex. While speaking of inducing neuroses in dogs by setting them a too difficult task, Pavlov mentioned that he had been led to these experiments by reading Freud's work. Pavlov added that Freud's thought had stimulated his own and that he anticipated a fusion of psychoanalysis and conditioned reflex studies would lead to a deeper understanding of human behavior.

Dr. Gerard then visited Freud and told him of this conversation. Freud responded: "It would have helped if Pavlov had stated that publicly a few decades ago."

Oli 44 yrs. . . .   Wed 19 February 1935

Presumably Oliver celebrated this birthday in France: I have found no evidence that he came to Vienna. Unable to find work in his own field as a civil engineer, Oliver was following Freud's advice to seek work elsewhere. He went instead into the photography business. As Freud commented: "In this way he has at any rate found work which satisfies his practical urges." (*Freud-Arnold Zweig 13.6.-1935*)

Minna to Meran . . .   Fri 22 February 1935

Another of Minna's regular visits to this resort, with the difference that in 1931 and 1932 she had gone there in autumn. The reason for this visit may be partly because of the trouble she had been having with her eyes, which made an operation for glaucoma necessary the following year.

+ Otto Fleischl (News) . . .   Thurs 28 February 1935

After two visits noted in June 1931 there was no further mention of Otto Fleischl, possibly because, shortly after that, he may have left for Lucerne, where

The Dolomites, not far from Meran, Minna's favorite resort. This photo was a record of Freud's holiday in San Martino di Castrozza in 1913.

he died. There is no mention how the news of his death reached Freud.

Ernstl comes of age . . .   Mon 11 March 1935

Ernstl's 21st birthday may well have been celebrated at Berggasse. Unfortunately W. Ernest Freud no longer has any memory of such an event.

House in Grinzing rented . . .   Sat 16 March 1935

This was the same beautiful villa they had rented the previous year—Strasser-gasse 47. They were lucky to get it again: only two days earlier Freud had written that he did not expect they would.

Universal conscription in Germany . . .   Sun 17 March 1935

Two decisive steps in Germany's rearmament had been taken over the previous week. First Goering proclaimed the new Luftwaffe on March 9, then on March 16 a new law on the reconstruction of the armed forces announced the necessity of universal conscription.

Over the following weeks preparations for war continued. On March 19 the first large-scale air-raid exercise was held in Berlin. The first "Day of the Luftwaffe" was celebrated on April 21, then, on May 21, conscription was actually introduced for all men from 18 to 45.

Operation with Pichler . . .   Sat 23 March 1935

The operation was relatively minor, using novocaine and orthoform and the familiar coagulation of tissue to be excised. Afterwards Anna wrote to Jones: "Times here are a little troubled again but we feel it less than one would suppose from the newspapers. Usually also some personal concern is in the foreground and obscures the more general one. Last week my father had to undergo a small operation in his mouth. This used to happen every few weeks but in the last year radium treatment had been tried instead. Well, it wasn't much and he withstood it very well with only half a day's interruption in work. Still it is always enough for me to worry about it." (*Anna Freud-Jones 29.3.1935*)

Electric clock . . .   Fri 29 March 1935

This was the day on which Jeanne Lampl-de Groot returned to Vienna from Holland, where she had gone because of her father's death. She was in analysis with Freud and a clock might seem an apt gift to one's analyst.

But Freud continued using clockwork timepieces, for Schur wrote: "He still followed a certain routine, and never forgot until the day before his death to wind either his watch or a desk clock which required winding once a week! In a way this tiny detail was typical of the disciplined organization of his mind." Martha Freud was later to give Schur one of Freud's clocks.

Minna back . . .   Sat 6 April 1935

Minna returned to Berggasse, after spending six weeks in the north Italian (or south Tyrolean) resort of Merano.

Ernst 43 yrs . . .   Sat 6 April 1935

Ernst and his family had been living in England since 1933 and he was now establishing himself there as an architect. Among others Ernest Jones was trying to provide contacts and recommendations. He had now contracted Ernst to design a new wing for his cottage, "The Plat," at Elsted near Midhurst in Sussex.

He wrote to Freud: "Although it is a small matter it is surprisingly complicated and that gives me an opportunity for the highest admiration of his extraordinary ingenuity and masterly efficiency. It is a rare treat to come across such a high standard of capacity in any work." (*Jones-Freud 27.6.1935*)

Not surprisingly Freud was delighted by this praise: "Your recognition of Ernst's capacity for work is balsam for my paternal heart. I wish my other son in Nice also had a fatherland and livelihood again." (*Freud-Jones 7.7.1935*)

New American Lectures . . .   Thurs 11 April 1935

The first English translation of the *Introductory Lectures* had been published in New York by Boni & Liveright in 1920, under the title *A General Introduction to Psychoanalysis*. This was now republished by Liveright Publishing Corporation.

Ernstl, mid-1930s. (Before the war Austrian cars were right-hand drive.)

Martin from Zurich . . .   **Sat 13 April 1935**

Martin paid a number of visits to Zurich over these years, not all of them recorded (for instance, he went there again in February 1936). By moving around his father's foreign assets, Martin was successful in saving the greater part of his fortune.

It is possible later trips to Zurich involved smuggling money and assets. There was an Austrian saying of this period: "Money alone does not make you happy. You have to have it in Switzerland."

Strassergasse . . .   **Thurs 18 April 1935**

This year the Freuds moved out to their summer residence in mid- instead of late April. But the weather remained wintry. A month later Freud was writing: "The garden outside and the flowers in the room are beautiful, but the spring is a *Fopperei* [mockery], as we say in Vienna. I am learning at last what it is to be cold. My doctor has ordered me to drink sugar water for my subnormal temperature, which makes one feel miserable." (*Freud-Lou Andreas-Salomé 16.5.1935*)

Reik & Landauer . . .   **Sat 20 April 1935**

Both Theodor Reik and Karl Landauer were now working in Holland. Reik had moved to The Hague from Berlin the previous year: Landauer and his family were forced to leave Frankfurt when the Nazis came to power in 1933 and they emigrated to Holland.[1] Both continued there as practicing psychoanalysts and they had come to Vienna to report on the state of psychoanalysis in Holland. The Dutch psychoanalytical association had split into two factions and Freud already knew (from Jeanne Lampl-de Groot) that they were at odds.[2]

Theodor Reik (1888–1969) was even more deeply indebted to Freud than most other pioneer analysts. At Vienna University he wrote a psychoanalytical study on Flaubert (*Flaubert and his Temptation of St. Antony*, published in 1912)—the first doctoral thesis on the new psychology. In 1910 Reik joined the Vienna Psychoanalytic Society. Freud became interested in his career and advised him not to study medicine but to take a training analysis with Karl Abraham in Berlin. Freud not only paid for this but also sent Reik and his wife a monthly allowance. Reik succeeded Rank as Secretary of the Vienna Psychoanalytical Society.

In 1926 legal action was brought against him for practising as an analyst without medical qualifications. It was this lawsuit that prompted Freud to write in his defense his booklet *The Question of Lay Analysis*. The action failed, but Reik subsequently found it hard to make a living in Vienna. In 1928 he moved to Berlin.

Easter, 49 yrs. practice . . .   **Sun 21 April 1935**

Freud's setting up in medical practice had been one of the preconditions of his marriage, which also occured in 1886. But whereas the practice is referred to six times in the diary, only two wedding anniversaries are mentioned.

Jones and family . . .   **Sun 21 April 1935**

Before the visit Freud wrote to Jones: "The prospect of your visit to Vienna at Easter makes me feel both joyful and melancholy. I know that as a result of the restrictions of age I shall only be able to fulfill the duties of hospitality very inadequately. Our Wolf too, who once behaved with such unfriendliness toward you is now an old man, in his doggy way as old as me i.e. over 11 years." (*Freud-Jones 24.2.1935*)

This was Jones's first visit with his family.[1] As it turned out Freud was in good health: "He surprised my little girl, aged five, by taking hold of her nose between two fingers, but ignoring this castrating symbolism she won his heart by immediately offering him her doll. To the boy, then aged thirteen, he presented some antiquities from his collection with the recommendation that archaeology would be an interesting career to choose, advice to which my son's literary bent did not respond. The proud father must record that Freud in his next letter said he had seldom met such delightful children; he always inquired about them afterwards. I have not often known a man so fond of children as he was."

Karl Landauer, 1930s.

Federn & Meng . . .   **Mon 22 April 1935**

It was at this time that Paul Federn decided to resign from the *Internationale Zeitschrift für Psychoanalyse* (the German journal of the psychoanalytical movement), of which he had been an editor since 1926. Edward Bibring now took over. Federn simply gave as his reason the fact that he had worked enough on the journal and was happy to resign his duties.

Heinrich Meng, Federn's friend and former analysand, was now living in Basel. He emigrated there after the Frankfurt Psychoanalytical Institute, which he and Karl Landauer were directing, was closed by the Nazis in 1933.

Schmiedeberg . . .   **Tues 23 April 1935**

While serving as an Austrian officer in World War I, Walter Schmideberg (1890–1954) was introduced to Freud by Max Eitingon. During the 1920s he lived and worked in Berlin with Eitingon; in 1932 he and his wife Melitta, daughter of Melanie Klein, emigrated to London, where he became an active member of the British Psycho-Analytical Society.

Now that psychoanalysis was effectively disappearing in Germany, Freud considered the relationship between the British and Viennese societies to be vital to the future of the movement. He wrote to Jones: "With patience and absorption we will naturally surmount our present theoretical differences. We—London and Vienna—must cling together, the other European groups play virtually no part and the centrifugal tendencies are at the moment very strong in our international meetings. And it would be a shame if it [the movement] were not to survive my personal existence." (*Freud-Jones 26.5.1935*)

As a way of bringing the two groups together Dr. Schmideberg and Jones came to Vienna, as representatives of the British Psycho-Analytical Society, to give guest lectures to the Vienna group. Schmideberg gave the first one today to the clinical seminar. In return, Robert Waelder, a "penetrating critic from Vienna," was invited to London and went there in November 1935 to give a lecture to the British Psycho-Analytical Society.[1]

Jones in the evening . . .   **Thurs 25 April 1935**

Jones had given his talk to the Vienna Psychoanalytical Society on the previous evening. This evening he discussed his theoretical viewpoint with Freud.

He wrote in Freud's biography: "About this time some differences had developed between some of the London analysts, including myself, and the Viennese. The latter, who adhered closely to Freud's teaching, had had the advantage of close contact and discussion with him. It seemed desirable to clarify the differences by more personal contact, and that was one of my objects of this visit. My own differences were partly doubt about Freud's theory of a 'death instinct' and partly a somewhat varying conception of the phallic stage in development, particularly in the female. So I read a paper on the latter topic before the Vienna Society on April 24, 1935. [. . .] In a long discussion with Freud I defended Melanie Klein's work, but it was not to be expected that at a time when he was so dependent on his daughter's ministrations and affections he could be quite open-minded in the matter."

Bowl from McCord . . .   **Fri 26 April 1935**

Clinton Preston McCord (1881-?) was an American psychologist turned analyst. He was a member of the New York Psychoanalytic Society. He first met Freud in Berchtesgaden in the summer of 1929. Nothing is known of this gift.

Mary Stuart from Zweig . . .   **Fri 26 April 1935**

Since Stefan Zweig's last contact with Freud in 1933, he had moved to London. It was there, three days after his arrival, that he had come upon the manuscript in the British Museum reporting Mary Stuart's execution. Although he had just finished his book on Marie Antoinette and had no intention of embarking on another biography, Zweig's curiosity was aroused and it led him to produce this study of her life, which Freud now received.[1]

Counterpiece to yellow dragon . . .   **Fri 26 April 1935**

There are only two matching dragons in the collection and these are small, carved jade figures, one pale and the other darker green. Also there is a larger *yellow*

Paul Federn, Freud's "Apostle Paul."

dragon, but without a companion piece. If it once had a counterpiece, Freud would hardly have given it away.[1] In Chinese folklore the dragon was a benevolent creature, an inhabitant of the heavens and the seas, a symbol of male vigor and vitality.

Letter to Thomas Mann . . .   Sun 28 April 1935

This letter—*To Thomas Mann on his Sixtieth Birthday*—was written at the request of the German publisher, Fischer Verlag, for a Festschrift to celebrate the novelist's birthday.[1] It is a brief message of respect, though Freud could not refrain from including jibes at the practice of celebrating birthdays.

He ends with the words: ". . . I wish to express the confidence that you will never do or say anything—an author's words, after all, are deeds—that is cowardly or base, and that even at a time which blurs judgment you will choose the right way and show it to others."

Ruth operated . . .   Mon 29 April 1935

No documentation of this operation is available. It may have been a sequel to the cervical surgery she had previously undergone. But her general health was poor, as Freud had had cause to complain.

Operation with Pichler . . .   Tues 30 April 1935

Since the March operation Pichler had as usual been keeping a close watch and had detected two suspect nodules which he now electro-coagulated.

Anna wrote to Jones: "My suspicions were right and my father had another little operation three days after you left. It was not much, but as an after-effect of a more mechanical nature he had a number of minor troubles with his prothese and a new one has to be made now. That brings a lot of disturbance and discomfort, of course." (*Anna Freud-Jones 9.5.1935*)

Beginning of prosthesis misery . . .   Sat 5 May 1935

This attack of pain, a consequence of the operation on April 30, was only one further episode in the long saga of suffering caused by the prosthesis. In a letter three years earlier Freud had talked of "the continual, never-ending misery of the prosthesis. . ." (*Freud-Eitingon 5.6.1932*) and any number of similar comments could be compiled from 1923 on.

Pichler noted tersely: "5.5.[1935] Patient has sudden violent pain when inserting prosthesis, therefore further reduction. 2 places, one with the small papilloma remnants mentioned before, the other higher above with dry brown eschar adhering."

79 yrs . . .   Sun 6 May 1935

The prosthesis trouble reached a crisis on Freud's birthday. Schur recorded the episode: "On his 79th birthday Freud was unable to insert it [the prosthesis] at all. Anna Freud and I tried to help him, and he kept at it to the point of exhaustion. Finally, we took him to Pichler's office. A new prosthesis had to be started that day. This was one of the very few occasions on which Freud felt somewhat desperate. Yet he soon regained control and in Pichler's office was again his composed, patient, polite self."

A week later Freud wrote with resignation: "Hesitantly a beautiful spring is unfolding before our eyes this year and I would not have too much to complain about if fate had not sent me as a birthday present for the May 6 the necessity of having the prosthesis remade, which naturally entailed an extraordinary amount of torture. A restriction of my analytical hours is also linked with that." (*Freud-Eitingon 12.5.1935*)[1]

Bullitt . . .   Mon 20 May 1935

Bullitt's reappearance—"as a meteor" again?—once again raised the unresolved question of the Wilson book, which had been set aside in 1932. Mention of the book had faded from Freud's correspondence by this time and it is possible he had given up hope that he and Bullitt could ever develop a manuscript he could accept.

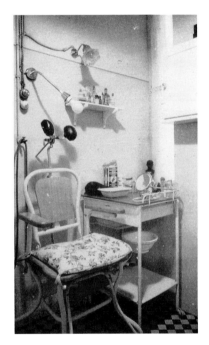

Jades from Freud's collection. WK

The lobby next to the consulting room where Freud underwent daily medical examination. EE

Honorary Member of Royal Society of Medicine* . . .   Mon 24 May 1935

In his letter of thanks the following day Freud wrote: "For many years my scientific work found no recognition among physicians. In the honour I am receiving from the Royal Society of Medicine I see a sign that psychoanalysis, which I have practised and recommended, can no longer escape recognition by the medical world." (*Freud-The Royal Society of Medicine 25.5.1935*)

To Arnold Zweig he wrote: "This will make a good impression in the world at large." (*Freud-Arnold Zweig 13.6.1935*). And to Jones he said: "Since this cannot have happened 'on account of my beautiful eyes' it must prove that respect for our psychoanalysis has made great progress among official circles in England." (*Freud-Jones 26.5.1935*) Jones assured him that the action of the Royal Society of Medicine had been spontaneous and without any intervention or lobbying by analysts, hence it did indeed prove Freud's point.[1]

Four Nation Conference in Vienna . . .   Sun 9 June 1935

The conference, which had begun the previous day, brought together analysts from Austria, Czechoslovakia, Hungary and Italy; its purpose was to give these isolated groups the opportunity of sharing ideas. There were to be no set talks apart from four main lectures on themes of particular interest: the problem of transference, character analysis, ego psychology and the death drive. Each of the national groups took one theme, which was followed by discussion. An evening for the discussion of organizational questions such as training and control analyses was also arranged. Robert Waelder gave the lecture for the Viennese on ego psychology.

Hollos . . .   Mon 10 June 1935

In 1933, after Ferenczi's death, Istvan Hollós succeeded him as president of the Hungarian Psychoanalytical Association. No account of this particular meeting with Freud has become available.[1]

Ed. Weiss . . .   Mon 10 June 1935

Freud afterwards wrote to Arnold Zweig: "At Whitsun we received a visit from our brave Italian colleague, Edoardo Weiss, from Rome. Mussolini is putting great difficulties in the way of psychoanalytic literature. Analysis can flourish no better under Fascism than under Bolshevism and National Socialism." (*Freud-Arnold Zweig 13.6.1935*)[1]

Chatterji . . .   Tues 11 June 1935

Maybe a member of the Indian Psychoanalytical Society—perhaps Suniti Kumar Chatterji who once interviewed Freud?

Minna 70 yrs. . . .   Tues 18 June 1935

Minna's continuing place in Freud's life is marked by the frequent references to her arrivals and departures. (Her name occurs, in fact, far more frequently than Martha's.) But none of her birthdays had been registered since the one in 1930, which Freud spoke of as a difficult problem, arguing that only birthdays that end in a zero should be recognized. It is not known how this important birthday was celebrated.

Anna to Prague . . .   Sat 22 June 1935

Anna Freud travelled to Prague to give two lectures to the psychoanalytical working group (*Arbeitsgemeinschaft*) there.

New prosthesis . . .   Sat 22 June 1935

This was Pichler's 17th visit since the "beginning of prosthesis misery" in May. The new prosthesis remained uncomfortable and impeded speech: five more fittings were needed before it was acceptable.

Ernstl Matura . . .   Thurs 27 June 1935

Ernstl was now 21 years old. He writes: "After the Easter holidays, 1933, I had

Minna Bernays.

---

* Freud first wrote, "London Medical Society" then crossed it out.

to decide whether to return to Scharfenberg to continue studying for the Abitur*
in the shadow of the Hitler regime or whether to continue my schooling in
Vienna. I decided for the latter and became a pupil of the RG VIII (Vienna
Realgymnasium in the 8th district of Vienna), where I finished school with the
Matura examination."

+ Albert Hammerschlag . . .   Mon 8 July 1935

Albert Hammerschlag (1863–1935), son of Freud's beloved teacher Samuel Hammerschlag, was a specialist for internal diseases and from 1893 a Privatdozent. He
had been one of the doctors consulted about Minna Bernays' condition in 1901.

Schuschnigg's accident . . .   Sat 13 July 1935

The new Austrian Chancellor, Kurt von Schuschnigg, and his family were being
driven to St. Gilgen to spend their holidays, when the car left the road near Linz
and crashed, killing his wife. He and his young son escaped with mild injuries.
Schuschnigg was seen as a cold and distant character. Unlike his predecessor
Dollfuss, he had no popular appeal. However, this accident may have won him
some sympathy. Freud's concern for him had obvious grounds—Schuschnigg
remained Austria's barrier against Nazism.

Th. Reik . . .   Sun 14 July 1935

Freud had a certain personal interest in Reik's career, which he had guided.
Perhaps because of a particular sense of responsibility, Freud's friendship with
Reik was occasionally tinged with exasperation.[1] One cause of Reik's difficulties
with colleagues was his notorious arrogance and his sensitivity about his status
as a lay analyst.

   In his New Year greeting Freud had expressed pleasure that Reik seemed to be
establishing himself in Holland. Around this period, however, Reik's wife, who
had been ill for a long time, died and he remarried.[2]

Heart attack, extra systole . . .   Wed 17 July 1935

Extra systoles were now a familiar heart symptom. The previous year Freud had
written to the American analyst Smith Ely Jelliffe (1866–1945): "The article
about chinidin was of particular interest to me since I myself use this medicine
for my irksome extra systoles, without any side effects by the way." (Freud-Jelliffe
2.8.1934)[1]

   Three days after this entry Anna Freud told Jones: "My father has had a few
bad days with irregularities of pulse etc. To-day it is better and I have the feeling
it is really over." (Anna Freud-Jones 20.7.1935). But when Smiley Blanton turned
up for psychoanalysis on August 3 Freud was too weak to work; the analysis
could not begin until August 5.

Princess . . .   Mon 22 July 1935

After spending Easter 1935 at her house in St. Tropez, Marie Bonaparte had
returned to Paris to find that her chow Topsy had developed a lymphosarcoma
of the lip. She began X-ray treatments at the Curie Institute (of which she had
been an important benefactor) and also began writing a book about the dog. She
now spent only a week in Vienna. It is more than likely that, among other things,
she and Freud would have discussed the X-ray treatment of cancer.

Martha 74 yrs. . . .   Fri 26 July 1935

Martin's traditional birthday poem for his mother includes a brief summary of
the correspondence she received:
>   "One values highly and holds dear
>   Those who bring greetings from afar,
>   For among their sixteen pages
>   Of lengthy and well-written phrases,
>   One can find the finest news,
>   What they are doing and getting up to:
>   A dog has barked at someone's puss,

---

*Abitur–school-leaving certificate, German equivalent of the Austrian *Matura*.

Ernstl, aged 18, with his grandmother,
Martha Freud, at Pötzleinsdorf.

The Isis with Horus from Freud's desk.
NB

The Nazi education Freud's grandsons
escaped. The blackboard reads: "The
Jew is our greatest enemy! Beware of
the Jew!" DOW

Jones has ordered a new house,
Levisons came for tea and cake,
Robert has the stomach ache,
Evchen writes like Emile Zola,
Henny's figure's getting fuller,
Luxchen is the best horsewoman,
And so on and so on and so on."

Rockefeller jr. . . .   Fri 2 August 1935

I can find no confirmation of any link between Freud and John Davison Rockefeller Junior (1874–1960). It is hard to imagine what was involved or what he and
Freud might have discussed if this was indeed a visit.[1] But they did have one
common interest—antiquities. Rockefeller's only hobby was collecting Chinese
porcelain.[2] Another, though unlikely, possibility is that Freud is referring to
Rockefeller Senior's married *daughter*, Mrs. Harold McCormick. She was involved in psychoanalysis, but was closely connected with Jung and the Zurich
group.

Isis with Horus . . .   Fri 2 August, 1935

This metal statuette of the goddess Isis suckling the infant Horus was among
Freud's favorites, selected to stand on his desk.

The Egyptologist Wallis Budge wrote of such figures: "And the bulk of the
masses in Egypt and Nubia who professed Christianity transferred to Mary the
Virgin the attributes of Isis the Everlasting Mother, and to the Babe Jesus those
of Horus."

The statuette is from the late period (c. 600 BC): the Isis figure bears a tripartite
vulture headdress surmounted by a horned sun disc. The dealer who sold it to
Freud, Robert Lustig, acquired it as junk from a country storekeeper who sold
it to him for its weight in metal!

How did such an exotic object find its way into a country store? Most likely
as a result of the postwar inflation in the early 1920s. Money was virtually
worthless and previously wealthy city dwellers were forced to barter their valu-
ables for farm produce. According to Stefan Zweig: ". . . on entering a Salzburg
farm-house one might find oneself, to one's amazement, under the gaze of an
Indian Buddha . . . ."

Robert 60 yrs. . . .   Sun 4 August 1935

Mathilde's husband, Robert Hollitscher (1875–1959). He is the Robert mentioned in Martin's birthday poem, who had a stomach ache. His birthday, the
only one of his that Freud records, has obviously found its way into the diary
because it is a round figure.

Eitingon . . .   Tues 6 August 1935

Anna Freud commented after this visit: "Eitingon left again two days ago and his
visit was a pleasant surprise. He is in a very good frame of mind, looks healthier
than for many years and is above all approachable and sensible in business
matters." (*Anna Freud-Jones 12.8.1935*)

This good mood was not to last. In late October Eitingon passed through
Vienna again and this time Anna Freud was dismayed to find him changed and
obstinate (*starrsinnig*).

Ernst with Lucian . . .   Wed 14 August 1935

On the annual visit to Vienna Ernst brought with him his middle son, Lucian,
who was now 13 years old. (Lucian's two brothers had already visited Freud
separately, Stephan in 1932 and Clemens in 1933.)

During the final years in Berlin, Lucian had been greatly affected by the
growing antisemitism. He was later to say that it was around 1929 when he
became aware of being a Jew. "Suddenly, one was an outsider, someone to be
hunted down. I rebelled, of course, and became very resentful. I would disappear
from home, and let no one know where I was. I was very secretive, and would
drive my parents wild."

But he was to remember his grandfather with affection, as "always very good,
very kind, very modest." [1]

Mother would have been 100! . . .   Sun 18 August 1935

During his mother's lifetime, her longevity was a cause of surprise and wonder for Freud; in 1928, for example, he was writing—"Mother is a miracle at 93!" (*Freud-Sam Freud 6.12.1928*) After her death he continued to note her birthdays. In 1932 he wrote to Eitingon: "My mother would have been 97 years old today." (*Freud-Eitingon 18.8.1932*)

The exact age of this "youthful mother" was a matter of lasting interest. When, in 1936, Freud's niece Lilly Marlé mistakenly wrote that his mother was 18 when he was born he replied: "Inveterately faithful to details I have only one thing to correct. Your grandmother was not 18 but 21 when she had her first child. She would have been 101 today!" (*Freud-Lilly Marlé 1.6.1936*)

Operation on scabs . . .   Mon 19 August 1935

Pichler performed the operation in the presence of Dr. Popper. One purpose was to eliminate some of the causes of prosthesis discomfort, but a suspect wart was also electrocoagulated. Novocain was used, without adrenalin. The pathologist Jakob Erdheim examined the extracted tissue and pronounced it free of malignancy, though with signs of pre-cancerous growth.

Freud did not suffer any pain for the first days after the operation but felt the effects later. Pichler noted: "[4.9.1935] As usual worse with distance from operation. Objectively all right, only lockjaw increased but not sufficient to prevent insertion [of prosthesis]."

Sarasin—Kempner . . .   Sun 1 September 1935

A visit from Freud's friend and former pupil, Philipp Sarasin of the Swiss Psychoanalytical Society, and the psychoanalyst Salomea Kempner, who had been a member of the German Psychoanalytical Society since at least 1920. But she was now forced to leave it because she was a "foreign Jew." (However she continued giving control analyses until 1938 in Berlin and eventually perished in the Warsaw Ghetto.) The two visitors were, apparently, lovers and they probably paid a combined visit on Freud.

Greeting to "Wien" B. B. on 40th Jubilee . . .   Tues 3 Sept. 1935

"B.B." refers to the B'nai B'rith—the "Sons of the Covenant"—an international order founded by German Jewish immigrants in New York in 1843. The *Wien* (Vienna) lodge was founded in 1895, at a time of rampant antisemitism, and Freud joined it on September 23, 1897.[1]

The society was ethical and educative, it aimed to combat prejudice by example rather than political intervention. The humanitarian interests of the organization attracted Freud. In the *B'nai B'rith Monatsblätter* of 1926 he wrote: "Our lodge is founded on a national basis and strives mainly toward ethical goals. My attitude to morality has not always been clearly understood among us. I believe that the search for its source and the exposure of its motives do not detract from the dignity or the value of human ethics." (*Freud 21.1.1926*)

Jade bowl and camel . . .   Thurs 5 September 1935

Freud had been collecting jade bowls for some time: during the early years of the century some of them were used as ashtrays during meetings of the Wednesday Psychological Society. To have rated mention this bowl would probably be above standard or one of those on the desk. Among the possibilities are three spinach-colored cup-shaped bowls (cut in China but originating from Lake Baikal), a polished jade pot (carved in China in the Mughal style especially for the Indian market) and a 19th-century nephrite wine cup in the form of a peach stone.

This was the second camel in the collection. The first one was a birthday present from Marie Bonaparte in 1933. Both are 20th-century forgeries in the early Tang style, 7th-8th century BC. Though both of them are well-modelled, one can be recognized as a fake by the applied paint which flakes off easily, while the other is stylistically suspect.

Emden . . .   Sun 15 September 1935

Jan van Emden (1868–1950) was a pupil and friend of Freud's. They first met in 1910 in Holland where Freud was spending his holidays and he and his wife

Freud's mother, a month before her death in 1930.

Jade bowls on the desk in London. NB

became personal friends of the Freuds.

While training in medicine van Emden became a member of the Vienna psychoanalytical society. At the same time he attended a course at the Vienna Medical School taught by an outspoken opponent of Freud's, Professor Raimann the Psychiatric Clinic. This, van Emden told Freud in 1912, would be a useful experience for him in facing the sort of opposition he anticipated on his return to Holland. Van Emden was one of the original members of the Dutch Psychoanalytical Association, founded in 1917. In 1935 van Emden replaced J. H. W. van Ophuijsen as President of the Dutch association

Stefan Zweig . . .   Sun 15 September 1935

As a resident of Salzburg, living within sight of Hitler's Berchtesgaden villa just over the border, Stefan Zweig had sensed the reality of the Nazi threat to Austria before most others. Already in October 1933 he had left the country for England and lived in voluntary exile in London until 1940. His work, like that of all other Jews, had been banned by Hitler.

Freud aired his current obsession at their meeting and afterwards apologized: "After your visit on September 15 I seriously reprimanded myself for having comprehensively set out the contents of the 'Moses' in front of you instead of letting you talk about your work and plans. The Moses will never see the light of day." (*Freud-Stefan Zweig 5.11.1935*)[1]

On Zweig's return to London he sent Freud an article for the *Sunday Times* which he had written on the English publication of Freud's *Autobiography*. The article hinted at the Nobel Prize, which immediately prompted Freud to scotch any rumors of such a possibility.

Willy Haas . . .   Sun 15 September 1935

Willy Haas (1891–1973) was a critic, essayist and film script-writer who had belonged to Kafka's circle. (It was Haas who edited Kafka's *Letters to Milena* in 1952.) Between 1925 and 1933 he was in charge of the publisher Rowohlt's series *Die literarische Welt* in Berlin, but in 1933 had emigrated to Prague.

Jeans . . .   Sun 29 September 1935

Could this have been a visit by the British physicist and astronomer Sir James Jeans (1877–1946)? Jeans was a member of the Royal Society and its secretary from 1919–1929: in 1936 Freud was himself to become a Foreign Member of the society.[1]

Large Kannon . . .   Mon [Tues] 1 October 1935

This is the second *Kannon* (the Bodhisattva Avalokitesvara, an attendant of the Buddha Amitabha) that Freud acquired and the most dramatic. It is probably a copy of a Sung period (979–1279 AD) Buddhist statuette. The figure is seated on a lion. Freud placed it on the study table with the large busts: it now stands on the library table at Maresfield Gardens, behind the smiling mummy case.

Beginning of war in Abyssinia . . .   Tues [Wed] 2 October 1935

Mussolini had been talking of a reborn Roman Empire for a long time; he needed foreign conquests to back up his claims. Preparations for an invasion of Abyssinia (now Ethiopia) had been going on for at least a year. On December 5, 1934 Italian troops attacked the Ethiopian oasis of Wal-Wal: in the Mussolini-Laval pact of January 7, 1935 France granted Italy's claim on Ethiopia. The actual attack began on October 3. On October 7 Italy was declared an aggressor by the League of Nations. Its economic sanctions were ineffective as Austria and Switzerland did not comply. On December 7 the Hoare-Laval pact consented to the surrender of Ethiopia.

Subtleties of a Faulty Action . . .   Thurs 10 October 1935

In this brief essay, *The Subtleties of a Faulty Action*, Freud examined a small mistake he made while writing a note to accompany a birthday present for Dorothy Burlingham. The gift was an engraved gem. In an accompanying note Freud explained that a certain jeweler would have the stone made into a ring. However, he mistakenly inserted the unecessary word "until" (in German *bis*) into the sentence.

One of Freud's two Tang style Chinese camels. NB

He eventually tracked down two concealed reasons for the mistake. The first was that an awkward repetition of another word in the sentence concerned him. The inserted *bis* reminded him of the French *bis* ["encore"] and also the Latin *bis*, meaning "a second time." By adding this word and then crossing it out, he was as if removing the unpleasant repetition. At that point Anna Freud offered a further hidden reason. This was not the first time Freud had given Dorothy Burlingham a stone for a ring. The *bis* criticized this repetition and, furthermore, seemed to provide an excuse for not giving the gift, which Freud would really have liked to have kept for himself.[1]

Pichler operation . . .   Fri 11 October 1935

This was a now standard operation, the removal of a papilloma using a diathermy needle and under novocain anesthetic. There were no notable side-effects and it was six weeks before Pichler's next checkup, when he found everything in order apart from the fact that Freud had had another bad cold.

Thornton Wilder . . .   Sun 13 October 1935

The following day Freud wrote to Arnold Zweig that he had had a visit from the author of "that delightful book *The Bridge of San Luis Rey*." In 1928 he had also recommended the book to his son Ernst as "unusually beautiful."

The meeting with the American writer Thornton Wilder (1897–1975) lasted an hour and a half.[1] Freud told Wilder that he had thrown away the novelist's latest book (*Heaven's My Destination*) and he asked him why he had written about an American fanatic, since that topic could not be treated poetically. But Minna Bernays had apparently liked a previous novel called *The Cabala* (Freud did not—Wilder suspected this was because a character in it made a slighting reference to Freud.)

On fiction in general, Freud told Wilder about such friends as Arnold Zweig, Stefan Zweig and Franz Werfel who were using psychoanalysis in their novels, but in such a way that it came out clinically or schematically. It would take centuries, Freud thought, until writers had assimilated it profoundly enough for it to emerge as "pure novel." Wilder objected that such a "pure novel" already existed—James Joyce's *Ulysses*.

Wilder reported that Freud then spoke of religion and his recent work, saying: " '. . . I like god . . . Just these last weeks I have found a *Formulierung* [formulation] for religion . . . Hitherto I have said that religion is an illusion; now I say it has a truth—it has an historical truth. Religion is the recapitulation and the solution of the problems of one's first four years that have been covered over by an amnesia.' "

Mathilde 48 yrs. . . .   Mon 16 October 1935

Mathilde had been in bad health this year. Because the climate of Bad Aussee was not good, Freud had recommended she and Robert go for the summer to Grafenberg, to Reinhold's sanatorium. Reinhold had a high reputation (Felix and Helene Deutsch respected him), and Freud offered to pay the costs.

Berggasse . . .   Fri 18 October 1935

The Freuds had now been exactly six months in Grinzing, the longest of their summer stays during these years.

+ Richard Wahle . . .   Tues 22 October 1935

The death of Richard Wahle (1857–1935), a philosopher and professor at the University of Czernowitz. He was the author of *The Tragicomedy of Wisdom: the Consequences and History of Philosophizing* (*Die Tragikomödie der Weisheit: Die Ergebnisse und die Geschichte des Philosophierens* Wien & Leipzig, 1915).

During the early 1880s he and his two brothers, Emil and Fritz, were among Freud's group of friends, the *Bund* which met weekly at the Café Kurzweil. Fritz Wahle was a friend of Martha Bernays and even, briefly, a rival for her affections during Freud's engagement.

Autobiographical Study . . .   Mon 28 October 1935

In June 1935 Jones had written to Freud asking whether he was willing to sell the rights of his *Autobiographical Study* (*Selbstdarstellung* 1925) and *Inhibitions, Symp-*

The large *Kannon* (Bodhisattva of Compassion). WK

toms and Anxiety (Hemmung, Symptom und Angst 1926) to the Hogarth Press, to be published in the International Psycho-Analytical Library Series. James Strachey would deal with the translation of the "excellent postscript" to the study.

Freud immediately agreed with this plan and added that Strachey was the "most desirable translator." The day after receiving his copy of the English translation Freud sent his thanks to Jones and Strachey.

+ Victor Dirsztay . . .   Wed 6 November 1935

Death of the German writer and novelist Victor Dirsztay. It is possible Freud notes this death because Dirsztay may once have been one of his analysands.

Visit from Yvette Guilbert . . .   Sun 10 November 1935

Yvette Guilbert's first concert in Vienna this year was entitled "La France qui chante" and the repertoire ranged from 15th-century French song to the present. The critic of the *Wiener Zeitung* commented: "Each of her *chansons* becomes a little theatrical play . . . ."

Since the diary entry makes it clear that she visited Freud, one assumes he was unable to attend her concert.

Though this is the last mention of Yvette Guilbert, it was not her final visit to Freud. She visited him again in May 1939, when she had three performances at the Wigmore Hall, London. (Her name appears in the dark blue notebook in which he listed his visitors during 1938-9. The dedicated photo she gave him is dated May 6, 1939).

Almanach 1936 . . .   Thurs 21 November 1935

The *Almanach der Psychoanalyse 1936* included three short contributions from Freud—the postscript to his *Autobiographical Study*, *The Subtleties of a Faulty Action* and *Letter to Thomas Mann* on his 60th birthday. There were 18 other international contributors to this collection of essays, from Franz Alexander in Chicago to Hans Zulliger in Ittigen (Switzerland). The themes of contributions are wide-ranging. There are not only case histories and general theory but also psychoanalytical studies of Poe, Schiller and Kierkegaard.

Oli from Nice . . .   Sat 23 November 1935

Oliver was in charge of a photography business in Nice. He now wished to buy a photography shop there, but to do this he would need to borrow money from his father. Freud had invited him to come to Vienna to discuss the matter.

Within the next week Martin, as the family business representative, had made the owner an offer which had been refused. Freud had decided that he could not go beyond 100,000 francs.

Anna 40 yrs. . . .   Tues 3 December 1935

This year Martin wrote two birthday poems. A longer one was written in the persona of a Hochrotherd chicken and it sings the praises of that place, the other was from the viewpoint of the notepaper on which Anna Freud was now writing a book (*The Ego and the Mechanisms of Defence*):

> "I am the sheets of manuscript
> Selected, dedicated, sanctified
> For the new book by Anna Freud."

Large Han box . . .   Tues 3 December 1935

Since this entry occurs on Anna's birthday, it may well have been a gift for her—a Chinese box from the Han dynasty (206 BC—220 AD), the era of Confucianism. (The following year Freud gave her a Han figurine for her birthday.)

Martin 46 yrs. . . .   Sat 7 December 1935

Though the diary records this birthday, it fails to mention all Martin's arrivals and departures at this period. For example, there is no mention that in early 1936 Martin once again travelled to Zurich on business.

Ernstl to Palestine . . .   Tues 10 December 1935

This year Ernstl had reached his majority and completed his school leaving certificate, but was still undecided about his future. Of this trip to Palestine, he

"To the *savant* Siegmund Freud, the greetings of an artiste, Yvette Guilbert"

wrote: "It was thought that my school career had not been brilliant enough for me to study, and I did not know what I wanted to become professionally. I thought that perhaps I might get some ideas if I visited countries like Palestine or Russia, to have a look round though my heart was not really in those places. Anyhow, I went to Palestine—I think for 6 months—staying partly with the Eitingons in Jerusalem, who, through their connections, enabled me to work briefly in some country place and to stay at a Kibbutz for a month. I was not too enthusiastic about the country and did not want to stay illegally, which at that time quite a few enthusiasts did. So I returned to Vienna when my permission to stay officially expired."

Three years earlier Freud declared his own interest in Palestine when he wrote: "I would very much like to travel and to nowhere more dearly than to Palestine, but I am an invalid . . . ." (*Freud-Velikovsky 26.2.1932*)

Masaryk resigned . . .   Sat 14 December 1935

Tomas Garrigue Masaryk (1850–1937) was founder and four times president of the Czechoslovak Republic. Born in Moravia (like Freud) he had a doctorate in philosophy from the University of Vienna and taught there as Privatdozent until 1881: in 1882 he became Professor Extraordinarius of Philosophy at the Charles University, Prague.

It was during World War I that he switched from philospher to leader of a national revolt against Austria-Hungary. He managed to interest President Wilson and the leading statesmen of the Allies in the idea of self-determination for the Central-European and Balkan peoples. Under his leadership the Czechoslovak Republic became a model democracy, surrounded by tyrannies.

By 1935 Masaryk was too old and ill to continue: on December 14 the head of his chancery read out his message of resignation, naming Dr. Eduard Benes as his successor.

Paul Hollitscher + . . .   Mon 23 December 1935

Paul Hollitscher was the brother of Mathilde's husband, Robert Hollitscher. Anna reported that Robert was greatly upset by the death.

Han box. NB

Oscar Nemon sketching Freud. Under pressure from colleagues, Freud consented to sit for him again in 1936.

1936

"When does any one of us have peace from their families? Never, until he finds eternal peace . . . " Freud once wrote to an American colleague.[1] Several events in 1936, including two anniversaries, illustrate the role that the family played in his life and work. Virtually his entire lifetime was spent within large families and for most of that time Freud was the main provider, or "money-earning machine," as he once put it.[2] He did not rebel against this role, on the contrary he revelled in it. He disliked solitude; the only time he lived alone was from the age of 27, when he left home for the first time, to the age of 30, when he married. For the whole of that period he was engaged and his courtship letters attest his loneliness. Later, in his married life, he tried going on holiday alone, but eventually gave this up: on a solitary trip to England in 1908 he wrote home " . . . this is my last attempt to enjoy freedom alone. Last year in Rome it was already hardly bearable."[3]

The two linked anniversaries in 1936 commemorated Freud's long years of married and working life. First, at Easter, there was the fiftieth anniversary of setting up in medical practice. This meant the beginning of financial independence, which was a precondition of marriage. Secondly, in September, he and his wife Martha celebrated their fiftieth wedding anniversary. Between these two dates, in May, came his eightieth birthday, which was the occasion for a deluge of congratulations and which brought in its wake one of the highest scientific honors bestowed on Freud, the title of corresponding member of the British Royal Society.

In a literal and metaphorical sense Freud had fathered large families. The figure of the father plays a central role in psychoanalysis; in his own experience Freud considered parenthood " . . . the most curious thing there is in life . . . ."[4] But one significant date remained unmarked in the diary for 1936—the fortieth anniversary of his father Jacob Freud's death in October. Yet the first work produced this year bore a close connection to his father's memory. A *Disturbance of Memory on the Acropolis*, written in January 1936, relates an incident from a trip to Athens in 1904 with his younger brother, Alexander. At the time Freud had experienced a sense of unreality on seeing the Acropolis. He afterwards attributed this to guilt at having gone beyond his father. Now, in 1936, he was one year short of his father's age when he died and was wondering whether that foreboded his own death.

It was also now thirteen years since his cancer had been diagnosed and and he had the first of many operations. Freud may not have considered the continued survival of an invalid a particular cause for rejoicing, but it was at least impressive, and especially so since he remained the chief breadwinner not only for his own household but also the extended family, for his sons had difficulty supporting their own families and often relied on their father. World-wide fame had not brought Freud a corresponding fortune. Moreover, his income also subsidized the psychoanalytical movement; for example, a large part of his royalties was invested in the publishing house. The various sums of money, whether donations or royalties, recorded in the diary are evidence of continuing anxiety about the financial state of the psychoanalytical cause. As far as family finances were concerned, both Freud and Anna had a number of foreign patients who brought in valuable hard currency. This kept their standard of living fairly high while the value of the local currency slumped. But family responsibilities, his generosity toward needy acquaintances or colleagues, his expensive habits (cigars and antiquities)—all this meant Freud could not amass any wealth. Instead he continued, like any provider for a large family, to be "set up for life with worries and interests."[5]

---

1. *Freud-Lehrman 27.1.1930* [Brill Library] ("Aber wann hat einer von uns Jeden Ruhe von seiner Familie? Niemals, solang er nicht die ewige Ruhe gefunden hat.")
2. *Freud-Lilly Freud 14.3.1911* [LoC] ("Wir Alten sind, wie du vielleicht ahnst, nur mehr Gelderwerbsmachiner . . . ")
3. *Freud-Meine Lieben 12.9.1908* [FM] (" . . . u weiss, dass dies mein letzter Versuch ist allein die Freiheit zu geniessen. Es war schon in Rom voriges Jahr kaum auszuhalten.")
4. *Freud-Binswanger 30.1.1911* in Binswanger, L., *Erinnerungen an Sigmund Freud*, Bern, 1956, p.39 (" . . . das Merkwürdigste, was es im Leben gibt . . . ")
5. *Freud-Lehrman 21.3.1929* [Brill Library] (" . . . mit Sorgen und Interessen für sein Leben versehen.")

Ernst . . .   Thurs 2 January 1936

In December 1935 the Vienna Psychoanalytical Society took over an apartment
a short way up the hill from Freud's house. This was to serve as its first independent premises, with seminar rooms, library and office space to be shared with the
International Psychoanalytical Press.

Anna Freud wrote to Jones: "A piece of good news. We have really taken the
apartment in Berggasse 7 that Martin told you about. Ernst will come after the
New Year to advise us about the division between our various institutions and
the furnishing. It will all have to be very simple but I am extremely happy about
it and so is the Society." (*Anna Freud-Jones 28.12.1935*)

Ernst departed . . .   Mon 13 January 1936

On returning to London, Ernst left behind his plans for the rooms at Berggasse
7. Anna told Jones: "Ernst has produced excellent designs. I hope that in this we
have not taken too much trouble upon ourselves. If it is successful it will be very
convenient. I think the Society is reckoning on you giving the opening lecture on
your spring visit." (*Anna Freud-Jones 22.1.1936*)

Disbelief on Acropolis finished . . .   Tues 14 January 1936

The poet Victor Wittkowski (1909–1960), who was organizing a festschrift in
honor of Romain Rolland on his 70th birthday, had appealed to Freud for a
paper. At first Freud apologized for being unable to help: ". . . the production
of something new in response to need and occasion is not forthcoming at this
time of life, at least not from me." (*Freud-Wittkowski 6.1.1936*)

But in the eight days between this disclaimer and the diary entry, an article
nevertheless did appear. Though he refers to it as "*Disbelief* on the Acropolis"
[*Unglaube*], the eventual title was to be "A *Disturbance of Memory* on the Acropolis" [*Eine Erinnerungstörung*]. The article analyzed Freud's sense of unreality on
seeing Athens for the first time in 1904. He concludes that the pleasure of the
occasion was disturbed by infantile guilt at having gone further than his father
ever did.

Princess departed . . .   Thurs 16 January 1936

Marie Bonaparte had spent Christmas and New Year at her villa in St. Tropez,
so this visit to Vienna must have been comparatively brief. Her arrival in Vienna
went unmentioned, and there is no further mention of her name in the diary this
year, although she was to return to Vienna in the last week of October, for six
hours of analysis with Freud.

Operation with Pichler . . .   Thurs 16 January 1936

The operation was performed under local anesthetic—novocaine without adrenalin. Afterwards Anna Freud told Jones: "We have had a couple of difficult days.
Today a week ago my father had a very painful operation. He had to have a fairly
large tumor removed. But since yesterday he has been all right again and the pain
has diminished." (*Anna Freud-Jones 22.1.1936*)

Georg V + . . .   Mon 20 January 1936

On the death of George V (1865–1936), his eldest son Edward, Duke of Windsor, was next in line to the English throne.

Freud had always been an anglophile, but now his interest in English affairs was
further justified by Ernst and his family's emigration there. When he heard they
had been to Southwold, Freud told them he had looked the place up on a map.

He added: "I regularly read English novels for an hour before going to sleep
and in this way I am becoming initiated into the charm of English landscapes."
(*Freud-Ernst Freud 6.6.1934*)

Nemon and Königsberger . . .   Tues 21 January 1936

Both artists, Oscar Nemon and David Paul Königsberger, had done busts of
Freud in the past. Nemon produced the one for his 75th birthday in 1931,
Königsberger did one that was presented to Freud on his 65th birthday in 1921.

Versions of each of their sculptures ended up as public monuments. Ernest
Jones donated a copy of the Königsberger bust to the University of Vienna. (On
February 4, 1955, this bust was ceremonially unveiled in the arcade walk of

*View of the Acropolis. A 19th c.
etching by Albert Linke, after George
Nestel, from Freud's print collection.*

*London Bridge. A memento of Anna's
visit to London in 1914, from Freud's
photo album.*

Vienna University.) Nemon produced a full-length statue which stands in the New York Psychoanalytic Institute. Another version with Freud seated is now situated near Freud's house, by Swiss Cottage Library in London.

van Wulfften . . .   Wed 22 January 1936

Perhaps a visit by the Dutch psychiatrist P. M. van Wulfften- Palthe. In 1935 he published a study of "disappearing penis" anxiety among the Batavian Chinese ("Koro. Eine merkwürdige Angsthysterie" *Internationale Zeitschrift für Psychoanalyse* XXI. Heft 2, 1935). Later he was to write *Neurologie en psychiatrie* (Amsterdam 1948).

One week Nemon . . .   Sat 1 February 1936

Freud's pupils decided to give him a bust for his 80th birthday and offered the commission to Nemon, who had done three busts of him five years earlier. Freud posed for 12 sessions. Nemon reports that Freud was initially bad-tempered, asking whether this gift from his pupils was really necessary. Then he began taking an interest in the work and questioning Nemon about his art.[1]

Max . . .   Sat 1 February 1936

Freud's son-in-law, the photographer Max Halberstadt, was paying a final visit before emigrating to South Africa.

Max's departure . . .   Tues 4 February 1936

Freud was able to provide Max Halberstadt with contacts in South Africa. The South African psychoanalyst Wulf Sachs proved to be very helpful. After Max Halberstadt had settled there with his second wife and their daughter, Wulf Sachs urged them to get Ernstl to follow as quickly as possible. In South Africa, as everywhere else, immigration was becoming progressively more difficult as time went on.

+ Rob. Breuer . . .   Sun 9 February 1936

Leopold Robert Breuer (1869–1936) was the eldest son of Josef Breuer, Freud's early mentor and co-author of the *Studies in Hysteria*. The son, too, was a doctor and worked in the hospital of the Jewish community in Vienna. By a strange coincidence his death is noted on the fifth anniversary of the death of his mother, Mathilde Breuer.

For Freud, the death of Robert Breuer may have brought to mind his own relationship with Josef Breuer. Though that friendship had finally turned sour, Josef Breuer had afterwards remained a sympathetic observer of Freud's subsequent career—Freud had been told this by Robert Breuer eleven years earlier.[1]

Bischowski . . .   Thurs 20 February 1936

Freud uses the German form of this Polish psychoanalyst's name. Gustav Bychowski (1895–1972) studied under Eugen Bleuler at the Burghölzli clinic after World War I. From 1921–3 he was in Vienna where he was analyzed by Siegfried Bernfeld and attended Freud's seminars. On returning to Poland in 1923 he pioneered the development of psychoanalysis there; from 1933 to 1939 he was Professor for Psychiatry and Neurology at the University of Warsaw. At the Marienbad Congress later this year he was to give a paper on relationships between ego and super-ego. Among his interests was the treatment of schizophrenia and psychosis. In 1939, on the outbreak of World War II, he emigrated to the United States.

Operation Pichler . . .   Thurs 20 February 1936

This was another cleaning-up operation: two places with brown crusts were cauterized with acid. Pichler was also not satisfied with some leukoplakia that interfered with the adjustment of the prosthesis, but did not remove it for the time being.

+ Pineles . . .   Tues 3 March 1936

The death of Friedrich Pineles (1868–1936), a doctor of internal diseases in Vienna and an early acquaintance of Freud's, who in 1899 called him "a pleasant and cultured, learned person . . . " (*Freud-Fliess 1.8.1899*)

An amateur snap of the professional photographer Max Halberstadt.

Josef Breuer, discoverer of the "talking cure," with his son Robert.

In summer 1892 Pineles had attended Freud's course on children's mental diseases ("*Über Nervenkrankheiten des Kindesalters*"). He later became Professor of Medicine at the University of Vienna and director of the Kaiser Franz Joseph Ambulatorium (outpatient clinic). He published work on neurology and endocrinology. Pineles was also a friend of Lou Andreas-Salomé, whom he had known since at least 1895.

Osiris group from Alex . . .   Tues 3 March 1936

This statuette, a gift from Freud's younger brother Alexander, stood on Freud's desk among his favorite antiquities. It shows a donor presenting a figure of Osiris. The authenticity of the piece is suspect; there is no other extant example of an Osiris and donor statuette where the Osiris figure actually dwarfs the presenter behind it.

In 1990 the group formed part of a British Museum exhibition on forgeries. It is made of black steatite and appears intact. But radiography reveals that the Osiris head is from another source and has been fitted to the front torso with a metal pin. The backrest is inscribed with the name of the donor—Padiwesir—and the name of the reigning king, Psammetichus I (26th Dynasty, ca. 600 BC).

Operation Pichler . . .   Tues 10 March 1936

The second operation within a month. Pichler now cauterized the remnants of the warts with acid and coagulated the leukoplakia after a novocaine injection.

Minna's glaucoma . . .   Wed 25 March 1936

Minna's eye trouble had been developing for some time and an operation for glaucoma was now performed. The following day Freud told Marie Bonaparte: "Yesterday Minna was operated on for bilateral glaucoma; she kept it a secret to the last minute. We hope for good results." (*Freud-Marie Bonaparte 26.3.1936*).

A letter from Lou Andreas-Salomé reflects the aftermath of the operation, and Freud's concern: " . . . Anna wrote of great and unexpected worries through your sister-in-law's eye trouble and the pain she suffered after the operation." (*Lou Andreas-Salomé—Freud 6.5.1936*)

Angela . . .   Wed 25 March 1936

Angela Seidmann, the young orphan daughter of Freud's niece Tom Seidmann-Freud, had been adopted by her aunt and uncle, the actors Arnold and Lilly Marlé. They fled from Germany in 1933, and now lived in Prague. The family visited Freud every year, but this was Angela's first visit to Vienna alone.

Confiscation of our books in Leipzig . . .   Wed 25 March 1936

The seizure of the press's stocks at Leipzig was in effect more damaging than the bookburning in Berlin three years earlier: "From Leipzig comes the news that the Gestapo has confiscated a large proportion of the psychoanalytic books in stock at Volkmar's, almost a catastrophe for the poor Verlag." (*Freud-Marie Bonaparte 26.3.1936*)

Migraine . . .   Wed 25 March 1936

In his letter to Marie Bonaparte the next day Freud added: "Yesterday I had a severe migraine, quite unusual for me, and today I am still doing all kinds of confused things, as you will have noticed from the letter and the address." (*Freud-Marie Bonaparte 26.3.1936*)

Schur points out that Freud had at first miswritten the address as "rue Adolphe-Yvon," corrected to "rue Yvon-Adolphe." He also notes that Freud is forgetting the part migraine played in his life during the 1890s—the Fliess period. (There is an undated draft manuscript on migraine among the Fliess letters.) It is as if he were superstitiously negating it, like the patient he mentions in a footnote to his 1925 paper on *Negation*.

Alexander Freud's gift, a hybrid statuette of Osiris and donor. NB

Arnold and Lilly Marlé, their son Omri and adopted daughter Angela Seidmann.

The Egyptian funerary barge bought on April 3, 1936. WK

Large funerary barge . . .   Fri 3 April 1936

This funerary barge is a large and fairly spectacular exhibit and was given pride of place in one of the study show-cases. Egyptian tombs frequently contained such model boats to convey the mummy of the deceased to Abydos.

However, this example may be a forgery. The style of the prow and stern are unusual and the body of the ship is composed of three separate pieces of wood. But the top of the canopy is possibly genuine. Often forgers would use fragments of real antiquities and ancient wood to construct their fakes.

This piece, like the plowing figures bought nine days later on April 12, was sold to Freud by one of his regular suppliers, the antique dealer Robert Lustig.

Henny with Eva . . .   Sun 5 April 1936

Since Freud only saw Oliver and Henny for the periods he was in Berlin or while they were on short visits to him, he could never become too attached to their daughter Eva. But it is clear he was extremely fond of her: in a way she was a substitute for Sophie's son Heinerle, whose death had left him heartbroken.

A letter 10 years earlier (three years after Heinerle's death) compares the two: "The strongest impression in Berlin is little Evchen, an exact repetition of Heinerle, square face with coalblack eyes, the same temperament, ease of speech, cleverness, luckily she looks stronger, was unwell and at first not kind." (*Freud-Anna Freud 27.12.1926*)

Ernst 44 yrs. . . .   Mon 6 April 1936

Ernst was not in Vienna for this birthday.

Easter 50 yrs practice . . .   Sun 12 April 1936

The anniversary of the medical practice is closely linked with Freud's wedding anniversaries. The beginning of the practice marked Freud's first step toward financial independence and therefore to the possibility of marrying Martha Bernays after the four long years of their engagement. This meant a sort of rebirth for Freud and that may have had some part in determining the date.

Egyptian plowing scene . . .   Sun 12 April 1936

Such figures found in Egyptian tombs had the magical function of ensuring that the deceased would be able to continue their daily work in the after-life. Since the group was acquired on the 50th anniversary of Freud's practice, one could consider it an apt gift for the occasion.

Like the other large Egyptian antiquity acquired nine days earlier (the funerary barge), it is of doubtful authenticity. Wooden figures cannot be dated by the age of the wood since forgers often used antique wood and artificially aged paints. But the shape of the plow is suspect, as are the markings of the oxen.

Minna still ill . . .   Sun 12 April 1936

Minna was suffering the after-effects of her operation. Anna wrote to Jones: "Here in our house we are not getting by without illness and worries, although my father has now had a quiet time. My aunt had a glaucoma operation from which she is still pretty ill." (*Anna Freud-Jones 3.4.1936*)

Henny Eva departed . . .   Wed 14 April 1936

The two had stayed nine days. Eva had to return to school in Nice. No correspondence between Freud and Eva appears to have survived, but his photo albums contained photos of her and her school friends in France, some of them personally dedicated to him. In one of them she is wearing a coat passed on from "Aunt Anna."

Minna to the sanatorium . . .   Wed 15 April 1936

Minna's failure to recover from her glaucoma operation seems to have made a stay in a sanatorium advisable.

Strassergasse . . .   Sat 18 April 1936

For the third year in succession the Freuds moved out for the summer to the beautiful villa at Strassergasse 47 in Grinzing.

#5000 from Brill . . .   Thurs 23 April 1936

It is possible this sum was a further donation to the press, perhaps raised by the New York Psychoanalytic Society. Presumably the "#" denotes dollars.

Egyptian statuettes in front of the ploughing scene in Freud's study. NB

Eva in her aunt Anna's coat.

Eva (left) with a friend, Nice c.1936.

Albert Schweitzer's postcard of his hospital at Lambarene. He wrote: "With all your friends I am glad you are celebrating in such vigorous health!"

Einstein's letter to Freud. "Princeton. 21.IV.36 Dear Mr Freud, I am glad that this generation will be granted the opportunity of expressing its respect and gratitude to you, as one of its greatest teachers, on the occasion of your 80th birthday. You have certainly not made it easy for the sceptical layman to arrive at an independent assessment of the correctness of your most important teachings. Until a short time ago I was only aware of the speculative force of your thought and of its powerful influence on our contemporary view of the world, and was unable to make up my mind about the intrinsic truth of your theories. However, I recently happened to hear about certain, as such insignificant, cases, which convinced me that any differing explanation (an explanation differing from the doctrine of repression) was excluded. This gave me pleasure, for it is always a source of pleasure when a great and beautiful idea proves to be correct in actual fact. With best wishes and deep respect Yours A. Einstein. Please do not reply. The joy of the event that occasioned this letter is entirely sufficient."

Minna from sanatorium . . .   Wed 29 April 1936

Minna had spent two weeks convalescing, possibly in the Sanatorium Löw or the Cottage Sanatorium. By mid-May the period of severe pain was over and she had completely recovered.

Addresses from Mann Wells Rolland et al. . . .   Mon 4 May 1936

A committee had organized greetings to Freud on his birthday. It consisted of Thomas Mann, Romain Rolland, Jules Romains, H. G. Wells, Virginia Woolf and Stefan Zweig. They collected the signatures of 350 eminent writers, artists and scientists. A set of celebratory addresses was collected and Freud received a handmade calligraphed presentation copy in a slipcase.

Romain Rolland was one of the contemporaries Freud most admired, as much for his moral stance as for his art. Earlier this year, when Freud was asked to contribute a work to Rolland on his 70th birthday on condition it was unpolitical, he answered that this made it impossible to praise "his courage of conviction, his love of truth and his tolerance." (*Freud-Wittkowski 6.1.1936*) In 1933, only a month after Hitler's coming to power, Rolland had been offered the Goethe Medal. In a letter to President von Hindenburg he declined any honor from a government that made antisemitism and the crushing of opposition its programme. Such a policy, he stated, was "a crime against humanity."

80th Birthday . . .   Wed 6 May, 1936

As early as July 1935 Freud been trying to prevent, or at least tone down, the inevitable celebrations. When he heard the British Psycho-Analytical Society was planning some festivity in his honour he first poured scorn on the idea of celebrating round-figure birthdays, arguing that such celebrations implied a small triumph over temporality, but that they only therefore made sense in cases where a person had in fact survived more or less intact.

In his case, he argued, there was no point in celebrating the survival of an invalid. He suggested instead that they simply compile an album of members' photographs.[1]

In the months preceding the event preparations increased. Jones wrote to Anna: "It was good news to hear that your Father is doing well. He would be horrified if he heard how widely the news of his eightieth birthday is spreading over the world and what a number of suggestions are being made in this connection. The last two are a general movement in America with its centre in St Louis of all strange places, which intends to work to get him the Nobel Prize in medicine, and another of a general address to be sent to him by literary persons from all over the world." (*Jones-Anna Freud 13.3.1936*)

Freud's attitude both toward the celebrations and the Nobel Prize remained unyielding: "The rumors that reach me about preparations for my birthday annoy me as much as the newspaper gossip about a Nobel prize," he wrote (*Freud-Marie Bonaparte 22.3.1936*).

Despite Freud's objections, a flood of honors and congratulatory messages poured in, among them the addresses signed by Thomas Mann, H. G. Wells, Romain Rolland etc. There was also a congratulatory letter from Albert Einstein and a postcard of Lambarene from Albert Schweitzer.

From Anna he received a copy of her new book, *Das Ich und die Abwehrmechanismen* (*The Ego and the Mechanisms of Defense*) which she had been working on over the previous year and had hurried to complete in time for the birthday.

Freud's niece Lilly Marlé sent him three specially written essays, which he afterwards declared were, of all his presents, the "most beautiful, because the most tender, most artistic and richest in feeling." (*Freud-Lilly Marlé 1.6.1936*)[2]

After the birthday Anna wrote that the celebrations had in no way harmed Freud: on the contrary, relief that it was all over had done him a great deal of good.

Conquest of Abyssinia . . .   Wed 6 May 1936

On May 5 the Italians took Addis Ababa and the Emperor Haile Selassie fled. Though it had taken longer than expected, the conquest of Abyssinia meant that Mussolini could at last achieve his long-held ambition and on May 9 his new Italian Empire was proclaimed.

In his diary entry for this day Thomas Mann wrote: "Entry of the Italians into

Princeton. 21. IV. 36

Verehrter Herr Freud!

Ich freue mich, dass dieser Generation das Glück zuteil wird, Ihnen als einem ihrer grössten Lehrer bei Gelegenheit Ihres 80. Geburtstages ihre Verehrung und Dankbarkeit ausdrücken zu können. Dem skeptischen Laien haben Sie es wahrlich nicht bequem gemacht, sich ein selbständiges Urteil über das Zutreffen Ihrer wichtigsten Lehren zu bilden. Bis vor Kurzem war mir nur die spekulative Kraft Ihrer Gedankengänge sowie der gewaltige Einfluss auf die Weltanschauung der Gegenwart klar geworden, ohne mir über den Wahrheitswert Ihrer Theorien klar werden zu können. In letzter Zeit aber hatte ich Gelegenheit, von einigen *an sich* geringfügigen Fällen zu hören, die jegliche abweichende Auslegung (von der Verdrängungs-Lehre abweichend) nach meiner Überzeugung ausschliessen, was empfand ich als beglückend; denn es ist stets beglückend, wenn eine grosse und schöne Idee sich als in der Wirklichkeit zutreffend erweist.

Mit den herzlichsten Wünschen in hoher Verehrung

Ihr
A. Einstein.

Bitte nicht antworten. Die Freude über die Gelegenheit zu diesem Briefe genügt völlig.

Addis Ababa, frenzied victory celebrations in Rome. Outmoded childishness—as will probably be proved."

Thomas Mann . . .   Thurs 7 May 1936

The previous day Freud had received the handwritten manuscript of the speech Thomas Mann was to deliver on May 8. Schur was there when it came. He wrote: "Freud opened it eagerly, but we discovered that Mann's handwriting was illegible. We tried to decipher the first few sentences, but had to give up." Presumably Mann paid a social call on Freud now.[1] Jones mentions a visit by Ludwig Binswanger and his wife on this day, but none by Mann.

Lecture Th. Mann . . .   Fri 8 May 1936

Freud was not fit enough to attend this lecture, but Max Schur did. He wrote: "Two addresses in honor of Freud were arranged by the *Akademischer Verein für Medizinische Psychologie*, an organization formed by a group of intelligent young doctors, mainly psychiatrists. The first was given by Freud's old friend Ludwig Binswanger, but the main event was Thomas Mann's speech. [. . .] Mann, who usually was rather detached and distant as a reader or speaker, rose to the occasion in the delivery of his address as well as in its content. It was a deeply moving experience for everyone present, giving us the feeling, which was rare in those days, that all was not yet lost."

After the talk Schur asked whether Mann could give the talk to Freud personally. Mann willingly agreed.

+ L. Braun . . .   Fri 8 May 1936

In his obituary to Ludwig Braun, Freud wrote: ". . . this high-minded man, outstanding in more ways than one, was one of my nearest and warmest friends. There was something predestined about our friendship. An older cousin of his, Heinrich Braun [1], had been my most intimate companion in our schooldays . . . [. . .] Then in the last few decades Ludwig Braun became my intimate friend, and, temporarily, my doctor, without my knowing of this relationship."

In the winter of 1887–88 Braun had attended Freud's university course on the *Medulla oblongata*. He became *Primärarzt* at the Vienna Rothschild Hospital. He was a fellow member of the B'nai B'rith and from 1933 on general president of the Austrian movement.

Visit to the new premises Berggasse 7 . . .   Fri 5 June 1936

Using Ernst Freud's plans, the premises at Berggasse 7 had been turned into a home for the Vienna Psychoanalytical Society and the International Psychoanalytical Press: it also included seminar rooms and a library. For both organizations it was their first stable base.[1]

At the opening ceremony a month earlier Jones, as President of the International Psychoanalytical Association, gave an address on the future of psychoanalysis.[2] Freud contrasted this occasion with the other ceremonies surrounding his birthday. He told Binswanger: "The opening of a new home for the Vienna Society will be the worthiest substitute for festivities. We regard the other events coldly."

Freud was not present at that occasion and today was presumably his first look at the place.

Thomas Mann lecture at our home . . .   Sun 14 June 1936

Dr. Schur, who had invited Mann, reported on this occasion: "With obvious emotion Mann read the speech, which in the meantime he had given in several other places, all, of course, outside Germany. Freud, who never liked to listen to praise of himself, was this time profoundly impressed. [. . .] It was to him a summary of his life's work, a vindication for the years of calumny and misunderstanding he had endured, and a confirmation that it really had been worthwhile to have lived that long.

"At tea and afterward, Freud and Mann engaged in a long and fascinating conversation, mainly about Joseph and Moses (Mann was then writing his *Joseph* tetralogy, and Freud, of course, was preoccupied with his *Moses*)."

Freud talked of the visit as a "great joy" ("*eine grosse Freude*") for himself and his family. He continued the discussion with Mann on the Joseph theme (with

Portrait of Freud by Wilhelm Krausz, 1936.

special reference to the life of Napoleon) in a long letter in November 1936.[1]

Minna 71 yrs. . . .   Thurs 18 June 1936

Although not a round-figure birthday, this one may have been included in the wake of Freud's own lengthy birthday celebrations, or because Minna's health was a cause of particular concern at this time. But in the following month, on July 26, Martha's 75th birthday is not registered.

Painter Krausz . . .   Mon 29 June 1936

The Viennese artist and engraver Wilhelm Krausz (1878-?) painted the portraits of many notable Viennese, and Freud's brother Alexander had now commissioned him to paint a portrait of Freud. Freud was extremely reluctant to sit once again for a portrait and told the artist that the sittings should not interfere with his five hours' daily work. He added: "Whatever remains in me of the vanity of former decades rises up against the surrender and even against fixing the present decay and hideousness." (*Freud-Krausz 22.5.1936*).

(According to Jones this portrait disappeared during the war but was rediscovered in the Vienna Art Museum with the caption *Portrait of an Unknown Gentleman*, and without the painter's name.)

Ella Braun . . .   Mon 29 June 1936

It is likely this was a visit by a relative of Ludwig Braun, possibly his widow.

Foreign Member Royal Society . . .   Tues 30 June 1936

The title of Corresponding Membership of the Royal Society was Freud's most treasured award to date. Jones wrote: "You have achieved the highest scientific honour in England and, I should suppose, in the whole world." He himself was indirectly responsible since the proposer in the Royal Society, the Cambridge astronomer and geophysicist Harold Jeffreys (b.1891), had been analyzed by him.

Also, a member of the Council of the Society, the surgeon Wilfred Trotter, was Jones's friend and brother-in-law. According to Jones, none of the other members were familiar with Freud's work, but ". . . Trotter had a way of convincing any committee."

Agreement with Germany . . .   Sat 11 July 1936

In March 1936 the Germans had established hegemony in Europe by reoccupying the Rhineland, thus undoing another article of the Treaty of Versailles. The next stage was to establish gradual control over Austrian politics.

This "agreement with Germany" obliged Schuschnigg to take two German sympathizers into his government and to conduct his foreign policy in conformity with German interests. All the Nazis involved in the unsuccessful coup of the previous year, in which Dollfuss had been murdered, were now to be granted amnesty, and Nazi papers, previously banned, could be freely sold in Austria.

Operation with Pichler . . .   Fri 14 July 1936

Anna, keeping Jones informed about Freud's condition, wrote: "The operation yesterday was not so small. It took an hour and was very painful. Pichler extracted a small growth on the upper back palate. Hopefully that will be it for a time. Afterwards there was no pain, my father rested yesterday and will be able to work again today. For three months we had been hoping that the tendency to form new growths had ceased, but it seems it is not so." (*Anna Freud-Jones 15.7.1936*).

After the operation Pichler submitted samples of tissue to the pathologist Erdheim.

Sanatorium operation . . .   Sat 18 July 1936

On July 16 Erdheim told Pichler he had discovered cancerous tissue (epithelial carcinoma). Pichler examined the slides and decided a further operation would have to be performed, this time at the Sanatorium Auersperg because of its better provisions for anesthetics. The clinical notes reveal another extremely unpleasant operation: "Isolation of formerly fulgurated soft tissue until bone exposed, then coagulation of base, with many interruptions because of pain. [. . .] Further, very thorough fulguration of surroundings causing state of excitation and complaints of very violent pain."

Minna Bernays, the Freud family's lifelong companion.

Lacework by Minna. One of the many intricate designs she produced.

Back with bandaged eye . . .   Sun 19 July 1936

After the operation Freud suffered an attack of double vision (two fields of vision oblique to each other), but without pain. The bandage was a measure for dealing with this temporary side-effect. The following day Pichler reported discomfort in speaking and several times a "kind of collapse." Freud was not in pain, but "disgruntled." Pichler advised two days' rest.

Out of grave illness . . .   Thurs 23 July 1936

The illness from which Freud was now emerging was a consequence of the latest operation, but it was made worse by fatigue and discouragement. This is reflected in a letter of Anna Freud to Ernest Jones: "Here it has not been a good week. The second operation was very severe and the after-effects quite different from usual. We are home again, but my father is very exhausted and tired this time. Prof. Pichler is satisfied with the scope of the operation; but I don't know whether one can stand many such operations." (*Anna Freud-Jones 23.7.1936*)

What for Freud and Anna was a qualitatively different reaction to surgery, Pichler simply characterizes twice as "disgruntled." One of the reasons why Freud valued Pichler's services was the surgeon's unbending objectivity in the face of illness and pain. Pichler's notes for this period exemplify this quality, to the extent of hardly recognizing this "grave illness." They mention only that Freud's general condition is worse and that he has migraine on July 24.

Anna Marienbad Congress . . .   Fri 31 July 1936

The 14th International Psychoanalytical Congress ran from August 2nd to 7th, but as Anna Freud was a vice-president of the International Psychoanalytical Association and one of the organizers of the congress, she arrived early. The venue—Marienbad (Mariánské Lázně) in Czechoslovakia—had been chosen not only because it was a convenient central European location, but also so that Anna should remain in reach of her father, in the event of an emergency.

Anna back from Congress . . .   Thurs 6 August 1936

According to the original plan Anna was to have chaired the session on August 6 and to have given her paper—On *a Particular Fate of Infantile Sexual Phantasies* (*Über ein bestimmtes Schicksal infantiler Sexualphantasien*)—on August 7, but both functions were shifted forward to allow her to leave earlier. She summarized her own paper extremely tersely for the booklet of conference paper abstracts: "The attempt was made to establish a link connecting certain sado-masochistic phantasies to the experience of the primal scene, the forms taken by the struggle to give up masturbation and particular attitudes towards life."

Arn. Zweig and H. Struck . . .   Fri 14 August 1936

Arnold Zweig had originally intended travelling from Palestine later in the month, but he embarked slightly earlier in order to accompany his friend Hermann Struck and his wife. Zweig's health and eyesight were not good and his doctor had warned him that a train journey could be a risk; their company was hence doubly welcome, since they would be able to assist him in case of need.

The painter and etcher Hermann Struck (1876–1944) moved to Palestine before Zweig. When Zweig visited the country briefly in 1932, a year before settling there, he stayed at Struck's house in Haifa.

Struck had known Freud for many years. At Karlsbad in August 1914 he gave him a sketch of an orchid they saw there. He also did an etching, which Freud liked, and a lithograph which he did not: "The Jewish aspect of the head has my full approval . . . " Freud wrote, but he still felt antipathy toward the portrait. He concluded that it had turned out as " . . . a hybrid image [*Mischfigur*], as in the *Interpretation of Dreams*, of Jew and orchid." (*Freud-Struck 7.11.1914*)

A view of Marienbad from Freud's album, recording his visit there in 1913.

"Orchibestia karlsbadiensis . . . a hybrid of Jew and orchid." Freud's description of Struck's print, done in 1914 at Karlsbad.

Moses with Arnold Zweig . . .   Tues 18 August 1936

The quality of his *Moses* manuscript had been depressing Freud. He valued Zweig's judgment and had been intending to show it to him for 18 months at least—ostensibly to persuade him it was worthless. In May 1935 he had written to him: "*Moses* will not let go of my imagination. I picture myself reading it aloud to you when you come to Vienna, despite my defective speech." (*Freud-Arnold Zweig 2.5.1935*). Ten days later Freud told Eitingon: ". . . the 'Moses' has become a fixation for me. I can't get away from it and I can't get on with it. If no new finds at Tel-el Amarna come to my aid I will hide it away forever." (*Freud-Eitingon 12.5.1935*)

Arnold Zweig had not only been kept informed about the progress of *Moses*, he had even participated in its creation by sending Freud ideas and suggestions. In June he had asked a neighbor of his, a historian of Judaism, to investigate references by earlier writers to Moses as an Egyptian. But Zweig had not yet seen the manuscript. In a July letter announcing his planned visit he asked Freud to read it to him. This then was the promised reading. Freud also gave Zweig a signet ring.[1]

Anna on the Rax . . .   Thurs 20 August 1936

Once again Anna returned to the Semmering area to recuperate. (The Rax is a mountain near the Semmering pass.) She had been running a temperature since May and was in bed with bronchitis for two weeks after her return from the Marienbad Congress. Two months later, although back at work, she was still lacking her usual energy.

Jones told Eitingon that he had "an anxious impression about Anna's health, both mentally and physically." (*Jones-Eitingon 2.10.1936*)

Plaquette by Willy Lévy . . .   Thurs 20 August 1936

Willy Lévy, the son of Dr. Lajos Lévy and the psychoanalyst Katá Lévy, became a sculptor. (After emigrating he was to work under the name Peter Lamda.) He had now made a plaquette of Freud: later he was to work on a life-size bust.[1]

Tandler + . . .   Tues 25 August 1936

Julius Tandler's earlier career had paralleled Freud's: he was also born in Moravia and came to Vienna as an infant, then studied medicine and taught anatomy at the university. But he had then become involved in social democratic politics. As a city councillor he set up a municipal, decentralized health system and laid down civic rights to health care and social security.

He was in China at the time of the Dollfuss putsch; on his return to Austria he was arrested and deprived of his university chair. After his release he travelled to the United States, China and finally Moscow, where he died soon after his arrival there.

Bullitt to Paris . . .   Tues 25 August 1936

Having served three years as United States Ambassador to the Soviet Union, Bullitt had become disillusioned with the Russians.[1] He had now been appointed American Ambassador to France. It is likely Freud had by now given up hope of seeing the Wilson book: Bullitt's duties could hardly allow sufficient time for lengthy discussions in Vienna with Freud.

Jones with family . . .   Fri 28 August 1936

Jones's visit with his wife and children the previous year had left a good impression. Both Freud and Anna referred to the children in their letters and when Jones's daughter fell ill they were concerned.

Anna said: "Nesta May seems one of those rare things in life that are as good as perfect; one hates to think of her as ill or suffering. My father asked me to give you and your wife his special sympathy and to tell you how glad he is that Nesta May is better again." (*Anna Freud-Jones 28.12.1935*)

The previous years of business collaboration had drawn Anna Freud and Jones closer. In their correspondence this is indicated not only by her switch from "Dear Dr. Jones" to "Dear Ernest," but also by the fact that from late 1935 on she began writing to him almost exclusively in German. Previously she had written largely in English.

Anna Freud's English was excellent (although she never lost her accent), but even so it represented a slight barrier and distancing. Also English had offered her the great advantage of not having to choose between familiar and polite forms of address. By now Anna had been using the familiar "*Du*" for some time with Jones. Earlier this year a longer than usual break in the correspondence had brought from her an admission of anxiety: "The idea that you are ill gives me an uncanny and abandoned feeling." (*Anna Freud-Jones 21.2.1936*)

Arnold Zweig and his wife Dita, who were now living in Haifa.

Anna Freud seated between Melanie Klein and Ernest Jones (Paris 1938?).

Ernstl to Russia . . .   Fri 28 August 1936

This trip was part of a grand tour Ernstl planned. After Palestine he wished to see more of the world. He writes: "I still did not know what to become professionally but decided to have a look at Russia anyhow. So I went for a week to Moscow as an ordinary Intourist traveller. My would-be contact there, a female analyst, I think, by name of Vera Schmidt, turned out to be away on holiday, and I found the atmosphere in Moscow rather oppressive even though at that time I myself did not know about the Stalin trials. I returned to Vienna, and as my father had emigrated from Hamburg to Johannesburg the Freud and the Halberstadt families thought it might be a good idea if I joined the latter in S. Africa. My father tried to get me a job at his firm in Johannesburg and to prepare myself for it I was apprenticed to the well-known portrait photographer in Vienna, Trude Fleischmann."

Kadimah . . .   Sun 6 September 1936

Kadimah was a Jewish nationalist organization created at the University of Vienna in 1883. (The word *Kadimah* means "forward" and "eastward.") At first it was a Jewish duelling fraternity, defending Jewish honor against antisemites. In 1892 a group of its alumni (*Alte Herren*) formed a Zionist group which in 1896 found its leader in Theodor Herzl.

When the *Kadimah* congratulated Freud on his 80th birthday, he replied that he would like to be one of their *Alte Herren*. Upon which they elected him an Honorary Member and a delegation came today to present him with the sash.

Martin Freud had joined the society as a student, when he saw that members of this society were the only Jews to fight back against antisemitic attacks. He was uncertain how his father would react to his joining, but Freud was delighted.

Ernst & Lux . . .   Sat 12 September 1936

Ernst and Lux came over from England to join the celebrations of the Freuds' 50th wedding anniversary. (Ernst and Lux's own very close marriage was to last exactly fifty years, until Ernst's death in 1970.[1])

Wolf again . . .   Sat 12 September 1936

Wolf was the first Freud dog—the Alsatian that had been bought for Anna Freud in 1925, so that she could go for walks alone in Vienna. By 1935 Freud was calling him "an old gentleman" ("*ein alte Herr*"), as Wolf was then 11 years old and therefore in canine terms roughly the same age as he himself.

This entry may mean Wolf had been in the kennels at Kagran and was now back. Since Anna had been ill and away from Vienna she could not have looked after him. On the other hand Anna speaks of Wolf as having shared the family's life for "more than ten years . . . ." Consequently his death must have occured around this time and there are no further references to him. It is possible this entry refers to the recurrence of some illness.

50 yrs marriage . . .   Mon 14 September 1936

Freud married Martha Bernays in 1886 when he was 30 years old and she 25, after a four-year engagement.[1] She belonged to an eminent Jewish family from Hamburg. Her mother would not allow her to marry until Freud had established himself in the world. The golden wedding celebrations were filmed by Ruth Mack Brunswick. It was a sunny day and the Freuds sat in the garden while a string of visitors came with flowers and gifts. Apart from numerous members of the extended Freud family, outsiders also paid their respects, for example the Faddenbergers who looked after Dorothy and Anna's country cottage, Hochrotherd.

This day is not the anniversary of the civil wedding, which had taken place at Wandsbeck on September 13, 1886, but of the religious ceremony that occured the following day and which, despite Freud's antipathy, was required by Austrian law. (The indignity was diminished by Martha's arranging it on a weekday, when few guests could attend, and at her mother's home to avoid formal evening dress: her uncle Elias Philipp had the task of coaching Freud in the required Hebrew responses.)

Ernst and Lux, 1920s.

Anna with Wolf, 1931. In 1927 he bit Jones. Freud said: "I had to punish him for that, but did so very reluctantly, for he—Jones—deserved it." (*Freud-Eitingon 13.9.1927*)

Berggasse . . .   Sat 17 October 1936

As always the move back took place on a weekend. The Freuds had now spent one day short of six months in Grinzing.

Beer-Hofmann . . .   Sun 18 October 1936

The poet and playright Richard Beer-Hofmann (1866–1945) was one of a galaxy of Viennese writers who rose to fame around the turn of the century—Arthur Schnitzler, Peter Alternberg, Hugo von Hofmannsthal, Hermann Bahr, Karl Kraus.

Beer-Hofmann was a patient of Max Schur. Knowing Freud's admiration for the poet, Schur apparently arranged their first meeting in 1930. But they had other common acquaintances, such as Lou Andreas-Salomé. She had known Beer-Hofmann since 1895: it was with her that he had attended Freud's lecture *Traumas of Childhood* on February 8, 1913.

On Freud's 80th birthday Beer-Hofmann sent Freud a gift of some intaglio-castings. In July Freud wrote a letter congratulating him on his 70th birthday and regretting they had not had a chance to become better acquainted: "From this you should not conclude that I have remained indifferent toward the majestic beauty of your writing. I have indeed gained the impression from things I have heard about you that you and I must share many significant points of agreement. But life sped by in the breathless excitement of demanding work and now that I enjoy more leisure there is not much of me left over." (*Freud—Beer-Hofmann 10.7.1936*). In September Beer-Hofmann sent Freud a dedicated copy of his latest work *Prologue to the Theatre of King David (Vorspiel auf dem Theater zu König David)*.

Arnold Zweig . . .   Thurs 22 October 1936

Earlier this year Zweig was toying with the idea of writing Freud's biography. Freud wrote to him in alarm: "Anyone who writes a biography is committed to lies, concealments, hypocrisy, flattery and even to hiding his own lack of understanding, for biographical truth does not exist, and if it did we could not use it." (*Freud-Arnold Zweig 31.5.1936*)

Meanwhile, Freud was not only discussing the identity of Moses with Zweig, he was also trying to persuade him that Shakespeare was Edward de Vere—an idea championed by Thomas Looney, author of *Shakespeare Identified in Edward de Vere, 17th Earl of Oxford* (London 1921). Zweig remained unconvinced.

Eitingon & date of Fliess's birthday . . .   Sat 24 October 1936

Eitingon and his wife Mirra had come to Europe for the International Psychoanalytical Congress at Marienbad in July-August.

This is the only time Freud mentions the birthday of his former friend Wilhelm Fliess.[1] He does not mention that the previous night was the 40th anniversary of his father Jacob Freud's death. The near coincidence of the two dates makes it likely that one virtually implied the other—in fact it was in the letter informing Fliess of Jacob Freud's death that Freud first mentioned his friend's birthday, the date of which he had only recently learned.

Certainly both numerical superstition and his father's death were on Freud's mind in this, his 81st year. Five weeks later he wrote: "At 81½ father and brother reached the limits of their lives. I am still one year short of that." (*Freud-Marie Bonaparte 1.12.1936*)

Nosebleed . . .   Tues 27 October 1936

Max Schur states that this severe nosebleed required a 24-hour packing of the nose. After the initial cancer surgery in 1923, Freud had suffered prolonged nasal trouble. A previous attack occured in 1931.

However, Freud experienced nasal problems much earlier. During the 1890s the nose specialist Wilhelm Fliess even thought Freud's heart trouble had a nasal origin. (The fact that this present nosebleed directly follows mention of Fliess's birthday could provide scope for speculation.)

New horse . . .   Fri 30 October 1936

This is probably the other large Chinese horse, similar to the one bought on June

Sigmund and Martha Freud, 1886. The photo is stuck to the menu of a celebration dinner for 18 guests on August 24, 1886.

The menu for the meal celebrating the Freuds' impending wedding on Tuesday, September 9, 1886.

28, 1932–both imitation antiquities. But it could also be a smaller striped, archaic Greek horse.

Meeting with Boehm . . .   **Sun 1 November 1936**

On March 8, 1936, Anna Freud travelled to Brunn for an urgent discussion with Felix Boehm on the future of psychoanalysis in Germany. Boehm had placed himself in the impossible situation of trying to save psychoanalysis while at the same time acquiescing to the demands of the authorities, who objected to the existence of a German psychoanalytical group and institute. He had been instructed to subordinate them to the (non-psychoanalytical) German Psychotherapeutic Society.

It was to report on the terms of this agreement that he visited Freud now. Richard Sterba, who was among those present, wrote: "Freud ended the meeting with an admonition to Boehm which I thought was in reality a tactful, indirect condemnation. He said 'You may make all kinds of sacrifices, but are not to make any concessions.' But Boehm had obviously made many concessions already."

Boehm's difficulties in trying to preserve psychoanalysis during the 1930s in Germany by compromising with the authorities led him to tell Anna Freud that "the worst thing about life over there [in Germany] is that today one already takes for granted what would have made one's hair stand on end last year."[1] (*Anna Freud-Jones* 10.3.1936)

Direktor v. Demel* . . .   **Sun 15 November 1936**

Hans A. Ritter von Demel, (1886–1951), Egyptologist, was the director of the Egyptian and Oriental collection of the Vienna Kunsthistorisches Museum from 1923 to 1951. He was also a valuer for the Dorotheum and himself an antique dealer. This is the only explicit reference to him in the diary and yet Freud often consulted him about his antiquities.

The documentation of Freud's collection includes 18 authentication notes signed by Demel during the period from 1933 to 1938. (It is possible some or all of these authentications may have been acquired through the intermediary of Ernst Kris, who also worked at the musem.) There are four Demel authentication slip from 1936, two in October and two in December. None is dated November 15 and there is no mention here of any antiquity. Consequently this entry may refer to a social visit or some other type of meeting.

Oliver . . .   **Sat 21 November 1936**

Why does Freud call his son *Oliver* here, for the only time in the diary? The full name seems to mark a coolness or distance. Because it was now two days short of a year since his previous visit? Five days later, when his son left, he was once again "Oli" as usual.

+ Etka Herzig . . .   **Sun 22 November 1936**

Etka Herzig was the sister of a schoolfriend of Freud's, Wilhelm Herzig (1853–1924), who became professor of pharmacological chemistry at the University of Vienna. He was one of Freud's group of friends who gathered once a week at the Café Kurzweil during the early 1880s.[1]

Oli departed . . .   **Thurs 26 November 1936**

Oliver returned home to France, where he was now proprietor of a photographic shop—*Paris photos* on the Boulevard Garnier in Nice.

Anna 41 years . . .   **Thurs 3 December 1936**

A birthday note from Freud states: "Miss *Han* (200 BC- 200 AD) Heartfelt greetings on 3 Dec. 1936. Perhaps also one of the ladies who like making themselves older." This note was evidently accompanied by the gift of a female Chinese figurine.

The "also" seems to imply that Anna welcomed middle age. At any rate, she was thriving in her professional life and Freud wrote: "The most pleasurable thing around me is Anna's love of work and uninhibited achievement." (*Freud-*

* Freud initially wrote *Dehmel*.

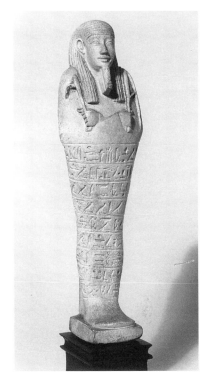

Demel's note of October 21, 1936, authenticating a *shabti* of Imhotep.

The *shabti* of Imhotep. NB

(*Opposite*) Freud, his mother and sisters, in mourning at his fathers grave, 1897.

(*Opposite bottom left*) Freud's father Jacob, aged 75, in 1890.

(*Opposite bottom right*) Wilhelm Fliess, Freud's closest friend during the 1890s. His birthday occurred the day after Jacob Freud's death.

Eitingon 5.2.1937) Freud told another correspondent that she was "a daughter who to an unusual extent satisfies all the needs of a father . . . ." *(Freud-Stefan Zweig 18.5.1936)*

One of the needs of the father in this instance was help in inserting and extracting the prosthesis. At this very time Anna noticed two suspicious pits in Freud's mouth, which she duly reported to Pichler, who examined him on December 7, but found nothing dangerous.

Martin 47 yrs. . . .   Mon 7 December 1936

Since Martin spent so many evenings at Berggasse, joining the card parties on Saturday evenings and bringing the family over on Sundays, it is highly likely he also celebrated this birthday there with his parents. Later this month he left Vienna to go on a skiing holiday with his son Anton Walter.

Edward VIII abdicated . . .   Thurs 10 December 1936

Edward VIII (1894–1972) had only reigned as British king since January 20, 1936. He was forced to abdicate because the British establishment objected to his proposed marriage to the American divorcée, Mrs Wallis Simpson.[1] (She divorced her previous husband on 27 October 1936). The abdication was a disappointment to the Nazis, who felt the ex-king had a favorable opinion of their regime.

Freud was not impressed by him. He wrote to Marie Bonaparte: "What is going on with the King? I think he is a poor fellow, no intellectual, none too bright, probably a latent homosexual who came to this woman by way of a friend and found his potency with her and therefore cannot get by without her." *(Freud-Marie Bonaparte 17.12.1936)*

Operation with Pichler . . .   Sat 12 December 1936

This operation involved coagulation of an ulcer under novocaine anesthetic. Even Pichler's studiously objective notes reveal that this was another particularly unpleasant operation: "Patient feels no pain at first, but says towards end that he cannot stand it any more. No real reason."

Prof. Otto Loewi . . .   Sun 20 December 1936

Otto Loewi (1873–1961) was Professor of Physiological Chemistry in Graz. He shared the 1936 Nobel Prize for Medicine and Physiology with the British scientist Henry Hallet-Dale for their studies of the chemical transmission of nerve impulses. (Another Austrian had also received a Nobel Prize this year— Viktor Franz Hess shared the Physics Prize with the American Carl David Anderson for their work on cosmic rays.) Loewi was sympathetic to Freud and supported his candidature for the Nobel Prize. At this meeting he told Freud about the recent award ceremony in Stockholm.

Christmas in pain . . .   Fri 24 December 1936

A letter to Marie Bonaparte one week earlier recounts Freud's suffering: ". . . I am ill myself and well and truly tortured as I will describe to you in detail. On Saturday 17th [12th]* Pichler stated that he was obliged to burn away a new place which seemed suspect to him. It happened, this time microscopic examination revealed harmless tissue, but the reaction was abominable. First great pain, in the following days severe lockjaw so that I could not eat and only drink with difficulty and give my hours with the help of a hot-water bottle renewed every half hour. Only short wave radiation, which really works wonders, brings relief but this does not last long enough. The prognosis says that I will have to put up with another week of this form of existence." *(Freud-Marie Bonaparte 17.12.1936)*

Stefan Zweig . . .   Sun 27 December 1936

Freud and Zweig were once again on good terms. Zweig's respect and admiration for Freud had never deviated despite their misunderstanding. Freud wrote of his portrait in Zweig's *Mental Healers (Die Heilung durch den Geist* 1931) that he was

Oliver Freud who was now living in Nice. MH

Martin on a skiing holiday with his son Anton Walter. A New Year Greetings card from Davos, December 30, 1936.

---

* [This letter is quoted from a handwritten transcription by Princess Marie Bonaparte. The dating of the operation as "Saturday 17th" is clearly a mistake for "Saturday 12th." Whether that mistake was hers or Freud's cannot be resolved without recourse to the original letter.]

not the book's most *interesting* character, but the only *living* one Zweig had drawn: "Perhaps I have that circumstance to thank for the warmth of your sympathy. Among biographers as among analysts there are phenomena which can be summarized by the term 'transference'." (*Freud-Stefan Zweig 18.5.1936*)

Freud and Jofi. "One cannot easily get over 7 years of intimacy."

1937

The opening entry for 1937—**Princess buys correspondence with Fliess** - connects two highly important friendships. The *Princess* was the French psychoanalyst Princess Marie Bonaparte, Freud's closest friend and confidante during the 1930s. She was a descendant of Napoleon's family and a member of the Greek royal family. Though she possessed the fascination of rank and wealth, Freud liked and respected her because she was "not at all an aristocratic lady, but rather a real person . . . ."[1] The second friend was the Berlin ear, nose and throat specialist Wilhelm Fliess, who had died ten years earlier.

During the 1890s, when Freud was evolving the basic ideas of psychoanalysis, one of his few sources of intellectual support came from his discussions and correspondence with Fliess. The correspondence offers vital insights into the background of Freud's discovery of psychoanalysis. It also reveals that Freud was strongly attached to Fliess. After the friendship ended around the turn of the century, the two did not meet again. When Freud heard that their correspondence had resurfaced, he did all he could to persuade Marie Bonaparte to destroy the letters. Because Freud's intellectual development was closely connected with his emotional life, it is hard to untangle the cause of this vehemence—whether it was his wish to erase the record of earlier mistakes and hypotheses, or to conceal his personal life.

One significant feature of the diary is that it documents Freud's relationships with his colleagues, friends and family. It shows that, to a great extent, Freud's family and professional life overlapped. Though only one of his six children, his daughter Anna, became a psychoanalyst, his son Martin was now in charge of the psychoanalytical press and another son, the architect Ernst, designed analysts' houses as well as the new premises of the Vienna Psychoanalytical Society, which opened in June 1936. Furthermore, a number of his analysands also became personal friends, or were even accepted as members of the family. The American psychoanalyst Dorothy Burlingham lived in the apartment above the Freuds and was Anna Freud's constant companion. Another friend, the young Dutch psychoanalyst Jeanne Lampl-de Groot, also fell into the role of adoptive daughter.

In his postscript to *An Autobiographical Study* Freud makes it clear he did not feel his personal life should be of any concern to the general public. This self-effacement denotes his own emotional reticence, rather than a condemnation of biographical research. Within his own circle Freud was of a gregarious nature and friendships played an important role throughout his life. However professionally isolated he may have felt during the 1890s at the time of his intense correspondence with Fliess, he was never socially isolated. Apart from his family, he had a circle of friends and acquaintances, many of whom survived until the 1930s. But from 1923 onward ill-health had restricted his social life. By 1937 Freud's contacts outside his immediate circle of family and friends was fairly limited. Death further limited social contact. Crosses next to familiar names designate the gradual passing of the old guard of school and student friends such as Willi Knöpfmacher or the archeologist Emanuel Löwy. An earlier generation of psychoanalyst colleagues was also disappearing. This year the diary marks the deaths not only of a good friend among them, Lou Andreas-Salomé, but also of one of Freud's antagonists and earliest defectors from the movement, Alfred Adler.

Moreover, the emigration of Freud's two sons and their families meant rarer family visits. In compensation, Freud had become a dog-lover in his old age. He compared their appeal to that of little children. After the death of a beloved grandson, he even wrote that Anna's Alsatian Wolf "almost replaced the lost Heinerle."[2] The first death recorded in 1937 is that of his chow, Jofi, who had lived at his side since 1930. She was immediately replaced by another chow, Lün. A simple affectionate relationship, whether with little children or dogs, was a welcome and necessary rest from the concerns and complexities of society or from the intricacies of practical and theoretical psychoanalysis.

---

1. *Freud-Ferenczi 18.10.1925* [FM] (" . . . gar keine Aristokratin, sondern ein richtiger Mensch . . . ")
2. *Freud -Lampl-de Groot 22.2.1927* [FM] ["... fast das verlorene Heinerle ersetzt."]

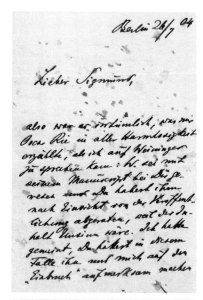

Wilhelm Fliess's final letter to Freud, July 26, 1904. It treats Otto Weininger's "theft" of the notion of bisexuality, obtained via Freud.

Freud's chow Jofi.

Princess buys correspondence with Fliess . . .   Sat 2 January 1937

These letters, covering the period 1887 to 1904, trace the intense intellectual and emotional relationship between Freud and Wilhelm Fliess, his closest friend during the 1890s, and they constitute the most revealing autobiographical source for Freud's development.

On December 30, 1936, Princess Marie Bonaparte wrote to Freud that she had been offered his letters to Fliess by a Herr Stahl from Berlin, at the low price of 12,000 francs. Fliess's widow had originally wished to donate them to the National Prussian Library, but decided against this when the Nazis burnt Freud's work. A stipulation of the sale was that the letters should not fall into Freud's hands.

In a note on this episode Marie Bonaparte wrote: "I told Freud that I had bought them. He was indignant that Mrs. Fliess had sold his correspondence. I did not hand them over to him, as I was afraid he would destroy them. I obtained permission from Freud to read them. I only read a few of the most important ones to him during my analytic hours, but without letting him have them.

"About the probable fate of these letters he told me the story of the 'Auerhahn' [capercaillie—a game bird]. (Some one asking how to cook that bird is told: 'You first bury it in the earth & then after a week take it out again.'—'And then?'—'Then you throw it away!')."

Two months later, on her way to Greece, Marie Bonaparte visited Freud to discuss the letters: "But when later, at the end of February or the beginning of March 1937, I saw him in Vienna and he told me he wanted the letters to be burned, I refused. [. . .] One day he told me: 'I hope to convince you to destroy them.' "

Jofi in hospital for operation . . .   Mon 11 January 1937

Freud had noted Jofi's sympathy with his own sufferings after his torturing operation on December 12, 1936: "I wished you could have seen with me what sympathy Jofi shows me during these hellish days, as if she understood everything." (Freud-Marie Bonaparte 17.12.1936) Jofi's operation was for two ovarian cysts. At first it seemed to have been successful.

+ Jofi from heart failure . . .   Thurs 14 January 1937

A dotted line connecting this entry with its date marks it as one of particular significance. Freud confided in Arnold Zweig: "It is a highly curious feeling, she was always so taken for granted and suddenly she is no longer there. Apart from any mourning it is very unreal and one wonders when one will get used to it. [. . .] But of course one cannot easily get over 7 years' of intimacy." (Freud-Arnold Zweig 10.2.1937).

Freud's intense affection for dogs was by no means exclusive to Jofi and it was similar to his love for children. Ten years earlier he had written: "How is it that these little beings [children] are so delightful? For we have learnt all sorts of things about them that do not correspond to our ideals and must regard them as little animals, but of course animals too seem delightful to us and far more attractive than the complicated, multistoried adults. I am experiencing this now with our Wolf who has almost replaced the lost Heinerle." (Freud- Lampl-de Groot 22.2.1927)

Thomas Mann . . .   Fri 15 January 1937

Thomas Mann arrived at the Hotel Imperial in Vienna from Budapest at 4 p.m. and left for his home at Küsnacht the following evening. His published diary for January 15 does not mention Freud at all, but speaks of many telephone calls. A meeting may nevertheless have taken place, but perhaps this entry refers to a phone call.

Freud had been reading Mann's novel Joseph and his Brothers and this had led him to write Mann a famous letter on November 29, 1936, in which he speculated on the significance of the Joseph myth for Napoleon.

Mann replied on December 13, 1936, announcing his forthcoming visit to Vienna in January 1937 and responding to the ideas of Joseph as Napoleon's avatar: "So they were no longer new to me but they retained their power to amaze and their striking verisimilitude, against which the question of their possible truth takes second place for me. This letter is a stimulating example of your genial flair in matters of the unconscious life of the mind and the effects arising from its depths, and I am greatly flattered to be able to count myself its recipient." (*Mann-Freud 13.12.1936*)

At this time Thomas Mann was living in exile in Switzerland. After an initial period of silence, he had begun his struggle against the Nazis and on February 3, 1936, he published a declaration of literature in exile in an open letter to the *Neue Zürche Zeitung*. On July 5, 1936, he wrote to the European Amnesty Conference declaring his solidarity with the victims of the freedom struggle in the Third Reich. In April 1937 Brecht, Arnold Zweig and Mann broadcast on the German Free Radio Station (*Deutscher Freiheitssender*) from Spain; in September, together with Falk, Mann founded the bimonthly journal *Mass und Wert* in Zurich.

Lün taken on . . .   Fri 15 January 1937

Lün was obscurely related to Jofi ("a sort of step-relationship"). She was much younger than Jofi and had originally been taken on at the same time. But because Jofi was "too nasty to her . . . " she had to be given away, first to Helene Deutsch and her husband, but when they emigrated to Boston she was handed over to the Burlinghams, who now restored her to Freud.

Freud characterized her as "very intelligent, much more trusty and tender towards many people than Jofi was, is very pretty, though without the lion's head she had." (*Freud-Arnold Zweig 10.2.1937*)

Heart condition . . .   Mon 18 January 1937

At Pichler's first checkup of the year on January 4 he recorded that both the objective and subjective condition of the patient had improved. But this present heart condition continued into February. Schur speaks of "anginal pain," Pichler mentions a "heart attack." Afterwards Freud suffered a severe catarrh followed by bronchitis. By March this had become a "permanent cold" (*"Dauererkältung"*: in a letter to Arnold Zweig in April, Freud said that the writer who invented that term must have been a great poet.)

Small Moses finished . . .   Wed 3 February 1937

This was the essay *Moses an Egyptian*. It was published later this year in *Imago* and was eventually to form the first chapter of *Moses and Monotheism*.

Two days later Freud told Eitingon: "Recovered from the latest damages and again capable of moderate enjoyment of smoking, I have even begun writing a little. Small things however; a fragment which I could free from the Moses work (known to you and A. Zweig) is finished. But the most essential things about it must remain unsaid." (*Freud-Eitingon 5.2.1937*)

Lou Salomé + died 5/2? . . .   Thurs 11 February 1937

The Freuds heard of Lou Salomé's death from her friend, Ernst Pfeiffer (who later edited her diary and correspondence), which explains the question mark about the exact day. The date is correct. She had died at her house in Göttingen at the age of almost 76, after a long period of ill-health that had prevented her meeting the Freuds.

Both Freud and Anna loved and respected her.[1] Freud wrote a brief obituary for the *Internationale Zeitschrift* in which he stated: "For the last 25 years of her life this remarkable woman was attached to psycho-analysis, to which she contributed valuable writings and which she practised as well. I am not saying too much if I acknowledge that we all felt it as an honour when she joined the ranks of our collaborators and comrades in arms, and at the same time as a fresh guarantee of the truth of the theories of analysis."

Wolf Sachs from Johannesburg . . .   Sun 28 February 1937

Wulf Sachs,[1] the leader of the South African Psychoanalytical Society, was now in Vienna, having spent three months in London. He was making himself very agreeable, Freud wrote to Jones. Also, he had been of help to Max Halberstadt who was now living in South Africa.

At the time of his visit to Europe, Wulf Sachs was having difficulties with his South African group, particularly with Fritz Perls, subsequently the founder of "Gestalt therapy" and the Esalen Institute. Jones told Eitingon: "At the moment he [Perls] is, in defiance of Sachs, avowedly training a number of very unsuitable

Lou Andreas-Salomé, mid-1930s. She had once been "muse and protecting mother" to Rilke. Freud was her "father-face which has presided over my life." (*Lou Andreas-Salomé-Freud 4.5.1935*)

candidates and at the same time his regression in the Reich direction is very pronounced. Sachs asked our Society for help . . . ." (*Jones-Eitingon 24.2.1937*)

Jul. Wagner 80 years . . .   Sun 7 March 1937

Julius Wagner Ritter von Jauregg (1857–1940) and Freud had studied together: as young doctors both had experimented on animals in Solomon Stricker's laboratory. Their careers had diverged: Wagner was to succeed Krafft-Ebing as director of the Psychiatric Clinic of the Vienna General Hospital and eventually he was awarded the Nobel Prize for malaria therapy in cases of general paresis.

But after World War I their paths crossed. In 1919 Wagner wrote a testimonial to the Medical Faculty of the University of Vienna recommending Freud be given the title of Professor Ordinarius. In 1920 the Austrian military authorities instituted a commission of inquiry into Wagner-Jauregg's handling of traumatized soldiers suspected of malingering, and Freud was asked to submit his assessment of the treatment (published as the *Memorandum on the Electrical Treatment of War Neurotics*).

Although Wagner was sceptical about psychoanalysis, he did not condemn it publicly and the two men remained on good terms. Wagner sent Freud congratulations in 1936 on his 80th birthday. Freud was presumably now returning the compliment.

Japanese medal . . .   Tues [Mon] 29 March 1937

One Japanese medal has been found, previously in the possession of Ernst Freud. However, it is dated 1938 (though it could conceivably have been struck in advance). It bears a portrait of Freud and is a Freud Prize award (*Freud Preis*) of the T.I.P.A. [Tokyo Institute of Psycho-Analysis?].

Montessori Nursery . . .   Tues [Mon] 29 March 1937

Anna Freud had decided to open a nursery school for children under the age of 2, where she could try out and study her own principles of early development. She rented space in an established Montessori Children's House, using funds donated by Edith Jackson, an American trainee in child analysis at the Vienna Institute.[1] Hilde Fischer, a teacher from the kindergarten, also helped out in her nursery. The nursery was on the Rudolfsplatz in the industrial Favoriten district and aimed to provide a service to working-class families.

The location in the Montessori *Haus der Kinder* also suited Anna, since she was in sympathy with the methods of their founder, Maria Montessori (1870–1952). She later wrote: "In a 'Montessori Children's House' (like the one in Vienna) the child was master in his own house. For the first time his interest in the material on hand could develop freely, instead of being arranged as in the usual kindergarten in a prescribed group activity. For the first time not the praise and disapproval of adults, but joy in the success of one's own work came into its own as a suitable impetus. Above all, not authoritarian discipline, but freedom within carefully placed limits was the principle of education."

Beer-Hofmann on visit . . .   Sun 4 April 1937

The previous year Freud and Richard Beer-Hofmann had met and exchanged gifts. Beer-Hofmann had also travelled to Palestine on the invitation of the Zionists, who saw in him a writer concerned with the essence of Jewish culture. In the light of Freud's present concern with Moses, this is a theme they could hardly have avoided discussing.

Schur, who was both Freud's and Beer-Hofmann's doctor, wrote about *Jacob's Dream*, Beer-Hofmann's play published in 1918: "I knew that Freud was particularly fond of this play, but I had not realized that he saw himself as having 'struggled with the Angel,' or that he had used this metaphor, along with those of the inner tyrant and the cancer, to describe the force of his drive toward making new discoveries decades before he had read *Jacob's Dream* [. . .] or met its author."

Children feeding each other at the Jackson nursery, Vienna in 1937. Part of a detailed photographic record shot by the analyst Willi Hoffer. WH

Play at the Jackson nursery, photographed by Willi Hoffer. WH

Ernst 45 yrs. . . . .   Tues 6 April 1937

Ernst's three sons, Stephan, Lucian and Clemens, were home from Dartington School for their Easter holidays. Martha called them the "three unoccupied wild boys" in her birthday greetings. While wishing Ernst "luck and joy" ("*Glück und*

Freude"), she added the hope that the children would at least give him some peace on his birthday.

Operation with Evipan . . .   Thurs 22 April 1937

Earlier this month Max Schur noticed a fast-developing growth which Pichler decided to excise and get a pathologist's report. Because of the violent pain during the previous operation he now used a general anesthetic—an Evipan injection. The operation was successful (in Pichler's terms) and the growth proved nonmalignant, but it was followed by almost complete lockjaw and weeks of pain.

The previous day Freud spent an hour with the Swiss analyst Arthur Kielholz. It was an achievement, Freud said, that he had now lived 15 years (actually 14 years) since his first operation.

From Sanatorium to Grinzing . . .   Sat 24 April 1937

This was the fourth and final summer move to the beautiful villa at Strassergasse 47. Freud was suffering severe after-effects from the operation—two days later he was still feeling ill and lockjaw was almost total. The move had been deferred because it had been cold and rainy around Easter.

Martha wrote at the beginning of April ". . . not even the Pessach [Passover] festivities which occured at the same time could save the weather . . ." (*Martha Freud-Ernst Freud 4.4.1937*)

Easter Sunday was March 28. This year Freud fails to note it—or the 51st anniversary of his setting up in practice.

+ Halban . . .   Sat 24 April 1937

Josef Halban (1870–1937) was the Viennese surgeon and gynecologist who had operated several times on Marie Bonaparte.

"Interminable Analysis" terminated . . .   Fri 30 April 1937

The German entry plays on the word "ending" ("*Unendliche Analyse beendigt*"). The pun relates to Freud's latest essay and it makes a serious point. This essay—*Analysis Terminable and Interminable*–deals with the aims and limitations of psychoanalysis and the qualifications of the analyst.

Freud is not over-optimistic about either: "It almost looks as if analysis were the third of those 'impossible' professions in which one can be sure beforehand of achieving unsatisfying results. The other two, which have been known much longer, are education and government."

Freud had been working on this essay for several months. The manuscript is dated January 18: the galley proof corrections were signed on May 21. Freud's own situation at the time reflected the split between therapy and theory within the essay, for only a reduction in his analytical workload freed him to write it.

In early February he referred to it in a letter to Eitingon: "A small technical essay which is slowly growing in my hands has the aim of helping me through the many free hours that the decrease in my analytical practice has granted me." (*Freud-Eitingon 5.2.1937*)

81 years! . . .   Thurs 6 May, 1937

At various times in his life since his first experience of heart trouble during the 1890s, Freud had expected a far shorter life span. In the *Interpretation of Dreams* he mentions fears of dying at 51: a letter to Jung of April 16, 1909, (when he was 52) speaks of a conviction he would die at 61.

But Freud's exclamation mark after the figure has a more specific sense. 81 denotes a fateful age—the age at which his father, Jacob Freud, had died in 1896 and Emanuel, his half-brother, in 1914.

In December 1936 Freud wrote twice to Marie Bonaparte citing 81½ years as the limit of his father's and half-brother's lives and, by implication, probably his own. To Arnold Zweig he stated explicitly: "My hereditary claim on life runs out, as you know, in November." (*Freud-Arnold Zweig 2.4.1937*)

Nevertheless he was determined that this birthday should be a low-key affair, even to the extent of his not acknowledging congratulations any more.[1]

Grinzing in 1900, from Freud's album. In the 1930s it was still a refuge from the city.

Coronation . . .   Wed 12 May 1937

Because of the abdication of his elder brother Edward VIII, the Duke of York (1895–1952) was now crowned King George VI.

Ernst departed . . .   Wed 12 May 1937

Before his visit to Vienna, Martha wrote to Ernst: "Do I guess right in supposing you planned your journey to Vienna for the beginning of May in order to evade the tumult of the Coronation?" (*Martha Freud-Ernst Freud 4.4.1937*) Ernst's arrival in Vienna is not noted. It seems likely that his father's birthday played as much a part in the timing of his visit as the coronation.

Antiquit. from Athens . . .   Thurs 13 May 1937

This entry is abbreviated and *Antiquit.* could be singular or plural. It probably refers to two excellent-quality Greek vases, probably a belated birthday present, from Marie Bonaparte, who in April had been touring Crete with her family. A letter three days later thanking her is a sad comment on Freud's condition: "A wonderful spring has come upon us. The garden has never been so beautiful. Unfortunately, the persistent pain interferes with my enjoyment . . . ." (*Freud-Marie Bonaparte 16.5.1937*)

Whitsun. Anna in Budapest . . .   Sun 16 May 1937

Over the weekend the second "Four Nation Conference" took place in Budapest—a gathering of analysts from Austria, Hungary, Czechoslovakia and Italy, as previously in June 1935.

Anna Freud chaired the first Sunday discussion: its theme was "Early Stages of Ego Development: Primary Object Love." She and Dorothy Burlingham both presented papers at the second symposium, on the revision of psychoanalytical pedagogy. Anna's presentation included a case history and remarks on the ego development of the child.

+ A. Adler in Aberdeen . . .   Fri 28 May 1937

Alfred Adler (1870–1937) was one of the founder-members of the Wednesday Psychological Society in 1902 and the first notable dissenter. However, he himself claimed never to have been a pupil of Freud's, but to have joined Freud's circle at his invitation and always to have expressed his own divergent point of view.

In 1911 he resigned from the editorial staff of Freud's *Zentralblatt* and founded his own "Society for Free Psychoanalysis" which in 1912 changed its name to the "Society for Individual Psychology," thus severing its connection with psychoanalysis.

Adler was a victim of his own popularity. During a punishing international tour in which he was to give 56 lectures in a month, he collapsed and died of a heart attack in Aberdeen. His popularity had also kept him in Freud's sight as an antagonist to be reckoned with. Freud continued to polemicize with his work. In 1936, on hearing that Adler's work was taught at the German Psychotherapeutic Institute, Freud said sarcastically: "Psychoanalysis one can teach for two years, for three years, for four years. But how can you teach Adler for two years? Adler's ideas and technique can be easily learned in two weeks because with Adler there is so little to know."

At the end of *Analysis Terminable and Interminable*, completed only a month previously, Freud argues that Adler's crucial term—masculine protest—would have been better expressed as "repudiation of femininity."

Oberholzer—Weil . . .   Sat 5 June 1937

This appears to be a visit by two child analysts, Mira Oberholzer and Annemarie Weil.[1] Dr. Mira Oberholzer was Polish by origin but lived in Switzerland; she had been analyzed by Freud and she was in turn analyst, and friend, of Otto Rank's first wife, Tola.

In March 1919 she, her husband, Dr. Emil Oberholzer, and Oskar Pfister were the founding members of the new Swiss Psychoanalytical Society, reconstituted to replace the prewar society led by Jung.

Ernst in a garden, 1937.

The "Four Nation Conference" at Budapest, May 1937. Anna Freud on the podium, between Otto Fenichel and Paul Federn.

Freud in the garden at Grinzing, 1937.

Anna's accident . . .   Fri 11 June 1937

The accident could not have been serious, whatever it was, for no other mention can be found. Perhaps it involved Dorothy's car (on the drive out to Hochrotherd?).

This entry, however, underlines Freud's constant concern for Anna and his reliance on her. A letter two months earlier to Arnold Zweig reflects his conflict at this time, between his own need for her and his wish to free her from her reliance on him. The crucial idea—her marriage—is left unspoken: "The child [*das Kind*] has become an able, independent person who has been granted knowledge of things that only confuse others. For her sake, of course, I would also like—but she must learn to get by without me . . . ." (*Freud-Arnold Zweig 2.4.1937*)

Pain . . .   Fri 11 June 1937

Probably this refers to the otitis (see following entry).

Great heat . . .   Fri 11 June 1937

The Freuds were now in their summer home where it was slightly cooler than in the city. Two days earlier the heat had been too great to allow Freud to visit Pichler for an examination. This day the wind remained in the south and the temperature in Vienna reached 30 degrees C.

Otitis . . . *   [Fri 11 June 1937]

Otitis (inflammation of the ear) was a perennial problem. This year there were only the two attacks, the previous one on April 30 after the operation. Max Schur attributes the ailment to "the direct spread of infection from the neighborhood of the Eustachian tube, the pharyngeal opening of which was quite close to the field of the last surgery."

Bust from McCord . . .   Sat 26 June 1937

Dr. Clinton McCord also presented copies of this bronze bust of Freud to the Psychoanalytical Institutes of New York, London, Paris and Vienna. The original was done by Marian Marvin and it was, apparently, the only American sculpture of Freud done during his lifetime.

Moses II . . .   July 1937

This was the essay *If Moses was an Egyptian* . . . which later formed the second chapter of *Moses and Monotheism*. The entry is written under July, but has no exact date. The manuscript in the Library of Congress is dated May 24, 1937, and Freud usually dated manuscripts from the time he began work. Presumably this entry means that Freud continued working on the essay throughout July.

The obsession with the figure of Moses was a dominant theme of the last decade of Freud's life. During this year Dr. Hans Ehrenwald had sent him his book *On the so-called Jewish Spirit* (*Über den sogenannten Jüdischen Geist*), and in his letter of acknowledgement Freud offers a partial explanation of this preoccupation: "Several years ago I began to apply myself to the question of how the Jew acquired his own particular character and in my habitual way I started out from the first origins. I did not get any further. I was surprised to find that already the first, so to speak embryonic experience of the people, the influence of the man Moses and the exodus from Egypt had laid down the entire further development until the present day—like a true trauma in early childhood in the history of a neurotic individual." (*Freud-Ehrenwald 14.12.1937*)

Eitingon . . .   Tues 27 July 1937

Earlier this year Eitingon reminded Freud that it was the 30th anniversary of their acquaintance. Freud replied: ". . . you have played a highly laudable role in our movement and few others have come closer to me personally on the most various occasions and in different respects. There has been no opportunity to make my thanks felt, apart from yielding to you the ring which I have myself

Moses with the Tablets of the Law. Engraving by Krüger, 1770, after Rembrandt's original, done in 1659. The print now hangs in the hall of Freud's London home.

---

*This entry is on an undated line by itself. It may be a continuation of 11 June, though it is strange that "Otitis" is not set next to "Pain"—unless that refers to the symptom of another ailment. On the other hand it could mean the otitis continued over several days in mid-June.

worn for many years on my finger." (*Freud-Eitingon 5.2.1937*) Moved by this letter and gift, Eitingon replied that it was like receiving the Committee ring once again.

Arn. Zweig . . .   Wed 28 July 1937

Arnold Zweig visited with his son Adam. Eitingon also came again. Marie Bonaparte filmed them together on this occasion. In a letter preceding this visit Zweig mentions both Moses and another of Freud's current preoccupations, namely the disputed authorship of Shakespeare's plays—both likely topics of conversation at this meeting. Freud demonstrated his affection for Zweig with the gift of a gold ring.

Two months later Zweig wrote: "You will believe me implicitly when I tell you that I think of you constantly, every day, not just when I am putting on or taking off your splendid ring. This time so much remained unsaid: my joy at finding you so well and your family so pleased was so great, and at being able to introduce my Adam to you on whom my heart hangs as Jacob's did on Joseph." (*Arnold Zweig-Freud 6.9.1937*)

Princess departed . . .   Wed 28 July 1937

Around the beginning of March Marie Bonaparte had visited Freud on her way to Greece and he had tried unsuccessfully to persuade her to burn the Fliess letters. (In the winter of 1937–38 she had them placed in a strongbox in the Vienna Rothschild Bank.) Probably Marie Bonaparte continued her analysis with Freud during these stopovers in Vienna.

After leaving she spent the summer in St Tropez. In one of her letters from there, she told Freud: "The greatest happiness of my life is to have met you, to have been your contemporary . . . ." (*Marie Bonaparte-Freud 6.9.1937*)

Moses II finished . . .   Sun 8 August 1937

The essay was published in *Imago* 23 (1937). Freud signed the galley proofs on October 21, 1937, adding a note in the margin for the typesetters: "Please take care to be consistent in the handling of the proper names!"

A letter to Marie Bonaparte just after its completion implies Freud was unsatisfied with the work: "I can answer you without delay, since I have little to do. Moses II was finished yesterday, and one forgets one's little troubles best in the friendly exchange of thoughts." (*Freud-Marie Bonaparte 13.8.1937*)[1]

Hematuria . . .   Wed 18 August 1937

Hematuria—the excretion of urine containing blood—may be caused by kidney, urether, bladder or prostate trouble.[1] Exactly a year later, in August 1938, Freud suffered a recurrence of this ailment. He wrote to Marie Bonaparte ". . . my handwriting has come back to what it used to be. For weeks it has been disturbed as the result of my last attack of urinary trouble which is now subsiding. There is an inner connection between urinating and writing . . . ." (*Freud-Marie Bonaparte 20.8.1938*).

But Freud's general health was otherwise good. He had not seen Pichler since early July and at the next consultation on September 20 Pichler registered: "No pain for several months. Patient looks well."

+ Kallich . . .   Tues 24 August 1937

Unknown.

Emanuel Loewy 80 yrs . . .   Wed 1 September 1937

Emanuel Löwy (1857–1938), professor of archaeology in Rome and later in Vienna, was among Freud's best and oldest friends. Forty years earlier Freud had called him "a mind as well-grounded as honest and a decent human being. . . ." (*Freud-Fliess 5.11.1897*)[1]

The warmth of this friendship remained and something of it comes through in a conversation of theirs captured on film during the 1930s in the garden of Freud's rented house in Grinzing. In her commentary to the scene Anna Freud says: "My father is here with a very old friend of his who already went to school with him in Vienna. He later became an archaeologist, Professor of Archaeology in Rome. He used to come to Vienna once a year in the autumn and then

Akhenaten, the Egyptian pharaoh credited with the discovery of monotheism. (This photo was found in Freud's copy of *An Egyptian Reading Book for Beginners* by Wallis Budge.)

inspected the new additions to my father's antique collection. And they stayed great friends all their lives. He was especially nice—lovable man.''

On Freud's 80th birthday Löwy had presented him with a Dürer etching[2] and Freud had been casting around in vain for something to give him. He thought of his own collected works, but Löwy's eyesight was by now too poor for reading.

+ Masaryk . . .   **Tues 14 September 1937**

Tomas Masaryk, the founder of the Czechoslovak Republic, had been living in retirement at Lány since resigning the presidency owing to illness in 1935. He had not responded to an invitation to sign the address on Freud's 80th birthday in 1936 (this may have been because of his poor health).

Meanwhile, Czechoslovakia remained of vital strategic importance in central Europe. A democracy with a strong armaments industry and an efficient army, a refuge for enemies of Nazism, it was, as Goebbels repeated, ''a dagger pointed at the heart of Germany.''

51 yrs. since marriage . . .   **Tues 14 September 1937**

No record of the celebration, if any, has been found. Freud appears to have regarded his own marriage as a successful and convenient arrangement. But a conversation of his in 1930, on marriage in general, illuminates some of his wider misgivings about the institution of marriage. Because girls nearly always identify with the mother, real or imaginary, (even if she be hated), Freud said it was hard to prophesy her later character. He told the American analyst, Smiley Blanton, '' '. . . where the girl is a virgin, there is generally a marked change in her character after marriage.' He paused a moment and then concluded, 'Picking a wife is one of the most difficult things in this civilization.' ''

Lou Jones . . .   **Wed 15 September 1937**

Loe Kann was a Dutchwoman who was analyzed by Freud in 1912–13. After having been the lover of Ernest Jones for several years (and a morphine addict), she married the American Herbert ''Davy'' Jones in 1914.[1]

During the years 1913–15 there had been a fairly regular and intimate correspondence between Freud and Loe Kann Jones. She was a vivacious personality and both Freud and Anna found her attractive.

Between September 1920 and this year there was a long break in their corresponence, ended by a note of thanks for what Freud had once done for her. It was written six days after this meeting with Freud, while she was still in Vienna, on notepaper of the Hotel Regina just around the corner from Berggasse, and she exclaims: ''What a perverse and capricious person I am! I don't write for 20 years and then when I *am* in Vienna I have to start!'' (*Loe Jones-Freud 21.9 1937*)

Idea about delusion and construction . . .   **Thurs 23 September 1937**

This paper was first published in the December 1937 issue of the *Internationale Zeitschrift für Psychoanalyse* under the title *Konstruktionenen in der Analyse*. (In 1938 James Strachey's translation appeared as *Constructions in Analysis* in the *International Journal of Psycho-Analysis*). The manuscript in the Library of Congress is signed and dated October 19, 1937. Other manuscript dates appear to mark the *beginning* of work. This may be an exception, or the entry for September 23 may refer to work on an earlier draft.

Freud's original title given in this entry is a wider description of its nature than the final one. It deals with the version of the past which patient and analyst together produce during the course of an analysis. The analyst digs and sorts through debris like an archaeologist trying to reconstruct the past: the analysand produces memories which may turn out to be delusions, but are in fact also an attempt to deal with traumatic events: ''The delusions of patients appear to me to be the equivalents of the constructions which we build up in the course of an analytic treatment—attempts at explanations and cure. . . .''

New teeth . . .   **Fri 15 October 1937**

During September/October Freud was undergoing dentistry which included a gold crown and a front tooth bridge.

Schmutzer's portrait of Freud's archaeologist friend, Emanuel Löwy.

Mathilde 50 yrs . . .   **Sat 16 October 1937**

Fifty years earlier, just after Mathilde's birth, Freud wrote a letter to Minna Bernays and his mother-in-law about this first child: "It weighs 3400 g., which is very reasonable, is terribly ugly, from its first moment on sucks its right hand, seems otherwise very good-tempered and behaves itself as if it were really at home." (*Freud-Mama & Minna 16.10.1887*)

Back to Berggasse . . .   **Sat 16 October 1937**

The final return to Berggasse.[1]

Queen Elisabeth of Belgium . . .   **Tues 19 Oct 1937**

Queen Elisabeth of Belgium (1876–1965), formerly Princess Elisabeth of Bavaria, was a Wittelsbach and the granddaughter of Ludwig II of Bavaria, the "mad king" who had been Wagner's patron. In 1900 she married Prince Albert of Belgium who reigned as a liberal constitutional monarch until his death in a climbing accident in 1934. She was unconventional and artistic, she played the violin and sculpted. Later she became friendly with Marie Bonaparte and did a bust of her in 1952.

This meeting with Freud may have come about through her mediation or through that of another mutual friend, Einstein. He had known her since 1929 and had often been invited to her palace at Laeken for musical evenings at which she would play second fiddle to him in their quartets.

Other mutual acquaintances were Roman Rolland and Stefan Zweig. The latter played the role of cultural intermediary several times for Freud (among others he introduced him to H.G. Wells and Salvador Dali).

+ Wilh. Knöpfmacher . . .   **Thurs 21 October 1937**

Freud and the Viennese lawyer Wilhelm Knöpfmacher (1853–1937) had been friends since their schooldays—in 1933 they both celebrated the 60th anniversary of their graduation from school.

Knöpfmacher was a founder-member of the same *Wien* branch of B'nai B'rith to which Freud belonged and in 1935 published an account of its history. He pointed out that it was antisemitism that had given rise to the need for such a union.

When Freud received greetings from the B'nai B'rith in late September on the 40th anniversary of his joining, he wrote back that he had now become a "relic of former days" ("*ein Derelikt alter Zeiten*") and would recognize nobody at their meetings apart from Wilhelm Knöpfmacher. But Knöpfmacher was already ill at this time. His son read him a copy of Freud's letter on October 6, his last day of full consciousness before death.

Dorothy fallen ill . . .   **Fri 22 October 1937**

Dorothy Burlingham had been helping Anna in the Jackson Nursery. However, she was now diagnosed as having tuberculosis. The disease was in the family and X-rays revealed tubercular scars from childhood. She was sent to the Cottage Sanatorium and remained there until April 1, 1938, after Hitler's invasion, when she left for Switzerland.

Eitingon . . .   **Fri 22 October 1937**

Eitingon may have been in Europe since at least July 27. After this visit he told Arnold Zweig that he had found Freud in good health. Since emigrating to Palestine in late 1933, Eitingon had only visited Freud three times and there had been relatively little correspondence between them. But they no longer had the business of the press and the International Psychoanalytical Association to discuss and Eitingon was busy establishing himself in his new country.

To bed with bronchitis . . .   **Fri 5 November 1937**

Though Freud's general health was quite good he suffered what Schur called "his usual November cold." In fact it had started in October. Freud mentions it already in a note eleven days earlier to the poet Victor Wittkowski—and incidentally sheds light on his attitude to lyric poetry at this period: "Thank you very much for the gift of your poems. I suspect that they are very beautiful but for many years now I have been unable to enjoy lyric poetry.

Dorothy Burlingham in the Jackson Nursery, 1937. WH

"My present state, a severe 'cold,' deters me from inviting you to pay a visit." (*Freud-Wittkowski 25.10.1937*)

+ Gärtner . . .   **Fri 5 November 1937**

Gustav Gärtner (1855–1937) worked in the laboratory of Salomon Stricker (1834–1898) as his assistant and, like Stricker, he too became Professor of Experimental Pathology in 1890. In 1884–5 Freud also worked in Stricker's laboratory and it was here, in 1884, that Gärtner witnessed Koller's first attempt to use cocaine as an eye anesthetic.

Oli . . .   **Thurs 11 November 1937**

This year, as also during the previous two years, Oliver timed his yearly visit from Nice for mid-November. Possibly this was a time when his photographic business was slack and he could afford to take a break.

Princess film show . . .   **Sun 14 November 1937**

During her visit in the summer Marie Bonaparte had filmed the visit of Max Eitingon and Arnold Zweig. These may be some of the scenes she now showed Freud.

In December of this year, when she and her daughter Eugénie were in Vienna for analysis with Freud, she had herself filmed nervously waiting for her hour in Freud's waiting-room. The camera tracks across the pictures, photographs and diplomas hanging on the walls and then across Freud's desk and antiquities. Together with Engelman's photographs, taken in May 1938, these scenes constitute the most important record of the interior of Berggasse 19.[1]

Lecture Dr. Bienenfeld . . .   **Tues 23 November, 1937**

Franz Rudolf Bienenfeld (1886–1961) was a prominent lawyer in Vienna. Martin Freud, a less successful lawyer, said: ". . . his sharp, clear voice and his personality filled and dominated the court." He had kept in close contact with Freud and the Vienna Psychoanalytical Society, though without becoming a member of the society. (An application to join in 1910 was unsuccessful as there were several objections from members.)

But he did join Freud's circle of card players. Martin Freud wrote: "His prudence and wit enchanted father, and he was much liked as a card partner."

On November 10, to mark the birthday of Friedrich Schiller, Bienenfeld gave a lecture entitled "The Religion of Irreligious Jews." It was held at the Society for Sociology and Anthropology of the Jews in Vienna and subsequently printed: Bienenfeld gave Freud a copy for Christmas in 1938 "in memory of Vienna."[1] Perhaps Freud attended a repeat of this lecture.

Stefan Zweig . . .   **Sun 28 November 1937**

Stefan Zweig had been living in self-imposed exile in England since 1934. Having by chance read an account in the *Evening Standard* of the Lord Halifax—Hitler talks he was convinced these could only concern the surrender of Austria to the Nazis. He took the next flight to Austria in order to see his mother, family and home for the last time.

At the time his Austrian friends mocked him, saying he was still the old "Jeremiah." Two weeks before this visit Zweig wrote: "If I had not been living here [in London] I would not have been able to work—happy are those who are blessed with 'Illusions'! [. . .] The real book that ought to be written would be the tragedy of the Jews, but I fear that reality, heightened to its extreme pitch, will exceed our wildest fantasies." (*Stefan Zweig-Freud 15.11.1937*)

Freud's reply was in the same mood: "The immediate future looks grim for my psychoanalysis as well. At any rate I will not experience anything joyful in the weeks or months that remain of my life." (*Freud-Stefan Zweig 17.11.1937*)

This was not Zweig's last visit to Freud but it is the last time the diary mentions his name. (He visited Freud several times in London in 1938 and 1939.)

Prosthesis broken . . .   **Tues 30 November 1937**

Max Schur noted this event as something extraordinary: "Around this time (December 1) Freud for the first and only time damaged the prosthesis by dropping it! He felt embarrassed about this 'slip,' and I remarked that I had often

Dorothy at Hochrotherd, 1937.

wondered why it had not happened before." The next day Pichler repaired the split caused by the fall.

His preceding note, for November 26, states: "This month it will be 14 years since first operation." (Like Freud he did not count the small earlier operations in 1923.) The note marks his success in keeping the cancer at bay for so long.

Anna 42 yrs . . .   Fri 3 December 1937

For her birthday Anna had asked Martin for old trousers for gardening. He responded with two poems, one in praise of Hochrotherd, the other lamenting the futility of writing poems and the impossibility of giving a more fitting present:

> "Other ladies are given lilac, roses,
> But you want nothing but old trousers [. . .]
> Nobody should frown on this account,
> My gifts already lie in store,
> A poem for five minutes' merriment,
> Old trousers for evermore . . . ."

Martin 48 yrs . . .   Tues 7 December 1937

Because of the near coincidence of dates, Martin's birthdays appear to be noted as an automatic corollary to Anna's.

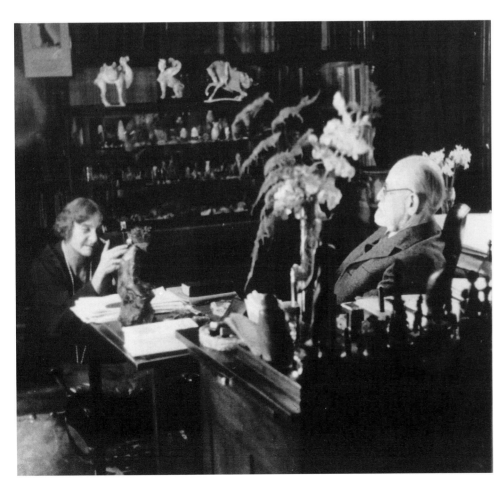

Anna, with Anna Faddenberger, at Hochrotherd, 1937.

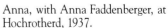

Marie Bonaparte filming Freud.

Freud in 1938. (Photograph by Marie Bonaparte.)

1938

During the summer of 1937 Freud had written a second part to his study of Moses. In early 1938 he began a third part and he prefaced it with a note that this section could not be published for fear of arousing the hostility of the Catholic Church. It now seemed that the Church was Austria's sole defense against the "almost prehistoric barbarism" of the Nazis.[1] Three months later Freud composed a new preface to this work. But this second preface was written "in lovely, free, magnanimous England."[2] Between these two prefaces, the first written in March and the second in June 1938, lay the most dramatic and dangerous period of his life.

Diary entries up to this year are mostly haphazard. Now the drama of events momentarily orchestrates the material, beginning with **Schuschnigg's speech**, on 24 February, the first indication of a political crisis. In March comes the German invasion and annexation, the end of Austria—**Finis Austriae**. From then until June everything focuses on the urgent necessity of escape: the diplomatic maneuvering to protect the Freuds from the Nazis and allow them to emigrate; the family's struggle to obtain various essential papers, passports and tax documentation; the departure of relatives; searches by the S.A. and S.S.; and, most frightening of all, Anna's brief arrest by the Gestapo. Viennese cafés, shops and businesses began proclaiming themselves "purely Aryan" immediately after the annexation, Jews were brutally attacked on the streets and the Nazis began mass arrests.

For almost three months the Freuds were trapped by bureaucracy in the hostile city. Under threat of arrest, Martin had to flee the country, leaving Anna to deal with the final formalities. Until the last moment everything remained in doubt. And even with their papers, there was no guarantee they would be able to bring out any possessions—the accumulated books, papers, furniture, antiquities. "They say that when the fox gets its leg caught in a trap, it bites the leg off and limps off on three legs," Freud wrote to his sister-in-law in late May. "We shall follow its example . . . ."[3]

While they waited, Freud was too preoccupied to be able to work seriously. But at last, on June 2, the authorities delivered the essential tax clearance and two days later the Freuds were finally able to set off for London. Here he was to spend the last year of his life in the freedom of exile.

In the peace of his new home in London, Freud's creativity returned. He completed the third part of *Moses and Monotheism* and began sketching out a new book, *An Outline of Psycho-Analysis*. The broad cultural questions of these later years had never diverted him entirely from his abiding concern, the technique and practice of psychoanalysis. After the *New Lectures* he had continued producing sporadic technical papers during the 1930s and this latest survey of psychoanalysis was a further attempt to consolidate his discoveries.

But it had to be abandoned, still uncompleted. Once again the cancer reasserted itself. In September the last operation, and one of the most serious, left him weakened and in pain. And even in the safety of England, international politics disrupted his life. The Munich crisis hung over the days during which the Freuds were moving into their final home at 20 Maresfield Gardens in the London suburb of Hampstead. Freud was concerned about the problems of other refugees, including his own relatives. Many came to him for assistance in finding work or obtaining papers. He and Anna wrote testimonials and requests. He was troubled by his limited ability to help and also the fate of those left behind weighed on him. After the "Kristallnacht" pogrom in November he realized something had to be done urgently for his sisters who remained in Vienna, but not even Princess Marie Bonaparte had enough influence to get them out.

More than ever before, Freud's fate was bound to that of the Jews. In the face of their persecution, he spoke of their mission as guardians of intellectual values.[4] For his own part, he knew that he was living on borrowed time and that he would not be able to enjoy his new home for long.

---

1. *S.E.*, XXIII.54.
2. *Ibid*, p.57.
3. *Freud-Minna Bernays 20.5.1938* [FM] ("Man sagt, wenn der Fuchs mit einem Bein in die Falle geraten ist, beisst er sich das Bein ab und hinkt auf drei Beinen davon. Wir werden seinem Beispiel folgen. . . .")
4. *Freud-Maitlis 30.11.1938* in Maitlis, Jaacob J., "Späte Begegnungen mit Sigmund Freud," *Neue Zürcher Zeitung*, 12.12.1964 ("We Jews have always cherished intellectual values, we have been held together by ideas . . . .")

Anna Lichtheim + . . .   [Sun] 9 January 1938

Anna Lichtheim (*née* Hammerschlag) was the daughter of Freud's schoolteacher and benefactor, Samuel Hammerschlag. She, too, had been a schoolteacher, having been widowed after a short marriage. Anna Freud, her goddaughter, was named after her.

She was one of the sources of the "Irma" figure in a vital dream Freud analyzes in the *Interpretation of Dreams*: at the time Freud was writing this work, she was a favorite patient of his.

Operation Auersperg—Atheroma, Evipan . . .   Sat 22 January 1938

Freud began the year in pain and with limited lockjaw. When Schur examined him on New Year's Day he discovered a suspect area. He alerted Pichler, who decided to operate, again under the general anesthetic Evipan. The operation was performed in the Sanatorium Auersperg.

The tumor was difficult to reach, dangerously close to the eye socket. A pathology report showed it to be cancerous. The atheroma was an unsightly sebaceous cyst on Freud's chin which he asked to be removed at the same time. After two days in the sanatorium and the usual pain Freud returned home.

Two weeks later he wrote to Eitingon: "My latest operation with Pichler gave rise to the usual reactions, but I have been working for a week and—I am chewing again. Since the histological condition of the removed tissue was suspect this time Pichler is threatening a follow-up operation in the near future but he has not yet decided on it. Obviously this is not comforting but thanks to the Evipan narcosis the operation itself has become ideally painless and safe and one need not think further than the next one." (*Freud-Eitingon 6.2.1938*)

+ Emanuel Loewy . . .   Fri 11 February 1938

With the death of the archaeologist Emanuel Löwy, Freud lost both a lifelong friend and one of his last links to his student days.

Operation Auersperg . . .   Sat 19 February 1938

Since the last operation Pichler had extracted a tooth, drilled and crowned another and worked on adjustments to the prosthesis. The discovery of suspect tissue made a follow-up operation necessary. It was also performed in the Sanatorium Auersperg, but was less severe than the previous operation.

Afterwards Anna informed Jones: "At first there was a lot of pain but then he recovered very quickly and perhaps we will be able to return to Berggasse today already. Perhaps a few better weeks will come now." (*Anna Freud-Jones 20.2.-1938*)

Schuschnigg's speech . . .   Thurs 24 February 1938

On February 12 Hitler had summoned Schuschnigg to Berchtesgaden for an ultimatum—Austria must subordinate itself politically to Germany, Nazis must participate in its government. On February 15 Austria accepted the demands and the next day the Nazi Seyss-Inquart was appointed Minister of the Interior. The following day jailed Nazis were amnestied and Seyss-Inquart was planning a coup d'état with Hitler. On February 20 Hitler made a speech in the Reichstag threatening Austria.

Many Jews had been making frantic efforts to leave the country. At the beginning of the week Anna wrote to Jones: "There was an atmosphere of panic in Vienna which has now calmed down a little. We have not joined in the panic. It is too early, one can not yet fully assess the consequences of what has happened. For the time being everything is as it was. It is perhaps easier for us than for others who are more mobile, we do not need to consider many decisions since for us hardly any come into consideration." (*Anna Freud-Jones 20.2.1938*)

On February 24, at 7 in the evening, Schuschnigg announced his reply to Hitler's threats in the Austrian Bundestag. Offices closed early so that patriotic organizations would have time to demonstrate and people could be home in time for the radio broadcast. The speech was long (the following day it spread over seven pages of the *Neue Freie Presse*) and it detailed Austrian economic achievements. Schuschnigg pledged that Austria would remain independent and announced his own willingness to form a united front with the left and the workers. He ended with the slogan: "Red-white-red until death! Austria!" ("*Bis in den Tod*

Schuschnigg broadcasting his speech in defiance of Hitler, under the "crutched cross" of his Fatherland Front party. DOW

Rot-Weiss-Rot! Österreich!"). This was at last an explicit challenge to Hitler and the Austrian Nazis.

Bad days . . .   [Thurs 24–Mon] 28 February 1938

This entry is linked to the entry for February 24 by a dash, which seems to imply that the "Bad days" covered the entire period from Thursday 24 to Monday 28. It apparently refers to Freud's physical health, rather than the political situation. This was a consequence of Freud's latest operation.

He wrote that it had been followed by " . . . unusually violent pain, so that I had to cancel my work for 12 days, and I lay with pain and hot-water bottles on the couch which is meant for others." (*Freud-Arnold Zweig 21.3.1938*)

Minna operation . . .   Wed 2 March 1938

This operation, as well as the one that followed nine days later, was for cataract. They were successful, but her health remained poor.

Schuschnigg in Innsbruck . . .   Wed 9 March 1938

In the evening, speaking from his hometown of Innsbruck, Schuschnigg announced a plebiscite on Austrian independence for Sunday, March 13. Since the vote was restricted to those over 24 years old, his victory appeared a foregone conclusion: much of the Nazi support came from the young. At Berchtesgaden on February 12, Hitler had challenged Schuschnigg to call a referendum.

This speech finally took up the gauntlet. It ended with the words of the Tyrol's national hero, Andreas Hofer, calling his forces to arms against Napoleon: "Men—the hour has struck!"

Wiley from American Embassy . . .   Thurs 10 March 1938

This visit to Freud by John Wiley, the Chargé d'Affaires at the American Embassy in Vienna, is the first evidence of a flurry of diplomatic activity on Freud's behalf. The political situation had become critical: Hitler now issued an ultimatum demanding the postponement of the plebiscite and Schuschnigg's resignation. The next day the Nazis invaded Austria. The Freuds, together with all Austrian Jews, were immediately in extreme danger.

Wiley's telegram on March 15 to Bullitt, the American Ambassador to France, alerted the U.S. authorities to Freud's plight. Bullitt was a friend of President Roosevelt and over the next few days the matter was followed through at the highest level. The President instructed the Secretary of State, Cordell Hull, to supervise the affair. The telegrams to Berlin and Vienna document the American diplomatic intervention and protection that was to guarantee Freud's safety over the next three months and finally to allow him and his family to emigrate.

Minna second operation . . .   Fri 11 March 1938

A further cataract operation. (This note could apply to the previous day—Thurs 10 March. The crowding of entries at this point makes it difficult to specify.)

Ernstl 24 yrs. . . .   Fri 11 March 1938

The events that broke out on this birthday convinced Ernstl he would have to leave Austria as soon as possible. He was able to do this before the other Freuds since he still had a German passport.

Schuschnigg's resignation . . .   Fri 11 March 1938

The plebiscite was cancelled in the morning, but that alone could not satisfy Hitler. Finally, on the radio at about 8 in the evening, Schuschnigg announced his resignation. Freud listened to the broadcast. (According to Martin Freud, this was the only occasion he could recall his father tolerating the radio.)

To avoid bloodshed Schuschnigg urged the armed forces not to oppose the imminent German invasion. His speech ended with the words: "God save Austria!" ("*Gott schütze Östtereich*"). Immediately afterwards jubilant Nazis appeared on the streets, chanting "*Ein Volk, ein Reich, ein Führer!*" and "Death to Judah" ("*Juda verrecke!*").

Finis Austriae . . .   [Sat 12 March 1938]

Finis Austriae (The end of Austria)—this Latin epitaph denoted the end of a very

"Fear Freud, despite age and illness, in danger." Wiley's telegram to the Secretary of State in Washington, 15.3.1938.

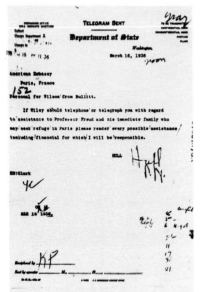

Nazis forced Jews to scrub the streets of
Vienna in preparation for Hitler's
arrival. DOW

"If Wiley should telephone or telegraph
you with regard to assistance to
Professor Freud and his immediate
family who may seek refuge in Paris
please render every possible assistance
including financial for which I will be
responsible." Bullitt's telegram to
Wilson, American Ambassador in
Berlin, 16.3.1938.

specific culture. Although the Habsburg Empire had ended with World War I,
Vienna remained a thriving cultural center. *Finis Austriae* meant not only political absorption into the German Reich but the destruction of Viennese intellectual life.[1] That culture was largely a Jewish and cosmopolitan phenomenon.

This entry stands on a line of its own. It could have been written directly after
the note about Schuschnigg's resignation. However, it is much more likely to
have been written the following day, which marked the true end of Austria, when
the Germans invaded and in the evening Hitler entered Linz. The Saturday
morning *Neue Freie Presse* had simply announced the formation of Seyss-
Inquart's government, but the evening edition bore the headline: "Proclamation
of Reichs Chancellor Hitler: A Historic Day." Hitler ended his proclamation of
the German invasion with the words—"Long live nationalsocialist German-
Austria." This must have been the paper that Freud flung aside, according to
Martin Freud's account: "Father kept on his desk a kind of unbound diary in the
form of large sheets of white paper upon which he recorded in a most laconic
way those events of each day that seemed to him of importance. On 12th March
1938 he wrote the words 'Finis Austriae,' the tragic climax which began building
itself up when urgent cries of newspaper sellers were heard in the usually quiet
Bergasse one Saturday afternoon. [. . .]

"After gently taking the paper from Paula's hands, he read through the head-
lines and then, crumpling it in his fist, he threw it into a corner of the room. Such
a scene might not be unusual in any happy land not enduring political convul-
sions; but father's perfect self-control seldom, or never, permitted him to show
emotion: and thus all of us remained silent in the livingroom, well aware that a
turn of events which would allow him to fling a paper from him in disgust and
disappointment must have alarming implications."

Since *Finis Austriae* almost certainly refers to Saturday, then the lack of any
date next to this entry takes on the significance of a deliberate suppression—an
accursed day

Anschluss with Germany . . .   Sun 13 March 1938

When the first Austrian republic was set up in 1918 it proclaimed itself the
"independent state of German-Austria" and "a constituent part of the German
republic." But the Treaty of St. Germain and the Treaty of Versailles forbade the
unification of the two German states without the approval of the Council of the
League of Nations.

When Hitler entered Linz on February 12, he had apparently intended impos-
ing a puppet goverment in Austria. It was his rapturous welcome from the
inhabitants which persuaded him to annex the country instead, for there is no
evidence that this tactic was a preconceived plan. But annexation was an ambition he had long cherished and one that is clearly stated on the opening page of
Mein Kampf: "German Austria must return to the great German mother country.. [. . .] One blood demands one Reich."

The actual "Anschluss" (unification of Austria with Germany) was publicly
announced in Berlin on the evening of March 13. Freud may have heard this on
the radio, as it was not published in the papers until the following day.

Meanwhile, a meeting of the Vienna Psychoanalytical Society was held at
Berggasse 19. Freud shook hands with all the members, saying, "There is nothing
one can do about it." It was decided to disband the society and reform wherever
Freud settled.

Hitler in Vienna . . .   Mon 14 March 1938

Vienna gave Hitler as ecstatic a welcome as had Linz. In preparation, local Nazis
had rounded up Jews and forced them to scrub hostile slogans off walls and
pavements. The Nazi Seyss-Inquart had now taken over office from Austria's
President Miklas and presented the Council of Ministers with the text of a law
on the "Reunificiation of Austria with the Reich." Meanwhile, von Papen arranged a meeting between Hitler and the Austrian Cardinal Innitzer, who could
sway the country's Catholic majority.

On March 15 Hitler spoke from the Hofburg to a vast crowd in the Helden-
platz on "the homecoming of my homeland into the German Reich."[1] Austria
was to be incorporated into the German *Gau* system, though for the time being
it would still have its own *Land* government.

But this was soon to to fade away. On 23 April Joseph Bürckel, *Gauleiter* of the Saarpfalz, became *Reichskommissar* with the task of reunifying Austria—or *Ostmark* as it was now called—with the Reich.

Among the diplomatic efforts now under way to protect Freud, Giovacchino Forzano, who had visited Freud in 1933, today wrote a note to Mussolini: "I recommend to Your Excellency a glorious old man of 82 who greatly admires Your Excellency: Freud, a Jew." (The "admiration" clearly alludes to Freud's book dedication on April 26, 1933 when he addressed him as a "culture hero." It is not known whether Mussolini did actually intervene with Hitler on Freud's behalf.)

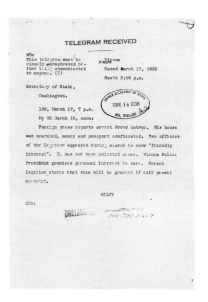

Search of press and house . . .   Tues 15 March 1938

Martin Freud was at the premises of the publishing house when it was raided by an irregular group of S.A. men, ". . . an odd medley shabbily dressed, including a fat boy of perhaps fourteen . . ." and also a haggard man who threatened to shoot him whenever he failed to cooperate.

During the raid Jones turned up, having just flown in from England. He, too, was threatened and held by the gang, but eventually released and left in order to appeal to higher authorities.

Martin bribed a guard and was covertly able to destroy some incriminating documents. "And so the day passed until finally there arrived in a breathless condition no less a person than a *Bezirksleiter*, the District Commander of nearby S.A. headquarters. . . . [. . .] The *Bezirksleiter* was correct, even polite; and I felt I was indeed awakening from a nightmare when sister Anna entered the room."

Meanwhile, a slightly more organized group of S.A. raiders was searching Berggasse 19. Martin Freud's second-hand account (he was being held at the time) stresses the effect his mother's *sang froid* had on the intruders: ". . . she treated them as ordinary visitors, inviting them to put their rifles in the sections of the hall-stand reserved for umbrellas and even to sit down. And although the invitation was not accepted, her courtesy and courage had had a good effect. Father, too, had retained his invincible poise, leaving his sofa where he had been resting to join mother in the living-room, where he had sat calmly in his armchair throughout the raid."

The intruders confiscated everybody's passports and took 6,000 schillings (about £300), leaving a receipt for this money. Freud supposedly commented: "I have never taken so much for a single visit."[1]

Jones . . .   Wed 16 March 1938

On March 14 a phone call from Dorothy Burlingham in Vienna alerted Jones to the critical situation. He rang Marie Bonaparte and they arranged to go to Vienna immediately. His diary records: "[15.3.1938] Flew to Vienna. Hitler parade. To Bauer's, whence Anna follows me to see Martin at Verlag. Arrested 3/4 hr. Bauers'. Dorothy. Freuds. Anna in despair."

Jones felt his mission was to persuade Freud to leave the country. He writes that at their meeting the previous day: ". . . he was still adamant, saying: 'This is my post and I can never leave it.' The image of a captain not leaving his ship gave me the idea of telling him the story of the officer who had been blown to the surface by the boiler explosion when the *Titanic* went down. On being sternly interrogated: 'At which moment did you leave the ship?' he proudly answered: 'I never left the ship, Sir; she left me.' Freud saw that was his case, that Austria had ceased to exist, and so consented to depart for England, the land of his early dreams."

Once Freud had consented, the question remained how many of the Viennese analysts could also come to England. Possibly now and certainly over the rest of the week, he and Anna discussed this problem. Anna wished to keep the Vienna group together: Jones insisted on limiting the numbers. Eventually they reached a compromise and Jones left Vienna on March 20.[1]

Princess . . .   Thurs 17 March 1938

Princess Marie Bonaparte remained in Vienna until April 10, staying at the Greek Legation but having her meals with the Freuds. Her presence represented additional protection. During this time she collected historical and biographical reminiscences from Freud and the family.

"Foreign press reports arrest Freud untrue. His house was searched, money and passport confiscated. Two officers of the Legation appeared during the search to show 'friendly interest'. He has not been molested since. Vienna Police President promises personal interest in case. French Legation states that visa will be granted if exit permit accorded." Wiley's telegram to Cordell Hull, Secretary of State, Washington, 17.3.1938

Ernest Jones, summer 1938.

She also helped Anna to go through Freud's papers and correspondence, burning whatever they considered not worth taking to London and rescuing things Freud would have destroyed.

Martin Freud said: "I think our last sad weeks in Vienna from 11th March until the end of May would have been quite unbearable without the presence of the Princess."

Anna with Gestapo . . .   Tues 22 March 1938

As a follow-up to the raid on March 15, the Gestapo now searched Berggasse 19 and took Anna with them back to headquarters for questioning. Apparently they suspected the International Psychoanalytical Association of being a subversive movement directed against them.[1] Marie Bonaparte was present and asked to be arrested with Anna, but even the S.S. were deterred by a royal passport.[2]

Max Schur spent this, the worst day for Freud, at Berggasse. "The hours were endless. It was the only time I ever saw Freud deeply worried. He paced the floor, smoking incessantly."

Meanwhile, Anna had been left waiting in a corridor in the Gestapo headquarters. She realized she might face deportation or be murdered if she remained there. She maneuvered herself into a room[3] where she was questioned and where she managed to persuade the interrogators that the International Psychoanalytical Association was nonpolitical and not an international terrorist organization.

At 7 in the evening she returned home. Freud was not told that Schur had previously given her (and Martin) "a sufficient amount of Veronal" in the event of their being subjected to torture.

Acceptance by England assured . . .   Mon 28 March 1938

Most countries' attitudes to Jewish refugees were now "ferociously inhospitable," as Jones says. It was due to his efforts that entry permits for the Freuds were obtained in so short a time.

In obtaining permits not only for Freud's own family group, but also for a number of Viennese co-workers (a total of 18 adults and 6 children in all), Anna Freud said that ". . . Ernest Jones did the near impossible." He achieved this firstly through the influence of his brother-in-law, William Trotter, who was on the council of the Royal Society. By this means he gained an introduction to its president, the physicist Sir William Bragg. Bragg then gave Jones a letter to Sir Samuel Hoare, the Home Secretary (whom Jones already knew slightly through the private skating club to which they both belonged).

Consequently on March 25 Jones was able to write in his diary: "Saw Hoare's secretary, A.S. Hutchinson, re Immigration. Success! First rain for 24 days. Amazing March."

Ernstl in Paris . . .   Mon 28 March 1938

With the help of Ernest Jones, Ernstl had obtained permission to come to England in transit to South Africa to join his father. He wrote: "Through the help of Princess Marie Bonaparte I could break my journey to London in Paris, where I stayed for 5 days at the Bonaparte's house in St. Cloud before proceeding to London. The princess herself was at that time in St. Tropez, but her daughter was in Paris, and her butler showed me the sights of Paris during that time."

Emigration appears possible . . .   Mon 28 March 1938

"Possible" ("*ermöglicht*": literally "made feasible") is still only a tentative hope based on the British entry permits and possibly indications from the Nazi authorities that they were aware of diplomatic maneuveres on Freud's behalf.

There were still important formalities to be overcome—namely the statement of no impediment (*Unbedenklichkeitserklärung*), which certified that the state had no further financial claim upon the holder, and the refugee tax (*Reichsfluchtsteuer*). Neither could be obtained before the assets of the press had been declared and its affairs liquidated.

Two Ernsts in London . . .   Fri 1 April 1938

Ernstl, Freud's grandson, had left Paris and now arrived safely in London, where his uncle Ernst had been living since 1933. He was supposed to continue his journey to South Africa but, as he writes, ". . . the work permit for S. Africa did

Engelman's portrait of Anna, after a harrassing visit to the emigration office. EE

not materialize, if I remember correctly, and I much preferred to stay in London anyhow." [1]

Ernst 46 yrs . . .   Wed 6 April 1938

Ernst was now a well-established architect. An article in *The Star* records one of the contracts he was working on: "Mr. Ernest Freud, son of Professor Sigmund Freud, has designed six unusual houses which have just been completed in Hampstead. They are in Frognal, not far from Finchley-road, and are of light brown brick in the modern Dutch style. Mr. Freud has included several labour-saving devices popular on the Continent and all the reception rooms communicate, making them suitable for big parties."

Ernst and his family were granted British nationality in autumn 1939, just in time to avoid being categorized "enemy aliens" and probably interned.

Topsy translation finished . . .   Sat 9 April 1938

In 1937 Marie Bonaparte had published a book about her chow—*Topsy, Chow-Chow au poil d'or.* Freud had already read the manuscript and commented: "I love it; it is so movingly real and true. It is, of course, not an analytic work, but the analyst's search for truth and knowledge can be perceived behind this creation. It really gives the reasons why one can love with such a strange depth an animal like Topsy or (Jo-fi): its affection without any ambivalency, the simplicity of its life free from the almost unbearable conflict with civilization, the beauty of an existence complete in itself. And in spite of the alien nature of its organic development nevertheless a feeling of intimate relationship—an undeniable sense of belonging together—exists between us." (*Freud-Marie Bonaparte 6.12.-1936*)

Freud began translating the work three years previously from manuscript—a partial draft translation is dated "May 1935–June 1936." In August 1937 he asked Marie Bonaparte—"Does Topsy realize she is being translated?" (*Freud-Marie Bonaparte 13.8.1937*)

During the last few months in Vienna Freud and Anna concentrated on this translation to distract themselves from the strain and uncertainty of waiting for their exit visas. The translation was published the following year as *Der goldenhaarige Chow.*[1]

Plebiscite . . .   Sun 10 April 1938

Since the Anschluss on March 13 (the date of Schuschnigg's cancelled plebiscite), German Reichs law had been introduced, which automatically included all the German antisemitic legislation. Cardinal Innitzer, the Archbishop of Vienna along with the Austrian bishops, had declared their loyalty to Hitler. Great Britain recognized the annexation on April 2, followed by France and the United States. (Only Chile, China, Mexico and the Soviet Union protested against the "rape of Austria.")

Hitler returned to Vienna on April 9 to build up enthusiasm for the *fait accompli* of unification. The plebiscite was linked to new elections to the Reichstag. The result was a 99.72% vote in favor—only 11,281 voted against, 4,939 of these in Vienna.

Bürckel, soon to be appointed *Reichskommissar* for the reunification of Austria with the Reich, crowed: "We are Germans and belong to Germany and to the Führer for all eternity."

Minna back from sanatorium . . .   Tues 12* April 1938

Minna had been away six weeks and undergone two eye operations in early March. Her return now, still in poor health, meant an additional responsibility for the household to bear during these already difficult days.

Easter Sunday 52 yrs practice . . .   Sun 17 April 1938

This is the last mention of the practice until its dissolution in the summer of 1939. (The anniversary is not mentioned the following year.) But Freud could not continue analyzing after the Anschluss. He told Smiley Blanton: " 'I had two patients, but I dismissed them and told them to go away. When the conscious

---

*Mon 11 has been crossed out.

Marie Bonaparte and her chow Topsy.

The entrance to Berggasse 19 decorated with a swastika. EE

mind is troubled, one cannot be interested in the unconscious mind.'
'Could you continue to write?' [Blanton] asked.
'Yes, I could write,' he said. 'There was some connection with the situation in Austria at that time and the material I was writing.' "

At this time Freud was working an hour a day on the third part of *Moses and Monotheism*, dealing with the peculiarities of the Jews and the nature of their claim to be the chosen people.

Alex 72 yrs . . .   Tues 19 April 1938

As a birthday present Freud "bequeathed" his brother one of his most precious possessions, his stock of cigars: "Your seventy-second birthday finds us on the verge of separating after long years of living together. I hope it is not going to be a separation forever, but the future—always uncertain—is at the moment especially difficult to foresee. I would like you to take over the good cigars which have been accumulating with me over the years, as you can still indulge in such pleasure, I no longer." (*Freud-Alexander Freud 19.4.1938*) Not that Freud had totally renounced smoking, but he could not longer "indulge himself."

Princess departed . . .   Tues 19 April 1938

Freud was not recording all of Marie Bonaparte's arrivals and departures at this period. After first coming to Vienna on March 17 she had stayed until April 10, then returned to Paris. On April 17 she returned to Vienna, and now she was leaving for Cracow to attend the wedding of the sister of her future son-in-law, Dominique Radziwill.

Not only had she rescued some of Freud's documents from the wastepaper basket, she also smuggled a few of the favorite antiquities to Paris, in case he could not take his collection with him.

Meal with engaged Radziwil couple . . .   Mon 18* April 1938

Marie Bonaparte's daughter Eugénie became engaged to Prince Dominique Radziwill on February 18, 1938. They were presumably now in Vienna en route for Cracow with Marie Bonaparte to attend his sister's wedding there. They themselves were to be married in Paris on May 30 at the church of Les Invalides.

Attack of deafness . . .   Tues 26 April 1938

When in 1934 the American Smith Ely Jelliffe told Freud about his hearing trouble Freud replied: "My hearing too is not what it was, but I get by and anyway at 78 years old I have a certain title to deafness which I would dispute with your age. [. . .] This last stage of my life is not being made easy for me." (*Freud-Jelliffe 2.8.1934*) Postoperative infections had so damaged Freud's hearing on his right side that he had had to reverse the position of his couch and chair in order to hear his patients.

Among his medical consultants Freud also had an ear specialist, Dr. Schnierer. It was, however, disturbing that Freud's health should be so fragile at this critical time.

He wrote to Jones: "I would much prefer to have come to England in better condition. I am travelling with a personal doctor, but I require specialized doctors and soon after my arrival I shall seek out an ear specialist and must find the jaw specialist whose name Pichler gave me. Sometimes one even says to oneself 'The game is not (no longer) worth the candle' and even though one is right in this, one cannot concede to being right." (*Freud-Jones 13.5.1938*)

Princess returned . . .   Fri 29 April 1938

This time Marie Bonaparte stayed in Vienna until May 4, when she returned to Paris to prepare for her daughter Eugénie's wedding.

Beer-Hofmann with Princess . . .   Sun 1 May 1938

Either before or after this visit to Freud, Marie Bonaparte went out into the street with her movie camera and recorded the May Day festivities. The Nazis had taken over the traditional celebrations and used them for their own pur-

Marie Bonaparte, summer 1938.

---

*This entry follows 19 April and is marked by an "X" in the margin, probably because it is erroneously placed rather than because of its importance.

poses. Scenes from her film show swastikas hung up along Berggasse 19, with a banner reading: "This First of May shall document that we do not wish to disrupt but mean to build." Then vast crowds are seen cheering Hitler, and finally a dazed stranger accidentally wanders into the frame.

Like Freud, Richard Beer-Hofmann had delayed emigrating. He did not get out until 1939. Soon afterwards his wife Paula died in Zurich. He then went to New York and in 1945, the year he died, he was granted U.S. nationality. Shortly before his death he was awarded the Prize of the American Institute of Arts and Letters.

Minna emigrated . . .   Thurs 5 May 1938

Minna, the first of the Viennese to receive her exit visa, was still too ill to travel alone. She was fetched by Dorothy Burlingham and taken to Switzerland.

Dorothy had been forced to leave Austria after the Anschluss by a new law compelling foreigners to convert their hard currency assets. Judging she would best be able to help the Freuds from outside, she had left for Switzerland with her daughter Mabbie. Mabbie went on to London with Simon Schmiderer, whom she married on May 8, but Dorothy remained in Lugano, ready to help the Freuds in any way possible.[1]

Negotiation with Gestapo . . .   Thurs 5 May 1938

After the Anschluss a Gestapo reign of terror had immediately begun. By mid-April over 7,500 arrests had occured. On April 1 the first trainload of political prisoners left for Dachau: thousands of Jews awaited deportation in Gestapo prisons.

Emigration depended on the consent of the Gestapo and the tax authorities—it was necessary above all to clarify the affairs of the press. As its director, Martin was banned from its offices and could not play a part in the negotiations, which were largely left to Anna.[1]

The Freuds were assigned a Nazi commissar, Dr. Anton Sauerwald, to super-vise the winding up of the press and their financial affairs. He turned out to have studied chemistry under one of Freud's old friends, Dr. Herzig: he soon devel-oped a respect and loyalty to Freud that was to be vital in the coming weeks.

Nevertheless, negotiations dragged on. One of the reasons for the delay was simply bureaucratic confusion resulting from the Anschluss. At the end of April Freud told Jones: "The delay is truly not our fault, it is connected with the wealth and property transactions and with the peculiarities of this transitional period during which the officials are no longer certain which rules they should be working by." (*Freud-Jones* 28.4.1938)

82 yrs . . .   Fri 6 May 1938

This year Freud was finally given an unassailable excuse for not celebrating his birthday. The problem of emigration obviously overshadowed everything else and it was decided that any eventual festivities would best be postponed until England: "We had decided that this birthday should not count, that it should be postponed until the 6 June, July, August etc., in short until a date after our liberation and I have in fact not answered a single one of the messages, telegrams and so on which have arrived." (*Freud-Jones* 13.5.1938)

Emigration within a fortnight? . . .   Tues 10 May 1938

In fact it was not until May 25 that the first essential step toward actual emigra-tion was taken—the payment of the Refugee Tax [*Reichsfluchtsteuer*]. This was a tax on the valued assets of the emigrant.

Meanwhile, Freud continued to be concerned with the emigration problems of others, for example a friend and analyst (in fact one of the earliest members of the Vienna Society) who was also the family dermatologist, Dr. Maximilian Steiner. Freud appealed to Jones to help him also in his efforts to leave Austria.

Anna was also active not only in negotiating with the authorities for the Freuds themselves but on behalf of many others as well. Looking ahead to England, Freud was aware that Anna's mere presence might appear threatening to Kleini-ans and he was therefore diplomatic in the way he commended her efficiency and energy to Jones: "Anna is untiringly active not only on our behalf but also for innumerable others. I hope she will also be able to do much for analysis in England, but she will not be obtrusive." (*Freud-Jones* 13.5.1938)

Portraits taken by the photographer Edmund Engelman in May 1938. The first became Freud's new passport photo. EE

The vital Refugee Tax payment
certificate, May 25, 1938 that opened
the way for the Freuds emigration.
Payment of 31,329 Reichs Mark, was
due on June 1.

Received passports . . .   Thurs 12 May 1938

The S.A. had confiscated the Freuds' passports during their raid on 15 March.
But these had been Austrian passports, which would have had to be replaced
anyway.[1] When the young photographer Edmund Engelman came to photograph the interior of Berggasse 19,[2] Freud asked him to take his passport photo
at the same time. Since Austria no longer existed as a sovereign state, the new
passports were German, bearing the insignia of the eagle and swastika.

Martin left . . .   Sat 14 May 1938

Martin's memoirs depict the devious background to his emigration: "I was
forced to leave Vienna two weeks before the others were ready to travel. During
that first Sunday rag-time raid on my offices, a number of incriminating (in Nazi
eyes) documents had been found and I had become a certain candidate for a
concentration camp, most probably Buchenwald, where a number of my friends
actually perished. Happily, the Vice-President of Police, a man with a criminal
record, was a close friend of my cook. Through this contact, I was able to buy
back the documents quite cheaply and, during the negotiations, I was given
timely warning of my projected arrest. Under these circumstances, it was decided
that any delay in my departure might only cause embarrassment, and I decided
to make for Paris to join my wife and two children, who had been sent there
some days earlier."[1]

Valuation of the collection . . .   Sat 21 May 1938

In April Freud had whiled away the time putting books and antiquities into
order, even though it remained uncertain whether he would be allowed to take
anything out with him to England. He told Jones in late April: "I am suffering
from the lack of occupation, am helping a bit in putting the library and collection
in order . . . ." (*Freud-Jones 28.4.1938*)

The high-level diplomatic negotiations on Freud's behalf assured him prefer-
ential treatment. Unlike most other refugees at this period who left the country
penniless, he was able to take with him not only personal belongings but furniture, library and, above all, his collection of antiquities.

However, he was kept in uncertainty until the last moment whether this would
be possible. It was for this reason that Princess Marie Bonaparte had smuggled
out his favorite statuette, the figure of Athena, after her recent visit to Freud.

Freud already knew Hans von Demel, the curator of the Vienna Kunsthistorisches Museum who now valued his collection, or rather, it seems, deliberately
undervalued it. Two days later Freud wrote to Minna: "The one good piece of
news is that my collection has been released. Not a single seizure, only a small
payment of 400 Reichsmarks. Director Dehmel of the Museum was very merciful, he assessed it all at only 30,000 RM but that leaves us far below the tax limit
for refugees. The removers can begin packing without delay." (*Freud—Minna
Bernays 23.5.1938*)

The "refugee tax" (*Reichsfluchtsteuer*) could now be estimated. On May 25
Freud's taxable assets were reckoned at 125,318 RM and he had to pay a 25
percent tax of 31,329 RM before being permitted to leave the country.

Mathilde & Robert left . . .   Tues 24 May 1938

Four days earlier Freud had written to his sister-in-law: "We are standing in the
doorway like someone who wants to leave a room but finds that his coat is
jammed. Mathilde and Robert are free already. [. . .] We are still caught up with
the tax. Anna is striving with great skill and good humor to get us out." (*Freud-
Minna Bernays 20.5.1938*).

Mathilde later described her departure to Jones: "Neighbours, friends, all our
tradesmen, came to say goodbye; housekeeper, charwoman, caretaker of the
house in Türkenstrasse, stood on the pavement weeping; a member of the firm
for whom Robert had been working during the last years, and a schoolmaster of
mine, came to the Westbahnhof—and so we left for the new life in England."
(*Mathilde Hollitscher-Jones n.d.*).

She and her husband phoned Freud the following day from Paris, where they
were stopping over with Marie Bonaparte on their way to London. Now that the
family was dispersing, Freud wrote ". . . [i]n a certain sense everything is unreal,
we are no longer here and not yet there." (*Freud-Minna Bernays 26.5.1938*)

+ Emilie Kassowitz . . .   Mon 30 May 1938

Emilie was the wife of Dr. Max Kassowitz (1842–1913), who had been in charge of the pediatric institute at which Freud had directed the department of neurology from 1886 to 1896. She was 84 years old and died of pneumonia, resulting from a flu caught off Karl Kassowitz from Milwaukee, whom Freud called the "most interesting of the farewell visitors."

Unbedenklichkeitserklärung . . .   Thurs 2 June 1938

The *Unbedenklichkeitserklärung* ("declaration of no impediment") certified that the authorities had no further claim upon its holder. This meant primarily that all debts and taxes had been paid. Since Freud's bank account and the assets of the press had been seized, he could not have paid any of the taxes demanded if Marie Bonaparte had not loaned him the money (which he was to pay back, after emigration, out of his foreign account).

In mid-May Freud had written to Minna: "Everything still depends on when we receive the *Unbedenklichkeitserklärung* from the tax authorities. Without it we are not certain of being able to cross the border. So this document is anxiously awaited. Until then we cannot buy our tickets either." (*Freud—Minna Bernays 14.5.1938*).

The arrival of this vital document meant that Freud was at last free to leave Vienna, his home for 78 years. Anna immediately set about buying the tickets from Thomas Cook, reserving sleeping places, fetching foreign currency. Freud told Minna: "You cannot imagine what sort of trivialities have now become of importance and all the most vital things as well as the inessential have to be taken care of by Anna alone." (*Freud-Minna Bernays 2.6.1938*)

Departure 3.25 Orient Express . . .   Sat 3[4]* June 1938

The party leaving Vienna consisted of Freud, Martha, Anna, Dr. Josefine Stross, Paula Fichtl and Lün. After the journey Freud reported to Max Eitingon: "My personal doctor Dr. Schur was to have accompanied us with his family but was inept enough to require an appendectomy in the eleventh hour so that we had to make do with the guarantee of the nice pediatrician Dr. Stross whom Anna is bringing with her. She looked after me well for in actual fact the difficulties of the journey produced an effect of painful cardiac weariness on me, against which I took ample doses of nitroglycerine and strychnine." (*Freud-Eitingon 6[7].6.-1938*)

3 3/4 am Kehl bridge . . .   Sat 3[4]** June 1938

Freud anticipated trouble at the border. He told Eitingon: "By some miracle we were spared the irksome customs inspection at Kehl. After the Rhine bridge we were free!" (*Freud-Eitingon 6[7?].6.1938*).

The treatment by Customs officials may have been influenced by the presence of a member of the U.S. Legation in Vienna, ordered to accompany the party. Schur, who eventually followed Freud to London, mentions the sense of "overwhelming relief" on crossing the Rhine into France. Paula Fichtl remembered Freud saying simply: "Now we are free." ("*Jetzt sind wir frei.*")

Paris 10h met by Marie Ernst Bullitt . . .   Sun 4[5] June 1938

Marie Bonaparte, Ernst Freud and William Bullitt,[1] now American Ambassador to France, were at the Gare de l'Est, together with a throng of journalists, waiting for the Freuds' arrival.

Freud's first letter after the journey conveys his impressions of the day in Paris: "The welcome at Paris—Gare de l'Est—was cordial, rather noisy with journalists and photographers. From 10 am to 10 pm we were with Marie at her house. She excelled herself in kindness and thoughtfulness, gave us a portion of

---

* This Saturday was actually 4th not 3rd June. The following two entries thus become 4th (instead of 5th) and 5th (instead of 6th) June. But the entry for Thursday 9th is once more correct. These three incorrect entries were probably written up in England after the journey: for Saturday's date Freud referred to the final preceding entry on June 2, not noticing it was for Thursday, not Friday. Afterwards he corrected the dates lightly in pencil. The error could be seen as an expression of impatience to leave the country.[1]

** The date is now doubly incorrect, since it was already the morning of Sunday 5 June.

Marie Bonaparte and the American Ambassador to Paris, William Bullitt, welcoming Freud at the Gare de l'Est.

our wealth back and would not let me travel further without new Greek terracottas." (*Freud-Eitingon 6[7?].6.1938*)

These new terracottas decorated Freud's otherwise empty desk during the two months in England before his collection arrived. The "portion of our wealth" refers to gold currency Freud had collected against inflation. Marie Bonaparte now told him she had managed to get it out of the country by means of the Greek Legation's diplomatic bag.

Marie Bonaparte filmed the Freud family, smiling and relaxed, on the terrace of her house, among friends, visitors and dogs. Freud afterwards wrote to her: "The one day in your house in Paris restored our good mood and sense of dignity; after being surrounded by love for twelve hours we left proud and rich under the protection of Athene."[2] (*Freud-Marie Bonaparte 8.6.1938*)

In the evening to London * . . . Sun 4[5] June

The Freuds left Paris for Calais in the evening and crossed the Channel by night ferry. Since 1936 train carriages had been loaded directly onto Channel ferries, so they did not have to get out of the train and Freud did not see the sea until the harbor at Dover, after a calm crossing.

9 am Dover-London . . . Mon 5[6] June 1938

At Dover Lün was taken into custody by a "friendly vet" to serve the obligatory six-month quarantine. But the Lord Privy Seal, Lord De La Warr, had granted the Freuds diplomatic exemption from Customs examination on arrival at Victoria Station in London. Also, their train had been rerouted to a different platform to avoid the journalists. Mathilde and Martin were there to greet them, with Jones and his wife.

New house. . . . Mon 5 [6] June 1938

Jones drove the Freuds from the station across central London, showing them the sights on the way, past Buckingham Palace, across Piccadilly Circus, along Regent Street and through Regent's Park. Anna, Paula and Ernst followed in two taxis with all the luggage.

At the edge of Primrose Hill they came to the house which Ernst had rented for them—39 Elsworthy Road. Freud wrote: "Ernst has rented a charming little house for us, my room looks out onto a verandah which overlooks our own garden framed with flower beds and gives onto a large tree-studded park. Naturally it is only a temporary measure for three months, Ernst still has to find the definitive solution which needs to fulfil all sorts of conditions which are seldom realized here. It is difficult for us to live vertically instead of horizontally." (*Freud-Lampl-de Groot 13.6.1938*)

Since the bedrooms were upstairs Freud had to be carried upstairs and downstairs every day, by Anna, Paula and Ernst, who was living nearby and visiting regularly.

Minna seriously ill . . . Mon 5[6] June 1938

Minna had contracted pneumonia and was in bed upstairs, too ill to see the new arrivals. Freud wrote to Jeanne Lampl-de Groot a week later that it would all have been nicer if Aunt Minna had not been lying seriously ill upstairs. But she was now out of danger, he added.

Columns in the newspapers . . . Mon 5[6] June 1938

It was not in fact until the following day—Tuesday, June 7—that the newspapers could report Freud's arrival. This was not the only form of welcome Freud received. The house was deluged with flowers[1], letters and telegrams of greeting and gifts, including antiquities.

Freud commented: "So now we have really arrived in England, it is very nice and the public, whether friends or strangers, has prepared us a warm welcome. (The climate is less warm.) [. . .] Of course everything is still uncustomary and as if unreal, a clear sense of alienation." (*Freud- Lampl-de Groot 13.6.1938*)

---

* *London* is written in the margin and underlined, a heavy ink line connects the word with this entry.

". . . we left proud and rich under the protection of Athene . . ." The bronze Roman statuette of Athena, a favorite antiquity. Marie Bonaparte smuggled it out of Vienna and Freud reclaimed it in Paris. NB

Houses of Parliament, London. A photo from Freud's album. He had not been to England since 1908.

(*Opposite top left*) Freud and Martha with Prince Waldemar of Denmark, uncle of Marie Bonaparte's husband, Prince George of Greece.

(*Opposite top right*) Marie Bonaparte, Martha, Ernst and Dr. Josefine Stross.

(*Opposite below*) Anna, Freud, Lün, Martha and Ernst on the terrace of Marie Bonaparte's Paris home, June 5, 1938.

The "ghost not laid." Moses continued to haunt Freud throughout 1938. (Michelangelo's statue of Moses at San Pietro in Vincolo, Rome. Print from Freud's collection.)

London, June 1938. Freud at work on the Moses book again, his desk empty now but for the new terracottas from Paris.

Sam from Manchester . . .   Thurs 9 June 1938

Just before leaving Austria, Freud sent a note (probably his last letter from Vienna) to his nephew Sam Freud: "Leaving Vienna for good today. Next address: 39 Elsworthy Road London NW3. Any chance of our meeting after so many years?" (*Freud-Sam Freud 4.6.1938*).[1]

Freud had last met Sam in Manchester 30 years earlier. Despite his anglophilia, Freud only came to England three times in his life, first at the age of 19 in 1875, next in 1908 and finally now in 1938, "to die in freedom."

Lün visited . . .   Fri 10 June 1938

From Dover Lün had been brought to the quarantine kennels at Ladbroke Grove, London. This visit to her, the first time Freud left the new house, was fully reported in *The Referee*, an Australian sporting newspaper: "Freud found his journey across London tiring. He seemed to find it a great effort even to walk up the path to the front door, supported by his daughter, Dr. Anna Freud. But nothing could have kept the great scientist away from his dog friend. And yesterday I was told by Mr. Kevin F. Quin, head of the quarantine kennels, how Lun leapt to meet him at his approach, glad recognition in every gesture. 'It was difficult to say which was more delighted,' Mr. Quin told me. 'I have never seen such happiness and understanding in an animal's eyes. [. . .] He played with her, talked to her, using all sorts of little terms of endearment, for fully an hour. And, though the journey is long for a man of his years, he said that he was resolute about coming to see Lun as often as he can.' In the daytime Lun can play with other dogs in a lovely, spacious garden at the back of Mr. Quin's house. She is happy there."

Visit of Jahuda . . .   Sat 11 June 1938

Abraham Shalom Yahuda (1877–1951) was a Jewish Bible scholar. His name heads Freud's list of visitors in England, and there, unlike in the diary, it is correctly spelled.

Freud had first come across this name the previous year, in connection with research on Moses, when Arnold Zweig wrote: ". . . a Professor Yahuda has promised to let me have his works on Egyptian influences on the Old Testament." (*Arnold Zweig-Freud 6.9.1937*)[1]

By coincidence Yahuda also lived on Elsworthy Road. His visit was not simply to pay his respects to his new neighbor. He was evidently keen to discuss the Moses book with Freud and primarily to try to dissuade him from publishing it. One of Yahuda's arguments was that Ernst Sellin's hypothesis of the murder of Moses—an important link in Freud's thesis—had been generally rejected and renounced by Sellin himself.

Minna seen for first time on her birthday . . .   Sat 18 June 1938

This was Minna's 73rd birthday and it seems she had now recovered enough from her bronchial pneumonia to come downstairs—or Freud was carried upstairs to see her.[1]

G.H. Wells . . .   Sun 19 June 1938

Wells had visited Freud in 1933 and inscribed the 80th birthday greetings in 1936. He was one of the few English authors Freud already knew personally. (According to Jones, he was also one of the very few who addressed Freud by his surname alone, the others being William Bullitt and Yvette Guilbert.)

Moses III begun again . . .   Tues 21 June 1938

This was a resumption of work Freud had already been wrestling with in April, before emigration, when he wrote to Jones: ". . . I also work for an hour a day at my Moses, which torments me like a *ghost not laid*.* I wonder if I shall ever complete this third part despite all the outer and inner difficulties. At present I cannot believe it." (*Freud-Jones 28.4.1938*)

Princess—Cypriot head . . .   Thurs 23 June 1938

It is virtually certain Marie Bonaparte would have brought Freud an antiquity on

* [in English in the original]

her first visit to him in London. This large bust is a suitably large and dramatic piece to compensate in part for the absence of his collection, still in storage in Vienna.

Martha reported the Princess's arrival the previous day, noting that she would be staying with them for three days, and adding: ". . . so there is not much sign of summer peace!" (*Martha Freud-Lilly Marlé 22.6.1938*)

Visit of R.S. . . .   Thurs 23 June 1938

The Times reported this occasion as follows: "HONOUR FOR PROFESSOR FREUD: One of the rare occasions when the charter book of the Royal Society is removed from the headquarters of the society at Burlington House is when it is taken to Buckingham Palace for the signature of the King, who is patron of the society. This special privilege was recently extended to Professor Sigmund Freud, now living in exile in London. Professor Freud, who has been a foreign member of the society since 1936, was unable, owing to his health, to visit the society offices to sign the book, and it was therefore taken to his home at St. John's Wood."

The Royal Society's *Notes and Records* also records the event: "On 23 June two officers of the Society, the Foreign Secretary and the Biological Secretary, with Mr Griffith Davies, who was in charge of the Charter Book, were heartily welcomed by Professor Freud. Madame Marie Bonaparte (H.R.H. Princess George of Greece) [. . .] and Dr. Anna Freud also received the deputation. [. . .] The simple, homely ceremony derived dignity and pathos from the heart-felt gratitude of the exiled psychologist to the Society which had done him honour."

Films . . .   Thurs 23 June 1938

The visit of the Royal Society officers with the book to Freud's home at Elsworthy Road was filmed by Marie Bonaparte. Anna Freud later added her commentary to the film and at this point she states: "And this is when three men of the Royal Society came to present the book of the Royal Society for signature to my father because he was not well enough to go there. [. . .] There was a very nice moment."

Anna drew attention to the signature of Charles Darwin on the same page of the Royal Society book—a fact that could hardly fail to gratify Freud, since Darwin was one of his heroes.

Mrs. Gunn with Egyptian antiquity . . .   Sat 25 June 1938

Mrs. Nicena Gunn trained at the Vienna Psychoanalytical Out-Patients clinic (*Ambulatorium*) during the 1920s but did not join the British Psycho-Analytical Society. She was married to Battiscombe George Gunn (1883–1950), an eminent Egyptologist who had taken part in the Amarna and Saqqara excavations during the 1920s and in 1924 had published his most important work—*Studies in Egyptian Syntax.*

Such visits and gifts as this contributed to Freud's sense of well-being at this period[1]: after the relief of the escape from Nazi Austria and the reunion with other family members, his reception by the English and the comfortable conditions at 39 Elsworthy Road were additional sources of pleasure.

He wrote: "Our circumstances here are good, I would say very good if it were not that the hideous news from Vienna and inevitable sympathy with the fate of so many others who are having a bad time cast a dark shadow over our happiness. Our reception in England was extremely amiable, we are not even thinking of moving to America." (*Freud-"Herr Doktor" 26.6.1938*)

Moses sold to America . . .   Fri 15 July 1938

Now that there was virtually no German market for psychoanalytical literature, the English, and above all the American sales, were vital. Freud was also now about to buy a new house. He was therefore eager to see the English translation and all the more sensitive about delays.

In November he was complaining to Eitingon about Jones: "The German edition will be brought out by Al[l]ert de Lange in Holland. The English (and American) ones depend on Jones unfortunately, who is putting off the translation

A "contemporary of Moses." Print of the legendary lawmaker, Hermes Trismegistus, from Freud's collection.

and sometimes behaves as if he wanted to sabotage the book. The friendliness with which he greeted us seems to be expended." (*Freud-Eitingon 3.11.1938*)

Mr. Kent? . . .   Fri 15 July 1938

The question mark after Mr. Kent's name may denote doubt whether a visit would take place. Perhaps the reference to him three days later means a promised visit occured then. The identity of Mr. Kent remains unknown.

In 1910 the psychologist G.H. Kent published a study of word association in insanity, together with A.J. Rosanoff. It is unlikely, though not impossible, this was the person in question.

Dr. Exner . . .   Fri 15 July 1938

George G. Exner (1902–1965), a South African now settled in London, was a distinguished oral surgeon. He had studied with the plastic surgeon Jacques Joseph in Berlin and with Pichler in Vienna and it was Pichler who had referred Freud to Exner. His Harley Street address is the second entry in Freud's green English address book, after the Royal Society.

Over the next two weeks Max Schur noticed some suspicious swellings in Freud's mouth. As he had difficulty convincing Exner of their significance, he wrote urgent letters to Pichler, requesting him to come to London.

House on Finchley Road viewed . . .   Sat 16 July 1938

Freud's eventual house was to be on Maresfield Gardens, a quiet avenue near Finchley Road, but not on it. Freud may perhaps have misunderstood the location or thought of Finchley Road as a district. He himself did not view it: it was Ernst who found the house, with the help of agents.

But it is likely this was another house, which turned out to be unsatisfactory, for the following day Freud wrote to his brother: "The next and most difficult problem is to find a house that corresponds at one and the same time to our complicated demands and to our modest means." (*Freud-Alexander Freud 17.7.-1938*)

Moses finished . . .   Sun 17 July 1938

The finishing of *Moses and Monotheism* did not mean its theme stopped obsessing Freud. Salvador Dali, who visited two days later, quotes a cryptic remark of Freud's: "Moses is flesh of sublimation."

And the day after that meeting Freud noted: "The individual perishes from his internal conflicts, the species perishes in its struggle with the external world to which it is no longer adapted.—This deserves to be included in *Moses*."

Will . . .   Sun 17 July 1938

The trustees and executors of the will were Anna, Ernst and Martin Freud. Anna inherited the collection of antiquities and the books on psychology and psychoanalysis. On April 5, 1943 the other two trustees transferred the freehold of 20 Maresfield Gardens to her name. A residuary trust fund formed from Freud's real estate and the remains of his personal estate was to provide Martha's income. The copyrights on his work went in trust to his grandchildren. Minna Bernays received an annuity of £300.

This was the last will and testament; it was not the first. There is a draft will, in the form of a letter to Martin dated October 30, 1923–immediately following his return home after the first major surgery on his jaw. A later will fell into the hands of the Nazis during the raid of March 15. It indicated Freud's assets abroad. This was illegal at the time. If the Nazi commissar Dr. Sauerwald had not suppressed this fact until after Freud had left the country it would have imperiled emigration.

Mr. Kent . . .   Mon 18 July 1938

The name "Kent" appears on Freud's list of visitors for this period, between those of "Mel. Klein" (who does not appear in the diary) and "Salvador Dali" (who does).

1200 Dutch gulden demanded . . .   Mon 18 July 1938

This money was in an account in Zurich. Freud's lawyer in Vienna, Dr. Alfred

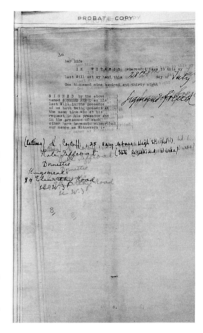

The will Freud drafted before his operations on October 30, 1923, in the form of a letter to Martin.

In England a new will was required. It was witnessed by a nurse and a housemaid and signed on July 28, 1938.

Salvador Dali's portrait of Freud
done after their meeting on July 19,
1938. It was only one of a number of
sketches, some done from newspaper
photographs earlier in 1938, before the
artist had even met him.

Martha Freud's Aliens Registration
Certificate, June 9, 1938, with the
passport photo taken by Edmund
Engelman in May, 1938.

Indra, wrote that the foreign currency office had demanded it, although the
Gestapo had previously promised Freud could keep it to build up ". . . a new
existence in a foreign country."

Neither the furniture nor the collection had yet arrived from Vienna and
might be held as ransom until the sum was surrendered. Freud therefore authorized Indra to forward the gulden as soon as he received their household effects.
But he really wanted the money to be transferred to the account of Marie
Bonaparte, to pay back the refugee tax which she had paid.

Deafness . . .   Tues 19 July 1938

Among the first addresses in the English address book is the *Ohrenarzt* (ear
specialist) F.W.Watkyn-Thomas of 8 Wimpole Street. Freud's ear trouble was
recurrent, being precipitated by other infections.

Two weeks later he wrote: "Since the day before yesterday catarrh has been
trying to affect my hearing again . . . " (*Freud- Anna Freud 3.8.1938*)

Salvador Dali . . .   Tues 19 July 1938

Freud was the most vital influence on Salvador Dali's life and art. It was Stefan
Zweig who arranged this meeting. Dali was accompanied by his wife Gala (his
"Gradiva") and the millionaire Edward James, who owned *The Metamorphosis of
Narcissus*, the painting they brought along to show Freud.

"It would be very interesting to investigate analytically how he came to create
that picture," Freud wrote to Zweig the following day. But to Dali he said: "In
classic paintings, I look for the sub-conscious—in a surrealist painting for the
conscious."—a remark that for Dali spelled the death sentence for surrealism.

During the meeting Dali was allowed to sketch Freud and produced a study for
an eventual sketch done on blotting paper.[1] Dali's written account of the meeting
refers to Freud's stare and apparent indifference to what he was saying—possibly
a result of the attack of deafness.

Dutch press . . .   Sat 23 July 1938

This probably refers to Allert de Lange in Amsterdam, who published German
émigré literature. It was they who brought out the Freuds' translation of *Topsy*
and they were to publish the first German edition of *Moses and Monotheism*.

Martha 77 yrs . . .   Tues 26 July 1938

Three weeks after their arrival in London, Martha had written: "So far I have
only been in two stores and three parks and see myself literally as a peasant who
has come to a city for the first time in his life. Everything is of an unimaginable
size and grandeur." (*Martha Freud-Lilly Marlé 22.6.1938*).

It was she, according to Freud, who adapted fastest to life in England. And
Jones said that she "never looked back to Vienna, only forward to her new mode
of life as if she were twenty-seven years old instead of seventy-seven. She insisted
on continuing her Vienna custom of doing all the shopping herself, a habit she
kept up till the very end of her long life . . . ."

Will signed . . .   Thurs 28 July 1938

For once Freud signed in full—"Sigmund Freud"—instead of just Freud, as he
did before coming to England, or "Sigm. Freud," an early form he had resumed
in England. The two witnesses to Freud's signature of the will were a nurse and
a domestic servant. When the will went to probate the gross value of the estate
came to £22,850.3s.2d, the net value of the personal estate £15,979.6s.4d.

House purchase concluded . . .   Thurs 28 July 1938

The new house, 20 Maresfield Gardens, London N.W.3, cost £6,500, which
required a loan of £4,000 from Barclays Bank. The mortgage was not redeemed
until 1943.

Freud had still not viewed the house. Three days later he wrote to Anna: "I
was able to learn from the newspaper that I have bought a house, I have not yet
seen it." (*Freud-Anna Freud 1.8.1938*).

Meanwhile, the public continued to take an interest in Freud's affairs. Two
days later he wrote again to Anna: "I have not yet been to my palace. My barber
has already read in the paper that I have bought a house." (*Freud-Anna Freud
3.8.1938*)

Anna to Congress in Paris . . .   Fri 29 July 1938

Anna had (with great difficulty, because she was an alien) obtained permission to travel to the 15th International Psychoanalytical Congress in Paris.

Freud wrote: "We expect that the congress will bring about the final release from the Americans who are a burden to us and thus establish clear relations. This time I am represented in absentia by my lecture." (*Freud- Lampl-de Groot 26.7.1938*)

The conflict with the Americans was over the question of lay analysis. Freud continued to insist on the necessity of independence from the medical profession ". . . in the face of the obvious American tendency to turn psycho-analysis into a mere housemaid of psychiatry." (*Freud-Schnier 5.7.1938*)

The lecture which "represented" Freud was, apparently, an extract from *Moses and Monotheism*–"The Advance in Intellectuality."

Greetings from the Paris Congress . . .   Mon 1 August 1938

A letter to Anna on this day shows that the greetings from the Paris Congress were not the only ones Freud had received: "Naturally it is not the same when you are not there, although telephone contact makes up for a lot. It is as if you had your rooms in Harley St. and came home dead tired in the evening . . . [. . .] The Oxford Psychotherapeutic Congress, chaired by Jung, has sent me the obligatory greetings telegram, to which I have responded with a cool answer prepared by Dr. Bennet. Somewhere I have become honorary president, I no longer know where." (*Freud-Anna Freud 1.8.1938*)

Prospectus of new press . . .   Thurs 4 August 1938

In March the Nazis destroyed the International Psychoanalytical Press and Freud's desire to re-establish it was now made possible by the poet, novelist and translator John Rodker (1894–1955).

Jones called him "a friendly, intelligent and enterprising publisher" (apart from Freud, he published James Joyce and T.S. Eliot). He founded the Imago Publishing Company. It brought out the new *American Imago* and began a new German edition of Freud's collected works. This was financed by Marie Bonaparte using the $4,824 she had advanced Freud to pay the refugee tax and which he had insisted on paying back to her. The German prospectuses advertised the 16-volume edition which was offered at £6.18s. (paperback) or £9.5s. (hardback).

News Bäumler of dispatch of things . . .   Fri 5 August 1938

The firm responsible for the packing and dispatch of Freud's collection and household goods, E. Bäuml of Vienna, specialized in moving art objects and antiquities. Their letter to Freud assured him that the packing had been carried out in a "first-class manner and with all due care by packers with many years' experience . . . ." (*Bäuml-Freud 4.8.1938*).

The packing had been supervised by the Freud's Nazi commissar, Dr. Sauerwald. His care in this matter was another example of his helpfulness.[1]

Anna back from Paris . . .   Fri 5 August 1938

Anna flew back from Paris in the evening. Even so, Freud had written her another letter on August 3. It shows him in good spirits. He was surprised how well he had stood up to the heatwave; a patient's check had enabled him to pay Dr. Schur's account (no money was left in the bank); there was confirmation that his sisters had gained access to the money in trust for them and that the things in Vienna had been dispatched.

Above all, Freud was still working on a manuscript begun on July 22: "My holiday job is turning out to be an amusing occupation. It has already grown to 26 sides, will fall into three parts. The overall view [*das Allgemeine*]—the practical task—the theoretical yield. I am still sticking to the fiction that it will not need to be printed." (*Freud-Anna Freud 3.8.1938*).

This was the unfinished *Outline of Psycho-analysis*, drafted in an abbreviated, telegraphic style and first printed posthumously in 1940. The manuscript in the Library of Congress consists of 66 fluently written folio sides: the date next to the title is "22/7." There are few corrections or crossings out and the handwriting is even.

Anna with Marie Bonaparte at the Paris Congress, August 1938.

Anna in the audience at the Paris Congress.

Marie Bonaparte, Anna Freud, Max Eitingon and Ernest Jones caught in an unusually cheerful photograph, in Paris.

NEUE AUSGABE

SIGMUND FREUD
GESAMMELTE SCHRIFTEN

IN CHRONOLOGISCHER FOLGE

16 BÄNDE

BROSCHIERT £ 6.18.0 : LEINEN £ 9.5.0

IMAGO PUBLISHING CO. LTD, 6 FITZROY SQUARE, LONDON W 1

Princess . . .   Sat 6 August 1938

Princess Marie Bonaparte's French Society had just played host to the Paris Congress where she delivered a paper on *Time in Life, Dream and Death.* Freud suggested linking the idea of time with the perceptual system. But he later conceded: "Your comments on 'time and space' have come off better than mine would have . . . " (*Freud-Marie Bonaparte 12.11.1938*)

Things arrived . . .   Sun 7-Mon 8 August 1938

Until this moment Freud had been justifiably sceptical whether he would ever see his collection and household goods again: as he told Eitingon ". . . the gangsters are unpredictable." (*Freud-Eitingon 15.6.1938*) Even after hearing that the things had been packed he still quoted the proverb "there's many a slip 'twixt cup and lip." Only on their arrival, he wrote, would he finally feel himself "free of the Nazis" ("*Nazifrei*").

Willi Lévy begun . . .   Sun 7-Mon 8 August 1938

The sculptor Willy Lévy, son of Freud's friends Lajos and Katá Lévy, had already done a plaquette of Freud in 1936. He was now beginning a bust.

Two weeks later Freud wrote: "Willy Levy has almost finished modelling me. Yesterday I sat for a photographer who is capable of notable masterpieces to judge by his folio. If he has succeeded you will receive a picture." (*Freud-Lampl-de Groot 22.8.1938*)

The bust was ready by October and Freud was keen to show it to Princess Marie Bonaparte when she visited. The photographer he mentions, who had come at Stefan Zweig's request, was the Austrian Marcel Sternberger and he did indeed produce a memorable portrait of Freud.

Own house viewed. 20 Maresfield Gardens . . .   Sat 13 August 1938

Their "own house" ("*eigenes Haus*")—Freud repeats the phrase from this entry in a letter to Jeanne Lampl-de Groot: "Well, *20 Maresfield Gardens* as, I hope*, our last address on this planet, but not to be used before the end of September. Our own** house! You can imagine the demands its purchase made on our shrunken savings. And far too beautiful for us; not far from here and from Ernst who has transformed the house into a ruin in order to restore it anew in a more suitable state for us. He is building in a lift, making two rooms into one or the other way round, sheer sorcery translated into architectural terms." (*Freud-Lampl-de Groot 22.8.1938*)

20 Maresfield Gardens is in Hampstead, a part of London that was closely associated with psychoanalysts. This was one of Ernst Freud's considerations in selecting the house.[1] Another was that it had large rooms and not too many of them. Ernst was now making one connected room from two downstairs to form Freud's future library and consulting room and was building a loggia at the back.

Ruth left . . .   Wed 24 August 1938

At the beginning of the month Freud had written: "Ruth [Mack Brunswick] . . . claims to be in a state of depression. What is true is that she is continually giggling." (*Freud-Anna Freud 1.8.1938*) Two days before she left he wrote: "Ruth is still here (until 24 of this month) and adding a bit of after-analysis which will probably be very good for her. How incomplete all my earlier analyses were." (*Freud- Lampl-de Groot 22.8.1938*)

Minna to nursing home . . .   Mon 29 August 1938

Minna's state of health was still alarming. As the Freuds had to leave Elsworthy Road at the end of the month, she was being sent to a nursing home and the others were to stay in a hotel until the renovated house was ready for them to move in.

A week earlier Freud wrote: "The joyful expectation of such a beautiful property is unfortunately darkened by all sorts of shadows, Aunt Minna's illness being the blackest of them. [. . .] We will be some weeks in a hotel, Aunt in hospital or so-called sanatorium which are all unbelievably inadequate here. A

Freud by Marcel Sternberger, "who is capable of notable masterpieces . . ." MS

Freud and Anna in their London garden. MS

Cover of the prospectus for Rodker's German edition of Freud's works, 1938. (See August 4, 1938.)

---

* "I hope"—*hoffentlich*: this word has been added in the margin.
** "Our own house"—*Ein eigenes Haus*. Freud first wrote *einiges* (*united*), then crossed it out.

land of contradictions, in many respects very backward." (*Freud- Lampl-de Groot 22.8.1938*)

Hotel Esplanade—Warrington Crescent . . .   Fri 2 September 1938

The Esplanade Hotel[1] was in Maida Vale, north London. The American, Smiley Blanton, who visited Freud at the hotel for his analysis, reported his wife's anxieties about the English cooking Freud might have to endure there: "He [Freud] replied that the hotel had a French chef and Margaret need not worry, as he would have excellent food. I said, 'English food is awful.' Freud agreed."

Alex Sophie Harry arrived . . .   Sat 4 September 1938

Freud's brother Alexander with his wife Sophie and son Harry had managed to leave Austria in March. They had been living in Switzerland. Harry, however, had already moved on to London by June and Freud had been trying to help him obtain a residence permit. He regretted being able to do no more than simply testify to the Home Office that Harry was his nephew and a trustworthy character: Freud himself had no personal influence and until now Jones had only been able to help psychoanalysts.

Sanat. London Clinic . . .   Wed 7 September 1938

At the end of August Max Schur spotted the beginning of a papilloma. He and Anna appealed to Pichler to come to London to operate and he arrived on September 7. The London Clinic, where the operation was to take place, was at 20 Devonshire Place.

Operation Pichler . . .   *Thurs 8 September 1938

This was another fairly radical operation. Under general anesthetic (Evipan) Pichler cut across the lip and along the nose to gain good access. Sections of tissue removed were examined microscopically during surgery, but without detecting anything more than precancerous.

Pichler flew back to Vienna the following day, having checked that the patient was recovering well. This was his final operation on Freud. It cost £325, including £25 travelling expenses (exchange value—4,420 RM).

Exactly a month later Freud was writing: "How am I doing? Slow recovery from the operation which was the worst since 1923, also because the incision was made from outside. I cannot yet eat or smoke properly, speak with effort, the pain is on the retreat, I am once again working 3 hours a day." (*Freud- Lampl-de Groot 8.10.1938*)

The extent of public interest in Freud is reflected by the number of newspaper reports—at least 20 British and Irish papers carried articles about this operation.

20 Maresfields Gardens** . . .   Tues 27 September 1938

On September 3 Freud was registered as owner: on September 16 Martha and Paula moved in. (Freud's own move coincided with the height of the Munich crisis and frantic preparations for war.)

Various letters contain delighted comments on the house: "Our own home. It is very beautiful [. . .] Light, comfortable, spacious . . . ." (*Freud- Lampl-de Groot 8.10.1938*) "Our new house was originally beautifully built and has been splendidly renovated by Ernst. We have it incomparably better than at Berggasse and even than Grinzing. 'From poverty to white bread' [*Aus Dalles Weissbrot*] as the proverb says." (*Freud-Eitingon 3.11.1938*)

Although the house was postwar (c.1920), the architect Albert G. Hastilow designed it to reflect an earlier, more sedate period (Ernst Freud called it "neo-Georgian").

Winter was, however, to reveal the disadvantages. The sash windows let in as much draft as light: "It is snowing here for the first time. It is bitterly cold, the plumbing has frozen up and British deficiencies in overcoming the heating problem are clearly evident." (*Freud-Eitingon 19.12.1938*)

"Our last address on this planet." 20 Maresfield Gardens, London.

"Light, comfortable, spacious. . . ." The study at Maresfield Gardens. NB

---

* A line links date and entry—a mark of its significance.
** On 13 August Freud spelled the road correctly—Maresfield Gardens. In this instance he appears to have originally written "Maresfield Garden," then overcorrected to "Maresfields Gardens."

Peace . . .   Fri 30 September 1938

On the day Freud moved into Maresfield Gardens, Neville Chamberlain had made his notorious broadcast: "How horrible, fantastic, incredible it is that we should be digging trenches and trying on gas masks here because of a quarrel in a far away country between people of whom we know nothing." Chamberlain had now brought back his "Peace with honour" from Munich, ending the war scare and causing Freud to scrawl the single ambivalent word "Peace" halfway across the page.[1]

In the first letter from the new house Freud wrote: ". . . now that the intoxication of peace has subsided, people as well as Parliament are coming back to their senses and facing the painful truth. We too of course are thankful for the bit of peace, but we cannot take any pleasure in it." (*Freud-Marie Bonaparte 4.10.1938*)

Minna in the house . . .   Sun 2 October 1938

In spite of her return home, Minna's health remained poor. Freud complained to Jeanne Lampl-de Groot: "Aunt Minna, a sad chapter. Still suffering from serious heart trouble and now also tortured by cystitis, and plagued by two nurses who are making my wife unhappy because they are occupying living and bath rooms on that floor. The housewife could be very content in the beautiful new house if it were not that windows, doors, central heating and lift constantly made craftsmen necessary whom one can only obtain with difficulty. In short it is a small example of émigré misery among greater ones. For all its glory England is a land for rich and healthy people. Also they should not be too old." (*Freud-Lampl-de Groot 8.10.1938*)

Minna's recovery was slow and it was not until November 19 that she was able to join the family at meals downstairs, with the help of the lift Ernst had installed.

Martin in hospital . . .   Sun 2 October 1938

Freud told Marie Bonaparte: "It strikes us as superfluous that at the moment Martin is also ill with a coli infection and a high temperature in the hospital which Minna has just left." (*Freud-Marie Bonaparte 4.10.1938*) By the end of the week Martin had recovered and was out of hospital.

Dr. Sauerwald . . .   Tues 11 October 1938

After the Freuds had escaped from Austria, it emerged that their Nazi Commissar, Dr. Sauerwald, had known about their foreign assets and kept this a secret from the Gestapo until after their departure. Anna said that not only had he "behaved very decently" toward them, but that it was "thanks to him that we came out alive."[1] It is not clear why he had now turned up in England. Schur thought it might be on a government spying mission.[2]

Arnold Zweig takes leave . . .   Wed 12 October 1938

Arnold Zweig had been in London since September 7, when he visited just before Freud left for the London Clinic. Afterwards he and Freud met several times: their discussions were intense, but sometimes left Freud exhausted.

On his return journey to Palestine Zweig wrote to Freud from Paris: "I am so happy to have seen you established in your temporary home with everything round you so bright and green. I am happy too that you are able to go on working at your own desk surrounded by your beautiful little gods. . . ." (*Arnold Zweig-Freud 16.10.1938*).

Zweig also apologized for having exhausted Freud with his problems. One of these was his plan to leave Palestine for the United States. (In 1948 Zweig was to return to (East) Berlin and from 1950–1953 he was President of the East German Academy of Arts.)

Mathilde 51 yrs . . .   Sun 16 October 1938

In Vienna Mathilde had been a dress designer and she now set up in business in London. An article in the *Jewish Chronicle* (6.1.1939) featured her new shop on Baker Street. The business had been set up in partnership with Mr. and Mrs. Stiassner, dress designers formerly of Innsbruck, and was called *Robell*. The premises and fittings had been designed by Ernst Freud.

Princess and Eugenie—Bronze Venus . . .   Sat 29 October 1938

Princess Marie Bonaparte visited Freud nine times in London. This visit with her

"Peace." Hitler seeing Mussolini off after the Munich conference. DOW

Mathilde, who had arrived shortly before her father, welcomed him to London.

daughter, Eugénie, was her first to Freud's new home in Maresfield Gardens.

Freud told Eitingon: "Princess Marie, always invigorating, was here for several days, took her leave yesterday. The young princess as well is blooming and thriving and is delightful to see. Her husband, the Radziwill, unfortunately creates an insignificant impression. They divided up their time here between us, the Duke and Duchess of Kent, Queen Mary and their own king. All the girls in the house were very proud that they were most frequently here and spent the longest time at our house." (*Freud-Eitingon 3.11.1938*).

Marie Bonaparte frequently—if not always—brought Freud gifts of antiquities for his collection and on this occasion it was an attractive little statuette of Venus holding a mirror. It had been bought from the antique dealer Ségrédakis on the Rue St. Honoré in Paris, her customary source of antiquities.[1]

A Comment on Antisemitism . . .   Mon 31 October 1938

Arthur Koestler's name appears on Freud's list of visitors for this day. As editor of a German émigré weekly published in Paris, Koestler asked Freud for an article on antisemitism. The article Freud wrote for him summarizes a defense of the Jews by a non-Jewish writer. Freud could not remember who that writer was. (It was probably Mark Twain in his essay *Concerning the Jews* [1899].)

The article appeared in Koestler's journal, *Die Zukunft* in November 1938. The editor noted: "The following article is the first publication from the pen of Siegmund Freud since his exile from Vienna."

Events in Germany and Austria meant this theme could not be forgotten, even though Freud was now "settled in relative security, glad to have escaped the furor teutoniens . . . ." (*Freud-Jelliffe 18.10.1938*). In July German Jews had been forced to carry identity cards, in August all had to add Israel or Sara to their names. Since the Anschluss the 192,000 Austrian Jews had been subjected to worse persecution than the German Jews had suffered during the previous five years. Internationally the Jews had been abandoned. The Evian Conference in July revealed they could expect no help from abroad.

Pogroms in Germany . . .   Thurs 10 November 1938

This entry is written in English, as if Freud had to distance himself even from the German language.[1] It refers to the infamous *Kristallnacht* ("the night of broken glass"). On November 7 Herschel Grynszpan, a 17-year-old Polish Jew, shot the Third Secretary of the German Embassy in Paris, Ernst vom Rath, as revenge for the deportation of his family. Two days later vom Rath died and that same evening the Nazi leadership unleashed the SS and SA. 267 synagogues and congregation buildings were razed; 7,500 Jewish shops damaged; 35 Jews murdered. Eventually the pogrom may have claimed the lives of between 2,000 and 2,500 men, women and children. In the following days 29,000 were deported to the Dachau, Buchenwald and Sachsenhausen concentration camps.

In the aftermath Eitingon wrote: "We are also receiving awful news from Germany. A synagogue my father founded in the 1920s has been burnt to the ground and the Jewish Hospital, the Eitingon Foundation also faces closure. Both chief doctors were arrested . . . ." (*Eitingon-Freud 12.12.1938*).

Freud wrote to Jeanne Lampl-de Groot in Holland: "The news from + + + Germany*, the waves of emigration that are breaking on these shores, the uncertainty what the immediate future might bring, all of this excludes any true comfort." (*Freud- Lampl-de Groot 20.11.1938*)

Ban in Franco Spain . . .   Thurs 10 November 1938

Franco was still not in control of the whole of Spain. The Spanish Civil War was not to end until March 28, 1939, with the fall of Madrid and the beginning of a long dictatorship.

Franco now announced a ban on 111 writers and ordered their books to be withdrawn from libraries. Apart from Freud, the list also included H.G. Wells, Carlyle, Goethe, Ibsen, Tolstoy and Victor Hugo.

H.G. Wells . . .   Tues 29 November 1938

Wells was as much preoccupied with the origin of culture and religion as Freud.

A Roman bronze Venus holding a mirror, a gift from Marie Bonaparte on her visit, October 16, 1938. NB

Return to the Middle Ages. German or Austrian women suspected of affairs with Jewish men were publicly mocked, their heads shaved. DOW

---

* " + + +"—Peasants chalked three crosses on doors as a defense against demonic forces. Here the sign denotes indescribable characteristics.

"Two devoted disciples." Marie Bonaparte and her daughter Eugénie.

It seems likely they would have discussed *Moses and Monotheism*. But the English translation was not to reach Wells until March: when it did he found its suggestions "immensely probable." (*Wells-Freud March 1939*)

Anna 43 yrs . . .   Sat 3 December 1938

This was Anna's first birthday in emigration and Freud was pleased by the speed with which she had adapted to England. Three weeks earlier he wrote to Marie Bonaparte: "Anna has given three public lectures which have been highly praised, even for their language."[1] (*Freud-Marie Bonaparte 12.11.1938*)

Anna, too, was optimistic about her future, though not without some misgivings. Some months earlier she had written to the American Clinton McCord: "England is indeed a civilised country and I am naturally grateful that we are here. There is no pressure of any kind or in any direction and there is a great deal of space and freedom ahead. Of course, it is strange still and I wonder whether an immigrant in England will ever be anything but an immigrant. But these are problems for the future and do not seem very important at the present moment." (*Anna Freud-McCord 28.8.1938*)

Princess on house visit . . .   Sun 4 December 1938

This was already the fourth visit Marie Bonaparte had paid on Freud since his arrival in England. One topic they had to discuss this time was the problem of Freud's four old sisters in Vienna.

Before her arrival he had written to her: "The latest horrifying events in Germany aggravate the problem of what to do about the four old women between seventy-five and eighty. To maintain them in England is beyond our powers. The assets we left behind for them on our departure, some 160,000 Austrian schillings, may have been confiscated already, and are certain to be lost if they leave. We have been considering a domicile on the French Riviera, at Nice or somewhere in the neighborhood. But would this be possible?" (*Freud-Marie Bonaparte 12.11.1938*)

Lün back . . .   Tues 6 December 1938

The dog-loving British press widely reported this event. Anna went to fetch the dog from its six-month quarantine.[1] Next day's *Daily Herald* carried a picture of her with Lün, while the *Daily Mail* showed the two of them being photographed by Marie Bonaparte. The *Evening Standard* (6.12.1938) reported a member of the kennel staff saying, "As soon as she saw her mistress she went wild with joy, [. . .] I have never seen a dog quite so excited."

Recital Engel Lund . . .   Tues 6 December 1938

The Icelandic folk singer Engel Lund (born 1900) was the author of *Engel Lund's Book of Folk Songs* (London 1936). It was on the invitation of Anna Freud, with whom she was already acquainted, that she came to Maresfield Gardens to give the Freuds a private recital of Icelandic and Jewish folk songs. Marie Bonaparte and Dorothy Burlingham also attended the recital. Freud told the singer about Lün's release from captivity.

Broadcasting   Wed 7 December 1938

On December 7 the BBC came to 20 Maresfield Gardens to record a short message from Freud. A transcript in Freud's handwriting concludes with the instruction: "A short sentence in German." The actual recording ends with the following sentence: *"Im Alter von 82 Jahren verliess ich in Folge der deutschen Invasion mein Heim in Wien und kam nach England, wo ich mein Leben in Freiheit zu enden hoffe.'* ("At the age of 82 I left my home in Vienna as a result of the German invasion and came to England where I hope to end my life in freedom.")

Freud's muffled voice on the recording demonstrates how difficult and painful the prosthesis made speaking. A letter from the BBC dated December 6 indicates that they would have preferred a much longer talk than the one he proposed and that they had wanted to record him reading a passage from the introduction of one of his books.

Anna and Lün, December 6, 1938. The *Daily Herald* report of Lün's liberation from quarantine.

Martin 49 yrs. . . .   Wed 7 December 1938

In England Martin was faced with the problem of making a living. There was no longer any opportunity for him to practice the business and legal skills he had used on behalf of the press and the Vienna Psychoanalytical Society. But he had gained experience of commerce, too, during the 1920s and now he started producing toiletries and a toothpaste called *Martin A.*[1]

Princess departed . . .   Thurs 8 December 1938

After her return, and in response to Freud's plea on behalf of his sisters in Vienna, Marie Bonaparte was to attempt to gain permission from the French authorities to bring them to France.

This was far from her only action in defense of the Jews. Apart from channelling funds into organizations to rescue Jewish scientists and doctors, four days after her return from England she wrote to President Roosevelt outlining a plan to buy Lower California from Mexico and establish a Jewish state there under United States protection.

Will. Brown . . .   Thurs 8 December 1938

The British psychologist William Brown (1881–1952) had studied at Oxford and Kings College Hospital and in 1910 under the mathematician Karl Pearson. During World War I he dealt with nerve shock cases at Edinburgh and the Maudsley Hospital. From 1921 to 1946 he was Wilde Reader in Mental Philosophy at the University of Oxford.

Jones wrote: ". . . William Brown, the psychologist and psychotherapist, visited Freud, but on my advice Freud declined to do any analytic work with him."

Marie Bonaparte photographing Anna with the liberated chow. *(Daily Mail* report)

"I discovered some new and important facts about the Unconscious in psychic life. . . ." Freud recording a BBC broadcast, December 7, 1938.

Freud in London, 1939.

1939

In spring 1939 *Moses and Monotheism* was finally published. "Quite a worthy exit . . ." Freud commented.[1] He was certain this would be his last book. His cancer was now inoperable and, despite radium and x-ray treatment, he knew it to be incurable. He was in constant pain and gradually forced to withdraw from the work which had been his life. Meanwhile, Anna's care and nursing had became indispensable to him. Over the final decade, she emerges as incomparably the most important person in his life—all her many arrivals and departures, her illnesses and her work, are recorded in the diary. In this final year, however, her name occurs only once (when she went on a brief holiday to Amsterdam), for the rest of the time she was constantly at his side.

Caring for her father over the previous sixteen years had not deflected Anna from making her own career as a psychoanalyst. She developed her own psychoanalytical practice, gave lectures and seminars, pioneered child analysis and ran a kindergarten, wrote articles and books, organized and participated in International Psychoanalytical Association Congresses. Freud was delighted by her "capacity for work and consistent achievement."[2] After emigration she had to start again from scratch in England. Undeterred, she threw herself into renewed activity, building up a new practice, writing, giving lectures and in general "energetically trying out how many lives one can live at the same time . . . ."[3]

It was primarily for Anna's sake that Freud had eventually consented to leave Vienna. Illness and age meant he was forced to remain an outsider, contenting himself with a distant view of the "promised land" which Anna was now entering. Visitors still called occasionally, but there were far fewer than in 1938. In March 1939 the British Psycho-Analytical Society celebrated its 25th anniversary. Since the destruction of the Central European psychoanalytical societies, England was for the moment the center of the psychoanalytical movement and Freud's hope for its future. But he was unable to attend the celebration dinner. Anna, however, was there, both as her father's representative and as an honored guest in her own right.

The drastically diminished number of diary entries this year indicates the narrowing of Freud's life. Many simply record birthdays, June is marked only by the anniversary of the arrival in England. Later that month Freud wrote to Marie Bonaparte that his world was now " . . . a small island of pain floating in an ocean of indifference."[4] Yet despite everything, Freud continued to treat four patients. It was not until the beginning of August, the last month of the diary, that he finally and formally disbanded his practice. The same day also brought a sudden spate of visitors, come to say their farewells. And the last entry marks a dispersal—Eva, the favourite granddaughter, returned to France, Dorothy, Anna's companion, left for the United States. The last entry—**War panic**—presages the imminent outbreak of World War II. At this critical turning point the diary is abandoned.

The eight months of entries for 1939 occupy most of the last page, leaving a blank space at the bottom, as if to express the total exhaustion of Freud's final month. During these last days his bed was set up in his study downstairs, among his beloved antiquities, and looking out onto the garden. He could no longer write, but for two more weeks Anna continued updating his list of correspondence received. She also slept in the study to be permanently at hand. When Max Schur became Freud's doctor eleven years earlier, Freud had made him promise not to let him suffer unnecessarily. On September 21, Freud decided that further pain would be senseless and asked Anna and Schur for their agreement to terminate the torture. An overdose of morphine was administered by Dr. Schur. After a coma lasting one and a half days, early in the morning of September 23, Freud died.

---

1. *Freud-Sachs 12[/14].3.1939* [FM] ("Ein ganz würdiger Abgang . . . .")
2. *Freud-Eitingon 5.2.1937* in *Letters*.
3. *Anna Freud-Arnold Zweig 11.5.1939* [SFC] ("Ich mache energische Versuche, wieviele Leben man auf einmal leben kann und habe verschiedene ganztagige Beschäftigungen auf einmal.")
4. *Freud-Marie Bonaparte 15.6.1939* in Schur, 524.

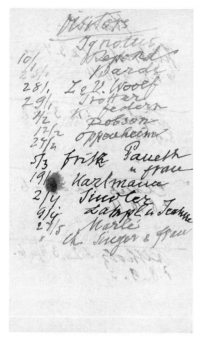

Freud's visitor list for January to May,
1939. Only the surgeon Trotter also
appears in the diary.

The front room, Maresfield Gardens.
NB

Lumbago—bone ache . . .   [Mon] 2–[Tues] 31 January 1939

Freud wrote "Lumbago" in English, perhaps to connect it with the English
weather and the faulty heating of which he had already complained. During
December there had been gales during the coldest spell in nine years and this was
followed by a white Christmas. It is impossible to say how long or continuous
the lumbago was during January. Schur does not even mention it. By contrast
with Freud's other ailments he must have considered it minor.

The "bone ache," on the other hand, was serious, and neither new nor temporary. A bone chip from the operation in September 1938 caused Freud intense
suffering before Schur was able to remove it on December 28. But an area of bone
necrosis remained and in mid-January 1939 Schur noticed a new swelling farther
back in Freud's mouth. He suspected renewed cancer, but Exner did not take his
anxieties seriously.

In March Freud told Eitingon: "I have developed a strong antipathy toward
the saviour of my life, Pichler, since his last operation left me with hideous bone
ache for six months afterwards. Perhaps I am doing him an injustice." (*Freud-
Eitingon 5.3.1939*)

The pain continued and a little later that month Freud was writing: "14/3 The
situation is that since my operation in September I have suffered continual pain
in the jaw which has even outlasted the discharge of a bone splinter." (*Freud-
Hanns Sachs 12.3.1939*)

Moses printed . . .   Thurs 2 February 1939

The German edition of *Moses and Monotheism* was first printed in its entirety by
Allert de Lange in Amsterdam. In November 1938 Freud was still correcting his
draft; he wrote to Eitingon on December 29 that he had finished his corrections.
However, he remained dissatisfied and conscious of the work's weaknesses.

When Eitingon told him of Martin Buber's critique of psychoanalysis he
replied: "Martin Buber's pious phrases will not do much damage to the *Interpretation of Dreams*. The Moses is far more vulnerable and I am prepared for the
Jewish attack on it." (*Freud-Eitingon 5.4.1939*)

Princess . . .   Sun 5 February 1939

Marie Bonaparte had spent January touring the near East with her husband. She
visited Eitingon in Palestine and then travelled on to Egypt. She then spent two
weeks in London, to deposit her papers and manuscripts in safekeeping at the
Rothschild Bank and to be with Freud.

Ernest Jones also came to visit this evening.

+ Pius XI . . .   Fri 10 February 1939

Cardinal Achille Ratti (1857–1939), the Archbishop of Milan, was proclaimed
Pope Pius XI in 1922. He negotiated the Lateran Treaty with Mussolini in 1929,
establishing the Vatican City as a neutral independent territory. In 1931 he
denounced Mussolini and the Fascists; the following year, however, the two met
and repaired their relationship. He supported Franco in Spain in 1936. In 1933
he signed a Concordat with the Nazis, but by 1937 was denouncing violations of
it and branding Nazism as anti-Christian.

There were two major aspects to Freud's interest in the Papacy during the
1930s. Ideologically Catholicism represented the arch-enemy of psychoanalysis,
science and reason. Politically it had seemed to be a protection against Nazism
in Austria until the Austrian church capitulated immediately after the Anschluss
in March 1938.[1]

Trotter . . .   Fri 10 February 1939

Wilfred Trotter, a Fellow of the Royal Society of Medicine, was Ernest Jones's
brother-in-law. In 1905 the two men had set up together for a short time as
Harley Street consultants. Jones wrote that they had discovered Freud's work at
the same time: " . . . Trotter and I fully realized that the secrets we wished to
discover were in a region of the mind outside consciousness—it was Freud who
drove home the conception of an unconscious mind and its biological nature,
just as Darwin had that of evolution . . . ." In 1908 they were the only British
members attending the first psychoanalytical congress at Salzburg. However,

Trotter subsequently became an eminent surgeon and distanced himself from psychoanalysis.

In January Max Schur had noticed a new swelling in Freud's mouth. Though Dr. Exner had thought it unsuspicious, Schur had insisted on a consultation. But Trotter only advised further observation and because of his eminence—he had been surgeon to the King since 1928–his opinion carried weight. But Schur, with his ten years' experience of Freud's cancer, was convinced a new malignancy had appeared and appealed to Pichler for his judgment.

Oli 48 yrs . . .   Sun 19 February 1939

Oliver had acquired French nationality in late 1938, the first of the immediate family to be naturalized. This, as Freud said, was ". . . a first step towards our internationalization." (*Freud-Eitingon 19.12.1938*)

In England it was warm enough to sit outside on Oliver's birthday. After the hard winter, February was turning out to be the sunniest hitherto recorded. The following day Ernest Jones (who, like Anna Freud, had an interest in gardens) noted early crocuses.

Princess with Lacassagne . . .   Sun 26 February 1939

After the previous consultation with Trotter on February 10, Schur had become convinced the swelling was malignant. An inconclusive further consultation with Exner and Trotter now led him to press for another opinion and on Marie Bonaparte's advice they called in Dr. Lacassagne, the successor to Rigaud at the Institut Curie in Paris. (It was Lacassagne who had treated the Princess's father and cured the chow Topsy.) Lacassagne asked for a biopsy of the suspect growth.

Marie Bonaparte later wrote that she came to London with Lacassagne by the night train. They both dined with Freud on February 27 and afterwards she and Anna Freud took the radiologist to see the art collection at Kenwood House on Hampstead Heath.

Trial excision and X-ray . . .   Tues 28 February 1939

X-ray photos were taken in profile and full-face, both with and without the prosthesis. They revealed graphically the extent of damage wrought by cancer and surgical intervention.

The trial excision provided a positive biopsy—"a typical malignant epithelioma." The site was too near the eye socket for a further operation to be feasible, even if Freud had consented.

Instructions from Paris . . .   Fri 3 March 1939

Since the cancer was now inoperable, Lacassagne suggested intensive X-ray treatment first, rather than radium, which was more likely to cause tissue damage. Freud was resigned: "A trial excision revealed that it is really a case of the carcinoma once again trying to put itself in my place. There was long hesitation between the various possibilities of defense. [. . .] and so we have all agreed on the use of X-rays from outside . . . ." (*Freud-Eitingon 5.3.1939*)

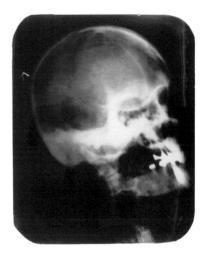

And to Arnold Zweig he wrote: "(There is now no further doubt that I have a new recurrence of my dear old cancer with which I have been sharing my existence for sixteen years. At that time naturally no one could predict which of us would prove the stronger.)"[1]

Pius XII . . .   Fri 3 March 1939

Cardinal Eugenio Pacelli (1876–1958) was proclaimed Pope Pius XII on March 2, his 63rd birthday. He was known for his diplomacy—he had, for example, held back an address by Pius XI denouncing the Nazi ban on mixed marriages.

As the Pope's delegate it was he who had signed the Concordat between the Vatican and Hitler's Reich on July 20, 1933, (only a week after the Germans had passed a eugenic law introducing compulsory sterilization in cases of hereditary illness). That treaty had been a propaganda victory for the Nazis; it was their first international agreement since the election of Hitler in March and it gave them legitimacy in the eyes of their own Catholics and of the world in general. Six months after the Concordat, on January 27, 1934, German bishops declared their loyalty to Hitler.

During the war Pius XII remained neutral.

Oliver Freud at the Pennsylvania Military College, Chester, Pennsylvania, after his escape with Henny from occupied France. The photo is "For Eva."

Freud, Lacassagne (?), Martha, Marie Bonaparte and Anna at Maresfield Gardens.

The X-ray photo of Freud's jaw on February 28, 1939, reveals the ravages of 16 years of cancer and constant operations.

Dr. Finzi . . .   Mon 6 March 1939

Dr. Neville Samuel Finzi (1881–1968), consulting radiologist at St. Bartholomew's Hospital, London, was the English radiologist recommended to undertake Freud's radiotherapy. The first visit, however, involved examining the patient. Freud wondered whether Finzi might also refuse to treat him, since Trotter had first refused to operate on him, then Lacassagne had advised against radium treatment.

But, as Freud said, ". . . X-ray is after all more sparing of me, it gives a kind of life insurance for several weeks, and probably permits the continuation of my analytic work during that time . . . " (*Freud-Eitingon 5.3.1939*)

25th anniversary of British Society . . .   Wed 8 March 1939

In a letter of congratulation to Ernest Jones on the anniversary of the British Psycho-Analytical Society, Freud commented on human lack of presentiment. When Jones had announced his intention of founding the Society just before World War I Freud had had no idea he would end up living so near, yet unable (through ill-health) to attend its celebrations.

He added: "The events of the past years have brought it about that London has become the main site and centre of the psycho-analytical movement. May the Society which discharges this function fulfil it in the most brilliant fashion." (*Freud-Jones 7.3.1939*)

Jones's own diary entry for this day is brief and jubilant:—"Un des jours de ma vie! Dinner at Savoy. 25 yrs." An anniversary dinner took place at the Savoy Hotel. Anna Freud had a place of honor, between Jones and the Rt. Hon. the Earl De La Warr P.C. (President of the Board of Education). Martin and Ernst were also present. Apart from psychoanalysts, the guests included Henry Moore, Virginia Woolf, H.G. Wells, Rebecca West and Professor Julian Huxley.

First X-ray—Finzi . . .   Thurs 9 March 1939

From now on Freud went for daily sessions at Finzi's Harley Street surgery. Schur reported that the journeys and the radiotherapy exhausted Freud; side-effects included headaches, dizziness, beard loss and bleeding from the mouth.

But he would not accept any stronger analgesic than aspirin. Finzi turns this into a reproach in his progress report to Lacassagne in July: "What he really requires is some psychological treatment to enable him to make a pact with some other medicament similar to that which he has with aspirin, but I dare not suggest this to him." (*Finzi-Lacassagne 5.7.1939*)

Anniversary of the Nazi invasion . . .   Sat 11 March 1939

This bitter anniversary of the end of Austria was also the day Hitler decided to crush Czechoslovakia. Keppler, Seyss-Inquart, Bürckel and a number of generals met in Bratislava to organize the fall of Prague, which took place four days later. The day after that, on March 16, Bohemia and Moravia—Freud's birthplace and childhood home—were declared German protectorates.

Moses with Lange . . .   Mon 13 March 1939

Freud received two copies of the new German edition of *Moses and Monotheism* from the publisher, Allert de Lange in Amsterdam. "Quite a worthy exit . . . " Freud commented in a letter to Hanns Sachs (12.3.1939). He gave one of the copies to Marie Bonaparte who was staying in the house with him at this time.

Princess with Lacassagne . . .   Mon 13 March 1939

Lacassagne returned to London with Marie Bonaparte in order to help in the application of radium the following day. Dr. Exner had prepared a special prosthesis for the application, which was to be administered by Dr. Finzi. Dr. Schur and Dr. Harmer, the ear, nose and throat specialist, were also in attendance.

Radium . . .   Wed 15 March 1939

Freud's letters reflect resignation and exhaustion. "*To cut a long story short*, it has turned out after many examinations that I have a recurrence of my old sickness.*

---

* [English in original]

Anna Freud seated between Ernest Jones and Earl De La Warr at the 25th anniversary celebration of the British Psycho-Analytical Society.

The treatment that was decided upon consists of a combination of external X-ray and internal radium which is at all events better than—cutting off my head, which would have been the other alternative [. . .] It is one way, like any other, to the inevitable end, if not that which one would have willingly chosen." (*Freud-Sachs 12–14.3.1939*).[1]

Despite tiredness caused by the treatment, Freud did not interrupt the analyses of his four patients.

Prague occupied . . .   Wed 15 March 1939

After the Munich agreement Dr. Eduard Benes resigned as president of Czechoslovakia. Soon afterwards autonomous governments were set up in Slovakia and the Carpathian Ukraine regions. The Nazi party took over its local equivalent, the Sudeten German Party, and Sudetenland was annexed by the Reich on November 21, 1938. On March 10, 1939 the pro-German regime in Slovakia was taken over by the Czech government and Hitler decided to crush Czechoslovakia. On March 14, Slovakia declared its independence, Hungary occupied the Carpathian Ukraine and the next day the Wehrmacht invaded and occupied Prague.

Ernst 47 yrs . . .   Thurs 6 April 1939

Ernst's presence in England had been invaluable to the Freuds. He had found them their accomodations, settled them in and designed "a re-erected Berggasse" at 20 Maresfield Gardens. (The expression is Ernst Freud's. In his diaries Ernest Jones also refers to Maresfield Gardens as "Berggasse.")

Ernst had always been the lucky one. On his 30th birthday his father had written: "Actually it is not necessary for me to wish you luck on your 30th birthday. You are the only one among my children who already possesses everything that one can have at your stage of life: a loving wife, a marvelous child, work, a livelihood and friends. You deserve it too and since not everything in life goes according to deserts, allow me to express the wish that luck remain true to you." (*Freud-Ernst Freud 3.4.1922*)

Summer time . . .   Sun 16 April 1939

In his 1916 and 1917 diary Freud had also noted the annual switching of clocks backward or forward to summer and winter times. But it is strange this is noted here, whereas Easter and the 53rd anniversary of Freud's practice, which occured the previous Sunday, are ignored. However, the banal fact becomes poignant in the light of Freud's knowledge that this would be his last summer.

Alexander 73 yrs. . . .   Wed 19 April 1939

Alexander Freud's son Harry had now gone to the United States and was trying to get visas for his parents to join him there.[1] They had meanwhile settled in England and during the coming months Alexander visited his brother almost daily.

Schur to New York . . .   Thurs 20 April 1939

Schur's application to emigrate to the United States was due to expire at the end of April. He had deferred going until Freud's condition improved at least slightly, but still felt guilty about abandoning his patient, knowing how reliant Freud had become on him. But he now had no alternative and therefore decided to take his family over, apply for his first papers and his New York medical license, and then return to Freud as soon as possible.

83rd birthday . . .   Sat 6 May 1939

The weather was fine and the birthday was celebrated in the garden and filmed by Princess Eugénie. In the loggia outside the dining room, a table of gifts was set up. They included a gold Greek ring (later stolen). Martin, Ernst, Mathilde and Anna were all present and Paula tied greetings around the dogs' necks to be delivered to Freud. He strolled among the family and guests, then retired into the peace of his study.

At this period he was beginning to enjoy the garden. The hanging couch from Grinzing had been set up and he would lie in it as often as the weather permitted.

"The lucky fellow", Ernst, with his wife Lux, on the beach near their former German holiday home.

Harry Freud in America.

Among the greetings was one from the poet and former analysand of his, H.D. (Hilda Doolittle), who spoke of the war threat: "It adds centuries to our life, but puts one back 25 years, a tricky 'relativity.' I can only hope that you feel secure and protected by the eternal verities and their symbolic, stabalized presences, your Egyptians and Greeks (the gods or 'goods') watch over you." (*H.D.-Freud 6.5.1939*)

Topsy published . . .   Fri 12 May 1939

Sigmund and Anna Freud's translation of Marie Bonaparte's book, *Topsy Chow-Chow au poil d'or*, was published in German by Allert de Lange, Amsterdam. Anna Freud later wrote a forward to the book, explaining her father's relationship to dogs: "Freud's interest in the world of dogs was a late acquisition. It began in the nineteen twenties with a relationship founded on mutual respect with a large and not undangerous Alsation which shared the family's life for more than ten years. It grew deeper and was transformed into tender sollicitude for an animal which had been specially acquired for him from Paris. [. . .] What Freud prized in his dogs was their grace, their devotion and loyalty; what he often commended—as a marked advantage in comparison to people—was the absence of any ambivalence. 'Dogs,' as he used to say, 'love their friends and bite their enemies, quite unlike people who are incapable of pure love and always have to mix love and hate in their object relations.' "

Moses in English . . .   Fri 19 May 1939

Both Freud and the American publisher, Knopf, had been impatient to see this translation. The translator was Katherine Jones. Ernest Jones and his wife only received the text at the end of August 1938. It was impossible to meet the publisher's first deadline at the end of October and since the next one was February 1939 there was no point in submitting earlier.

Freud, not understanding this, thought Jones was delaying and should pass the work to someone else, even though—as Jones pointed out—the only properly qualified translators (James Strachey and Joan Riviere) would in fact work more slowly than he and his wife.

Before publication the British editor Leonard Woolf (on behalf of Hogarth Press) asked Freud to alter the book's title to *Moses*: "From the publishing point of view it is, I am sure, a great mistake to have a long title, for in England many people will be frightened by the word MONOTHEISM. Would you, therefore, agree to its appearing under the shorter title?" (*Woolf-Freud 15.3.1939*).

Freud not only refused this alteration, but (alarmed, apparently, by Woolf's proposal) he wrote to his American editor, Blanche Knopf, asking for an assurance that she would not try to change the title *Moses and Monotheism* either.

Anna to Amsterdam . . .   Sat 20 May 1939

Anna Freud took a short break to visit her friends, Hans Lampl and Jeanne Lampl-de Groot, in Amsterdam. As before, she was combining the professional life of a training analyst with the duties of nurse to her father, at the same time preparing a seminar on child analysis for the summer and an introductory lecture to be given on June 30 to the British Psycho-Analytical Society on "Sublimation and Sexualization."

She wrote to Arnold Zweig: "I am energetically trying out how many lives one can live at the same time and have several full time occupations at the same time." (*Anna Freud-Arnold Zweig 11.5.1939*)

One year in England . . .   Tues* 6 June 1939

This is the correct anniversary although the entry for the arrival in England was at first mistakenly recorded as 5 June 1938.

Princess birthday with us . . .   Sun 2 July 1939

Princess Marie Bonaparte was born July 2, 1882 and had come to London to celebrate her 57th birthday with the Freuds. She had been in London for Freud's

Freud in the garden at Maresfield Gardens, 1939.

* For the first time the day is given in an English abbreviation—*Tue*. Following this date there are three more English weekdays—another *Tue* and two *We* (Wednesday). But the months for 1939 are all written in English, apart from February.

birthday, which she and her daughter had filmed. Then she had spent part of June at her home in St. Tropez. Her chow Tatoun died and Freud began a letter of condolence to her which turned into an account of his own agony.

No doubt it was the realization of Freud's imminent death which now brought her back to England. Freud had written: "The radium has once again begun to eat away at something, causing pain and toxic manifestations, my world is what it was previously: a small island of pain floating on an ocean of indifference." (*Freud-Marie Bonaparte 10.6.1939*)

Havelock Ellis + . . .   Mon 10 July 1939

The sexologist Henry Havelock Ellis (1859–1939) was among the first in the English-speaking world to greet Freud's work; in 1898 he published a paper accepting Freud's sexual etiology of hysteria in *Studies on Hysteria* (1895). But Ellis retained a certain distance between his own position and that of psychoanalysis. He declined joining the London Psychoanalytical Society when it was formed in 1913.

Ellis had once described Freud as "an artist," which Freud took as evidence of resistance to the scientific force of his theories. However, he valued Ellis's opinions and respected him.[1]

The poet H.D. had been trying to set up a meeting of the two at this time. But Ellis, although not actually ill, had been feeling too tired to attempt the journey from his home to meet Freud.

Schur back . . .   Wed 12 July 1939

Schur's account records his impression of Freud's state: "I took my New York State Boards during the last week of June, and sailed on the first boat back to England, arriving in London on July 8, 1939. I found Freud looking much worse. He had lost weight and was somewhat apathetic, at least as compared with his usual mental vigor. The skin over the right cheekbone was slightly discolored. He had lost most of his beard on the right side due to the X-ray treatments. In the region of the last lesion there was foul necrotic tissue."

+ Bleuler . . .   Sat 15 July 1939

Like Havelock Ellis, Eugen Bleuler had been among the very first significant foreigners to recognize psychoanalysis. As Professor of Psychiatry in Zurich and director of the Burghölzli sanatorium, he had contacted Freud in autumn 1904, informing him that he and his staff (which included Jung) had been studying and applying psychoanalysis for two years already.[1]

Despite their differences they had remained sporadically in contact. Ten years earlier Bleuler had written Freud a letter about aging, saying that although he himself was older than Freud he was risking travelling to the United States. (But he was actually a year younger than Freud.)

Evchen . . .   Mon 24 July 1939

This was the final visit of Freud's favorite grandchild, Oliver's daughter Eva. In 1929 when she was five years old, he had called her "an unalloyed pleasure ("*ein ungestörtes Vergnügen*"). In the ten years since then he had acquired a small collection of photos of her in France, portraits or with friends, some dedicated to "Grosspapa" (Grandpa). She was now a pupil at the Lycée Calmette in Nice.

Wells in citizenship . . .   Mon 24 July 1939

Ten days earlier H.G. Wells had written to Freud: ". . . a number of us want you to do us that honour [of becoming a British citizen]." (*Wells-Freud 14.7.1939*). In his reply Freud said that the idea of becoming an Englishman was for him "an intense wish phantasy" nurtured since his first visit to England at the age of 19.[1]

The British Member of Parliament, Commander Oliver Locker-Lampson, was now about to propose a bill to confer British nationality on Freud.[2] But the attempt failed, since Parliament was not willing to waive the period of residence rules in Freud's case, for fear of setting a dangerous precedent.[3]

Apart from the discussion of citizenship, Wells also gave Freud a copy of his tract *The Fate of Homo Sapiens*.

A dedicated photo Eva Freud sent her grandfather in August 1938.

13, HANOVER TERRACE, REGENT'S PARK, N. W. 1.

TELEPHONE, PADDINGTON 6204.

July 14. 39

Dear Doctor Freud.

How are you? Would it
be possible for the Baroness Budberg and myself
to call one afternoon & see you? Any
afternoon next week (except the 18th) or the week
after is free for us.

Since I saw you last I have
been making inquiries & stirring up people
about your becoming naturalized as a British
citizen. I believe you had a note from

13, HANOVER TERRACE, REGENT'S PARK, N. W. 1.

TELEPHONE, PADDINGTON 6204.

that anyhow a number of us want
you to do us that honour. The normal
method of naturalization is too slow; it
takes five years or more. But it is
possible with the consent of the Government
to pass a special act of parliament
setting aside the customary delays (in your favour) & I
have every reason now to hope that this
will shortly be done.

My salutations to your family.

Yours,
H. G. Wells

Martha 78 yrs . . .   Wed 26 July 1939

Earlier this year Martha had written to a friend that she was slowly beginning to feel her age. But she was still generally healthy and active (unlike Minna, who was only slowly recovering after her long months of illness the previous year).

After Freud's death, Oskar Pfister was to pay tribute to Martha's part in Freud's life and career: ". . . you, with your gentle, kindly nature, kept putting fresh weapons into your husband's hands in the fierce battle of life. The more human beings struck him as trash (he used that expression once in his letters), the more the 'grim divine pair Ananke and Logos' (that is his own phrase too) forced him into their grim service, the more need he had of you, and without you even the giant that he was would have been unable to achieve the tremendous task on behalf of good-for-nothing humanity that his life-work represents." (*Pfister-Martha Freud 12.12.1939*)

Disbanding of the practice . . .   Tues 1 August 1939

On coming to England, Freud had complained that no new patients were finding their way to him because he was old and liable to die soon. However, he did build up a restricted but regular practice. Between June 1938 and July 1939 he had four regular analysands, whose payments and hours he recorded in a dark blue notebook.[1]

But during the summer he had been growing progressively weaker. In July he had suffered "cardiac asthma" with failure of the left ventricle—an emergency from which Schur had rescued him. He was no longer sleeping well, his appetite was declining and the fetid odor from his mouth was growing unbearable—a result of bone necrosis. There was no alternative but to take what Schur called "the most painful decision of all," to disband his practice, thus marking the end of 53 years' work.

Visitors Ruth, Prince George & Marie, Segredakis, Sachs . . .
                                                Tues 1 August 1939

This gathering included Freud's two most loyal friends of the 1920s and 1930s—Ruth Mack Brunswick and Marie Bonaparte—and one of his early champions, Hanns Sachs. The Princess and her husband, Prince George of Greece, had come to London on July 30 and were to stay until August 6.

Ségrédakis was the antiquities dealer whose shop on the Rue St. Honoré in Paris was one of Marie Bonaparte's sources of antiquities. He supplied the bronze Venus she brought Freud on October 10, 1938, and also a pair of 5th-century BC Greek rhyta with women's heads, one of which he may have brought on this occasion.

Freud lay in his hanging couch, while the visitors sat around him on chairs in the garden.

Ruth taken leave . . .   Wed 23 August 1939

Ruth Mack Brunswick returned to the United States. In 1946 she died in New York.

Money from bank . . .   Thurs 24 August 1939

Freud's bank in London was Barclays, which also dealt with his house mortgage. But Freud's letter list reveals no correspondence with them at this time, and the bank no longer has his records. Perhaps this entry relates to money transferred from the Swiss account.

Eva to Nice . . .   Fri 25 August 1939

Schur wrote of their parting: ". . . I remember the utter tenderness with which he took leave of his granddaughter Eva in August, 1939, knowing full well that he would never see her again."

In 1944 Eva died of septicemia in France. After her death Martha wrote to a friend: "To write to you about Evchen, here my pen falters. The sweet child, of all my grandchildren the closest to my heart, was torn from us and her poor parents after a terrible illness (brain tumor). She died in Nice, Oli's previous home, where they had left her behind, well looked after by friends, while they themselves took flight at risk of their lives across the Pyrenees." (*Martha Freud-Elsa Reiss 2.12.1945*)

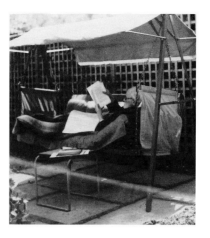

Freud in the garden, summer 1939.

Marie Bonaparte, Prince George of Greece and Hanns Sachs on a final visit to Freud, August 1, 1939.

(*Opposite top*) H. G. Wells letter to Freud on obtaining British citizenship, July 14, 1939. "Dear Doctor Freud. How are you? Would it be possible for the Baroness Budberg and myself to call one afternoon & see you? Any afternoon next week (except the 18th) or the week after is free for us. Since I saw you last I have been making enquiries & stirring up people about your becoming naturalized as a British citizen. I believe you had a wish for that and anyhow a number of us want you to do us that honour. The normal method of naturalization is too slow; it takes five years or more. But it is possible with the consent of the Government to pass a special act of parliament setting aside the customary delays in your favour & I have every reason now to hope that this will shortly be done. My salutations to your family. Yours H.G. Wells."

(*Opposite*) Two women's head rhyta in Freud's study showcase. WK

Dorothy N. York . . .   Fri 25 August 1939

Dorothy Burlingham was going to the United States in order to be there for the birth of Mabbie and Simon Schmiderer's child, her first grandchild. While waiting at Southampton for the steamer *New Amsterdam* to leave, she wrote a letter to Anna Freud, which conveys not only her mood but that of the times: "How I hope there will be no war. I felt so sure as I was in the train going through those green fields but tonight I feel depressed & fearful. I do so hope that days will get gradually better for your father. How I hope that." (*Dorothy Burlingham-Anna Freud 25.8.1939*)

She believed she could get back to England before either war broke out or Freud died, but she was mistaken.

War panic . . .   Fri 25 August 1939

Ever since the Munich agreement, Germany had been putting increasing pressure on Poland. The primary demands had been rights over the Polish corridor to East Prussia, the surrender of Danzig and the entrance of Poland into the Anti-Comintern Pact. Poland had resisted these demands and had been backed up by guarantees of help from France and Great Britain. During 1939 preparations for war had continued steadily: Hitler had brought Hungary and Spain into the Anti-Comintern Pact, signed the *Steel Pact* of military alliance with Italy in May and in August a military pact with Japan. Finally, on August 23 von Ribbentrop signed the nonagression pact with Stalin and this had been a signal that war was now virtually inevitable.

On August 25 Britain declared its support for Poland. In a last-ditch attempt at appeasement, Chamberlain proposed direct talks between the Germans and Poles: the Germans responded by proposing a new set of demands including the handing over of the Polish corridor and Upper Silesia and special rights for *Volksdeutsche*. On September 1 the Germans invaded Poland; Britain sent an ultimatum to which there was no response and on September 3 war was declared.

Postscript: Freud's Death   Saturday 23 September 1939

During September Freud's condition worsened progressively. Putrid secondary infections ate a hole through his cheek—the smell drove away his beloved chow, Lün. Even though exhausted, Freud refused sedation until the last few days.

On September 21 he reminded Schur of their pact, saying "Now it's nothing but torture and makes no sense any more." At Freud's request Schur discussed the tacit decision with Anna. She eventually agreed with Schur, that there was no point in prolonging dying. Schur gave Freud a morphine injection, twice repeated the following day. At 3 a.m. on September 23 Freud died in a coma.

The funeral and cremation took place on September 26 at Golders Green Crematorium. Ernest Jones read a funeral oration in English, followed by a German tribute from Stefan Zweig.[1]

Anna wrote a month later to Arnold Zweig: "It is curious, but I cannot mourn him properly as one otherwise does and as people expect you to do. Mourning is somehow no adequate feeling for the fact that he has died. Perhaps my bond with him was more serious than the separation from him. At any rate, what one has received from him is always much more than what other people even possess. So I carry on living, which I previously could never imagine. He seems to have imagined it like that, for he did not worry at all about that point." (Anna Freud-Arnold Zweig 28.10.1939)

In a later letter Anna denied having any religious feelings, but added: "But as far as my feelings are concerned, it seems to me as if this whole separation were something temporary, something transient during which one has to keep everything in order. Rather, something like in earlier years when my father was away on journeys." (Anna Freud-Arnold Zweig 13.2.1940)

Martha was, of course, differently affected by the loss. She told Paul Federn: "I cannot even complain, for I have been granted more than a lifetime in which I have been allowed to look after him, to shield him from the troubles of everyday life. That my life had now lost sense and content is only natural." (Martha Freud-Federn 5.11.1939)

Martha standing at the gate of 20 Maresfield Gardens.

Kürzeste Chronik
[The German Text]

1929
31 Okt.   Kürzeste Chronik
im Nobelpreis übergangen

So. 2 Nov.   Erste Tarokpartie—Besuch
Rickman

Di 4 Nov.   mit Fingereiterung bei Schnitzler
Mi 5 Nov.   Almanach
Vorwort für Eitingon

Do 6   Kris u Montirungen, Flournoy
Fr 7   Antisemit. Unruhen—
Dioscurenring—

Mo 11   Neuralgie. Adda weggeben
Do 14   Herz-Warmanfall. Dr Altmann
Sa 16   Rothschildspital, Anna's Buch
Mi 20   Erster Abend Yvette
Do 21   Im Hotel bei Yvette
Fr 22   Widmung Th. Mann. Yvette
zweiter Abend

Sa 23   bei Gottlieb.
Blinder Lärm bei Pichler

Mo 25   Adda geholt
Sa 30   Prinzessin abgereist, Eitingon's
Mutter +

Di 3 Dez   Anna's Geburtstag. 34 J.
Sa 7 Dez   Martin 40 J.
Sa 7—Di 10—   Schlechte Herztage
Mi 11   Smaragdring
Do 12   Vereinsabend
Di 17   Anna nach Essen—
geschnittene Steine gekauft

Sa 21   Anna zurück
Di 24   Weihnacht—Eitingon
"Unbehagen"

Fr 27   Perlen für Martha
Mo 30   Adda gestorben

1930
Fr 3 Jan   Zigarren von Landauer
Mo 6 Jan   Konferenz Martin—Drucker
Do 9 Jan   Vereinsabend.
Fr u Sa 10 u 11   geschnittene Steine
Mitt 15 Jan   Montirte Thonfiguren
gekommen

Sa 18 Jan   Felix Wiener in NY +
Do 16 Jan   Bücher von R. Rolland
Die 21 Jan   Mrs London, Gallenanfall
Fr 24 Jän   Schur. Museum. Akrobat
gekauft

Mon 3 Febr   Besuch Prof. Rojas B-Aires
Do/Fr 6/7 Feb   Traum von Nestroy
Sa 8 Feb   Tom +
So 9 Febr   Arnold Zweig
Do 13 Febr   Abend mit Alexander—Staub
Fr 14   Jadekette für Anna.
Hypnoanalyse

Sa 15   Agypt. Halbbüste.
So 16   Ruth Geburtstag, Opalkette.
M 17   Margaretl's todtes Kind,
Roheim's Buch

So 23   Mitzi in Wien
Mi 26   Prof Berman Cordoba Argent.
Fr 28   Dr Trebitsch u ohne Prothese
Eisinger über Angela

So 2 März   Kongestion Darmzustand
Di 4 M.   Jade gekauft
Mi 5 M.   Anfrage preuss.
Kultusministeriums.

So 9 M.   Jo-Fi angekommen
Di 11 M.   Ernstl 16 Jahre.
So 16 M/Mo 17 M.   Yvette
Mitt 19 M.   Neue Vorlesungen. Verlag $1000
Do 20 M.   Abend über Unbehagen
~~Di 25 M~~   ~~Norwegische Vorlesungen~~
Mi 26 M.   Anna nach Bpest. Elkuss +
Do 27 M.   Anna zurück—Eitingon aus
Paris

Fr 28 M.   Mela schwer erkrankt.
Sa 29 M.   Martha nach Berlin
So 30 M.   Lajos auf Besuch—Bei Rie

Mi 2 April $5000 Martin zum Ankauf
Do 3 "   Walter 9 Jahre.
Sa 5   Nächtlicher Herzanfall. Braun.
Mo 7 "   Bob operirt. Dr Hans Zweig
Do 10 "   Rob, Math. abgereist. Dr Stefan
Zweig Witz französisch

Sa 12—   Ferenczi über Sonntag.
So 13   Martha zurück, Ferenczi.
Prinzess abends—

Mo 14—   Feder gebrochen. Illus. russ.
Die 15   Anna u Dorothy nach Paris
Do 17   Anna u Dorothy zurück
Fr 18   Sachs—Caligula
Di 22   CottageSanator.
Fr 25   Tabakabstinenz
Mai Fr 2   Japan. Übersetzg. "Jenseits
Lustprinz."

Sa 3   Zurück v. Sanator.
Berlin [in red]—Mo
5   Ankunft in Tegel
Do 6   74 Jahre
Mi 7   Yabe aus Japan—Lederer 1
Besuch

So 11   Lederer 2 Besuch
Mi 14   Operation an Prinzessin
Martha nach Kärnten

Sa 17   Besuch in Caputh—Bullitt.
So 25   Max auf Besuch.
Mo 26   Lederer 3 Besuch
Do 29/Sa 31   Hiddensee

Juni 1930
Mi 4   Dritter Besuch bei Lederer
So 8   Robert Fliess
Fr 13   Frau Mercedes—Miete in
Grundlsee.
Trude Hammerschlag +

Sa 14   Vierter Besuch Lederer
Di 17   Dr Alexander
Mi 18   Dr Weinmann   Minna's
Geburtstag

Fr 20   Dr Staub.
Sa 21   Lucie—Jackson u David B.
entlassen.

Di 24   Zeppelin nachts.
Max angekommen, Dorothy
abgereist

Mi 25   Traumdeutung 8 Aufl.
Mo 30   Anfall Herzneuralgie mit
Diarrhoe

Juli
Di 1—   Letzter Besuch b. Lederer.
Honorar Traumdeutung
verteilt

Do 3   Arnold Zweig—Goethepreis
aufgetaucht.

Fr 11   Liebman £20 Hogarth f.
Unbehagen

Mo 14   Neuländer £81 Hogarth f.
Collect Pap.

Mi 23   Abschied v. Schröder
—[red line] Fr 25   Ankunft in Wien
—[blue line] So 27   Ankunft in Grundlsee
Di 29   Goethepreis
August
Sa 2   Besuch Federn, Meng, Hollos
Mi 6   Mathilde angekommen
Fr 8   in Ischl bei Mutter
Sa 16   F. Salten—Alex Sophie Harry
So 17   Ischl bei Mutter G. 95 J.
Di 19   Ständchen
So 24   Dr Michel u Goethepreis
Abschied v. Mutter

Mo 25   Mela Rie +
Do 28   Anna in Frankfurt
Fr 29   Nachricht Martin Blinddarm.
Anna zurück.

Sa 30   Math. abgereist
So 31   Simmel u Laforgue
Sept
Di 2   Sachs.
Mi 3   Bernfeld abends, Paquet dazu
So 7   Eitingon, Simmel, Federn,
Weinmann

Fr 12   + Mutter gestorben 8h früh
So 14   Anna bei Mutters Begräbnis.
Mi 15   Anna mit Dorothy abgereist
Di 16   Prinzess abgereist
Mi 17   Dolfi angekommen.
Do 18   Ernst u Jofi nach Wien   Eva
eingezogen

—[blue line] So 28   Ankunft in Wien
Mo 29   Anna zurück. Dr Bondy
Do 30   Röntgen bei Schwartz

Okt Fr 3   Alle Ärzte bei Pichler, neue
Vitrine

Di 14   Operation bei Pichler.
Fr 17   Fieberhafte Erkrankung—Bullitt
Mi 29   Arbeit aufgenommen

Nov So 2   Erste kleine Zigarre
Mi 5   Fortsetzg des Grabreliefs von
Rom

Do 6   Im Nobelpreis endgiltig
übergangen.

So 9 — Wahlen—Ferenczi
Do 20 — Relief montirt
Di 25 — Erster Abend Yvette
Sa 29 — Eitingon
So 30 — bei Yvette Hotel
Dez Mi 3— — Anna 35 J.
Do 4 — Wilson beendigt
Do 11 — Ed. Weiss—Sitzung
Sa 13 — Anna nach Bpest
So 14 — Halsmann in N. Presse Hebraeische Vorreden
Mi 17 — Bei Max Pollack
Fr 26 — Unbehagen f. 2 Aufl. korrigirt
Di 30 — Japanisches Alltagsleben.

1931

Jan Do 8 — Ernst u Lux, Kette für Lux.
Sa 10 — Ernst abgereist. Jofi Niederkunft.
Mo 12 — Einladung London, Huxley Lecture
Mi 14/Do 15 — Periostit. Schmerzen Nachts
Sa 17 — Anna in Prag
Mo 19 — Prinzess eingetreten
Di 20 — Röntgen bei Dr Presser
Mi 21 — Martha Grippe
So 25 — Martha ausser Bett

Febr Mi 4 — Korinth Vase bei Fröhlich
Sa 7 — Electrocution bei Pichler
Mo 9 — + Mathilde Breuer
Mi 11 — Mundsperre. St. Zweig Heilung d. Geist
Mo 16 — Arbeit aufgenommen
Do 19 — Oli 40 Jahre.
Fr 20 — Gutachten f. Bernfeld
Sa 28 — Eitingon Besuch
Fr 27 — Abend Bernfeld

März Fr 20 — Lux Operation erfahren.
Sa 21 — Ehrenmitglied Ges Ärzte
Fr 27 — Abend mit Radó

April Fr 3 — Poetzleinsdorf gemietet
So 12 — Tansley—Ernstl nach Scharfenberg
Di 14 — Consil Pichler
Mi 15 — Republik in Spanien
Di 22 — Consil Holzknecht
Do 24 — Auersperg Operation

Mai Di 5 — nach Hause zurück
Mi 6 — 75 Geburtstag
Sa 9 — Sitzung Poetzl—Gomperz
Do 14 — Oli's Besuch.
Juni
P—[in red] Mo 1 — Übersiedlung Poetzleinsdorf
Di 3 — Edith Rischawy Begräbnis
Sa 6 — Japan. Übersetzg—Otto Fleischl
Sa 13/Mo 15 — Eitingon
Sa 20/Di 23 — Ernst
So 28 — Storfer—Tarok mit Fleischl

Juli Di 14 — Bildhauer Juran für Freiberg
Sa 19 — + Johanna Rie
Do 23 — bei Alfred Rie—v.d.Hoop
Fr 24 — Bildhauer O.Neumann— Graf'sches Portrait—Alex u Lilli abd.— Kongress abgesagt
So 26 — Martha 70 J.
Di 28 — + Forel
Fr 31 — Armenier Zahnarzt aus Boston

August Sa 1 — Anna krank. Neue Prothese Kazanjean
Fr 7 — Dr Stein wegen Nasenbluten
Mo 10 — Kazanjian Arbeit begonnen
Do 13 — Ernstl in Scharfenberg

— angenommen
Di 25 — Tegel wird sperren
Do 27 — Wendepunkt
Fr 28 — Ricarda Huch Goethepreis
Sa 29 — Kazanjian abgereist. Neue Prothesen

Mo 31 — Minna's Unfall auf Strasse.
Sept Di 1 — Oscar Rie erkrankt.
Mi 2 — Libidinöse Typen begonnen.
Mo 7 — Dr Alexander
Fr 11 — Eitingon
Sa 12 — Prinzess abgereist
So 13 — Nunberg verabschiedet. Putsch in Steiermark, Eitingon abgereist
Mi 16 — Minna nach Meran
Do 17 — + Oscar Rie, Emden
Fr 18 — bei Nunberg
*—Sa 26 — in Berggasse
Mi 30 — Weibl Sexualität beendigt —Rickman—

Okt So 4 — Lampl—Friedjung
Mo 5 — + Tattoan
Di 6 — Kwannon u Tangfigur gekauft
Do 8 — Federn—Priester gekauft
Fr 9 — Devisenordnung
Mo 12 — Juran Gipsplakette Album v. Poetzleinsdorf
Mi 14 — Gold eingewechselt
Do 15 — Minna zurück Reiter u Wächter gekauft

Fr 16 — Mathilde 44 J.
Sa 17 — Ernst angekommen.
Mi 21 — Arthur Schnitzler +
Do 22 — Albr. Schaeffer u Frau
So 25 — Feier in Freiberg
Mi 28 — Ferenczi—Martin nach Zürich
Do 29 — Drei Büsten von Nemon
Sa 31 — Holzknecht +—Nepenthe— Jeanne abgereist

Do 5/Fr 6 XI — Magendarmzustand
So 8/XI — In Hochrotherd
Di 10/XI — Kolik—Bondi
Fr 13 — Obras XIV u XV—Einkäufe Kameeltreiber, Jade
Mi 18 — Marianne Kind u Operation
Do 19 — Perlen u Ringe gekauft.
Sa 21 — Bleuler—Martin nach Berlin
So 22 — Oppenheimer—Prometheussage.
So 29 — Tandlerbrief in N.Presse
Mo 30 — Yvette
Dezember
Do 3 — Perlen f. Anna z. 36 Geburtstag—Scharlach bei Ernst's Kindern.
Fr 4 — Lou Salomé's Dank
Mi 9 — Vishnu von Calcutta.
Di 22 — Japanische Übersetzgen.

1932 Januar
Fr 1 — Langer Magenanfall—Schritt gegen Reich
Sa 16 — Eitingon—Martin an Stelle Storfer's.
So 17 — Anna Grippe—Erste portug. Übersetzg.
Mo 18 — £2500 von Bullitt.
Di 26 — Anna auf Semmering
Sa 30 — $1000 von Jackson u von Brill.
Februar
Mo 1 — Anna zurück
Fr 5 — Chinesische Reiterin
Mi 10 — Vorrede zu neuen Vorlesungen.
Do 18 — Geschenk Fuziyama von Kosawa
Fr 19 — Morator. Verlag
Mo 22 — Infekt. Schnupfen bei Anna u mir

Di 23 — Projekt d. Büste im Goethehaus. März
Mo 7 — Operation bei Pichler
Do 8 — Briand +
So 13 — Grosse Kelebe von Fröhlich gekauft Selbstmord Kreuger
Mo 14 — Wal in Deutschland unentschieden
Do 17 — Besuch Thomas Mann
Di 22 — Goethetag—Französ. Illusion

Ostern 1932
27 März — 46 J. Praxis. Rundbrief für Verlag
Mo 28/3 — Dr Stockert, Enkel v Meynert, Rundbrief fertig
April
Mo 4/4 — Martha nach Berlin—Vier Krankengeschichten
Mi 6/4 — Roheim auf Besuch. Martha bei Ernst's Geburtstag.
So 10/4 — Hindenburg gewählt
Sa 16/4 — Rivista italiana—Ed Weiss
So 17/4 — In Hochrotherd.
Di 19/4 — Martha von Berlin, Martin nach Leipzig
Fr 22/4 — Binswanger
Mai
Fr 6/5 — 76 Geburtstag
So 8/5 — Tag in Hochrotherd
Mi 11/5 — Redaktionssitzung
Sa 14/5 — Poetzleinsdorf
Mo 23/5 — Ungarische Übersetzungen
Di 31/5 — Psa. Quarterly—Mitzi abgegangen—
Juni
Mo 6/6 — Unbehagen schwedisch
Mi 15/6 — Liebesleben japanisch
Di 21/6 — Aufforderung Steinig—Einstein
Fr 24/6 — Lux u Gabi
Di 28/6 — Grosses Pferd gekauft. $2000 v Jackson
Juli
Mo 11/7 — Jakob Bernays von Fränkel
Mi 13/7 — Mathilde Haiberstadt +
Sa 16/7 — Eva Scharlach in Mallnitz—Jofi zurück
Di 26 — Geburtstag in Hochroterd
August
Mo 1/8 — Steinig mit Einstein's Brief
Mi 10/8 — Martin Nierenkolik
So 14/8 — Geometrische Pyxis
Mo 15/8 — Jeanne als Gast.
Mi 22/8 — Brill
Di 23/8 — Ferenczi's Absage
Sa 27/8 — Ernst's Besuch—Radó
Di 30/8 — Ernst abgereist
Mi 31/8 — ~~Sept~~ Vorlesungen fertig
Sept.
Do 1/9 — Anna nach Göttingen— Kongress
Fr 2/9 — Ferenczi mit Brill.
So 4/9 — Kongress Wiesbaden
Di 6/9 — Discussion Einstein beendigt
Do 8/9 — Anna zurück
Fr 9/9 — + Chr Ehrenfels
Mo 12/9 — Obras XV u XVI
Sa 17/9 — Berggasse

Di 20 — Mathilde krank
Sa 24/9 — Minna nach Meran—Martin zurück
So 25/9 — Hochrotherd
Di 27/9 — bei Anna in Imperial. Urenkel Brücke's
Oktober
So 2/10 — Hochrotherd mit Ruth u Mark
Di 4/10 — Anna nach Berlin geflogen—

	Fetisch Jackson
Do 6/10	Anna zurück—Gerstberg—
	Tüchtige Operation b.
	Pichler
Fr 14/10	Minna von Meran
Sa 29/10—So 30/10	Alfred Rie + Unfall u. Tod.
	November
Di 1/XI	Grippe und Ohrenentzündung
Do 3/XI	Parazentese Ruttin
Di 8/XI	Roosevelt in USA gewählt.
Mi 30/XI	bei Yvette im Hotel
	Dezember
Sa 3/XII	Anna 37 J.—Neue Vorlesungen.
Do 8/XII	Operation bei Pichler

1933
Januar

Mi 4/1	Dr May—Martin nach Berlin
Do 5/1	G. Anton +
Mi 18/1	L. Tiffany + New York
Fr 27/1	Eitingon
So 29/1	Ruth Grippe, Hitler
	Reichskanzler
Di 31/1	Galsworthy +; JoFi Kagran
	Februar
So 12/2	Arnold Zweig
Mo 13/2	Brill—Traumdeutung
Di 14/2	vier japan. Übersetzungen
Fr 17/2	Eiserner Buddha
Di 21/2	Leonardo czechisch
Di 28/2	Parlament Berlin in Brand
	März
Sa 4/3	Dollarmorator—Roosevelt
So 5/3	Hitlerwahl in Deutschland.
Mo 13/3	Egypt. Stoffmalerei
Mi 15/3	Harry Promotion—
Fr 17/3	farbige Chinesin—
Mi 22/3	Warum Krieg?
Sa 25/3	Setzerstreik
Mo 27/3	Pourquoi Guerre?—Nachricht
	Ferenczi—Jofi Verletzg
Mi 29/3	Besuch Barilari
Fr 31/3	Bryher

April

So 2	Ernstl von Berlin—Arn.
	Zweig—.
Mo 3	Jofi's gefährliche Geburt—
	Norman Douglas
Mi 5	Ernstl, Bob, Mabbie nach Sizilien
Sa 8	Oli—Henny aus Berlin
Mo 10	Moses italienisch—Why War?
So 16	Ostern. 47 J Praxis
Mo 17	Boehm u Federn
Sa 22	Klemperer
Di 25	Dr Ed Weiss—Forzano
	Mai
Mo 1	Sperre der Stadt gegen Umzüge.
Do 4	Umzug Hohe Warte
Fr 5	Ernst u Klemens
Sa 6	77 Geburtstag—Schwindelanfall
Do 11	Verbrennung in Berlin
Di 15	Ernst abgereist. Operation P.—
	Arn. Zweig
Mi 16	Jeanne Hausbesuch
So 21	Colitis. Jeanne abgereist—van
	Vriesland
Mo 22	Ferenczi +. Serbische Vorlesgen
Di 23	Japan Zeitschrift N–I
Mi 24	Ruth u Mark von Paris
Do 25	Anna u Martin von Bpest
Fr 26	Diathermie a Unterkiefer—
So 28	Oli—Henny in Paris
Mo 29	Poe von Marie Bonaparte
Di 30	Budha Kopf
	Juni
So 4	Nachruf Ferenczi beendigt
Mo 5	H.G. Wells auf Besuch
Fr 16	Eitingon

Mo 26	Paul Hammerschlag +, Wittels'
	Reise.
Fr 30	Ernstl's Tonsillenoperation
	Juli
Sa 8	Ruth Operation—Martin's
	Furunkulose.
So 9	60 Jahre Matura mit
	Knöpfmacher u Wagner
	August
Di 1/8	Ferien—Hochroterd
Mi 2	Bullitt
Do 10	Blindeninstitut
Fr 11	Eitingon
Sa 12	Hochrotherd—Stephen Wise
Do 17	Prinzessin—Essais de psych.
	appliquée.
Fr 18	Dorothy zurück u Lampl
Do 24	Jeanne operirt
Fr 25	Ruth nach Amerika

So 3	September 1933
	Laforgue—Stiftung Bryher
Di 5	Operation—Herzanfall—Beginn
	d. Krankheit
Sa 16	Ernst u Lux gekommen.
Di 19	Pichler z. Consilium. Lux
	abgereist.
Sa 30	Berggasse
	Oktober 1933
Di 3	Attentat auf Dollfuss.
Mi 4	Dr Ludwig Bauer
Do 5	Martin Anwaltprüfg. bestanden.
Mo 9	Erste Ausfahrt—Zwergfigur u
	Jade f. Dorothy
Sa 14	Deutschland will aus Völkerbund
	aus.
Mo 16	Mathilde 46 J.
Do 19	Martin nach Zürich
	November
Sa 4	Martin zurück
Do 8	Stomatitis—Pichler Besuch
So 12	10 Jahre seit Operation—
	deutsche Wahlen
Di 14	Nachricht Simmel's Verhaftung.
Do 16	New Lectures (Sprott)—
	cyprische Siegel u Funde
	Ernst von Berlin abgereist.
Sa 25	Eitingon
	Dezember
So 3	Anna 38 J.—Mitzi Herzanfall
Mo 11	Fall bei der Lampe

1934
Januar

Di 2	Hebraeische Vorlesungen I.
Fr 5	Martin's Nierensteinoperation
Sa 6	Prinzess abgereist—Oscar
	Philipp.
Mi 24	Röntgen im Hause.
	Februar
Mi 7	Silberne Hochzeit Math—Robert
	u Alex—Soph
Sa 10	Martin nach Hause
Mo 12	Generalstreik
Sa 17	Ehrenfels jun.
So 18	Burlingham's nach Italien
Mo 19	König Albert +
	März
Sa 3	Lux Autounfall erfahren.
Do 8	G. Earle—Mumienmaske
Fr 9	Mumienhülle
M 12	Katarrh
Mi 14	+ Läufer
Fr 23	Radium

1934
April

Do 5/4	Volkszählungscommission
Fr 13/4	Wohnung Strasserg gesehen u
	gemietet
Fr 20/4	Oli aus Paris.
Sa 21/4	Daly
Mo 23/4	Zweites Radium
Di 24/4	Nestroy's Werke
Mi 25/4	Jekels' Abschied
Do 26/4	Ur Excavations—Oli abgereist—
	vdLeeuw abds
Sa 28/4	Strassergasse 47
	Mai
Di 1/5	Neue Verfassung
So 6/5	78 Jahre Gisela Ferenczi—
Mo 7/5	Elfenbeinbuddha u stein. Fohund
Fr 18/5	Gardenia
	Juni
Mo 4/6	Sarapis und Brunnenstier
Do 14/6	+ Groddeck und + Frau Zweig
Sa 30/6	S. A. Revolte in Deutschland
	Juli
Mi 4/Do 5	Migraine ophthalm. mit
	Krankheit
Mo 9	Meteorstein—Harry Karlsbad
Do 12	Ernstl auf Wanderung—
	Löwendrache
Fr 13	Sarasin
Mon 16	Chinesisch Vorlesgen.
Di 17	Dr Sachs, Johannesbg.
Sa 21	Ernst v Berlin
Mi 25	+ Dollfuss; Putsch im Ballhaus
Do 26	Martha 73 J.—Sohn bei
	Marianne
August	
Do 2/8	+ Hindenburg.
Sa 18/8	Eitingon
Mo 20/8	Nunberg
Mi 22/8	Jones
Sa 25/8	Alexander—Anna nach Luzern
Mi 29/8	+ v.d. Leeuw
September	
Sa 1/9	Anna von Luzern
Di 3/9	Radó
Mi 6/9	Eros Myrina
Fr 14/9	XII Band Ges. Ausgabe
So 23/9	Moses beendigt

Di 9/10	Oktober 1934
	Attentat in Marseille
Sa 13/10	In Berggasse
Di 16/10	Mathilde 47 J.
	Nov 1934
Sa 3/XI	Lux
Mo 26/XI	Dozentur erloschen—
	Hormoninjektion
	Dezember 1934
Mo 3/XII	Anna 39 J.
Fr 7/XII	Martin 45 J.
Fr 14/XII	Flimmern—Dr ~~Fischer~~ Fleischer
So 16/XII	Vagusanfall

1935
Januar

Di 1/1	Magenanfall—Erbrechen
Mi 9/1	Martin zurück von Nizza
So 13/1	Saarabstimmung
Mi 23/1	+ Anna v Vest—Anna's Vortrag
So 27/1	Nachschrift zu Selbstdarstellung.
	Februar
Mi 6/2	Levy-Brühl. Anna's II Vortrag
Di 18/2	Dr Gerard
Mi 19/2	Oli 44 J.
Fr 22/2	Minna nach Meran
Do 28/2	+ Otto Fleischl (Nachricht)
	März

Mo 11/3	Ernstl grossjährig		Dezember	
Sa 16/3	Haus in Grinzing gemietet	Di 3/XII	Anna 40 J.—Grosse Hanbüchse	Sa 17/10	Berggasse
So 17/3	Allgemeine Wehrpflicht in	Sa 7/XII	Martin 46 J.	So 18/10	Beer-Hofmann
	Deutschland	Di 10/XII	Ernstl nach Palaestina	Do 22/10	Arnold Zweig
Sa 23/3	Operation bei Pichler	Sa 14/XII	Masaryk zurückgetreten	Sa 24/10	Eitingon u Datum v Fliess'
Fr 29/3	Elektrische Uhr.	Mo 23/XII	Paul Hollitscher +		Geburtstag.
	April			Di 27/10	Nasenblutung.
Sa 6/4	Minna zurück. Ernst 43 J.		1936	Fr 30/10	Neues Pferd.
Do 11/4	Neue amerik. Vorlesungen.				Nov
Sa 13/4	Martin aus Zürich	Do 2/1	Ernst	So 1/11	Versammlung mit Boehm
Do 18/4	Strassergasse	Mo 13/1	Ernst abgereist	So 15/11	Direktor v. Dehmel
Sa 20/4	Reik u Landauer	Di 14/1	Unglaube auf Akropolis fertig	Sa 21/11	Oliver
So 21/4	Ostern, 49 J. Praxis—Jones u	Do 16/1	Prinzess abgereist. Operation b	So 22/11	+ Etka Herzig
	Familie		Pichler	Do 26/11	Oli abgereist
Mo 22/4	Neuralgie—Federn u Meng	Mo 20/1	Georg V +		Dezember
Di 23/4	Schmiedeberg	Di 21/1	Nemon u Königsberger	Do 3/12	Anna 41 Jahre.
Do 25/4	Jones abends	Mi 22/1	van Wulfften	Mo 7/12	Martin 47 Jahre.
Fr 26/4	Schale von McCord. Maria		Februar	Do 10/12	Eduard VIII abgedankt
	Stuart von Zweig—	Sa 1/2	Eine Woche Nemon—Max	Sa 12/12	Operation bei Pichler
	Gegenstück zu gelb Drachen	Di 4/2	Abschied von Max.	So 20/12	Prof. Otto Loewi
So 28/4	Brief an Thomas Mann	So 9/2	+ Rob. Breuer	Fr 24/12	Weihnacht in Schmerzen
Mo 29/4	Ruth operirt	Do 20/2	Bischowski-Operation Pichler	So 27/12	Stefan Zweig
Di 30/4	Operation bei Pichler		März		
		Di 3/3	+ Pineles.—Osirisgruppe von		
			Alex.		1937
	Mai	Di 10/3	Operation b Pichler	Sa 2/1	Prinzessin kauft Korrespondenz
S 5/5	Anfang des Prothesenelends	Mi 25/3	Minna's Glaukom.—Angela		mit Fliess
Son 6/5	79 Jahre.		Konfiskation unserer Bücher in	Mo 11/1	Jofi in's Spital zur Operation
Mo 20/5	Bullitt		Leipzig	Do 14/1	+ Jofi an Herzschwäche
Fr 24/5	Ehrenmitglied des ~~London~~		Migraine	Fr 15/1	Thomas Mann—Lün
	~~Medical Society~~		April		angenommen
	Royal Society of Medicine	Fr 3/4	Grosser Totenschiff	Mo 18/1	Herzzustand
	Juni	So 5/4	Henny mit Eva.		Februar
So 9/6	Vierländertagung in Wien	Mo 6/4	Ernst 44 J.	Mi 3/2	Kl. Moses beendet
Mo 10/6	Hollos Ed. Weiss	So 12/4	Ostern 50 J. Praxis—Aegypt.	Do 11/2	+ Lou Salomé, gest. 5/2?
Di 11/6	Chatterji		Ackerszene	So 28/2	Wolf Sachs aus Johannsburg
Di 18/6	Minna 70 Jahre		Minna noch immer krank		März
Sa 22/6	Anna nach Prag. Neue Prothese	Di 14/4	Henny Eva abgereist	So 7/3	Jul. Wagner 80 Jahre
Do 27/6	Ernstl Matura	Mi 15/4	Minna in's Sanatorium	Di 29/3	Japanische Medaille—
	Juli	Sa 18/4	Strassergasse		Montessorikrippe
Mo 8/7	+ Albert Hammerschlag	Do 23/4	#5000 von Brill		April
Sa 13/7	Unfall Schuschnigg	Mi 29/4	Minna aus Sanat.	So 4/4	Beer-Hofmann auf Besuch
So 14/7	Th. Reik		Mai	Di 6/4	Ernst 45 Jahre
Mi 17/7	Herzanfall Extrasystol	Mo 4/5	Adresse von Mann, Wells,	Do 22/4	Operation mit Evipan
Mo 22/7	Prinzessin		Rolland u A.	Sa 24/4	von Sanat. nach Grinzing, +
Fr 26/7	Martha 74 J.	Mi 6/5	80st Geburtstag-Eroberung v.		Halban
	August		Abessinien	Fr 30/4	"Unendliche Analyse" beendigt
Fr 2/8	Rockefeller jr.—Isis mit Horus	Do 7/5	Thomas Mann		Mai
So 4/8	Robert 60 J.	Fr 8/5	Vortrag Th. Mann + L.	Do 6/5	81 Jahre!
Di 6/8	Eitingon		Braun—	Mi 12/5	Coronation—Ernst abgereist
Mi 14/8	Ernst mit Lucian			Do 13/5	Antiquit aus Athen
So 18/8	Mutter wäre 100 Jahre!			So 16/5	Pfingsten, Anna i Bpest
Mo 19/8	Operation der Krusten.		1936	Fr 28/5	+ A. Adler in Aberdeen
	September		Juni		Juni
So 1/9	Sarasin—Kempner	Fr 5/6	Besuch im neuen Lokal Bergg. 7	Sa 5/6	Oberholzer—Weil
Di 3/9	Begrüssung der "Wien" B.B. z. 40	So 14/6	Vorlesung von Thomas Mann bei	Fr 11/6	Anna's Unfall—Schmerzen—
	Jubil.		uns.		Grosse Hitze Otitis
Do 5/9	Jadeschüssel und Kameel	Do 18/6	Minna 71 Jahre	Sa 26/6	Büste von McCord
So 15/9	Emden—Stefan Zweig—Willy	Mo 29/6	Maler Krausz, Ella Braun		Juli
	Haas	Di 30/6	foreign member Royal Society	Di 27/7	Moses II
So 29/9	Jeans		Juli	Mi 28/7	Eitingon
	Oktober	Sa 11/7	Verständigung mit Deutschland		Arn Zweig, Prinzess abgereist
Mo 1/X	Grosse Kwannon.	Fr 14/7	Operation bei Pichler		August
Di 2/X	Beginn d. Krieges in Abessinien.	Sa 18/7	Sanatorium Operation	So 8/8	Moses II beendigt
Do 10/X	Feinheit e. Fehlleistung	So 19/7	Zurück mit verbundenem Auge.	Mi 18/8	Haematurie
Fr 11/X	Operation b Pichler	Do 23/7	Aus schwerem Kranksein	Di 24/8	+ Kallich
So 13/X	Thornton Wilder	Fr 31/7	Anna Marienbad, Congress		
Mo 16/X	Math 48 Jahre		August		
Fr 18/X	Berggasse	Do 6/8	Anna zurück von Congress		Sept 1937
Di 22/X	+ Richard Wahle	Fr 14/8	Arn. Zweig und H. Struck	Mi 1/9	Emanuel Loewy 80 J.
Mo 28/X	Autobiographical Study	Di 18/8	Moses mit Arn. Zweig	Di 14/9	+ Masaryk—51 J. seit Heirat
	November	Do 20/8	Anna auf Rax—Plaquette von	Mi 15/9	Lou Jones
Mi 6/XI	+ Victor Dirsztay		Willy Levy	Do 23/9	Idee über Wahn u Konstruction
So 10/XI	Besuch von Yvette Guilbert	Di 25/8	Tandler +—Bullitt nach Paris		Okt
Do 21/XI	Almanach 1936	Fr 28/8	Jones mit Familie—Ernstl nach	Fr 15/X	Neue Zähne
			Russland	Sa 16/X	Mathilde 50 J.—Zurück
			Sept.		Berggasse
		So 6/9	Kadimah	Di 19/X	Königin Elisabeth v. Belgien
Sa 23/XI	Oli von Nizza	Sa 12/9	Ernst u Lux—Wolf noch einmal	Do 21/X	+ Wilh. Knöpfmacher
		Mo 14/9	50jährige Ehe		
			Okt		

Fr 22/X	Dorothy erkrankt—Eitingon
	November
Fr 5/XI	mit Bronchitis zu Bett.
	+ Gärtner
Do 11/XI	Oli
So 14/XI	Prinzessin Kinovorstellung
Di 23/XI	Vortrag Dr Bienenfeld
So 28/XI	Stefan Zweig
Di 30/XI	Prothese gebrochen,
	Dezember
Fr 3/XII	Anna 42 J.
Di 7/XII	Martin 48 J.
	1938 Januar
9/1	Anna Lichtheim +
Sa 22/1	Operation Auersperg—Atherom.
	Evipan
	Februar
Fr 11/2	+ Emanuel Loewy.
Sa 19/2	Operation Auersperg
Do 24/2	Schuschnigg's Rede
—28/2	Schlechte Tage
	März
Mi 2/3	Minna Operation
Mi 9/3	Schuschnigg in Insbruck
Do 10/3	Wiley von amerik. Gesandtschaft
Fr 11/3	Minna zweite Operation.
	Ernstl 24 J.—Abdankung
	Schuschnigg
	Finis Austriae
So 13/3	Anschluss an Deutschland
Mo 14/3	Hitler in Wien
Di 15/3	Kontrole in Verlag u Haus
Mi 16/3	Jones
Do 17/3	Prinzessin
Di 22/3	Anna bei Gestapo
Mo 28/3	Aufnahme in England
	gesichert—Ernstl in
	Paris.—Ausreise scheint
	ermöglicht
	April
Fr 1/4	Zwei Ernste in London
Mi 6/4	Ernst 46 J.
Sa 9/4	Topsy's Übersetzung beendigt
So 10/4	Abstimmung
Di 12/4	Minna aus Sanator zurück
So 17/4	Ostersonntag 52 J. Praxis.
Di 19/4	Alex 72 J. Prinzessin abgereist
X Mo 18/4	Malzeit mit Brautpaar Radziwil
Di 26/4	Anfall von Taubheit
Fr 29/4	Prinzess wiedergekommen.
	Mai
So 1/5	Beer-Hofmann mit Prinzess
Do 5/5	Minna ausgereist—Verhandlg mit
	Gestapo.
Fr 6/5	82 Jahre
Di 10/5	Ausreise innerhalb 14 Tage?
Do 12/5	Pässe bekommen.
Sa 14/5	Martin abgereist
Sa 21/5	Schätzung der Sammlung
Di 24/5	Mathilde u Robert abgereist.
Mo 30/5	+ Emilie Kassowitz
	Juni
Do 2/6	Unbedenklichkeitserklärung
Sa 3/6	Abreise 3h 25. Orient Express—
	3 3/4 am
	Brücke von Kehl
So 4/6	Paris 10h, von Marie Ernst,
	Bullit empfangen. Abft nach
London	London
Mo 5/6	9h früh Dover-London. Neues
	Haus. Minna schwer krank.
	Columnen in Zeitungen.
Do 9/6	Sam aus Manchester
Fr 10/6	Lun besucht
Sa 11/6	Besuch Jahuda

Sa 18/6	Minna z. Geburtstag zuerst
	gesehen
So 19/6	G.H. Wells
Di 21/6	Moses III neu begonnen
Do 23/6	Prinzess—Cyprischer Kopf
	Besuch der R.S.—Filme
Sa 25/6	Mrs Gunn mit aegypt Antiq.
	Juli 1938
Fr Mi 15/7	Moses nach Amerika verkauft—
	Mr Kent?
	Dr Exner.
Sa 16/7	Haus in Finchley Road besichtigt
So 17/7	Moses beendigt. Testament.
Mo 18/7	Mr Kent—12000 Hollandg.
	angefordert.
Di 19/7	Taubheit—Salvador Dali
Sa 23/7	Holländischer Verlag.
Di 26/7	Martha 77 J.
Do 28/7	Testament unterschrieben
	Hauskauf abgeschlossen.
Fr 29/7	Anna zum Kongress nach Paris
	August
Mo 1/8	Begrüssung von Paris Kongress
Do 4/8	Prospekt des neuen Verlags
Fr 5/8	Nachricht Bäumler v. Abgang d.
	Sachen.
	Anna zurück von Paris
Sa 6/8	Prinzessin
So 7/8 Mo 8/8	Sachen angekommen. Willi Lévy
	begonnen
Sa 13/8	Eigenes Haus besichtigt 20
	Maresfield Gardens
Mi 24/8	Ruth verabschiedet
Mo 29/8	Minna in's nursing home
	September
Fr 2/9	Hotel Esplanade—Warrington
	Crescent
Sa 4/9	Alex Sophie Harry angekommen
Mi 7/9	Sanat London Clinik
Do 8/9	Operation Pichler
Di 27/9	20 Maresfields Gardens
Fr 30	Friede
	Oktober
So 2/10	Minna in's Haus. Martin im
	Spital
Di 11/10	Dr Sauerwald
Mi 12/10	Arnold Zweig z. Abschied
So 16/10	Mathilde 51 J.
Sa 29/10	Prinzess und Eugenie—Bronze
	Venus
Mo 31/10	Ein Wort z. Antisemitismus.
	November
Do 10/11	Pogroms in Germany—Verbot in
	Franco-Spanien
Di 29/11	H.G. Wells
	Dezember
Sa 3/XII	Anna 43 J.
So 4/XII	Prinzessin auf Hausbesuch
Di 6/XII	Lün zurück—Vortrag Engel Lund
Mi 7/XII	Broadcasting—Martin 49 J.
Do 8/XII	Prinzess abgereist—Will. Brown
	1939
	January
2/—1	Lumbago.
—31/1	Knochenschmerzen
	Februar
Do 2/2	Moses imprimiert
So 5/2	Prinzessin
Fr 10/2	+ Pius XI—Trotter
So 19/2	Oli 48 J.
So 26/2	Prinzess mit Lacassagne
Di 28/2	Probexzision u Röntgen
	March
Fr 3/3	Bescheid von Paris—Pius XII
Mo 6/3	Dr Finzi

Mi 8/3	25 Jahrfeier d. British Society.
Do 9/3	Erster Röntgen—Finzi
Sa 11/3	Jahrestag der Nazi-invasion
Mo 13/3	Moses bei Lange—Prinzess m
	Lacassagne.
Mi 15/3	Radium—Prag besetzt
	April
Do 6/4	Ernst 47 J.
So 16/4	Sommerzeit
Mi 19/4	Alexander 73 J.
Do 20/4	Schur nach New York
	May
Sa 6/5	83st. Geburtstag
Fr 12/5	Topsy erschienen
Fr 19/5	Moses englisch
Sa 20/5	Anna nach Amsterdam
	June
Tue 6/6	Ein Jahr in England
	July
So 2/7	Prinzessin Geburtstag bei uns.
Mo 10/7	+ Havelock Ellis
We 12/7	Schur zurück
Sa 15/7	+ Bleuler
Mo 24/7	Evchen—Wells in citizenship
Mi 26/7	Martha 78 J.
	August
Tue 1/8	Auflösung d. Praxis. Besucher.
	Ruth Prinz
	Georg u Marie, Segredakis.
	Sachs.
We 23	Ruth verabschiedet
Do 24	Geld von Bank
Fr 25	Eva nach Nizza. Dorothy N. York
	Kriegspanik

NOTES & REFERENCES

The notes are dated as the diary entry to which they refer.

Works consulted and sources of quotations are listed in order of occurrence. (Where footnotes also occur, their sources are included in the listing.)

Where archival documents have been used, the transcription and translation are my own. The German original of unpublished archival quotations is provided in the notes.

Unless otherwise stated, the source material is either the original document or a photocopy of the original. There are three important exceptions:

1. *Freud-Ferenczi* correspondence. The Freud Museum possesses both sides of this correspondence in a typewritten transcript which has been used here. The translation is mine.

2. *Freud-Eitingon* correspondence. The Freud Museum has a typewritten transcript of Freud's letters to Eitingon. By courtesy of Sigmund Freud Copyrights, this has now been supplemented by photocopies of Eitingon's letters to Freud. Translations and transcriptions are mine.

3. Pichler Notes. Freud's surgeon, Professor Pichler, kept detailed notes of his treatment. My reference is to the handwritten English translation of his notes kept in the Freud Museum. (For a history of these notes, see Jones III.497 Appendix B.)

ABBREVIATIONS

(Where translated books or later editions are used, original publication date appears in square brackets. This is not a complete bibliography: works not listed below appear unabbreviated in the notes.)

1. Archives:

[Baeck]—Leo Baeck Institute, New York.

[Brill Library]—Abraham A. Brill Library, New York Psychoanalytic Institute, New York.

[FM]—Freud Museum, London.
(File details given only for out of series material.)

[IN]— Freud Museum Photograph Catalogue Reference.

[Inst of PsA]—Archives of the British Psycho-Analytical Society, Institute of Psycho-Analysis, London.

[LDFRD]—Freud Museum Collection Catalogue Reference.

[LoC]—Sigmund Freud Archive, Manuscript Division, Library of Congress, Washington.
(Container details given only for out of series material.)

Pichler Notes—English transcription of original notes kept by Professor Hans Pichler. Copy in Freud Museum, London.

[SFC]—Archive of Sigmund Freud Copyrights, Wivenhoe, Colchester, England.

2. Books & Journals:

Bergschicker—Heinz Bergschicker, *Deutsche Chronik 1933-1945: Ein Zeitbild der faschistischen Diktatur*, Verlag der Nation, Berlin, 1985 [1981].

Bertin—Celia Bertin, *Marie Bonaparte: A Life*, (Translator: not credited), Quartet Boooks, London Melbourne New York, 1983 [1982].

Bonin—Werner F. Bonin, *Die grossen Psychologen*, Hermes Handlexicon, ECON Taschenbuch Verlag, Düsseldorf, 1983.

Burlingham—Michael John Burlingham, *The Last Tiffany: A Biography of Dorothy Tiffany Burlingham*, Atheneum, New York, 1989.

Clark—Ronald W. Clark, *Freud: The Man and The Cause*, Granada, London Toronto Sydney New York, 1982 [1980].

Engelman—Edmund Engelman, *Berggasse 19: Sigmund Freud's Home and Offices, Vienna 1938*, Basic Books Inc., New York, 1976.

Freud & Art—Lynn Gamwell and Richard Wells (Eds.), *Sigmund Freud and Art*, State University of New York and Freud Museum London, Binghampton, 1989.

Gay—Peter Gay, *Freud: A Life for Our Time*, Dent, London Melbourne, 1988.

Grinstein—Alexander Grinstein, M.D., *Sigmund Freud's Writings: A Comprehensive Bibliography*, International Universities Press Inc., New York, 1977.

Jones—Ernest Jones, *Sigmund Freud: Life and Work*, (Three Volumes) Hogarth, London, Vol. I—1980 [1953]: Vol. II—1955: Vol. III—1980 [1957].

Hier geht . . . —Karen Brecht, Volker Friedrich, Ludger M. Hermanns, Isidor J. Kaminer, Dierk H. Juelich (Hrsg.), *Hier geht das Leben auf eine sehr merkwürdige Weise weiter . . . ": Zur Geschichte der Psychoanalyse in Deutschland*, Verlag Michael Kellner, Hamburg, 1985.

Int. J. PsA—*International Journal of Psycho-Analysis*.

Int. Z. Psa—*Internationale Zeitschrift für Psychoanalyse*.

Letters—Ernst L. Freud (Ed.), *Letters of Sigmund Freud*, (Translators: Tania & James Stern), Basic Books, New York, 1960.

Martin Freud—Martin Freud, *Glory Reflected*, Angus & Robertson, London, 1957.

Masson—Jeffrey Moussaieff Masson (Ed.), *The Complete Letters of Sigmund Freud to Wilhelm Fliess 1887-1904*, (Translator: Jeffrey Moussaieff Masson), Belknap Harvard, Cambridge (Mass.) & London, 1985.

Peters—Uwe Henrik Peters, *Anna Freud: Ein Leben für das Kind*, Kindler, München, 1979.

Pfeiffer—Ernst Pfeiffer (Ed.). *Sigmund Freud and Lou Andreas-Salomé: Letters*. The Hogarth Press & the Institute of Psycho-Analysis, London, 1972 [1966].

Pfister Letters—Heinrich Meng & Ernst Freud (Eds.), *Psychoanalysis and Faith: The Letters of Sigmund Freud and Oskar Pfister*, (translator Eric Mosbacher), Hogarth and Institute of Psycho-Analysis, London, 1963.

Pictures & Words—Ernst Freud, Lucie Freud and Ilse Grubrich-Simitis (Eds.). *Sigmund Freud: His Life in Pictures and Words*, (Translator: Christine Trollope), W.W.Norton & Co., New York London, 1985 [1978].

Psychoanalytic Pioneers—Franz Alexander, Samuel Eisenstein & Martin Grotjahn (Eds.), Basic Books, New York & London, 1966.

Romm—Sharon Romm, *The Unwelcome Intruder: Freud's Struggle with Cancer*, Praeger, New York, 1983.

Schur—Max Schur, *Freud: Living and Dying*, The Hogarth Press and the Institute of Psycho-Analysis, London, 1972.

Schröter—Jeffrey Moussaieff Masson (Hrsg.), *Sigmund Freud: Briefe an Wilhelm Fliess 1887-1904*, (Deutsche Fassung: Michael Schröter), Fischer, Frankfurt/Main, 1986.

S.E.—James Strachey (Ed.), *Standard Edition of the Complete Psychological Works of Sigmund Freud*, Vols. I-XXIV The Hogarth Press and the Institute of Psycho-Analysis, London, 1953-74.

Stefan Zweig—Stefan Zweig, *Ueber Sigmund Freud* (Hrsg), Lindken, Hans-Ulrich, Fischer, Frankfurt/Main, 1989.

Sterba—Richard Sterba, *Reminiscences of a Viennese Psychoanalyst*, Wayne State University Press, Detroit, 1982.

Young-Bruehl—Elisabeth Young-Bruehl, *Anna Freud: A Biography*, Summit Books, New York, 1988.

Zweig Letters—Ernst L. Freud (Ed.), *The Letters of Sigmund Freud and Arnold Zweig*, (Translators: Professor and Mrs. W.D. Robson-Scott), The Hogarth Press and the Institute of Psycho-Analysis, London, 1970 [1968].

1929

31 October 1929
1. The award of a Nobel Prize would obviously have signified international, "official" approval for psychoanalysis. But the repeated efforts of Freud's friends to secure him the prize actually annoyed him. The apparent futility of these efforts could only aggravate his resentment at continuing and powerful opposition to psychoanalysis.

There was also the question:—which category of Nobel Prize would Freud have received? Not for Physics, Chemistry or Peace. Nor Medicine and Physiology—the opposition here was far too strong. That only left Literature. When the Austrian novelist Stefan Zweig tried to enlist Heinrich Mann's support for Freud's claim, Mann replied: "I am obliged to dissuade you from any act which, even unintentionally, would lead to depriving literature of its own great prize . . . ." (*Heinrich Mann-Stefan Zweig 30.1.1930*)
Freud-Ferenczi 31.10.1915 in Jones, II.213.
Freud-Lou Andreas-Salomé 13.7.1917 in Pfeiffer.
Heinrich Mann-Stefan Zweig 30.1.1930 in *Freudiana* (Exhibition Catalogue), Jerusalem, 1973, p.x.

2 November 1929 (Tarock)
1. Freud's ophthalmologist friend Leopold Königstein (1850–1924) began the ritual around 1890. The practice was already established by 1891 when Freud wrote that a certain Dr. Arthur Schmerz would complete their tarock party. Other early card companions were the pediatrician Ludwig Rosenberg (died 1927) the surgeon Julius Schnitzler (1865–1939). When the old guard began dying off, Freud's son Martin and daughter Anna sometimes made up the party. "She was a good card player; I was not," Martin wrote, and added: "A few newcomers also came - all Jewish."
2. Some tarock cards came with Freud to England when he emigrated in 1938. During the packing Freud laid them to one side and the housemaid Paula Fichtl claimed to have secretly rescued them.
Jones, I.362.
Freud-Minna Bernays 11.8.1891 [LoC].
Masson, p.55 n.1.
Freud, Anton Walter, Telephone communication, 29.7.1989.
Freud, Martin, "Who was Freud" in Fraenkel, Josef (ed.), *The Jews of Austria*, London, 1970 (1967), p. 205.
Berthelsen D., *Alltag bei der Familie Freud*. Hamburg, 1987, p.81.

2 November 1929 (Rickman)
Jones-Freud 14.10.1929 [Inst. of PsA].
Freud-Ferenczi 13.12.1929 [FM].
Freud-Ferenczi 11.1.1930 [FM].

4 November 1929 (Schnitzler's)
1. In April 1923 Hajek performed the first operation on a growth in Freud's mouth. It was conducted casually, in an out-patient clinic. Afterwards Freud was left unattended and nearly bled to death.
Romm, p.5.
Schur, p.337, 351.
Jones, III.95.

4 November 1929 (Almanach)
Storfer, A. J. (Ed.), *Almanach der Psychoanalyse 1930*, I.P.V., Wien, 1930 [FM].

4 November 1929 (Preface)
1. In the years before World War I a number of prominent members of the psychoanalytical movement, among them Alfred Adler, Wilhelm Stekel and Carl Gustav Jung, left it to go their own ways. Freud was worried that the movement might disintegrate entirely after his death. Consequently he welcomed the suggestion that his closest followers should form a committee to assure the survival of psychoanalysis. Freud insisted that the group be strictly secret, but admitted that there was "a

boyish and perhaps romantic element in this conception . . . ."
Jones, II.172–4.
S.E., XXI.257.
Freud-Radó 7.11.1929 [FM].
Hier geht . . . p.70,74.
Eitingon-Freud 22.10.1929 [FM].
Freud-Jones 1.8.1912 in Jones, II.172.

6 November 1929 (Kris)
1. In 1927 Kris presented Freud with the catalogue of cameos in the Vienna Kunsthistorisches Museum, which he and Fritz Eichler had produced.
Psychoanalytic Pioneers passim.
Kris, Anton O. - Molnar 1.6.1990 [FM].
Eichler, Fritz, & Kris, Ernst, *Die Kameen im Kunsthistorischen Museum*, Wien, 1927 [FM].

6 November 1929 (Flournoy)
"Obituary", *Int. J. PsA*, 1956.

7 November 1929 (Disturbances)
Freud-Dwossis 15.12.1930 [FM: ARC/40].
Carsten, F.L., *The First Austrian Republic 1918–1938*, Aldershot, 1986.
Neue Freie Presse (Abendblatt), 7.11.1929.

7 November 1929 (Ring)
Jones, II.174–5.

11 Nov 1929 (Neuralgia)
Sterba, p.105.

11 Nov 1929 (Adda)
Anna Freud-Jones 19.9.1929 [Inst. of PsA CFA/FO1/14] ("Ich möchte sehr gerne, dass wir wieder eine neue Lün haben. Mein Vater will vorläufig noch nichts davon wissen.").

14 November 1929 (Heart)
Ferenczi-Freud 21 & 26.2.1926 [FM].
Freud-Ferenczi 3.3.1926 [FM].
Freud-Fliess 19.4.1894 in Masson.
Schur, Max, Interview R.S.Stewart, 28.5.1966.

14 November 1929 (Altmann)
1. It is unlikely this was the historian and doctor of philosophy Adolf Altmann (1879–1944), who was rabbi of Salzburg from 1907 to 1915 and from 1920 on chief rabbi of Trier. But Freud possessed a three-volume edition of the Philippson Bible from the Rabbi Altmann's collection, acquired perhaps via a bookseller or intermediary.
Encyclopaedia Judaica Year Book 1983/5.
Altman, Dr. Manfred, Telephone communication, 11.5.1990.
Burlingham, pp.297–8.

16 November 1929 (Hospital)
"*Wer ist's*" (Hrg.) Degener, (10 Ausg.) 1935.
Fichtner-Molnar 21.5.1990 [FM].

16 November 1929 (Anna)
1. Another book by Anna Freud—*Einführung in die Technik der Kinderanalyse* (I.P.V. 1929)—was published in 1929. However, this was a second edition. The book first appeared in 1927 and had already been published in English in 1928 as *Introduction to the Technique of Child Analysis* (Nervous and Mental Disease Publishing Co. New York & Washington D.C.).
Young-Bruehl, pp.197–8.
Peters, p.178.
Ferenczi-Freud 5.1.1930 [FM] ("Annas Buch las ich mit ungemischter Freude; es vereinigt alle Vorzüge ihrer Schreibweise: Überlegenheit, Klugheit, Masshalten, Geist und Menschlichkeit. Ihre Reife ist geradezu bewundernswert.").
Peltzman, Barbara R., *Anna Freud: a Guide to Research*, New York & London, 1990.

20 November 1929
Macinnes, Colin, "Yvette," *New Statesman*, 22.4.1966.
Brécourt-Villars, Claudine, *Yvette Guilbert l'Irrespectueuse*, Paris, 1988.
Knapp, Bettina, & Chipman, Myra, *That was Yvette*, London, 1966 [1964], p.263.

Freud-Ferenczi 13.12.29 [FM] ("In diesem November habe ich meine liebe Yvette, - Sie wissen wir stehen sehr gut zu einander - mit ihrer unvergleichlichen Betonung wieder hören:
  J'ai dit tout ça? C'est possible, mais
  je ne me souviens pas.").

21 November 1929
1. The invitation to Freud is actually undated, and could apply to the following year when she returned to Vienna. At any rate, her tea parties at the Bristol were a regular ritual.
Brécourt-Villars, Claudine, *Yvette Guilbert l'Irrespectueuse*, Paris, 1988.

22 November 1929 (Mann)
Freud-Andreas-Salomé 28.7.1929 in Pfeiffer.
Mann, Thomas, *Die Forderung des Tages: Reden und Aufsätze aus den Jahren 1925 - 1929*, Fischer, Berlin, 1930. [FM: LDFRD 2534] ("Sigmund Freud. in grosser Verehrung München 17.XI.29 Thomas Mann").
Mann, Thomas, "Die Stellung Freuds in der modernen Geistesgeschichte" *Die Forderung des Tages: Reden und Aufsätze aus den Jahren 1925–1929*, Berlin, 1930, p.224.

22 November 1929 (Yvette)
Wiener Zeitung, 22.11.1929.

23 November 1929 (Gottlieb)
1. There is, however, another possibility, namely Bernhard Gottlieb (1885 - ?), who lived very near Freud on the Türkenstrasse and who was a dentist specializing in oral tumors and growths. If this was a consultation with him, it was "unofficial," for it is not mentioned in the Pichler notes.
Photo album [FM: LDFRD 3148].
"University Papers," (Beilage II), [LoC].
Fichtner-Molnar 21.5.1990 [FM].

23 November 1929 (Pichler)
Romm, p.14.
Pichler Notes, 1929–39, *passim* [FM].
Jones, III.507.
Young-Bruehl, p.480 n.18.

30 November 1929 (Princess)
1. Her arrival is not recorded, but she was present at a meeting of the Vienna Psychoanalytical Society on November 6, when Wilhelm Reich gave a paper on psychoanalysis in the Soviet Union.
Martin Freud, p.202.
Bonaparte, Marie, *Journal d'analyse 7.10.1925* in Bertin, p.155 & 179.
Int. Z. Psa. ("Jahresberichte 1929").

30 November 1929 (Eitingon)
Freud-Eitingon 1.12.1929, [FM & *Letters*].

3 December 1929
Freud-Arnold Zweig 25.2.1934 in *Zweig Letters*.

7 December 1929
1. Actually *Jean Martin* Freud, named after Freud's early mentor, the eminent Parisian neurologist Jean Martin Charcot (1825–1893).
Freud, Anton Walter, Telephone communication, 30.8.1989.

7–10 December 1929
Freud-Ferenczi 13.12.1929 [FM] ("Privatim steht es so, dass ich den grössten Teil meiner Tätigkeit auf die Behauptung jenes Stück Gesundheit verwenden muss, dass ich für die festgehaltene tägliche Arbeit brauche. Ein wahres Mosaik von Massnahmen, mit denen die widerspenstigen Organe in ihren Dienst gezwungen werden sollen. Zuletzt ist das Herz dazu gekommen mit Extrasystolen, Arrythmien, Flimmeranfällen. Mein weiser Leibarzt, Prof. Braun, sagt zwar, das alles hat keine ernsthafte Bedeutung. Fängt er schon an mich zu beschwindeln?").

11 December 1929
1. On Freud's final, 83rd birthday in London, he was himself given a golden Greek ring. This, according to Anna Freud's commentary, was subsequently stolen from the house by burglars. Possibly that was also

the fate of this emerald ring.
Freud-Simmel 11.11.1928 [FM].
Burn, Lucilla, in *Freud and Art*, p.123.
Anna Freud, (Commentary to "Home Movies")
[FM].

12 December 1929
1. One of the participants of these meetings, Richard
Sterba, contrasts their relatively relaxed atmosphere
with the more formal structure of the Vienna
Psychoanalytical Society, as recorded in the published
minutes. Freud was far more inclined to illustrate his
remarks with jokes or anecdotes. Sterba surmises that
one reason for this was that psychoanalysis was no
longer an embattled cause, the other factor was the
prohibition of minutes or other records at these
smaller meetings.
Waelder, Robert, Interview R.S. Stewart, 29.7.1966.
Sterba, pp.106–7.

17 December 1929
Pfeiffer, p.211.
Lou Andreas-Salomé - Anna Freud 1.12.1929 [FM:
LS206] (" . . . Ich hätte am liebsten jeden Tag deinem
Vater erzählt und tat es auch im Gedanken.").

21 December 1929
Anna Freud-Freud 18.12.1929 & 19.12.1929
(Telegrams) [FM].

24 December 1929 (Christmas)
Freud, Martin, "Who was Freud?" in Fraenkel, Josef
(ed), *The Jews of Austria: Essays on their Life, History
and Destruction* (1967), p.203.
Martha Freud-Lucie Freud 7.12.1934 [FM: Lucie Freud
Papers] ("Ich richte schon für Weihnachten, der uns
immer viel Geld kostet, aber auch sehr viel Freude
macht.").

24 December 1929 (Eitingon)
Freud-Eitingon 8.7.1929 [FM] ("Meine Arbeit könnte,
wenn sie überhaupt einen Namen braucht, vielleicht
heissen: Das Unglück in der Kultur. Sie wird mir
nicht leicht.").
Freud-Eitingon 13.12.1929 [FM] ("Selbstverständlich
wollen wir Sie gerne auch zwischen Weihnacht u
Neujahr sehen. Ich mache am 24 - 26 frei.
Wahrscheinlich kann ich Ihnen auch ein
unbehagliches Weihnachtsgeschenk machen.").
Jones-Eitingon 18.11.1929 [Inst. of PsA CEC/FO1/41].
Eitingon-Freud 10.3.1930 [FM].

27 December 1929
Freud-Mathilde Freud 26.3.1908 [LoC & *Letters*].

30 December 1929
1. Professor Fichtner suggests this may be a reference
to Ada Elias, born Hirsch (ca. 1885) who was the
niece of Emma Eckstein, an early patient of Freud's,
and who attended his lectures.
Freud's grandson W. Ernest Freud writes: "I only
know of one Adda, who was a friend of Mathilde
Hollitscher's. Once I was at a party at the
Hollitschers and the said Adda showed us proudly
how she could waggle her ears. Much to her surprise
I was in a position to impress her with an equally
impressive series of ear wagglings, which took her
down a peg." But neither suggestion will explain the
entry "Adda given away", nor the record of death
lacking the customary " + ".
Fichtner-Molnar 21.5.1990 [FM].
Freud, W. Ernest - Molnar 17.5.1990 [FM].

1930

3 January 1930
Hier geht . . . p.56.
Freud-Eitingon 3.2.1930 & 15.2.1930 [FM].

6 January 1930
1. Esti was a speech therapist and had worked in the
Neumann clinic of the Vienna Allgemeines
Krankenhaus retraining the voices of soldiers injured
in the vocal cords. She studied in Professor Fröschels
Department of Speech Theraphy and in later life
practised her profession successfully in Paris and New
York and published a number of specialist papers.
Freud, Anton Walter, Telephone conversations,
30.7.1989, 30.8.1989.
Freud-Sam Freud 27.10.1919 & 31.12.1930 [FM].
Freud, Esti D., *Vignettes of my Life*, 1979 (Typescript)
[Baeck].

9 January 1930
1. In his memoirs Richard Sterba recalls another
discussion in which Reich stubbornly persisted in
holding the floor until Freud silenced him—the only
time Sterba saw Freud adopt an authoritarian
attitude. He speculates that it was general disapproval
of Reich's socio-political views which alienated him
from psychoanalysis.
Waelder, Robert, Interview R.S. Stewart, 29.7.1966.
Sterba, pp.110–12.

15 January 1930
"Authentication slips" [FM].
Jones, II.195.
Kris, Marianne, Oral communication to R.S. Stewart.

18 January 1930
1. During Freud's only visit to the United States in
1909 to give a series of lectures at Clark University,
Worcester, Massachusetts, he visited his relations. He
was not impressed with Felix Wiener and wrote
home to his newly-married daughter Mathilde: "My
son-in-law has gained a great deal by comparison with
hers . . . ." (*Freud-Mathilde Freud 23.9.1909*)
Lange, Hanns-Walter, *Family Tree* [FM].
Freud-Mathilde Freud 23.9.1909 [LoC] ("Mein
Schwiegersohn hat durch den Vergleich mit ihrem
sehr gewonnen . . . .").

16 January 1930
Rolland, Romain, *Les Léonides*, Paris, 1928 [FM:
LDFRD 2324].
Rolland, Romain, *Liluli*, Paris, n.d. [FM: LDFRD
2325].
Freud-Rolland 20.7.1929 [FM].
Freud-Ernst Freud 14.3.1923 [LoC] ("Reizender Brief u
Buchaustausch mit Romain Rolland. Man ist immer
erstaunt, dass nicht alle Leute Gesindel sind.").

21 January 1930
Schur, 409–410 & passim.
Freud-Schur 19.9.1929 [FM: MISC (Typescript)] ("Die
Gallenanfälle - oder was es ist - sind selterner und
leichter geworden.").

24 January 1930 (Schur)
1. After Schur had promised never to hide the truth
from his patient, he relates that Freud " . . . then
added, looking searchingly at me: 'Versprechen Sie
mir auch noch: Wenn es mal so weit ist, werden Sie
mich nicht unnötig quälen lassen.' ['Promise me one
more thing: that when the time comes, you won't let
me suffer unnecessarily.'] All this was said with the
utmost simplicity, without a trace of pathos, but also
with complete determination. We shook hands at this
point." A further condition was that Freud should
not be given professional courtesy, i.e., cheaper
treatment between doctors, but should be charged
normal fees. At the time of this meeting Freud had
recently received Schur's first bill. In a letter of
January 10 he wrote to Schur complaining that the
bill was unprofessionally low. Reminding Schur of
the contract between them, he advised him to submit

a more realistic bill.
Schur, 407–9.
"University Papers," (Beilage III) [LoC].
Freud-Schur 10.1.1930 in Schur 557–8.

24 January 1930 (Acrobat)
Bernhard-Walcher - Neufeld 17.12.1987 [FM].

3 February 1930
Gran Enciclopedia Argentina, Buenos-Aires, 1961.
Fichtner-Molnar 21.5.1990 [FM] (With thanks to
Professor Fichtner for help with this note).

6/7 February 1930
1. On the morning of the 7th, after this dream, it was
raining and Freud could not take the Alsatian Wolf
for his customary walk (the dog had a tendency to
suffer from eczema when it got wet). Instead, he
wrote a letter to his old friend, the Swiss pastor
Oskar Pfister, defending his pessimistic hypothesis of
a death drive. One metaphor Freud uses would not
have been out of place in a play of Nestroy's: "I
could also say that I have made a marriage of
convenience with my dismal theories, others live with
theirs in a marriage of love. I hope that they will be
happier in them than I." (*Freud-Pfister 7.2.1930*).
Freud-Pfister 20.8.1930 in *Pfister Letters*.
Jones, II.57.
Janik, Allan, & Toulmin, Stephen, *Wittgenstein's
Vienna*, N.Y., 1973, pp.86–7.
Freud-Pfister 7.2.1930 [FM: Typescript copy 1-F8–16].

8 February 1930
1. The children's books that Tom wrote and
illustrated during the 1920s were translated into other
languages, including English. One of her last books,
Buch der erfüllten Wünsche ("Book of wishes come
true"), is described in the *Brockhaus Encyclopaedia*
(1967) as the picture book in which the
"breakthrough of psychoanalytic thought" into
children's literature first occured.
Young-Bruehl, p.193.
Freud-Sam Freud 6.12.1929 [FM].
Freud, Anna: Quoted in Murken, Barbara "Tom
Seidmann-Freud" *Die Schiefertafel. Zeitschrift für
historische Kinderbuchforschung* IV, Heft 3, Dezember
1981, pp.163–202.

9 February 1930
1. But Zweig had come across Freud's ideas much
earlier than 1927, through the pioneer analyst Otto
Gross (1877–1920) whom he had met before the war
in the *Café des Westens* in Berlin. It was Gross who
also introduced Ernest Jones to the practice of
psychoanalysis. Gross was associated with artists and
radical politics in Berlin and Munich. Freud had a
high opinion of his work, as also did Jung, who tried,
unsuccessfully, to cure Gross of the drug addiction
from which he eventually died.
Arnold Zweig-Jones 22.2.1956 [SFC].
Zweig, Arnold, "Freud und der Mensch" in *Die
psychoanalytische Bewegung*, Juli-August 1929, p.102.
Jones, II.33.

13 February 1930
1. In all likelihood their papers would have been
based on their latest book. In 1929, Alexander and
Staub had published a psychoanalytically-based
criminological study - *Der Verbrecher und seine Richter*
("The Criminal and his Judges") of which Freud had
approved, though with certain reservations. He wrote:
"I have now read the book by Alexander-Staub. It
seems that with it the long-planned breakthrough of
analysis into criminology has succeeded. The
psychological expositions and formulations are almost
without exception apt. The work deserves to arouse
great interest. I have communicated some misgivings
to the authors. The denigratory triumphal tone
employed against the judicial system seems to me
factually pointless and moreover unjustified. Analysis,
which cannot explain everything, which cannot
influence everything it explains and from which no
direct path leads to practical measures, has reason to
adopt a more modest stance."(*Freud-Eitingon
14.12.1928*).
2. After Hitler came to power, Staub left Germany
for Paris, but in 1935 came to England and

eventually, despite opposition, was accepted by the British Psycho-Analytical Society. In 1940 he was interned by the British as an "enemy alien" but managed to escape to America.
Freud-Eitingon 15.2.1930 [FM] ("Ich danke Ihnen für die mit Alexander übersandten Zigarren, ich hatte sie schon sehnsüchtig erwartet. Der Abend bei mir verlief sehr angeregt, Alex. benahm sich im Vortrag einigermassen einfältig, Staub machte einen sehr klugen Eindruck.").
Freud-Eitingon 14.12.1928 [FM] ("16/XII Das Buch von Alexander-Staub habe ich jetzt auch gelesen. Der lang geplante Einbruch der Analyse in die Kriminalistik scheint hiemit gelungen. Die psychologischen Ausführungen und Formulirungen sind fast ohne Ausnahme zutreffend. Das Werk verdiente es, eine grosse Aufmerksamkeit zu erwecken. Ich habe den Autoren einige Bedenken mitgeteilt. Der geringschätzig triumphirende Ton gegen die Rechtspflege scheint mir faktisch unzweckmässig und überdies unberechtigt. Die Analyse, die nicht alles erklären kann, nicht alles beeinflussen kann, was sie erklärt und von der kein direckter Weg zu praktischen Massnahmen führt, hat Grund bescheidener aufzutreten.").
Eitingon-Jones 12.3.1935 [Inst. of PsA CEC/FO2/42].
Jones-Eitingon 17.11.[1940?] [Inst. of PsA CEC/FO2/69].

14 February 1930 (Jade)
1. A gossipy newspaper interview celebrating Anna's birthday in 1932 offered a tongue-in-cheek "explanation" of her style of dress. It reports Anna as saying: " . . . in child analysis two sharply differentiated movements have emerged, which are represented by Melanie Klein in London on the one hand and me in Vienna on the other. Since Mrs. Klein, although she is—please bear this in mind!—a grandmother, usually goes around in deeply-decolleté́d, ankle-length silk slips of dresses, I have chosen the severe style of dress which caught your attention; naturally I do not intend by this to underline any sort of personal opposition!" The accuracy of this interview is questionable, but it does highlight the real and important rivalry between the Vienna and London approaches to child psychoanalysis.
Die Stunde, 3.12.1932.

14 February 1930 (Hypnoanalysis)
Freud-Eitingon 15.2.1930 [FM] ("Ich erhielt durch Sie ein Heft 'Hypnoanalyse' von Lifschitz in Moskau. Haben Sie es gelesen? Kennen Sie den Mann u haben Sie ein Urteil darüber, wieweit er der Wahrhaftigkeit verdächtig werden darf? Unzweifelhaft scheint mir, dass er ein Esel ist und seine Arbeit den Normen einer Kultur unterworfen hat, in der die Reflexologie offiziell anerkannt, die Psychologie aber verboten ist. Seine Kenntnis der PA ist nicht weit her nach seinen Zitaten zu schliessen, den einzigen, etwas abgetragenen Autor, den er erwähnt, heisst er Spengler, meint wol Sperber. Er bestätigt all ps Charaktere des Traumes, die ich beschrieben habe, doch ist für ihn der Traum sinnlos. Dass diese Charaktere nur unter der gegenteiligen Voraussetzung gefunden werden konnten, genirt ihn nicht. Glücklicher Schwachkopf! Und dabei geht ihm alles gut aus, offenbar auf das Kommado der Sowjets. Die Übersetzung ist fürchterlich u lässt ihn noch mehr Unsinn sagen als sein Auftrag rechtfertigt - Aber ich werde noch einmal meine Eingeweide aufreissen, um der Welt etwas zu beweisen wie der Traum einen Sinn hat!").
Eitingon-Freud 19.2.1930 [FM].

15 February 1930
Engelman, Plate 35.
Reeves, Dr. C.N., in *Freud and Art*, p.62.

16 February 1930
1. She analyzed him for five months from October 1926 to February 1927 and in 1928 published her results in the *International Journal of Psycho-Analysis*, IX (1928), 439 under the title: - "A Supplement to Freud's 'History of an Infantile Neurosis'."
Freud-Ernst Freud 28.4.1927 [SFC] (. . . sie gehört fast zur Familie")

Gardiner, Muriel (Ed.), *The Wolf-Man and Sigmund Freud*, Hogarth Press, London, 1973, pp.263–307.
Bertin, p.159.
Jones, III.148, 153, 173.

17 February 1930 (Magaretl)
Young-Bruehl, p.52.
Nunberg, Herman, *Memoirs N.Y.*, 1969, p.20 & 55.

17 February 1930 (Róheim)
Psychoanalytic Pioneers, p. 274.

26 February 1930
1. On the same day he met Professor Berman, Freud also wrote an important letter on the Palestine problem. (Incidentally, the name "Berman" links his visitor to two significant Jewish figures for Freud, his father-in-law Berman Bernays, and Dr. Hugo Berman, the first rector of the Jewish National University in Jerusalem.) At this period Palestine was in a state of crisis. In August 1929 160 Jews had been killed by Arabs in the riots over the issue of the Jews' right to worship at the Western Wall. The British Prime Minister had appointed a committee which was in favour of limiting Jewish immigration. The Jewish Agency was now appealing for support to eminent Jews, including Freud. His reply to their request was guarded: "Whoever wants to influence the masses must have something sonorous and enthusiastic to say to them and my sober judgement of Zionism does not allow this. Certainly I have great sympathy for its aims, am proud of our University in Jerusalem and am delighted with our settlements' prosperity. But, on the other hand, I do not believe that Palestine could ever become a Jewish state, nor that the Christian and Islamic worlds would ever be prepared to leave their holy places in Jewish care. It would have seemed more sensible to me to found a Jewish homeland on a historically unburdened land. [. . .] I concede with regret that the unworldly fanaticism of our people bears part of the blame for the awakening of Arab distrust." (*Freud-Koffler 26.2.1930*).
Garcia, Germán, *Oscar Masotta y el psicoanálisis del castellano*, Editorial Argonauta, Barcelona, 1980.
Fichtner-Molnar 21.5.1990 [FM].
Freud-Chaim Koffler 26.2.1930 [FM] ("Wer eine Menge beeinflussen will, muss ihr etwas Volltönendes, Enthusiastisches zu sagen haben und das gestattet meine nüchterne Beurteilung des Zionismus nicht. Ich habe gewiss die besten Sympathien für seine Bestrebungen, bin stolz auf unsere Universität in Jerusalem und freue mich des Gedeihens unserer Siedlungen. Aber anderseits glaube ich nicht, dass Palästina jemals ein jüdischer Staat werden kann und dass die christliche wie die islamitische Welt ja bereit sein werden ihre Heiligtümer jüdischer Obhut zu überlassen. Mir wäre es verständiger erschienen ein jüdisches Vaterland auf einem historisch unbelastetem Boden zu gründen . . . [. . .] Auch gebe ich mit Bedauern zu, dass die wirklichkeitsfremden Fanatismus unserer Volksgenossen sein Stück Schuld trägt an der Erweckung des Mistrauens der Araber.").

28 February 1930 (Trebitsch)
Freud-Eitingon 6.3.1930 [FM] ("Ich war nahe daran, meine Prothese wegen schon im März nach Berlin zu kommen, aber ein Assistent Schroeder's, Dr. Trebitsch, der auf Urlaub hier war, hat mir soviel vorläufige Besserung gebracht, dass ich den Termin vielleicht um vieles - verschieben kann.").

28 February 1930 (Eisinger)
1. The need to take Angela into care had arisen even before her mother's death three weeks previously. After Angela's father had committed suicide in October 1929, Anna Freud described the girl's situation to her friend Eva Rosenfeld:
"He hanged himself yesterday and in doing so I think he committed the first bad act of his life, certainly the first unloving one. He was a young Eastern Jew, very friendly, very brotherly and of a totally Russian nature. She is the most difficult person one could imagine, melancholic, forever thinking of suicide. In the middle is a 7 year old girl who looks like a little elf. Now he is dead, she in a sanatorium so that she

can be watched and for the moment the child is with the Lampls. Now the break up of the business is coming and what will survive among the ruins remains to be seen.
   I would have liked best to have taken the child in the night to granny,* but she knows the Lampls and one doesn't want to expose her to more shocks than necessary.
   I don't know to what end there has to be so much unhappiness." (*Anna Freud-Eva Rosenfeld 20.10.1929*)
* "Granny" (Omi) - Eva Rosenfeld's mother. (With thanks to W. Ernest Freud for this information.)
2. Another reason why Angela should not come to Vienna, according to Freud, was that the climate there was bad for such a sickly child. (Actually Angela was a healthy girl.) He cited the fact that both his daughter Sophie's children, Heinerle and Ernstl, had contracted TB there, and instead he advised a 'reliable country upbringing'. Freud wrote the ungrammatical phrase *'verlässliches [sic] Landerziehung'* (*Freud-Mitzi Freud 15.2.1930*). In his transcription of this letter, Dr. H. Lobner (30.6.1973 LoC) suggests that the grammatical slip indicates Freud intended to say "a reliable country children's home" ["*ein verlässliches Landerziehungsheim*"]. Freud may well have balked at the idea of sending the child to a children's home. If he already knew of Tom's intentions, he may have been angry that the mother had denied her daughter a home in Vienna with Anna and might have wanted to cover this up.
Harari, Mrs. Aviva, Interview, 10.7.1991.
Anna Freud-Eva Rosenfeld 20.10.1929 [FM: Transcript P. Heller] ("Er hat sich gestern Abend erhängt und hat, glaube ich, damit die erste böse Tat seines Lebens getan, sicher die erste lieblose. Er war ein junger Ostjude, sehr lieb, sehr brüderlich und ganz russisch in seinem Wesen. Sie ist die [?] schwierigste Mensch, den man sich denken kann, melancholisch, seit jeher mit Selbstmordgedanken. Dazwischen ein 7 jähriges Mäderl, das aussieht wie eine kleine Elfe. Jetzt ist er tot, sie in einem Sanatorium, damit man sie bewachen kann und das Kind für den Augenblick bei Lampls. Jetzt kommt noch der geschäftliche Zusammenbruch über sie und was dann noch aus dem Trümmerhaufen bleibt, wird man erst sehen.
   Ich hätte das Kind am liebsten noch in der Nacht zu Omi gebracht, aber die Lampls kennt es und man will es ja nicht mehr Schocks aussetzen als nötig.
   Ich weiss nicht, wozu so viel Unglück nötig ist.).
Freud-Mitzi Freud 15.2.1930 [LoC].
Lobner, Dr. Hans, 30.6.1973, [Transcript of above: LoC].
Young-Bruehl, pp.193–4.

2 March 1930
Jones, II.66, 436–7.
Schur, 58.

4 March 1930
Bernfeld, Suzanne Cassirer, "Freud and Archaeology," *The American Imago* 8, June 1951.
Clark, p.217.
Pope Hennessy, Una, *Early Chinese Jades*, London, 1923 [FM].

5 March 1930
Hier geht . . . pp.46–9.
Freud-Hermann 28.2.1936 [Baeck (Typescript)] ("Es war alles so verführerisch, ich war in der Stadt gern gesehen, der sozialdemokratische Minister Dr. Becker hatte mir einen freundlichen Besuch in Tegel gemacht von zwei seiner Räte begleitet . . . .").

9 March 1930
Freud-Martha Freud 1.4.1930 [FM] ("JoFi erobert sich täglich mehr Sympathien, legt sich vor eine Hausthür anstatt es sich bequem zu machen.").
Freud-Martha Freud 9.4.1930 [FM].
Freud-Meine Lieben 9.5.1930 [FM] ("P.S. Besucht jemand einmal Jofi? Sie fehlt mir sehr. Die Schildkröte ist ein schwacher Ersatz.").
Freud-Ferenczi 12.9.1929 [FM].

Anna Freud-Eva Rosenfeld 2.8.1929 [FM: Typescript P. Heller].
Anna Freud-Jones 19.9.1929 [Inst. of PsA. CFA/FO1/14].

11 March 1930
1. Ernstl's first memory of his grandfather related to an earlier birthday: "He was sitting in the bathtub and holding a tin drum in his hand, on which he was beating with the drumsticks. That was his birthday present for me."
S.E., XVIII.14–15.
Freud, W. Ernest, "Brief Biography" (ms.), 1989, [FM].
Freud, W. Ernest-Molnar 6.8.1989 [FM].
Freud-Max Halberstadt 9.8.1928 [LoC] ("Er ist doch das einzige Vermächtnis unserer Sophie. Freilich, man kann sich nicht enthalten daran zu denken, was an Heinele verloren gegangen ist.").
Freud, W. Ernest, "Die Freuds und die Burlinghams in der Berggasse: Persönliche Erinnerungen" (*Sigmund Freud-Vorlesung, gehalten an der Universität Wien, am 6.Mai 1987*) in *Sigmund Freud House Bulletin*, Vol.11/1, Summer 1987, p.3.

16/17 March 1930
1. For Freud's own admirers, his appearance at these concerts aroused considerable attention. Margaret Blanton, wife of the American psychoanalyst Smiley Blanton, wrote:
"Amusingly enough, Guilbert played entirely to the professor, and the audience hardly saw Guilbert for watching him. But Freud did not seem conscious of the excitement he was causing, and his poise remained unshaken."
Neue Freie Press, 17.3.1930, (" . . . dessen Züge von allen menschlichen Leidenschaften gemeisselt zu sein scheinen . . . ")
Margaret Blanton in Blanton, Smiley, *Diary of my Analysis with Sigmund Freud*, N.Y., p.49 n.

19 March 1930
1. In the typescript copy of Freud's letter to Eitingon the sum given is $10,000, not $1,000 as in the diary. Without consulting the original letter, it is impossible to say whether this piece of "megalomania" originates in the transcriber's or Freud's parapraxis.
Freud-Eitingon 25.3.1930 [FM] ("Storfer hat in einem Anfall von Grössensucht mir einen Scheck auf $10000 [sic in typescript copy] als Abschlagszahlung geschickt.").

20 March 1930
1. Though no minutes were kept, at this meeting Richard Sterba surreptitiously took notes, published in part in his memoirs. Freud himself was not very happy about the discussion this particular week. Afterwards he reported to Eitingon: "Last Thursday they had a meeting at my house on the *Discontents*. Actually only Federn expressed an opinion, it was not very inspiring and so once again I had to talk, talk, talk." (*Freud-Eitingon 25.3.1930*)
Waelder, Robert, Interview R.S.Stewart, 29.7.1966.
Sterba, pp.113–7.
Freud-Eitingon 25.3.1930 [FM] ("Letzten Donnerstag tagten sie bei mir über das "Unbehagen". Eigentlich äusserte sich nur Federn, es war nicht sehr grossartig und so musste ich wieder reden, reden, reden.").

25 March 1930
Freud, *Forelaesninger Til Indførelse I Psykoanalyse*, (transl. Kristian Schjelderup), Gyldendal Norsk Forlag, Oslo, 1929, (Hardback edition with translator's dedication) [FM].
Freud, *Forelaesninger Til Indførelse I Psykoanalyse* (transl. Kristian Schjelderup), Gyldendal Norsk Forlag, Oslo, 1930, (Paperback) [FM].

26 March, 1930 (Anna)
Frankwood E. Williams-Freud 3.12.1929 [FM: Filed in Eitingon letters].
Peters, p.183.

26 March 1930 (Elkuss)
Eitingon-Freud 22.10.1929 [SFC].

27 March 1930
Freud-Ferenczi 30.3.1930 [FM] ("Ich kann nicht unterlassen, Ihnen herzlich zu danken für die Aufnahme, die Sie Anna bereitet, und die Ehrung, die Sie erwiesen haben. Mir erscheint ihre Entwicklung so erfreulich, dass mir auch Widerhall sehr wohltut.").

27 March 1930
Eitingon-Freud 19.3.1930 [FM].
Eitingon-Freud 7.4.1930 [FM] (" . . . bei meinem letzten, sehr melancholischen Besuch in Wien . . . .").

28 March 1930
Freud-Martha Freud 1.4.1930 & 9.4.1930 [FM].

29 March 1930
Freud-Eitingon 25.3.1930 [FM].
Freud-Martha Freud 1.4.1930 [FM] ("Ich bin sehr zufrieden damit, dass du dein guter Zimmer im Hotel behalten hast. Wir sind zu alt um zu sparen. [. . .] . . . und schaff dir 'a good time,' wie man in Amerika sagt.").

30 March 1930
Schur, 358 n.
Young-Bruehl, p.79.

30 March 1930
Freud-Martha Freud 1.4.1930 [FM] ("Sonntag waren wir bei Rie. Ich habe nur ihn gesprochen. Er ist sehr bedrückt obwol man die böse Diagnose auf Kopfgrippe bei ihr aufgegeben hat u das Ganze viel freundlicher aussieht. Es scheint mir nicht ausgeschlossen, dass die Zustand nach einigen Wochen ablaufen kann, ohne viel Schaden zu hinterlassen. Margarete sieht nicht gut aus. Der Pechvogel Nunberg hat eine tüchtige Grippe.").

2 April 1930
1. Was this sum the gift of an American benefactor? In February one former American patient, hearing that one of Freud's concerns was in danger, sent him $500. (Figures sometimes get muddled in transcription—could this have been the $5,000?). The concern in question was the Berlin Tegel clinic. But Freud decided to put that sum towards the press, which was also in a critical situation. Curiously, in 1929 Edward Bernays had suggested to the American publisher, Liveright, that they publish Freud's autobiography and they had offered $5,000. Freud responded: " . . . it is American naiveté on the part of your publisher to expect a hitherto decent person to commit so base a deed for $5,000." (*Freud-Edward Bernays 10.8.1929*).
Freud-Eitingon 24.2.1930 [FM].
Freud-Edward Bernays 10.8.1929 in *Letters*.
Bernays, Edward L., "Uncle Sigi," *Journal of Hist. of Med.*, April 1980, p.219.

3 April 1930
1. Anton Walter and his father both emigrated to England in 1938 and were both interned as enemy aliens in June 1940. Martin was sent to the Isle of Man, Anton to Australia aboard the *Duneira*. He was released in October 1941. On returning to England, he joined the Pioneer Corps. After about two years he joined S.O.E. (Special Operations Executive, whose mission was to liaise with resistance movements behind enemy lines). In early 1945 he was parachuted into Austria near Judenburg and captured the airfield of Zeltweg single-handedly. After the war he was involved in the War Crimes Commission and was demobbed with the rank of Major in September 1946.
Freud, Anton Walter, Telephone conversations 29 July 1989 & 19 November 1990.

5/6 April 1930
Jones, III.127.
Freud-Martha Freud 9.4.1930 [FM] ("Ich bin am letzten Samstag spät abends durch einen Herzanfall alarmirt worden, aber Braun hat nichts daraus gemacht und ich habe endlich die Überzeugung bekommen, dass das freie Rauchen nicht mehr vertrage, habe mich seither auf 3 1/2 Zigarren

eingeschränkt u fühle mich seither wirklich wie ein anderer Mensch. Nur dass dieser andere auch die fehlenden Zigarren sehr vermisst.")

7 April 1930 (Bob)
1. Afterwards all the other Burlingham children suffered attacks of appendicitis and were operated on in succession. The youngest daughter Katrina ("Tinky") remembers being ill for much of the summer of 1931 until Dr. Julius Schnitzler, who was a specialist in abdominal disorders, was consulted. He instantly diagnosed correctly and it was he who operated on her, and probably on the others, too.
Young-Bruehl, p.132.
Burlingham, pp.151–2.
Freud-Martha Freud 9.4.1930 [FM].
Freud-Martha Freud 26.6.1930 [FM] (" . . . wie ein junger Gott . . . ").
Valenstein, Mrs K., Interview, 14.5.1990.

7 April 1930 (Zweig)
Fichtner-Molnar 21.5.1990 [FM].

10 April 1930 (Rob)
Freud, Anna, "Obituary" *Sigmund Freud House Bulletin*, Vol.2, 1. 1978 p.2.
Freud-Sam Freud 26.6.1923 & 6.12.1929 [FM].

10 April 1930 (Zweig)
1. When challenged by Freud, Zweig explained that he had only glanced at Maylan's book and written the author some general words of encouragement, which Maylan had then misused in the advertisement. Nevertheless, Freud was justifiably angry that Zweig had laid himself open to this abuse of confidence. Even the most cursory glance at Maylan's book would have revealed its hostility. The offense rankled: in September 1930 Freud spoke of the incident as having occured in the previous half year, whereas it actually took place in December 1929.
Janik, Allan, & Toulmin, Stephen, *Wittgenstein's Vienna*, N.Y., 1973, p.45.
Zohn, Harry, "Three Austrian Jews in German Literature: Schnitzler, Zweig, Herzl" in Fraenkel, Joseph, *The Jews of Austria*, London, 1970, [1967], p.74.
Freud-Arnold Zweig 21.8.1930 & 10.9.1930 in *Zweig Letters*.
Freud-Stefan Zweig 4.12.1929 in Stefan Zweig.
Stefan Zweig, p.206, N.146. (Thanks for help to Dr. Ludger Hermanns.)

10 April 1930 (Jokes)
1. *Der Witz und seine Beziehung zum Unbewussten*:
-"Mot d'Esprit" captures only the specific connotation of "*Der Witz*" as "witticism", as did the first English translation by A. A. Brill - *Wit and its Relation to the Unconscious* (N.Y. 1916). But the English word "*jokes*" loses the general sense of "wit" as intellectual subtlety.
Freud, Sigmund, *Le Mot d'Esprit et ses Rapports avec l'Inconscient*, Gallimard, Paris, 1930 [FM: LDFRD 2972].
Translation list [FM: I-F8-17-26].

12 April 1930
Freud-Ferenczi 7.2.1909 in Jones, II.61.
Psychoanalytic Pioneers.

13 April 1930 (Martha)
Freud-Martha Freud 9.4.1930 [FM] ("Mit Respekt u Bewunderg habe ich von deinen gesellschaftlichen Leistungen in Berlin gehört und gelesen. Ich werde es dir nicht nachthun.").
Freud-Ernst Freud 13.4.1930 [LoC] ("Mama ist heute in bester Verfassung, sehr zufrieden mit ihrem Berliner Eindrücken und Erlebnissen zurückgekommen. Es was gewiss sehr richtig, dass sie allein gereist ist und nicht auf mich gewartet hat. Alle Teile haben mehr davon gehabt.").

13 April 1930 (Ferenczi)
Ferenczi-Freud 30.4.1930 [FM] ("Oft und oft denke ich an die freundliche und gemütliche Stimmung während den Stunden, die am vorletzten Sonntag in Ihrem mir so trauten Arbeitszimmer verlebte. Ich schied mit der Überzeugung, dass meine Angst die

etwas zu selbständige Arbeits- und Denkweise könnte mich in einen, mir so peinlichen Gegensatz zu Ihnen bringen, in hohem Grade übertrieben war. Ich setze also meine Arbeit mit gehobenem Mut fort und hoffe sicherlich, dass diese kleinen Umwege mich nie von der Hauptstrasse ablenken können, auf der ich nunmehr seit fast 25 Jahren an Ihrer Seite wandle.")

13 April 1930 (Princess)
Bertin, pp.140–1, 173.

14 April 1930
1. Ironically underlining his subservience to this mechanical device, Freud wrote to Eitingon, just before his departure for Berlin in May: "Of course the prosthesis urgently needs the change of air." (*Freud-Eitingon 1.5.1930*)
Pichler Notes, 1927–8.
Freud-Eitingon 1.5.1930 [FM] ("Die Prothese braucht den Luftwechsel natürlich dringend.").

14 April 1930 (Illusion)
Translation list, [FM: I-F8–17-30].
Jones, III.102.

15 April 1930
Burlingham, *passim.*
Berthelsen, Detlef, *Alltag bei der Familie Freud,* Hamburg, 1987, pp.24–6.

17 April 1930
Valenstein, Mrs K., Interview, 14.4.1990.

18 April 1930
Jones, II.39.
Freud-Sachs 22.1.1933 [FM] ("Ihre Arbeitsabsichten erregen meine Spannung, lieber Narzismus als Caligula.").

22 April 1930
1. In the same year, Urbantschitsch joined the Wednesday Society. But since his public support for Freud threatened the existence of the sanatorium, he was forced to leave. In the mid-1920s, however, he left the sanatorium and began training as a psychoanalyst, despite reservations about his suitability expressed by Freud and members of the Vienna Society.
Freud-Ernst Freud 19.4.1930 [LoC].
Nunberg, Herman and Federn, Ernst (Eds.), *Minutes of the Vienna Psychoanalytic Society* Vol.1, xxxvii & 204.
Urbantschitsch, Rudolf, *Wiener Cottage-Sanatorium,* Wien o.J. [1910?].

25 April, 1930
1. The term "*autotomy*"—literally "cutting into oneself"—is repeated in letters to Eitingon and Ferenczi: the expression brings to mind the operation Freud performed on himself in his "Irma dream" in *The Interpretation of Dreams.* As for the gruesome image of himself as a fox biting off its own leg, this was to recur in a letter to Minna Bernays (20.5.1938) in connection with his escape from Nazi Vienna in 1938. The fact that flight from his native land and abstinence from smoking could arouse the same imagery is one small indication—if any more were needed—of the importance of Freud's tobacco addiction.
Total abstinence did not last. In August Freud wrote to his brother: "I permit myself one cigar daily and torment myself like a malefactor if I exceed the quota." (*Freud-Alexander Freud 8.8.1930*) Later on that year he complained " . . . since I am no longer allowed to smoke I am also only working with difficulty." (*Freud-Radó 26.9.1930*). Smoking and working were inextricable: this theme is a refrain in Freud's letters: " . . . since I am not smoking I will hardly write anything at all . . . " (*Freud-Arnold Zweig 25.10.1933*).
Freud-Ferenczi 7.5.1930 [FM] ("Dies als Bericht: Herz- und Darmbeschwerden hatten mich am 22/4 genötigt, mich ins Cottage Sanat. zu flüchten. Mit der schmerzlichen Erkenntnis, dass eine am 25/4 gerauchte Zigarre für längere Zeit die letzte sein müsse, fieng der Umschwung an. Am 4 Mai konnte ich fast hergestellt nach Berlin reisen. Es geht mir nun

hier recht gut, aber es war ein Stück Autotomie, wie es der Fuchs vollbringt, wenn er sich in der Falle ein Bein abbeisst. Ich fühle mich auch nicht sehr glücklich, eher deutlich depersonalisirt.").
Freud-Alexander Freud 8.8.1930 [LoC] ("Ich gestatte mir täglich eine Zigarre u quäle mich wie ein Missethäter wenn ich das Quantum überschreite")
Freud-Radó 26.9.1930 [FM] (" . . . und seitdem ich gar nicht mehr rauchen darf, arbeite ich auch sehr schwer.").
Freud-Arnold Zweig 25.10.1933 in *Zweig Letters.*

2 May 1930
1. Yabe was a psychologist to the government railways of Japan and had been sent to Europe for three months to investigate psychoanalysis. In London he did a brief training analysis with the English psychoanalyst Edward Glover. Jones was highly impressed by his intelligence and recommended accepting the small Japanese group Yabe had formed into the International Psychoanalytical Association.
2. The situation in Japan was complicated by the fact that during the 1930s two Tokyo publishers were simultaneously bringing out rival editions of Freud's work—the Shinyodo Press and the "Ars" publishing house, each representing opposing psychoanalytical groups.
Eitingon-Freud 30.4.1930 [FM].
Translation list [FM: I-F8–17-29].

3 May 1930
Freud-Jones 12.5.1930 [Typescript Inst. of PsA.] ("Dort machte ich bald die Entdeckung, dass ich eine absolute Intoleranz gegen die Zigarre erworben hatte, und für den Verzicht auf diesen langgewohnten Genuss erwarb ich eine rasche und weitgehende Besserung, die andauernd ist. Nur der Magen arbeitet noch nicht ohne Beschwerden.").
Freud-Jones 19.5.1930 [Typescript of PsA] ("Ich habe eben gestern die schüchterne erste und vorläufig im Tag einzige Zigarre versucht.").

5 May 1930
Schultz, U., Hermanns, L.M.: "Das Sanatorium Schloss Tegel Ernst Simmels—Zur Geschichte und Konzeption der ersten Psychoanalytischen Klinik." *Psychotherapie. Psychosomatik Medizinische Psychologie.* 2. Feb. 1987, pp.37–82.
Freud-Meine Lieben 6.5.1930 [FM] ("Das Wichtigste ist Schroeder. Anstatt die Prothese ausbessern, will er eine neue machen. Wie lange habe ich Zeit? Ich bin heute 74 . . . [. . .] Also dass wir bald heimkommen ist nicht wahrscheinlich. Aber bei der raffinirten Zärtlichkeit hier im Haus der Ruhe u der Schönheit des Frühlings ist es für mich u Anna eine Verlängerung der Ferien.").

6 May 1930
Freud-Meine Lieben 6.5.1930 [FM] ("Es war natürlich keine Möglichkeit dem Unsinn des Geburtstags zu entgehen. Ich ersticke in Rosen, Orchideen u Tlgr. wie in Wien, Besucher sind dort weniger. Überwältigend ist ein Rosenbuschen von Eitingon, ich glaube, es sind 74, andere meinen: 120. Das netteste ist ein Gedicht im Namen von Jofi, natürlich von Anna in Begleitung einer lebenden kleinen Schildkröte. Aber Ihr wollt wahrscheinlich anderes wissen.").
Jofi, *Jo Fie, die Hüpfende* [FM: SOH9–3 (HG 2)] ("Jo Fie, die Hüpfende,—durch Tore Entschlüpfende,—die der Leine Entgleitende,—mit Feinden sich Streitende,—die zum Grusse sich Streckende,—die Hände Beleckende,—schickt anbei—zum 6. Mai—ein Symbol,—das anzeigen soll,—wie sie will sich verwandeln—und bedächtiger handeln: will bei offenen Türen—nur wenig sich rühren,—will nicht bellen,—will nicht springen, nicht laufen,—will kaum fressen und saufen.
    So spricht Jo Fie, die Trauende,—die Trennung Bedauernde.")

7 May 1930 (Yabe)
1. The day after this meeting Yabe received his certificate entitling him to practice psychoanalysis. He was not the only Japanese psychologist to come to

Europe: in 1933 Professor Marui visited Freud and worked with Federn. Anna Freud was as favorably impressed by the Japanese as was Jones. In 1934, contrasting them to other groups and particularly the Americans or the Dutch who had been causing a great deal of trouble (not to speak of the German group), she wrote: "*Japan. This seems to be a country where people are ideal to deal with. I got a great wish to go there.*" (*Anna Freud-Jones 30.1.1934*)
Yabe, Yaekichi, *A Meeting with Professor Freud,* p.11 [LoC: English translation transcript. Originally published in Japanese in appendix to Vol. V of Freud's *Collected Works on Psychoanalysis,* Shunyudo Publishing Company, Tokyo, 1931 pp.1–9].
Anna Freud-Jones 30.1.1934 [Inst. of PsA: CFA/FO1/66].

7 May 1930 (Lederer)
Adressbuch, Berlin, 1936 ("Dr. Philipp Lederer, Numismatik, Alte Münzen u. archäologische Objekte, Berlin N.24, Am Kupfergraben 4") [With thanks to Eberhard Stein and Brigitte Molnar.].
Freud-Meine Lieben 18.9.1929 [FM] ("Die Nachricht von Dr. Lederer's Tod stellt sich nach Mark Twain's Ausdruck als stark übertrieben heraus. Ich bin überzeugt, er wird sich ebenso geldgierig zeigen wie die früheren Male, u das ist doch ein starkes Lebenszeichen.").
Freud-Meine Lieben 9.5.1930 [FM] ("Nur die Zigarre fehlt, was man dagegen versucht, Weintrinken, Briefschreiben, Dattelbeissen, ist kein Ersatz. Antiquitäten waren es vielleicht, aber soviel kann man nicht kaufen.").

11 May 1930
Freud-Meine Lieben 12.5.1930 [FM] ("Schön wäre es, wenn alles heuer so gut ausgieng, wie meine Einkäufe bei Lederer. Schade, dass dann die langen Ferien kommen, in denen man sich von ihnen trennen muss. Hier in Tegel stehen sie alle auf dem Tisch versammelt. Es ist denn freilich so als hätte der Verlag mir nichts bezalt. Aber das hätte auch leicht sein können.").

14 May 1930 (Operation)
Bertin, p.140, 180–1.

14 May 1930 (Martha)
Freud-Martha Freud 19.5.1930 [FM] ("Es thut mir doppelt leid, dass deine tapferen Unternehmungen erfolglos geblieben sind. Was machen wir nun? Man könnte glauben, dass der liebe Gott, der bekanntlich eine Lilienbekleidungs - Anstalt leitet, auch eine Sommerwohnungs - Agentur führt, aber man kann sich darauf doch nicht verlassen.")

17 May 1930 (Visit)
Freud-Meine Lieben 12.5.1930 [FM].
Freud-Anna Freud 29.12.1926 [FM] ("Einstein war sehr interessant, heiter, glücklich, wir haben 2 St. gesprochen, auch diskutirt, mehr über Analyse als über Relativ. Er liest grade, hat natürlich keine überzeugung. Er sieht älter aus als ich, erwartet 48J!")
Freud-Eitingon 22.12.1930 [FM].
Jones, III.164.
Clark, Ronald W., *Einstein: The Life and Times,* London, 1973, p.389.

17 May 1930 (Bullitt)
Freud, Sigmund & Bullitt, William C. *Thomas Woodrow Wilson, Twenty-eighth President of the United States: a Psychological Study,* London, 1967, pp.vii-viii.
"Obituary," *New York Times,* 15.2.1967.

25 May 1930
Freud-Marie Freud 20.7.1912 [LoC] (" . . . gehört zu unserer entferntesten Verwandtschaft in Hambg. ist sehr ernsthaft, vertrauenswürdig, beide scheinen recht verliebt in einander zu sein. Die Verhältnisse sind bürgerlich anständig, kein Reichtum, keine Vornehmheit, woran uns ja auch nichts liegt.").

26 May 1930
Freud-Jones 19.5.1930 [Typescript Inst. of PsA].

29 - 31 May 1930
Anna Freud-Eva Rosenfeld 3.6.1930 [FM: Typescript P.

Heller] ("Jetzt weiss ich ganz genau, was mir die ganze Zeit gefehlt hat: eine Insel. Schon zwei Tage Insel haben mich ganz gesund gemacht und jetzt bin ich wieder so bei mir, dass ich gar nichts mehr von mir zu wissen brauche. Das ist das Beste. Hiddensee ist ein wirkliches Paradies, eine Vereinigung von allem, was schön ist, auf einem kleinen Fleck und dazu Luft und Wind und Sonne und Freiheit.")
Freud-Meine Lieben 1.6.1930 [FM] ("Die Wiederkehr des Anfalles hat meinen Zuversicht natürlich sehr gestört u lässt mich manchmal glauben, ich hätte für einen Sommeraufenthalt nicht mehr viel Verwendung, für seine Gesundheit leben anstatt von ihr, ist aber etwas sehr dummes.").
Freud-Martha Freud 4.6.1930 [FM] ("In Wirklichkeit mahnen mich meine Herzbeschwerden sehr an die Zeit vor 35 Jahren als ich zuerst das Rauchen aufgeben musste. Aber ich gestehe, mein Übermut ist gebrochen, ich fühle mich nicht mehr sicher, getraue mich keiner gewagteren Unternehmung und wäre mit einem anspruchslosen Sommer zufrieden. Nebenbei fühle ich mich wie betrogen, da die grosse Besserung seit dem Aufgeben des Rauchens nicht gehalten hat u mit der Entbehrung und den Beschwerden der elend vernachlässigten Prothese, bin ich grade nicht beneidenswert.").

4 June 1930
1. Later, when recalling this time, Freud explicitly mentions Lederer's premises on the "Kupfermarkt" (Kupfergraben). But there is an outside possibility that Lederer, like the Viennese dealers, might sometimes have come to Freud. However, if there had been three visits *by* Lederer and three *to* him, most of these would have gone unrecorded, which is unlikely, given their importance and the fact they are otherwise consecutively numbered.
Freud-Hermann 28.2.1936 [Baeck].

8 June 1930
Sulloway, Frank J., *Freud: Biologist of the Mind*, Fontana Paperbacks, 1980, [1979] pp.190–1.
S.E., V.643–4
Robert Fliess-Bernfeld 28.8.1944 in Masson, p.3.

13 June 1930 (House)
Freud-Meine Lieben 14.6.1930 [FM] ("Also wir haben eine Sommerwohnung, dank Mama's Energie, und ich nur zufrieden, dass es nicht Ischl oder Reichenau ist (Huhn u Blumenkohl), verspreche mich nicht öfter als einmal über jeden kleinen Mangel zu beklagen, der sich vielleicht zu der Burg in Grundlsee findet.")

13 June 1930 (Trude)
Freud-Meine Lieben 14.6.1930 [FM] (" . . . das entsetzlich ungeschickte Ende von Trude H. hat auch mich sehr erschüttert.).
Swales-Molnar 21.4.1990 [FM].
Fichtner-Molnar 21.5.1990 [FM].
Stross, Dr. J., Interview, 13.6.1990.

17 June 1930
1. Initially Freud had not been wholeheartedly in favor of Alexander's appointment because others he considered better qualified, such as Eitingon, Sachs, Radó, Nunberg or Federn, had not been offered the post. But by autumn 1930 he was saying that psychoanalysis in the United States was facing better times and that one could set hopes by Alexander's influence.
Freud-Jelliffe 12.10.1929 [FM: 1-F8–74-1]
Freud-Lehrmann 5.10.1930 [Brill Library]
Alexander-Freud 1.2.1930 [FM: SOH–9–17] ("Im ganzen scheint es mir, dass dieser Ausflug in die akademische Welt und medizinische Fakultät nur ein neue Beweis sein wird, dass die Psychoanalyse von der Medizin noch immer nicht angenommen werden kann. Mc Lean hat mir gesagt, dass an dieser Sitzung hat er erst wirklich gesehen, was für tiefer Widerstand gegen die Analyse herrscht und dass die Menschen aufhören korrekt zu handeln unter dem Einfluss dieses Widerstands.").

18 June 1930 (Weinmann)
Romm, p.92.
Freud-Meine Lieben 19.6.1930 [FM] ("Gestern hatte ich wieder einen Zustand mit Schwindligkeit, übelen

Magen, Beklemmung, ganzen Tag über Herz unbeteiligt. Merkwürdiger Weise hatte Anna ganz derselbe, die Übligkeiten sogar ärger als ich, so dass unsere Diagnose zwischen einer Hitzerwirkung und einer leichten Speiservergiftung (womit?) schwankt, heute fast vorüber. Der Schaden bei Schr. ist wieder gutgemacht, die Arbeit heute festgesetzt. Dr. Weinmann hat uns gestern besucht, unseren Dank eingeheimst.").

18 June 1930 (Minna)
Freud-Meine Lieben 14.6.1930 [FM] ("Minna's Geburtstag ist ein schweres Problem. Eigentlich bin ich für Abschaffung aller Geburtstage, die nicht auf eine Null ausgehen, aber sie soll sich darüber frei äussern.).
Freud-Meine Lieben 19.6.1930 [FM].

20 June 1930
1. When Staub came to England in 1935 he was keen to continue working on criminal cases and was disconcerted when the British Psycho-Analytical Society would not permit this, since they had only accepted him on condition he worked in research, not private practice.
Berliner Tageblatt 23.5.1930.
Eitingon-Jones 12.3.1935 [Inst. of PsA: CEC/FO2/42].
Jones-Eitingon 21.3.1935 [Inst. of PsA: CEC/FO2/43].

21 June 1930 (Lucie)
Lange, H.W., *Freud Family Tree* [FM].
Jones, I.132.
Freud-Meine Lieben 22.6.1930 [FM] ("Zärtlich u vernünftig wie immer, doch der einzige Mensch in der ganzen Linie.").

21 June 1930 (Jackson)
Freud-Meine Lieben 22.6.1930 [FM] ("Ich habe gestern die Jackson u den David entlassen, nur Dorothy wird noch eine Woche aushalten. Also wirklich Ferien.").
Roazen, Paul, *Freud and his Followers*, New York 1984 [1971] pp.423–5.
Wessel, Morris A., "Edith B. Jackson, M.D.," in *The Journal of Pediatrics*, July 1978 pp.165–6.

21 June 1930 (Zeppelin)
1. Freud's flight was reported in the Berlin newspaper *Tempo* (29.10.1928) in an issue whose main story was the transatlantic flight of the airship *Graf Zeppelin*. In the final pages of the *New Introductory Lectures* (1932) the sinister connotations of the low-flying airship emerge: "...in the night during which (in peace-time and on an exercise) a German Zeppelin cruised over London the war against Germany was no doubt a foregone conclusion."
Freud-Meine Lieben 22.6.1930 [FM] ("Gestern nach 12 h wurde ich durch ein sich immer verstärkendes Geräusch aus dem Schlaf gerissen, weckte Anna, wir öffneten die Thür auf den Balkon, eilten in den Garten u sahen grade noch der Zeppelin ganz niedrig über unserem Haus als ob er uns einen speziellen Besuch abgestattet hätte.").
Freud-Sam Freud 6.12.1928 [FM].
Bryher, *The Heart to Artemis*, London, 1963, p.245.
Tempo, 29.10.1928.
S.E., XXII.178.

24 June 1930
Anna Freud-Eva Rosenfeld 25.6.1930 [FM: Transcript P. Heller].
Burlingham, p.211.
Freud-Meine Lieben 26.6.1930 [FM].

25 June 1930
1. Though bored by its revision, Freud always regarded *The Interpretation of Dreams* as his most essential work and the foundation of psychoanalysis. After its first publication on November 4, 1899 (the publisher, however, printed 1900 as its publication date), the book went through four expanded editions, in 1909, 1911, 1914 and 1930. The 6th and 7th editions in 1921 and 1922 were identical with the 5th.
Freud-Ferenczi 13.12.1929 [FM] ("Nun, ich habe als öffentlich interessant nur mitzuteilen, dass die neue Schrift gleich nach Neujahr erscheinen wird u dass ich mich mit der 8er Auflage der Trdeutung langweile.").

Jones, I.395.

30 June 1930
Freud-Meine Lieben 14.6.1930 & 30.6.1930 [FM].

1 July 1930 (Lederer)
Freud-Ernst Freud 20.9.1931 [LoC] ("Ich bitte Dich heute, Lederer noch M 300 zu schicken – wahrscheinlich zum letzten Mal . . . ")
Freud-Hermann 28.2.1936 in Mattenklott, Gert " ' . . . dass wir nicht auch gestorben sind' " *Neue Rundschau*, 1987, 3, p.18.

1 July 1930 (Royalties)
Freud-Meine Lieben 26.6.1930 & 2.7.1930 [FM].

3 July 1930 (Zweig)
Freud-Meine Lieben 5.7.1930 [FM] ("Donnerstag abds war Arnold Zweig mit Frau bei uns. Der arme Junge ist halb erblindet, er kann nicht mehr selbst lesen. Im Spiegel solcher Schicksale schweigt man von seinem. Aber hoffentlich dauert es jetzt nicht mehr lange.").
Arnold Zweig-Jones 3.2.1956 [SFC].
Freud-Ernst Freud 19.4.1930 [LoC].

3 July 1930 (Prize)
Kuratorium des Goethe-Preises - Freud 26.7.1930 [FM: VAR SF 109](" . . . soll der Preis einer mit ihrem Schaffen bereits zur Geltung gelangten Persönlichkeit zuerkannt werden deren schöpferisches Wirken einer dem Andenken Goethes gewidmeten Ehrung würdig ist.").
Berliner Tageblatt, 9.7.1930.
Freud-Martha Freud 10.7.1930 [FM: Postcard].

11 July 1930 (Liebman)
1. More than this cannot at present be discovered about Liebman: however, in the Library of Congress there is an interview with a Julius Liebman which will become accessible in 2007.
Freud-Meine Lieben 26.6.1930 [FM].
Eissler-Molnar 20.5.1990 [FM].

11 July 1930 (Hogarth)
Woolf, Leonard, *Downhill all the way: An Autobiography of the Years 1919–1939* Hogarth, London, 1967, pp.64–5, 163–8.
Meynell, G.G., "Freud translated: an historical and bibliographical note," *Journ. of R. Soc. Med.* 74, April 1981.

14 July 1930 (Neuländer)
Fichtner-Molnar 21.5.1990 [FM].

14 July 1930 (Hogarth)
Woolf, Leonard, *Downhill all the way: An Autobiography of the Years 1919–1939*, Hogarth, London, 1967 p.167.

23 July 1930
Freud-Martha Freud 4.6.1930 [FM] ("Es wird gewiss ein Meisterstück sein und es ist noch nicht vorherzusagen auf welche Art es mir das Leben verderben wird. Das schwer zu Ertragende ist die Abhängigkeit von einem Menschen, den man eigentlich nicht erreichen kann. Dass mir die neue Prothese Selbständigkeit schenken wird, darf ich nicht erwarten.")
Freud-Meine Lieben 7.6.1930, 30.6.1930, 11.7.1930 [FM].

25 July 1930
Freud-Meine Lieben 11.7.1930 [FM].

27 July 1930
Freud-Eitingon 31.7.1930 [FM] ("Grundlsee ist wunderschön, das Haus bequem, das Wetter wie überall regnerisch und unfreundlich.")
Freud-Ernst Freud 31.7.1930 [SFC].
Freud-Jones 13.8.1930 [Typescript Inst. of PsA].

29 July 1930
Freud-Eitingon 31.7.1930 [FM].
Kuratorium des Goethe-Preises - Freud 26.7.1930 [FM: VAR SF 109]. ("Ihre Psychologie hat aber nicht nur die ärztliche Wissenschaft, sondern die Vorstellungswelt der Künstler und der Seelsorger, der Geschichtsschreiber und Erzieher aufgewühlt und

bereichert.").
Freud-Arnold Zweig 21.8.1930 in Zweig Letters.

2 August 1930
1. Hollós' work on psychotics had elicited a curious antipathy in Freud which he tried to explain in a letter: "I finally admitted to myself that it was because I did not like these sick people, that I was angry with them at finding them so far from myself and everything human. A curious type of intolerance which of course makes me unfit to be a psychiatrist.

"In the course of time I have ceased to find myself interesting, which is of course analytically incorrect. Can you understand me better? Am I here behaving as previous doctors did toward hysterics, is it the result of an ever more clearly discernible partisanship for the primacy of the intellect, the expression of a hostility toward the id?" (*Freud-Hollós 10.4.1928*).
Leupold-Loewenthal, Harald, *Handbuch der Psychoanalyse*, Wien, 1986.
Psychoanalytic Pioneers.
Hier geht . . . p.52.
Meng, Heinrich: "Sigmund Freud in Brief, Gespräch, Begegnung und Werk." *Psyche* Heft 9, December 1956 p.525 ("Es war für uns ergreifend, zu spüren, wie stark von Freude erfüllt und tief berührt er war von der Tatsache der kommenden ersten öffentlichen Ehrung seines Werkes.")
Freud-Hollós 10.4.1928 [FM: 1-F8-18-3 (Copy)] ("Ich gestand mir endlich, es komme daher, dass ich diese Kranken nicht liebe, dass ich mich über sie ärgere, sie so fern von mir und allem Menschlichen empfinde. Eine merkwürdige Art von Intoleranz, die mich gewiss zum Psychiater untauglich macht.

"Im Laufe der Zeit habe ich aufgehört, mich selbst interessant zu finden, was gewiss analytisch inkorrekt ist, und bin darum in der Erklärung dieser Einstellung nicht weiter gekommen. Können Sie mich besser verstehen? Benehme ich mich dabei wie frühere Ärzte gegen die Hysteriker, ist es die Folge einer immer deutlicher gewordenen Parteinahme für den Primat des Intellekts, den Ausdruck einer Feindseligkeit gegen das Es?")

6 August 1930
Freud, Anna, "Mathilde Hollitscher-Freud. 1887–1978," *Sigmund Freud House Bulletin*, Vol.2, 1. 1978 pp.2–3.
Augenfeld-Lobner 8.2.1974 [FM: Copy].

8 August 1930
1. But debts, whether of gratitude or otherwise, demand repayment. Throughout his life Freud paid regular Sunday visits on his mother at her home on the Gymnasiumsgasse. Beyond that his sense of indebtedness to her is hinted at in a cryptic comment from a letter to Eitingon:
"Since, as you know, one must pay and atone some time for every unasked thing that one has received and enjoyed, the love of a mother as well . . . "
(*Freud-Eitingon 8.11.1929*).
2. At this moment, in August 1930, while he was writing his Goethe Prize speech, which would be read in the house where Goethe was born, Freud's fate had symbolically intersected that of Goethe.
Freud-Ernst Freud 23.8.1930 [LoC].
Freud-Eitingon 8.11.1929 [FM] ("Da man, wie Sie wissen, für alles, was man ungebeten bekommen und genossen hat, auch für die Liebe einer Mutter einmal zu zalen und zu büssen hat . . . .")
S.E., XVII.156.

16 August 1930 (Salten)
1. The actual greeting to Salten is as follows:
"Dear Mr. Salten!
As soon as I heard of the intention to celebrate your 60th birthday, I felt determined to take part. Not to vaunt your services, to honor your position in literature and the public eye—and whatever other gruesome caresses there may be—but just to speak a single friendly word on the date, that does not in itself impress me much. And that is, that you belong among those writers for whom one immediately feels a personal affection if one likes something of theirs. And since there are only a few of them, that means a lot."

Freud, "Felix Salten zum 60. Geburtstag" Cited in: Hemecker, W.W., *Ein Geburtstagsgruss an Felix Salten*, (ms.) ("Sobald ich hörte, dass man Ihren 60. Geburtstag zu feiern beabsichtigt, stand bei mir fest, dass ich dabei sein müsse. Nicht etwa um Ihnen Ihre Verdienste vorzuhalten, Ihre Stellung in der schönen Literatur und zur Öffentlichkeit zu würdigen - und was dergleichen grausame Liebkosungen mehr sein mögen - sondern nur, um Ihnen zum Datum, das mir an sich nicht sehr imponiert, ein einziges freundliches Wort zu sagen. Und das ist, dass Sie zu den Dichtern gehören, die man sofort persönlich lieb gewinnt, wenn man etwas von ihnen liebt. Und da es nur wenige solche gibt, bedeutet das viel.") (With thanks to Dr. W. Hemecker for bringing this work to my attention.).

16 August 1930 (Alex)
1. Another brother, Julius, had been born when Freud was one year old but died the following year. In a letter to Wilhelm Fliess (3.10.1897) Freud admitted his own—magically fulfilled—death-wish against this brother. In his 1917 essay on the childhood memory from *Dichtung and Wahrheit*, Freud inferred that the infant Goethe was angry with his mother because of the birth of a rival sibling. According to this analysis the logic of the narrative sequence in Goethe's *Dichtung und Wahrheit* betrays an infantile train of thought relating to the rival's subsequent death: " . . . destiny removed my brother, so that I did not have to share my mother's love with him . . . ."
2. As adults, the brothers frequently went on holiday together: the *Disturbance of Memory on the Acropolis* (1936) records their trip to Athens in 1904 and, of course, documents a case of family rivalry—but with the father.
S.E., XVII.156.
Lange, Hanns W. *Family Tree* [FM].
Freud-Alexander Freud 8.8.1930 [LoC].

17 August 1930
Freud-Ernst Freud 23.8.1930 [LoC] ("Am 17 u 18 dM waren wir bei Grossmutter in Ischl. Über sie ist nicht mehr viel Gutes zu sagen. Man hebt es dankbar hervor, wenn sie aus der Apathie erwacht, uns erkennt und sich teilnehmend zeigt.").
Freud-Sam Freud 21.8.1925 [FM].

24 August 1930 (Michel)
Freud-Eitingon 26.8.1930 [FM] ("Sonntag hat Stadtrat Dr. Michel Diplom u Preis überbracht. Ein noch junger, charmanter, liberal denkender Mann. In seiner Begleitung befanden sich seine Frau u - merkwürdiger Weise! - die Frau des kl. Hans, der jetzt Kapellmeister in Frankfurt ist. Der Oberbürgermeister der Stadt Dr. Landmann ist ein beiderseitiger Jude, obwol getauft! Das erklärt doch manches.").

24 August 1930 (Parting)
Freud-Eitingon 26.8.1930 [FM] ("Mit meiner Mutter steht es schlecht, wir sind froh, dass sie mit Hilfe von Federn lebend von Ischl nach Wien gekommen ist.").

25 August 1930
Nunberg, Herman, *Memoirs: Recollections, Ideas, Reflections*, New York, 1969, p.55.
Swales-Molnar 21.4.1990 [FM].
Fichtner-Molnar 21.5.1930 [FM].

28 August 1930
1. It was this "poem", as the *Wiener Zeitung* incorrectly reported, " . . . which Freud heard as an 18-year old youth at a lecture and which was to determine his entire career." This is an interesting variation on the story, that it was an (apocryphal) *essay* by Goethe which played that role.
Wiener Zeitung, 28.8.1930.
Jones, I.31.

29 August 1930 (Martin)
Freud-Eitingon 30.8.1930 [FM] ("Martin musste plötzlich am Blinddarm operirt werden, es geht ihm gut.").

29 August 1930
Freud-Eitingon 30.8.1930 [FM] ("Anna ist zurück u sagt, es war sehr schön und ehrenvoll für die Psychoanalyse . . . .").
Freud-Jones 15.9.1930 [Typescript: Inst. of PsA] ("Sie haben vielleicht gehört oder selbst gelesen, dass ausländische Zeitungen alamirende Nachrichten über mein Befinden bringen. Ich glaube, das sind Folgen des Goethepreises, den die feindliche Öffentlichkeit nicht ohne Zeichen von Sträuben hinnehmen kann. So bringen sie mich eiligst um. Nun, sie müssen ja einmal Recht behalten.").

31 August 1930
1. In 1928, in gratitude to Simmel for his personal kindness and for his contribution to psychoanalysis, Freud gave him an intaglio ring, such as he had previously given the members of the Committee. (This ring was kindly donated to the Freud Museum by Dr. K. R. Eissler.)
Hier geht . . . pp.46–8.
Girard, Claude, "Histoire de la formation dans la Société psychanalytique de Paris," *Revue Internationale d'Histoire de la Psychanalyse* 2, 1989, pp.303–342.
Mijolla, Alain de, *Psychoanalysis in France*, I.A.H.P., 1986.
Bertin, pp.139–40.
Freud-Simmel 11.11.1928 [FM].
Freud and Art, p.123.

2 September 1930
1. Freud was not alone in his antagonism toward America and the state of psychoanalysis there. After Ernst Simmel had also emigrated, Jones reported that he had apparently "undergone some regression as a result of the peculiarly ennervating influence of America." (*Jones-Eitingon 24.2.1937*).
Freud- Lampl-de Groot 8.6.1933 [FM] ("Sachs habe ich kurz gesprochen. Ungünstiger Eindruck, das Vulgare was er immer gehabt hat, um soviel greifbarer. Wie ein nouveau riche, dick, selbstzufrieden, eingebildet, snobbisch, entzückt von Amerika und beseeligt von seinen grossen Erfolgen dort. Anna hat Recht gehabt die Frage aufzuwerfen, was man den Leuten wünschen soll. Das Unglück that ihnen nicht wol und den Erfolg vertragen sie nicht.").
Jones-Eitingon 24.2.1937 [Inst. of PsA CEC.FO2/61].

3 September 1930
1. The only book by Paquet in Freud's library (the travel book *Städte, Landschaften und ewige Bewegung*) bears an authorial dedication dated 21 August 1930. It is likely Dr. Michel presented it to Freud on Paquet's behalf, during his visit of August 24.
Freud-Eitingon 27.5.1920 [FM] (" . . . .kommt noch Dr. Bernfeld in Betracht, ein trefflicher Mensch glänzender Lehrer der aber dem Pathologischen ferner steht . . . .").
Paquet-Anna Freud 26.7.1930 [FM: VAR SF].
Paquet-Freud 5.8.1930 [FM: VAR SF 110].

7 September 1930
Eitingon-Freud 8.8.1930 [SFC].
Romm, p.92.
Freud- Lampl-de Groot 14.3.1931 [FM].
Schur, p.414.
Freud-Schur 9.9.1930 [FM].

12 September 1930
1. Freud's sense of obligation to his mother was seen by those around as one of the fundamental traits of his character. In 1923, at the time when he was facing his first operation for cancer, Jones was discussing with others how to persuade Freud to accept treatment: "Someone, I think it was Eitingon, asserted that the final and most potent appeal that could be made to you was 'for your mother's sake'." (*Jones-Freud 10.9.1930*)
Freud-Sam Freud 12.9.1930 [FM].
Freud-Abraham 29.5.1918 [FM: Typescript] ("Meine Mutter wird heuer 83 J alt u. ist nicht mehr recht solid. Manchmal denke ich, es wird ein Stück Freiheit mehr für mich sein wenn sie stirbt, denn die Annahme, dass man ihr mitteilen muss, ich sei gestorben, hat etwas, wovor man zurückschreckt.").
Freud-Jones 15.9.1930 in Jones, III.162.
Jones-Freud 10.9.1930 [Inst. of PsA].

14 September 1930
1. When Jakob Seidmann, husband of Freud's niece Tom, was buried in Berlin, Freud wrote home: "But I shall not be going to the funeral, I pass such ceremonies by in Vienna too." (*Freud-Meine Lieben 21.10.1929*)
Freud-Ferenczi 16.9.1930 [FM] ("Kein Schmerz, keine Trauer.. [. . .] Irgendwie werden sich in tieferen Schichten die Lebenswerte merklich geändert haben.").
Freud-Meine Lieben 21.10.1929 [FM] ("Zum Begräbnis gehe ich aber nicht, ich lasse solche Feierlichkeiten auch in Wien an mir vorübergehen.").

15 September 1930
Anna Freud-Sigmund Freud 15.9.1930 [FM] ("Statt in der Scala sind wir schon im Bett, denn der erste Tag war so voll wie eine ganze Ferienzeit. Reise ausgezeichnet, nach dein Motto: 'Mann kann es auch viel billiger haben, nur . . . '. Mastkur im Speisewagen, pünktlichst angekommen, nicht fühlbarer als Wien-Berlin.").

16 September 1930
Freud-Eitingon 18.9.1930 [FM] ("Das Haus verödet sich allmälich. Anna ist heute mit Dorothy zwischen Sulden u Trafoi.") .

17 September 1930
1. In 1883 Freud wrote to Martha: "She [Dolfi] is the sweetest and best of my sisters, has such a great capacity for deep feeling and alas an all-too-fine sensitiveness." (*Freud-Martha Bernays 9.9.1883*).
2. Freud's mother had a dictatorial temperament and there were family anecdotes of the humiliations to which she sometimes subjected Dolfi, supposedly treating her all her life as if she were still an adolescent. Freud appreciated the sacrifices Dolfi made for their mother. In a note attached to her (cash) birthday gift this year Freud spoke of his " . . . profoundest thanks for your inestimable work over all these years." (*Freud-Adolfine Freud 22.7.1930*).
Dolfi was to continue in an occasional nursing role. In 1933, for example, she was looking after the Marlés' children and home in Prague while they were on tour abroad.
Freud-Eitingon 18.9.1930 [FM] ("Schwester Adolfine erholt sich bei uns von dem Erlebnisse der letzten Woche. Die Natur hat die 95 Jahre der Mutter nicht als Milderungsgrund gelten lassen; die Schmerzen von der Gangrän des Beines machten das Morph. der letzten Tage unentbehrlich.")
Freud-Martha Bernays 9.9.1883 in *Letters*.
Waldinger, Ernst M. *Über die Familie Freud*, pp.10–11 [Typescript: Inst of PsA].
Freud-Adolfine Freud 22.7.1930 in *Letters*.
Martha Freud-Lucie Freud 7.12.1933 [FM].

18 September 1930 (Ernst)
Gardner, Muriel (Ed.), *The Wolf Man and Sigmund Freud*, Hogarth, London, 1973, p.144.
Freud-Anna Freud 19.9.1930 [FM] ("Heutige Nachricht, sie hat eine Darmstörung u spielt lustig mit Wolf. Das Tierchen fehlt natürlich auf Schritt und Tritt.").

18 September 1930 (Eva)
Young-Bruehl, pp.135–6.
Freud-Anna Freud 19.9.1930 [FM].

28 September 1930
1. Freud had resigned himself to his marriage of convenience with the city of Vienna and was no longer expressing his hatred of it in such strong terms as 30 years previously: "I have an almost personal hatred for Vienna and, in contrast to the giant Antaeus, I gather fresh strength as soon as I lift my foot from the ground of my father city [*vom vaterstätdischen Boden*]" (*Freud-Fliess 11.3.1900*).
Freud-Alexander Freud 8.8.1930 [LoC] ("Allgemeines Urteil, dass wir noch nie so schön gewohnt haben.")
Freud-Viereck 20.8.1930 [Brill Library] (" . . . ich habe nichts Ernsthaftes zu thun, bin menschenfreundlicher aufgelegt als sonst . . . ")
Freud-Fliess 11.3.1900 in Schröter.

29 September 1930 (Anna)
Anna Freud-Eva Rosenfeld 18.9.1930 [FM: Transcript P. Heller] ("Wir sind der Sonne um 1500 m nähe als sonst und das spürt man. Sie brennt langsam alles weg, was an einem überflüssig ist.
Es ist sehr schön und an jeder Station lasse ich ein bisschen Unruhe zurück.
Ich war bei einer Bäuerin, die noch selber spinnt und Loden webt.
Aber sie macht keine Analysen dabei
Ich habe alles im Rucksack, was ich brauche. Vielleicht braucht man nie mehr.").

29 September 1930 (Bondy)
Freud-Mitzi Freud 15.2.1930 [LoC] ("Wir hören zB. sehr gutes von dem eines Dr. Bondy bei Hamburg.")

30 Sept 1930
Freud-Ernst Freud 30.9.1930 [LoC]
Urbantschitsch, Rudolf von, *Wiener Cottage-Sanatorium*, Wien, o.J.

3 October 1930 (Pichler)
Schur, 424.
Pichler Notes, 3.10.1930 [FM].

14 October 1930
Pichler Notes, 14.10.1930 [FM].
Freud-Eitingon 15.10.1930 [FM] ("Während also Magen- und Herzbeschwerden von dem Eingreifen der Therapie langsam zurückweichen, hat Pichler's Initiative den Zustand im Mund in den Vordergrund gerückt. [. . .] . . . es war reichlich unangenehm, als Operation nimmt es natürlich keinen hohen Rang ein. Die Prothese wird nun 3 - 4 Tage lang nicht abgelegt, sie soll das Hautstück an die Wunde anpressen. Solange kann ich nicht kauen und nur schlecht sprechen, habe also Arbeitsferien u nähre mich von flüssigem Stoff. Gestern hatte ich auch heftige Mundschmerzen, heute nur mehr den Druck.").

17 October 1930 (Sickness)
Freud-Ferenczi 5.11.1930 [FM].

17 October 1930 (Bullitt)
Stewart R.S., "Posthumous Analysis" N.Y. *Times Book Review*, 29.1.1967.
Freud-Eitingon 15.11.1931 [FM].

29 October 1930
Freud-Arnold Zweig 7.12.1930 in *Zweig Letters*.

2 November 1930
Freud-Eitingon 3.11.1930 [FM] ("Ich habe gestern die Spuren des Krankenexistenz verwischt . . . ").
Freud-Meine Lieben 26.6.1930 [FM].
Freud-Radó 26.9.1930 [FM] (" . . . und seitdem ich gar nicht mehr rauchen darf, arbeite ich auch sehr schwer.").
Freud-Schur 9.9.1930 in Schur, 558.
Freud-Eitingon 16.11.1930 [FM] ("Ich arbeite 4 Stunden u konsumire 2 Zigarren täglich").
Freud-Eitingon 22.11.1930 [FM] ("Rauche ich doch unter dem Beifall meines Leibarztes Braun 3–4 Zigarren täglich.").

5 November 1930
1. The relief represents an incident from Homer's *Iliad*. After Achilles had slain the Trojan hero Hector in revenge for his slain comrade Patroclus and dragged the body round the tomb, Hector's father Priam, the King of Troy, ransomed his son's body and brought it back for burial. (According to Anna, Freud thought the frieze represented "The Death of Patroclus" rather than the ransoming of Hector). A curious side-effect of the systemic cataloguing of Freud's antiquities by the Freud Museum has been the "rediscovery" of this object. Recent publications on Roman sarcophagi refer to this relief as "lost". It was previously well-documented; in fact an account of this sarcophagus relief was printed in 1926 before it even came into Freud's possession (in the *Jahresheft des Oesterreichen Archaeologischen Institutes in Wien*, Band XXIII, 1926). (I have to thank Dr. A. Bernhard-Walcher of the Vienna Kunsthistorisches Museum, Vienna, for having pieced together the

fragments of this story.)
Ransohoff, R., in Engelman, p.61.
Jahresheft des Oesterreichen Archaeologischen Institutes in Wien, Band XXIII, 1926.
Archaeologischer Anzeiger, Berlin, 1976: *Römische Sarcophage*, G. Koch und H. Sichtermann, München, 1982.
Burn, Lucilla in *Freud and Art* pp.114–5.
Bernhard-Walcher - Neufeld 6.2.1987 [FM].

6 November 1930
Jones-Eitingon 26.7.1930 [Inst. of Psa. CEC/FO1/49].
Freud-Einstein 10.5.1931 in *Freudiana*, Jerusalem, 1973, p.x.

9 November 1930 (Elections)
Kitchen, Martin, *The Coming of Austrian Fascism*, Montreal, 1980, p.32.
Bergschicker, p.12.
Wiener Zeitung, 11.11.1930.

9 November 1930 (Ferenczi)
Ferenczi-Freud 23.11.1930 [FM] ("Die Wiener Reise hat mir wohl getan. Es freute mich zu sehen, dass die Dinge, an denen ich arbeite, am Ende gar nicht so revolutionär sind; Sie wissen, wie ungerne ich Meinungsverschiedenheit mit Ihnen, auch in Detailfragen habe. Ich hoffe, es geht Ihnen nach wie vor gut; mein Eindruck über Ihren Gesundheitszustand war ein ausgezeichneter.")

20 November 1930
Engelman, Plate 17.
Burn, Lucilla, in *Freud and Art* pp.114–5.

25 November 1930
Wiener Zeitung, 29.11.1930 ("Guilbert ist diesmal stimmlich indisponiert. Aber der Gesang war ja bei ihren Vortrag nie das Wichtigste. Sie hat immer nur so getan, als ob sie sänge.")
Guilbert-Freud n.d. [FM: GUIL 19] ("Merci mille fois des adorables fleurs reçues, et combien je reste flattée et heureuse que le Grande Homme ait pris quelque plaisir à mon concert!").

29 November 1930
1. Freud was well aware of difficulties in the Berlin group, as can be deduced from a comment in a letter home from Berlin the previous year:
"Today Anna, Lou and Simmel are going to a Berlin society meeting, I think the visit to the monkeys at the zoo in the morning was a preparation."
(*Freud-Meine Lieben 19.3.1929*).
Freud-Meine Lieben 19.3.1929 [FM] ("Heute gehen Anna, die Lou u Simmel in die Berliner Sitzung, ich glaube der Besuch bei den Affen im Zoo heute vormittags war schon Vorbereitung.").
Eitingon-Freud 19.11.1930 [SFC] (". . . . nur allzu nahe lag die Frage, ob das wirklich nur Zufall ist.").

30 November 1930
1. Max Schiller's reply to Freud's letter ends with the statement that Freud is wrong in thinking an "unwarranted analysis" might disturb their friendship. He assured Freud that his wife ardently desired an analysis and hoped that the next summer would bring them together to make this possible.
Freud-Guilbert 8.3.1931 [FM].
Freud-Max Schiller 26.3.1931 in *Letters*.
Schiller-Freud 3.4.1931 [FM: SOH9–17 "S"].

3 December 1930
Freud-Jones 15.9.1930 (Typescript Inst. of PsA).

4 December 1930
1. It was not in fact until April 1932 that Bullitt was to announce the book's completion, and even at that date it still needed editing and abbreviation. He eventually decided not to bring the book out until after the death of Woodrow Wilson's widow and in the end it was not to be published until 1967. Thus, the book on Wilson was to betray hopes in the same way as the man himself had done in 1919, when Freud wrote: "For us the defeated, President Wilson was a disappointment which will not so soon be forgotten." (*Freud-Viereck 28.8.1919*).
Freud, Sigmund & Bullitt, William C. *Thomas*

Woodrow Wilson, Twenty-eighth President of the United States: a Psychological Study, London, 1967, p.ix.
Freud-Arnold Zweig 7.12.1930 in Zweig Letters.
Freud-Eitingon 16.4.1931 [FM] ("Der Verlag hat übrigens glänzende Aussichten, wenn er nur das neue Wilsonbuch (das erst halb fertig ist) von mir erhält.").
Gay, p.557.
Freud-Viereck 28.8.1919 [FM: MISC] ("President Wilson war für uns Unterlegene eine Enttäuschung, die nicht so bald in Vergessenheit geraten wird.")

11 December 1930 (Weiss)
Freud-Weiss 29.6.1919 [FM].
Freud-Weiss 28.11.1930 [FM] ("Sie sind der richtige, zähe Pionier.").

11 December 1930
Waelder, Robert, Interview, R.S. Stewart, 29.7.1966.

13 December 1930
Int. J. PsA, Vol. 12, 1931 (Reports), p.255.
Freud-Eitingon 22.12.1930 [FM].

14 December 1930
1. The *Neue Freie Presse*, the newspaper Freud read regularly, was the only Viennese daily with an international reputation. Moritz Benedict, the main editorial writer, was considered among the most influential men in Austria and his presence guaranteed the paper's excellence in culture and literature.
"The Expert Opinion in the Halsmann Case" *S.E.*, XXI.251–3.
Spiel, Hilde, *Vienna's Golden Autumn: 1866–1938*, London, 1987, p.109.
Zweig, Stefan, *The World of Yesterday*, London, 1944 [1943], p.84.

14 December 1930
1. Freud continues querying the problem of his own Jewishness in the preface to *Totem and Taboo*: "If the question were put to him: 'Since you have abandoned all these common characteristics of your countrymen, what is there left to you that is Jewish?' he would reply: 'A very great deal, and probably its very essence.' He could not now express that essence clearly in words . . . .'
A letter to J. Dwossis [Y. Dvosis], the Hebrew translator, accompanied the prefaces. It is of great interest since it further elaborates the fascinating question of Freud's attitude to Judaism in general:
"It is a source of extraordinary joy and satisfaction to me that some of my books are going to be published in Hebrew. My father spoke the sacred language as well as German or better. He let me grow up in total ignorance of everything to do with Judaism. Only as a grown man did I begin to reproach him about this. But I had felt myself to be a Jew even before this - under the influence of German antisemitism of which repeated outbreaks occured during my university years.
Zionism aroused in me great sympathy which I continue to feel to this day. From the very beginning I connected it with those anxieties which the present situation seems to justify. I would prefer to be mistaken." (*Freud-Dwossis 15.12.1930*).
S.E., XV.11.
S.E., XIII.xv.
Freud-Dwossis 15.12.1930 [FM: ARC/40] ("Es ist mir eine ausserordentliche Freude und Genugthuung, dass einige meiner Bücher in hebräischer Sprache erscheinen werden. Mein Vater sprach die heilige Sprache wie deutsch oder besser. Mich liess er in voller Unwissenheit über alles, was das Judentum betrifft, aufwachsen. Erst als reifer Mann begann ich ihm darob zu grollen. Ich hatt aber schon früher mich als Jude gefühlt - unter dem Einfluss des deutschen Antisemitismus dessen neuerlicher Ausbruch in meine Universitätszeit fiel.
Der Zionismus erweckte meinen stärksten Sympathien, die ihm noch heute treu anhängen. Von allem Anfang an knüpfte ich an ihn jene Besorgnisse welche die heutige Lage zu rechfertigen scheint. Ich möchte mich gerne geirrt haben.").

17 December 1930
1. The 1914 Pollack portrait was exhibited at the gallery of Hugo Heller, the bookseller and publisher. When Freud received the print, he wrote to Karl Abraham: "Pollack's etching arrived a few days ago. I like the pose very much. It takes some time to get used to the facial expression, but one comes to like it in the end." (*Freud-Abraham 2.4.1914*).
Freud-Eitingon 5.10.1930 [FM] ("Es ist keine Zeit sein Gesicht verewigen zu lassen, ausserdem meine ich, dass die Schmutzersche Radierung nicht zu übertreffen ist. Das 'letzte Gesicht' habe ich Max Pollak in Wien zugesagt.").
Reik, Theodor, *From Thirty Years with Freud* Hogarth, London, 1942, pp.9–10.
Freud-Abraham 2.4.1914 [FM].

30 December 1930
Translation list [FM: I-F8–17-29].
Freud-Jones 4.1.1931 [Typescript Inst. of PsA] ("Vor kurzem erhielt ich die japanische Übersetzung des Alltagslebens, aber nicht von der Seite Yabe's. Ich habe da eine kleine Verwirrung angerichtet.")
Jones-Freud 15.1.1931 [Inst. of PsA].

1931

8 January 1931
Freud-Eitingon 14.6.1920 [FM].
Pictures and Words, p.216.
Freud-Ernst Freud 18.3.1931 [LoC].

12 January 1931
1. On hearing of the invitation Jones wrote:
"It happens to be one of my few remaining ambitions to receive a similar invitation myself some day, Huxley having been the chief hero of my youth. As you doubtless know, he was nicknamed 'Darwin's bulldog', and you would perhaps agree that my identification with him has not been entirely fruitless." (*Jones-Freud 15.1.1931*).
Forsyth-Freud 7.1.1931 [FM: SOH9–17].
Freud-Eitingon 18.1.1931 [FM].
Jones-Freud 15.1.1931 [Inst. of PsA].

14/15 January 1931
Freud-Eitingon 22.12.1930 [FM] ("Wenn die Prothese nicht wäre, das richtige Muster eines notwendigen Übels, könnte ich einen Versuch wagen, mich des Lebens zu freuen.").
Freud-Jones 4.1.1931 [Typescript Inst. of PsA] ("Trotz fortgesetzter Quälereien mit der Prothese geht es mir mit der Gesundheit nicht schlecht; ich habe in Berlin u. hier im Ganzen 6 1/2 Kilo zugenommen. Der Rauchgenuss bleibt dauernd eingeschränkt.").
Freud-Eitingon 18.1.1931 [FM] ("Ich habe jetzt besonders schlechte Zeiten mit Kiefer und/oder Prothese.").

17 January 1931
Freud-Ernst Freud 1.2.1930 [LoC] (" . . . aber ich will nicht, dass sie sich weiter verbindlich macht, sie hat genug auf sich und wird noch 35 Jahre lang in Übung bleiben.").

19 January 1931
1. Marie Bonaparte's daughter, Princess Eugénie, continued to arouse concern. She had spent two months of the winter in bed and only joined her mother in Vienna on February 20. Both stayed in the Cottage Sanatorium, where Eugénie received X-ray treatment, until the end of March when they left for Cannes.
Freud-Eitingon 8.2.1931 [FM] ("Die Prinzessin ist seit 2 Wochen hier u will bis Anfangs März bleiben. Sie ist sehr brav, recht geteilt zwischen verschiedenen Interessen. Die Tochter leidet wieder unter ihrer Tbc. Schleimbeutelaffektion, soll hieher kommen, um eine Röntgenbehandlg. zu haben. Sie will selbst noch eine plastische Operation bei Halban vornehmen lassen, um ihre Idee von der anatomischen Fundirung der Frigidität bis zum letzten Ende durchzuführen.").
Bertin, p.182.

21 January 1931
Freud-Eitingon 27.1.1931 [FM] (" . . . theile ich Ihnen mit, dass wir so ziemlich alle leidend sind an Erscheinungen, die wir der Grippe zuschreiben. Auch meine Frau ist mehrere Tage mit Feber und Darmsymptomen zu Bett gelegen.").

4 February 1931
1. "Fröhlich" means happy. Two other of Freud's dealers at this period were called Lustig ("merry") and Glückselig ("blissful"). Freud could hardly have overlooked the reference to his own name ("joy") - or perhaps to his delight in his collection. These names are coincidental but there is an example of more deliberate play on his name to be found on a piece of furniture in the Freud Museum collection. Among the items of furniture brought to England is a peasant-style Austrian bridal wardrobe, dated 1850. On its doors the artist painted inscriptions which, with their reference to Freud's name, may have amused and attracted the buyer, for example: "The first joy began when I received my spouse." ("*Wo fang sich die Erste Freude an wie ich meinen Breudigam bekomen hab*").

"And I have my joy forever, I remain true until
death." ('Und ich hab mein Freude imer ford, ich bleibe
im getreu bies in den Tod')
Burn, Lucilla, in Freud and Art, p.83.
Wardrobe inscription [FM].

7 February 1931
Pichler Notes, 7.2.1931 [FM].
Freud-Eitingon 8.2.1931 [FM] ("In letzter Woche
haben die Sachkundigen wiederum gefunden, eine
bestimmte Schleimhautwucherung in meiner Narbe
sei ja gewiss nicht bösartig aber doch suspekt, man
könne nicht wissen, was sie anstellen werde und
darum müsste sie weg. Mit Aufbietung all meiner
Passivität habe ich mich gefügt und so gestern eine
neue kleine Operation bei Pichler durchgemacht.
Diesmal eine Electrocoagulation, ich bin weniger
hergenommen als im Oktober, schon heute fast
schmerzfrei, rauche während ich Ihnen schreibe und
werde wahrscheinlich, wenn ich der Grippe und der
Schluck -pneumonie entgehe, nur noch 2–3 Tage die
Arbeit aussetzen.").

9 February 1931
1. Breuer's fatherly kindness put Freud in a position
of dependence he could eventually no longer tolerate.
He turned from him to his new friend Wilhelm Fliess
for a more equal relationship. After a visit to Fliess
and his wife in 1893 he wrote to Minna Bernays:
"One always has a place for a friend who does not,
like Breuer, mix too much compassion with his
affection." (Freud-Minna Bernays 17.4.1893).
Jones, I.183.
Hirschmüller, Albrecht, The Life and Work of Josef
Breuer, New York University Press, 1989 [1978],
p.189.
Freud-Minna Bernays 17.4.1893 in Schröter, p.33 n.3.

11 February 1931 (Lockjaw)
Pichler Notes, 13.2.1931 [FM].

11 February 1931 (Zweig)
Freud-Stefan Zweig 17.2.1931 in Stefan Zweig p.154.

16 February 1931
Freud-Ferenczi 22.2.1931 [FM] ("Die Wunde von
meiner letzten Operation ist noch nicht verheilt. Alle
diese Eingriffe werden mir als unvermeidlich, dann
aber doch als notwendig ausgegeben. Ihre Folgen
füllen die nächsten Wochen mit Elend aus.").

19 February 1931
1. Oli's birthdays for the following two years are not
noted, but Ernst received instructions both times to
send him and Henny money from the account.
Freud-Sam Freud 21.8.1925 [FM].
Freud-Ernst Freud 9.2.1931, 6.2.1932, 10.2.1932 [LoC]

20 February 1931
1. But over the following two years Bernfeld entered
a phase of emotional confusion caused by separation
from his wife, Liesl Neumann. This came to light
through Freud's analysis of Bernfeld's future wife,
Suzanne Cassirer Paret, and radically altered his
assessment: "I have a more definite judgment of
Bernfeld for he was once with me and I can compare
his behavior then with what I found out about what
he is doing and saying from P.[Paret] who is in love
with him. And it is not to his credit, he speaks and
acts as if suffering a psychosis, madly contradictory,
completely insincerely against me. P. asserts that he is
gradually coming to his senses and admitting his
distortions. No word he speaks about P. or analysis is
to be believed. . . ." (Freud- Lampl-de Groot 10.2.1933)
Freud-Olden 22.1.1931 in Psychoanalytic Pioneers p.425.
Bernfeld-Archiv (Repertorium Blatt Nr. 190),
Zentrales Staatsarchiv Merseburg. (With thanks to
Dr. Johannes Reichmayr for information leading to
this note.)
Freud- Lampl-de Groot 10.2.1933 [FM] ("Ein sicheres
Urteil habe ich aber über Bernfeld, denn er war
einmal bei mir und ich kann sein Verhalten damals
mit dem, was ich über sein Benehmen u seine Reden
von der (in ihn verliebten) P. erfahren, vergleichen.
Nun es ist nicht zu seinen Gunsten, er redet u
handelt wie in einer Psychose, wirr widerspruchsvoll,
gegen mich ganz unaufrichtig. Die P. behauptet, dass

er jetzt allmälich zu sich kommt und auch seine
Entstellungen eingesteht. Kein Wort, was er über die
P. u die Analyse sagt, verdient Glauben . . . .").

28 February 1931
Eitingon-Storfer 4.3.1931 [Transcript: SFC].
Eitingon-Freud 8.4.1931 [SFC].
Eitingon-Freud 13.4.1931 [SFC] ("Ich musste ihn also
einfach kaufen für dieses Jahr . . . ").

27 February 1931
Freud-Eitingon 20.2.1931 [FM].

21 March 1931
1. Freud spoke of wanting to leave it as early as 1888
(Freud-Fliess 4.2.1888). At the opening of the
Introductory Lectures Freud warns any doctor in the
audience who might want to take up psychoanalysis:
" . . . he would find himself in a society which did
not understand his efforts, which regarded him with
distrust and hostility, and unleashed upon him all the
evil spirits lurking within it." But he remained a
member, and letters from the society's librarian thank
him for sending them copies of the Interpretation of
Dreams and the Psychopathology of Everyday Life.
Freud-Marie Bonaparte 10.5.1926 [FM: F8/CON 14]
("Ich hätte ihre Glückwünsche und Auszeichnungen
doch nicht für ehrlich gehalten.").
Freud-Eitingon 20.3.1930 in Jones, III.185.
S.E., XV.16.
Letters from Librarian of Ges. Aerzte to Freud [FM:
SOH9–17 (Filed under "K")].

27 March 1931
1. An incidental effect of this appointment was to
deepen Ferenczi's sense of isolation within the
movement. Radó had just turned down a post in
Philadelphia that Ferenczi had offered him (the post
had initially been offered to Ferenczi), without telling
him he was going to New York. When Freud told
Ferenczi about Radó's other appointment, Ferenczi
was upset: he felt that as potential president of the
international society he should have been kept
informed. At the same time he blamed himself for his
situation.
Bonin, p.258.
Freud-Radó 20.3.1931 [FM].
Freud-Eitingon 3.4.1931 [FM].
Freud-Radó 11.5.1927 [FM].

12 April 1931 (Tansley)
Freud-Jones 6.4.1922 [Inst of PsA: CFG/F03/06].

12 April 1931 (Ernstl)
Freud-Ernst Freud 21.4.1931 [LoC].
W. Ernest Freud-Molnar 6.8.1989 [FM].

14 April 1931
Pichler Notes, 14.4.1931 [FM].
Schur, 424–5.

15 April 1931
Thomas, Hugh, The Spanish Civil War, Penguin, 1986
[1961], p.32.
Freud, S., [ed. Walter Boehlich], Jugendbriefe an
Eduard Silberstein 1871–1881, Fischer, Frankfurt/
Main, 1989, pp.231–2.

22 April 1931
Romm, pp.49–52.
Freud-Eitingon 21.4.1931 [FM].
Sterba, pp.104–5.

24 April 1931
1. Pichler reported after the operation:
"Evening: some drowsiness as during operation.
Temporary confusion. Pulse good. Fluids can be
drunk without difficulty. 24.4. Patient feels well, of
course in pain, catches himself attempting to remove
prosthesis. Still, pain does not appear intolerable."
Cathrin Pichler-Molnar 22.8.1988 [FM].
Schur, 428.
Freud-Eitingon 7.5.1931 [FM].
Pichler Notes, 23–24.4.1931 [FM].

5 May 1931
Freud-Eitingon 7.5.1931 [FM] ("Nach Hause habe ich
eine eigenartige Müdigkeit oder Erschöpfung

mitgebracht . . . ")
Freud-Jones 2.6.1931 [Typescript Inst. of PsA] ("Die
letzte Erkrankung hat die Sicherheit aufgehoben, die
ich durch 8 Jahre genossen.").
Schur, 428.

6 May 1931
1. Eitingon, who for the first time was not present at
a birthday, sent a check for 20,000 M to pay off a
loan due to Storfer. He also sent another check for
15,000 M and one for 20,00 Swiss francs, both for
Freud himself, since he had borne approximately half
the debts of the press. More than 50,000 M had now
been collected to help rescue the press: this sum was
presented to Freud as a birthday gift.
Freud-Eitingon 7.5.1931 [FM] ("Ich war sehr froh am
Geburtstag zu Hause zu sein, es war leichter und
schöner für meine geplagten Pflegerinnen. Der Tag ist
übrigens erfreulich verlaufen . . . ").
Wolf-Jofie-Tattoun "Als Überraschung . . . " 6.5.1931
[FM: SOH9–3].
Freud-Marie Bonaparte 6.5.1931 in Jones, III.169.
Eitingon-Freud 9.5.1931 [SFC].
Int. J. PsA, Vol. XII. Part 4, 1931, p.508.

9 May 1931
1. The 1919 edition of the Interpretation of Dreams
mentions a paper of Pötzl's on the experimental
arousal of dream imagery. During the 1920s Pötzl
taught at Prague University and in 1926 he published
a psychoanalytical study of the déjà-vu phenomenon.
Pötzl had been an assistant to Wagner von Jauregg.
Afterwards he was to be Jauregg's successor as
Chairman of the Department of Psychiatry at the
University of Vienna. He devoted himself to
neuropathology during these later years, but never
lost his enthusiasm for psychoanalysis and remained a
member of the Vienna Psychoanalytical Society. In
1937 he told Freud: "My own researches, which I
cannot boast of being more than an honest
investigation of pathological data in the brain, - the
results of which are perhaps not worth the effort -
have only brought me constantly to the borderland of
psycho-analysis. The teaching I do, however, I cannot
imagine without psycho-analysis; in it I and my
audience are your enthusiastic followers!" (Pötzl-Freud
15.11.1937). After the Anschluss, when Freud was
under threat from the Nazis, Pötzl was one of those
who used his influence to try to assist him.
2. Theodor Gomperz had edited John Stuart Mill's
collected writings in German and employed Freud in
1879 as one of his translators, at a time when Freud
was badly in need of money. In 1892 Gomperz's wife,
Elise, was treated hypnotically by Freud. In 1900 she
tried to use her influence to gain Freud's promotion
to the rank of Professor Extraordinarius.
Pötzl, Otto, "Experimentell erregte Traumbilder in
ihren Beziehungen zum indirekten Sehen," Z. ges.
Neurol. Psychiat. 37, 278.
S.E., IV.181–2.
Schur, 497.
Wortis, Joseph, "Fragments of an Analysis" in
Ruitenbeek, H.M., Freud as we knew him, Detroit,
1973, p.286.
Eissler, Kurt, Freud und Wagner-Jauregg vor der
Kommission zur Erhebung militärischer
Pflichtverletzungen, Vienna, 1979, p.299 note 71.
Masson, p.388 n.3.
Pötzl-Freud 15.11.1937 in Jones, III.229–30.

1 June 1931
Freud-Eitingon 1.6.1931 [FM] ("Es ist nicht bequem,
sich in die Hinterlassenschaft eines Kenners u
Sammlers von alten Möbeln u österr. Folklore
hineinzusetzen, aber es ist gegangen und manche
Stücke der neuen Einpassung werden Ihnen sicherlich
gefallen. Jedenfalls, wenn ich meine Thüre öffne, bin
ich in einem weitläufigen parkartigen Garten, der zur
Sicherheit unserer morgen erwarteten Wolf u Jofi
durch einen Zaun geteilt ist. Akazien duften noch,
Linden fangen eben an, Amseln u Lerchen gehen oder
fliegen spazieren, kein Lautsprecher oder
Autogehuppe stört die Ruhe. Man könnte hier sehr
wol sein. Ich bin es natürlich nicht. Meine Kräfte
sind noch nicht beisammen, die Wunde noch nicht
ganz geheilt, die Prothese noch nicht definitiv

aufgebaut. Ich gebe wieder fünf Stunden.").

3 June 1931
Freud-Meine Lieben 18.9.1929 [FM] (" . . . stark
meschugge, ganz unzugänglich, von der Überzeugung
beherrscht, dass sie sich umbringen muss und
thöricht genug die Mittel dazu von anderen zu
verlangen.")
Young-Bruehl, p.193.

6 June 1931
Translation list [FM: I-F8–17–29].

6 June 1931
Swales-Molnar 21.4.1990 [FM].
Fichtner-Molnar 21.5.1990 [FM].
Jones, I.99–101.

13/15 June 1931
1. This letter to Eitingon deserves quoting fairly
fully: "I too do not say it very often, but I never
forget what you in your quiet and thus irresistible
way have achieved over these years, even after the
founding of your exemplary Berlin Institute, for our
cause which is also unconditionally yours. Nobody
apart from me knows this and perhaps nobody
thanks you for it. For there has been no task too
difficult or thankless for you to have taken it on
during your time as president and to have effectively
dealt with it. My dearest wish would be to see you as
president for life in order to assure the future of my
child of tribulation, the International Society and the
press. In a sense I imagine that you have done all this
for me and am therefore tempted, because there is no
rational reason for it, to treasure it more than
anything. Is it not true that our heartfelt harmony has
never been seriously troubled?" (*Freud-Eitingon June
1931*).
Freud-Eitingon 12.5.1931 [FM] (" . . . dass er in allem,
was er beginnt, tüchtig u zuverlässig ist.")
Freud-Eitingon June 1931 [FM] ("Auch ich sage es ja
nicht oft, aber ich vergesse nie daran, was Sie in
diesen Jahren auch nach der Gründung des
mustergiltigen Berliner Instituts für unsere Sache, die
ja uneingeschränkt die Ihre ist, in Ihrer stillen und
dabei unwiderstehlichen Art geleistet haben, Niemand
ausser mir weiss es und niemand vielleicht dankt
Ihnen dafür. Es gab doch keine noch so schwierige
und undankbare Aufgabe, die Sie in der Zeit Ihrer
Präsidentschaft nicht auf Sich genommen und -
glücklich erledigt hätten. Am liebsten sähe ich Sie als
Präsident auf Lebenszeit, um die Zukunft meines
Schmerzenskindes, der Internationalen Vereinigung
und des Verlags zu sichern. Einigermassen, bilde ich
mir ein, haben Sie das Alles auch meinetwegen
gethan, was man grade darum, weil es keinen
vernünftigen Grund hat, am meisten zu schätzen
versucht ist. Unser herzliches Einvernehmen - nicht
wahr? - war auch niemals ernsthaft getrübt.").

20/23 June 1931
1. After the birth of Ernst's third son, Freud wrote
to him: "So now you too have three sons and soon
you will also be able to be dissatisfied that you hear
so little from one or the other of them." (*Freud-Ernst
11.5.1924*).
Freud-Ernst Freud 11.5.1924 [LoC] ("Jetzt hast du also
auch drei-Söhne u bald wirst du auch unzufrieden
sein können, dass du von dem einem anderen [sic] so
wenig erfährst").

28 June 1931
1. In his autobiography Martin Freud summarizes the
situation and gives his own opinion of Storfer as
manager of the press: " The period of the world
economic crisis in 1933 saw father's publishing press
in serious difficulties. This firm, established in 1918
with the help of a generous donation, had lost money
continuously, not only depriving father of all income
from his writings, but also threatening to use up his
savings. A crisis in the business side of the press
risked the discrediting of psychoanalysis in the eyes
of the world.
    "The manager of the press had great artistic talent,
His deep devotion to his employer allowed his
friends to regard him in an amiable light, but did not
permit them to place much dependence on his

business ability. Financial considerations were alien to
him. If he needed money he borrowed it; when a
debt became due he endeavoured to prolong it or
borrowed from someone else to meet it. Father
appreciated all this, but the man was dependent on
him and all he would say was 'Lass ihn machen!' -
'Let him carry on.' "
Ferenczi-Eitingon 31.5.1931 [FM: Copy in
"Freud-Ferenczi Correspondence"].
Freud-Eitingon 20.3.1931 & 16.4.1931 [FM].
Ferenczi-Freud/Eitingon/Anna Freud 30.11.1930 [FM].
Martin Freud, pp.199–200.

28 June 1931
1. A *bon mot*, ascribed to Freud's tarock partner
Julius Schnitzler, refers to the pleasures of this card
game (in contrast to *Civilization and its Discontents*) as
"contentment in the uncivilization" (*Behagen in der
Unkultur*).
Eissler, K.R., quoted in Romm, p.5.
Leupold-Loewenthal, Harald: "Das Behagen in der
Unkultur (1930:1984)," *Sigmund Freud House Bulletin*,
Vol.8/No.2 Winter, 1984, p.2.

14 July 1931
Anna Freud-Eva Rosenfeld n.d. [FM: Typescript P.
Heller] ("Papa spielt Karten und mann kann durchs
Fenster hineinschauen und draussen geht ein Wind
und kühlt die schreckliche Hitze ab. Ein Bildhauer
war den ganzen Tag da und hat ein Bild von Papa für
sein Geburtshaus in Freiberg gemacht. Es ist sehr
ähnlich geworden.").

19 July 1931
Swales-Molnar 21.4.19 [FM]) (With thanks to Peter
Swales).

23 July 1931 (Rie)
Swales-Molnar 21.4.1990 [FM].

23 July 1931 (Hoop)
1. According to Jones, van der Hoop's study of
psychoanalysis was either incomplete or did not
involve a personal analysis. He complained to Anna
Freud in 1934: "Van der Hoop is completely
unanalysed and more Jungian than Jung." (*Jones-Anna
Freud 25.11.1934*).
Lindebroom (Ed), *Dutch Medical Biography*.
Jones-Anna Freud 25.11.1934 [Inst. of PsA:
CFA/FO2/18].

24 July 1931
1. According to the sculptor, Freud had initially been
distant. The first words he spoke to him were "I am
sure that you know your profession is the oldest in
the world." When the sculptor expressed surprise
Freud added "Did not God create man from clay?".
Freud-Eitingon 3.8.1931 [FM] (" . . . macht jemand
eine Büste von mir, ein Bildhauer Oscar Neumann
aus Brüssel, seinem Gesicht nach ein slavischer
Ostjude, Chazare oder Kalmük udgl. Federn hat ihn
mir aufgedrängt, der sonst eine höchst unglückliche
Hand im Aufspüren von noch unerkannten Genies
hat. Diesmal aber etwas daran oder eher viel. Der
Kopf, den der hagere ziegenbärtige Künstler aus
Dreck - wie der liebe Gott - geformt hat, ist sehr gut
und einem Eindruck von mir überraschend ähnlich.
Wie er das Werk verwerten will, verschweigt er, ich
habe es ja nicht bei ihm bestellt.")
Meng, H. "Freud and the Sculptor" in Ruitenbeek,
H.M., *Freud as we knew him*, Detroit, 1973, p.351.

24 July 1931 (Graf)
1. The other portrait, that of an older bearded man,
had been bought before 1922, for 600 florins. Both
are well documented, in Buberl, the standard
catalogue of the Graf collection, which Freud had in
his library.
Reeves, C.N. in *Freud and Art*, p.78.
Buberl, P., *Die griechisch-aegyptischen Mumienbildnisse
der Sammlung Th. Graf*, Vienna, 1922.
Parlasca, K., *Repertorio d'arte dell'Egitto greco-romano.
Serie B - Vol. II. Ritratti di mummie*, Rome 1977.

24 July 1931
Lange, H-W, *Family Tree* [FM].
Freud-Ernst Freud 24.8.1930 [LoC].

24 July 1931 (Congress)
Int. J. PsA, Vol. XII. Part 4, 1931, p.508.
Jones, III.171.
Freud-Eitingon 3.8.1931 [FM] ("Wenn wir einen guten
Anlass haben, die Veröffentlichung des Buches der
Melanie Klein aufzuschieben und endlich von uns zu
weisen, sollten wir ihn wirklich nützen. Ich bin durch
die Rücksicht auf Anna in der Parteinahme gehemmt,
aber in den letzten Studien über die Entwicklung des
weiblichen Kindes, habe ich doch die Überzeugung
erwerben müssen, dass die Resultate der Klein'schen
Spieltechnik irreführend und ihre Folgerungen
unrichtig sind. Wir brauchen uns dafür wirklich nicht
einzusetzen.").

26 July 1931
Freud-Martha Bernays 21.10.1885 & 19.6.1884 in
Letters.

28 July 1931
1. In 1911 Forel sent Freud the 6th edition of his
Hypnotismus. Freud respected Forel and was
correspondingly annoyed by Forel's "feeble-minded"
('*schwachsinnig*') arguments against psychoanalysis. He
wrote to Ferenczi:
"His arguments, e.g., against sexuality, are truly
depressing for a man who has written a thick book
on the sexual question." (*Freud-Ferenczi 21.5.1911*).
Bonin, pp.97–8.
Freud-Ferenczi 21.5.1911 [FM] ("Seine Argumente zB.
gegen die Sexualität sind wirklich betrübend für einen
Mann, der ein dickes Buch über die sexuelle Frage
geschrieben hat.").

31 July 1931
Romm, pp.100–1.
Freud-Eitingon 3.8.1931 [FM] ("Er ist ein sehr
vertrauenerweckender scheuer Mann mit einem
Lächeln wie Charlie Chaplin.").

1 August 1931 (Anna)
Anna Freud-Ferenczi 29.7.1931 [FM: in
"Freud-Ferenczi Correspondence"] ("Jetzt kann man
es sich wenigstens gönnen, müde zu sein.").

1 August 1931 (Prosthesis)
Freud-Eitingon 3.8.1931 [FM] ("Und jetzt hat sich das
Unglaubliche ereignet! In 1 1/2 Tagen—Freitag und
Samstag—heute ist Montag, hat der Zauberer eine
provisorische Prothese fertig gebracht, die nur *halb* so
gross und schwer ist wie meine früheren, mit der ich
kauen, reden und rauchen kann, mindestens ebenso
gut wie bisher. "
Freud-Eitingon 3.8.1931 [FM] ("Keine Sicherheit, alle
bisherigen Bemühungen und Versprechungen sind
doch nur in Enttäuschung ausgelaufen.").
Eitingon-Freud 5.8.1931 [Telegram: SFC].

7 August 1931
Freud-Abraham 21.7.1925 in *Letters*, p.362.
Freud-Ferenczi 16.7.1924 & 6.8.1924 [FM].
Freud-Fliess 20.6.1898 in Masson.

10 August 1931
1. Ruth certainly *offered* to pay the doctor's fees, but
Freud refused and paid them himself (*Freud-Ernst
Freud 30.8.1931*). However, they may have shared
travel and incidental expenses.
In his notes Pichler claims "American friends" paid
for the treatment: a footnote from Anna Freud insists
Freud paid himself. Schur's footnote to her footnote
claims Dr. Brunswick paid it "mainly" (Pichler Notes,
8.9.1931). In his 1958 interview with Dr. Eissler,
Kazanjian speaks of Ruth Brunswick as having paid
his income.
Freud-Ernst Freud 30.8.1931 [LoC] (" . . . mit Frau
und Tochter gleichsam an der Leine . . . .").
Freud- Lampl-de Groot 11.8.1931 [FM] ("Durch die
vieljährigen Quälerei mürbe gemacht . . . .").
Pichler Notes, 8.9.1931 [FM].
Kasanjian [sic]: Interview Dr. K. Eissler 26.10.1958
[Transcript LoC].

13 August 1931
W. Ernest Freud-Molnar 6.8.1989 [FM].

25 August 1931
1. Eitingon's letter is dated August 26. Freud may

have heard about the closure by telephone on August 25 (the day of the decision and of his diary entry) from one of the participants at the meeting—Ernst Simmel or Eva Rosenfeld. Otherwise this entry was filled in retrospectively.
Eitingon-Freud 26.8.1931 [SFC].
Hier geht . . . pp.46–9.

27 August 1931
Freud-Eitingon 8.8.1931 [FM] ("Die schwere Hitze der letzten Woche hat mein Allgemeinbefinden nicht günstig beeinflusst.").
Neue Freie Presse, 27.8.1931.
Anna Freud-Eva Rosenfeld n.d. [FM: Typescript P.Heller] ("Ich liege heute schon im Garten, in Dorothys grünem Schubkarren und versuche, wieder gesund zu sein. Jetzt habe ich keine erhöhte Temperatur und wenn sie Nachmittag nicht wiederkommt, dann ist es vielleicht vorbei. Der Hals ist noch nicht ganz frei und die Galle, die ein bischen gereizt war, auch noch nicht vollständig, aber im Ganzen ist mir viel besser. Komisch ist das Ganze.").

28 August 1931
1. Two years later she demonstratively resigned from the Prussian Academy of Arts when the president, von Schilling, required members to refuse to engage in any open political opposition to the regime. She explained her resignation as a protest against the suppression of free speech rather than against the upsurge of German nationalism.
Bergschicker, p.100.

29 August 1931
1. Kazanjian later claimed that changes in the device required modification and said: "I doubt that the physicians in Vienna performed those changes adequately."
Freud-Eitingon 30.8.1931 [FM] ("Der Zauberer hat mich gestern verlassen. Ich befinde mich nicht gar grossartig, immerhin ist die Sprache besser. Von der Gewöhnung an das neue Stück soll ich weitere Fortschritte erwarten. Es scheint nicht möglich mehr bei mir auszurichten.").
Freud-Marie Bonaparte 18.9.1931 in Schur, 560.
Freud-Eitingon 27.10.1931 in Schur, 560.
Pichler Notes, Sept.-Dec. 1931 [FM].
Kasanjian [sic]: Interview Dr. K. Eissler, 26.10.1958 [Transcript LoC].

1 September 1931
Freud-Marie Bonaparte 18.9.1931 in Schur, 430.
Freud-Ernst Freud 20.9.1931 [LoC].

2 September 1931
1. A letter to Jung indicates that Freud probably placed himself in the narcissistic-obsessional category: "If a healthy man like you regards himself as a hysterical type, I can only claim for myself the 'obsessional' type, each specimen of which vegetates in a sealed-off world of his own." (*Freud-Jung 2.9.1907*).
S.E., XXI.217–220.
Freud-Jung 2.9.1907 in McGuire, William (Ed.) *The Freud/Jung Letters,* London, 1979 [1974].

7 September 1931
1. Another opportunity was the Rosenwald Fund. Its director E.R. Embree was interested in psychoanalysis and willing to finance the analysis of criminals, which was Alexander's speciality. Alexander wanted to discuss with Freud this possibility of opening a psychoanalytical institute in the United States. Earlier that year he had told Freud: "Resistance here is naiver and less malicious than in Europe . . . ." (*Alexander-Freud 18.1.1931*)
Alexander-Freud 6.7.1931 [FM: SOH9–17].
Embree, Edwin J., & Waxman, Julia, *Investment in People: The Story of the Julius Rosenwald Fund,* New York, 1949.
Alexander-Freud 18.1.1931 [FM: SOH9–17] ("Der Widerstand ist hier naiver und weniger boshaft, als in Europa . . . .").

11 September 1931
Freud-Eitingon 27.1.1931 [FM].
Eitingon-Freud 29.5.1931, 26.8.1931, 14.10.1931 [SFC].

12 September 1931
Bertin, p.183.

13 September 1931 (Nunberg)
Nunberg, Herman, *Memoirs: Recollections, Ideas, Reflections,* N.Y., 1969, p.57.
Young-Bruehl, pp.193, 200.

13 September 1931 (Putsch)
Stadler, Karl R., *Austria,* London, 1971, pp.132–3.
Schuschnigg, Kurt v., *The Brutal Takeover,* London, 1971, pp.55–6.

13 September 1931 (Eitingon)
Eitingon-Storfer 26.10.1931 [SFC].

17 September 1931 (Rie)
1. Three weeks later Freud's niece Lilly Marlé sent him an album of family photos, among which he was glad to discover two pictures of himself together with Oskar Rie—the only ones he possessed.
Freud-Marie Bonaparte 18.9.1931 in Schur, 430.
Freud-Ernst Freud 20.9.1931 [LoC].
Freud-Lilly Marlé 12.10.1931 [LoC].

17 September 1931 (Emden)
1. Despite friendship, he might have slightly overstayed his welcome in that instance. Freud wrote to Ernst: "Emden has been sharing our meals for the same period [a week], is a bit of a burden for us all." (*Freud-Ernst Freud 10.8.1929*).
Jones, II.89, 95.
Freud-Ernst Freud 10.8.1929 [LoC] ("Emden theilt seit ebensolang [eine Woche] unsere Malzeiten, lastet ein wenig auf uns allen.").

18 September 1931
Nunberg, Herman, *Memoirs: Recollections, Ideas, Reflections,* N.Y., 1969, p.57.

26 September 1931
1. Freud officially registered himself resident at Berggasse 19 on September 23, 1891. However, he had already been living there at least eleven days, for on September 12 he wrote to his sister-in-law: "We are now living at IX Berggasse 19 after many troubles." (*Freud-Minna Bernays 12.9.1891*).
Freud-Eitingon 3.8.1931 [FM] (" . . . ein in dieser Zeit kaum erlaubtes Idyll.").
Freud-Eitingon 3.8.1931 [FM] ("Zur Freude in Poetzldf tragen—lachen Sie nicht—unsere Hunde sehr viel bei, die ihre Freiheit im Garten intensiv geniessen. Meine Jofi ist ein entzückendes Wesen, eine Erholung gegen die meisten menschlichen Besucher, ihr schwarzer Sohn ein erfreulicher Schelm. Ich mag mir den Sommer ohner diese Thiere nicht mehr vorstellen.").
Freud-Fliess 17.8.1891 & 11.9.1891 in Masson.
Berggasse 19, Visiting card: 1891 [FM: I/F8–73].
Freud-Minna Bernays 12.9.1891 [LoC] ("Wir wohnen jetzt IX Berggasse 19 nach vielen Mühen.").

30 September 1931 (Female)
1. Freud had been working on this theme at least a year. In a letter of September 1930 to Viereck, Freud states that he was just at that time working on a version of femininity that would be "as distant from the poetical as from the pseudo-science of Hirschfeld." (*Freud-Viereck 21.9.1930*) The essay was published in German later in 1931 (in the *Internationale Zeitschrift für Psychoanalyse*) and in English the following year.
2. The different approaches of Anna Freud and Melanie Klein (or the Viennese and English psychoanalytical societies in general) is one of the concerns behind *Female Sexuality.* In 1928 Freud wrote to Jones: "The more I find out about these things, the more I believe that Melanie Klein has taken a false track and Anna the right one. "Everything we know about female early development seems to me unsatisfactory and uncertain." (*Freud-Jones 22.2.1928*).
The correspondence following the publication of *Female Sexuality* aired these differences. Jones implied Freud might now be in danger of undervaluing the father as he had previously undervalued the role of the mother. Freud replied that there was risk of this—he had simply been concerned with stages of

development before the father plays any role. He criticized the Kleinians for ignoring chronology and Jones for distinguishing between "clitoridic" and "phallic" stages, the two being identical for Freud. "Some Psychical Consequences of the Anatomical Distinction between the Sexes" S.E., XIX.243. "Female Sexuality" S.E., XXI.221.
Freud-Viereck 21.9.1930 [Brill Library] (" . . . von der poetischen ebenso weit entfernt ist wie von der pseudowissenschaftlichen Hirschfelds.").
Freud-Jones 22.2.1928 [Typescript Inst. of PsA] ("Je mehr ich von den Dingen erfahre, desto mehr glaube ich, dass Melanie Klein einen falschen Weg geht und Anna den richtigen.
"Alles was wir von der weiblichen Frühentwicklung wissen, kommt mir unbefriedigend und unsicher vor.").
Jones-Freud 10.1.1932 [Inst. of PsA].
Freud-Jones 23.1.1932 [Typescript Inst. of PsA].
Jones-Freud 12.2.1932 [Inst. of PsA].

30 September 1931 (Rickman)
Jones-Freud 15.11.1931 & 2.6.1932 [Inst. of PsA].

4 October 1931
"Obituary," *Int. J. PsA,* 1960.
Young-Bruehl, pp.95–6.

5 October 1931
1. Martin Freud writes of one of Freud's puppies dying of a disease that decimated the Austrian dog population: "No expense was spared and everything possible was done to save his [Freud's] pets. Their loss caused much grief."
2. The canine record is confused, for the chows' names (variously spelled) are all recycled on new dogs. On the Freuds' passage through Paris in June 1938, the chow Lün (named after their first chow) met and hid from the Bonapartes' much larger Tattoun. Subsequently several generations of Hampstead chows were to be named Jofi.
H.D., p.166.
Freud-Eitingon 3.8.1931 [FM].
Bertin, pp.174, 192.
Martin Freud, p.191.

6 October 1931
Hansford, S.H., *A Glossary of Chinese Art and Archaeology,* London, 1961.
Reischauer, Edwin O., & Fairbank, John K., *East Asia: The Great Tradition,* Boston, 1958 & 1960, pp.144–5.
Spinks' evaluation [FM].
Engelman, Plate 25.

8 October 1931
Psychoanalytic Pioneers, p.150.

9 October 1931
1. The financial restrictions did little to alleviate the crisis. By December 1931 the National Bank could cover only 25 per cent of circulating money: foreign capital was withdrawn and production continued to fall. Meanwhile, the business of the International Psychoanalytical Press suffered under these restrictions. In addition, Freud's important income from foreign analysands was diminished by adverse exchange rates.
Wiener Zeitung, 10.10.1931.
Kitchen, Martin, *The Coming of Austrian Fascism,* Montreal, 1980, pp.92–3.

12 October 1931
Leaflet of Freud House [FM: AF I/F8–58].

15 October 1931 (Minna)
Freud-Ernst Freud 20.9.1931 [LoC] ("Tante Minna hat in Meran die Sonne angetroffen, die wir hier nicht zu sehen bekommen.").

15 October 1931
Portal, Jane, in *Freud and Art,* p.126.

17 October 1931
Anna Freud-Ernst Freud 22.11.1931 [FM: Lucie Freud Papers] ("Ich habe grosse Freude an dem Bau und es tut mir nur schrecklich leid, dass ich nicht täglich draussen sein kann und alles mitmachen.").

Anna Freud - Lou Andreas-Salomé 22.10.1930 in Pfeiffer, p.286.
Young-Bruehl, p.191.
gestanden - und hat mich auch in dieses Land her begleitet.").
Letters, p.460.
Letter list 1938–9 [FM].

25 October 1931
1. In his letter to his English nephew Sam Freud, brother of his first playmate John, Freud wrote more enthusiastically about the honor:
"Think what a treat it would have been for your grandfather and your father to witness that ceremony! But of course grandfather had to be 116 years at the time! I do not appreciate old age, I have no reason to do so!" (*Freud-Sam Freud 1.12.1931*).
In 1990 Freiberg (Příbor) also decided to rename its main square after Freud.
S.E., XXI.259.
Freud-Eitingon 27.10.1931 [FM] ("Ich stelle mir nach einigen Andeutungen vor, dass die guten Freiberger in Unkennntnis meiner Stellung in der Welt sich einen überreichen Besuch aus aller Herren Länder erwartet hatten.").
Eitingon-Freud 27.10.1931 [FM].
Federn, Paul, "Freud Amongst Us" in Ruitenbeek, H.M., *Freud as we knew him*, Detroit, 1973, p.218.
Freud-Sam Freud 1.12.1931 [FM].
Stadlen, Anthony, Oral communication 24.9.1990.

28 October 1931 (Ferenczi)
Freud-Eitingon 1.11.1931 [FM] ("Ferenczi habe ich in den drei Tagen seines Aufenthalts viel gesehen. Am ersten war er zurückhaltend verstopft, hatte auch die dem entsprechende Darmstörung, am zweiten fühlte er sich entspannt ('relaxirt') und hörte mich ruhig an, während ich ihm so ziehmlich alles sagte, was ich ihm zu sagen hatte, am dritten antwortete er mit seiner gewohnten Bonhommie und Aufrichtigkeit. Da er aber auf einen gewissen Punkt, seine persönliche Entfremdung von mir, nicht einging, bin ich über die Lokalisation der Störung ziemlich orientirt. [. . .]. Von den Gefahren seiner Technik abgesehen, thut es mir leid, ihn auf einem Weg zu wissen, der wissenschaftlich wenig fruchtbar sein dürfte. Das Wesentliche scheint mir aber doch seine neurotisch bestimmte Regression zu sein. Es ist aber mit den Menschen nicht anders. Was kann man da machen?").
Freud-Ferenczi 13.12.1931 [FM] ("Aber da Sie die zärtliche Mutterrolle gern gegen andere spielen, dann vielleicht auch gegen sich selbst. Und dann sollen Sie von brutaler väterlicher Seite die Mahnung hören, dass—nach meiner Erinnerung - die Neigung zu sexueller Spielerei mit Pat. Ihnen in voranalytischer Zeit nicht fremd war, so dass man die neue Technik mit der alten Verfehlung in Zusammenhang bringen könnte. Daher sprach ich in meinem früheren Brief von einer neuen Pubertät . . . .").
Freud-Eitingon 18.4.1932 [FM].
Ferenczi-Freud 5.12.1931 [FM].

28 October 1931 (Martin)
Martin Freud-Jones 5.12.1952 [Inst. of PsA CFB/FO3/O8].
Eitingon-Storfer 26.10.1931 [FM].
Eitingon-Freud 29.10.1931 [FM].

29 October 1931
Freud-Eitingon 1.11.1931 [FM] ("Mein Zimmer ist mir gegenwärtig unheimlich, es beherbergt ausser mir drei Köpfe auf hohen Säulen, die mir ähnlich sein wollen, unter denen ich zu wälen habe . . . ").
Freud-Federn 1.11.1931 [SFC] (" . . . die mit ihren lebendigen und freundlichen Ausdruck ein angenehmer Zimmergenosse zu werden verspricht.").

31 October 1931 (Holzknecht)
1. Holzknecht's obituary in the *Neue Freie Presse* (31.10.1931) called him "a modern Mucius Scaevola" (referring to the Roman hero who burnt away his own right hand). A year after his death a monument was unveiled to him in the Bürgerpark in Vienna.
Neue Freie Presse, 31.10.1931.

31 October 1931 (Nepenthe)
Fichtner-Molnar 21.5.1990 [FM] (With thanks to Professor G. Fichtner for suggesting this plant.)

31 October 1931 (Jeanne)
Freud- Lampl-de Groot 29.11.1931 [FM].

5/6 November 1931
Freud-Eitingon 15.11.1931 [FM] ("Wenn ich von mir selbst reden soll, ich habe mehr gehabt als eine einfache Magenverstimmung, es war eine arge Magendarmrebellion—unbekannt woher—in deren Verlauf ein mehrstündiger Kolonkrampf mich sogar zwang, eine Analysenstunde plötzlich abzubrechen, was mir bisher nur einmal im Leben zur Not geworden war.").
Freud, Anna, *Photograph Album* [FM: IN 632] ("Die Aussicht, die immer gleich schön ist, im Frühling, Sommer und Herbst. Winter ist noch nicht ausprobiert. 8 Nov. 1932.).
ibid [FM: IN 633] ("Der leere Armstuhl unter dem Sonnenschirm wartet auf jemanden, der sich in ihm niederlässt. 8 Nov. 1932.).

10 November 1931
Rice, Emanuel, *Freud and Moses: The Long Journey Home*, Albany N.Y., 1990 pp.207–8 n.3.
Kürschners Deutscher Gelehrten-Kalender 1931 (With thanks to Prof. Dr. G. Fichtner for this reference).

18 November 1931
"Obituary" [by Ernst Federn] *Sigmund Freud House Bulletin*, Vol.4/No.2 Winter, 1980, p.57.
Freud- Lampl-de Groot 20.5.1931 [FM].
Anna Freud-Ernst Freud 22.11.1931 [FM: Lucie Freud Papers].
Freud- Lampl-de Groot 29.11.1931 [FM] ("Ich war selbst in mehrfacher Weise leidend u wir waren alle schwer in Anspruch genommen durch die gefährliche Erkrankung, von Marianne Kris' neugeborener Tochter - an Melaena neonatorum. Jetzt ist das Kind durch eine Bluttransfusion gerettet worden u ich selbst wieder soweit wol um schreiben zu können.").

21 November 1931 (Bleuler)
1. The conquest of the Swiss was the first great step out of the ghetto of Jewish Viennese culture. Freud experienced it as a breakthrough and wrote to Jung in 1906: "I must own that whenever a work such as yours or Bleuler's appears it gives me the great and to me indispensable satisfaction of knowing that the hard work of a lifetime has not been entirely in vain." (*Freud-Jung 7.10.1906*).
Bonin, p.49.
Freud-Jung 7.10.1906 in McGuire, William (Ed.,) *The Freud/Jung Letters*, London, 1979 [1974].
Bleuler-Freud 17.5.1925 [LoC] ("Ihre *wesentlichen* Theorien waren für mich selbstverständlich . . . .").
Bleuler-Freud 7.12.1931 [LoC].
Binswanger, Ludwig, *Erinnerungen an Sigmund Freud*, Bern, 1956, p.104.

21 November 1931 (Martin)
Freud- Lampl-de Groot 29.11.1931 [FM] ("Sie wissen von Martin's Besuch in Berlin. Ja, den Tagen hatte ich also in dieser Stadt drei gesunde und arbeitsfähige Söhne von denen keiner einen Heller erwerben kann. Heitere Zeiten.").

22 November 1931 (Oppenheimer)
Exhibition Catalogue, "The Freud Centenary Exhibit," May 1956, pp.74–5 [FM: IV/F29–51].
Weiss, Edoardo "Paul Federn" in *Psychoanalytic Pioneers*, pp.142.
Fichtner-Molnar 21.5.1990 [FM] (With thanks to Prof. G. Fichtner for suggesting Carl Oppenheimer).

22 November 1931 (Prometheus)
S.E., XXI.90.
Schaeffer, Albrecht, "Der Mensch und das Feuer," *Psychoanal. Beweg.*, Vol.2. 201.
S.E., XXII.187–193.

29 November 1931
1. It is possible there was some sort of contact between Freud and Tandler during the days following this entry, for Tandler wrote a private memorandum,

titled and dated 'Freud 9.XII.31', giving his view of Freud's character and personality. The following extracts from this document show how deep and complex an impression Freud could make:
"The level of the drives is of unprecedented strength in him, this person is never free of his drive. Even in a spiritual state of mind he is not free of drives. [. . .].
"A hard person. It is uncanny in such an old man, this vital strength, this sexual strength, this saturation of his vessels with sap. This person is so rooted in his physical being that the intellect has repeatedly to find points of contact with the physical. That must be expressed in his intellectual work. [. . .].
"He is a person who is only accountable to his own law, who only lives according to its direction and who cannot subordinate himself to rules. He is incapable of adapting to a mould because of his proportions. Without doubt a person who influences his time. If he were not a Jew he might be Bismarck."
Eissler, Ruth S., & Eissler, K.R., "A Letter by Freud to Professor Tandler (1931), *International Review of Psycho-Analysis*, Bd. 10, Nr. 1, S.1–11.
Neue Freie Presse, 29.11.1931 ("Hoffentlich finden sich viele, die sich ihrer sozialen Pflichten in einem so hohen Masse bewusst werden, wie dieser internationale Wiener Gelehrte.").
Freud, S., *Gesammelte Werke. Nachtragsband.*, Fischer, 1987, pp.718–9.
Sablik, Karl, "Sigmund Freud and Julius Tandler: eine rätselhafte Beziehung" *Sigmund Freud House Bulletin*, Vol 9/No.2, Winter 1985 p.17.
Federn, Ernst, "Die Beziehung ist nicht so rätselhaft" *Sigmund Freud House Bulletin*, Vol. 10/1, Summer 1986.
Freud-Tandler 8.3.1925 [FM: SFVAR]. (With thanks to Dr. Christine Diercks and Dr. Johannes Reichmayr for having brought to my attention information leading to this note.)

30 November 1931
Neue Freie Presse, 1.12.1931 (" . . . immer dieselbe und doch niemals dieselbe.").
Yvette Guilbert-Freud 2.12.1931 [FM].

3 December 1931 (Pearls)
1. A number of these poems from Martin to Anna on her various birthdays survive. Anna, too, wrote such *vers d'occasion* at times. On her father's birthdays Freud generally received a poem written by the dogs—with Anna's help. The earliest surviving example is the one attached to the picture of Anna's alsatian Wolf, presented to Freud on his 70th birthday in 1926.
Martin Freud-Anna Freud 3.12.1931 [FM].
"Wolf Photograph & Poem" [FM].

3 December 1931 (Ernst)
Martha Freud-Lucie Freud 2.1.1932 [FM: Lucie Freud Papers].
Freud-Ernst Freud 13.12.1931 [LoC].
Lucie Freud-Ernst Freud 7.1.1932 [FM: Lucie Freud Papers]. ("Sie sind die Treppen hinunter geflogen und gesprungen, dass mir angst und bange wurde.").

4 December 1931
Lou Andreas-Salomé -Freud (soon after 3 April 1931) in Pfeiffer.
Lou Andreas-Salomé - Freud mid-July 1931 in Pfeiffer.

9 December 1931
1. Freud's pleasure in the Vishnu was unfeigned. In a letter to Ernst he describes it as "delightful." But he was worried that the wood and ivory had developed cracks - perhaps the God could not stand the Viennese climate? It was still at the center of the desk in March 1933, as the American poet H.D. noticed at the start of her analysis, but by 1937 it had shifted to the left-hand corner.
Freud-Bose 13.12.1931 [FM: copy 1-F8–30].
Bose Freud Correspondence, Indian Psycho-Analytical Society, Calcutta-9, n.d. [FM: VI/F29–187].
Kakar, Sudhir "Considérations sur l'histoire et le développement de la psychanalyse en Inde," *Revue Internationale d'Histoire de la Psychanalyse* 2, 1989, pp.499–503.

Freud-Eitingon 14.12.1931 [FM].
Freud-H. Gomperz 21.1.1921 [FM: SFVAR 52] ("In indischen Dingen bin ich leider ebenso unwissend wie in philosophischen, wogegen aber nichts mehr zu machen ist.").
H.D., p.147.
Freud-Ernst Freud 13.12.1931 [LoC].

22 December 1931

1. Repeated references to translations indicate Freud's interest in the progress psychoanalysis was making worldwide. A year later he wrote to Marie Bonaparte: "The Scandinavians are of course hard-working folk but the most backward in their acceptance of analysis, far behind the Indians and the Japanese. (Yesterday I received the 12th volume of my Japanese translation.)" (Freud-Marie Bonaparte 21.12.1932).
Int. Z. Psa 1931 XVII. Heft 1. p.160.
Freud-Marie Bonaparte 21.12.1932 [FM: F8/CON 19] ["Die Skandinaver sind gewiss tüchtige Leute, aber in der Aufnahme der Analyse am meisten rückständig, weit hinter den Indern und Japanern. (Ich habe gestern den 12 ten Band meiner Japanischer Übersetzung erhalten.)"].

1932

1 January 1932 (Gastric)
Freud- Lampl-de Groot 17.1.1932 [FM] ("Mein Magen ist wieder in Bedienung u damit mein Allgemeinbefinden gebessert. Mit der Prothese kommt man nicht weiter. ").

1 January 1932 (Reich)

1. Reich continued to be a member of the I.P.A. until 1934, but in the interim was viewed by Freud and others as more and more of a danger to the psychoanalytic movement in general. In spring 1933 he briefly visited Vienna and gave talks at Communist meetings, in which political matters were discussed in psychological terms. Freud considered that in the unstable, proto-fascist political situation of Austria at that time, this was harmful and irresponsible. Anna commented: "My father's remark on this is: if psychoanalysis is to be forbidden, let it be forbidden as psychoanalysis, but not as the mixture of politics and analysis that Reich represents." (Anna Freud-Jones 27.4.1933).
Reich–Int. Z. Psa n.d. [1932] in Reich, W. Reich speaks of Freud, London, 1975 [1967], pp.134–7.
Reich, W., "Der masochistische Character," Int. Z. Psa, XVIII (1932).
Bernfeld, S., "Die kommunistische Diskussion um die Psychoanalyse und Reichs 'Wiederlegung der Todestriebhypothese'," Int. Z. Psa, XVIII (1932).
Freud-Ferenczi 24.1.1932 [FM] (" . . . in dem Unsinn gipfelte, was man für Todestrieb halte, sei die Tätigkeit des kapitalistischen Systems.").
Freud-Eitingon 9.1.1932 [FM] ("Ärgelich, eigentlich mehr als das, ist die Häufung der Erfahrung, dass mit immer mehr Leuten nichts zu machen ist. Bald der bald jener stellt sich als unbrauchbar oder unlenkbar heraus. Ferenczi's Beharren bei seiner bedenklichen Technik, Reich's und Fenichel's Versuch die Zeitschriften für bolschw. Propaganda zu misbrauchen [. . .] alles zeigt, dass unter dem ätzenden Einfluss dieser Zeiten sich die Charaktere rasch zersetzen.")
Anna Freud-Jones 27.4.1933 [Inst. of PsA: CFA/FO1/30] ("Der Ausspruch meines Vaters darüber ist: wenn die Psychoanalyse verboten wird, so soll sie als Psa. verboten werden, aber nicht als das Gemisch von Politik und Analyse, das Reich vertritt.").

16 January 1932 (Eitingon)
Freud- Lampl-de Groot 17.1.1932 [FM] ("Es scheint, dass uns dies gelungen ist, mit grossen Geldopfern allerdings, die nötig sind am Storfer's persönliche Schulden zu bezalen und ihn zum Verzicht auf seine Stellung zu bewegen. Seine Miswirtschaft hat alles ruinirt. So wertvoll er als Redakteur und geistiger Lector war, so unheimlich haben seine Narrheit, Unordentlichkeit und Grossmannsucht geschäftlich gewirkt.").
Eitingon-Freud 17.2.1932 & 19.6.1932 [FM].

16 January 1932 (Martin)
Martin Freud, pp.199–200.
Freud-Eitingon 19.1.1932 [FM] ("Mein armer Junge geht mit sorgenschweren Mienen herum, nimmt sich aber seiner Aufgabe tüchtig an. Storfer soll an ersten Tag nach seinem Sturz von tadelloser Gefügigkeit gewesen sein. Für wie lange? Martin hat ihm in wol berechneter Höflichkeit das Chefzimmer überlassen.").

Sun 17 January 1932 (Anna)
Freud-Ferenczi 24.1.1932 [FM].

17 January 1932 (Portuguese)
Translation list [FM: I-F8–17-32].
Freud, Cinco Lições de Psicanalise, São Paulo, n.d. [FM].

18 January 1932

1. As a farewell gift, after a visit the previous summer, Bullitt had given Freud ("unfortunately" for this was at a time Freud could not smoke) " . . . a

beautifully worked leather case with the finest Havanas." But, Freud added, "I can at least treat my guests." (Freud-Eitingon 25.7.1931).
Freud-Eitingon 19.1.1932, 12.2.1932, 25.7.1931 [FM].

26 January 1932
Jones, III.155.

30 January 1932
Freud- Lampl-de Groot 6.2.1932 [FM].
Freud-Eitingon 12.2.1932 [FM] ("Der Verlag hat bisher an Zuweisungen bekommen:
   M 5000 - bei Ihnen
   M 6000 - Beitrag von Ihnen
etwa S 6000 - Institutionsgelder, die in Wien vorhanden waren
   1000 - Sammlung von Brill
   1000 - Geschenk Dr. Edith Jackson
   200 - Alexander, Dr. Putnam, Boston
   2500 - von mir, die mein Mitarbeiter am Wilson-Buch von den erwarteten amerikan. royalties vorgestreckt hat.
Weitere $3000 halte ich bereit, um sie Martin allmälich für den Betrieb zufliessen zu lassen.").
Bonin, p.57.
Leupold-Loewenthal, Harald, Handbuch der Psychoanalyse, Wien, 1986, p.72.
Wessel, Morris A., "Edith B. Jackson M.D.," The Journal of Pediatrics, July 1978, p.165.

1 February 1932
Freud- Lampl-de Groot 6.2.1932 [FM] (" Anna hat sich auf dem Semmering rasch erholt, zu rasch eigentlich, ich hätte gewunscht, dass sie länger geblieben wäre. Es ist jetzt Mode die Grippe nach kurzem Intervall wieder zu bekommen.").

10 February 1932
Freud- Lampl-de Groot 2.3.1932 [FM].
Freud- Lampl-de Groot 18.2.1932 [FM] ("Ich trage mich mit dem Plan in Sommer Neue Vorlesungen als Ergänzung zur Einführung zu verfassen, die Gnade des Schicksals natürlich vorausgesetzt. Vielleicht werde ich für einige Kapitel Hilfe brauchen, Literatur, Vorschläge. Darf ich dabei auch auf Sie rechnen? Aber halten Sie die Sache vor allen geheim. Hier wissen nur Anna u Martin davon.").
Neue Vorlesungen (ms.) [LoC].

18 February 1932
Kosawa-Freud 15.4.1925 [LoC].
Earle, J. 19.1.1990 [FM: Fax].
Freud-Kosawa 20.2.1932 [LoC] (" . . . das schöne Bild, das mir vor Augen führt, worüber ich soviel gelesen habe und was mir selbst zu sehen nicht vergönnt war.")
Freud-Kosawa 16.3.1932 [LoC].
Int. J. PsA, 1935, p.531.

19 February 1932
Freud- Lampl-de Groot 2.3.1932 [FM] (" . . . auf ehrenvolle Weise.").
Freud-Eitingon 27.4.1932 [FM].
Freud-Eitingon 12.2.1932 [FM] ("Sie wissen, ich bin nicht reich geworden, habe $7000 für ein verunglücktes Experiment mit dem Armenier ausgegeben usw.").
Pichler Notes, 8.9.1931 [FM].

22 February 1932

1. Freud's comment on his condition is matter-of-fact: "I have no reason to be satisfied with the prosthesis, but this time the fault is more an infectious catarrh that I have caught at the same time as Anna and which has as little desire to finish with me as with her. In general an operative correction of the scar is again necessary apparently and has only been postponed because of the catarrh but it should be carried out next Monday. It shouldn't be serious, Pichler thinks." (Freud- Lampl-de Groot 2.3.1932).
Freud-Eitingon 22.2.1932 [FM].
Freud- Lampl-de Groot 2.3.1932 [FM] ("Mit der Prothese zufrieden zu sein, habe ich keinen Grund, aber die Schuld ist diesmal mehr am infektiosen Katarrh, den ich gleichzeitig mit Anna bekommen habe u der bei mir sowenig zu Ende kommen will wie bei ihr. Übrigens soll wieder eine operative Korrektur an

der Narbe notwendig sein, der nur des Katarrhs
wegen aufgeschoben wurde aber nächsten Montag
gemacht werden soll. Es soll nicht arg werden, meint
Pichler.").

23 February 1932
1. By the following year, when the Nazis came to
power, the idea of Freud's bust in the Goethe House
would be out of the question. But their shadow also
fell over the 1932 centenary celebrations. An event at
the Marxist Workers' School in Berlin, at which
Georg Lukacs and Dr. Wimmfogel were to have
discussed "Goethe from a Marxist Viewpoint", was
cancelled at the last moment by the police as a
"threat to public order."
Freud-Lilly Marlé 11.5.1932 [LoC] (" . . . dass meine
Büste im Goethehaus aufgestellt wird oder wurde ist
glaub ich nur ein Gerücht . . . ").
Frankfurter Zeitung, 23.3.1932 (Nos.221–222).

7 March 1932
Freud- Lampl-de Groot 19.3.1932 [FM] ("Meine
Operation und die erste Woche nachher waren
wirklich weniger arg als sonst, in der zweite Woche
die jetzt abläuft, sind die Schmerzen stärker gewesen
und haben im Verein mit Magen-darmstörungen eine
recht unbehagliche Zeit geschaffen.").
Freud- Lampl-de Groot 25.3.1932 [FM].
Freud-Eitingon 20.3.1932 [FM].
Anna Freud-Groddeck 25.3.1932 [Typescript FM] ("
. . . er überwindet alle körperlichen Schwierigkeiten,
die sich entgegenstellen, immer wieder mit
wunderbare Energie und Frische.").

8 March 1932
Bertin, pp.112–5, 131.

13 March 1932
1. After Kreuger's death John Maynard Keynes said
of him that he had been "maybe the greatest financial
intelligence of his time."Kreuger himself stated: "I've
built my enterprise on the firmest ground that can be
found—the foolishness of people." J.K. Galbraith's
judgment of him differed from that of Keynes: "He
was, by all odds, the biggest thief in the long history
of larceny—a man who could think of embezzlement
in terms of hundreds of millions."
Kreuger intrigued the public, not only because of his
great wealth and influence but also through his
enigmatic character. He was not married and
journalists persistently speculated on his private life
or lack of it; Graham Green modelled the millionaire
Krogh in *England Made Me* on him; the Swedish
psychoanalyst Poul Bjerre published a study of his
character.
A further ground for speculation is what aspect of
this event intrigued Freud enough to report it in his
diary.
Shaplen, Robert, *Kreuger: Genius and Swindler*,
London, 1963, pp.9, 23 & 135.

14 March 1932
Wiener Zeitung, 15.3.1932.
Eitingon-Freud 16.3.1932 [FM].

17 March 1932
Freud- Lampl-de Groot 19.3.1932 [FM].
Mann, Thomas, *Tagebücher 1935–1936*, Fischer, 1979,
p.506 n.140.
Freud-Eitingon 20.3.1932 [FM] ("Thomas Mann's
Besuch war sehr erfreulich. Er benahm sich echt und
ungezwungen, man war sofort mit ihm vertraulich, u
was er sagte war verständig, es klang nach
Hintergrund. Die Frauen haben uns natürlich nicht
lang allein gelassen. Sie lieben ihn sehr als halben
Landsmann.").

22 March 1932 (Goethe)
1. Goethe remained an authoritative figure
throughout Freud's life. In his *Autobiographical Study*
Freud said that a reading of Goethe's essay on Nature
had decided his choice of career. (However, Goethe
scholars now consider this essay to have been written
by the Swiss writer Christoph Tobler.) Wittels noted
how lovingly Freud handled a volume of *Faust II* he
was consulting for a reference and concluded: - "I
realized that he had a special relationship to Goethe."

Frankfurter Zeitung, 23.3.1932 (Nos.221–222).
Gay, p.24 & note p.658.
Wittels, Fritz, *Sigmund Freud*, Leipzig/Wien/Zürich,
1924, p.10.

22 March 1932 (French)
Translation list [FM: I-F8–17-27].

27 March 1932 (Practice)
Jones, I.157, 158.

27 March 1932 (Circular)
1. At the Wiesbaden International Psychoanalytical
Congress in September 1932, members agreed to
subscribe $3 monthly for at least the next two years
toward the maintenance of the press, and an
international committee was formed to take
responsibility for its affairs. Another consequence of
the congress was that at the end of 1932 Ernest Jones
and Anna Freud decided to resume the practice of
circular letters (*Rundbriefe*). They had previously been
a regular form of communication within the
movement but had been largely discontinued in
recent times.
Freud, Sigmund, *An die vorsitzenden der
psychoanalytischen Vereinigungen!* (Brochure) Vienna
1932 [FM].
Freud-Eitingon 12.2.1932, 22.2.1932, 27.3.1932 [FM].
Freud-Jones 26.4.1932, 1.6.1932, 8.6.1932 [Typescripts:
Inst. of PsA].

28 March 1932 (Stockert)
Wiener Zeitung, 28.12.1929.
Fichtner-Molnar 21.5.1990 [FM].

28 March 1932 (Circular)
Freud-Eitingon 20.3.1932, 8.4.1932, 11.4.1932 [FM].
Jones-Freud 21.4.1932 [Inst. of PsA].

4 April 1932 (Martha)
Freud-Martha Freud 12.4.1932 [FM].
Jones, III.179.
Eitingon-Freud 12.4.1932, 18.4.1932, 26.4.1932 [FM].

4 April 1932 (Histories)
S.E., VII. 3–122.
S.E., X. 3–149 & 153–318.
S.E., XII. 3–82.

6 April 1932 (Róheim)
"Die Psychoanalyse primitiver Kulturen" *Imago,*
XVIII, 3/4, 1932.
"Psycho-Analysis of Primitive Cultural Types" *Int.
PsA, XIII, Jan.-Apr. 1932.*

6 April 1932 (Martha)
Freud-Martha Freud 12.4.1932 [FM].
Freud-Ernst Freud 1.4.1932 [LoC].

10 April 1932
1. Von Papen resigned on November 17, 1932 and
the next day Hitler asked Hindenburg for dictatorial
power. A group of financiers and industrialists
demanded his immediate instatement. Eventually von
Papen and Hitler agreed on a Nazi-lead coalition
government. Finally, on January 30, 1933,
Hindenburg appointed Hitler Chancellor. On
February 1 the Reichstag was dissolved and new
elections set for March 5.
Bergschicker, p.12.

16. April 1932
1. 'In 1936 Freud said of the Italian movement that
the " . . . name Edoardo Weiss assures it a rich
future." Unfortunately this prediction did not take
politics into account. After two years the fascists
banned the journal and in 1938 antisemitic laws
forced Weiss to emigrate to the USA and virtually
suppressed the Italian movement.
Freud-Eitingon 18.4.1932 [FM].
Freud-Eitingon 27.4.1932 [FM] ("Die Person des
Führers ist eine sichere Garantie für die Entwicklg.
der Gruppe, er allein ist eine Gruppe wert und an
eine Gesellschaft, die eine Rivista heraus giebt,
braucht man keine weiteren Forderungen zu
stellen.").
Freud-Weiss 24.4.1932 [FM] ("Das Journal Ihre Rivista
macht einen sehr respektabele Eindruck äusserlich

wie inhaltlich. Auch die Zivilisten drin scheinen recht
zweckmässig. Ihr Mitarbeiter Berroti verspricht eine
tüchtige Kraft zu werden. Hoffentlich bleiben Ihnen
die unvermeidlichen Entäuschungen an Mitarbeitern
auf lange hinauf erspart.").
Rovigatti, Franca (ed.), *Italy in Psychoanalysis*, Rome,
1989.

17 April 1932
Freud-Martha 12.4.1932 [FM] ("Anna ist selig mit
Hochrotherd stolz auf die Lobsprüche ihrer Besücher:
Onkel Deutsch, Marlé u. A. Mein Besuch draussen
ist vom Sonntagwetter noch nicht zugelassen
worden.").

19 April 1932 (Martha)
Freud- Lampl-de Groot 24.4.1932 [FM] ("Meine Frau
hat den Berliner Aufenthalt sehr genossen,
wenngleich nicht alles schön war, was sie gesehen hat.
Die Zeiten sind eigentlich fürchterlich schlecht und
ganz ohne Garantie einer erträglicheren Zukunft.").
Freud-Martha Freud 12.4.1932 [FM] ("Der neue Anzug
von Stefan ist widerum tadellos, ich werde ihn fragen,
ob er nicht auch Prothesen macht.").

19 April 1932 (Martin)
Jones, III.201.
Freud-Martha Freud 12.4.1932 [FM].

22 April 1932
Bonin, p.48.
Binswanger, Ludwig, *Erinnerungen an Sigmund Freud*,
Berne, 1956, p.104.
Freud-Binswanger 8.10.1936 in *Letters.*

6 May 1932
1. Nevertheless, Freud could not refrain from
grousing on this subject: "Birthdays are one of those
things which can adequately be described only by the
English word *nuisance*. Their sole excuse is that they
can only occur once a year and that not for long."
(*Freud-Lou Andreas Salome 8.5.1932*).
Freud-Eitingon 4.5.1932 [FM] ("Ihr Ausbleiben an
meinem diesjährigen Geburtstag—unerwünscht genug
in seiner Begründung—wird mir wenigstens den
Anlass geben, den Tag so zu begehen, wie ich es
immer wollte, also als gemeinem Wochentag.
Morgens Besuch in Kagran mit den Hunden,
nachmittags der gewohnte Besuch bei Pichler, 4
Stunden analytische Arbeit und harmloses
Kartenspiel am Abend. Zweifel, ob man sich freuen
soll, das Datum erlebt zu haben und dann
Resignation.").
Freud-Lou Andreas Salome 8.5.1932 in Pfeiffer.
Freud- Lampl-de Groot 9.5.1932 [FM].

8 May 1932
Anna Freud-Eva Rosenfeld n.d. [FM: Transcript P.
Heller] (" . . . in HRE musst Du auch eine Wurzel
schlagen, damit wir im selben Boden wachsen.").

11 May 1932
Freud-Radó 10.5.1932 [FM] ("Natürlich haben wir hier
Sie schwer vermisst. Was ich Ihnen nun mitteile,
dürfen Sie als eine Folge Ihrer Abwesenheit auffassen.
Ich konnte mit Ihren Ersatzmann Fenichel nicht
zufrieden sein und unter mitwirkender Rücksicht auf
Ersparung und den Vorteil der Konzentration habe
ich mich entschlossen, die Redaktion beider
Zeitschriften nach Wien zu verlegen. Federn u
Hartmann sollen die Internationale, Kris u Waelder
(zwei Nichtärzte) die Imago übernehmen. Es wird
natürlich damit gerechnet, dass Sie wieder in die
Redaktion eintreten, wenn Sie es wollen. Sonst
beschäftigt uns, wie Sie wissen, die Sorge um den
Verlag, dessen Führung mein Sohn Martin
übernommen hat. Die verhängnisvolle Wirtschaft
Storfer's konnte nicht länger fortgesetzt werden.").
Jones, III.181
Freud- Lampl-de Groot 12.4.1932 [FM].

14 May 1932
Freud-Ferenczi May/June 1932 [FM] ("Ich glaube, ich
komme hier langsam zu Kräften. Unser Wohnort in
Poetzleinsdorf ist ideal schön und angenehm. Hunde
und Menschen befinden sich hier wol. Man vergisst,
dass man eigentlich im XVIII Bezirk einer Grossstadt

lebt. Ich gebe alle fünf Stunden, ringe mit den letzten Resten meiner Antwortsverschuldung, u bin noch nicht zu eigentlicher Arbeit gekommen.").

23 May 1932
Translation list [FM: I-F8–17-30].
Grinstein, p.99.

31 May 1932 (Quarterly)
1. The foundation of this new American journal was to lead to a sharp exchange of letters between Jones and Freud. Jones's initial response to the journal was alarm and indignation that it had been launched without due consultation. He felt it might threaten the existence of his *Journal*.
Jones's complaints eventually brought to the surface Freud's exasperation and tiredness with handling the politics of the movement. He responded: "Once again one feels the collapse of the committee and the termination of the circulars through which it maintained contact with members as a great loss. Since then Ferenczi has isolated himself, since then the English group has gone its own ways and lost sight of events on the continent. I have gradually grown tired of the efforts it costs to keep together such different and not very willing people."
(*Freud-Jones 17.6.1932*).
Editorial, *The Psychoanalytic Quarterly* 1, 1932.
Jones-Freud 2.6.1933 [Inst. of PsA].
Freud-Jones 17.6.1932 [Typescript Inst. of PsA] ("Man empfindet wieder einmal den Zerfall des Komités und die Einstellung der Rundbriefe, durch die es den Kontakt der Mitglieder aufrecht hielt, als einen schweren Nachteil. Seither hat sich Ferenczi isolirt, seitdem geht die englische Gruppe ihre besonderen Wege und verliert die Vorgänge auf dem Kontinent aus den Augen. Ich bin der Anstrengungen, die das Zusammenhalten so verschiedener und nicht sehr williger Personen kostet, allmählich müde geworden.").

31 May 1932 (Mitzi)
Freud-Mitzi Freud 20.3.1931 [LoC] ("Jetzt bist auch du, als vierte von uns, über die Schwelle getreten, die die leichtsinnige Jugend vom gesetztem Alter scheidet.").

6 June 1932
Translation list [FM: I-F8–17-31].
Grinstein, p.94.

15 June 1932
1. Freud referred to his plan of writing something on the psychology of love in an early letter to Jung: "When I have totally overcome my libido (in the common sense), I shall undertake to write a "Love-life of Mankind"." (*Freud-Jung 19.9.1907*).
2. In the *Chronologie* [LoC B19]—a chronological list of his own writings and the translations, which Freud himself drew up—the only translator mentioned for his Japanese works is Otsuki: "Liebesleben 1932 Ohski [sic].
Technik   1932 Ohtski [sic]."
Translation list [FM: I-F8–17-29].
Freud-Jung 19.9.1907 in *Freud-Jung Letters*, London, 1979 [1974], pp.81–2.
Freud, *Chronologie* Ms. [LoC].

21 June 1932
Clark, Ronald W., *Einstein: The Life and Times*, London, 1973, pp.346–9.

24 June 1932
1. After the birth of the youngest son, Freud wrote to Ernst: "If he is to be an archangel as well, then there is only Raphael left over for him, Uriel is too uncustomary." (*Freud-Ernst Freud 11.5.1924*).
Lucie Freud-Jones 23.1.1956 [Inst of PsA CFB/FO2/04].
Freud-Ernst Freud 11.5.1924 [LoC] ("Wenn er auch ein Erzengel sein soll, so bleibt nur Raphael für ihn übrig, Uriel ist zu ungebräuchlich.").

28 June 1932
Freud-Eitingon 3.7.1932 [FM].
Jones-Freud 5.5.1932, 28.5.1932, 16.6.1932 [Inst. of PsA].

11 July 1932
1. Later this year Freud sent a copy of Fränkel's book to Arnold Zweig with the words: "I had a hand in editing the book which is going off to you at the same time as this. They are the letters of an uncle of my wife's who was a famous classical scholar and, it appears, an outstanding personality. His attitude towards the Jewish and Christian faiths is worthy of attention." (*Freud-Arnold Zweig 27.11.1932*).
Fränkel, Michael, *Jacob Bernays: Ein Lebensbild in Briefen,*Marcus, Breslau, 1932.
Freud-Ernst Freud 20.9.1931 [LoC] (". . . ein Akt der Dankbarkeit, denn mit der Erbschaft nach ihm haben wir seinerzeit unser Haus begründet.").
Freud-Arnold Zweig 27.11.1932 in *Zweig Letters*.

16 July 1932
Freud-Eitingon 21.7.1932 [FM] ("Meine kleine Lou* ist nach Mallnitz (Kärnten) mit einem scheinbar sehr leichten Scharlach gekommen, aber ich fürchte, man ist nicht genug vorsichtig mit ihr. Das Heer meiner kleinen Beschwerden wächst . . . ")
[*sic in typescript. Almost certainly a misreading of "Eva".].

16 July 1932
Bernfeld-Liesl Neumann-Bernfeld 14.9.1932 in Reichmayr, Johannes, *Im Zwischenraum von Theorie und Praxis*, Frankfurt a. M. 1990 [Quoted from ms. by courtesy of the author] ("Ich war heute bei Anna F. Prof. hinreissend liebenswürdig; hat weder mit den Hunden noch über sie gesprochen, sondern sehr lieb mit mir. ").

26 July 1932
Martha Freud-Ernst Freud 30.7.1932 [FM: Lucie Freud Papers] ("Überhaupt bin ich einmal wieder mit Blumen & Aufmerksamkeiten zu meinem Geburtstag überschüttert worden.").
Freud- Lampl-de Groot 30.7.1932 [FM] ("Auch ich bin wenigstens fleissig, unter vielen kleinen Beschwerden und Behandlungen. Unser Wetter scheint viel gnädiger gewesen zu sein als Ihres. Am 26 st. haben wir einen vollkommen schönen Halbtag in Hochroterd verbracht.").

1 August 1932
Einstein-Freud 30.7.1932 [FM] ("Ich möchte diese Gelegenheit dazu benutzen, um Ihnen privaten herzlichen Grüsse zu senden und Ihnen zu danken für so manche schöne Stunde, die ich der Lektüre Ihrer Werke verdanke. Es ist für mich immer so amüsant zu beobachten, dass auch die Menschen, welche sich Ihren Lehren gegenüber als 'Ungläubige' betrachten, Ihren Ideen so wenig Widerstand entgegenzusetzen vermögen, dass Sie in Ihren Begriffen zu denken und zu reden pflegen, wenn sie sich—gehen lassen.").
Clark, Ronald W., *Einstein: The Life and Times*, London, 1973, pp.346–9.

10 August 1932
Anna Freud-Eva Rosenfeld n.d. [FM: Transcript Peter Heller].
Freud-Eitingon 5.6.1932 in *Letters*.

15 August 1932
Freud- Lampl-de Groot 30.7.1932 [FM].
Freud- Lampl-de Groot 8.9.1932 [FM: Typescript].

22 August 1932
1. Two years later Anna Freud said of Brill's struggle: "I really think it is terrible what Brill has to go through. I cannot understand how that athmosphere [sic] of continual quarrel can lead to anything like a real analytic movement in America. And it certainly is a bad sign for effect of analysis on the analysts. It is beyond me to understand all these matters." (*Anna Freud-Jones 27.6.1934*).
Freud-Eitingon 27.4.1932 [FM] ("In keinem Land—unglaublich—stösst Organisation und Zusammenarbeit auf solche Widerstände wie in Amerika. Es wäre schon sehr recht, wenn es Brill gelänge, eine Einheit mit Untergruppen herzustellen, aber es ist keine überragende Persönlichkeit da, die NY Gesellschaft geniesst keine Achtung bei den anderen. Brill hat den in seiner Latenz riesen-grossen amerika. Antisemitismus gegen sich. Somit sollten

wir, wenn Brill seine Absicht nicht durchsetzt, aufnehmen, was sich uns anträgt u nicht auf einer Form bestehen, die diese Rothäute ablehnen.")
Freud-Eitingon 4.5.1932 [FM].
Anna Freud-Jones 27.6.1934 [Inst of PsA: CFA/FO1/97].

23 August 1932
Jones, III.126, 164.
Ferenczi-Freud 25.12.1929 & 1.5.1932 [FM].
Freud-Ferenczi 12.5.1932 [FM].
Ferenczi-Freud 21.8.1932 [FM] ("Nach langem qualvollen Zögern habe ich mich entschlossen, auf die Präsidentschaftskandidatur zu verzichten. Zu den Motiven, über die ich Ihnen bereits berichtete, gesellte sich seither der Umstand, dass ich im Laufe der Anstrengung meine Analyse tiefer und effektvoller zu gestalten, in ein entschieden kritisches und selbstkritisches Fahrwasser geraten bin, das in einiger Hinsicht nicht zu Ergänzungen, sondern auch Korrekturen unserer praktischen und stellenweise auch unserer theoretischen Ansichten notwendig zu machen scheint. Ich habe nun das Gefühl, dass eine solche geistige Verfassung zur Würde eines Präsidenten, dessen Hauptsorge das Konservieren und die Befestigung des Bestehenden sein soll, garnicht passt und mein inneres Fühlen sagt mir, dass es nicht einmal ehrlich wäre, diese Stellung zu okkupieren. . . .").

27 August 1932 (Ernst)
Freud, Ernst, Interview R.S.Stewart, 10.6.1966.

27 August 1932 (Radó)
Freud-Eitingon 29.8.1932 [FM] ("Ferenczi soll elend aussehen, kreidebleich, tief deprimirt sein. Radó, dessen Verstand scharf ist wie ein Rasirmesser, meint er befinde sich in vorgeschrittener sklerotischer Degeneration. Ich möchte viel von dem Eindruck auf den Konflikt schieben, der ihn erschüttert, die Loslösung fällt ihm offenbar sehr schwer.").

30 August 1932
1. In view of the demands made on this fund, it is rather surprising to find Freud complaining to Ernst in 1933: "I too find it depressing that the Goethe Prize did not hold out longer than 2 1/2 years." (*Freud-Ernst Freud 15.1.1933*).
Freud-Ernst Freud 15.1.1933 [LoC] ("Auch ich finde es betrübend, dass der Goethepreis nicht länger als 2 1/2 J. vorgehalten hat.").

31 August 1932
Freud-Jones 17.6.1932 [Typescript Inst. of PsA].
Freud- Lampl-de Groot 15.7.1932 [FM] ("Ich schreibe emsig, finde es nicht leicht, meine Arbeitshemmung dürfte recht gut physiologisch begründet sein. Ich ärgere mich auch jedesmal, wenn ich Worte auslasse oder entstelle. Dergleichen gab es früher einmal nicht.").
Freud-Eitingon 24.8.1932, 21.7.1932, 18.8.1932 [FM].

1 September 1932
Freud-Lou Andreas-Salomé 11.12.1927 [LoC] ("Anna ist prächtig, gut und geistig selbstständig, aber kein Sexualleben. Was wird sie ohne Vater anfangen?").

2 September 1932
Freud-Anna Freud 3.9.1932 [FM] ("Ferenczi's kamen also vor 4 h. Sie liebenswürdig wie immer, von ihm gieng eine eisige Kälte aus. Ohne weitere Frage oder Begrüssung, begann er: Ich will Ihnen meinen Vortrag vorlesen. That er auch und ich hörte erschüttert zu. Er hat eine volle Regression gemacht zu aetiologischen Ansichten, die ich vor 35 Jahren geglaubt und aufgegeben, dass die regelmässige Ursache der Neurosen grobe sexuelle Traumen der Kindheit sind, sagt es fast mit den nämlichen Worten wie ich damals. Kein Wort über die Technik, mit der er sich dieses Material verschafft, mitten drin Bemerkungen über die Feindseligkeit der Pat. und die Notwendigkeit ihre Kritik anzunehmen und seinen Fehler vor ihnen zu bekennen. Die Folgerungen daraus verworren, unübersichtlich verkünstelt. Das Ganze eigentlich dumm oder es scheint so, weil es so unaufrichtig und unvollständig ist.").

4 September 1932
Jones-Freud 9.9.1932 [Inst. of PsA].
Jones, III.181.

6 September 1932
Freud-Eitingon 18.8.1932 [FM] ("Leider betrifft sie die Frage, wie man das Verhängnis der Kriege vermeiden kann. Ich glaube nicht, dass ich für meinen Beitrag den Friedensnobelpreis bekommen werde.").

8 September 1932
Burlingham, pp.237–8.
Peters, p.189.
Leitsätze der Kongressvorträge. 12 Int. Psa Kong. 23–7 Sept. 1932 [LoC].

9 September 1932
Nunberg, Herman, & Federn, Ernst (Eds.), *Minutes of the Vienna Psychoanalytic Society* Vol.2.
S.E., IX. 181.
S.E.,VIII.111.
Hemecker, Wilhelm *Ehrenfels* [Typescript. By courtesy of the author].
Hemecker, Wilhelm: " 'Ihr Brief war mir sehr wertvoll . . . ' Christian von Ehrenfels und Sigmund Freud - ein verschollene Korrespondenz," in Clair, Pichler, Pircher (Hrsg.), *Wunderblock: (Eine Geschichte der modernen Seele,)* Wien, 1989, pp. 561–570.

12 September 1932
Translation list [FM: I-F8-17-38].

20 September 1932
Freud-Ernst Freud 7.10.1927 [LoC] ("Mathilde ist elend u macht uns zum ersten Mal ernste Sorge.").

24 September 1932
Freud-Anna Freud 3.9.1932 [FM].

25 September 1932
Freud, Martin, *"Gelb ist das Haus . . . "* [FM] ("Still ruht das Land, als wär" ihm Glück beschieden,/Als wär' die Welt nicht hass- und angstverzerrt,/Rings um das Haus voll Anmut, Ruh und Frieden,/Die schöne, grüne Insel: HOCHROTHERD.").

27 September 1932 (Anna)
Lange H.W. *Family Tree* [FM].
Freud-Fliess 23.3.1900 in Masson.

27 September 1932 (Brücke)
S.E., XX.252.
Swales-Molnar 21.4.1990 [FM].
Fichtner-Molnar 21.5.1990 [FM].

2 October 1932
1. Mark Brunswick was in analysis with Freud. When the American psychoanalyst Smiley Blanton once asked Freud whether their social relations made it more difficult to analyze him, Freud agreed, but said that this could be overcome.
Bernfeld-Neumann 21.11.1932 [Quoted by kind permission of Frau Elisabeth Neumann-Viertel & Dr. Johannes Reichmayr] ("Das Haus von Anna F. und Dorothy Burlingham sehr sauber . . . mit vielen erstklassigen bunten Bauernmöbeln, schönen Vorhängen, Öfen, Truhen, Halle. Stall mit Kuh, vielen eierlegenden Hühnern, Buttermaschinen, Gemüsegärten, Mistbeeten - eine sehr geschmackvolle, teure Primitivität. Aber wirklich behaglich.").
Blanton, Smiley, *Diary of My Analysis with Sigmund Freud*, Hawthorn Books, N.Y., 1971, p.79.

4 October 1932 (Anna)
Freud-Ernst Freud 12.5.1929 [LoC] ("Es soll ein grossartige Eindruck gewesen sein.").

4 October 1932 (Jackson)
1. In his paper on "Fetishism" (1927), Freud wrote: " . . . the normal prototype of fetishes is a man's penis . . . ". There are a number of small (probably Roman) phallus amulets in Freud's collection. But the male organ itself is not the fetish. Only if Freud were using the term allusively could these amulets be considered possible "fetishes".
S.E., XXI.157.
Phallus amulets [FM: LDFRD 3408, 3409, 3392, 3413,

3499, 4144].

6 October 1932 (Anna)
1. Since no talk by her was recorded in the yearly report of the Berlin Psychoanalytical Society, it must be assumed that this was either unofficial or an outside event.
Eitingon-Freud 19.10.1932 [FM] ("Sie haben gewiss gehört was für einen schönen Erfolg Annas auftreten in Berlin war. Diesmal war es eine Riesenversammlung.").

6 October 1932 (Pichler)
1. As an example not only of Pichler's thoroughness as a surgeon but also as a meticulous recorder of his own work, it is worth reproducing his notes for this operation:
"After 1 allonal and 1 litran and after infiltration at palate, attempt at subbasal anaesthesia of ramus III. Excision of 2 bolsters, at first under and inside residual antrum (piece No.1) and then directly at inferior posterior edge including small piece of nasal mucous membrane. This includes removal of whole thickness of old scar. In second place some bone exposed with intention to remove chip. Base of processor pteryoideus. Intention not carried out since bone without doubt healthy. After this both places slightly diathermised and bridge between them cut with linear 3mm basal diathermy cut to provide for scar from right to left. Third remaining red bolster at outer edge thoroughly destroyed with diathermy only. Some jodoform-gauze on bone in upper wound-hole, otherwise only orthoform and prosthesis."
Freud- Lampl-de Groot 8.10.1932 [FM] (" . . . .dass Pichler vorgestern wieder eine jener kleinen Operationen in meinen Mund vorgenommen hat, die er zur Vorsicht notwendig hält, diesmal weit energischer, als die letzten Male. Es ist aber alles sehr gut verlaufen, ich habe nur 3 Stunden Wundschmerzen gehabt u alle Injektionen gut vertragen. Heute gehe ich aus, Montag arbeite ich wieder. Garantien, dass es das letzte der Art sein wird, giebt es natürlich nicht.").
Freud- Lampl-de Groot 23.10.1932 [FM].
Pichler Notes, 6.10.1932 [FM].

14 October 1932
Anna Bernays-Stefan Zweig 23.11[?].1932 [SFC].

29/30 October 1932
Eitingon-Freud 17.11.1932 [FM].
Freud-Eitingon 20.11.1932 [FM] ("An Stelle von Alfred Rie ist Jekels einberufen worden.").

1 November 1932
Schur, 433.
Freud-Radó 22.11.1932 [FM].
Freud-Eitingon 4.12.1932 [FM].
Freud-Eitingon 20.11.1932 [FM] ("Mit der Otitis bin ich zwar durch, aber abscheuliche Katarrhe halten an u erniedrigen das Existenzniveau um ein weiteres Stück.").

3 November 1932
Freud- Lampl-de Groot 7.11.1932 [FM] ("Nach einer gar nicht angenehmen Woche von Grippe und Fieber, Otitis, Paracentese usw. nehme ich heute die Arbeit in eingeschränktem Verhältnis von 2 - 5 wieder auf. Natürlich nicht sehr kräftig geworden. Aber doch wieder menschlich.").

8 November 1932
Freud-Eitingon 20.11.1932 [FM] ("Am 1 Dez etwa erwarte ich auch meinen Mitarbeiter nach den Wahlen in U.S.A. und werde von ihm hören, wann das Wilson-Buch in die Öffentlichkeit geschickt werden kann.").
Freud-Marie Bonaparte 21.12.1932 [Transcript by Marie Bonaparte. FM: F8/CON 19–20] ("Er erwartet mit einer wichtigen politischen Position betraut zu werden, gesteht aber zu, dass er auch leicht übergangen werden kann. In diesem Fall könnte unser Wilsonbuch ohne Verzögerung erscheinen.").

30 November 1932
Wiener Zeitung 30.11.1932 ("Mit einigen geistvollen

Worten leitet sie jedes kleine Drama ein. Spricht diesmal vor einem Tisch wie ein witzige, geistreicher, dabei gelehrter Dozent.").
Yvette Guilbert en Caricatures, Concert programme, "Au temps du Chat Noir" 24.12.1932 [FM: LDFRD 1749].

3 December 1932 (Anna)
1. True to the general tone of the paper, the report is frothy and simpering, but it does contain references to her collaboration with Paul Federn in organizing the movement and also refers to the rivalry between Anna Freud's techniques of child therapy and those of Melanie Klein.
Freud-Anna Freud 3.12.1932, 3.12.1924, 3.12.1925 [FM].
Die Stunde, 3.12.1932 ("Anna Freud - 37 Jahre alt - Besuch bei Sigm. Freuds Tochter, der berühmten Heilpädagogin.").

3 December 1932 (Lectures)
Freud-Eitingon 20.11.1932 & 4.12.1932 [FM].

8 December 1932
Pichler notes (1.12.1932. 8.12.1932) [FM].
Freud- Lampl-de Groot 11.12.1932 [FM] ("Es heisst dann jedesmal, das Entfernte hatte ganz harmlose Charakter, aber Sie wissen ja, wenn man ihm Zeit gelassen hätte, vielleicht usw. Es geht seit dem wie immer, zuerst wenig Schmerzen und Beschwerden und nach einigen Tagen die Unannehmlichkeiten der entzündlichen Reaktion und nicht kauen, kaum Sprechen, sonderbarer Weise auch kaum Schreiben.").
Anna Freud-Eva Rosenfeld 15.12.1932 [FM: Transcript: P. Heller].
Pichler Notes, 24.12.1932 [FM].

1933

4 January 1933 (May)
Freud-May 1.1.1933 in Swales, Peter, "Brief eines Landarztes," *Werkblatt* 1/2 1987, Salzburg, p.7. "Letter from a Country Doctor," *Die psychoanalytische Bewegung*, Jan./Feb. 1933.

4 January 1933 (Martin)
Freud-Eitingon 5.1.1933 [FM].
Freud- Lampl-de Groot 8.1.1933 [FM].

5 January 1933
Wiener Zeitung (Obituary), 5.1.1933.

18 January 1933
Bernfeld, Suzanne Cassirer, "Freud and Archaeology," *The American Imago* 8 (June 1951), pp.107–128.
Burlingham, p.236, 238.

27 January 1933
Freud- Lampl-de Groot 1.2.1933 [FM] ("Eitingon sah nicht gut aus, wir fanden ihn aber umgänglicher und gesprächiger als sonst.").
Freud-Eitingon 5.1.1933 & 5.2.1933 [FM].

29 January 1933 (Ruth)
Freud- Lampl-de Groot 23.10.1932 [FM] ("Ruth ist eine sehr unregelmässige Patientin und durch organischen Komplikationen schwer fassbar.").
Freud- Lampl-de Groot 1.2.1933 [FM].

29 January 1933 (Hitler)
Freud- Lampl-de Groot 1.2.33 [FM] ("Wir sind alle gespannt darauf, was aus dem Programm des Reichskanzler Hitler werden wird, dessen einzige politischer Punkt ja die Judenhetze ist.").
Wiener Zeitung, 31.1.1933.

31 January 1933 (Galsworthy)
S.E.,XXI.105 note 2.
"New Introductory Lectures" S.E., XXII.49.

31 January 1933 (Jofi)
1. In July Freud wrote to H.D.: "There has been much commotion in the dog-state. Wulf had to be shipped off to Kagran, because both ladies were in heat, and the fierce antagonism between Yofi and Lün, which is rooted in the nature of women, resulted in good, gentle Lün's being bitten by Yofi. Thus Lün, too, is at present in Kagran and her future is uncertain." (*Freud-H.D. 20.7.1933*).
Martin Freud, p.195.
Freud-H.D. 20.7.1933 in H.D. p. 191.

12 February 1933
Arnold, *Zweig-Freud 30.12.1932, 1.5.1932, 29.5.1932* in *Zweig Letters*.
Arnold, *Zweig-Freud 27.11.1932* ibid.
Arnold, *Zweig-Freud 30.11.1932* ibid.

13 February 1933
S.E.,IV.xxxii.

14 February 1933
1. Though the rival "Ars" publishers in Tokyo also published Hayashi's translation of the *Metapsychology* this year, it is improbable they that would have arrived with the same post.
Translation list [FM: I-F8–17-29].

17 February 1933
1. Freud does not seem to have done any special research either into oriental antiquities or cultures. However, his library does contain a work on the concept of the Buddha. As a memory of the last psychoanalytical congress Freud attended, in Berlin in September 1922, Eitingon gave him the book *Der Ewige Buddho* by Leopold Ziegler.
Portal, Jane, in *Freud and Art*, p.124.
Ziegler, Leopold, *Der Ewige Buddho*, Otto Reichl, Darmstadt, 1922 [FM].

21 February 1933
Translation list [FM: I-F8–17-37].

28 February 1933
1. Apparently, few believed the Nazi version of events. At that time a film was being shown, based on a novella by Stefan Zweig. Its title was *Burning Secret* (*Brennendes Geheimnis*). On the day after the burning, the Gestapo noticed people pointing at the placards and winking or laughing. By that evening, according to Zweig, performances were banned and advertisements for both book and film had disappeared.
Zweig, Stefan, *Die Welt von Gestern*, Fischer, 1979 [1944], p.264.

4 March 1933 (Dollar)
Wiener Zeitung, 4.3.1933.

4 March 1933 (Roosevelt)
1. When Vienna finally decided to honor Freud by naming a square after him during the 1980s, part of Rooseveltplatz was renamed Sigmund-Freud-Platz. The various previous names of this square by the Votivkirche (not far from Berggasse) reveal buried strata of Austrian history. Originally Maximilianplatz, the square became Freiheitsplatz (Freedom Square) after World War I, then in the 1930s Dollfussplatz. In 1938 it was renamed Adolf-Hitler-Platz. [With thanks to Dr. Johannes Reichmayr for this information].

5 March 1933
Bergschicker, p.22.
Freud- Lampl-de Groot 9.3.1933 [FM] ("Mit unserem Kleinstaat Österreich ist irgend etwas Unheimliches los; man weiss natürlich nicht, was.").
Freud- Lampl-de Groot 8.4.1933 [FM] ("Wir halten an zwei Punkten fest, am Entschluss uns nicht wegzurühren und an der Erwartung, dass es bei uns nicht entfernt so werden kann, wie in D. Wir sind auf dem Weg zu einer Diktatur der Rechtsparteien die sich mit den Nazi verbünden werden. Allers eher als schön, aber Ausnehmsgesetze gegen eine Minorität sind bestens durch den Friedensvertrag ausdrücklich verboten, den Anschluss an Deutschl. werden die Siegerstaaten nie zulassen und unser Pöbel ist ein Stück weniger brutal als der stammverwandte Deutsche.").

13 March 1933
Reeves, Dr. C. N. in *Freud and Art*, p.75, 76.

15 March 1933
Lange, Hanns W. *Family Tree* [FM].
Freud-Sam Freud 1.12.1931 [FM].

22 March 1933
Freud- Lampl-de Groot 10.2.1933 [FM] ("Meine Diskussion mit Einstein ("Warum Krieg") ist zu Ende korrigirt und kann noch im Febr. erscheinen. Auch sie wird die Menschheit nicht retten. Ja, warum macht Einstein solche Dummheiten wie mit dem Glaubensbekenntnis u andere Überflüssigkeiten? Vielleicht weil er so gutmütig und weltfremd ist.").

25 March 1933
Arbeiter-Zeitung 26.3.1933 in Klusacek, Christine, & Stimmer, Kurt (Hrsg.), *Dokumentation zur Oesterreichischen Zeitgeschichte*, Wien, München, 1982, Bd. 1928–1938, S.232.

27 March 1933 (Pourquoi)
Freud-Eitingon 3.4.1933 [FM].

27 March 1933 (Ferenczi)
Ferenczi-Freud 27.11.1932 [FM].
Ferenczi-Freud 29.3.1933 [FM] ("Zwei aktuelle Momente drängen mich heute dazu, dass kindische Schmollen endlich zu unterbrechen und den Kontakt mit Ihnen, als wäre nichts geschehen, aufzunehmen. [. . .]. Vielleicht hörten Sie durch Dr. Lévy, dass ich in den letzten Wochen einen neuerlichen Rückfall in der Symptomatik meines Leiden (Anaem. pernic.) zu erfahren hatte, diesmal aber weniger in einer Verschlimmerung meines Blutbefundes als in einer Art nervösen Zusammenbruchs, aus dem ich mich nur langsam erhole.").

Freud-Eitingon 3.4.1933 [FM].

29 March 1933
Fichtner-Molnar 21.5.1990 [FM] (With thanks to Professor G. Fichtner for this suggestion).

31 March 1933
1. Bryher recorded Freud's reactions to their first visit: "He asked us first several questions about Ellis whose courage as an investigator he admired, but then an amazing life came into his eyes as he questioned us about flying: why had we chosen to come by air, what did it feel like, how high had the pilot taken us, what did a landscape look like from above? We told him about the storm and the strange impression that we had had of seeing lightning sideways and I knew that he wished that he had been with us himself."
H.D., p.176.
Bryher, *The Heart to Artemis*, London, 1963, p.245.

2 April 1933
Freud-Eitingon 3.4.1933 [FM] ("Unser Ernstl ist heute auf "verfrühte" Osterferien eingetroffen. In Dresden hat er seine erste Berührung mit der Zeitgeschichte erlebt.").
Freud, W. *Ernest-Molnar 6.8.1989* [FM].

3 April 1933 (Jofi)
Freud- Lampl-de Groot 8.4.1933 [FM] ("Jofi hat eine gefährliche Geburt gehabt, ist aber jetzt wol u stolz auf ihre zwei kleinen, rattenähnlichen Kinder.").
Freud- Lampl-de Groot 14.7.1933 [FM] ("Fo u Tattoun haben sich glänzend entwickelt, sind fast so gross wie ihre Mutter, sehr übermütig u stellen allerlei an.").
Freud-H.D. 20.7.1933 in H.D., p.191.
Ibid p.166.

3 April 1933 (Douglas)
Freud-Douglas 10.4.1933 in Holloway, Mark, *Norman Douglas: A Biography*, London, 1976, pp.399–400.

5 April 1933
Freud, W. *Ernest-Molnar 6.8.1989* [FM].

8 April 1933
Freud-Jones 7.4.1933 [Typescript Inst. of PsA] ("Mein Sohn Oliver, den ich seit einem Jahr als Arbeitslosen erhalte, kommt morgen nach Wien, um über seine Zukunft zu sprechen. Es ist wenig zweifelhaft, dass er in Berlin nie mehr eine Anstellung finden wird. (Er ist Tiefbauingenieur.)").
Freud- Lampl-de Groot 15.4.1933 [FM] ("Der Eindruck von Oli's Besuch war niederdrückend. Er benimmt sich gut, jammert nicht, sieht sich um und ist bereit sich zu plagen. Aber seine Aussichten sind doch so schlechte. Er schwankt zwischen Spanien und Palästina, hat aber noch an keinem Punkt einen Anhalt.").

10 April, 1933
1. In actual fact the solitary visit to Rome was in 1912: on his visit there in September 1913 he was accompanied by Minna Bernays. Freud possessed a guidebook, published in 1912 - *Rom und die Campagna* by Dr. Th. Gsell Fels - which he probably took with him on that first occasion. In it he has marked in blue crayon the section on the Moses statue, incidentally the only marking in the entire book. Here Gsell Fels stresses the fact (which was to be a key point in Freud's argument) that Michelangelo has depicted not an outburst of wrath but a moment of self-restraint. Gsell Fels also points out that Roman Jews regarded this particular statue as a religious image of their leader. Freud's critical analysis of that image later developed into the attack on Judaism implicit in *Moses and Monotheism*.
Freud-Weiss 12.4.1933 in *Letters*.
Gsell Fels, Dr. Th., *Rom und die Campagna* (7th ed.), Leipzig & Wien 1912, p.754 [FM: Lucie Freud Papers].

10 April 1933
Freud- Lampl-de Groot 15.4.1933 [FM].

16 April 1933
Jones, I.158.
Freud- Lampl-de Groot 15.4.1933 [FM]

("... nebenbei der letzte Tag einer 47 jährigen ärztlichen Praxis.").

17 April 1933
1. Eitingon afterwards wrote that the episode reminded him of a recent political incident. Two ministers told von Papen that they would only give way to violence, whereupon von Papen politely asked them what type of violence they would prefer.
Jones, III.195, 198.
Peters, p.193.
Clark, p.491.
Freud-Eitingon 17.4.1933 [FM].

22 April 1933
1. Other names suggested by Peter Swales, are Viktor Klemperer, a Viennese poet, and Karl Klemperer or Dr. Alois Klemperer, both fellow members of the B'nai B'rith.
Eissler, K.R., *Talent and Genius* N.Y., 1971, p.140 n.5.
Psychoanalytic Pioneers, p.157.
Jones, II.88–9.
Swales-Molnar 21.4.1990 [FM].

25 April 1933
1. 'Benito Mussolini mit dem ergebenen Gruss eines alten Mannes der im Machthaber den Kulturheros erkennt. Wien 26.4.1933 Freud."
There is no reason to interpret these "respectful greetings" as admiration. Indeed the choice of book in which they were inscribed (*Why War*) could be taken as a pointed comment on Mussolini's foreign policy. In a letter of 1928 Freud had spoken of his utter lack of sympathy for "despots like Lenin and Mussolini." (*Freud-Viereck 20.7.1928*).
Freud-Weiss 12.4.1933 [FM].
Lobner, Hans, "Some additional remarks on Freud's library," *Sigmund Freud House Bulletin*, Vol.1 No.1, 1975, p.23.
Freud-Viereck 20.7.1928 in *Letters*.
Carloni, Glauco, "Freud and Mussolini" in Rovigatti, Franca (Ed.), *Italy in Psychoanalysis*, Rome, 1989, pp.51–60, pp.58–9.

1 May 1933
Freud-Eitingon 3.4.1933 [FM] ("Unsere politische Lage versteht hier niemand, man hält es nicht für wahrscheinlich, dass die Entwicklung ähnlich sein wird wie bei Ihnen, das Leben verläuft hier ungestört bis auf Umzüge, welche die Polizei beschäftigen. Es fehlt nicht an Versuchen, Panikstimmungen zu suggeriren, aber ich werde ganz wie Sie erst im allerletzten Moment den Platz räumen und wahrscheinlich auch dann nicht.").
Wiener Zeitung, 3.5.1933.

4 May 1933
Anna Freud-Jones 27.4.1933 [Inst.of PsA: CFA/FO1/30] ("Wir übersiedeln am 3. Mai nach Wien XIX. Hohe Warte 46. Manchmal wundert mich, dass auch in solchen Zeiten wie den jetzigen der Frühling und Sommer kommt, als wäre nichts geschehen.").

5 May 1933
Knoepfmacher, Hugo "Zwei Beiträge zur Biographie Sigmund Freuds," *Jahrbuch der Psychoanalyse*, Bd. XI p.61.
Freud-Jones 7.4.1933 [Typescr. Inst. of PsA].
Jones, III.193.

6 May 1933 (Birthday)
Freud-Jones 7.5.1933 ("Ich glaube, ich habe entdeckt, dass die Sehnsucht nach der endgiltigen Ruhe nichts elementar primäres ist, sondern der Ausdruck des Bedürfnisses, das Gefühl der Unzulänglichkeit los zu werden, das den Alten besonders bei all den kleinen Aufgaben des Lebens überfällt.").
Freud-Jones 7.5.1933 in Jones, III.192.
Freud-Jones 7.5.1933 [Typescript Inst. of PsA].
Jones-Freud 16.5.1933 [Inst. of PsA].
Freud-Marie Bonaparte 9.5.1933 in Schur, 445.
Eitingon-Freud 27.4.1933 [FM].

6 May 1933 (Vertigo)
Freud-Marie Bonaparte 9.5.1933 in Schur, 444–5.

11 May 1933
Neuköllner Tageblatt, 12. Mai 1933, (Auszug) in Bergschicker, p.100.
Jones, III.194–5.

15 May 1933 (Ernst)
Jones-Freud 3.6.1933 [Inst. of PsA].
Freud-Eitingon n.d. (June 1933) [FM].

15 May 1933 (Operation)
Pichler Notes, 28.2.1933, 6.4.1933, 15 & 16.4.1933 [FM].

15 May 1933 (Zweig)
1. Zweig's book attacks German antisemitism with Freudian weapons: *Mein Kampf* is compared to Daniel Schreber's *Memoirs of my Nervous Illness* [*Denkwürdigkeiten eines Nervenkranken*], the book which served as a basis for Freud's study of the sources of paranoia. Zweig compares Nazi Germany to a psychotic individual, its life centered around the demonic drive of its own disease and determined to destroy the surrounding world which denies its manic wishes.
Arnold Zweig-Freud 15.2.1936 in *Zweig Letters*.
Zweig, Arnold, *Bilanz der deutschen Judenheit 1933. Ein Versuch*," Amsterdam, 1934, pp.71–5, 101–4, 232.

16 May 1933
Freud-Lampl-de Groot 25,2,1933, 9.3.1933, 8.4.1933 [FM].

21 May 1933 (Jeanne)
Freud-Lampl-de Groot 27.7.1933 [FM].
Lampl-de Groot, Jeanne, n.d. [FM: SF/LG 70].

21 May 1933 (Vriesland)
Salten, Felix, *Neue Menschen auf alter Erde: Eine Palästinafahrt*, Berlin - Wien - Leipzig, 1925, pp.111–2.
Eitingon-Freud 2.11.1933 [FM].

22 May 1933
Freud-Lampl-de Groot 26.5.1933 [FM] ("Ein verworrenes Gefühl einerseits der Erlösung, dass er dem schrecklichen Zerfall nun entzogen ist - er konnte in den letzten Wochen nicht mehr stehen oder gehen und der Wahn war viel ärger gewesen, als wir gewusst hatten - anderseits doch erst jetzt der Schmerz über den Verlust von altem, was er uns bedeutete, obwol er ja schon seit Jahren uns abgestorben war. Aber die endgiltige brutale Tatsache hat ihre besondere Gewalt.").
Freud-Jones 29.5.1933 [Typescr. Inst. of PsA] ("Im Mittelpunkt stand die Überzeugung, dass ich ihn nicht genug liebte, seine Arbeiten nicht anerkennen wollte, auch dass ich seine Analyse schlecht gemacht hätte. Damit standen seine technische Neuerungen in Zussamenhang, er wollte mir zeigen, wie liebevoll man seine Patienten behandeln müsse, um ihnen zu helfen.").

23 May 1933
Freud-Ohtski 20.5.1935 in *Zeit. f. Psa. Tokio*, V3.5 1935 [LoC].

24 May 1933
Freud-Jeanne Lampl-de Groot 15.4.1933 [FM] ("Ruth ist ewig krank, hustet, fiebert ....").

25 May 1933
Freud-Lampl-de Groot 26.5.1933 [FM] ("Anna ist ganz erschüttert wiedergekommen.").

26 May 1933
Pichler Notes, June 1933 [FM].

28 May 1933
Freud-Pfister 28.5.1933 in *Pfister Letters*.
Arnold Zweig-Freud 21.1.1934 in *Zweig Letters*.

29 May,1933
Freud, "Forward" in Bonaparte, Marie, *Edgar Poe: étude psychanalytique*, Denoël et Steele, Paris 1933. [FM 2770–2771].
Bonaparte, Marie: Handwritten dedication (*ibid*) ("à mon maître aimé, ces pages inspirées par son oeuvre et son esprit, et ou l'auteur s'est complu, pour pénétrer en l'un des psychismes les plus sinistres qui

furent, à suivre longuement les voies ouvertes par celui qui, le premier, pénétra l'inconscient des hommes.").

4 June 1933
1. Freud's internal struggle is reflected in the crossings out and alterations in the manuscript. (Up to the very end of his life Freud usually wrote fluently, with very few changes.) For example, the printed version contains the sentence: "From unexhausted springs of emotion the conviction was borne in upon him that one could effect far more with one's patients if one gave them enough of the love which they had longed for as children."
In manuscript the first part of the sentence originally read: "From the unexhausted springs of his childlike inner life ...."
Freud- Lampl-de Groot 4.6.1933 [FM] ("Die Pfingstzeit war von dem Nachruf für Ferenczi in Anspruch genommen, in keinem Sinn eine leichte Arbeit. Jetzt fühle ich nur noch die Leere, die vom Ganzen übrig geblieben ist.").
Freud-Eitingon 7.6.1933 [FM] ("Den Nachruf an Ferenczi habe ich fertig gemacht, er war schwer zu schreiben u hinterliess eine schwere Stimmung.").
S.E.,XXII.229 (G.W.XVI.269)
Nachruf Ferenczi, Ms. [LoC] ("Aus unversiegten affektiven Quellen floss ihm die Überzeugung, dass man bei den Kranken weit mehr ausrichten könnte, wenn man ihnen genug von der Liebe gäbe, nach der sie sich als Kinder gesehnt hatten.").
ibid ("Aus unversiegten Quellen seines kindlichen Gemütsleben ... ").

5 June 1933
1. Jones dates Freud and Wells' first encounter to 1931, but there is no other record of any meeting that year. The meeting now was organized (at Wells' request) by Stefan Zweig, whom Wells visited in Salzburg.
Jones, III.171.
Freud- Lampl-de Groot 8.6.1933 [FM].
Stefan Zweig-Freud June 1933 in Stefan Zweig, p.167.

16 June 1933
Freud-Eitingon 7.6.1933 & 17.4.1933 [FM].
Eitingon-Freud 31.5.1933 [FM] ("Es ist mir ein grosses Bedürfnis, mit Ihnen über all diese Dinge bald zu sprechen.").

26 June 1933 (Hammerschlag)
Schröter, p.60 n.4, p.468 n.1.

26 June 1933 (Wittels)
1. Freud only rarely wrote in books, at most he simply drew a line in the margin to mark particular passages. But the vast majority of his library, including his most valued books, are entirely free of notes or marks.
"Letter to Fritz Wittels" S.E., XIX.286.
Freud-Wittels 19.11.1933 [FM: I/F8–33-1–14] ("Zu Ihren Grubeln und Bedenken betreffs der Wiedergutmachung Ihrer Missetat vor zehn Jahren lassen Sie mich bemerken, dass restloses Ungeschehenmachen überhaupt eine schwere Sache ist, wirklich am Besten der Magie überlassen bleibt. Wenn Sie darüber hinaus ein anderes persönliches Verhältnis zu mir anstreben, so lassen Sie sich doch mahnen, dass solche Umstellungen sich für mich nicht mehr lohnen. Sie würden bei meinem Alter nicht zur Auswirkung kommen.").
Wittels, F. *Sigmund Freud: Der Mann, die Lehre, die Schule*, Leipzig/Wien/Zürich, 1924 [FM].

30 June 1933
Freud, W. Ernest-Molnar 6.8.1989 [FM].

8 July 1933 (Ruth)
Freud- Lampl-de Groot 14.7.1933 [FM].

8 July 1933 (Martin)
Freud, Anton Walter, Telephone interview, 30.8.1989.
Freud- Lampl-de Groot 14.7.1933 [FM].
Martin, Freud-Jones 18.8.1933 [Inst. of Psa: CFB/FO3/01].

9 July 1933
1. "Wolf" should be "*Wilhelm Knöpfmacher*". The invitation to the celebration also included some of the exam questions, among them a passage from Sophocles' *Oedipus Rex* and the essay theme: "*What considerations should be taken into account when choosing one's career?*"
"Invitation to Matura celebration 1933" [FM: SOH9–17 "B"].
Knoepfmacher, Hugo, "Zwei Beiträge zur Biographie Sigmund Freuds" *Jahrbuch der Psychoanalyse*, Bd. XI p.61 [FM: Author's copy dedicated to Anna Freud, with erroneous dates hand corrected.)
ibid. p.53.

1 August 1933
Anna Freud-Jones 23.8.1933 [Inst. of PsA: CFA/FO1/39].

2 August 1933
Freud- Lampl-de Groot 1.2.1933 [FM] ("Bullitt ist wieder als Meteor erschienen.").
Freud- Lampl-de Groot 10.2.1933 [FM].
Freud- Lampl-de Groot 16.2.1933 [FM] ("B. ist der einzige Amerikaner, der etwas von Europa versteht und etwas für Europa thun will. Darum getraue ich mich nicht zu hoffen, dass er wirklich auf den Posten gestellt werden wird, wo er in seinem Sinn wirken kann.").
Freud-Marie Bonaparte 7.12.1933 in Schur, 562.

10 August 1933
1. It is also possible this visit had some connection with the Braille *Introductory Lectures* published by the Hohe Warte press (no publication date). The following year Dr. Altmann sent Freud a book of sculpture done by the blind at his institute: Ludwig Münz & Viktor Löwenfeld, *Plastische Arbeiten Blinder*, Brünn, 1934. The dedication is dated 8.11.1934.
2. Three years later, on his 80th birthday, the children sent Freud a pseudo-Braille congratulatory message - that is, one in embossed, but normal alphabet letters.
Burlingham pp.297–8
Guestbook, Jewish Institute for the Blind, "Hohe Warte" in Siegfried Altmann Collection [Baeck: AR-C.1107. 2899].
Ludwig Münz & Viktor Löwenfeld, *Plastische Arbeiten Blinder*, Brünn, 1934 [FM].
Blinden-Institut, Hohe Warte (*80th Birthday Congratulatory Message*) [SFC]. (My thanks to Drs. Karl Fallend and Johannes Reichmayr for information leading to this note).

11 August 1933
Freud-Eitingon 29.7.1933 & 5.8.1933 [FM].

12 August 1933 (Hochrotherd)
Freud- Lampl-de Groot 12.8.1933 [FM].

12 August 1933 (Wise)
1. When Freud's brother-in-law Eli Bernays came to the United States, he apparently improved his English by listening to Stephen Wise's talks.
Wise, Stephen, *Challenging Years: The Autobiography of Stephen Wise*, London, 1951.
Freud Bernays, Hella, *All in the day's work*, Talk to Altrusa Club, Columbus, Ohio, 21.9.1978 [LoC].

17 August 1933
1. Later that year, to help establish an institute of psychoanalysis in Paris, Marie Bonaparte put her previous apartment, (137 Boulevard St. Germain), at the disposal of the French Pyschoanalytical Society.
2. Jones had reservations on account of French hostility to lay analysis: "It would also be amusing to have a President who was a woman as well as being a lay analyst, though I feel the latter point would cause local opposition." (*Jones-Anna Freud 2.12.1933*).
Freud-Eitingon 29.7.1933 [FM].
Freud-Jones 23.8.1933 [Typescript Inst. of PsA].
Marie Bonaparte-Jones 20.10.1933 [Inst. of Psa GO7/BE/FO1/04].
Jones-Anna Freud 2.12.1933 [Inst. of PsA CFA/FO1/56].

18 August 1933 (Essais)
Translation list [FM: I-F8–17-26].
Freud, Sigmund, *Essais de Psychanalyse appliquée*, Gallimard, Paris, 1933 [FM: LDFRD 2927].

18 August 1933 (Dorothy)
Burlingham, p.240.
Freud- Lampl-de Groot 8.4.1933 & 27.7.1933 [FM].
Young-Bruehl, p.96.

24 August 1933
Valenstein, Mrs. K., Interview, 14.5.1990.
Freud-Jeanne Lampl-de Groot 27.7.1933 [FM] ("Der Krankenstand bessert sich bei uns aber die Nachricht, dass Sie ihn vergrössern wollen, ist unleidlich. Es gehört wenig Medizin dazu um bei Ihrer Beschreibung an Blinddarm zu denken . . . ").
Freud-Jeanne Lampl-de Groot 12.8.1933 [FM].

25 August 1933
Anna Freud-Jones 31.10.1933 [Inst. of PsA: CFA/FO1/49].
Freud- Lampl-de Groot 27.7.1933 [FM].

3 September 1933 (Laforgue)
1. This is the last noted visit by Laforgue, but he called on Freud again, for example in early 1937. On that occasion he tried to persuade Freud to leave Austria. Freud responded: "The Nazis, I'm not afraid of them. Just help me in my battle against my great enemy." When Laforgue asked in amazement who that was, Freud replied: "Religion, the Catholic church."
2. By 1938 the situation had changed, as Anna Freud found to her cost when she had to haggle with Jones to bring even a few of the Vienna group with her to England.
Anna Freud-Jones 27.11.1933 [Inst. of PsA: CFA/FO1/55].
Laforgue, Dr. "Persönliche Erinnerungen an Freud," *Die Vorträge der 5 Lindauer Psychotherapiewoche 1954*, Stuttgart, n.d., p.51 [FM: VI/F29–165].
Waelder, Robert, Interview R.S.Stewart, 29.7.1966.

3 September 1933 (Bryher)
1. Bryher continued to be involved in the psychoanalytical movement: she attended the congresses at Lucerne in 1934, Marienbad in 1936 and Paris in 1938. Her last visit to Freud (not recorded in the diary) was after the Marienbad Congress in 1936. When the political situation deteriorated, she moved to Switzerland, where she worked on a refugee committee helping Jews and political dissidents to cross the border from Germany. Before being forced to leave Switzerland, she claimed to have aided 105 people to escape the Nazis (among them the ill-fated German critic Walter Benjamin, who afterwards committed suicide on being refused entry into Spain).
Robinson, Janice S., *H.D.:The Life and Work of an American Poet*, Boston, 1982, pp.303–4.
Grosskurth, Phyllis, *Melanie Klein: Her World and Her Work*, London, [1989], p.369.
Bryher, *The Heart to Artemis: A Writer's Memoirs*, London, 1963, pp.269–70, 278.

5 September 1933
1. One. of Freud's analysands at this time, Dr. Roy R. Grinker, saw Freud before and after this episode and reported a radical change: "I met Freud for the first time in the late summer of 1933 at his villa. He impressed me as extremely energetic, with long fingers and hands, constantly moving about. He appeared much younger than his actual age. [. . .] This Freud I never saw again. [. . . .] At his advanced age, and with this serious illness, Freud resumed analytic work in only a few weeks, but physical liveliness was gone. He walked very slowly and the abounding energy in his movements had disappeared."
Pichler Notes, 15.9.1933 [FM].
Freud-Jones 15.10.1933 [Typescript Inst. of PsA] ("Ich bin ausser Bett, habe schon eine Woche lang in bescheidenem Anfang gearbeitet, fühle mich "moderately" well, aber die Folgen der Thrombose sind noch nicht überwunden und einen ersten Versuch meine Stiege zu steigen habe ich mit einem

tüchtigen Rückfall bezalt.").
Anna Freud-Jones 18.10.1933 [Inst. of PsA: CFA/FO1/45].
Freud-Arnold Zweig 25.10.1933 in *Zweig Letters*.
Grinker, Roy R., M.D., "Reminiscences of a Personal Contact with Freud," *The American Journal of Orthopsychiatry*, Vol. X. Oct. 1940, No. 4 p.850.

16 September 1933
Freud-Liebe Kinder [Oli & Henny Freud] 2.9.1933 [FM] ("Wir werden die Freude haben, dass Lux mit den Jungen uns vom 12–18 Sept, ehe sie nach London gehen besucht u wir verlängern darum den Aufenthalt der Hohe Warte. Gern hätten wir Euch auch gehabt, aber in unserer Vorstellung bleibt Ihr uns näher in Frk als sie in England . . . ").

19 September 1933 (Pichler)
Pichler Notes, 19–20.9.1933 [FM].

19 September 1933 (Lux)
Freud, Stephen, Personal communication, 23.3.1990.
Freud-Lucie Freud 20.10.1933 [SFC].

30 September 1933
Mathilde Freud-Ernst Freud 1.11.1933 [FM: Lucie Freud Papers]. ("Du weisst wohl, dass Papa ziemlichen argen Schnupfen hatte und Mama direkte Herzmüdungserscheinungen nach der Übersiedlung von der Hohen Warte; ich habe mir jetzt in den Kopf gesetzt, ein Haus für das ganze Jahr zu finden, aber was man sieht, ist alles so unmöglich!").

3 October 1933
Neue Freie Presse, 4.10.1933.
Schuschnigg, Kurt v., *The Brutal Takeover*, London, 1971, p.49, 90.
Freud- Lampl-de Groot 14.7.1933 [FM] ("Politik erst nach den Hunden. Ruhe vorläufig. Wir dürfen annehmen, dass wir einen besonderen bodenständigen Faschismus entgegengehen, der nicht so brutal sein wird wie der deutsche. Ob es schön sein wird in Wien zu leben? ").

4 October 1933
1. When Bauer died in 1935, Freud could still not forgive him: "It was not just that he abused his role as a journalist but also the base way in which he defended what he had done. It was a painful disillusionment, yet another." (*Freud-Arnold Zweig 13.2.1935*).
Freud-Arnold Zweig 28.1.1934 & 13.2.1935 in *Zweig Letters*.

5 October 1933
Freud, Martin, *Reifezeugnis* [FM: Photocopy—Courtesy A.W.Freud).
Freud, Esti, *Vignettes of my Life*, Nov. 1979 (ms.), [Baeck].
Martin Freud, p.200.

9 October 1933 (Outing)
Martha Freud-Lucie Freud 13.11.1933 [FM: Lucie Freud Papers]. ("Papa geht leider gar nicht aus, trotz dem wir schon einen Tragsessel bereit stehen haben. Teils ist es sein eigene, teils die Ängstlichkeit seiner Ärzte. Aber merkwürdige Weise fehlt es ihm kaum.").
Martha Freud-Lucie Freud 13.11.1933 [FM: Lucie Freud Papers]. (" . . . ich kann schon wieder rennen und mich bucken wie sonst, die Maschine arbeitet wieder, Gott s. Dank!!").

9 October 1933
Reeves, Dr. C.N., in *Freud and Art*, p.59.
H.D., p.174.

14 October 1933
Neue Freie Presse, 15.10.1933.

16 October 1933
Freud-Mathilde Hollitscher 16.10.1933 [LoC] ("Von Papa mit herzlichen Wünsche u Versicherung gegen Kursverlust.").
Freud-Mathilde Hollitscher 16.10.1924 [LoC].

19 October 1933
Freud-Ernst Freud 3.12.1933 [LoC].

Martin Freud-Jones 5.12.1952 [Inst. of PsA: CFB/FO3/O8].

4 November 1933
Freud-Ernst Freud 3.12.1933 [LoC].

8 November 1933 (Stomatitis)
Anna Freud-Ernst Freud 7.11.1933 [FM: Lucie Freud Papers]. ("Papa geht es im Ganzen gut, mit sehr vielen kleinen täglichen Beschwerden und Quälereien . . . ").

8 November 1933 (Pichler)
Pichler Notes, 9.11.1933 [FM].

12 November 1933 (Operation)
1. Actually, the operation of November 12 was not the first one in 1923, nor was it even the first one performed by Pichler. The trouble had begun early in 1923 when Freud noticed "a leucoplastic growth on my jaw and palate right side . . . " (*Freud-Jones 25.4.1923*). On April 20 the rhinologist Marcus Hajek, Julius Schnitzler's brother-in-law, performed an unskilful operation, which was followed by a dangerous hemorrhage. A pathology report revealed the growth to be malignant. In the following month Holzknecht gave Freud X-ray and radium treatments.

After creating an oral prosthesis, Pichler performed his first operation on Freud in two stages—the first on October 4, 1923, the second on the 11th. But a month later he received a pathologist's report showing that malignant tissue remained and on November 12 further radical surgery was necessary. It is that final operation in 1923, which is commemorated here.
2. At a meeting on March 20, 1930, to discuss *Civilization and its Discontents* Freud argued that his devotion to truth did people no harm, saying: "The death of each of you is certain, mine obviously in a shorter time, and you do not let yourself be disturbed by this. Seven years ago I was told that I would have a maximum of five years to live, and since I took it rather well, I can also tell mankind the most unpleasant things; it does not touch them." *Freud-Rank 26.11.1923* [FM: MISC] ("Ich habe mich ja wirklich gefülsmässig sehr an Prof. Pichler angelehnt, mit der zweiten Operation kam eine Entäuschung, Lockerung der homosexuellen Bindung. Zurück zu den Frauen."). *Martha Freud-Ernst/Lucie Freud 29.11.1933* [FM: Lucie Freud Papers]. ("Ist ausserdem durch die Prothese so gequält, wie eigentlich nur in der ersten Zeit der ersten Operation."). Sterba, pp.115–6.

12 November 1933
Neue Freie Presse, 12 & 13.11.1933.

14 November 1933
1. After his escape, Simmel went to Brussels to await a visa to the United States, where a post had been promised in Los Angeles. In April 1934 he was able to leave Europe. In the United States he transformed the Los Angeles Study Group into a psychoanalytic society. He also wrote works on self-preservation and the death instinct, antisemitism and mass psychology. *Anna Freud-Jones 23.11.1933* [Inst of PsA: CFA/FO1/55]. *Martha Freud-Ernst/Lucie Freud 29.11.1933* [FM: Lucie Freud Papers]. Fliess, Robert, "In Memoriam," *The Psychoanalytic Quarterly*, N.Y., Vol. 17, 1948 pp.1–5. Schultz, U., Hermanns, L.M., "Das Sanatorium Schloss Tegel Ernst Simmels—Zur Geschichte und Konzeption der ersten Psychoanalytischen Klinik." *Psychotherapie. Psychosomatik Medizinische Psychologie.* 2. Feb. 1987, p.65. Hermanns, Dr. Ludger, Oral communication, 22.7.1990.

16 November 1933 (Lectures)
Meisel, Perry, & Kendrick, Walter (eds.), *Bloomsbury/Freud: The Letters of James and Alix Strachey 1924–1925*, N.Y., 1985, p.46. *Jones-Freud 17.7.1933* [Inst. of PsA]. *Freud-Jones 23.7.1933* [Typescr. Inst. of PsA].

16 November 1933 (Cypriot)
Jones, III.222.
Arnold Zweig-Freud 2.3.1936 in *Zweig Letters.*

16 November 1933 (Ernst)
1. During his first year in England, Ernst was appalled by British ignorance of the situation in Germany. When people wanted to be friendly, he later said, they would say something nice about Hitler: "They had absolutely no idea." *Martha Freud-Lucie Freud 13.11.1933* [FM: Lucie Freud Papers]. Freud, Ernst, Interview R.S.Stewart, 10.1.1966.

25 November 1933
Freud-Eitingon 5.10.1933 [FM]. *Int. J. PsA*, January 1934, Vol.XV, I pp.108–9. *Eitingon-Freud 2.11.1933* [FM]. *Martha Freud-Ernst/Lucie Freud 29.11.1933* [FM: Lucie Freud Papers].

3 December 1933 (Anna)
Freud-Anna Freud 3.12.1933 [FM] ("Chinesischer Schmuck (voriges Jahrh.) die beiden durch eine Nadel verbundene Scheiben können getrennt u gesondert verwendet werden. Die Zierraten sind Feingold. z. 3 Dez. 1933 Herzlich Papa."). *Martha Freud-Ernst/Lucie Freud 29.11.1933* [FM: Lucie Freud Papers].

3 December 1933 (Mitzi)
1. She survived another nine years. On June 29, 1942, she and two of her sisters, Adolfine and Paula, were deported to Theresienstadt. From there she and Paula were transported on September 23, 1942, to be murdered at the extermination camp at Malyi Trostinets. *Martha Freud-Lucie Freud 7.12.1933* [FM: Lucie Freud Papers]. Leupold-Loewenthal, Harald: "L'émigration de la famille Freud en 1938," *Revue Internationale d'Histoire de la Psychanalyse* 2, 1989, p.459.

11 December 1933
1. Could this *"Fall"* have been the incident of the falling lamp, which W. Ernest Freud recounts in the note for Friday, June 30, 1933? If so, it would mean Ernstl was in hospital now for further treatment. *Dorothy Burlingham-Lucie Freud 17.1.1934* [FM: Lucie Freud Papers].

1934

2 January 1934
S.E., XV.11.
Freud, Sigmund, *Shiurim be-mavo le-psikhoanalizah* Vol.1. (Authorized Hebrew translation by Y. Devosis), Stybel, Tel Aviv, 1933/34. [FM: LDFRD 5358].

5 January 1934
Freud, Anton Walter, Telephone interview, 30.8.1989.
Martha Freud-Ernst/Lucie Freud 15.1.1934 [FM: Lucie Freud Papers].

6 January 1934 (Princess)
Bertin, p.190.
Anna Freud-Jones 24.10.1934 [Inst. of PsA: CFA/FO2/15].

6 January 1934 (Philipp)
1. During the summer of 1934 Oscar Philipp's son Elliot, then a student at Cambridge, visited Martha and Freud at their summer home in Grinzing. Freud's first question to him was, "Is your father still orthodox?" — a question Elliot's father had predicted, knowing how much Freud disapproved of his Judaism. His father should read the *Future of an Illusion*, Freud continued, to which Elliot replied that his father had read it and it had only strengthened his faith. *Martha Freud-Ernst/Lucie Freud 15.1.1934* [FM: Lucie Freud Papers]. Philipp, Elliot, "Souvenirs de rencontres avec Sigmund Freud," *L'Ecrit du Temps* 6, Les Editions de Minuit, Paris, [1984?], pp.45–6.

24 January 1934
Schur, 486.
Engelman, pl.19.
Anna Freud-Jones 30.1.1934 [Inst.of PsA: CFA/FO1/66].
Martha Freud-Lucie Freud 12–14.2.1934 [FM: Lucie Freud Papers].
Pichler Notes, 9.2.1934 [FM].

7 February 1934
Young-Bruehl, p.45.
Martha Freud-Ernst/Lucie Freud 3.2.1934 [FM: Lucie Freud Papers].
Martha Freud-Lucie Freud 12.2.1934 [FM: Lucie Freud Papers] ("Kurz, sie haben Beide gestrahlt, was man ja von Rob. bekanntlich nicht *täglich* behaupten kann!").

10 February 1934
Anna Freud-Jones 14.1.1934 [Inst. of PsA: CFA/FO1/63].
Anna Freud-Jones 30.1.1934 [Inst. of PsA: CFA/FO1/63].
Anna Freud-Brill 28.2.1934 [FM: Transcript GENERAL file].
Freud-Ernst Freud 2.3.1934 [SFC].
Martha Freud-Lucie Freud 12.2.1934 [FM: Lucie Freud Papers].

12 February 1934
1. Martha Freud broke off in the middle of writing a letter because the electricity was turned off. Trams stopped and telephones did not work, but gas and water continued. On the evening of the next day she resumed her letter. There was no theater or cinema, the house doors were locked at 8 o'clock, martial law had been declared and there were bloody battles between government forces and the Social Democrats. Furthermore, there were barbed-wire entanglements separating the Freuds from their supplier, Papst on Schlickgasse. "Even during the war we experienced nothing like this!" she wrote. Stadler, Karl R., *Austria*, London, 1971, pp.130–1. Spiel, Hilde, *Vienna's Golden Autumn: 1866–1938*, London, 1987, p.231. *Freud-H.D. 5.4.1934* in H.D. p.192.

Kitchen, Martin, *The Coming of Austrian Fascism*,
Montreal, 1980, p.6 & 279.
Freud-Ernst Freud 20.2.1934 in *Letters*.
Freud-Eitingon 1.3.1934 [FM].
Mann, Thomas, *Tagebücher 1933–34*, Fischer, 1977,
p.324.
Martha Freud-Lucie Freud 12/13/14.2.1934 [FM: Lucie
Freud Papers].

17 February 1934
Hemecker, Dr. Wilhelm, Oral communication,
30.5.1990.

18 February 1934
Burlingham, p.243.

19 February 1934
Dumont, Georges-Henri, *Elisabeth de Belgique*, Paris,
1986, p.265.

3 March 1934
1. Jones wrote to Freud: "On the momentous motor
trip she was disturbed by the fact that the man was
not able to drive and very apprehensive, with right,
about the woman's driving. She begged a man to take
her place in driving, but this could not be done. Five
minutes before the accident she sent off a postcard at
a stopping place and thought to herself it would
probably be the last postcard she would ever send; I
think it was to her mother. This seems to me already
excessive. When the accident happened she went off
into a pleasant dream that everything was all right
and she was very happy. I read this as a strong
Reizschutz with vigorous denial of reality, based on
the assertion that her infantile fears (?danger from the
mother) could never come true in reality. She was in
fact astonishingly well and only the bleeding from the
ear revealed that there was trouble." (*Jones-Freud
26.3.1934*)
Jones-Freud 26.3.1934 & 12.6.1934 [Inst. of PsA].
Jones-Anna Freud 28.2.1934 [Inst. of PsA:
CFA/FO1/70].
Anna Freud-Jones 4.3.1934 [Inst. of PsA:
CFA/FO1/72].

8 March 1934
Freud-Ernst Freud 11.3.1934 [LoC].

8 March 1934
Reeves Dr. C.N. in *Freud and Art*, p.73.

9 March 1934
Ransohoff, Rita, "Sigmund Freud: Collector of
Antiquities and Student of Archaeology,"
Archaeology, Vol.28, No.2, 102–111, p.106

12 March 1934
Wittels, F., *Sigmund Freud: Der Mann, die Lehre, die
Schule*, Leipzig/Wien/Zürich, 1924 p.21 (margin note)
[FM].
Freud- Lampl-de Groot 25.1.1933 [FM].

23 March 1934
Pichler Notes, 22–3.3.1934 [FM].

5 April 1934
Wiener Zeitung, 4.4.1934 (With thanks to Dr.
Johannes Reichmayr for this reference).

13 April 1934
Freud-Eitingon 14.4.1934 [FM] ("Nach einer besonders
langen und schwierigen Suche haben wir gestern
Wohnung für den Sommer gemietet. Es ist XIX
Strassergasse 47 also halbwegs auf dem Hügel, der
oben 'Himmel' heisst, nicht weit von Kobenzl usw.
Das Haus scheint bequem, der alte Garten hat einen
ebenen und einen ansteigenden Teil, an dem ich
Terrainkur üben kann. Vorläufig kann ich noch sehr
wenig leisten, bezale jedes kleine Muskelunternehmen
mit Herzsensationen.").
Freud-Lou Andreas-Salomé 16.5.1934 in Pfeiffer.
Martha Freud-Lucie Freud 8.5.1934 [FM] ("Das Haus
ist altmodisch, aber riesig behaglich und der Garten
einfach herrlich, vielleicht noch schöner, als der
Poetzleinsdorfer.").

20 April 1934
Freud-Lucie Freud 20.10.1933 [SFC] ("Von der Pariser

Zweig der Familie nichts Hoffnungsvolles.").
Martha Freud-Lucie Freud 13.11.1933 [FM]
(" . . . jetzt sitzen sie schon über ein halbes Jahr in
Paris und nicht der Schimmer einer Aussicht!").

21 April 1934
J.R. "Obituary" [for Daly], *Int. J. PsA*, vol. 31, 1950,
pp. 290–1.
Freud-Ferenczi 14.4.1925 [FM] ("Daly is ein einfältiger
Mensch, sieht aber richtig u ist ein guter Kerl.").
Lupton, Mary Jane, Ph.D., "Claude Dagmar Daly:
Notes on the Menstruation Complex" *American
Imago* Vol.46, Spring 1989, No.1, pp.1–2.

23 April 1934
Pichler Notes 7 & 23.4.1934 [FM].

24 April 1934
Nestroy, Johann, *Sämtliche Werke: historisch-kritische
Gesamtausgabe* (ed. Fritz Brukner and Otto Rommel),
Wien, 1924–1930) 15 vols. [LDFRD 1072].
Beer-Hofmann, Richard, *Gesammelte Werke*, Fischer,
Frankfurt a. Main, 1963, p.637.

25 April 1934
1. Problems in Sweden led Jekels to consider going
to London in 1936. Jones, however, was not
encouraging and wondered why he did not go to
Warsaw instead to help the young group there. In
1937 he returned to Vienna, but when the Nazis
invaded in 1938 he emigrated to the United States,
via Australia. Freud remained concerned for his
welfare and wrote to Smith Ely Jelliffe: "Among the
immigrants in N. York there is one man Dr. Jekels
not only a distinguished analyst but also a very good
friend of mine. I would like to hear that you can do
something to ease his situation by sending him
patients etc." (*Freud-Jelliffe 18.10.1938*).
Mühlleitner, Elke, *Die Männlichen Mitglieder der
Wiener Psychoanalytischen Vereinigung 1937/38*,
(Typescript) (With thanks to Elke Mühlleitner).
Freud-Eitingon 20.11.1932 [FM].
Freud-Jelliffe 18.10.1938 [FM: I-F8–74-25].

26 April 1934 (Ur)
1. At this period Freud was analyzing H.D. In her
Tribute to Freud she records a remark made on March
20, 1933, that epitomizes the connection between his
analytical work and the collection of antiquities: "He
said his little statues and images helped stabilize the
evanescent idea, or keep it from escaping altogether."
But Freud's fascination with antiquity could
sometimes disturb his analytical composure. Reik
says Freud once had to break off treating a
well-known Egyptologist, because his own wish to
learn more about archaeology interfered with the
analysis.
Wooley, Sir Charles Leonard, *The Royal Cemetery: a
report on the predynastic and Sargonid graves excavated
between 1926 and 1931*, London, 1934, 2 vols.
[LDFRD 1573].
H.D. p.175.
Reik, Theodor, *The Inner Experience of a
Psychoanalyst*, London, 1949, p.128.

26 April 1934 (Oli)
Freud-Oli/Henny Freud 2.9.1933 [FM].
Freud-Arnold Zweig 25.10.1933 in *Zweig Letters*.
Freud-Sam Freud 31.7.1933 [FM].

26 April 1934
H.D. p.xiii & 5.
Freud- Lampl-de Groot 15.4.1933 [FM].

28 April 1934
Martha Freud-Lucie Freud 8.5.1934 [FM]
(" . . . alle seine Bilder und auch ein Grossteil seiner
Antiquitäten waren an ihrem Platz!").
Freud-Lou Andreas-Salome 16.5.1934 in Pfeiffer.
Anna Freud-Jones 7.5.1934 [Inst. of PsA:
CFA/FO1/85].
Anna Freud-Jones 11.5.1934 [Inst. of PsA:
CFA/FO1/87].
Freud-Eitingon 27.5.1934 [FM].
Freud-Ernst Freud 15.4.1934 [LoC].
Kitchen, Martin, *The Coming of Austrian Fascism*,
Montreal, 1980, p.278.

Wiener Zeitung, 1.5.1934 (No. 120).

6 May 1934
Freud-Eitingon 27 .5.1934 [FM] ("Fast alle, die mir
heuer zum Geburtstag gratulirt haben, werden
vergeblich auf Dank u Annererkennung warten. Ich
will sie durch diese Technik dazu erziehen, dass sie es
das nächste 'Mal' nicht wieder thun.")
Martha Freud-Lucie Freud 8.5.1934 [FM] ("Das
Geburtstag brachte wieder einen Blumenregen, aber
alle Besuche hatten wir energisch verboten, sogar die
Familie.").

6 May 1934
Freud-Anna Freud 3.9.1932 [FM].
Freud- Lampl-de Groot 26.5.1933 [FM].
Martha Freud-Lucie Freud 8.5.1934 [FM].

7 May 1934
Portal, Jane in *Freud and Art*, p.130.

18 May 1934
1. The previous year, on Freud's 77th birthhday,
H.D. had seen Freud's desk cleared of antiquities and
covered with vases of orchids. But people also gave
Freud other flowers. Thanking Mathilde for her
flowers in 1930, Freud mentions that, apart from
orchids, there were roses and lilies of the valley on
his desk " . . . reminding me [. . .] how impossible
it is to flee one's fate." (*Freud-Mathilde 9.5.1930*). It is
not known who gave him the gardenia. Mirra
Eitingon had given Freud gardenias three times
already by 1932, but as she was now in Jerusalem,
this flower unlikely to be from her. In 1933 Freud
had confided to H.D. his memories of Rome, the
Spanish Steps and gardenias, adding: " 'In Rome even
I could afford to wear a gardenia.' " She had then
searched Vienna in vain for these flowers. But she,
too, was not in Vienna at this time.
Freud-Meine geliebte Alte [Martha Freud] 20.9.1912
[FM] ("Ich habe mich auch noch nie so gepflegt und
so arbeitslos und nach Wunsch und Behagen gelebt.
Heute habe ich sogar eine Gardenia gefunden und
gekauft, deren Duft mich in beste Stimmung gebracht
hat. Minna kennt die Blume, sie ist noch edler als die
Datura.").
Freud-Mathilde Hollitscher 9.5.1930 [LoC] ("Deine
Blumen stehen vor mir während ich dir herzlich
danke und erinnern mich mit den anderen, - Rosen,
Orchideen, Maiglöckchen, wie unmöglich es ist,
seinen Schicksal zu entfliehen").
Eitingon-Freud 6.7.1932 [FM].
Freud-H.D. 28.11.1938 in H.D. p.11.
Ibid p.9.

4 June 1934
1. Freud rarely refers to small items from his
collection in the diary. Perhaps a large bust of a
bearded male figure may have been the "Sarapis" in
question here. This piece appears in Engelman's 1938
photos of Berggasse 19, but has since disappeared.
Otherwise he may have mentioned the small Sarapis
figure because of the curious fact that he bought two
bull figures together on one day. (His astrological
sign, incidentally, was Taurus.)
Wallis Budge, E.A., *Osiris and the Egyptian
Resurrection*, N.Y., 1973 [1911], Vol.I, p.61.
Hart, George, *A Dictionary of Egyptian Gods and
Goddesses*, London, 1987 [1986], pp.188–9.

Thurs 14 June, 1934
1. Jones and Anna Freud were both concerned about
the paper Groddeck had applied to deliver at the
Lucerne Congress in August. Jones wrote to her that
it would surely be nonsense, to which she replied
even more dismissively: " . . . my impression is it
may be more than nonsense, the kind of thing that
makes everybody who listens uncomfortable because
one does not feel sure that the author is quite in his
right mind." (*Anna Freud-Jones 12.4.1934*).
Groddeck's death eliminated this problem.
Freud-Jones 16.6.1934 [FM: SFVAR 76] ("Das
Gerücht sagt, dass Groddeck zuletzt wegen
psychischen Störungen internirt war. Die Parte theilt
mir dass er in Zürich gestorben; was hätte er in Z. zu
suchen? War er also in Burghölzli? Die Zeit verlangt
Opfer. Menschen sterben, vielleicht bereitwilliger als

sonst.")
Ibid ("Gestern erfahren wir dass Frau Stella Zweig,
Martin's unschätzbare Hilfskraft im Verlag einem
Anfall von Poliomyelitis vom Laudry'schen Typus
erlegen ist. Eine grosse Verlegenheit für den Verlag.
Es ist schön hier in Grinzing, aber man wird seines
Lebens nicht froh. Die Fundamente schwanken.").
Jones-Anna Freud 9.4.1934 [Inst. of PsA:
CFA/FO1/81].
Anna Freud-Jones 12.4.1934 [Inst. of PsA:

30 June 1934
Freud-Arnold Zweig 15.7.1934 in *Zweig Letters*.

4/5 July 1934
Pichler Notes, 6.7.1934, 23.3.1934 & 9.8.1934.
Schur, p.450.

12 July 1934
Freud, W. Ernest-Molnar 6.8.1989 [FM].

12 July 1934
Portal, Jane in *Freud and Art* p.130.

13 July 1934
Freud-Jones 17.6.1932 [Typescript Inst. of PsA]
("Sarasin steht mir als persönlicher Schüler nahe, ich
würde ihn auch für jeden Vertrauensposten
vorschlagen, nur grade geschäftliche Einsicht suche
ich nicht bei ihm.").
Sarasin, Philipp, *Lebenslauf* [FM: S9 Offprints].

16 July 1934
Translation list [FM: I-F8-17-29].

17 July 1934
1. After J. H. W. van Ophuijsen resigned from the
Dutch group he spent some time working in South
Africa. Sachs' helpfulness to him greatly impressed
Jones and Anna Freud, both tired of dealing with the
warring factions in the European and American
groups: "I also enclose Wulf Sachs' letter which is
indeed charming, as nice as the Japanese ones. Is it
the distance from Europe that does that?" (*Anna
Freud-Jones* 9.5.1935).
J.R. "Obituary" [Wulf Sachs] *Int. J. PsA* 31, 1950,
288–9
Jones-Anna Freud 29.4.1935 [Inst. of PsA:
CFA/FO2/36]
Anna Freud-Jones 9.5.1935 [Inst. of PsA:
CFA/FO2/37]

21 July 1934
Martha Freud-Lucie Freud 8.5.1934 [FM: Lucie Freud
Papers].

25 July 1934
1. Freud's suspicions about Mussolini were only
partly justified. Mussolini managed to get Hitler to
agree that Austrian independence should be
maintained, but could not get him to guarantee it.
2. Martin Freud, who was at Dollfuss's funeral,
wrote: "Few Viennese people attended the funeral.
The majority of the Viennese population were now
Socialists who had become hostile to the Dolfuss
regime after their defeat in the first civil war. A fair
proportion were Nazis who regretted that the coup
designed to bring down the Government had failed."
Freud-Jones 16.6.1934 [Typescript Inst. of PsA]
("Vielleicht grade jetzt hat uns der Intriguant M. in
Venedig an den Räuberhauptmann H. verkauft.").
Clare, George, *Last Waltz in Vienna*, London, 1981,
pp.131–3.
Martin Freud, p.197.

26 July 1934 (Martha)
Freud-Liebe Kinder[Oli/Henny] 31.7.1933 [LoC]
Freud-Ernst Freud 11.3.1933 [LoC]

26 July 1934 (Marianne)
1. Marianne Kris was later to become influential as a
child analyst. In 1938 she and her husband emigrated
to New York. After her husband's death in 1957 she
continued his research on problems of childhood and
adolescence. Her son, Dr. Anton O. Kris, is now a
psychoanalyst practising in the United States.
[Ernst Federn] "Obituary" (Marianne Kris), *Sigmund
Freud House Bulletin*, Vol.4/No.2, Winter 1980, p.57.

Kris, Anton O.-Molnar 1.6.1990.

2 August 1934
Freud-Jelliffe 2.8.1934 [FM: 1-F8–74-15] ("Wir würden
hier schöne Sommerruhe in einem reizenden Vorort
von Wien geniessen, wenn die politischen
Verhältnisse diese erlauben würden. Eben heute ist
die Nachricht vom Tod des deutschen Präsidenten
Hindenburg eingetroffen und niemand kann erraten,
welche Folgen die Entwicklung in Deutschland für
unser arme Österreich haben kann.").

18 August 1934
Eitingon-Freud 21.7.1934 [FM].

20 August 1934
1. In 1932, Huber, in collaboration with the
International Psychoanalytical Press, published
Nunberg's *Allgemeine Neurosenlehre auf
psychoanalytische Grundlage*, a work that Freud
recommended as " . . . the most complete and
conscientious presentation of a psychoanalytical
theory of neurotic processes which we at present
possess."
Nunberg, Herman, *Memoirs*, N.Y., 1969, pp.59–63.
Freud, Sigmund, Advertising circular I.P.V. 1932
[FM] (" . . . die vollständigste und gewissenhafteste
Darstellung einer psychoanalytischen Theorie der
neurotischen Vorgänge, die wir derzeit besitzen.").

22 August 1934
1. In his Freud biography, Jones misdates this visit.
He writes: "*After* the Congress I flew to Vienna for
three days to visit Freud in Grinzing. I had not seen
him for five years. . . ." [My italics].
Anna Freud-Jones 18.8.1934 [Inst. of PsA:
CFA/FO2/10].
Jones-Anna Freud 24.1.1934 [Inst. of PsA:
CFA/FO1/65].
Jones-Anna Freud 2.4.1935 [Inst. of PsA:
CFA/FO2/35].
Jones, III.205.
CFA/FO2/13].
Freud-Redaktion der I.P.Zeitschrift 11.2.1933 [LoC].

5 September 1934
Burn, Lucilla in *Freud and Art*, p.103.

23 September 1934
1. Curiously enough, Eitingon, unaware of this
subtitle, independently suggested subtitling the work
A Historico-psychological Novel (*Ein
geschichtspsychologischer Roman*), in order to disarm
dangerous opponents. In Freud's own chronological
list of his writings, *Moses* is registered at the
beginning of 1935. But this list was probably
compiled retrospectively, not month by month. The
title is recorded in brackets, indicating its
unpublished and provisional nature.
Freud-Arnold Zweig 18.8.1933 in Schur, 563 [Passage
not included in *Zweig Letters*, but no cuts indicated].
Freud-Arnold Zweig 30.9.1934 in *Zweig Letters*.
Freud-Lou Andreas-Salome 6.1.1935 in Pfeiffer.
Freud-Arnold Zweig 16.12.1934 in *Zweig Letters*.
Yerushalmi, Yosef Hayim, "Freud on the 'Historical
Novel': From the Manuscript Draft (1934) of *Moses
and Monotheism*." *Int. J. PsA*. (1989) 70. p.375.
Eitingon-Freud 14.10.1934 [FM].
Freud, *Chronologie* [LoC].

9 October 1934
1. Although the French politician was not the
primary target, it was his death which Arnold Zweig
mentioned in a letter to Freud, since this once more
implicated Europe in the perennial Balkan problem:
"Barthou's assassination has made things in the
immediate future very uncertain. It is frightful:
violence begets violence and stupidity stupidity. I was
quite shattered yesterday. Clearly the Yugoslavs have
a troubled history behind them to feel compelled to
perpetuate it like this. Though Hitler is the only one
to benefit, it will be hard to prove that he had a hand
in this. But if there were the slightest hint that this
were the case, it might give rise to a new torrent of
events which would put an end to the Hitler epoch.
But shall we have this joy?" (*Arnold Zweig-Freud*
11.10.1934).

Seton-Watson, Hugh, *Eastern Europe between the Wars:
1918–1941*, N.Y., 1967, p.228 & 231.
Arnold Zweig-Freud 11.10.1934 in *Zweig Letters*.

25 August 1934 (Alexander)
Roazen, Paul, Review of "Howard J. Faulkner &
Virginia D. Pruitt (Eds.) "The Selected
Correspondence of Karl A. Menninger, 1919–1945"
(Yale University Press 1988)" *Psychoanalytic Books*,
Fall 1990, p.448.
Freud-Eitingon 21.7.1932 [FM] ("Zu Alexander möchte
ich gern unbeirrtes Zutrauen haben; es, gelingt mir
nicht ganz. Seine echte oder vorgespielte Einfalt
macht ihn mir fremd. Oder mein Mistrauen gegen
Amerika ist nicht zu besiegen.").

25 August 1934 (Anna)
Anna Freud-Jones 15.6.1934 [Inst. of PsA:
CFA/FO1/95].

29 August 1934
H.D., pp.5–6.

1 September 1934
Anna Freud-Jones 20.9.1934 [Inst. of PsA:
CFA/FO2/11].
Eitingon-Freud 18.9.1934 [FM]
Leitsätze der Kongressvorträge, 13 Int. Psa Kon. 26–31
Aug. 1934 [FM]
Anna Freud-Jones 24.10.1934 [Inst. of PsA CFA/FO].

[Mon] 3 September 1934
1. In 1933 Freud had sent a message to the editorial
board of the *Zeitschrift* that henceforth only names of
those actively involved should be listed on its letter
head. An exception was made for Radó, firstly
because he had been such an excellent editor for 7
years from 1924 to 1931, and secondly "weil er rabiat
ist" ("because he has a furious temper") and it was
not worth angering him over a point of principle.
Anna Freud-Jones 20.9.1934 [Inst. of PsA:
CFA/FO2/11].
Jones-Anna Freud 24.9.1934 [Inst. of PsA:

13 October 1934
Anna Freud-Jones 24.10.1934 [Inst. of PsA:
CFA/FO2/15].
Martha Freud-Lucie Freud 12.10.1934 [FM: Lucie
Freud Papers] ("Wir waren dies Mal genau 5 1/2
Monate fort, da sammelt sich allerlei! Und ich freu
mich direkt auf die Winterfahrordnung.").
Freud-Eitingon 27.10.1934 [FM] ("Berggasse ist nicht
ganz so schön wie Grinzing. Die fälschlich so
genannte Gesundheit könnte erfreulicher sein.").

3 November 1934
Martha Freud-Ernst Freud 27.10.1934 [FM: Lucie
Freud Papers].

26 November 1934 (Dozent)
Dekan-Freud 23.11.1934 [FM: SOH9–17 "D"].
Austrian laws cited in above letter:
  Staatsgesetzblatt Nr. 415. #21, Absatz 1. Punkt 4.
                                          (2.9.1920)
  Bundesgesetzblatt 1934 Stück 16, Nr. 34 [Artikel
  4].   (23.5.1934)
(My thanks to Dr. Johannes Reichmayr for help
with this note.)

26 November 1934 (Hormone)
1. On November 17, 1923, just after the main cancer
operation, Freud underwent a Steinach operation—a
vasectomy—which had been recommended by Rudolf
von Urbantchitsch as a method of rejuvenation and
thus of delaying any recurrence of the cancer. He
reported no effect the following year, but defended
the surgery in a later interview with the American
journalist George Viereck. To the question whether
he approved Steinach's attempts to lengthen life,
Freud responded: "Steinach makes no attempt to
lengthen life. He merely combats old age. The
Steinach operation arrests untoward biological
accidents in its [sic] early stages. It makes life more
livable. It does not make it worth living. Secretly
every living being, no matter how intense life burns
with him, longs for the cessation [of] 'the fever called
living.' " [*London Weekly Dispatch* 28.7.1927].
Pichler Notes, 22.11.1934 [FM].

Schur, 450.
London Weekly Dispatch 28.7.1927 [Transcript LoC: B28].
Jones, III.104.
Freud-Ferenczi 22.1.1924 & 6.8.1924 [FM].
Romm, pp.73–85.

3 December 1934
Freud, Martin, "Birthday poem 3.12.1934" [FM: MOB 16] ("Der alte Anzug kommt aufs Land/ Und findet dort bei Huhn und Kuh/ Die wohlverdiente Altersruh.").

7 December 1934
Freud, Esti D., *Vignettes of my Life*, Nov. 1979 (ms.), [Baeck].
Freud, Anton Walter, Telephone communication, 30.8.1989.

14 December 1934
Freud-Fliess 19.4.1894 in Masson.
Freud-Ferenczi 13.12.1929 [FM].

16 December 1934
Schur, 57–8.

1935

1 January 1935
Schur, 409–410.

13 January 1935
Jones-Federn 4.12.1934 [Inst. of PsA: GO7/BC/FO5/07].

23 January 1935
Freud-Anna v. Vest 26.3.1925 in Goldmann, Stefan, (1985): "Eine Kur aus der Frühzeit der Psychoanalyse. Kommentar zu Freuds Briefen an Anna von Vest." *Jahrbuch der Psychoanalyse*, Bd. XVII. S. 296–337 ("Ich bekomme für eine Anna eine andere."). (With thanks to Prof. Fichtner and Peter Swales for information leading to this note.)

23 January 1935
1. Freud's pride was tempered with a familiar anxiety. The letter continues: "Of course there are certain worries; she takes things too seriously. What will she do when she has lost me? Will she lead a life of ascetic austerity?" (*Freud-Lou Andreas-Salomé* 6.1.1935).
Peters, pp.199–200.
Anna Freud-Jones 14.1.1935 [Inst. of PsA: CFA/FO2/26].
Freud-Lou Andreas-Salomé 6.1.1935 in Pfeiffer.
Sterba, p.70.

27 January 1935
1. When Freud received, via his American relative Edward Bernays, an American offer to write a "real" autobiography, he responded: "A psychologically complete and honest confession of my life, on the other hand, would require so much indiscretion (on my part as well as on that of others) about family, friends, and enemies, most of them still alive, that it is simply out of the question. What makes all autobiographies worthless is, after all, their mendacity." (*Freud-Edward Bernays* 10.8.1929).
"Postcript to An Autobiographical Study" S.E.,XX.71.
Freud-Edward Bernays 10.8.1929 in *Letters*.

6 February 1935
1. The work Lévy-Bruhl gave Freud was fifth in the following series of books: - *How Natives Think*, *Primitive Mentality*, *The Soul of the Primitive*, *Primitives and the Supernatural*, *Primitive Mythology*, *Mystical Experience and Symbols among Primitives*. Unlike the Hungarian ethnologist Géza Róheim, Lévy-Bruhl was not trying to apply psychoanalysis to native cultures, but to redefine the interrelation of individual and society. He summarized that difference in his *Notebooks*: "It is only recently that the existence and importance of the unconscious (Freud) has been recognized, and it has still only been studied in the individual. Now what we have to describe never presents intself to the mind of philosophers and psychologists who have not had experience of individuals who, although individuals, feel themselves to be the members, the elements of a social body which is felt and represented as the true individual; which, without doubt, is composed of its members but which, at the same time, makes them exist . . . ."
Freud-Marie Bonaparte 7.2.1935 in Jones, III.208.
Lévy-Bruhl, Lucien, *La mythologie primitive: le monde mythique des Australiens et des Papous*, Paris, 1935 [FM: LDFRD 1013].
Lévy-Bruhl, Lucien, *The Notebooks on Primitive Mentality*, Oxford, 1975, p.80.

6 February 1935
Anna Freud-Jones 25.2.1935 [Inst. of PsA Soc: CFA/FO2/31].
Freud-Arnold Zweig 13.2.1935 in *Zweig Letters*.

18 February 1935
Kubie, Lawrence S., "Pavlov, Freud and Soviet Psychiatry" in Sarason, I. G. (ed), *Psychoanalysis and the Study of Behaviour*, N.Y., 1965 p.32. (My thanks to Peter Swales for this reference.)

19 February 1935
Freud-Arnold Zweig 13.6.1935 in *Zweig Letters*.

22 February 1935
Lou Andreas-Salomé - Freud 6.5.1935 in Pfeiffer.

28 February 1935
Swales-Molnar 21.4.1990 [FM].

11 March 1935
Freud, W. Ernest-Molnar 6.8.1989 [FM].

16 March 1935
Freud-Arnold Zweig 14.3.1935 in *Zweig Letters*.

17 March 1935
Bergschicker, p.130.

23 March 1935
Pichler Notes, 23.3.1935 [FM].
Anna Freud-Jones 29.3.1935 [Inst. of PsA: CFA/FO2/34].

29 March 1935
Schur, 527.
Lucie Freud-Ilse Grubrich-Simitis (End letter n.d.[After 1969]) [FM: Lucie Freud Papers (Marbled notebook p.4)].

6 April 1935
Jones-Freud 27.6.1935 [Inst. of PsA].
Freud-Jones 7.7.1935 [Typescript Inst. of PsA] ("Ihre Annerkennung für Ernst's Leistungsfähigkeit ist Balsam für mein väterliches Herz. Ich wollte, mein anderer Sohn in Nizza hätte auch wieder Vaterland und Erwerb.").

11 April 1935
Grinstein, p.98.

13 April 1935
Freud-Pfister 31.1.1936 in *Pfister Letters*.
Freud, Martin, "Who was Freud" in Fraenkel, Josef (ed.) *The Jews of Austria*, London, 1970 [1967], p. 206.
Sterba, p.163.
Freud, Martin-Jones 5.12.1952 [Inst. of PsA: CFB/FO3/O8].

18 April 1935
Freud-Lou Andreas-Salomé 16.5.1935 in Pfeiffer.

20 April 1935
1. In 1943 Landauer was arrested during one of the final Nazi raids in Holland and was interned. In January 1945, three months before the liberation of the camp, he died in Bergen-Belsen. His family survived.
2. Landauer was the person most closely involved in the split of the Dutch Psychoanalytical Association, since the new group was formed largely for his benefit. After the split, however, he felt uncomfortable about the situation and also about the resignation of van Ophuijsen, the previous leader. He felt he should try to reunite the two. The result was that others in his new group now felt bitter that he was making overtures to the opposition. At this period the conflict between the two groups had still not been resolved.
   In the circular reporting the visit of Reik and Landauer, Anna Freud afterwards noted that the news from Holland was not particularly favorable, for the two groups were now "in a state of war with each other." The Dutch Psychoanalytical Association was reunited in 1938 under the chairmanship of S.J.R. de Monchy.
Anna Freud-Jones 29.3.1935 [Inst. of PsA].
Anna Freud-Jones 24.10.1934 [Inst. of PsA: CFA/FO2/15].
Reik, Theodor, *Fragment of a Great Confession*, N.Y., 1965, p.301.
Freud-Jones 20.11.1933 [Typescript Inst. of PsA].
Jones-Freud 1.12.1933 [Inst. of PsA].
Freud-Reik n.d. [FM: 1-F8-16-6].
Hier geht . . . p.56.
Note to Hollós-Federn 17.2.1946, *Sigmund Freud House Bulletin*, Vol. 3/No. 2, Winter 1979, pp.70–71.
Freud, Anna *Rundbrief* 9.5.1935 [Inst.of PsA: CFA/FO2/37] (" . . . im Kampfzustand miteinander").

"Obituary" (S.J.R. de Monchy), *Int. J. Psa.* (1971), 52, 201.

21 April 1935
1. Jones was accompanied by his second wife and two children. His first wife, the composer and pianist Morfydd Llwyn Owen, died after an operation on September 7, 1918. He met his second wife, Katharina Jokl, in Zurich in October 1919. They became engaged within three days of the meeting and married after three weeks.
Their first daughter had died in 1928—this was the occasion on which Freud had tried to console Jones by suggesting that he engage in some Shakespeare research to distract himself from his grief.
Freud-Jones 24.2.1935 [Typescript Inst. of PsA] ("Die Aussicht auf Ihren Besuch in Wien zur Osterzeit stimmt mich freudig und auch wehmütig. Ich weiss, dass ich infolge der Hemmungen des Altes die Pflichten der Gastfreundschaft nur sehr ungenügend werde erfüllen können. Auch unser Wolf, der sich dereinst so unfreundlich gegen Sie benommen hat, ist jetzt ein alter Herr, in seiner Hundeart so alt wie ich, d.i.: über 11 Jahre.").
·Jones, III.209.
Jones-Freud 2.5.1935 [Inst. of PsA].
Davies, T.G., *Ernest Jones 1879–1958* University of Wales Press, 1979, pp.43–5.
Jones, III.149.

22 April 1935
Anna Freud-Jones 29.3.1935 [Inst. of PsA: CFA/FO2/34].
Hier geht . . . p.52.
Psychoanalytic Pioneers.

23 April 1935
1. After the Anschluss in 1938, when Jones was deciding which Viennese analysts he was prepared to invite to London, he rejected Waelder. Apparently, a place might only be found for him in Newcastle, not London. As a result, Waelder emigrated to the United States. He remained convinced that it was his critical lecture to the London society which had made him unwelcome.
Glover, Edward, "Obituary" (Schmideberg), *Int. J. PsA 26*, 1955, pp.213–5.
Freud-Jones 26.5.1935 [Typescript Inst. of PsA] ("Mit Geduld und Vertiefung werden wir gewiss über unsere gegenwärtigen theoretischen Differenzen hinwegkommen. Wir—London u Wien—müssen zusammenhalten, die anderen europäischen Gruppen spielen kaum eine Rolle und die zentrifugalen Tendenzen sind derzeit sehr stark in unserer Internationalen. Und es wäre schade, wenn sie meine persönliche Existenz nicht überleben sollte.").
Anna Freud (Rundbrief), 9.5.1935 [Inst. of PsA: CFA/FO2/37].
Jones-Freud 2.5.1935 [Inst. of PsA].
Freud-Jones 7.7.1935 [Typescript Inst. of PsA].
Waelder, Robert, Interview R.S. Stewart, 29.7.1966.

25 April 1935
Jones, III.210.

26 April 1935 (Bowl)
McCord, Clinton, "Freud—The Man" (Reprint), *The Psychiatric Quarterly*, Vol. 14, Jan. 1940.

26 April 1935 (Stuart)
1. No mention of the book is found in the published correspondence with Zweig, though it is possible Freud spoke of it at their meeting in September. Thomas Mann had just read the book and expressed a damning opinion of it in his diary: "[24.4.1935] St. Zweig's 'Maria Stuart' is an inferior and trivial book, with all its blood, passion and history, sentimentally written, with persistent commonplace asides. This type of writing that spoils good material is a plague." Zweig, Stefan, *Die Welt von Gestern*, Fischer, 1988 [1944], p.434.
Mann, Thomas, *Tagebücher 1935–1936*, Fischer, 1978, p.89.

26 April 1935
1. No collector would give away half a matching set. Otherwise Freud was generous with his antiquities.

To the poet Albrecht Schaeffer, who benefitted from that generosity, he had once said:
"A collector does not give his best piece away, but he is ashamed to give his worst . . . ."
Schaeffer-Freud 21.6.1939 [FM] ("Sein bestes Stück giebt ein Sammler ja nicht weg; aber sein schlechtestes schämt er sich zu geben").

28 April 1935
1. Mann's 60th birthday was on June 6, 1935. Shortly afterwards he went on an American tour. On the return Atlantic crossing he met Dorothy's son, Bob Burlingham on board the "Berengaria" on July 10–11 and wrote: "The visit of the young Broulingham [sic] yesterday was the most humanly beneficial impression of the whole journey. Nineteen, almost twenty years old. Wants to become a correspondent for American papers in Germany or Austria where he has spent 9 years. Apparently I have already met him at Siegm. Freud's in Vienna when I visited him 3 or 4 years ago."
S.E., XXII.255
Freud-Mann June 1935 in *Letters* (The published date of "June 1935" is probably intended to coincide with Mann's birthday of June 6.).
Mann, Thomas, *Tagebücher 1935–1936*, Fischer, 1979, p.140.

Tues 30 April 1935
Pichler Notes, 30.4.1935 [FM].
Anna Freud-Jones 9.5.1935 [Inst. of PsA: CFA/FO2/37].

5 May 1935
Freud-Eitingon 5.6.1932 (" . . . das ständige nicht abzuschliessende Elend der Prothese.").
Pichler Notes, 5.5.1935 [FM].

6 May 1935
Schur, 457.
Freud-Eitingon 12.5.1935 [FM] ("Zögend entfaltet sich heuer ein schöner Frühling vor unseren Augen und ich hätte nicht zuviel zu klagen, wenn nicht das Angebinde des Schicksals zum 6 Mai die Nötigung gewesen wäre, die Prothese neu machen zu lassen, was natürlich ein ungewöhnliches Mass von Quälerie bedeutet. Auch eine Einschränkung der analytischen Stundenarbeit ist damit verbunden.").

24 May 1935
1. Though the most important, this was not the last honor Freud was to receive from official medical circles in England. In May 1937 he wrote to Jones: "I have just received a solemn diploma as 'Honorary Member' of a 'Royal Medico Psychological Association, London.' Could you let me know in a couple of lines what sort of a thing that is and what sort of reaction is expected from me. I think it is nothing special." (*Freud-Jones 18.5.1937*)
Jones replied that this society consisted of the "official Group of Psychiatrists in Great Britain, chiefly of course Asylum doctors. [. . .] The honour in question is a considerable one. Actually, it must have been bestowed on you some time ago because I remember referring to it in my last Congress address." (*Jones-Freud 22.5.1937*)
Freud-The Royal Society of Medicine 25.5.1935 [FM: II/F8–105].
Freud-Arnold Zweig 13.6.1935 in *Zweig Letters*.
Freud-Jones 26.5.1935 [Typescript Inst. of PsA] ("Da dies nicht 'wegen meiner schönen Augen' geschehen sein kann, muss es beweisen, dass der Respekt vor unserer Psychoanalyse in den offiziellen Kreisen Englands grosse Fortschritte gemacht hat.")
Freud-Jones 18.5.1937 [Typescript Inst. of PsA] ("Ich habe soeben ein feierliches Diplom als Ehrenmitglied einer "Royal Medico Psycholog. Association, London" erhalten. Wollen Sie mich mit zwei Zeilen wissen lassen, was das für ein Ding ist und welche Reaktion von mir erwartet wird. Ich meine, es ist nichts Besonderes.").
Jones-Freud 22.5.1937 [Inst. of PsA].

9 June 1935
Anna Freud-Jones 7.6.1935 [Inst. of PsA].
Anna Freud (Rundbrief), 9.5.1935 [Inst. of PsA: CFA/FO2/37].

10 June 1935
1. In 1945 Hollós and his wife narrowly escaped murder by the Hungarian Fascists. He related this experience in a moving letter to Paul Federn after the war (*Hollós-Federn 17.2.1946*).
Hollós-Federn 17.2.1946 in *Psyche 28* (1974), pp. 266–268. [English version] *Sigmund Freud House Bulletin*, Vol. 3/No. 2, Winter 1979, pp. 70–71.

10 June 1935
1. The writer Giovacchino Forzano (who had visited Freud together with Weiss in 1933) was a confidant of Mussolini and attempted to intercede on behalf of Weiss and psychoanalysis. In 1934 Weiss was granted an audience with Mussolini's son-in-law, the future Foreign Minister Galeazzo Ciano, about the suppression of the journal *Rivista Italiana di Psicoanalisi*, but with no result. Freud suspected that his enemy, the reactionary Austrian priest Father Wilhelm Schmidt, had used his influence to procure the ban.
Freud-Arnold Zweig 13.6.1935 in *Zweig Letters*.
Carloni, Glauco, "Freud and Mussolini," in Rovigatti, Franca (ed.), *Italy in Psychoanalysis*, Rome, 1989 pp.51–60.
Freud-Arnold Zweig 30.9.1934 in *Zweig Letters*.
Freud-Weiss 7.7.1935 [FM].

11 June 1935
My thanks to Prof. Fichtner for expert assistance in deciphering this name, and to Peter Swales for the reference to the interview [LoC. Container D 11, Item 1194].

18 June 1935
Freud-Meine Lieben 14.6.1930 [FM].

22 June 1935
Anna Freud-Jones 19.6.1935 [Inst. of PsA: CFA/FO2/42].

22 June 1935
Pichler Notes, (Summer 1935) [FM].

27 June 1935
Freud, W. Ernest-Molnar 6.8.1989 [FM].

8 July 1935
Freud-Fliess 30.1.1901 p.477 n.1 Schröter.

13 July 1935
Neue Freie Presse, 14.7.1935.
Clare, George, *Last Waltz in Vienna*, London, 1981, p.133.

14 July 1935
1. In 1928, before Reik left for Berlin, Freud wrote to Eitingon: "A few days ago I had a talk with Reik that left me with a painful impression. I reproached him about certain things which he did not refuse to accept, but I could not promise him any help out of his difficult situation." (*Freud-Eitingon 17.11.1928*). And ten years later, when Reik asked for a testimonial, Freud replied from London: "When I think of you sympathy and anger conflict within me. I could feel at home in England if all possible demands made upon me did not continually show me my helplessness to assist others." (*Freud-Reik 3.7.1938*).
2. The diary records no further visits, but in fact Reik visited Freud for the last time in 1938, shortly before emigrating to the United States. He wrote: "I found him greatly changed, his skin withered and his eyes deep-sunken. His hands, as he opened a cigar case, seemed no more than skin and bones. But his eyes, his curious and penetrating eyes, were as lively and kindly as always."
Psychoanalytical Pioneers, p.250.
Freud-Reik 4.1.1935 [FM: I-F8–18].
Sterba, pp.82–3.
Freud-Eitingon 17.11.1928 [FM] ("Vor einigen Tagen hatte ich ein Gespräch mit Reik, aus dem mir ein peinlicher Eindruck zurückblieb. Ich hielt ihm manches tadelnd vor, was er anzunehmen nicht verweigerte, konnt ihm aber für seine schwierige Situation keine Hilfe versprechen.").
Freud-Reik 3.7.1938 [FM: Copy 1-F8–18-7] ("Wenn ich an Sie denke, streiten bei mir Sympathie und

Ärger. Ich könnte mich in England wohl fühlen, wenn ich nicht durch alle möglichen Anforderungen unausgesetzt an meine Ohnmacht, anderen zu helfen, gemahnt würde.").
Reik, Theodor, *From Thirty Years with Freud*, London, 1942, p.34.

17 July 1935

1. "Chinidin" is a heart relaxant derived from quinine. Apart from that, Freud was also given amyl nitrite at some time, but did not like its effect: "I hated it because it gave me such upleasant sensations of congestion in the head." (*Freud-Arnold Zweig 20.12.1937*).
Freud-Jelliffe 2.8.1934 [FM: 1-F8–74-14] ("Der Aufsatz über Chinidin hatte mein besonderes Interesse, da ich eben selbst wegen meiner lästigen Extrasystolen das Mittel gebrauche, ohne Nebenerscheinungen übrigens.").
Anna Freud-Jones 20.7.1935 [Inst. of PsA: CFA/FO2/48].
Blanton, Smiley, *Diary of My Analysis with Sigmund Freud*, N.Y., 1971, p.61.

22 July 1935
Bertin, pp.191–2.

26 July 1935
Martin Freud, 26.7.1935 [FM: MISC] ("Gratulanten aus der Ferne,
Schätzt man sehr und hat man gerne,
Denn in ihren 16 Seiten
Langen hübsch geschriebnen Schreiben
Steh'n die schönsten Neuigkeiten,
Was sie tun und was sie treiben:
Hund hat Katze angebellt,
Jones hat neues Haus bestellt,
Levison's war'n da zum Tee,
Robert tut der Magen weh,
Evchen schreibt wie Emile Zola,
Henny wird im Umfang voller,
Luxchen ist der beste Reiter,
Und so weiter und so weiter.").

2 August 1935
1. Was the possibility of a psychoanalysis under discussion? Freud had already encountered other famous multimillionaires, but his dealings with them had come to nothing. In 1920 the head of the London Rothschilds had visited him. Freud wrote afterwards: "He is meschugge [mad] enough and probably beyond any assistance, anyway he refuses treatment." (*Freud-Anna Freud 12.10.1920*). Two years later, in 1922, Mrs. Guggenheim had called, but Freud put her off: "But through open rudeness and various dark threats I persuaded the multimillionairess, who is supposed to be even more "exact" (mean *) than rich, to refuse." (*Freud-Anna Freud 17.7.1922*). * English in the original.
2. Six months previously Freud had met Dr. Gerard who was travelling on behalf of the Rockefeller Foundation. And curiously enough the name Rockefeller begins recurring in Freud's correspondence with Arnold Zweig in December 1935. Zweig had heard that Moses had been a pupil of the sun temple of Re-Aton and a younger contemporary of Amenophis III: the source of this information was a Professor Smith of the "Rockefeller Museum at Luxor." Freud could not at first discover any trace of a "Rockefeller Museum," but eventually found out that there was an "Oriental Institude of the University of Chicago" at Luxor of which Rockefeller was the patron.
Collier, Peter, & Horowitz, David, *The Rockefellers*, London, 1976, p.146 note.
Puner, Helen Walker, *Freud: His Life and His Mind*, N.Y., 1947, p.236.
Hannah, Barbara, *Jung: His Life and Work*, N.Y., 1976, p.130 (Thanks to Sonu Shamdasani for this reference).
Freud-Anna Freud 12.10.1920 [LoC] ("Er ist meschugge genug u wahrscheinlich jenseits aller Hilfe, lehnte auch die Behandlg ab.").
Freud-Anna Freud 17.7.1922 [LoC] ("Ich habe es aber durch offene Grobheit u verschiedene dunkle Drohungen dahingebracht, dass die Multimillionärin,

die noch mehr "genau" (mean) als reich sein soll, verzichtet hat.").
Arnold Zweig-Freud End Dec. 1935 in *Zweig Letters*.

2 August 1935
Wallis Budge, E.A., *Osiris and the Egyptian Resurrection*, N.Y., 1973 [1911], Vol.II, p.306.
Lustig, Robert, Interview Lynn Gamwell, 5.9.1988 [FM: FAR/41/37] (With thanks to Lynn Gamwell for interview transcript).
Bonnet, Hans, *Reallexicon der Aegyptischen Religionsgeschichte*, Berlin, 1952.
Reeves, Dr. C.N. in *Freud and Art*, p.53.
Zweig, Stefan, *Die Welt von Gestern*, Fischer, 1979 [1944], p.211.

6 August 1935
Anna Freud-Jones 12.8.1935 [Inst. of PsA: CFA/FO2/51] ("Eitingon ist vor zwei Tagen wieder abgereist und sein Besuch war eine angenehme Überraschung. Er ist in sehr guter Verfassung, sieht gesünder aus als seit Jahren und ist vor allem viel zugänglicher und einsichtiger in den Geschäften.").
Anna Freud-Jones 1.11.1935 ibid.

14 August 1935
1. Lucian was to become a leading British artist. He thus fulfilled his father Ernst's own early ambition to be an artist. Freud's patient Sergei Pankejeff (the "Wolf Man"), who also painted, remembered being told ".... that his [Freud's] youngest son had also intended to become a painter, but had then dropped the idea and switched over to architecture. 'I would have decided on painting,' he had told his father, 'only if I were either very rich or very poor.' The grounds for this decision were that one should either regard painting as a luxury, pursuing it as an amateur, or else take it very seriously and achieve something really great, since to be a mediocrity in this field would give no satisfaction. Poverty and the 'iron necessity' behind it would serve as a sharp spur goading one on to notable achievements. Freud welcomed his son's decision and thought his reasoning well founded."
Green, John, "The relentlessly personal vision of Lucian Freud," *Art News*, April 1977, pp.60–3.
Martha Freud-Gabriel Freud 29.7.1935 [FM: Lucie Freud Papers].
Gardiner, Muriel (Ed.), *The Wolf Man and Sigmund Freud*, Hogarth, London, 1973, pp.144–5.

18 August 1935
Freud-Sam Freud 6.12.1928 [FM].
Freud-Eitingon 18.8.1932 [FM] ("Meine Mutter wäre heute 97 alt geworden.").
Freud-Lilly Marlé 1.6.1936 [FM: MISC] ("Nur eines muss ich mit eingewurzelte Detailtreue verbessern. Deine Grossmutter war nicht 18, sondern 21 Jahre alt als sie ihr erstes Kind bekam. Sie wäre heute 101!").

19 August 1935
Pichler Notes, 19.8.1935, 26.8.1935, 4.9.1935 [FM].

1 September 1935
Hier geht . . . p.80.
Roazen, Paul, *Helene Deutsch*, N.Y., 1985, p.246 n.
Roazen-Molnar 17.12.1990 [FM].

3 September 1935
1. This date, September 23, 1897, marked a turning point in Freud's career: two days earlier he had admitted to Fliess that he had abandoned his seduction theory, thus taking the first step toward the theory of infantile fantasies and the Oedipus complex. (*Freud-Fliess 21.9.1897*).
Freud gave his first lecture to members—"The Intepretation of Dreams"—on December 7, 1897, followed by a second lecture on the same theme on February 3, 1899. According to the minutes "the audience showed its gratitude by frantic applause." Over the next 20 years he delivered a further nineteen lectures. They were frequently connected with his professional work. For example, in 1899 he gave a lecture on "The Psychology of Forgetting," in 1900 one on "The Psychic Life of the Child" and in 1901 "Chance and Superstition" at the very time he was working on the *Psychopathology of Everyday Life*.

He gave his final talk, on "Phantasy and Art," in 1917. The society gave him access to his first non-specialist public—it was, in effect, his "first audience."
Rozenblit, Marsha L., *The Jews of Vienna 1867–1914*, Albany, 1983, pp.149–50.
Knoepfmacher, Hugo, "Sigmund Freud and the B'nai B'rith" in Knoepfmacher, Hugo "Zwei Beiträge zur Biographie Sigmund Freuds" (Offprint from *Jahrbuch der Psychoanalyse* Bd. XI).
"Address to the members of B'nai B'rith" *S. E.* XX. 273–275.
Freud, 21.1.1926 in *Freudiana: From the Collection of the Jewish National and University Library* (Exhibition catalogue), Jerusalem, 1973, p.ix.
Freud-Fliess 21.9.1897 in Masson.
Klein, Dennis B. *Jewish Origins of the Psychoanalytic Movement*, University of Chicago Press, 1985 [1981], pp.156–163.

5 September 1935
Bernfeld, Suzanne Cassirer, "Freud and Archaeology," *American Imago*, Vol.8, No.2, p.110.
Martin Freud, quoted in Clark, p.217.
Portal, Jane in *Freud and Art*, p.127.

15 September 1935
Jones, II.122.
Emden-Freud 12.4.1912 [FM: SOH9–17].
Int. J. PsA, Jan. 1935, Vol. XVI, part 1, (Reports).

15 September 1935
1. But while Freud's letter apologizes for having ridden one of his hobby horses, a postscript brings another one of them out of the stable: "P.S. I also forgot to ask you at the time whether you wanted to interest yourself in the Shakespeare-Oxford problem. I am virtually convinced that Edward de Vere, 17th Earl of Oxford was the real Shakespeare."
Freud-Stefan Zweig 5.11.1935 in Stefan Zweig.
Zweig, Stefan, *Die Welt von Gestern*, Fischer, 1988 [1944], p.432.

15 September 1935
Meyers Enzyk. Lexikon, Bibliog. Inst. 1974.
Fichtner-Molnar 21.5.1990 [FM].

29 September 1935
1. This visit has not been confirmed from other sources. But if this was indeed Sir James Jeans, one might suppose the possibility of membership of the Royal Society for Freud could have been a topic of discussion. Freud had one of Jeans' books in his library - *Eos or the Wider Aspects of Cosmology*, London, 1929—but it bears no dedication.
Milne, E.A., *Sir James Jeans*, 1952.
Royal Society Yearbooks [FM].
Jeans, J., *Eos or the Wider Aspects of Cosmology*, London, 1929 [FM].

1 October 1935
Roger Keverne (Spinks of London: unofficial assessment).

2 October 1935
Bergschicker, p.112.
Natkiel, Richard, *Atlas of 20c History*, London, 1982.

10 October 1935
1. The first ring Freud had given Dorothy Burlingham was of gold, inset with an ancient Greek black jasper intaglio representing a chariot and driver. However, the stone cracked and this second gem was offered as a replacement. It was also black jasper and showed a Viking long boat.
"The Subtleties of a Faulty Action," *S.E.*, XXII. 232–235.
Burlingham, p.192.

11 October 1935
Pichler Notes, 11.10.1935 [FM].

13 October 1935
1. Thornton Wilder apparently paid another visit to Freud in London on June 21, 1938[?]. On one of these visits Freud supposedly made a remark Wilder recorded in his journals—"that it might some day be shown that cancer is allied to 'the presence of hate in

the subconscious.' "
Freud-Arnold Zweig 14.10.1935 [SFC: Typescript copy]
(" . . . jenes reizendes Buches) *The Bridge of San Luis
Rey . . . .*").
Freud-Ernst Freud 16.12.1928 [LoC] ("Thornton
Wilder The Bridge of San Luis Rey müsst Ihr lesen,
es ist etwas ganz ungewöhnlich schönes.").
Simon, Linda, *Thornton Wilder: His World*, Garden
City, N.Y., 1979, pp.118–9.
Gallup, Donald (Ed), *The Journals of Thornton Wilder
1939–1961*, Yale, 1985, p.282.
Goldstone, Richard H., *Thornton Wilder: An Intimate
Portrait*, New York, 1975, pp.147–8.

16 October 1935
Freud-Mathilde Hollitscher 16.7.1935 [LoC].

22 October 1935
Jones, I.123–7, 179.

28 October 1935
Jones-Freud 27.6.1935 [Inst. of PsA].
Freud-Jones 7.7.1935 [Typescr. Inst. of PsA].
Freud-Jones 29.10.1935 [Typescr. Inst. of PsA].

6 November 1935
Mottled notebook [FM: F8.104].

10 November 1935
Wiener Zeitung, 12.11.1935 (No. 313).
Visitor list 1938–9 [FM: LDFRD 5238].
Macinnes, Colin, "Yvette" *New Statesman*, 22.4.1966.

21 November 1935
Almanach der Psychoanalyse 1936 [FM].

23 November 1935
Freud-Arnold Zweig 13.6.1935 in *Zweig Letters*.
Freud-Ernst Freud 21.11.1935 & 29.11.1935 [LoC].

3 December1935
Martin Freud, 3.12.1935 [FM: MOB 8A]
    ("Ich bin das Manuskriptpapier
    Gewält, gewidmet und geweiht,
    Dem neuen Buch von Anna Freud.").

7 December 1935
Freud-Pfister 31.1.1936 in *Pfister Letters*.

10 December 1935
Freud, W. Ernest-Molnar 6.8.1989 [FM].
Freud-Velikovsky 26.2.1932 [LoC].

14 December 1935
Hruby, Karel in Capek, Milic, & Hruby, Karel, *T.G.
Masaryk in Perspective*, S.V.U. Press, 1981, p.vii.
Zeman, Zbynek, *The Making of
Czechoslovakia*, London, 1976, p.155.
Herben, Jan, *T.G. Masaryk*, Prague, 1947, pp.470–1.

23 December 1935
Anna Freud-Ernst Freud 30.12.1935 [FM: Lucie Freud
Papers].

1936

2 January 1936
Anna Freud-Jones 28.12.1935 [Inst. of PsA.
CFA/FO2/61].

13 January 1936
Anna Freud-Jones 22.1.1936 [Inst. of PsA:
CFA/FO2/62] ("Ernst hat die Pläne ausgezeichnet
gemacht. Hoffentlich haben wir uns nicht zu viel
Sorgen damit aufgeladen. Wenn es gelingt, wird es
sehr angenehm werde[n]. Ich glaube, die Vereinigung
rechnet darauf, dass Du, bei Deinem Besuch im
Frühjahr den Eröffnungsvortrag halten wirst.").

14 January 1936
Freud-Wittkowski 6.1.1936 in *Letters*.
Freud-Wittkowski 15.1.1936 [FM: I F8–34-1–4].
"A Disturbance of Memory on the Acropolis" *S.E.*,
XXII.238–248.

16 January 1936 (Princess)
Bertin, pp.194–5.

16 January 1936 (Pichler)
Pichler Notes, 16.1.1936 [FM].
Anna Freud-Jones 22.1.1936 [Int. of PsA:
CFA/FO2/62] ("Wir haben hier ein paar schwierige
Tage gehabt. Heute vor eine Woche hatte mein Vater
eine sehr schmerzhafte Operation. Man hat ihm eine
ziemlich grosse Wucherung nehmen müssen. Aber
seit gestern geht es ihm wieder gut und die
Schmerzen haben nachgelassen.").

20 January 1936
Freud-Ernst Freud 6.6.1934 [LoC].

21 January 1936
Jones, III.26 & 221.
Meng, H. "Freud and the Sculptor" in Ruitenbeek,
H.M., *Freud as we knew him*, Detroit, 1973, pp.350 &
351.

22 January 1936
NLM Cat.
Fichtner-Molnar 21.5.1990 (With thanks to Prof.
Fichtner for this suggestion).
van Wulfften-Palthe, P.M., "Koro. Eine merkwürdige
Angsthysterie" *Int. Z. Psa*, XXI. Heft 2, 1935, pp.
249–257.

1 February 1936
1. In later years Nemon settled in Britain. As a
successful portrait sculptor he was to produce statues
of, among others, Queen Elizabeth II and her mother,
as well as Lord Beaverbrook, Lord Montgomery,
Winston Churchill and Dwight D. Eisenhower.
Jones, III.221.
Nemon, Mrs., Telephone communication, 29.5.1990.
Nemon, Oscar, "Comment j'ai fait le buste de
Freud" *Psyche*, Paris, Vol. 10, 1955, p.483.

4 February 1936
Freud-Jones 2.3.1937 [Typescript Inst. of PsA].

9 February 1936
1. After his father's death in 1925, Robert Breuer
told Freud: "He followed your work, dear Professor,
with untiring interest and often with real pleasure,
and even though he may sometimes have had factual
objections to make, I have again and again heard him
name you in the highest terms, with almost
marvelling recognition at the abundance of your gifts
and the greatness of your achievement." (*Robert
Breuer-Freud 25.6.1925*).
Hirschmüller, Albrecht, *The Life and Work of Josef
Breuer*, New York University Press, 1989 [1978], p.30.
Robert Breuer-Freud 25.6.1925 [FM: SF/Breuer ("Ihre
Arbeit, verehrter Herr Professor, hat er mit nie
ermüdenden Interesse und oft mit heller Freude
verfolgt, und wenn er auch manchmal vielleicht
sachliche Einwände zu machen hatte, so habe ich ihn
doch immer und immer wieder mit Worten der
höchster, fast bewundernder Annerkennung für die
Fülle von Begabung und für die Grösse der Leistung

Ihrer Namen nennen hören.").

20 February 1936 (Bischowski)
*XIV Internationaler Psychoanalytischer Kongress:
Leitsätze der Kongressvorträge: Marienbad 2 bis 7 August
1936* [FM: SOH9–2].
Kardiner, Abram, *My Analysis with Freud*, Norton,
1977, p.85.
Mühlleitner, Elke, *Die Männlichen Mitglieder der
Wiener Psychoanalytischen Vereinigung 1937/38*,
(Diplomarbeit: Vienna University, 1990 unpubl.).
Ehrenwald, Jan, M.D., "Gustav Bychowski: An
Appreciation" *American Imago*, Vol.30, Spring 1973,
No.1.

20 February 1936 (Pichler)
Pichler Notes, 20.2.1936 [FM].

3 March 1936 (Pineles)
Freud-Fliess 1.8.1899, Schröter p.399 n.2.
University Papers Beilage 3. [LoC].
Pfeiffer, p.231 n.142 & footnote.

3 March 1936 (Osiris)
Jones, Mark et al. (Eds.), *Fake? the art of deception*,
London, 1990, p.270.
Reeves, Dr. C.N., *Notes on LDFRD 3132* ms. [FM].

10 March 1936 (Pichler)
Pichler Notes, 10.3.1936 [FM].

25 March 1936 (Minna)
Lou Andreas-Salomé - Freud 6.5.1936 in Pfeiffer.
Freud-Marie Bonaparte 26.3.1936 in Schur, 478.

25 March 1936
Interview, Mrs. Aviva Harari, 10.7.1991.

25 March 1936 (Books)
Freud-Marie Bonaparte 26.3.1936 in Schur, 478.

25 March 1936 (Migraine)
Freud-Marie Bonaparte 26.3.1936 in Schur, 478.
Schröter, p.155.
S.E.XIX.236 n.1 (N.B. The English version translates
the *Migräne (migraine)* of the German original as
headache.).
Schur, 99.

3 April 1936
Reeves, Dr. C. N., *Notes on LDFRD 3852* ms. [FM].
Ransohoff-Shamdasani 27.11.1987 [FM].

5 April 1936
Freud-Anna Freud 27.12.1926 ("Der stärkste Eindruck
von Berlin ist das kl. Evchen, eine genaue
Wiederholung von Heinerle, viereckiger Gesicht mit
kohlschwarzen Augen, dasselbe Temperament,
Leichtigkeit im Reden, Gescheitheit, sieht zum Glück
kräftiger aus, war unwol u zuerst nicht gnädig.").

12 April 1936 (Egyptian)
Reeves, Dr. C.N., *Notes on LDFRD 3275* ms. [FM].
Ransohoff-Shamdasani 27.11.1987 [FM].

12 April 1936 (Minna)
Anna Freud-Jones 3.4.1936 [Inst. of PsA:
CFA/FO2/70] ("Bei uns im Haus geht es auch nicht
ohne Krankheit und Sorgen, obwohl mein Vater jetzt
eine ruhige Zeit gehabt hat. Meine Tante hatte eine
Glaukomoperation, von der sie sich noch recht elend
ist.").

29 April 1936
Freud-Lou Andreas-Salomé [c. 20th] May 1936 in
Pfeiffer.

4 May 1936
Rolland-von Hindenburg 20.4.1933 in Doisy, M.,
Romain Rolland 1866–1944, Bruxelles, 1945, p.84.
Freud-Wittkowski 6.1.1936 in *Letters*.
Meng, Heinrich "Sigmund Freud in Brief, Gespräch,
Begegnung und Werk" *Psyche*, J.X. Heft 9 Dez. 1956,
p.529.

6 May, 1936 (Birthday)
1. When Jones agreed, Freud even had second
thoughts about this alternative: "I am now offended
by an aesthetic monstrosity, some 400 photographs of
mostly hideous people and of whom a good half I do

not know at all, whereas a considerable number want to know nothing of me." (*Freud-Jones 21.7.1935*)
2. The essays were entitled: *Sigmund Freud in seinem Heim*[Sigmund Freud at home] *Meine Begegnung mit Rainer Maria Rilke* [My Meeting with Rainer Maria Rilke] and *Mein Freund H. Ch. Andersen* [My Friend H. C. Andersen]. Freud only interrupted his thanks to correct a mistake in the first essay about the age of his mother at his birth.
Jones-Anna Freud 13.3.1936 [Inst. of PsA: CFA/FO2/69].
Freud-Marie Bonaparte 22.3.1936 in Jones, III.216.
Freud-Lilly Marlé 1.6.1936 [FM: MISC Typescript copy] (" . . . das schönste, weil das zärtlichste, kunstvollste, an Empfindung reichste.").
Anna Freud-Jones 28.5.1936 [Inst. of PsA: CFA/FO2/73].
Freud-Jones 21.7.1935 [Typescript Inst. of PsA] (" . . . ich nehme jetzt Anstoss an einer ästhetischen Ungeheuerlichkeit, etwa 400 Bilder von meist hässlichen Leuten, und von denen ich gut die Hälfte überhaupt nicht kenne, während eine beträchtliche Anzal von mir nichts wissen will.").

6 May 1936 (Conquest)
Mann, Thomas, *Tagebücher 1935–1936*, Fischer, Frankfurt/M., 1978, p.299.

7 May 1936
1. Thomas Mann mentions travelling to Vienna on May 6, but unfortunately there is a gap in his published diaries from 6 to 13 May.
Schur, 479.
Jones, III.218.
Mann, Thomas, *Tagebücher 1935–1936*, Fischer, 1979, p.299.

8 May 1936 (Mann)
Schur, 480.

8 May 1936 (Braun)
1. The personality of Heinrich Braun (1854–1927) made a lasting impression on the young Freud. Later he became a prominent journalist active in the German Social-Democratic movement.
Freud, "Zum Ableben Professor Brauns," *Mitteilungsblatt der Vereinigung jüdischer Aerzte*, No. 29, May 1936, Vienna p.6., quoted in *Pictures and Words* p.274.
"University papers: Beilage II" [LoC].

5 June 1936
1. In 1920, the future Vienna Psychoanalytical Ambulatorium (out-patient clinic) was refused permission to use the premises of the General Hospital. The Vienna Municipal General Polyclinic allowed it to use their premises on Pelikangasse 18, but only on condition no lay analysts practised there. The Vienna Psychoanalytical Society also met there fortnightly, as did their teaching institute at which Anna Freud ran technical seminars from 1935 on.
2. Richard Sterba reports Jones's opening remarks: "His first sentence betrayed the ambivalence so often noticable in his behavior: 'It is a significant sign of the honorable poverty that the Vienna Psychoanalytical Society, the mother of all others, has suffered, that it took more than thirty years until it found a decent home of its own.' "
Anna Freud-Ernst Freud 30.12.1935 [FM: Lucie Freud Papers].
Binswanger, Ludwig, *Erinnerungen an Sigmund Freud*, Bern, 1956, p.108.
Anna Freud-Jones 3.4.1936 [Inst. of PsA: CFA/FO2/70].
Jones, III.216.
Pictures and Words, p.335.
Diercks, Dr. Christine, "Exhibition at Berggasse 19," (Exhibition, Sigmund Freud Haus, Summer 1988).
Sterba, p.153.

14 June 1936
1. In his diaries Thomas Mann calls Freud "the Old Man" (*der Alte*—in the final years of Austria-Hungary the term applied to Kaiser Franz Josef). He mentions tea and ice on the terrace before the reading and speaks of Freud's emotion and of his reply concerning Napoleon, evidently in connection with

the Joseph theme. Afterwards "the American lady" (presumably Dorothy Burlingham) took Mann back to the Hotel Imperial where he was staying.
Schur, 481.
Freud-Arnold Zweig 17.6.1936 in *Zweig Letters*.
Freud-Mann 29.11.1936 in *Letters*.
Mann, Thomas, *Tagebücher 1935–1936*, Fischer, 1979, p.316.

29 June 1936
Freud-Krausz 22.5.1936 [FM] ("Was in mir von der Eitelkeit früherer Jahrzehnte noch vorhanden ist, sträubt sich gegen die Preisgabe und gar gegen die Fixirung der gegenwärtigen Verwitterung und Hässlichkeit.").
Jones, III.216.

30 June 1936
Jones-Freud 6.7.1936 [Inst. of PsA].
Jones, III.220.

11 July 1936
Stadler, Karl R., *Austria*, London, 1971, p.148.

14 July 1936
Anna Freud-Jones 15.7.1936 [Inst. of PsA: CFA/FO2/78] ("Die Operation gestern war nicht so klein. Sie hat eine Stunde gedauert und war sehr schmerzhaft. Pichler hat ein kleines Geschwür am oberen hinteren Gaumen weggenommen. Hoffentlich ist damit für eine Weile wieder Ruhe. Nachher waren dann keine Schmerzen, mein Vater hat gestern ausgeruht und wird heute wieder arbeiten können. Wir hatten jetzt durch drei Monate gehofft, dass die Tendenz zur Neubildung zur Ruhe gekommen ist, aber es scheint docht nicht so zu sein.").

18 July 1936
Pichler Notes, 16, 17 & 18.7.1936 [FM].

19 July 1936
Pichler Notes, 19 & 20.7.1936 [FM].

23 July 1936
Pichler Notes, 20, 22, 24, 27.7.1936 [FM].
Anna Freud-Jones 23.7.1936 [Inst. of PsA: CFA/FO2/80] ("Bei uns war keine gute Woche. Die zweite Operation war sehr arg und die Nachwirkung ganz anders als sonst. Wir sind wieder zu Hause, aber mein Vater ist diesmal sehr erschöpft und müde. Prof. Pichler ist mit dem Umfang der Operation zufrieden; aber ich weiss nicht, ob man sehr viele solche Operationen aushalten kann.").

31 July 1936
XIV. Internationaler Psychoanalytischer Kongress: Leitsätze der Kongressvorträge, Jakob Weiss, Wien, n.d. [FM: SOH9–16].
Jones, III.223.

6 August 1936
XIV. Internationaler Psychoanalytischer Kongress: Leitsätze der Kongressvorträge. Jakob Weiss, Wien, n.d. [FM: SOH9–16] ("Es wird der Versuch gemacht, für bestimmte sado-masochistische Phantasien eine Verknüpfung zwischen dem Erlebnis der Urszene, den Formen des Onanie-Abgewöhnungskampfes und speziellen Lebenshaltungen herzustellen.").

14 August 1936
Arnold Zweig-Freud 16.2.1932 in *Zweig Letters*.
Freud-Struck 23.10.1914. [FM: SF VAR 114].
Pictures and Words, pp.210–11.
Freud-Struck 7.11.1914 [FM: SF VAR 115 Typescript & Letters].

14 August 1936 (Moses)
1. This was a fairly rare honor. After the "Committee" (the original fellowship of the ring) disbanded in 1925 with the death of Abraham and the defection of Rank, Freud had revived the custom by giving Ernst Simmel a ring in 1928, in gratitude for his help and hospitality during Freud's stay at the Tegel Sanatorium. After that a number of friends or relatives, mostly women, received rings as gifts.
Freud-Arnold Zweig 13.2.1935 & 2.5.1935 in *Zweig Letters*.
Freud-Eitingon 12.5.1935 ("Auf Ihre Frage antworte

ich, dass der "Moses" für mich eine Fixirung geworden ist, ich komme nicht von ihm weg und mit ihm nicht weiter. Wenn nicht neue Funde in Tel-el Amarna mir zu Hilfe kommen, werde ich ihn wohl für immer sekretiren.").
Arnold Zweig-Freud 8.6.1936 & 16.7.1936 in *Zweig Letters*.
Freud-Simmel 19.11.1928 in *Letters*.
Freud and Art, p.123.
Jones, III.223–4.

20 August 1936 (Anna)
Jones-Eitingon 2.10.1936 [Inst. of Psa: CEC/FO2/59].

20 August 1936 (Levy)
1. The following year Freud was to discuss Moses, Jewish and Egyptian art in a letter to Willy Lévy. Freud was speculating why the Jews did not take over the art of Amarna, whether this was because of Moses' own attitude or because it could not be transported across the desert. In Mosaic law art is sacrificed to religion.
Pictures and Words, p.335 n.311.
Freud-Willi Lévy 1.10.1937 [LoC: Filed under *Freud-Unknown*].

25 August 1936 (Tandler)
Sablik, Karl, *Julius Tandler: Mediziner und Sozialreformer*, Wien, 1983.

25 August 1936 (Bullitt)
1. After World War II Bullitt campaigned on the necessity of stopping Soviet aggression and called for democracy in the Soviet Union, to be achieved through a World Bill of Rights and a World Federal Government.
'Obituary: W.C. Bullitt," *New York Times* 15.2.1967.
Bullitt, W.C., *The Great Globe Itself: A Preface to World Affairs*, London, 1947.

28 August 1936 (Jones)
Anna Freud-Jones 28.12.1935 [Inst. of PsA: CFA/FO2/61].
Anna Freud-Jones 21.2.1936 [Inst. of PsA: CFA/FO2/65] ("Die Idee, dass Du krank bist, gibt mir ein unheimliches und verlassenes Gefühl.").

28 August 1936 (Ernstl)
Freud, W. Ernest-Molnar 6.8.1989 [FM].

6 September 1936
Rozenblit, Marsha L., *The Jews of Vienna 1867–1914*, Albany, 1983, pp.161–4, 171.
Clark, p.499.
Martin Freud, pp.163–5.

12 September 1936 (Ernst)
1. Lux attempted suicide after Ernst's death, but was saved. From having been an aggressive woman, she changed radically and became docile. A result of this was a change in her relationship with her son Lucian. He found he could now paint her and began a long series of paintings of his mother, extending until her death in 1989.
Gruen, John, "The relentlessly personal vision of Lucian Freud," *Art News*, April, 1977.

12 September 1936 (Wolf)
Freud-Jones 24.2.1935 [Inst. of PsA].
Freud, Anna, "Introduction" in Bonaparte, Marie, *Topsy, Der goldhaarige Chow*, Fischer, Frankfurt am Main, 1981, pp.8–10.

14 September 1936
1. Freud once commented to a visitor: "Yes, nature tells a man to marry at 18; and society tells him to marry at 28." In a letter to his eldest daughter, Mathilde, on the factors involved in the choice of a wife, Freud wrote: "I know that the decisive factor in making my choice was to find an honourable name and a warm atmosphere at home and surely others too will think as I did when I was young."
(*Freud-Mathilde Freud 26.3.1908*).
"Home Movies" [FM].
Jones, I.164–5.
G.W.Allport Recalls a Visit to Sigmund Freud, July 1920 [LoC].
Freud-Mathilde Freud 26.3.1908 [FM: MISC & in

Letters (misdated 19.3.1908).]

18 October 1936
Andreas-Salomé, Lou, *The Freud Journal*, London, 1987 [1958], p.91.
Schur, 208. n.14.
Freud - Beer-Hofmann 10.7.1936 [FM: SF VAR 5] ("Dabei sollen Sie nicht meinen, dass ich gleichgiltig geblieben hingegenüber der hoheitsvollen Schönheit Ihrer Dichtung. Ich nahm sogar an, nach manchem, was ich über Sie hörte, dass viele bedeutsame Übereinstimmungen zwischen Ihnen und mir bestehen mussten. Aber das Leben ist so vorbeigerauscht in den atemlosen Spannungen anspruchsvoller Arbeit und jetzt, wo ich mehr Musse geniesse, ist nicht mehr viel von mir übrig.").

22 October 1936
Arnold Zweig-Freud 16.4.1936 in *Zweig Letters*.
Freud-Arnold Zweig 31.5.1936, ibid.
Arnold Zweig-Freud 22.6.1936, ibid.

24 October 1936
1. Although Freud's friendship with Fliess had ended more than 30 years earlier, and not without rancor, according to Martin Freud Fliess's picture remained in Freud's study and in a place of honor. Did Freud really keep a visible reminder of that friendship and everything it meant permanently in front of him? The most comprehensive photographs of Freud's study, taken by Edmund Engelman in 1938, fail to reveal any photo of Fliess, let alone one in "a place of honor". Martin admits that he seldom met Fliess and cannot remember any details about him. It seems likely he was confusing Fliess with *Fleischl* (Ernst Fleischl von Marxow)—another bearded mentor—whose photo does indeed hang in a place of honour, not however in the study but in the consulting room, above the couch.
Freud-Fliess 26.10.1896 in Masson.
Freud-Marie Bonaparte 1.12.1936 in Schur, 485 ("81 1/2 war die Lebensgrenze die Vater und Bruder erreicht haben: mir fehlt dahin noch ein Jahr . . . ").
Martin Freud, p.110.
Engelman, Pl. 12.

27 October 1936
Freud-Ferenczi 16.7.1924 & 6.8.1924 [FM].
Schur, 484.
Freud-Fliess 18.10.1893 & note 5, Schröter.

1 November 1936
1. Paradoxically, in these hard times psychoanalysis appeared to be thriving in Germany. Anna Freud told Jones: "Strange to say the work is flourishing. New candidates are arriving, the courses are attended, the various hospitals are sending patients galore for treatment. Even official bodies believe in the seriousness of analysis and in its therapeutic efficacity. This bit of success in the outside world naturally makes it really difficult for him [Boehm] to dissolve everything and give up." (*Anna Freud-Jones 10.3.1936*).
    Boehm's efforts at negotiating with the Nazi authorities evoked some sympathy from Jones. He responded to Anna: "I cannot but admire Boehm for choosing the stormier side of life and think it is probably the more honourable and excellent way." (*Jones-Anna Freud 13.3.1936*). Boehm's speciality was research on homosexuality and he became an adviser to the Nazis on this topic in the armed forces. Initially he opposed their punitive methods, including sterilization, internment and the death penalty. However, after December 1944, he consented to such practices.
Sterba, pp.155-7.
Anna Freud-Jones 10.3.1936 [Inst. of PsA: CFA/FO2/68] (" . . . das Ärgste am Leben dort [in Deutschland] ist, dass einem heute schon als natürlich vorkommt, wobei sich einem voriges Jahr die Haare gesträubt haben.").
Jones-Anna Freud 13.3.1936 [Inst. of PsA: CFA/FO2/69].
Anna Freud-Jones 10.3.1936 [Inst. of PsA: CFA/FO2/68] ("Merkwürdiger Weise floriert die Arbeit. Es kommen neue Kandidaten, die Kurse werden besucht, die verschiedenen Krankenanstalten

schicken im Überfluss Patienten zur Behandlung. Sogar die offiziellen Stellen glauben an die Ernsthaftigkeit der Analyse und an ihre therapeutische Wirksamkeit. Dieses Stück Erfolg in der Aussenwelt macht es ihm natürlich erst recht schwer, alles aufzulösen und aufzugeben.").

15 November 1936
Freud Collection Authentication Notes [FM].
Berhard-Walcher - Neufeld 17.12.1987 [FM].

22 November 1936
1. There was a curious epilogue to Freud's relationship with Wilhelm Herzig. In 1938 the Nazis appointed a commissar to take charge of the Freuds' affairs. This man (Dr. Sauerwald) turned out to have been a former student of Professor Herzig's. His respect for Herzig was transferred to Freud. As a result, Sauerwald was of great service to the Freuds in facilitating their emigration.
Pictures & Words, pp.274, 335.
Jones, I.179 & III.238.

26 November 1936
Bourgeron-Molnar 28.10.1990 [FM] (With thanks to Dr. Bourgeron for this information)

3 December 1936
Freud-Anna Freud 3.12.1936 [FM] ("Frl Han (200 B.C.-200 A.D.) Gratuliere herzlich zum 3 Dez 1936, Vielleicht auch eine der Damen, die sich gern älter machen.").
Freud-Eitingon 5.2.1937 [FM] ("Das Erfreulichste in meiner Nähe ist Anna's Arbeitslust und ungehemmte Leistung.").
Freud-Stefan Zweig 18.5.1936 in Stefan Zweig.
Pichler Notes, 7.12.1936 [FM].

7 December 1936
Freud, A.W., Telephone interview, 29.7.1989.

10 December 1936
1. On June 3, 1937 the ex-King, now Duke of Windsor, married Mrs. Simpson in France. They spent their honeymoon in Austria, at Schloss Wasserleonburg in Carinthia. The last few days, in mid-September, were spent in Vienna where they were mobbed by enthusiastic crowds. On October 27, 1937, they paid a visit to Germany as guests of Hitler.
Freud-Marie Bonaparte 17.12.1936 [FM: F8/CON 12 Transcr. M.B.]. ("Was es mit dem King auf sich hat? Ich glaube, er ist ein armer Kerl, kein Intellektueller, nicht über gescheit, wahrscheinlich ein latent Homosexueller der auf dem Weg über einen Freund zu dieser Frau gekommen ist, bei der [er] seine Potenz gefunden hat und darum nicht um[sic] ihr loskommt.").
Bloch, Michael, *The Secret File of the Duke of Windsor*, London, 1988, p.112.

12 December 1936
Pichler Notes, 12.12.1936 [FM].

20 December 1936
Jones, III.224.
Schur, 506 note 4.

24 December 1936
Freud-Marie Bonaparte 17.12.1936 [FM: F8 CON 11 Transcript M.B.] (" . . . und zweitens bin ich selbst krank und recht gequält wie ich Ihnen ausführlich beschreiben werde. Am Samstag 17ten erklärte sich Pichler genötigt, eine neue Stelle, die ihm verdächtig schien, wegzubrennen. Es geschah, die mikroskopische Untersuchung ergab diesmal harmloses Gewebe, aber die Reaktion war abscheulich. Heftige Schmerzen zunächst, in dem nächsten Tagen arge Mundsperre, so dass ich nichts essen nur mit Mühe trinken kann und meine Stunden mit Hilfe ein halbstündig erneuerten Wärmflaschen gebe. Eine Erleichterung bringt die Kurzwellenbestrahlung, die in der That Wunder wirkt, welche aber nicht lange genug anhalten. Die Prognose meint, ich werde mich noch eine Wochelang mit dieses Existenzform abfinden müssen.).

27 December 1936
Freud-Stefan Zweig 18.5.1936 in Stefan Zweig.

1937

2 January 1937
Schur, 486.
Marie Bonaparte, 8.11.1951 (Transcript notes M.B.) [FM: II/F8-102].
Marie Bonaparte (Notebook): Quoted in Masson p.9.

11 January 1937
Freud-Marie Bonaparte 17.12.1936 [FM: F8-CON 11 Transcript M.B.] ("Ich hätte Ihnen gewünscht mitanzusehen, welche Sympathie Jofi nur während diese Heidenstage bezeigt, nicht anders, als ob sie alles verstünde.").
Jones, III.226.

14 January 1937
Freud-Arnold Zweig 10.2.1937 [SFC Typescript copy] ("Es ist ein höchst merkwürdiges Gefühl, sie war immer so selbstverständlich da und mit einem mal ist sie nicht mehr da. Von aller Trauer abgesehen, ist es sehr unwahrscheinlich und man fragt sich wann man sich daran gewohnen wird. [. . .] Aber natürlich über 7 Jahre Intimität kommt man nicht leicht hinweg.").
Freud- Lampl-de Groot 22.2.1927 [FM] ("Woher es kommt, dass diese kleine Wesen [Kinder] so reizend sind? Wir haben doch allerlei von ihnen erfahren, was nicht zu unseren Idealen stimmt und müssen sie als kleine Tiere ansehen, aber freilich erscheinen uns auch die Tiere reizend und weit anziehender, als die komplizierten, mehrstöckigen erwachsenen Menschen. Ich erlebe das jetzt an unserem Wolf, der mir fast das verlorene Heinerle ersetzt.").

15 January 1937 (Mann)
Mann, Thomas, *Tagebücher 1937–1939*, Fischer, 1980, pp.10–11.
Jones, III.492-3.
Thomas Mann-Freud 13.12.1936 [FM: VAR SF 98] ("Sie waren mir also nicht mehr neu, aber sie behalten ihr Überraschendes und ihre schlagende Wahrscheinlichkeit, gegen welche die Frage ihrer einstigen Wirklichkeit für mich zweiter Ordnung ist. Für ihren genialen Spürsinn in Dingen des unbewussten Seelenlebens und seiner aus der Tiefe kommenden Wirkungen ist dieser Brief jedenfalls ein erregendes Beispiel, und ich tue mir nicht wenig darauf zu gute, mich seinen Empfänger nennen zu dürfen.").

15 January 1937 (Lün)
Freud-Arnold Zweig 10.2.1937 [SFC Typescript copy] (" . . . eine Art von Stiefverwandschaft." " . . . weil Jofi zu garstig gegen sie war." " . . . . sehr intelligent, viel zutraulicher und zärtlicher mit mehreren als Jofi war, ist sehr hübsch, obwohl sie nicht den Löwenkopf hat wie sie.").

18 January 1937
Pichler Notes, 4 & 14.1.1937, 12.2.1937, 17.3.1937 [FM].
Schur, 489.
Freud-Arnold Zweig 2.4.1937 in *Zweig Letters*.

3 February 1937
"Moses ein Aegypter," *Imago* 23 (1937), pp.5-13.
Freud-Eitingon 5.2.1937 in *Letters*.
Yerushalmi, Yosef Hayim, "Freud on the 'Historical Novel' " *Int. J. PsA.*, 1989, 70, p.384.

11 February 1937
1. Many years later Anna Freud was to say of Lou Andreas-Salomé: "I knew her very well myself and I know what a wonderful woman she was." (*Anna Freud-Stewart 11.12.1972*).
S.E., XXIII.297.
Pfeiffer, p.240.
Anna Freud-Stewart 11.12.1972 (With thanks to R.S. Stewart for the use of this quote.)

28 February 1937
1. Wulf Sachs founded and ran the left-wing journal *The Democrat*. In addition to his involvement in

social issues, he was a staunch Zionist and active in the South African Zionist Federation. After the publication of *Moses and Monetheism*, he wrote to Freud arguing that the creation of a Jewish nation state would diminish hatred of Jews since it would normalize them as a race and destroy the false mystery surrounding them, which was the source of antisemitism.
Freud-Jones 2.3.1937 [Typescript Inst. of PsA]. Bonin, p.245.
Jones-Eitingon 24.2.1937 [Inst. of PsA: CEC/FO2/61].
Wulf Sachs-Freud 1.8.1939 [FM: SOH9-16].

7 March 1937
"Memorandum on the Electrical Treatment of War Neurotics" *S.E.* XVII.211
Eissler, Kurt, *Freud und Wagner-Jauregg vor der Kommission zur Erhebung militärischer Pflichtverletzungen*, Wien, 1979.

29 March 1937
1. Dr. Jackson, who had been studying child analysis with Anna Freud at the Vienna Psychoanalytical Institute, had returned to Yale in 1936, as director for the Psychiatric Services for Children. But she had negotiated the opening of the nursery with the Vienna city authorities. (Had Anna done so, antisemitism could have given rise to a refusal.) She was also involved, with her friend Muriel Gardiner, in helping clandestine socialist organizations and in assisting Jews to emigrate. According to Dr. Josefine Stross, a co-worker at the nursery, Dr. Jackson founded in gratitude for her analysis with Freud: she deputized for Dr. Stross when the latter was on holiday. One of the nursery's famous experiments was a study of feeding disturbances which (as Dr. Stross puts it) distressed Viennese parents as much as bedwetting does elsewhere.
Young-Bruehl, p.219-20.
Freud, Anna "Forward" in Kramer, Rita, *Maria Montessori*, Oxford, 1978, p.5.
Stross, Dr. Josefine, Interview, 13.6.1990.

4 April 1937
Schur, 208.

6 April 1937
Martha Freud-Ernst Freud 4.4.1937 [FM: Lucie Freud Papers] (" . . . dreier unbeschäftigten, wilden Buben . . . ").

22 April 1937
Schur, 490.
Pichler Notes, 19/22/24/26.4.1937 [FM].
Kielholz, Arthur, "Persönliche Erinnerungen an Freud," *Schweizer Archiv für Neurologie und Psychiatrie*, Bd. 79, Heft 2 (1957), p.402.

24 April 1937 (Grinzing)
Pichler Notes, 26.4.1937 [FM].
Martha Freud-Ernst Freud 4.4.1937 [FM: Lucie Freud Papers] (" . . . nicht einmal die gleichzeitig gefallenen Pessach Feiertage konnten das Wetter retten . . . ").

24 April 1937 (Halban)
Bertin, pp.140-1.

30 April 1937
"Analysis Terminable and Interminable,"
S.E.,XXIII.248.
Unendliche Analyse Typescript ms. & galleys [LoC].
Freud-Eitingon 5.2.1937 in *Letters*.

6 May, 1937
1. In contrast to the previous birthday, this was a family affair. In the established tradition Martin Freud composed one of his birthday poems entitled *No sensation today!* that ends:
"Therefore in strict confidence we communicate
The next 8 birthdays we shall also meditatively
celebrate!
Until then goodbye!"
Schur, 186, 231.
Freud-Marie Bonaparte 6.12.1936 in Jones, III.226.
Freud-Marie Bonaparte 1.6.1936 in Schur, 563.
Freud-Arnold Zweig 2.4.1937 in *Zweig Letters*.
Freud-Jones 18.5.1937 [Typescript Inst. of PsA]

Martin Freud, *Heute keine Sensation!* [FM: SOH9-5] ("Darum verkünden wir streng vertraulich:/ Die nächsten acht Geburtstage feiern wir gleichfalls beschaulich!/ Bis dahin auf wiedersehen!").

12 May 1937
Martha Freud-Ernst Freud 4.4.1937 [FM: Lucie Freud Papers] ("Vermute ich recht, wenn ich annehme, dass Du Deine Reise nach Wien auf Anfang Mai beabsichtigst, um den Rummel der Coronation zu entgehen?").

13 May 1937
Freud-Marie Bonaparte 16.5.1937 in Schur, 490.
Bertin, p.198.

16 May 1937
Peters, p.222.
Leitsätze; Budapest 15–17 May 1937 [LoC].

28 May 1937
Sterba, pp.155-7.
Analysis Terminable and Interminable, S.E.XXIII.250.
Orgler, Hertha, *Alfred Adler: The Man and His Work*, London, 1973, pp.7, 200–201.

5 June 1937
1. At first sight this entry would seem to refer to the Swiss analysts, Emil Oberholzer and Frédéric Weil. But in 1927 Emil Oberholzer (Mira Oberholzer's husband) had split the Swiss society over the issue of lay analysis, which he opposed, and founded a Society of Medical Analysts (*Verein ärtzlicher Analytiker*). Frédéric Weil was in training with him. Both may still have been persona non grata with Freud. (During a meeting with the Swiss analyst Kielholz on April 21, 1937 Freud called Oberholzer self-willed and asked if he was still the same.)
Fichtner-Molnar 21.5.1990 [FM].
Roazen, P., "Tola Rank" *Revue AIHP*, 1990, 3 p.446.
Int. J. PsA., Vol.1 No.3., 1920 pp.365-9.
Eissler, K.R., "Obituary. F.S. Weil," *Int. J. PsA*, Vol 41, 1960, pp.633-40.
Kielholz, Arthur, "Persönliche Erinnerungen an Freud," *Schweizer Archiv für Neurologie und Psychiatrie*, Bd. 79, Heft 2 (1957), p.402 & note.

11 June 1937 (Anna)
Freud-Arnold Zweig 2.4.1937 in Freud, Ernst L. (Hrsg.), *Sigmund Freud/Arnold Zweig: Briefwechsel* Fischer, Frankfurt/Main, 1984, [1968]

11 June 1937 (Heat)
Neue Freie Presse, 11.6.1937.
Pichler Notes, 9.6.1937 [FM].

11 June 1937 (Otitis)
Schur, 490-1.
Jones, III.229.
Pichler Notes, 6.7.1937 [FM].

26 June 1937
McCord, Clinton, "Freud—The Man," *The Psychiatric Quarterly*, Vol. 14, Jan. 1940.

July 1937
Gay, p.605 n.
*Freud-Ehrenwald 14.12.1937** [FM: Typescript copy 1-F8-18-4]
* Published in *Letters* as "*Freud-Anonymous 14.12.1937.*"

27 July 1937
Eitingon-Freud 24.1.1937 [FM].
Freud-Eitingon 5.2.1937 [FM] & *Letters*.
Eitingon-Freud 24.2.1937 [FM].

28 July 1937 (Zweig)
Arnold Zweig-Freud 6.9.1937 in *Zweig Letters*.

28 July 1937 (Princess)
Marie Bonaparte-Freud 6.9.1937 in Bertin, p.198.
Jones, I.316.
Marie Bonaparte 8.11.1951 [FM: II/F8-102].
Marie Bonaparte (Notebook), in Masson, p.9.

8 August 1937
1. In Jones's version of the letter to Marie Bonaparte (13.8.1937), Freud says he finished the Moses

"yesterday": in Ernst Freud's edition of the letters this becomes: "Two days ago.". Probably one translator read *Gestern* (yesterday), the other *Vorgestern* (the day before yesterday). According to these versions of the letter, Freud either finished the work on August 11 or 12. But neither date tallies with August 8, the date given in the diary entry.
Freud-Marie Bonaparte 13.8.1937 in Jones, III.494-5.
Wenn Moses ein Aegypter war . . . (Galley proof), [LoC] ("Bitte auf konsequente Behandlung der Eigennamen zu achten!").

18 August 1937
1. In his biography Jones writes: "In August [1937] he had for three days a disagreeable attack of haematuria without any ascertainable cause. Freud was under the impression, ever since his visit to America in 1909, that he was afflicted with prostatitis, but his medical reports do not confirm this."
Freud-Marie Bonaparte 20.8.1938 in Jones, III.252.
Pichler Notes, 20.9.1937 [FM].
Jones, III.229.

1 September 1937
1. The word used for "mind" (*Kopf*) occurs fortuitously in another of Freud's characterizations of Löwy 11 years afterwards. On Freud's tour round the National Portrait Gallery in London on September 13, 1908, he made jotted notes, including one in which he speaks of Shakespeare as "a typical thinker" ("*ein typischer Kopf*"), like Homer, Gomperz, Em. Löwy and Socrates. Certainly Löwy's head does bear some resemblance to the accepted image of Socrates.
Schmutzer, who did a portrait of Freud in 1926, also drew the portrait of Löwy in Freud's collection.
2. Two Dürer prints hang in Freud's study at Maresfield Gardens: a small etching of *The Betrayal of Christ* and a larger portrait of Philip Melanchthon.
Freud, Anna, "Home Movies" commentary [FM].
Freud-Fliess 5.11.1897 in Schröter.
Freud-Martin Freud 16.8.1937 in *Letters*.
Freud, 13.9.1908, *Bemerkgn. über Gesichter u Männer National Portrait Gallery* [FM: I/F8-73-4].

14 September 1937 (Masaryk)
Freud-Arnold Zweig 22.6.1936 in *Zweig Letters*.
Zeman, Zbynek, *The Masaryks: The Making of Czechoslovakia*, 1976, p.155.
Seton-Watson, Hugh, *Eastern Europe between the Wars: 1918–1941*, N.Y. 1967, p.391.

14 September 1937 (Marriage)
Blanton, Smiley, *Diary of my Analysis with Sigmund Freud*, N.Y., 1971, p.41, (Entry for 23.1.1930).

15 September 1937
1. Herbert Jones sent Anna his poetry. One example of his work is the meditation of a wife blissfully awaiting her husband's return from work, and entitled *Why Feminism has no Future*. Another, a vapid fantasy called *The Greek Flute Girl*, Anna translated into German. When a letter from him to Anna arrived while she was away from home, Freud sent it on to her opened, because "she would have shown it to him anyway." He added that Herbert Jones was charming ("*liebenswürdig*") but clearly shifted personal relationships into literature.
Young-Bruehl, pp.65-8.
Loe Jones-Freud 21.9 1937 [FM: SOH9-11] ("Bin ich ein perverse u eigensinnige Mensch! Schreibe nicht für 20 Jahre, und wenn ich dann in Wien bin, muss ich anfangen!").
"The Greek Flute Girl" in Jones, Herbert, *The Blue Ship*, Bodley Head, London, 1921.
Freud, Anna, *Die Griechische Flötenbläserin* [FM: AM 56].
"Why Feminism has no Future" in Jones, Herbert, *Finlay*, Bodley Head, London, 1923.

23 September 1937
"Constructions in Analysis" [ms. LoC].
"Constructions in Analysis" S.E.,XXIII.268.

15 October 1937
Pichler Notes, 14.10.1937 [FM].

16 October 1937 (Mathilde)
Freud-Mama & Minna [Bernays] 16.10.1887 [LoC]
("Es wiegt 3400 gr, was sehr anständig ist, ist furchtbar hässlich, lutscht von seinem ersten Moment ab an seiner rechten Hand, scheint sonst sehr gutmütig als ob es wirklich zu Hause wäre.").

16 October 1937 (Berggasse)
1. There had once been a move to have Berggasse renamed after Freud, but nothing came of it. In an undated letter from Pötzleinsdorf [1931 or 1932], Freud wrote to Max Halberstadt:
"Furthermore Berggasse is supposed to be changing its name in my honour. If it really happens, imagine how proud I will be." (*Freud-Max Halberstadt n.d.*).
Freud-Max Halberstadt n.d. [LoC] ("Die Berggasse soll übrigens mir zu Ehren ihren Namen ändern. Wenn es wirklich geschieht, stell' dir vor wie stolz ich sein werde.").

19 October 1937
Clark, Ronald W., *Einstein: The Life and Times*, London, 1973, pp.396–7.
Bertin, p.242.
Dumont, Georges-Henri, *Elisabeth de Belgique*, Paris, 1986.

21 October 1937
Knöpfmacher, W., *Entstehungsgeschichte und Chronik der Vereinigung "Wien" B'nai B'rith in Wien, 1895–1935*, B'nai B'rith, Wien, 1935.
Klein, Dennis B. "The Prefiguring of the Psychoanalytic Movement: Freud and the B'nai B'rith," in *Jewish Origins of the Psychoanalytic Movement*, University of Chicago Press, 1985.
Freud-B'nai B'rith Vienna [End September] 1937 in Knoepfmacher, Hugo "Sigmund Freud und B'nai B'rith," *Jahrbuch der Psychoanalyse*, Band XI S.70.

22 October 1937 (Dorothy)
Burlingham, p.257, 262.

22 October 1937 (Eitingon)
Arnold Zweig-Freud 27.10.1937 in *Zweig Letters*.

5 November 1937 (Eitingon)
Schur, 49.
Freud-Wittkowski 25.10.1937 [FM: SFVAR] ("Ich danke Ihnen sehr für das Geschenk Ihrer Gedichte. Ich vermute, dass sie sehr schön sind, aber ich kann Lyrik seit langen Jahren nicht mehr geniessen.
"Mein gegenwärtiger Zustand von akuter 'Erkältung' hält mich ab, Sie zu einem Besuch einzuladen.").

5 November 1937 (Gärtner)
Jones, I.58, 60, 95.
Schröter, p.336 n.3.
Byck, Robert (Ed.), *The Cocaine Papers*, N.Y., 1974, p.284.

14 November 1937
1. Apart from the Princess, Dr. Mark Brunswick also filmed the Freuds during the 1930s. A number of clips from their films were put together in 1972 for the 20th Birthday Celebrations of the Hampstead Clinic, forming a short chronological film with Anna Freud as the live narrator. Subsequently the film was professionally re-edited to include Anna Freud's commentary and was shown for the first time at the International Psychoanalytical Congress in New York in July 1979. (It is now regularly shown at the Freud Museum in London.)
"Home Movies" [FM].
Yorke, Clifford: October 1986 (Typescript Introduction to "Home Movies") [FM].

23 November, 1937
1. In 1937, under the *nom de plume* Anton von Miller, he published the book *Deutsche und Juden*, which appeared in English in 1939 as *The Germans and the Jews*. As the Nazi threat to Austria increased, Bienenfeld helped many people (though not Freud himself) get their money out of the country. He was trusted implicitly, for such transactions involved handing over cash without receipts. Bienenfeld also

moved to London. His address there is the final one written into Freud's small green English address book.
Freud, Martin, "Who was Freud" in Fraenkel, Josef (ed.), *The Jews of Austria*, London, 1970 [1967], p.205.
Nunberg, H., and Federn, Ernst (eds), *Minutes of the Vienna Psychoanalytic Society*, New York, 1962, Vol. III, p.59.
Bienenfeld, Rudolf, *Die Religion der Religionslosen Juden*, Wien, 1938 [FM] (Inscribed: "Zur Erinnerung an Wien").
Waelder, Robert, Oral communication R.S. Stewart.
Green address book [FM:5238].

28 November 1937
Zweig, Stefan, *Die Welt von Gestern*, Fischer, 1979 [1944], p.288.
Stefan Zweig-Freud 15.11.1937 in Stefan Zweig.
Freud-Stefan Zweig 17.11.1937 Ibid, p.175.

30 November 1937
Schur, 491.
Pichler Notes, 26.11.1937 & 1.12.1937 [FM].

3 December 1937
Martin Freud, 2.12.1937 [FM: MOB 13].
("Andere Damen kriegen Flieder, Rosen,
Aber Du willst nichts als alte Hosen [. . .].
Niemand soll darob die Stirne runzeln
Meine Gaben liegen schon bereit:
Ein Gedicht für fünf Minuten schmunzeln
Alte Hosen für die Ewigkeit . . . ").

1938

9 January 1938
Young-Bruehl, p.28, 46, 65.
Jones, II.429.
Jones, I.179, 245.

22 January 1938
Schur, 492–3.
Pichler Notes 22/23.1.1938 [FM].
Freud-Eitingon 6.2.1938 [FM] & *Letters*.
Anna Freud-Jones 25.1.1938 [Inst. of PsA: CFF/FO1/01].

19 February 1938
Anna Freud-Jones 20.2.1938 [Inst. of PsA: CFF/FO1/02] ("Zuerst waren sehr viel Schmerzen, aber dann hat er sich sehr schnell erholt und wir werden vielleicht schon heute in die Berggasse zurückgehen können. Vielleicht werden jetzt wieder einige bessere Wochen kommen.").

24 Feburary 1938
Anna Freud-Jones 20.2.1938 [Inst. of PsA: CFF/FO1/02] ("In Wien war Panikstimmung, die sich jetzt wieder etwas beruhigt. Wir machen die Panick nicht mit. Es ist zu früh, man kann die Folgen des Geschehenen noch nicht voll beurteilen. Vorläufig ist alles wie es war. Es ist vielleicht auch für uns leichter als für andere, die beweglicher sind, wir brauchen nicht vieler Entschlüsse zu überdenken, denn es kommen für uns kaum welche in Betracht.").
Clare, George, *Last Waltz in Vienna*, London, 1981, pp.170–1.
Bergschicker, pp.228–233.
Neue Freie Presse, 25.2.1938.

24–28 February 1938
Freud-Arnold Zweig 21.3.1938 in *Zweig Letters*.

2 March 1938
Freud-Arnold Zweig 21.3.1938 in *Zweig Letters*.

9 March 1938
Clare, George, *Last Waltz in Vienna*, London, 1981, pp.173–4.

10 March 1938
Telegrams, Vienna, March 15 [1938], Washington, March 16 [1938] (2) [FM].

11 March 1938 (Ernstl)
Freud, W. Ernest-Molnar 6.8.1989 [FM].

11 March 1938 (Schuschnigg)
Martin Freud, p.121.
Clare, George, *Last Waltz in Vienna*, London, 1981, pp.176–7.

13 March 1938
Jelavich, Barbara, *Modern Austria; Empire and Republic, 1815–1986*, Cambridge University Press, 1987, pp.156–7.
Hitler, Adolf, *Mein Kampf*, (transl. Ralph Manheim), London, 1969, p.3 ("Deutschösterreich muss wieder zurück zum grossen deutschen Mutterlande . . . [. . .] Gleiches Blut gehört in ein gemeinsames Reich.").
Stadler, K.R., *Austria*, London, 1971, p.150.
Neue Freie Presse, Nr. 26403S 13.3.1938 & Nr. 26404A 14.4.1938.
Waelder, Robert, Interview R.S.Stewart, 29.7.1966.
Jones, III.236.
Schuschnigg, Kurt von, *The Brutal Takeover*, London, 1971, p.269.

14 March 1938
1. The *Neue Freie Presse* reported: "He was greeted by cries of enthusiasm ringing out from a hundred thousand throats." Letters posted on March 15 bore a swastika stamp with "*Der Führer in Wien*" inscribed around it. (One such letter was from Freud to Dr. Abrahamsen. Ignoring the political furore, the letter deals with Freud's own history, namely the facts of his relationship with Otto Weininger at the turn of

the century.) Stefan Zweig's memoirs express the sadness of Vienna's fate: "Only the coming decades will show the crime that Hitler perpetrated against Vienna when he sought to nationalize and provincialize this city, whose meaning and culture were founded in the meeting of the most heterogeneous elements, and in her spiritual supernationality. For the genius of Vienna—a specifically musical one—was always that it harmonized all the national and lingual contrasts. Its culture was a synthesis of all Western cultures."
Stadler, Karl R., *Austria*, London, 1971, p.182.
Carloni, Glaucom, "Freud and Mussolini" in Rovigatti, Franca [ed.], *Italy in Psychoanalysis*, Rome, 1989, pp.51–60.
Freud-Abrahamsen 14.3.1938 [LoC].
Neue Freie Presse, 15.3.1938.
Zweig, Stefan, *The World of Yesterday*, London, 1944, pp.28–29.
Clare, George, *Last Waltz in Vienna*, London, 1981, p.196.

15 March 1938
1. It was after the raid that Ernest Jones found Freud "adamant" about not leaving Vienna. Probably this unyielding mood reflected his reaction to the Nazi raids, which had aroused his fighting spirit. By this time it was blatantly obvious he would have to leave. In fact, as Jones himself reports, at the board meeting the previous Sunday Freud had already agreed to disband the Vienna society and emigrate.
Martin Freud, pp.207–211.
Jones, III.234.
Jones, I.323 & III.234–5.
Waelder, Robert, Interview R.S.Stewart, 29.7.1966.

16 March 1938
1. There were several reasons why Jones wished to limit the numbers of Viennese who could be accepted into the British Psycho-Analytical Society. One was the danger of swamping the British society with immigrant psychoanalysts. Already a year earlier, Jones had written to Freud: "Our Society is becoming distinctly verdeutscht, there being some seventeen members who have reached us from abroad in the last few years." (*Jones-Freud 23.2.1937*). But there was also the question of Jones's Kleinian sympathies and his sense that the emigrés might challenge his ideological leadership or the society's integrity. Anna Freud understood his difficulties. She later wrote: "It cannot have been easy to persuade the British Society to open their doors [. . .] to colleagues who held different scientific views from their own and could only be expected to disrupt peace and internal unity."
   This March diary entry is, incidentally, the last actual mention of Jones, though he was to be a frequent visitor once the Freuds were established in England. He played an invaluable role in securing their entry permits into England and both Freud and Anna were grateful. She wrote in April: "In quieter times I hope to be able to show you that I understand in its entirety what you are now doing for us. [. . .] I think it through with you and sense completely what it all means." (*Anna Freud-Jones 3.4.1938*).
Jones's Diary, 15.3.1938 [Inst. of PsA].
Jones, I.323.
Waelder, Robert, Interview R.S.Stewart, 29.7.1966.
Freud-Jones 28.4.1938 in Jones, III.240.
Jones-Freud 23.2.1937 [Inst. of PsA].
Freud, Anna, "Personal Memories of Ernest Jones," (1979) *The Writings of Anna Freud: Vol. VIII* Hogarth, London, 1982, p.350.
Anna Freud-Jones 3.4.1938 [Inst. of PsA: CFF/01/03] ("In ruhigeren Zeiten hoffe ich, Dir zeigen zu können, dass ich im ganzen Umfange verstehe, was Du jetzt für uns tust. [. . .] Ich denke es mit Dir durch und ich spüre ganz, was es alles bedeutet.").

17 March 1938
Jones, III.238.
Bertin, p.200.
Berthelsen, Detlef, *Alltag bei der Familie Freud*, Hamburg, 1987, p.81.
Martin Freud, p.214.

22 March 1938
1. When questioned in 1966 why it was the Gestapo had arrested her in particular, Anna Freud responded: "Oh but they arrested everybody!"
2. Berthelsen's memoirs of Paula Fichtl claim that the Gestapo initially wanted Freud himself to accompany them up to the offices at Berggasse 7. At that point Anna intervened, saying Freud could not climb stairs. Instead her offer to go with them to Berggasse 7 was accepted. According to Paula, it was there that she was held by the Gestapo. This version appears to confuse the first raid of March 15 with Anna's arrest on March 22. But there remained the possibility the Gestapo might arrest Freud. On March 22 Pichler wrote a report, testifying that Freud was his patient, that his heart was too weak for him to climb even a few steps and that any excitement could be dangerous for him. According to Martin Freud it was Anna who obtained this certificate from Pichler. If so, she must have done this before she herself was arrested that day, or else she sent someone round to the surgeon's. Paula also asserted that in the days following Anna's arrest, Marie Bonaparte sat on the stairs leading to the Freuds' apartment, to guard against further raids.
3. According to Martin Freud it was through "the influence of friends" that she managed to leave the corridor in the Gestapo headquarters, where she had been left waiting with many others. In Anna Freud's account to Jones she speaks of a "mysterious phone call" (indicating outside maneuvering on her behalf) which promoted her to the inner room. After her arrest Dorothy Burlingham had phoned Wiley at the American Embassy and a cable was sent to the American Secretary of State.
Martin Freud, pp.212–4.
Schur, 498.
Berthelsen, Detlef, *Alltag bei der Familie Freud*, Hamburg, 1987, pp.78–9.
Pichler, Prof. Hans, 22.3.1938 [FM].
Cathrin Pichler-Molnar 29.11.1990 [FM].
Martin Freud, p.215.
Freud, Anna, Interview R.S.Stewart, 17.1.1966.
Gay, p.626 n.
Clark, p.507.

28 March 1938 (Acceptance)
Jones, III.234–5, 237.
Freud, Anna, "Personal Memories of Ernest Jones," (1979), *The Writings of Anna Freud: Vol. VIII*, Hogarth, London, 1982, p.350.
Jones diary, 25.4.1938 [Inst. of PsA].

28 March 1938 (Ernstl)
Freud, W. Ernest-Molnar 6.8.1989 [FM].
Freud, W. Ernest, *Brief Biography* (ms.), 1989 [FM].

1 April 1938
1. After his father's death Ernstl assumed his mother's surname. He spent the war and postwar years in London and received his psychoanalytic training in adult and child analysis at the London Institute of Psycho-Analysis and the Hampstead Child Therapy Clinic (now known as the Anna Freud Centre). He became a training analyst at both institutes, where he taught mother-infant observation for several years. At Hampstead he was head of the Well-Baby Research Group, which was created for working out his idea of the Baby Profile, together with Anna Freud, Dorothy Burlingham and members of the Well-Baby Clinic staff. He has published and lectured widely on the psychosocial aspects of perinatal care and especially of neonatal intensive care. By agreeing to forego the inheritance of Freud's house in Maresfield Gardens, which had been earmarked by Anna Freud as his inheritance, he enabled her to initiate the creation of the Freud Museum in London. After her death he relocated in West Germany, where he has been in psychoanalytic and supervisory practice in Cologne.
   In his 1987 Freud lecture at Vienna University W. Ernest Freud has presented a unique picture of the home life of the Freud and Burlingham households during the 1930s and of the effect they had on each other—the one old-fashioned and Viennese, the other progressive and American.
Freud, W. Ernest-Molnar 6.8.1989 [FM].

Freud, W. Ernest, *Brief Biography* (ms.), 1989 [FM].
Freud, W. Ernest "Die Freuds und die Burlinghams in der Berggasse: Persönliche Erinnerungen" (Sigmund Freud-Vorlesung, gehalten an der Universität Wien, am 6.Mai 1987), *Sigmund Freud House Bulletin*, Vol.11/1, Summer 1987, 3–18.

6 April 1938
The Star, 5.7.1938 [FM: F29–58-24].

9 April 1938
1. Marie Bonaparte wrote the book between May 1935 and June 1936. It was prompted by Topsy's sickness—a cancerous tumor in the dog's mouth which was eventually cured by X-ray treatment. The book is not frivolous; it is in fact a meditation on sickness, love and death. The translators could not have avoided drawing parallels with Freud's own situation, when working on such passages as the following: "The verdict on Topsy has been delivered: there is a lympho-sarcoma beneath her lip which is once again beginning to swell, a tumour which will grow, spread, proliferate, burst open and kill her. In a few months she has been condemned to die the most terrible of all deaths."
Freud-Marie Bonaparte 6.12.1936 in Jones, III.225–6.
"Topsy" ms. [LoC].
Freud-Marie Bonaparte 13.8.1937 in *Letters*.
Jones, III.239.
Bonaparte, Marie, *Der goldenhaarige Chow*, Allert de Lange, Amsterdam, 1939, p.19 [German translation: Anna & Sigmund Freud].

10 April 1938
Stadler, Karl R., *Austria*, London, 1971, pp.183–4.
Bergschicker, pp.228–233.

17 April 1938
Blanton, Smiley, *Diary of my Analysis with Sigmund Freud*, N.Y., 1971, pp.106–7.

19 April 1938 (Alex)
Freud-Alexander Freud 19.4.1938 in *Letters*.

19 April 1938
Bertin, p.201.
Berthelsen, Detlef, *Alltag bei der Familie Freud*, Hamburg, 1987, p.81.

18 April 1938
Bertin, p.199, 201.

26 April 1938
Freud-Jelliffe 2.8.1934 [FM: 1-F8–74-14] ("Auch mein Gehör ist nicht mehr, was es war, aber ich reiche aus und habe jedenfalls mit 78 Jahren ein gewisses Anrecht auf Taubheit, während ich es Ihrem Alter bestreiten würde. [. . .] Mir wird dieses letzte Abschnitt des Lebensablaufs nicht bequem gemacht.").
Jones, III.100–1.
Freud-Jones 13.5.1938 [Typescript Inst. of PsA] ("Gern wäre ich in besseren Zustand nach England gekommen. Ich reise zwar mit einem Leibarzt, aber ich habe Bedürfnis nach näheren Ärzten und bald nach meiner Ankunft werde ich einen Ohrenarzt ausfindig machen und den Kieferarzt aufsuchen müssen, dessen Namen mir Pichler angegeben hat. Manchmal sagt man sich auch "Le jeu ne vaut (plus) pas la chandelle", und obwol man damit Recht hat, darf man sich nicht Recht geben.").

29 April 1938
Bertin, p.201.

1 May 1938
"Home Movies" [FM] ("Dieser erster Mai er soll dokumentieren, dass wir nicht stören wollen sondern aufzubauern gedenken").

5 May 1938 (Minna)
1. While in Switzerland Dorothy kept in daily contact with the Freuds by telephone. It was not until May 28, when she felt reasonably certain of their safety, that she left with Minna for London. That same day, in the United States, her estranged husband, Dr. Robert Burlingham, committed suicide. In his condolence letter the following day, Freud said

that the death meant " . . . release for an unhappy
man . . . " and a relief for their four children.
Valenstein, Mrs K., Interview, 14.5.1990.
Freud-Dorothy Burlingham 1.5.1938 [LoC].
Burlingham, pp.261–5.
Freud-Dorothy Burlingham 29.5.1938 [LoC] (" . . . eine
Erlösung für einen Unglücklichen . . . ").

5 May 1938 (Gestapo)
1. Nine days later Freud wrote to Minna: "Almost
everything that had to be done, Anna took care of.
The men like Robert [Hollitscher] and Martin were
useless, semi-idiotic . . . ." (*Freud-Minna Bernays
14.6.1938*).
Stadler, Karl R., *Austria*, London, 1971, p.184.
Jones, III.238.
Schur, 498–9 n.3.
Martin Freud, p.214.
Freud-Jones 23.4.1938 [Typescript Inst. of PsA].
Freud-Jones 28.4.1938 ibid ("Die Verzögerung ist
wahrlich nicht unsere Schuld, sie hängt an den
Vermögens- und Besitzabhandlungen und an den
Eigentümlichkeiten dieser Übergangszeit, in der die
Behörden noch nicht sicher sind, nach welchen
Bestimmungen sie arbeiten sollen.").
Freud-Minna Bernays 14.6.1938 [FM] ("Fast alles
was zu thun war, hat Anna besorgt. Die Männer
wie Robert u Martin waren unbrauchbar halb
närrisch . . . ").

6 May 1938
Freud-Jones 13.5.1938 [Typescript Inst. of PsA] ("Wir
hatten beschlossen, dass dieser Geburtstag nicht
gelten soll, dass er auf den 6. Juni, Juli, August usw.,
kurz auf ein Datum nach unserer Befreiung
verschoben wird und ich habe in der That keine der
eingetroffenen Zuschriften, Telegramme u dgl.
beantwortet.").

10 May 1938
Reichsfluchtsteuerbescheid [FM].
Freud-Jones 13.5.1938 [Typescript Inst. of PsA]
("Anna is unermüdlich thätig, nicht nur für uns, auch
für unbegrenzt viele andere. Ich hoffe sie wird in
England auch viel für die Analyse thun können, aber
sie wird sich nicht aufdrängen.").

12 May 1938
1. Stefan Zweig noted bitterly, on becoming stateless
after the Anschluss: "And I was continually reminded
of words spoken to me years ago by a Russian exile:
'Formerly man only had a body and soul. Today he
needs a passport as well, otherwise he will not be
treated like a man.' "
2. It was the Viennese psychologist August Aichhorn
who had asked Engelman to record the interior of
Berggasse 19 for posterity, so that, as he put it, " . . .
a museum can be created when the storm of years is
over."
Engleman, E., Oral communication, 3.2.1989.
Zweig, Stefan, *Die Welt von Gestern*, Fischer, 1979
[1944], p.294.
Engelman, p.134.

14 May 1938
1. Freud offers a slightly different version of the
story: "Martin will probably leave before us with his
family, leave wife and daughter in Paris, go to
London with the boy. He hopes, and we all join him
in this, that this will in practice be the end of his
unhappy marriage. She is not only maliciously
meshugge but also mad in the medical sense. But
what will he do in England? He cannot live without a
wife (women) and there he won't find again the type
of freedom he allowed himself here." (*Freud-Ernst
Freud 12.5.1938*).
Martin Freud, p.215.
Freud-Ernst Freud 12.5.1938 [Inst. of PsA:
CFB/FO2/O1] ("Martin wird mit den Seinigen
wahrscheinlich vor uns weggehen, Frau u. Tochter in
Paris lassen, mit dem Buben nach London kommen.
Er hofft, und wir alle mit ihm, dass dies praktisch das
Ende seiner unglücklicher Ehe sein wird. Sie ist nicht
nur bösartig meshugge, sondern auch im ärztlichen
Sinn verrückt. Aber was fängt er denn in England an?
Er kann ohne Frau(en) nicht leben u. die Art Freiheit,

die er sich hier gestattet hat, findet er dort nicht
wieder.").

21 May 1938
Freud-Jones 28.4.1938 [Typescript Inst. of PsA] ("Ich
leide unter dem Mangel an Beschäftigg., helfe ein
wenig bei der Ordnung der Bibliothek u. der
Sammlung . . . ").
Freud-Minna Bernays 23.5.1938 [FM] ("Die eine gute
Neuigkeit ist dass meine Sammlung frei gegeben
wurde. Keine einzige Beschlagnahme, eine geringe
Abgabe von RM 400. Direktor Dehmel vom
Museum war sehr gnädig, er hat das Ganze zwar auf
RM 30,000 geschätzt, aber das damit sind wir noch
weit unter der Steuerfluchtgrenze. Der Spediteur kann
ohne Aufschub mit der Verpackung beginnen.").
Reichsfluchtsteuerbescheid [FM].

24 May 1938
Freud-Minna Bernays 20.5.1938 [FM] ("Wir sind
zwischen Thür und Angel wie jemand der ein Raum
verlassen möchte aber seinen Rock eingeklemmt
findet. Mathilde und Robert sind schon frei. [. . .]
Wir hängen noch an der Steuer. Anna bemüht sich
mit viel Geschick und guten Humor, uns
loszumachen.").
Mathilde Hollitscher-Jones n.d. in Clark, p.511.
Freud-Minna Bernays 26.5.1938 [FM] ("Alles ist in
gewissen Sinn unwirklich, wir sind nicht mehr hier
und noch nicht dort.").

30 May 1938
Freud-Minna Bernays 20.5.1938 [FM] ("Der
interessanteste von den Abschiedsbesuchern . . . ").
Freud-Minna Bernays 28.5.1938 & 2.6.1938 [FM].

2 June 1938
Jones, III.238.
Freud-Minna Bernays 14.5.1938 [FM] ("Alles hängt
noch davon ab, wann wir die
Unbedenklichkeitserklärung von der Steuer
bekomme. Ohne sie sind wir der
Grenzüberschreitung nicht sicher. Auf dieser Papier
wird also ängstlich gewartet. Vorher können wir auch
keine Fahrkarten bestellen.").
Freud-Minna Bernays 2.6.1938 [FM] ("Du kannst dir
nicht vorstellen, was für Kleinigkeiten jetzt eine Rolle
spielen und alles das Wichtigste wie das
Unwesentliche muss Anna allein besorgen.").

3[4] June 1938 (Departure)
1. Freud did have another, correctly dated, record of
the journey. This is in a small black notebook,
afterwards stored in his desk drawer. It is entirely
unused apart from four entries apparently jotted
down en route: "Saturday 4 June. *Departure*. Sunday
5 June *Paris evening Dover* Monday 6 June *London*".
Freud-Eitingon 6[7].6.1938 [FM] & *Letters*.
Black notebook [FM 5233] ("Sonnabend 4. Juni
Abreise Sonntag 5. Juni *Paris abds Dover* Montag 6.
Juni *London*").

3[4] June 1938 (Kehl)
Freud-Eitingon 6[7?].6.1938 [FM] & *Letters*.
Clarke, p.513.
Schur, 502.
Berthelsen, Detlef, *Alltag bei der Familie Freud*,
Hamburg, 1987, p.86.

4[5] June 1938 (Paris)
1. Freud was indebted to Bullitt for all the diplomatic
pressure he had exerted on the Nazis. When they met
at the station, Bullitt suggested they resume
discussion of the Wilson book in London. By now
Freud may have already given up the book as beyond
hope of improvement. Bullitt visited him twice in
London and produced a text to which
Freud—according to Bullitt—did not object. He
apparently agreed to let Bullitt publish the book after
the death of Wilson's widow.
2. "Athene" refers to the statuette which Marie
Bonaparte had already smuggled out for Freud
because it was his favorite piece, the one that stood
directly in front of him on his desk. The figurine is a
1st or 2nd century A.D. Roman copy of a Greek 5th
century B.C. original. It represents Athena, goddess
of wisdom and war, her left hand raised, her right

hand carrying a libation bowl. The breastplate bears a
medusa head. It had been in the collection since at
least 1933, which is when he showed it to H.D.:
" 'She is perfect,' he said, 'only she has lost her
spear.' "
Freud-Eitingon 6[7?].6.1938 [FM] & *Letters*.
Jones, III.243.
"Home Movies" [FM].
Freud-Marie Bonaparte 8.6.1938 in Schur, 504 & 564.
Freud, Sigmund & Bullitt, William C., *Thomas
Woodrow Wilson, Twenty-eighth President of the United
States: A Pychological Study*, London & Boston, 1967,
pp.ix-x.
Burn, Lucilla, in *Freud and Art*, p.110.
H.D., p.74.

4[5] June 1938 (London)
Freud-Eitingon 6[7?].6.1938 [FM].
Berthelsen, Detlef, *Alltag bei der Familie Freud*,
Hamburg, 1987, p.88.

5[6] June 1938 (Dover)
Jones, III.243.
Freud-Eitingon 6[7?].6.1938 [FM].

5[6] June 1938
Jones, III.243.
Freud- Lampl-de Groot 13.6.1938 [FM] ("Ernst hatte
ein reizendes Häuschen für uns gemietet, mein
Zimmer geht auf eine Veranda, die auf einen eigenen
Garten, Rasenplatz von Blumen eingerahmt und der
Blick in einen grossen mit Bäumen besetzten Park. Es
ist natürlich erst ein Provisorium für drei Monate,
Ernst hat das Definitive noch zu suchen, das allerlei
selten hier verwirklichte Bedingungen zu erfüllen hat.
Es ist schwer für uns vertikal anstatt horizontal zu
leben.").
Berthelsen, Detlef, *Alltag bei der Familie Freud*,
Hamburg, 1987, p.89, 92.

5[6] June 1938 (Minna)
Schur, 505.
Freud- Lampl-de Groot 13.6.1938 [FM].

5[6] June 1938 (Columns)
Freud- Lampl-de Groot 13.6.1938 [FM] ("Wir sind jetzt
also wirklich in England angekommen, es ist sehr
schön und die Öffentlichkeit, Freunde wie Fremde,
bereitete uns einen warmen Empfang. (Das Klima
weniger warm.) [. . .] Natürlich ist noch alles
ungewohnt u wie unwirklich, ein deutliches
Entfremdungsgefühl.").
Jones, III.244–5.

9 June 1938
1. Although Sam is the first visitor noted in the
diary, his name comes seventh in Freud's notebook,
where he listed his visitors. The preceding names are:
"Yahuda, St. Zweig, Mrs. Eder, B. Low,
Schmiedeberg, Glover & Frau." But the diary records
"Jahuda" [sic] as visiting two days after Sam, on June
11. This seems to indicate that the visitor list may
have been filled in retrospectively, like the diary, and
not necessarily in strict chronological order.
Freud-Sam Freud 4.6.1938 [FM].
Freud-Ernst Freud 12.5.1938 in Schur, 499.
Dark blue notebook [FM: LDFRD 5238].

10 June 1938
Freud-Eitingon 6[7?].6.1938 [FM].
The Referee, 18.6.1938 [FM].

11 June 1938
1. The books Arnold Zweig had in mind are in
Freud's library: *The Accuracy of the Bible: the Stories of
Joseph; the Exodus and Genesis Confirmed and Illustrated
by Egyptian Monuments and Language* (London 1934)
and *The Language of the Pentateuch in its Relation to
Egyptian*; vol.1 (London 1933).
Dark blue notebook [FM: LDFRD 5238].
Arnold Zweig-Freud 6.9.1937 in *Zweig Letters*.
Jones, III.250. 396, 400.

18 June 1938
1. According to Jones, she was later taken to a
nursing home: this probably refers to another illness
in late August.
Jones, III.246.

19 June 1938
Jones, III.91.

21 June 1938
Freud-Jones 28.4.1938 [Jones, III.240 & Typescript
Inst. of PsA] (" . . . finde auch eine Stunde täglich,
um am Moses weiter zu arbeiten, der mich plagt wie
ein ghost not laid.").

23 June 1938
Martha Freud-Meine Theuern [Lilly Marlé] 22.6.[1938]
[LoC (Filed under "Martin F.—Lilly F. Marlé")] ("
. . . also von Sommerruhe nicht viel zu spüren!").

23 June 1938
The Times, 5.9.1938.
Royal Society, *Notes and Records,* 2 October 1938.

23 June 1938
Freud, Anna, Commentary to "Home Movies" [FM].

25 June 1938
1. Freud's English address book contains the name of
an antiquities dealer in north London, showing he
was still interested in the search for new pieces. He
was also visited by the art dealer Hans Calmann,
Ernst Freud's brother-in-law, and from him acquired
a wooden refectory table, now in the study at
Maresfield Gardens.
"Rechte und Pflichte der Mitarbeiten 1924," *Archiv
des Psychoanalytischen Ambulatoriums, Wien* [FM:
SOH9–6 (P67–8)].
Dawson, Warren R., *Who was who in Egyptology,* The
Egypt Exploration Society, London.
Dawson, Warren R., *Battiscombe George Gunn:
1883–1950,* From the Proceedings of the British
Academy, Vol.XXXVI, London n.d.
Freud-"Herr Doktor" 26.6.1938 [FM: I/F8–41-2] ("Uns
geht es hier gut, ich würde sagen, sehr gut, wenn
nicht die abscheulichen Nachrichten aus Wien und
die unabweisbare Teilnahme am Schicksal sovieler
Anderer, denen es schlecht geht, einen tiefen Schatten
auf unser Glück werfen würden. Unsere Aufnahme in
England war äusserst liebenswürdig, wir denken nicht
daran, nach Amerika zu übersiedeln.").
Calmann, Mrs G., Oral communication, 1990.
Freud-Ernst Freud 12.5.1938 in *Letters.*

15 July 1938
Freud-Eitingon 3.11.1938 ("Die deutsche Ausgabe wird
bei Alert de Lange in Holland erscheinen. Die
englische (u amerikanische) hängt leider von Jones ab,
der die Übersetzung verzögert u sich manchmal
benimmt, als ob er das Buch sabotieren wollte. Die
Freundlichkeit, mit der er uns empfangen, scheint
sich verausgabt zu haben.").
Freud-Eitingon 19.12.1938 & 29.12.1938 [FM].

15 July 1938
Kent, G.H., & Rosanoff A.J., "A Study of
Association in Insanity," *Amer. J. Insan.* 67:37–96,
317–390, cited in: Burnham, John Chynoweth,
"Psychoanalysis and American Medicine,
1894–1918," *Psychological Issues* Vol.V/No.4 (With
thanks to Sonu Shamdasani for this reference).

15 July 1938
Romm, p.123.
Green address book [FM: LDFRD 5238].
Schur, 507–8.

16 July 1938
Freud, Ernst, Interview R.S.Stewart, 10.1.1966.
Freud-Alexander Freud 17.7.1938 [LoC] ("Das nächste
und schwierigste Problem ist ein Haus zu finden, das
unseren komplizirten Ansprüchen und unseren
bescheidenen Mitteln gleichzeitig gerecht wird.").

17 July 1938 (Moses)
Dali, Salvador, *The Secret Life of Salvador Dali,*
London, 1961, p.398.
"Findings, Ideas, Problems," *S.E.,XXIII.*299.

17 July 1938 (Will)
Probate copy of Freud's will [FM].
Schur, 497.
Jones, III.238.

18 July 1938 (Kent)
Dark blue notebook [FM: LDFRD 5238].

18 July 1938 (Gulden)
Freud-Indra 20.7.1938 in *Letters.*

19 July 1938 (Deafness)
Green address book [FM: LDFRD 5238].
Freud-Anna Freud 3.8.1938 [FM] ("Seit vorgestern will
der Katarrh wieder mein Gehör stören . . . ").

19 July 1938 (Dali)
1. Dali did a number of sketches of Freud. A sketch
now in the collection of François Petit appears to
have served as a study for the portrait now in
Maresfield Gardens. But another set of sketches are
inscribed "morphologie of Sigmund Freud's cranium
according to the principle of the volute and of the
snail. Drawn from life two years before his death."
These also influenced the portrait. However, it is
unclear whether they were all produced on this
occasion or earlier, under the combined influence of
a snail dinner, a conversation about Marie
Bonaparte's book on Poe and a newspaper
photograph of the exiled Freud arriving in Paris.
Stefan Zweig-Freud 18.7.1938 in Stefan Zweig.
Freud-Zweig, Stefan 20.7.1938 in Jones, III.251.
Dali, Salvador, *The Secret Life of Salvador Dali,*
London, 1961, pp.23–5 & 397–8.
Zweig, Stefan, *The World of Yesterday,* London, 1943.
p.318.
Romm, Fig.42, p.124.

26 July 1938
Martha-Meine Theuern [Lilly Marlé] 22.6.[1938] [LoC
(Filed under "Martin F.-Lilly F. Marlé")] ("Ich war
bis jetzt nur in zwei Warenhäusern und drei Parks
und komme mir buchstäblich wie ein Bauer vor, der
zum erstem Mal in seinen Leben in eine Stadt
kommt. Alles ist von einer unvorstellbarer Weite und
Grossartigkeit.").
Jones, III.248.

28 July 1938 (Will)
Probate copy of Freud's will [FM].

28 July 1938
Ellis, Donald, Report 26.6.1986 [FM: MAG/41/5].
Freud-Anna Freud 1.8.1938 [FM] ("Aus der Zeitung
konnte ich erfahren, dass ich ein Haus gekauft habe,
ich habe es noch nicht gesehen.").
Freud-Anna Freud 3.8.1938 [FM] ("Im meinen Palais
war ich noch nicht. Mein Friseur hatte schon in der
Zeitung gelesen, dass ich ein Haus gekauft habe.").

29 July 1938
Freud- Lampl-de Groot 26.7.1938 [FM] ("Wir
erwarten, der Kongress wird die endgiltige Lösung
von den für uns lästigen Amerikanern bringen und so
klare Verhältnisse schaffen. Diesmal bin auch ich in
Absentia durch mein Vortrag vertreten.").
Freud-Schnier 5.7.1938 in Jones, III.323.
Peters, p.231.
S.E.,XXIII.111–115.

1 August 1938
Freud-Anna Freud 1.8.1938 [FM] ("Es ist natürlich
nicht dasselbe, wenn du nicht da bist, obwol der
telephonische Kontakt vieles gut macht. Es ist wie
wenn du dein Rooms in Harley Str hättest u am
abend totmüde nach Hause kämest. [. . .] Der
Oxforder Ps therapeut. Kongress, dem Jung präsidirt,
hat mir das obligate Begrüssungstelegram geschickt,
das ich mit einen von Dr. Bennet vorbereiteten
kühlen Antwort erwiedert habe. Irgendwo bin ich
Ehrenpresident geworden, weiss nicht mehr wo.").

4 August 1938
Jones, III.249.
Bertin, p.200.
Prospectus cover [FM: V/F29–80].

5 August 1938 (Bäumler)
1. In the third paragraph of the letter, the firm's
representative states: "Dr. Sauerwald has directed me
to charge all costs as far as the destination in London
to the account here, however the costs of clearance
and delivery in London will be charged to your

account there." (*Bäuml-Freud 4.8.1938*).
Bäuml-Freud 4.8.1938 [FM] (" . . . in erstklassiger
Weise unter Beobachtung aller Vorsicht durch meine
langjährig geschulten Packer . . . ").
Bäuml-Freud 4.8.1938 [FM] ("Herr Dr. Sauerwald hat
mich angewiesen alle Kosten bis Ankunftsstation
London hier zu verrechnen, dagegen werden die
Kosten der Abfertigung und Zustellung in London
mit Ihnen dort verrechnet werden.").

5 August 1938 (Anna)
Freud-Anna Freud 3.8.1938 [FM] ("Meine Ferienarbeit
erweist sich als eine amusante Beschäftigung. Sie ist
schon 26 Seiten stark gewachsen, wird in drei Teile
zerfallen. Das Allgemeine—die praktische
Aufgabe—der theoretische Gewinn. Noch immer
bleibe ich bei der Fiktion, dass sie nicht gedruckt zu
werden braucht.").
Abriss der Psychoanalyse (ms.) [LoC].

6 August 1938
Freud-Marie Bonaparte 21[22?].11.1938 in Jones,
III.496.
Freud-Marie Bonaparte 12.11.1938 in Schur, 508 n.5.
Bertin, p.203.

7-Mon 8 August 1938 (Things)
Freud-Eitingon 15.6.1938 [FM] (" . . . die Gangsters
sind nicht zu berechnen.").
Freud- Lampl-de Groot 26.7.1938 [FM].
Freud-Anna Freud 3.8.1938 [FM].

7/Mon 8 August 1938 (Levy)
Freud- Lampl-de Groot 22.8.1938 [FM] ("Willy Levy
hat mich modellirt beinahe fertig. Gestern sass ich
einem Photographen, der nach seinem Musterproben
besondere Kunststücke kann. Wenn es ihm gelungen
ist, bekommen Sie ein Bild.").
Freud-Willy [Lévy] 19.10.1938 [LoC (Filed under
"Unknown")].
Zweig, Stefan-Freud [August 1938] in Stefan Zweig.

13 August 1938
1. At that time Hampstead had only recently
developed into a psychoanalysts' haven. Ernst Freud
states that when he came to London in 1933, it was
impossible for a psychoanalyst to live farther out
than Regents Park. However, Ernest Jones found a
house for Melanie Klein in St. John's Wood and this
encouraged the drift out toward Hampstead.
Freud- Lampl-de Groot 22.8.1938 [FM] ("Also 20
Maresfield Gardens als unsere hoffentlich letzte
Adresse auf diesem Planeten aber nicht vor Ende
Sept zu gebrauchen. Ein einiges eigenes Haus! Sie
können sich vorstellen, mit welchen Ansprüchen an
unser eingeschrumpftes Vermögen angekauft. Und
viel zu schön für uns; nicht weit von hier und von
Ernst, der das Haus in eine Ruine verwandelt, um es
für uns besser passend neu entstehen zu lassen. Er
baut einen Lift ein, macht aus zwei Zimmer eines
oder umgekehrt, das reine Hexeneinmaleins ins
Architektonische übersetzt.").
Freud, Ernst, Interview R.S.Stewart, 10.1.1966.

24 August 1938
Freud-Anna Freud 1.8.1938 [FM] ("Ruth [. . .]
behauptet in einer Depression zu sein. Dazu stimmt,
dass sie unausgesetzt kichert.").
Freud- Lampl-de Groot 22.8.1938 [FM] ("Ruth ist noch
hier (bis 24 dm) u nimmt eine Portion Nachanalyse zu
sich, die ihr wahrscheinlich sehr wolthun wird. Wie
unvollständig doch alle meine früheren Analysen
waren.").

29 August 1938
Freud- Lampl-de Groot 22.8.1938 [FM] ("Die freudige
Erwartung eines so schönen Besitzes wird leider
durch allerlei Schatten getrübt, Tante Minna's
Krankheit der schwarzeste unter ihnen. [. . .] Wir
wochenlange in einem Hotel, Tante in Spital oder
sog. Sanatorium die hier alle unglaublich unzulänglich
sind. Ein Land der Gegensätze, in manchen Punkten
sehr rückständig.").

2 September 1938
1. Freud's version—Hotel Esplanade—harks back to
at least two continental hotels of that name in which

he or members of the family had stayed. One was in Hamburg, the other in Berlin. Freud stayed in the latter from December 1926 to January 1927. A postcard to Anna dated December 29, 1926 bears its picture and reports a meeting with Einstein during which the two men discussed psychoanalysis rather than relativity.
Blanton, Smiley, *Diary of my Analysis with Sigmund Freud*, N.Y., 1971, p.107.
Freud-Anna Freud 29.12.1926 (postcard) [FM].

4 September 1938
Freud-Alexander Freud 22.6.1938 in *Letters*.
Freud-Alexander Freud 17.7.1938 [LoC]

7 September 1938
Anna Freud-Arnold Zweig n.d. [SFC 7433].
Schur, 508–9.

8 September 1938
Pichler Notes 8/9.9.1938 [FM].
Pichler-Anna Freud n.d. [FM: SAF 276]
Freud- Lampl-de Groot 8.10.1938 [FM] ("Wie es mir geht? Langsame Erholung von der Operation, die die ärgste war seit 1923, auch weil Schnitt von aussen gemacht wurde. Kann noch nicht ordentlich essen und rauchen, spreche mit Anstrengung, die Schmerzen sind im Rückzug, ich arbeite wieder 3 Stunden täglich.").

27 September 1938
Freud- Lampl-de Groot 8.10.1938 [FM] ("Das eigene Heim. Es ist sehr schön [. . .] Hell, bequem, geräumig . . . ").
Freud-Eitingon 3.11.1938 [FM] ("Unser neues Haus war ursprünglich schön gebaut u ist von Ernst prächtig hergerichtet worden. Wir haben es ungleich besser als in der Berggasse und selbst in Grinzing. 'Aus Dalles Weissbrot' sagt ein Spruch.").
Freud-Eitingon 19.12.1938 [FM] ("Hier schneit es grade zum ersten Mal. Es ist bitter kalt, Wasserleitungen sind eingefroren und die britischen Mängel in der Bewältigung des Heizungsproblems sind ganz evident.").

30 September 1938
1. After this withdrawal from the brink of war, this day was one of general rejoicing. Even such a pessimist as Stefan Zweig was carried away by the mood. But it could not last. One British historian, Hugh Seton-Watson, has stated that Munich was " . . . the greatest defeat and the greatest blow to prestige suffered by Britain since the loss of the American colonies. All over Europe it was assumed, with anguish and horror, that Britain had handed the Continent to the Axis."
Chamberlain, Neville, Broadcast speech, 27.9.1938.
Freud-Marie Bonaparte 4.10.1938 in *Letters*.
Zweig, Stefan, *The World of Yesterday*, London, 1943, p.313.
Seton-Watson, Hugh, *Eastern Europe between the Wars: 1918–1941*, N.Y., 1967, pp.396–7.

2 October 1938 (Minna)
Freud- Lampl-de Groot 8.10.1938 [FM] ("Tante Minna, ein trauriges Kapitel. Noch immer schwer leidend an ihrem Herzen und jetzt noch einer Cystitis gequält, von zwei·Nurses geplagt, die meine Frau unglücklich machen, weil sie Wohn- und Badezimmer im Stock belegen. Die Hausfrau könnte im neuen schönen Haus sehr zufrieden sein, wenn nicht Fenster, Thüren, Zentralheizung und Lift fortwährend Handwerker notwendig machten, die man so schwer bekommt. Kurz, es ist ein Stück kleines Emigrantenelend neben dem grossen. England ist bei all seiner Herrlichkeit ein Land für reiche und gesunde Leute. Auch sollen sie nicht zu alt sein.").

2 October 1938 (Martin)
Freud-Marie Bonaparte 4.10.1938 in *Letters*.
Freud- Lampl-de Groot 8.10.1938 [FM].

11 October 1938
1. After the war Sauerwald was put on trial by the Austrian government as a war criminal. He was acquitted, partly thanks to affidavits from Anna Freud and Marie Bonaparte testifying to his

helpfulness in their dealings with him.
2. Schur says Sauerwald turned up in England in 1939, but it is likely he is confusing the date of this visit in 1938. Though this would not exclude a "spying mission" or even a private holiday, it may be that Sauerwald came to England to discuss Freud's financial affairs. One catches perhaps an echo of this visit in a statement by Freud's nephew, Ernst Waldinger: "The Gestapo had graciously left him [Freud] in possession of a sufficient sum of money to tide him over the first days of his exile. Shall we call it naiveté or shamelessness when a Nazi official [Sauerwald?] visited him in London a long time afterward and demanded this amount back?"
Freud, Anna, Interview R.S.Stewart, 17.1.1966.
Jones, III.237–8 .
Schur, 498–9. n.3.
Waldinger, Ernst, "My Uncle Sigmund Freud," *Books Abroad*, Vol. 15 No. 1, Jan. 1941, p.4.

12 October 1938
Blue notebook [FM: LDFRD 5238].
Schur, 511
Arnold Zweig-Freud 16.10.1938 in *Zweig Letters*.

16 October 1938
Jewish Chronicle, 6.1.1939.

29 October 1938
1. Ségrédakis also supplied her with an authentication note dated October 28, 1938—i.e., twelve days after her visit to Freud—so it is possible Freud requested information about the piece. The note states that the object is "an antique bronze—Hellenistic age (3rd, 2nd c. BC)." However the statuette is in all probability Roman, from the 1st or 2nd c. AD. Ségrédakis' footnote, that the statuette was said to have been found at Valence, France, further supports a Roman attribution.
Freud-Eitingon 3.11.1938 [FM] ("Prinzess Marie, immer eine Erquickung, war einige Tage hier, hat sich gestern verabschiedet. Auch die junge Prinzessin blüht u gedeiht, ist erfreulich anzusehen. Ihr Mann, der Radziwill macht leider einen unbedeutenden Eindruck. Sie haben ihre Zeit hier zwischen uns, dem Herzogspaar von Kent, Queen Mary und ihrem eigenen König geteilt. Alle Mädchen im Haus waren sehr stolz, dass sie am meisten u längsten bei uns waren.").
Burn, Lucilla in *Freud and Art*, p.112.

31 October 1938
Die Zukunft, No.7., 25.11.1938 ("Der nachstehende Aufsatz ist die Veröffentlichung aus der Feder Siegmund Freuds seit seiner Verbannung aus Wien.").
Richmond, Marion, "The Lost Source in Freud's 'Comment on Antisemitism': Mark Twain," *Journal of the American Psychoanalytic Association*, (Vol. 28, No. 3, p.563).
Freud-Jelliffe 18.10.1938 [FM: 1-F8–74-25].
Clare, George, *Last Waltz in Vienna*, London, 1981 [1980] pp.208–9.
Klepper, Jochen, *Unter dem Schatten deiner Flügel*, Stuttgart, 1962 [1955], p.631, p.24.

10 November 1938 (Pogroms)
1. Five days later Viscountess Rhonnda, editor of the weekly review *Time and Tide*, invited Freud to contribute an article on antisemitism. In his response Freud detailed the persecutions he personally had suffered—the destruction of the psychoanalytic movement and its press, his children's expulsion from their professions, he and his family driven from home—and ends with the request that the journal find contributions from non-Jews, less personally involved than he.
Thalmann, Rita, & Feinermann, Emmanuel, *Crystal Night: 9–10 November 1938* (Transl. Gilles Cremonesi), Holocaust Library, N.Y., 1974 [1972].
Clare, George, *Last Waltz in Vienna*, London, 1981, p.228.
Eitingon-Freud 12.12.1938 [FM] ("[Aus] Deutschland haben auch wir grauenhafte Nachrichten. Eine Synagogue, die mein Vater in den zwanziger Jahren gestiften hat, ist völlig niedergebrannt worden und

das Jüdische Krankenhaus, die Eitingon-Stiftung steht auch vor seinem Ende. Die Chefärzte waren beide verhaftet . . . ").
Freud- Lampl-de Groot 20.11.1938 [FM] ("Die Nachrichten, aus + + + Deutschland, die Emigrationswellen, die an diese Küste schlagen, die Unsicherheit, was eine nahe Zukunft bringen kann, das alles schliesst ein wirklicher Behagen aus.").

10 November 1938 (Ban)
Freies Deutschland, Antwerp, 1.12.1938 [FM: Press cuttings].

29 November 1938
Wells-Freud March 1939 in Jones, III.259.

3 December 1938
1. Anna's three lectures, on child psychology, were part of a program run by the London County Council Education Committee and they were designed to keep teachers in touch with the latest developments in their subject.
Freud-Marie Bonaparte 12.11.1938 in *Letters*.
Anna Freud-McCord 28.8.1938 [FM 5044].

4 December 1938
Freud-Marie Bonaparte 12.11.1938 in *Letters*.
Jones, III.246.

6 December 1938 (Lün)
1. While Lün was in quarantine the Freuds bought a little Pekinese - Jumbo - as a "temporary replacement". The dog became very attached to Paula, but for Freud it was no substitute. As Anna Freud said: "I think he remained very loyal to Lün." Press clippings 6/7.12.1938 [FM].
Freud, Anna, Commentary "Home Movies" [FM].

6 December 1938 (Recital)
Lund, Engel, Telephone communication, 20.6.1990 (With thanks to Dr. J. Stross for information leading to this note).

7 December 1938
BBC-Freud 6.12.1938 [FM].
BBC recording (Cassette) [FM].

7 December 1938 (Martin)
1. The outbreak of war terminated this business because the government requisitioned the necessary chemicals. During and after the war, Martin worked for the Dock Labour Board as an auditor. This involved much travelling and staying in hotels in places like Hull and Grimsby and he hated the work. Then he had a tobacconist shop near Tottenham Court Road. It had a back room rented out to a hairdresser. He used to travel there on his Vespa from his home in Highgate and one day was knocked off. Afterwards he never properly recovered from this accident.
Freud, A.W., Telephone interview, 30.8.1989.

8 December 1938 (Princess)
Jones, III.246.
Bertin, p.201, 204.

8 December 1938 (Brown)
Who Was Who, Vol. 5, London, 1964.
Jones, III.254.

1939

2–31 January 1939
Jones Diary, 18/25.12.1938 [Inst. of PsA].
Schur, 512, 517.
Freud-Eitingon 5.3.1939 [FM] ("Gegen meinen Lebensretter Pichler habe ich eine starke Antipathie entwickelt, seitdem mir seine letzte Operation abscheuliche Knochenschmerzen durch sechs Monate hinterlassen hat. Vielleicht thue ich ihm Unrecht.").
Freud-Sachs, Hanns 12.3.1939 [FM] ("14/3 Der Tatbestand ist der, dass ich seit meiner Operation im Sept. an unausgesetzten Kieferschmerzen gelitten habe, die auch die Ablösung eines Knochensplitters überdauerten.").

2 February 1939
Freud-Eitingon 3.11.1938, 19.11.1938, 29.12.1938 [FM].
Freud-Eitingon 5.4.1939 [FM] ("Martin Buber's fromme Redensarten werden der Traumdeutung wenig schaden. Der Moses ist weit vulnerabler und ich bin auf den jüdischen Ansturm gegen ihn vorbereitet.").

5 February 1939
Bertin, p.206.
Jones Diary, 5.2.1939 [Inst. of PsA].

10 February 1939
1. A month after Dolffuss had crushed the opposition in 1934 Freud wrote to Ernst: "The progress of the Catholic reaction is unbelievably rapid and far-reaching. But even that itself holds a certain guarantee that the Hitlerite barbarity, from which we would have fled, will not cross the border. The Catholic Church as our protection!" (*Freud-Ernst Freud 11.3.1934*).
Kelly, J.N.D., *Oxford Dictionary of Popes*, Oxford & New York, 1986.
Freud-Arnold Zweig 30.9.1934 in *Zweig Letters*.
Freud-Ernst Freud 11.3.1934 [LoC] ("Die Fortschritte der katholischen Reaktion sind unglaublich rasch und ausgiebig. Aber selbst darin liegt eine gewisse Garantie, dass die Hitler'sche Barbarei vor der wir geflohen wären, nicht über die Grenze kommen wird. Die katholische Kirche als unser Schutz!").

10 February 1939
Jones, Ernest, *Free Associations*, Hogarth, London, 1959, p.160.
Brome, Vincent, *Ernest Jones: Freud's Alter Ego*, London, 1982.
Schur, 517–8.

19 February 1939
Freud-Eitingon 19.12.1938 [FM] ("Oli ist endlich Franzose geworden, ein erster Schritt zu unserer Internationalität.").
Jones Diary 19/20.2.1939 [Inst. of PsA].

26 February 1939
Schur, 517–8.
Marie Bonaparte [Inst. of PsA: CBC/FO8/20].

28 February 1939
Schur, 518.

3 March 1939
1. Max Schur, has seized on two interesting mistakes in the final sentence of the letter to Zweig: an ungrammatical "würd" (an amalgam of "würde"["would have been"] and "wird" ["will be"]) and the substitution of "damals" ["in the past"] for "diesmal" ["this time"]. Thus, in Schur's translation, the passage reads: "(There no longer is any doubt that it is a new advance of my dear old cancer, with which I now have been sharing my existence for 16 years. Who in the *past will be* [or: *would have been*] the stronger, one of course cannot foresee.)" (*Freud-Arnold Zweig 5.3.1939*). Schur, interprets these slips as an expression of the wish to live in conflict with the death wish.
Freud-Eitingon 5.3.1939 [FM] ("Eine Probeexzision hat

ergeben, dass es sich wirklich um einen Versuch des Carcinomas handelt, sich wieder an meine Stelle zu setzen. Man schwankte lange zwischen verschiedenen Möglichkeiten der Verteidigung. [. . .] und nun haben wir uns alle auf Röntgenbestrahlung von aussen geeinigt . . . ").
Freud-Arnold Zweig 5.3.1939 in *Zweig Letters*.
Freud-Arnold Zweig 5.3.1939 in Schur, 520–1 ("Es ist kein Zweifel mehr, dass es sich um einen neuen Vorstoss meines lieben alten Carcinoms handelt, mit dem ich seit jetzt 16 Jahren die Existenz teile. Wer damals der Stärkere sein würd, konnte man natürlich nicht vorhersagen.)").
Schur, 520–1.

3 March 1939
Kelly, J.N.D., *Oxford Dictionary of Popes*, Oxford & New York, 1986.

6 March 1939
Who was Who, Vol. VI., London, 1979 (2nd ed.).
Freud-Eitingon 5.3.1939 in Schur, 520.

8 March 1939
Freud-Jones 7.3.1939 in Jones, III.260.
Jones diary 8.3.1939 [Inst. of PsA].
Programme: 25 anniversary dinner [FM].

9 March 1939
Schur, 518–9.
Finzi-Lacassagne 5.7.1939 in Schur, p.525 n.15.

13 March 1939
Freud-Sachs, Hanns 12[/14].3.1939 [FM] ("Ein ganz würdiger Abgang . . . ").

13 March 1939
Lacassagne-Marie Bonaparte 28.12.1954 (Ms. copy by Marie Bonaparte) [FM].
Schur, 518.

15 March 1939
1.Six days later his mood remained the same in a letter to Eitingon: "My doctors here seem quite pleased by the success so far of the combined X-ray and radium treatment. Subjectively I am feeling fairly bad. My overall state of health has suffered greatly, the localized symptoms are very disturbing. I am told that is part of it. So we will carry on waiting. One cannot do anything else anyway." (*Freud-Eitingon 20.4.1939*).
Freud-Sachs 12[14].3.1939 [FM] ("14.3. [. . .] To cut a long story short, es hat sich nach vielen Untersuchungen ergeben, dass ich eine Rezidive meines alten Leidens habe. Die Behandlung, zu der man sich entschloss, besteht in einer Kombination von Röntgen von aussen und Radium von innen, die immerhin schonender ist als ‑ Kopfabschneiden, was die andere Alternative gewesen wäre . . . [. . .] Es ist eben ein Weg zum unvermeidlichen Ende wie ein anderer, wenngleich nicht der, den man sich gerne ausgesucht hätte.").
Anna Freud-Arnold Zweig 11.5.1939 [SFC].
Freud-Eitingon 20.4.1939 [FM] ("Meine Ärzte hier scheinen vom bisherigen Erfolg der kombinirten Röntgen-Radiumbehandlung recht befriedigt zu sein. Mir geht es subjecktiv schlecht genug. Mein Allgemeinbefinden hat sehr gelitten, die lokalen Symptome sind sehr störend. Man sagt mir, das gehört dazu. Also warten wir ab. Anderes kann man ohnehin nicht thun.").

15 March 1939
Bergschicker, pp.228–233.

6 April 1939
Freud, Ernst, Interview R.S. Stewart, 10.1.1966.
Jones diaries [Inst. of PsA].
Freud-Ernst Freud 3.4.1922 [LoC] ("Es ist eigentlich nicht nötig, dass ich dir zum 30sten Geburtstag Glück wünsche. Das einzige unter meinen Kindern besitzest du jetzt schon alles, was man auf deiner Lebensstufe haben kann: ein zärtliches Weib, ein prächtiges Kind, Arbeit, Erwerb u Freunde. Du verdienst es alles auch und da nicht alles im Leben nach Verdienst geht, lass mich den Wunsch aussprechen, dass das Glück dir treu bleiben möge.").

16 April 1939
Prochaskas Familien-Kalender, 1916 & 1917 [LoC].

19 April 1939
1. Though Harry submitted his parents' application to emigrate to the United States in spring 1939, a year later they were still in England waiting for their visas.
Alexander Freud-Ernst Freud 17.2.1940 & 28.4.1940 [FM: Lucie Freud Papers].
Harry F.-Mizzi,Dolfi & Pauli F. 25.9.1939 [LoC]

20 April 1939
Schur, 522.

6 May 1939
"Home Movies" [FM].
Anna Freud-Arnold Zweig 11.5.1939 [SFC].
H.D.-Freud 6.5.1939 [FM: VAR SF 20–21].

12 May 1939
Freud, Anna, (1981) in Bonaparte, Marie, *Topsy, Der goldhaarige Chow*, Fischer, Frankfurt am Main, 1981 [1939], pp.8–10.

19 May 1939
Freud-Jones 1.11.1938 [Inst. of PsA].
Jones-Freud 2.11.1938 [Inst. of PsA].
Leonard Woolf-Freud 15.3.1939 [FM: SOH9–16].
Blanche Knopf-Freud 31.3.1939 [FM: SOH9–16].

20 May 1939
Young-Bruehl, pp.236–7.
Peters, p.237.
Int. J. PsA., vol. 21., 1940, p.121.
Anna Freud-Arnold Zweig 11.5.1939 [SFC] ("Ich mache energische Versuche, wieviele Leben man auf einmal leben kann und habe verschiedene ganztagige Beschäftigungen auf einmal.").

2 July 1939
Freud-Marie Bonaparte 10.6.1939 in Schur, 524.
Bertin, p.207.

10 July 1939
1. Freud's respect for Havelock Ellis was, however, qualified. H.D. knew Ellis and spoke of him during her analysis with Freud in 1933. In her account of this analysis she reports one of his sceptical comments about Ellis: "The Professor said he had always wondered why a man so situated and not dependent on outside criticism should spend his enormous energy on a superficial documentation of sex. Now the Professor said he felt from my reactions that his own opinion was not unjustified. He said he had been puzzled. 'He records so many funny things that people do but never seems to want to know *why* they do them. You see I *lose* him a little, but I always thought there was something immature about his *Psychology of Sex.*' "
Freud-Ellis 8.11.1925 [FM: SFVAR 132].
H.D.-Freud 6.5.1939 [FM: VAR SF 22].
H.D., p.148.

12 July 1939
Schur, 525.

15 July 1939
1. This first important conquest beyond Vienna marked the end to "years of honorable but painful isolation." In 1907, Freud wrote to Jung: " . . . calm assurance [. . .] finally took possession of me and bade me wait till a voice from the unknown answered mine. That voice was yours; I also realize now that Bleuler can be traced back to you. Let me thank you for this . . . ." (*Freud-Jung 2.9.1907*).
Bleuler-Freud 23.10.1929 [LoC].
Freud-Jung 2.9.1907 in Schur, 253.

24 July 1939
Freud-Meine Lieben 17.3.1929 [FM].
Bourgeron-Molnar 28.10.1990 [FM].

24 July 1939
1. The following paragraph of Freud's letter to Wells, however, shifts the ground away from the first trip to England. Freud now talks of the desire for British nationality as "an infantile phantasy," thus

invoking the departure of his half-brothers to
Manchester when he was three years old. For the
young Freud this event signified the loss of his
playmates, John and Pauline Freud, his own
departure from Freiburg and the reduction of the
extended Freud clan to a two-parent family. In this
phantasy, England may have stood for paradise
regained.

2. This was Locker-Lampson's second attempt to
influence parliament on Freud's behalf. In April 1938
he had proposed a bill extending Palestine nationality
in order to assist Jews to escape death in Germany.
During the debate, Freud was specifically referred to
as an example—though "old and dying," yet a victim
of the "Nazi monsters." The terms must have
reminded Freud uncomfortably of Ludwig Braun's
"defence" of his cause in 1933. The bill did not get
through parliament.

3. In an interview after Freud's death, Wells returned
to the question of bestowing British nationality: " 'A
number of us,' Wells said, 'did all we could to satisfy
that desire, for it was a great honour to Britain. But
we were unable to do it. All that was necessary was a
small private bill which could have been passed in
half an hour with the consent of the Government,
but it was not done. I am extraordinarily sorry that it
couldn't be done.' "

Wells-Freud 14.7.1939 [FM: VARSF].
Freud-Wells 16.7.1939 [FM: SFVAR & *Letters*].
Clark, p.508.
Locker-Lampson - Freud 6.9.1938 [FM: VARSF].
South African Jewish Times, 3.11.1939.
Wells, H.G., *The Fate of Homo Sapiens*, London, 1939
[Dedicated copy: Private collection].

26 July 1939
Martha Freud-Elsa Reiss 23.2.1939 [LoC].
Pfister-Martha Freud 12.12.1939 in *Pfister Letters*.

1 August 1939
1. Apart from the ordinary patients, there was
Dorothy Burlingham's training analysis—99 hours
between June 13, 1938, and January 1, 1939. There
were also two brief analyses, one of them being the
American analyst Smiley Blanton, who had eight
hours from August 30 to September 7, 1938, at 4
guineas an hour. (The rate varied between £3 and 6
guineas an hour.)
Dark blue notebook [FM: LDFRD 5238].
Schur, 526.

1 August 1939
Photograph Album [FM: IN 87]
Bertin, p.207.

23 August 1939
Young-Bruehl, pp.278–9.

24 August 1939
Letter list 1938–39 [FM].
Ellis-Neufeld 26.6.1986 [FM: MAG/41/5].

25 August 1939
Schur, 360.
Roudinesco, Élisabeth, Oral Communication.
Oliver Freud-Jones 16.4.1953 [Inst. of PsA:
CFB/FO5/02].
Martha Freud-Elsa Reiss 2.12.1945 [LoC] ("Ihnen von
Evchen zu schreiben, da stockt meine Feder. Das
süsse Kind, mir von all meinen Enkeln am meisten
an's Herz gewachsen, ist uns und den armen Eltern
nach einer furchtbaren Krankheit (Gehirnstumor)
entrissen. Sie starb in Nizza, Oli's früherem
Wohnort, wo sie sie gut aufgehoben bei Freunden
zurückliessen, während sie selbst über die Pyränaen
die lebensgefährliche Flucht unternahmen.").

25 August 1939
Dorothy Burlingham-Anna Freud 25.8.1939 [FM].
Valenstein, Mrs K., Interview, 14.5.1990.
Burlingham, p.271.

23 September 1939
1. Stefan Zweig's funeral oration at the Golders
Green Crematorium on September 26, 1939, was a
heartfelt expression of thanks to Freud. Zweig stated:
"Each of us, people of the twentieth century, would

have been different in our manner of thinking and
understanding without him, each of us would think,
judge and feel more narrowly, less freely, less justly
without that powerful stimulus inwards which he
gave us. And wherever we seek to advance into the
labyrinth of the human heart, henceforth his
intellectual light will shine upon our path."
Schur, 529.
Anna Freud-Arnold Zweig 28.10.1939 [SFC] ("Es ist
merkwürdig, aber ich kann nicht so richtig um ihn
trauern wie man es sonst tut und wie die Menschen
es von einem erwarten. Trauern ist für die Tatsache,
dass er gestorben ist, irgendwie kein adäquates
Gefühl. Vielleicht ist auch nur meine Verbundenheit
mit ihm ersthafter als die Trennung von ihm.
Jedenfalls ist das, was man von ihm bekommen hat,
immer noch sehr viel mehr als das was andere
Menschen überhaupt haben. So lebe ich also weiter
fort, was ich mir vorher nie vorstellen konnte. Er
scheint es sich so vorgestellt zu haben, denn er hat
sich über diesen Punkt gar keine Sorgen gemacht.").
Anna Freud-Arnold Zweig 13.2.1940 [SFC] ("Aber so
weit es mein Gefühl angeht, stellt es sich mir so dar
als wäre diese ganze Trennung etwas Vorläufiges,
etwas Vorübergehenedes währendessen man alles in
Ordnung halten muss. Eher so wie in früheren
Jahren, wenn mein Vater auf Reisen war.").
Martha Freud-Federn 5.11.1939 [SFC] ("Ich darf ja
nicht einmal klagen, war es mir doch vergönnt mehr
als ein Menschenalter ihn betreuen zu dürfen, ihm
die Misere des Alltags fern zu halten. Dass nun mein
Leben Sinn u Inhalt verloren, ist nur
selbstverständlich.").
Zweig, Stefan, *Worte am Sarge Sigmund Freuds* in
Stefan Zweig, p.250.

Index

The index includes references to all the diary entries, people, places and subjects discussed. Subheadings for major entries are arranged: 1. the diary entries in chronological order; 2. general subjects in alphabetical order; 3. publications, where applicable, in alphabetical order, and 4. illustrations, in some cases arranged in page number order. Page references to illustrations are given in *italic*.

Photo Credits

Where no photograph credit appears in the
caption, the photograph forms part of the
Freud Museum photograph archive and has
been reproduced by kind permission of
A.W. Freud et al.

The following sources and photographers
are also thanked for permission to use their
photographs (the caption abbreviation
appears in brackets above their names):

(NB)
  Nick Bagguley
(DOW)
  Dokumentationsarchiv des
  Osterreichischen Widerstandes
(EE)
  Edmund Engelman
(TG)
  Tim N. Gidal
(MH)
  Max Halberstadt: By courtesy of
  W. Ernest Freud
(WH)
  Willi Hoffer
(WK)
  Walter Kaufmann
(MS)
  Marcel Sternberger